Praise for the First Edition of *GWT in Action*

"The thoroughness with which the authors designed examples to illustrate every concept dealt with in the book, and the scope of the topics addressed in it, make *GWT in Action* a valuable addition to any web developer's library."

—JavaLobby.com

"… *GWT in Action* is packed with practical information on a wide range of GWT topics."

—Michael J. Ross, Slashdot.org

"How to 'think in GWT.' The code: concise, efficient, thorough, and plentiful."

—Scott Stirling, AT&T

" Impressive quality and thoroughness. Wonderful!"

—Bernard Farrell, Kronos, Inc.

"Perfect for Java developers struggling with JavaScript."

—Carlo Bottiglieri, Sytel-Reply

"A real nitty-gritty tutorial on the rich features of GWT."

—Andrew Grothe, Eliptic Webwise, Inc.

"I was very impressed with the quality of the writing as well as the depth of coverage. The authors explain the examples well and it is easy to follow them."

—YongSung Kim, Amazon reader

GWT in Action

SECOND EDITION

ADAM TACY
ROBERT HANSON
JASON ESSINGTON
ANNA TÖKKE

MANNING
SHELTER ISLAND

For online information and ordering of this and other Manning books, please visit www.manning.com. The publisher offers discounts on this book when ordered in quantity. For more information, please contact

Special Sales Department
Manning Publications Co.
20 Baldwin Road
PO Box 261
Shelter Island, NY 11964
Email: orders@manning.com

Manning Publications Co.
20 Baldwin Road
PO Box 261
Shelter Island, NY 11964

Development editor: Jeff Bleiel
Copyeditor: Linda Recktenwald
Technical proofreader: Levi Bracken
Proofreaders: Tara Wlash, Tiffany Taylor
Typesetter: Marija Tudor
Cover designer: Marija Tudor

ISBN: 9781935182849
Printed in the United States of America
2 3 4 5 6 7 8 9 10 – MAL – 18 17 16 15 14 13

To my parents.
Simply, thank you once again,
for everything.

—A. Tacy

To my father.
Thank you for every computer and video game
you bought me when I was a kid.
Without them I would have never found
my true passion in this world.

—R. Hanson

To my wonderful husband Peter and daughter Elektra.
Thank you for allowing me the time to do this.
Love you both.

—A. Tökke

brief contents

contents

preface

Since the first edition of this book, the Google Web Toolkit (GWT) has grown, transformed, and emerged from a promising toolkit for web applications into a toolkit that truly supports 1) developers and managers in delivering web applications that can push the boundaries of the possible and 2) the application of well-tread engineering principles (deliver better user experience while reducing your development/maintenance costs).

This second edition of *GWT in Action* builds on our view of the first edition. It's fully updated to look at the latest version, 2.5, of GWT, covering all the new techniques and tools—we even take a sneak look at the experimental items (such as super dev mode and the Elemental library). Perhaps the largest change between editions is that each technique is demonstrated with individual examples, rather than the monolithic example from the first edition. We hope this allows more focused examination and offers a simpler Ctrl+C/V mechanism to get those techniques into your own applications.

We said back in 2005 that we had noticed the web was reinventing itself with terms such as Ajax and Web 2.0 being created to help define the new technologies and ideas. As time has gone by, snippets of those techniques are on most modern websites—few websites require a page refresh to the server when updating information nowadays. Some sites have even harnessed the techniques in more depth and become full web applications, for example, Google Docs.

Now, in 2012, we stand at the beginning of the next reinvention, one that will further push the complexity of web applications. As we move toward the "cloud," users will begin to expect web applications to be equivalent to the desktop ones they'll be replacing. As more people gain access to smartphones, tablets, and related devices, there are opportunities to harness HTML 5 to provide web applications giving the same functionality as native apps, but you only have to write once rather than per device. These applications must be more robust than ever and will need the stability, speed, and responsiveness that at least matches native applications, if they're to be taken seriously.

To reach that point, we'll see a maturing from ad hoc web development that includes a sprinkling of Ajax toward the use of solid, well-tread, and proven engineering techniques that are commonly available in desktop development—such as applying architectural patterns such as MVP as well as harnessing dependency injection. At the same time, the flexibility of design, so well established in the web with separation of functionality from styling, needs to be maintained and harnessed.

But there are still the same challenges in the development world that we saw seven years ago around how to effectively manage a project using JavaScript—where we're missing the ease of development that comes with typed languages, testing, and powerful IDEs with debugging capabilities. As we said in the first edition, it's possible to manage a successful JavaScript project, but the need to develop and maintain several different versions of code for differing browsers is a headache, even with the use of modern libraries such as JQuery and the like. We can add to that the additional headaches we've experienced when trying to maintain all those versions over the lifecycle of the project, especially in the maintenance phases.

It also remains, in our experience, a challenge to find enough JavaScript developers who are aware of the necessary browser issues and nuances and who are also at a sufficient comfort level with production-quality development processes to deliver a large project (compared to the number of Java programmers).

Step forward the latest versions of the Google Web Toolkit. GWT provides the support necessary for industry-grade techniques—event busses, the model-view-presenter (MVP) pattern, together with a reference implementation that can be built on activities and places, as well as the ability to harness dependency injection through Guice/GIN.

We get access to efficient paging through large datasets with cell-based data presentation widgets and can harness Editors to ensure that updates in UI items are automatically reflected in the model—and if that model is stored on a server, we can batch together updates to increase efficiency. Generators can be employed to minimize the amount of boilerplate code a developer needs to write and get it generated automatically at runtime.

GWT handles browser differences for us, and the compiler is aggressive about code removal to ensure the download is as small as possible for the user. Using GWT's code-splitting approach together with bundling resources further increases the speed of downloads and efficiency—smaller and more efficient downloads all increase the user's experience.

The toolkit allows us to separate the user interface from functionality by using the declarative UiBinder approach. CSS styling can be applied to all widgets to give the style needed, and it's also possible to have some primitive themes, three of which are built in; beyond that your designer is free to apply the look you've agreed upon.

Because we're developing in Java, we get access to all the Java tooling that's available as well as robust IDEs in which to develop and debug. We can harness Ant and/or Maven to build the application and use Hudson to perform continuous builds and drive automated JUnit testing, ensuring team development quality is measurable and actionable. GWT's development modes (original and super) enable us to user test in our browser of choice while debugging live in the IDE. There's much more to say about that in this preface!

Let's be clear: GWT won't solve every problem you have when it comes to creating rich web applications. But GWT takes massive steps toward maturing the process of developing and maintaining Ajax applications. Couple that with a strong architect and development processes, and you can push those web application boundaries while being sure to excite and engage the user—just look at Rovio's very popular Angry Birds version on Chrome, which is written in GWT (http://mng.bz/xbYP).

The first version of this book summed up by saying, "We don't even want to think about the amount of effort that would be required to program, let alone debug, any issues or perform maintenance across six different browsers for an application such as Dashboard [the monolithic application in the first edition] directly in JavaScript." That view hasn't changed, except to say there are more browser combinations, and the latest version of GWT brings more industry-grade techniques to the table to help us.

GWT has proven to be a viable alternative to pure JavaScript development. Each major release of GWT brings new features and bug fixes yet leaves relative stability to legacy code. Because it's open source, you can contribute your own patches or see if patches in future releases are going to be helpful with any issue you might be having. With a wide user community it's also easy to get answers to problems.

We hope that through this book we can share our enthusiasm for GWT and make it easier for you to get the most out of this technology.

acknowledgments

There are four names on the cover as authors, but, as ever, writing and producing this book has been a tremendous undertaking by a large cast.

We'd like to begin our thanks with Michael Stephens from Manning for getting this project started and for his continuing support and honesty about the amount of work the book would take, even though at least two of us should have known better!

Our thanks also to publisher Marjan Bace for greenlighting the project and heading up a great team at Manning. That team included some familiar faces and some new ones, but always of the same outstanding quality and helpfulness. This includes the fantastic work from Jeff Bleiel, Mary Piergies, Linda Recktenwald, Tara Walsh, Tiffany Taylor, and Marija Tudor. Thanks to all of you for being part of this team and seeing yet another edition of *GWT in Action* smoothly through the publication process.

We also want to thank Levi Bracken for being our technical proofreader. We'll never underestimate the work that a technical review takes in terms of time and effort, and we also acknowledge the invaluable improvements the output required us to make!

As reviewers ourselves we know the effort required to review manuscripts, so special thanks go to the following: A.O. Van Emmenis, Christian Goudreau, Dale Gregory, Ernesto Cullen, James Hatheway, Jeffrey Chimene, Jeroen Benckhuijsen, Jérôme Baton, John Pedersen, Michael Glenn Williams, Michael Moossen, Mike Bailey, Nathan Workman, Olivier Nouguier, Olivier Turpin, Orhan Alkan, Patrick Steger, Peter Hannaway, Ramnivas Laddad, Rick Wagner, and Bradley Jones.

Thank you all for the free time that you gave up to review our chapters and the very useful comments and questions you provided.

We feel it's also important to thank our readers of the MEAP (Manning Early Access Program) versions of the book for their comments and questions and for their patience in reading chapters that had not gone through the final editing and proof-reading processes at the time that they were reading them. Your comments and insights were most helpful.

about this book

Google Web Toolkit, or GWT, works on a simple but powerful idea. You write a web application in Java, and GWT cross-compiles it into JavaScript. This free, open source collection of tools is both supported and used by Google.

The latest version, GWT 2.5, includes a library of high-quality interface components, an easy-to-use UI designer, and a set of productivity tools that make using GWT a snap, and it supports industry-grade development techniques such as MVP, dependency injection, and event busses. And yes, the JavaScript it produces is really, really good, especially if you turn on the optional Closure compiler!

GWT in Action, Second Edition is a completely revised edition of the best-selling GWT book. It covers all the new features introduced in GWT 2.5, as well as the best development practices that have emerged in the GWT community. It begins with a rapid-fire introduction to GWT and Ajax to get you up to speed with GWT concepts and tools. Then, you'll explore key concepts like managing events, interacting with the server, creating UI components, building your user interface declaratively using UiBinder, and more.

As you move through the engaging examples, you'll pick up the skills you need to stay ahead of the pack. You'll absorb the latest thinking in application design and industry-grade best practices, such as these:

- Writing code that handles internationalization and localization; you can make your applications usable by as many people as possible while keeping the download size as small as it can be (and small download sizes mean quicker starts and better user experience).

- Driving out browser differences in your coding; why worry that IE does things differently than other browsers requiring you to pepper your code with `if/then/else` statements? GWT does away with those concerns for you in the majority of cases, and when you implement your own functionality you can harness the same approaches to minimize your final application code size as well as have an easily maintainable code base (cutting your maintenance costs).
- Implementing the MVP pattern becomes easy in GWT with the arrival of `Activity`s and `Place`s, though you're not forced to implement MVP or forced to use `Activity`s and `Place`s to do so.
- Using dependency injection to manage dependencies between various aspects of your application; you'll see how to use the GIN library, which is based on the popular Guice library, to do dependency injection within GWT client-side code.
- Harnessing event busses to further loosely couple your application.
- Presenting large data sets in the new lightweight cell-based widgets, which support paging, sorting, and data retrieval while giving the best GUI performance possible.
- Editing data by using Editors, allowing the GWT compiler to take the strain of ensuring that code is produced to keep presentation and models in sync.
- Optimizing your code by implementing code splitting; even though GWT produces fantastically compact JavaScript code, it also supports you in pushing the complexity boundaries of your functionality. That probably will increase your code size, and so you can split up your application so that only necessary code segments are downloaded when appropriate. GWT also comes with a lightweight metrics mechanism and compiler reports to allow you to further tweak and optimize your code.

Any substantial application requires server-side components, and many books can tell you about all the server-side development techniques (Java, PHP, and so on) for which GWT is highly flexible and which it can plug into. Our approach in *GWT in Action* is to concentrate several chapters on ensuring you get a thorough understanding of GWT's client/server communication techniques. For example:

- JSON processing
- GWT-RPC
- Form handling
- Traditional Ajax communication
- RequestFactory

Although we don't have a dedicated section on security, we do highlight GWT techniques as and where appropriate, for example, using SafeHtml when creating new widgets, manipulating the DOM, or using i18n; using SafeHtmlTemplates in Cell widgets; and protecting against cross-site forgery requests in GWT-RPC.

We've substantially updated and rewritten the examples from the first edition, splitting them into examples that focus purely on the topic of the chapter. Our hope is that these new examples give you a much more focused view of how to use GWT as well as show off what GWT can do. By breaking out into examples per chapter, it should be much easier to see the techniques in use and then employ them directly in your applications as needed.

Who should read this book

The book is aimed at anyone with an interest in

- Understanding GWT initially and in more detail
- Pushing the boundaries of web application functionality in a controlled manner
- Reducing the headache of maintaining web applications
- Reducing the lifecycle costs of web applications that continuously excite your users

We appreciate that the readership will come from varied backgrounds—JavaScript programmers looking to see what the fuss is about or wanting, just as we did, to give better structure to their web applications; Java programmers learning that they can now program Ajax applications simply; server-side developers interested in understanding how GWT would affect them (it doesn't have to); web designers looking to see how this useful development approach fits in with their approach (and to see how to guide programmers to use GWT's built-in approaches to ensure their life is easier); managers/technicians looking to see how to get the web application beast under control; and many others.

In the first edition we spent a lot of time selling GWT itself. In this edition we no longer feel a need for that; rather we can spend the time on the exciting array of techniques and tools in GWT and get going more quickly.

Readers looking for an introduction to GWT concepts and components should find it in chapters 2 and 3. Here we go through using the tools to create a simple GWT `HelloWorld` application and show how to run in various modes (developer and super dev) as well as how to compile and debug problems. We then look at a more complex GWT application to show how to use concepts such as widgets, panels, history management, and styling. By the end of these two chapters, you should be familiar with creating a basic application, enhancing it to give some real complexity, as well as running/debugging the application in development mode and compiling it for web mode.

The middle part of the book covers techniques you'd use in everyday applications: building your own widgets, using client bundles, separating design from coding with UiBinder, communicating with the server in various ways, using widgets as editors, efficiently displaying/sorting/paging through large data sets, and interfacing with JavaScript (JSNI/fast JSON parsing with overlay objects).

More advanced readers will find that the book addresses the industry-grade approaches GWT supports that you may well have thought of but perhaps haven't yet implemented—and we hope a few things you haven't thought of yet! We cover MVP, dependency injection, deferred binding, generators, and using metrics and code splitting to squeeze out the most performant code possible.

You should be familiar with the concept of Java classes and packages, although we feel this is something you can pick up as you read the book, follow the code examples, and use an IDE, such as Eclipse. A lot of GWT (and Java) issues revolve around classpaths and GWT's package structure, so we recommend a good read of chapter 2 if you get stuck.

Roadmap

Part 1 "Basics" consists of chapters 1 through 3. It aims to get you going in GWT and producing a first real-world example. We would suggest reading it in the order it is presented:

- ***Chapter 1*** provides an introduction to GWT. We begin by defining what GWT is and how it fits into this new ecosphere of rich-client web development. Then for readers new to GWT we provide an overview of what GWT means and some explanation of the more popular components of the toolkit. The chapter then explains how to set up your development environment so that you can begin writing applications using GWT.
- ***Chapter 2*** starts our journey with GWT. We look at how to use the Google Plugin for Eclipse to create a basic GWT application and then examine its structure and what we can do with it. It's a hands-on chapter where you can create the application yourself as we reinforce the points (or you can just download the result). We also show how to run the application in development mode (and touch on the new experimental super dev mode), how to use standard debug tools to hunt problems, and how to compile the application for web mode, as well as clarify a number of GWT concepts such as modules and client- and server-side code.
- ***Chapter 3*** takes the next step in building a real application. Typically you perform the steps in chapter 2 to get a base structure and then build your application on that result. In this chapter we look at an application that has been through those steps and examine the concepts of widgets, panels, event handling, managing history, and styling components to get from a mockup introduced at the start of the chapter to the actual implementation at the end.

Part 2 we have called "Next Steps" and covers chapters 4 through 13. Here we discuss the usual technologies that you will often use when taking your application to the next level. You can read this part in order or jump directly to the topics that you are interested in:

- ***Chapter 4*** is where we really start to dig into GWT. We look at widgets (which include panels) in detail, covering their lifecycle and three ways to create new widgets should GWT not contain something you need (including creating composite widgets). We also spend a moment looking at the GWT 2.5 Elemental library and examine Layout panels because they're the future of GWT panels.

- ***Chapter 5*** introduces you to client bundles, a unique tool that allows you to create bundles of images, binary documents, stylesheets, and more and have them optimized by the GWT compiler. In this chapter you'll also learn about GWT's extension to CSS, which allows you to include runtime-evaluated expressions in your styles including constants and conditional statements.
- ***Chapter 6*** is where we dive into UiBinder, one of the defining features of GWT. In this chapter we provide a superior method of creating complex composite widgets. We begin the chapter by showing you how to transform HTML into a UiBinder template and bind that template to a Java class. Next, we explain how to bind events to methods in the Java class and then how to apply CSS styles to the template elements.
- ***Chapter 7*** introduces you to GWT-RPC, the first of several methods of communicating with the server. In this chapter we explain how you can send Java objects between the client and server, as opposed to using some other message format like JSON or XML. We then look at how you can debug client/server communications and how to protect your users from cross-site request forgery attacks.
- ***Chapter 8*** examines RequestFactory, an alternate method of client/server communication. Whereas GWT-RPC is more general purpose, RequestFactory specifically targets the communication of domain objects that will ultimately be persisted in a database. In this chapter we provide an overview of the architecture and show you how to build the interfaces and objects required to use this tool and how to integrate it with Java's Bean Validation specification (JSR-303).
- ***Chapter 9*** The Editor framework supports editing of any bean-like object holding a bunch of properties using widgets. It reduces the amount of code needed to glue bean objects to widgets. Values are moved back and forth between the widget and the bean object with ready-to-use controllers called drivers. There are two types of drivers: the `RequestFactoryEditorDriver` that is used to edit remote objects and the `SimpleBeanEditorDriver` used for editing beans residing on the client. In this chapter you start by learning how to construct editors to support both remote and local beans. You'll find out how the framework can be used in both simple and complex situations. The chapter ends by presenting generic logic provided by the framework for even more effective ways to use the framework.
- ***Chapter 10***'s data-presentation (aka `Cell`) widgets allow efficient display of large datasets and support paging and sorting through that data both locally and from the server. In this chapter we look at the provided underlying cells and how to create them, including via the GWT 2.5 UiBinder approach. Then we explore the six built-in widgets—including `Lists`, `Tables`, and `Trees`—and how they can be used, finishing off by writing your own builders to create more complex table layouts.
- ***Chapter 11*** looks under the hood at GWT as we examine how to interface to JavaScript to interact with the browser (if you can't do it another way in GWT),

how to wrap an existing JavaScript library, how to handle JSONP return objects, and how to expose your application as an API.

- *Chapter 12* covers a collection of communication and data-parsing tools. In this chapter we look at how to create and parse JSON and XML messages and how to pass these messages between the client and the server. In addition we explore GWT's `FormPanel` widget, which can be used to transmit traditional form data to the server in a slightly less traditional way.
- *Chapter 13* covers all the aspects you need to know to internationalize your application with different messages/constants, to manage plurals and user-defined changes in messages, and to drive localization (date, time, and currency formats). We also cover GWT 2.5's approach to accessibility to make sure your application is as widely usable as possible.

Part 3 is "Advanced Topics." In chapters 14 through 19 we cover topics that are more involved or complicated. As with the previous part, you can read in the order presented or dive into the chapters as you want.

- *Chapter 14* moves us into the advanced part of the book, and we start off by looking at advanced event handling—creating your own events, preventing event propagation, and how GWT avoids browser differences. The second half of the chapter looks at how event busses can be used to loosely couple your application and shows a user-defined event in action.
- *Chapter 15* considers how the MVP pattern can be applied to GWT applications in two ways: building the pattern yourself or by using GWT's `Activitys` and `Places`.
- *Chapter 16* examines how dependency injection (DI) can be used in GWT applications to manage dependencies. We look more at how DI is supported on the client side using the Guice library but build on an examination of the GIN library that can be used server side (and we discuss why it's different on the client and server sides).
- *Chapter 17* is the first of two chapters that look at manipulating code at compile time. Here we consider the deferred-binding approach to use different defined code implementations depending on particular values of properties. You create your own property and see how to generate the property provider that determines the property value.
- *Chapter 18* finishes our look at compile-time code manipulation started in the previous chapter by showing how generators can create new code that's then used in the compilation.
- *Chapter 19* introduces you to several tools related to finding and fixing performance-related issues. The chapter starts with a discussion of lightweight metrics, a tool that will allow you to capture performance information about your application, and then moves on to the compile report so that you can better understand the size of the JavaScript files generated by the GWT compiler. The

chapter then explains how you can use code splitting to break your application into smaller parts, leading to improved performance for your users.

Code conventions and downloads

The following typographical conventions are used throughout the book:

- `Courier` typeface is used in all code listings.
- `Courier` typeface is used within text for certain code words.
- *Italics* are used for emphasis and to introduce new terms.
- Code annotations are used in place of inline comments in the code. These highlight important concepts or areas of the code. Some annotations appear with numbered bullets like this ❶ that are referenced later in the text.

Source code for the examples in this book is available for download from the publisher's website at www.manning.com/GWTinActionSecondEdition.

Author Online

The purchase of *GWT in Action, Second Edition* includes free access to a private forum run by Manning Publications where you can make comments about the book, ask technical questions, and receive help from the authors and other users. You can access and subscribe to the forum at www.manning.com/GWTinActionSecondEdition. This page provides information on how to get on the forum once you're registered, what kind of help is available, and the rules of conduct in the forum.

Manning's commitment to our readers is to provide a venue where a meaningful dialogue among individual readers and between readers and authors can take place. It's not a commitment to any specific amount of participation on the part of the authors, whose contribution to the book's forum remains voluntary (and unpaid). We suggest you try asking the authors some challenging questions, lest their interest stray!

The Author Online forum and the archives of previous discussions will be accessible from the publisher's website as long as the book is in print.

About the title

By combining introductions, overviews, and how-to examples, the *In Action* books are designed to help learning and remembering. According to research in cognitive science, the things people remember are things they discover during self-motivated exploration.

Although no one at Manning is a cognitive scientist, we are convinced that for learning to become permanent, it must pass through stages of exploration, play, and, interestingly, retelling of what is being learned. People understand and remember new things, which is to say they master them, only after actively exploring them. Humans learn in action. An essential part of an *In Action* book is that it is example driven. It encourages the reader to try things out, to play with new code, and to explore new ideas.

There is another, more mundane reason for the title of this book: Our readers are busy. They use books to do a job or solve a problem. They need books that allow them to jump in and jump out easily and learn just what they want, just when they want it. They need books that aid them in action. The books in this series are designed for such readers.

About the authors

ADAM TACY is a digital channels client service manager for CGI based out of the Nordics with over 14 years experience in IT. He coauthored the first edition of *GWT in Action* with Robert Hanson in 2007 and has particular interest in how GWT 2.5 reduces the costs (development, maintenance, and management) of complex web projects while allowing the complexity boundaries of such applications to be aggressively challenged.

ROBERT HANSON is the applications development manager for Quality Technology Services and has spent over 15 years developing high-performance web applications. He released the first open source library of GWT tools and widgets in 2006 and coauthored the first edition of *GWT in Action*. Robert is also a member of the planning committee for the Philadelphia ETE conference, where he is a frequent speaker on GWT and other topics.

ANNA TÖKKE is a consultant for CGI Sweden with over 20 years of experience in IT development, the last 13 years as a lead programmer and solution architect. She educates developers in good programming practices and in object-oriented analysis and design. In recent years she has worked with GWT on a daily basis.

JASON ESSINGTON is a Java software engineer for Calypso Technology with over 12 years of experience in treasury and financial industries. He has been an advocate of GWT since its public release and is an active member of the GWT community, contributing to both the mailing list and the GWT IRC channel.

about the cover illustration

The figure on the cover of *GWT in Action, Second Edition* is captioned a "Janissary in Ceremonial Dress." Janissaries were an elite corps of soldiers in the service of the Ottoman Empire, loyal only to the Sultan. The illustration is taken from a collection of costumes of the Ottoman Empire published on January 1, 1802, by William Miller of Old Bond Street, London. The title page is missing from the collection, and we have been unable to track it down to date. The book's table of contents identifies the figures in both English and French, and each illustration bears the names of two artists who worked on it, both of whom would no doubt be surprised to find their art gracing the front cover of a computer programming book...200 years later.

The collection was purchased by a Manning editor at an antiquarian flea market in the "Garage" on West 26th Street in Manhattan. The seller was an American based in Ankara, Turkey, and the transaction took place just as he was packing up his stand for the day. The Manning editor did not have on his person the substantial amount of cash that was required for the purchase, and a credit card and check were both politely turned down. With the seller flying back to Ankara that evening, the situation was getting hopeless. What was the solution? It turned out to be nothing more than an old-fashioned verbal agreement sealed with a handshake. The seller simply proposed that the money be transferred to him by wire, and the editor walked out with the bank information on a piece of paper and the portfolio of images under his arm. Needless to say, we transferred the funds the next day, and we remain grateful and impressed by this unknown person's trust in one of us. It recalls something that might have happened a long time ago.

The pictures from the Ottoman collection, like the other illustrations that appear on our covers, bring to life the richness and variety of dress customs of two centuries ago. They recall the sense of isolation and distance of that period—and of every other historic period except our own hyperkinetic present. Dress codes have changed since then, and the diversity by region, so rich at the time, has faded away. It is now often hard to tell the inhabitant of one continent from another. Perhaps, trying to view it optimistically, we have traded a cultural and visual diversity for a more varied personal life. Or a more varied and interesting intellectual and technical life.

We at Manning celebrate the inventiveness, the initiative, and, yes, the fun of the computer business with book covers based on the rich diversity of regional life of two centuries ago, brought back to life by the pictures from this collection.

Part 1

Basics

In part 1 we introduce you to the Google Web Toolkit, providing an overview of the toolkit's contents. We then explore the typical two-step process you'd use to create a GWT application: using the tools to create a base application and then expanding it to create a real-world-complexity application. Along the way we'll look at development mode, where you'll spend a lot of time during production cycles, as well as how to compile for web mode, harnessing Google's built-in Closure compiler if you wish.

We suggest reading this part in chronological order, and if you're new to GWT, spend some time playing with the code download to get a better understanding—there's nothing that helps you gain knowledge more than making changes and resolving errors. We also include some suggestions at the end of chapters 2 and 3 on what you might want to do to the code, but you can easily invent your own enhancements.

1 GWT

This chapter covers

- Understanding GWT's place in the world
- Introducing some of GWT's more notable features
- Preparing your development environment

This book is about empowerment. If you're like 99% of us, you're sinking in the relentless waves of new tooling in what has become a vast ocean of web development. What you seek is a way to escape the churning waters and land on solid ground.

As the cover says, this is a book about the Google Web Toolkit, pronounced "gwit" by the cool kids at Google, and although GWT might not put you on the perfect tropical island it will get you out of the water and give you a dry place to rest your head for awhile.

But *what* is GWT? GWT isn't a "way," or a framework, or a language. It's a toolkit. It's a set of tools that provide the means to easily write sophisticated and reliable Ajax applications using Java. It's not meant to take advantage of the Java runtime, but instead it makes use of the Java language and existing Java tooling.

So what does this mean? Oversimplifying a bit, it means that you'll write your code in Java and then compile it to JavaScript. The obvious question is, why would you want to do that? The answers are numerous. One possible answer might be that the world contains many more skilled Java developers than seasoned JavaScript developers, but that isn't why GWT came to be. GWT was created in order to facilitate the development of large client-side browser applications with a focus on providing a great user experience, and its creators felt that the Java universe was a good fit to accomplish that goal.

But the ability to write your code in Java isn't the only reason to adopt GWT; it also comes with a lot of bling: things like a full widget set, flexible RPC support, built-in internationalization, a template language, obfuscation, minification, image bundling, integration with server-side persistence, and more. And beyond the bling GWT comes with all of the freebies, too. We aren't talking about T-shirts; we're talking about open source libraries like PlayN (http://code.google.com/p/playn/). PlayN is a gaming engine, the same one that Angry Birds Chrome uses.[1]

Many alternatives to GWT exist, so let's add one more reason to use it: maturity. GWT has been publicly available since 2006, and during the intervening years it has grown and stabilized. You might think this means GWT has become the old fart of web tooling, but that isn't the case. The latest version of GWT includes a lot of the HTML5 goodies, like client-side storage, canvas, audio, and video.[2] And for mobile developers GWT also supports touch events.

But enough talk; let's get into it and see what GWT can do for you. In this chapter we'll provide a high-level overview of all that is GWT and help you set up your development environment. Our overview will provide a glimpse into each tool in the toolkit and include references to sections or chapters in the book where we cover each tool in detail.

Our purpose in this chapter is to give you a better understanding of what GWT provides to have you ready to start coding in the next chapter. But let's begin with a brief history of browser application development to give you an understanding of where GWT fits in.

1.1 Unplanned consequences (or the road to GWT)

If you have kids, you know that sometimes things happen. But sometimes you need to roll with the changes because not even Google with its massive amounts of processing power can predict the future (yet?). And the web, as with most other things in our lives, evolved over time into what it is today. But how did we get here? Let's take a moment to reflect on the lineage of the modern web.

What we call "the web" got its start in the mid-1990s, but in computing time (and dog years) that's ancient history. What we need to do is look at more recent history. We'll fly our time machine past the invention of HTML, past the beginnings of CSS, beyond the browser wars,[3] and land at a place known as Mountain View on April Fools' Day 2004. That was the day Gmail was released to the public.[4]

---

1 Angry Birds Chrome is found at http://chrome.angrybirds.com/.

2 GWT's HTML5 support is documented at https://developers.google.com/web-toolkit/doc/latest/DevGuideHtml5.

3 History of the browser wars on Wikipedia: http://en.wikipedia.org/wiki/Browser_wars.

4 Many people thought Gmail was an April Fools' Day joke because it provided 1 gigabyte of storage for free, which was completely unheard of at that time.

Gmail developers didn't invent anything new; they used what was already available. In Gmail the development team made use of what's now referred to as XHR or XMLHttpRequest. XHR is an API created by Microsoft that allows JavaScript to run in the browser to initiate direct communication with the server. Gmail was designed to use this tool, which was available in all major browsers, to change the paradigm of how we interact with websites in a visual and forceful way.

In Gmail you could list the emails in your inbox, as you could with all email web clients, and then click an email to load it into the browser. But what would happen, which was different from traditional web applications, was that the contents of the email were loaded into the page without having to load an entirely new page. Gmail did this by using XHR to load the contents of the email in the background and then using Dynamic HTML (DHTML) to alter the contents of the page and insert the email's contents.

Gmail content still had to be loaded from the server, but this new paradigm did speed up things like page loading, because only new content had to be loaded, not the entire page. In addition, with some smart caching on the client side, you could cache already viewed content so you didn't need to reload it if you went back to that same email. If you haven't used Gmail, take a look at the current version, a full-featured email client on the web, as shown in figure 1.1.

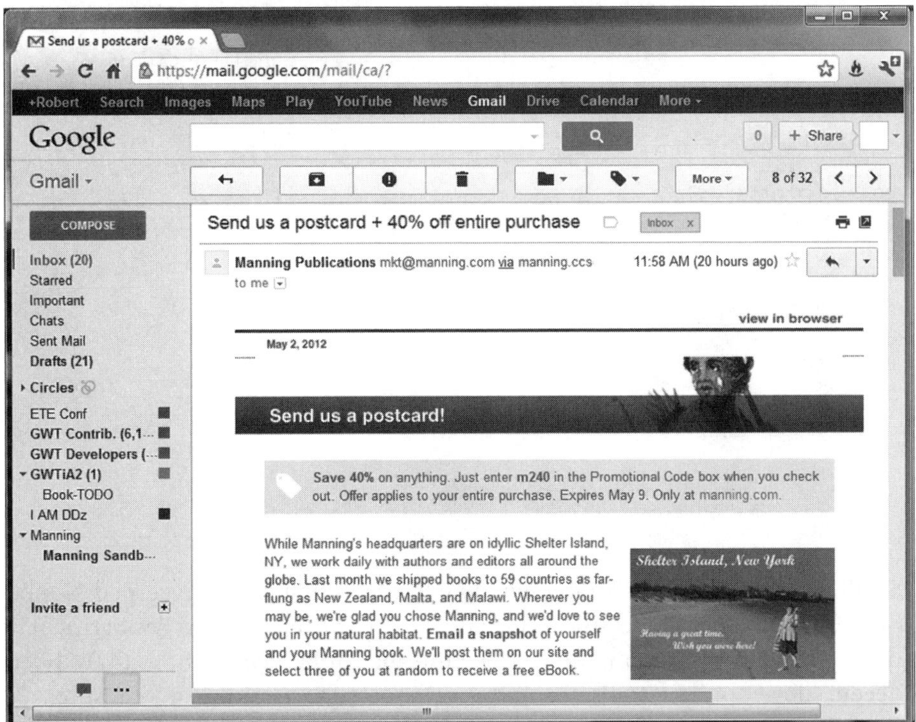

Figure 1.1 Gmail was launched on April 1, 2004, and was one of the early web applications to influence the new paradigm of web applications that work like a traditional desktop application.

These advancements were super innovative, but they were still hard for the average developer to wrangle, because each browser on the market implemented things a little differently, and using XHR wasn't exactly trivial.

But like all difficult development problems, the solution was to build an API and abstract away the hard parts. Lots of libraries hit the scene, like Prototype, jQuery, DWR, and others. These libraries all provided diversity to the process and allowed web developers to create some interesting web applications.

For example, take a look at table 1.1, where we compare using only JavaScript (on the left) to using jQuery (on the right). The jQuery example shows a substantial amount of code reduction.

Table 1.1 Comparing the use of plain-old JavaScript versus jQuery to make a call to the server using XHR. Which one do you think looks easier to read?

Using XHR with JavaScript only	Using XHR with jQuery

`var xhr;`
`if (window.XMLHttpRequest) {`
`  xhr = new XMLHttpRequest();`
`}`
`else if (window.ActiveXObject) {`
`  xhr =`
`    new ActiveXObject("Microsoft.XMLHTTP");`
`}`
 	
`xhr.onreadystatechange = function()`
`{`
`  if(xhr.readyState == 4) {`
`    if (xhr.status == 200)`
`      alert(msg);`
`    else`
`      alert("error!");`
`  }`
`};`
 	
`xhr.open("POST", "register.jsp", true);`
 	
`xhr.setRequestHeader("Content-Type",`
` "application/x-www-form-urlencoded");`
 	
`xhr.send("title=Dr.&name=Blackwood&"`
`  + "profession=surgeon");`
	`$.ajax({`
	`  type: "POST",`
	`  url: "register.jsp",`
	`  data: {`
	`   title: "Dr.",`
	`   name: "Blackwood",`
	`   profession: "surgeon"`
	`}})`
	`.done(function(msg) {`
	`  alert(msg);`
	`})`
	`.fail(function() {`
	`  alert("error");`
	`});`

So all is well, right? Not completely. The libraries that were developed helped in their own way, but all of them still required that you develop using JavaScript. That might not sound like a problem, but understand that only recently have there been halfway decent development tools for JavaScript, both for editing and testing. And even though we currently have some good tooling available, it can't compare to what the average Java developer has available to them.

No doubt you can see where we're going, but let's dig a little deeper. When GWT was first released, the JavaScript community created a lot of backlash. In general it seemed that the amount of hate developers had for GWT was inversely proportional to their love of JavaScript. At the time, both GWT's lovers and haters generated considerable public debate.

But that was then. As time passed, the web continued to evolve. Today many other tools like GWT exist, which allow you to use alternate languages for developing client-side applications: Pyjamas, Vaadin, ZK, Dart, CoffeeScript, Echo3, ClojureJS, and Script#, to name a few. Some of them run most of the code on the server (thin client), typically with lots of client and server communication, whereas others compile everything to be run in the browser (thick client). As you can see, GWT has plenty of company.

So why use GWT? As we mentioned in the beginning of this chapter, GWT is a toolkit that allows you to write code in Java, compiling everything to JavaScript to be run in the browser, without assistance from the server (a thick client). The toolkit includes a widget set and lots of tools to ease the development of massively rich and interactive applications. This last statement leads us into the next section, where we start to look at some of the details of these tools.

1.2 Exploring the toolkit

In this section we'll explore from the top down, starting with the GWT compiler, which is the most important and exciting part of what GWT has to offer. From there we'll introduce a few other key pieces that make the toolkit hum, including templates, events, remote server calls, internationalization, and more.

1.2.1 Compiling and optimizing

At the heart of the toolkit is the compiler, which takes your Java code and compiles it into JavaScript. During the process it will analyze your code in order to optimize it and remove any code that isn't reachable by your application. It then generates JavaScript code that's minified so that the file size is as small as possible. And this is only part of what the compiler does.

The compiler is a busy bee, and throughout this book we'll show you some of its secrets. One of these is a code *generator*, which generates Java source code for you in certain cases. The compiler may kick off one or more code generators based on what it finds in your code. This could be the generator that produces the code to serialize Java objects and send them to the server (chapter 7, "Communicating with GWT-RPC"), or it could be the generator that converts your templates into working code (chapter 6, "Interface design with UiBinder"). It could also be the generator that takes external files like CSS or images and optimizes them in a way that allows the browser to load them more quickly (chapter 5, "Using client bundles"). Or perhaps you'll create your own custom generator to fill a specific need (chapter 18, "Generators").

Figure 1.2 shows the work performed by the compiler, where the generators are kicked off near the beginning of the compilation process.

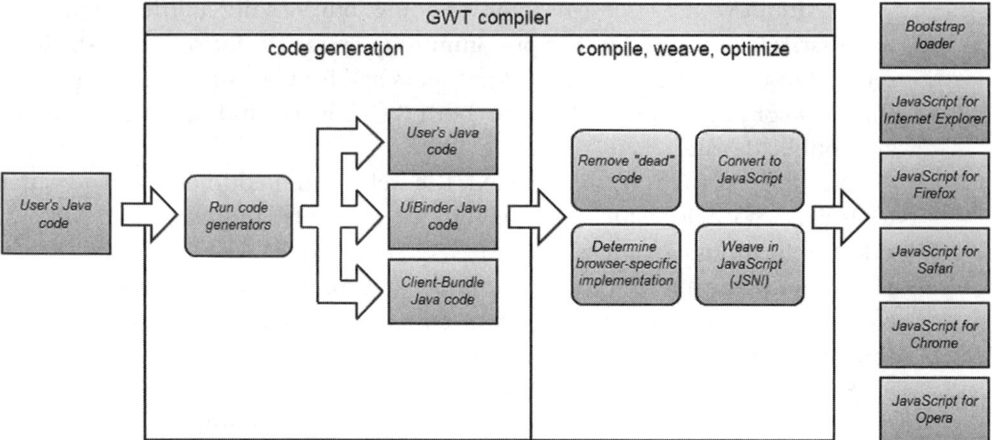

Figure 1.2 This is an artist's rendering of what the GWT compiler is responsible for. This figure doesn't cover everything the compiler does, but it does provide a high-level overview of how Java code (on the left) is compiled into JavaScript code.

Another cool feature of the compiler is the ability to weave your Java code with existing JavaScript code. The compiler does this via the use of the JavaScript Native Interface (JSNI), which allows you to embed JavaScript code within your Java classes in order to facilitate Java-to-JavaScript communication (chapter 11, "Using JSNI—JavaScript Native Interface"). It all ends up as JavaScript when the compiler weaves everything together.

But using JavaScript can be tricky because each browser has its own idiosyncrasies. That's where *deferred binding* comes in. Deferred binding allows you to create multiple implementations of the same functionality, perhaps one for Internet Explorer and one for all others. The compiler will generate multiple JavaScript output files, one for each browser (chapter 17, "Deferred binding").

With multiple JavaScript files for different browsers, the compilation process also generates a bootstrap loader. This loader is a JavaScript file that will run in your browser and load the correct application code file for that browser type.

As you can see, the compiler is the key to everything in GWT. But when someone looks at your application, they don't care about how you wrote the code; they care about what it looks like.

1.2.2 Powerful widgets and a template binding engine

In GWT the fundamental building block of the user interface is the `Widget`, and its subclasses come in all shapes and sizes. To group these widgets you use a specialized type of widget called a `Panel`, which is a widget that has the ability to contain other widgets, including other panels. Next is the `Composite`, which is a specialized widget that can hide its internal implementation from outside callers. These widgets will be covered throughout this book.

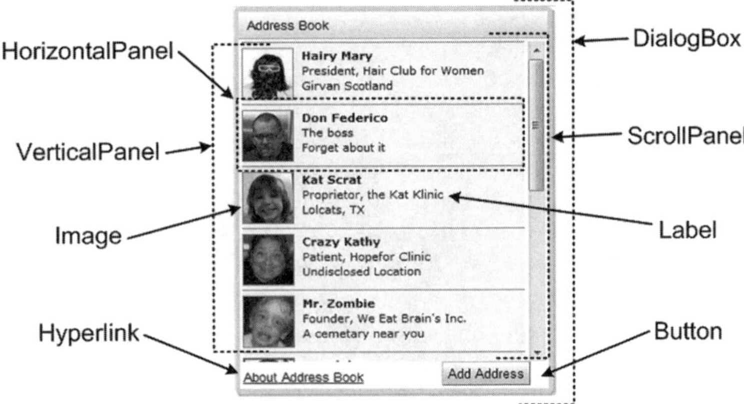

Figure 1.3 An example of a user-built `AddressBook` widget. It's made up of at least eight different types of widgets and dozens of instances. Some of the widgets are used for layout, like the `VerticalPanel`, and others will react based on user events, like the `Button`.

Together, widgets, panels, and composites allow you to piece together your user interface. GWT also provides a special class of widgets called data-presentation widgets (or `Cell` widgets) that are designed to make it easy to display data to the user in a series of pages, like a search result listing (chapter 10, "Data presentation (Cell) widgets"). These are designed to be fast, to conserve memory in the browser, and to make it easy for you as the developer to provide access to extremely large data sets.

But not all widgets are as full featured as the data-presentation widgets. Some are building blocks that you can use to build more complex widgets, like the `Image`, `Button`, and `Hyperlink` widgets. When you use GWT to build your interface, you'll combine basic widgets into complex composites and then reuse them (chapter 4, "Creating your own widgets"). Figure 1.3 shows a "simple" Address Book dialog box, but as you can see, it's far from simple and contains dozens of widget instances.

If you find that your custom-built composites are useful, you may even bundle them in a JAR file and share them with other GWT developers. Or perhaps you'll want to take advantage of the work of others and use third-party widget libraries in your own project. One popular library is the Google API Libraries for GWT,[5] which provides APIs for communicating with Google+, Google Calendar, Google Latitude, and other Google services. In addition you'll also find third-party libraries for drag and drop,[6] Google APIs (maps, search, and so on), dependency injection containers, additional widget libraries, and much more. If you want to see what else is available, you can go to code.google.com and search for "label:GWT."

---

[5] The Google API Libraries for GWT are located at http://code.google.com/p/gwt-google-apis/.

[6] The GWT Drag-and-Drop Libraries can be found at http://code.google.com/p/gwt-dnd/.

A word or two on drag and drop

Back in 2007 a smart guy named Fred Sauer created the gwt-dnd project (http://code.google.com/p/gwt-dnd/), making it trivial to add drag and drop to your GWT application. But since that time many browsers have included built-in support for drag and drop. As of version 2.5, GWT provides some built-in support for this, but at the time of this writing it isn't a replacement for the gwt-dnd library. First of all, it doesn't support all browsers (such as IE9 and Opera), and even when it does, issues have been reported. Because of this we've decided to not cover it in this book.

The bottom line is that if you do use the built-in support, you need to be cautious and thoroughly test the feature on all browsers that you need to support.

Returning to the example layout, one thing that initial versions of GWT taught the early adopters was that it's hard to build large interfaces with dozens and dozens of widgets. The amount of code required made it time-consuming to build an interface. This changed when a new tool was added to the toolkit called UiBinder (chapter 6), which allows you to define your interface in XML code that looks a lot like HTML. This is more compact than Java code, allowing you to define complex interfaces using markup instead of code.

Developing what your user sees is only part of the work involved in developing an interface; you need to handle user-driven events as well.

1.2.3 Event handling beyond JavaScript

At one end of the spectrum, GWT allows you to register for plain-old JavaScript events. This includes clicks on a button, focusing on a check box, and mouse movements over a widget. In GWT these are called *native* events.

On the other end are events that are specific to a particular widget. For example, when a user clicks a date in the `DatePicker` widget, it fires a `ValueChangeEvent`. These events are called *logical* events. As you develop more advanced widgets you'll create your own logical events (chapter 14, "Advanced event handling and event busses").

In addition, GWT provides a tool called the `HandlerManager`, which you can use as an event bus. An *event bus* is a messaging channel where an event producer sends an event, and any number of event listeners can receive the event and act on it. The important distinction between an event bus and basic event handling is that with an event bus the event producer and recipient don't know about each other; they only know about the message channel. This is a popular pattern that allows you to develop an architecture where components are loosely coupled.

An event bus works similarly to Internet Relay Chat (IRC), where you send a message to the channel and everyone else connected to the channel will see your message. Figure 1.4 shows how the event bus works using the paradigm of pipes to illustrate how producers and recipients know about the pipe (message bus), but not each other.

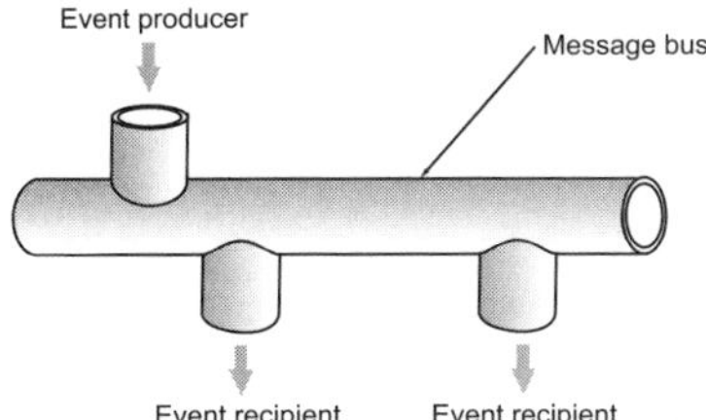

Figure 1.4 An event bus is like a messaging channel or a pipe. A producer puts an event onto the bus, and any number of recipients can handle it. Producers and recipients are decoupled from each other because they connect to the message bus and not to each other.

Speaking of communication, one type of communication that's vital to most GWT applications is the ability to pass data to and from the web server.

1.2.4 *Client/server communication*

In a perfect Java-centric world you'd be able to use Java on the server, use Java to write your GWT-based application, and pass Java objects between the browser and the server. This is where GWT-RPC fits in (chapter 7). It provides the tooling required to handle the serialization and transmission of Java objects to and from the server, even though the client-side code in this is JavaScript.

This can be a relatively difficult problem given the mismatch in languages. On the server this isn't so hard because of Java's reflection capabilities. On the server the application can inspect the Java object to determine its field types and values. In the browser this isn't possible; reflection won't work.

In order to solve this problem, GWT-RPC uses a code generator, as mentioned in section 1.2.1. This allows GWT to generate all of the serialization and communication code at compile time. But still, it isn't a magical process, and you'll need to use some annotations to help the code generator determine what to do. We'll cover all of that in great detail in chapter 7.

But for those of you interested in communicating with the server Ajax style, GWT can do that, too. The tool for that job is `RequestBuilder`, and it allows you to send `GET` and `POST` requests to the server (chapter 12, "Classic Ajax and HTML forms").

`RequestBuilder` alone isn't particularly useful when you consider that most remote services send either JSON,[7] JSON with Padding (JSONP), or XML[8] data. To allow the use of these formats, GWT provides an API for reading and writing JSON data and an XML parser for reading XML. We'll cover both of these APIs in the `RequestBuilder` chapter and provide an example of using JSONP with Picasa in chapter 11, where we discuss the JavaScript Native Interface.

Figure 1.5 shows a graphical representation of the separation of the client application, the various languages that you might use on the server, and the various types of communication for which GWT provides support.

---

7 The JavaScript Object Notation (JSON) specification can be found at www.json.org/.

8 The Extensible Markup Language (XML) introduction and specification can be found at www.w3.org/XML/.

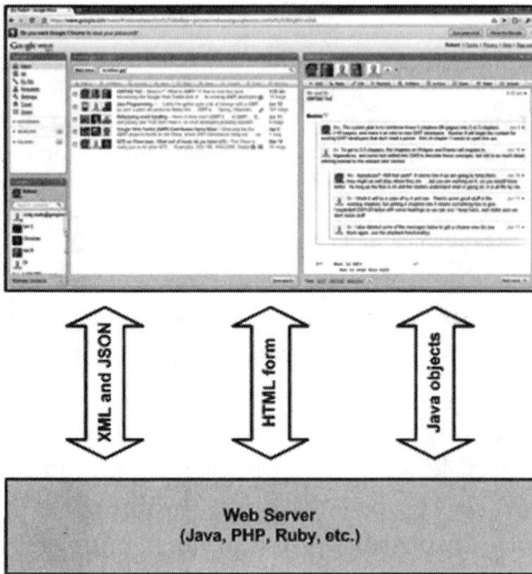

Figure 1.5 GWT provides a number of tools for passing data between the server and browser. This includes Ajax-style communication for passing XML and JSON data, HTML forms for form data, and GWT-RPC for passing serialized Java objects.

GWT also has support for the original client/server communication tool that the browser uses, the HTML form (chapter 12). But we should highlight some differences on how GWT handles form submissions. For example, in a standard form submission the page in the browser changes. In GWT we don't usually want to load another page into the browser, and GWT provides a way to do this. We'll cover all of this when we discuss forms.

At this point we hope you'll agree that GWT provides some serious tools for developing a rich user interface. But there's more to it than that. GWT also provides you, the developer, with the tools you need to develop your application rapidly.

1.2.5 Simplified development and debugging

When you're doing traditional Java development, some things are less than optimal. When you modify the code for a servlet (Spring Controller, Struts Action, and the like) you need to recompile your code, deploy it to a server, and then start the server. That can take a lot of time, depending on what you're doing.

Now think about how you might test a change in GWT. You need to compile your client-side code to JavaScript, compile your server-side Java code, deploy all of it to a server, and start the server.

Besides testing being a slow prospect, how might you handle debugging an application that lives as Java on the server and as JavaScript in the browser? How do you debug clicks to the user interface and remote calls to the server?

To solve this problem, GWT has a closely related project named the Google Plugin for Eclipse. This tool provides support for GWT as well as support for the Google App Engine.[9] For GWT the plug-in provides wizards, single-click compiling,

---

9 Google App Engine can be found at http://code.google.com/appengine/.

autocompletion support, and one-click access to development mode, where you can test your application without deploying it to an external server.

If you're a fan of an Integrated Development Environment (IDE) that competes with Eclipse, we understand how you might not be excited by this news. And although you can develop GWT code using any IDE (or no IDE at all), we strongly recommend that, until you get your feet wet with GWT, you use Eclipse. In section 1.3 we'll cover installing both Eclipse and the Google Plugin for Eclipse, and in chapter 2 ("Building a GWT application: saying "Hello World!"), we'll show you how to use it.

We mentioned that the Google Plugin for Eclipse provides autocompletion support. One area where it provides that support is when you're writing code to bridge the gap between Java and JavaScript.

1.2.6 Integration with JavaScript

For the most part you can write your GWT applications using only Java, but you'll always have exceptions to the rule. One example would be when you're starting the move to GWT and you have hundreds or thousands of lines of JavaScript code that you want to reuse. Or perhaps you need to access some new JavaScript API that GWT doesn't directly support yet. Or maybe you need to use a third-party JavaScript API. GWT supports all of these use cases with the JavaScript Native Interface, also known as JSNI (chapter 11).

JSNI works by allowing you to embed JavaScript code right inside your Java code through the use of a Java comment block, along with the `native` Java keyword. The purpose of the `native` keyword in Java is to denote that a method is implemented in another language like C, C++, or even assembly. And although GWT isn't using the keyword in the way that its creators envisioned, it's a creative solution to our needs.

Even without any background knowledge of JSNI, this example should be easy to follow. It prints a specified message a precise number of times in the browser.

Listing 1.1 An example of a JSNI method

```
public native String printMessageTimes (String msg, int times)    <- Java signature
/*-{
    for (x = 1; x <= times; x++) {                                 JavaScript body
        var prefix = '#' + x + ' - ';
        $doc.write(prefix + msg + '<br />');
    }
}-*/;
```

If you look closely, you can see that in the previous code the method is inside a Java comment block. And to prove that it's JavaScript, the example code fails to declare the variable `x`, uses `var` to declare the variable `prefix`, and uses single quotes around string constants. The only thing that isn't standard JavaScript is the `$doc` variable, which is an alias GWT uses to represent the JavaScript `document` object.

In the Java IDE this code is ignored because the code has been hidden in a Java comment, and by declaring the method as native the IDE doesn't expect a method body. But although this code may be hidden to the standard Java compiler, the GWT compiler will extract this JavaScript code and weave it into the final output.

But this is only part of what you'll want to know about JSNI. Besides being able to call JavaScript code from Java, you can also call your Java code from JavaScript. In addition, GWT has a feature called JavaScript Overlay Types, which allows you to wrap a JavaScript object in a Java class. Because JSNI is a complex topic, we've dedicated a whole chapter to explaining it all.

At this point you can see that GWT isn't about only widgets and provides a full solution to building rich user interfaces. One such feature GWT provides is a solution to the broken Back button.

1.2.7 History support

When Ajax was conceived in 2005,[10] one thing it did was to break the Back button. What this means is that typical browser users are accustomed to the idea of using the Back button in the browser to go back to the last page they were viewing. Ajax has the convention of not changing the page you're looking at, and instead it manipulates the page with JavaScript to alter its contents.

When typical browser users employed one of these Ajax applications and clicked the Back button, because that was the natural thing for them to do, they were surprised to not be directed to the last thing they were looking at within the Ajax application. Instead they were directed to what they were looking at before they came to the Ajax application.

This isn't a new problem, but it became noticeable in 2005 when many developers rushed to deploy Ajax applications. That's why, with its release in 2006, GWT came with history support built in (chapter 3, "Building a GWT application: enhancing Hello World").

GWT's solution isn't new and is simple when you think about it. GWT uses a hidden HTML iFrame, and each time you go to another "page" in your application, it changes the URL of the hidden frame. Your browser considers this URL change as you going to another page and adds it to your browsing history. So when you click the Back button in your browser, all you're doing is changing the URL of the hidden frame to the last URL it had in the history. This in turn triggers an event in your application that you can handle.

It's far from automatic, but with proper deployment you can allow your users to use the browser's Forward and Back buttons to navigate through your GWT application. In chapter 3 we provide everything you need to know to use this feature.

Another feature that makes GWT a complete solution is its support for internationalization.

---

[10] Ajax is an acronym for Asynchronous JavaScript and XML, coined by Jesse James Garret in his essay "Ajax: A New Approach to Web Applications"; www.adaptivepath.com/ideas/essays/archives/000385.php.

1.2.8 Internationalization—Sprechen sie Deutsch?

GWT doesn't provide any translation capabilities, but it does provide a framework where you can deploy your application in any number of languages (chapter 13, "Internationalization, localization, and accessibility"). In Java the typical way this is handled in a web application is to have the web framework you're using detect the language requested by the browser and use a properties file with messages specific to that language.

This works great on the server but has some failings when you try to do this for a browser application. For example, if you want to support 10 languages, your application now needs to hold 10 translations of every phrase used in the application. This means a larger download and slower application startup for the user.

GWT's approach is to handle this the same way it handles the multiple browser-specific implementations of the same Java code, which we discussed in section 1.2.1. And that is to generate a separate JavaScript file for each language. Doing this allows you to support 1 language, or 100, with no output file size penalty.

In figure 1.6 you can see the `DatePicker` widget, which makes use of GWT's internationalization tooling to provide different views for the same month based on the locale. This not only includes the month and weekday names but also extends to the day the week starts on (for example, Sunday versus Monday).

And you mustn't forget that supporting different locales is more than simply translating text. You must accommodate the fact that not all languages are written left to right and are instead written right to left, like Arabic. Many of GWT's widgets and panels provide built-in support for this, like the `TextBox` and `HorizontalPanel`. So regardless of your internationalization (i18n) needs, GWT should be able to provide it out of the box.

> **DEFINITION** The word *internationalization* is long, weighing in at 20 letters. Imagine getting in trouble at school and having to write that on the board 100 times. At some point someone decided that it needed to be shortened a bit. The term *i18n* is a numeronym, or a number-based word. The term *i18n* literally means the letter *i*, plus 18 other letters, plus *n*.

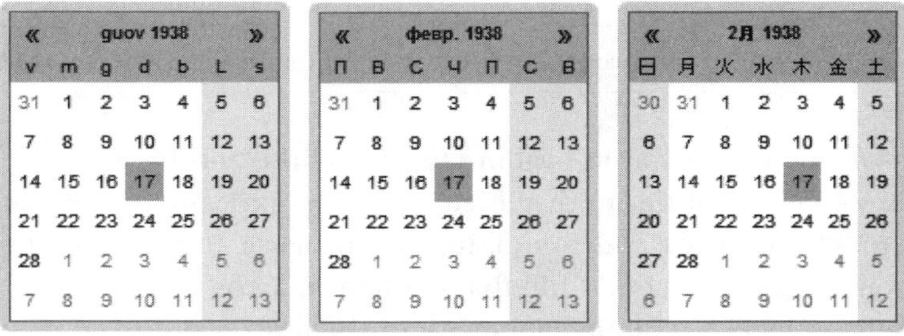

Figure 1.6 GWT's `DatePicker` widget, using three different locale settings. From left to right are calendars for Northern Sami, Russia, and Japan.

With that we wrap up the whirlwind tour of GWT. As you can see, GWT is a robust toolkit, and new features will be added over time. Let's switch gears now and prepare to do some coding (which you'll begin to do in the next chapter). In order to do that you first need to set up your development environment.

1.3 Setting up your development environment

We understand that everyone is different, with different needs and affinities, but unfortunately, we can't cover every IDE or "way" to work with GWT. In this book we'll use the tools that are at the time of this writing the best fit for use with GWT. If you're new to GWT we strongly suggest that you follow our lead and use the tools we recommend. As you gain proficiency in GWT, you'll find it's much easier to use other tooling that we don't cover in this book.

For this book the "way" is to use the Eclipse IDE along with the Google Plugin for Eclipse, which provides many wizards as well as code completion for GWT-specific files. And best of all they're both free.

In addition to Eclipse and the mentioned plug-in you'll need to install the Java JDK as well as the Development Mode Browser Plugin. In this section we'll walk you through installing these tools, providing you with a good development environment for working with GWT.

Table 1.2 is a summary of the tools you'll install in this chapter.

Table 1.2 Development tools for use with Eclipse and the Google Plugin for Eclipse

Tool	Download site
Java Development Kit (JDK)	Windows / Linux / Mac OS X / Solaris: www.oracle.com/technetwork/java/javase/downloads/index.html
Eclipse IDE	www.eclipse.org/downloads Recommended version: Eclipse IDE for Java EE Developers
Google Plugin for Eclipse	http://code.google.com/eclipse/docs/download.html
GWT SDK	http://code.google.com/webtoolkit/download.html Can also be installed via the Google Plugin for Eclipse update site
Development Mode Browser Plugin	http://gwt.google.com/missing-plugin/MissingPlugin.html Allows you to run GWT in development mode with your browser

If for some reason you can't or aren't willing to use Eclipse and the mentioned plugins, your journey will be a little more difficult but not impossible. GWT provides a command-line tool for creating and compiling GWT projects. In addition, the project-creation tool generates an Ant build file that contains macros for compiling, testing, and packing your project. A modified summary of the tools you'll need if you follow that path is shown in table 1.3.

Table 1.3 Development tools for use with non-Eclipse environments

Tool	Download site
Java Development Kit (JDK)	Windows / Linux / Mac OS X / Solaris: www.oracle.com/technetwork/java/javase/downloads/index.html
GWT SDK	http://code.google.com/webtoolkit/download.html
Apache Ant	http://ant.apache.org/bindownload.cgi Used for compiling and launching development mode when not supported by the IDE
An IDE	Optional
Development Mode Browser Plugin	http://gwt.google.com/missing-plugin/MissingPlugin.html Allows you to run GWT in development mode with your browser

In addition to the core development tools that you'll need to work with GWT, you might want to include other useful tools in your environment, some of which we make reference to throughout this book. Perhaps it's best for you to install these after you have a working GWT environment, so we present them merely as a reference in table 1.4.

Table 1.4 Optional development tools

Tool	Download site
GWT Designer	http://code.google.com/webtoolkit/tools/download-gwtdesigner.html A visual design tool for building GWT applications
Speed Tracer	http://code.google.com/webtoolkit/download.html A diagnostic plug-in for Chrome
Firebug	http://getfirebug.com/ A diagnostic plug-in for Firefox
Firebug Lite	http://getfirebug.com/firebuglite A diagnostic tool for non-Firefox browsers
Gwt4nb	https://github.com/gwt4nb/gwt4nb A NetBeans GWT plug-in
Maven	http://maven.apache.org/ A build-management tool, often used in place of Ant (When using Maven with GWT it's recommended to use the GWT Maven Plugin: http://mojo.codehaus.org/gwt-maven-plugin/.)
Spring Roo	www.springsource.org/roo A code-generation tool that includes support for GWT
SpringSource Tool Suite	www.springsource.com/products/sts An Eclipse-based IDE with built-in support for Spring and Roo

We hope a lot of these tools will look familiar, and if not, we recommend that you explore what they have to offer. So without delay, let's run through the detailed installation of the recommended environment. We begin with the Java Development Kit.

1.3.1 Installing the JDK

The first thing you'll need is the latest version of Java. We've made the assumption that our readers know the basics of Java, so it's likely that you already have the JDK installed. For developing with GWT we suggest using the latest version of Java, although GWT is currently compatible as far back as Java 5. The JDK for Windows, Linux, and Mac OS X can be downloaded from www.oracle.com/technetwork/java/javase/downloads.

If you already have Java installed, you should verify that you have the JDK installed. This differs from the Java Runtime Environment (JRE) in that it includes tools for compiling Java code. This isn't strictly needed for compiling GWT applications because the GWT compiler will handle that, but it will be required if you plan on using Java on the server side of RPC calls, which we discuss in chapter 7.

If you're unsure what you have, open a command prompt and run the command `javac -version`. If you don't find `javac`, then you don't have the JDK installed, or it's not on your path. If you do have `javac`, it will let you know what version you have with output that looks like the following:

```
C:\>javac -version
javac 1.7.0_05
```

If you have the JDK installed but it isn't in your path, you may want to consider adding it. In particular, if you plan on using an IDE other than Eclipse, you'll need to run command-line tools, and these tools will expect the `java` command in your path.

Next, you'll need to install Eclipse.

1.3.2 Installing Eclipse

Eclipse is an open source IDE with support for Java, PHP, C++, and many other languages. In addition it has a rich plug-in ecosystem, including a wide range of tools useful for web developers.

You can download Eclipse from www.eclipse.org/downloads/. Several packages for Eclipse are available. Each comes with the core Eclipse workbench, along with a set of plug-ins that are typically appropriate for a specific kind of developer. You can use any of these, but we suggest installing the Eclipse IDE for Java EE Developers, which has a good assortment of tools for Java developers.

Installing Eclipse couldn't be easier: uncompress the distribution, and place the directory somewhere on your hard drive. There's no installation, and if you're running Eclipse on Windows it won't alter your registry file. If you have problems downloading or uncompressing the distribution, consult the Eclipse installation guide for help, located at http://wiki.eclipse.org/FAQ_Where_do_I_get_and_install_Eclipse%3F.

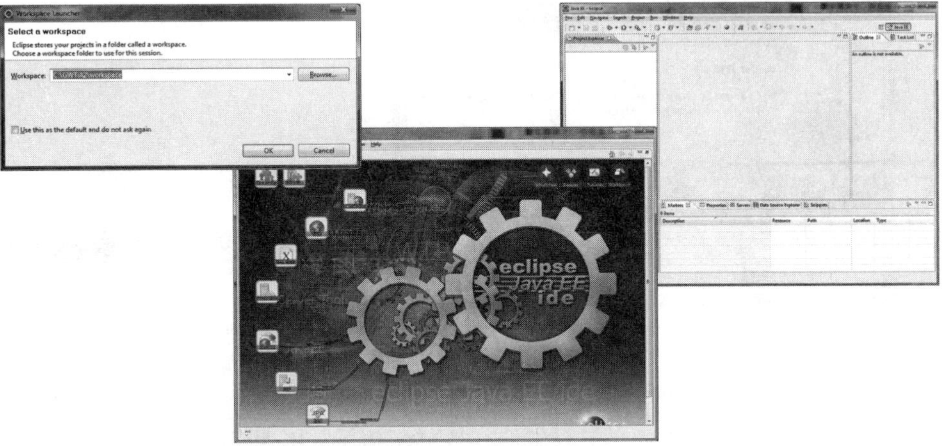

Figure 1.7 When you run Eclipse for the first time, it will ask you for the location to store your projects (left), also known as your workspace. After selecting a location you'll see a Welcome screen that contains Eclipse documentation (center). Closing the Welcome tab will bring you to the editor (right).

When it's downloaded and uncompressed, you should run the Eclipse executable to verify that it's working properly. On startup it will ask you the location of your workspace, as shown in figure 1.7. This is a directory where Eclipse will store configuration information and is usually where you'll store your projects. Select a suitable empty directory when prompted. This will bring you to the Welcome screen.

Once you're at the Welcome screen, you may want to explore some of the documentation provided, or you can close the Welcome tab to go to the editor.

When you've made your way to the editor, you can work on installing the Google Plugin for Eclipse.

1.3.3 *Installing the Google Plugin for Eclipse*

When you install plug-ins for Eclipse, you use the Install New Software tool. In Eclipse you'll find this wizard under the Help menu. In this section we'll walk you through how to use this tool.

The first step is to find the location of the update site. An update site is a URL to a web server that's providing the Eclipse plug-in. The Google Plugin for Eclipse has different update site URLs depending on which version of Eclipse you're running. You'll need to visit the Google Plugin for Eclipse website, located at http://code.google.com/eclipse/docs/download.html, to find the appropriate URL.

The download page will list different update URLs for different versions of Eclipse. The easiest way to know which version of Eclipse you're running is to look at the splash screen when you start Eclipse, which will display the version name.

If you're unable to determine the version from the splash screen, which could happen if you're using a distribution of Eclipse from another vendor (for example, the SpringSource Tool Suite), you'll need to find it in the Help menu. To find the version

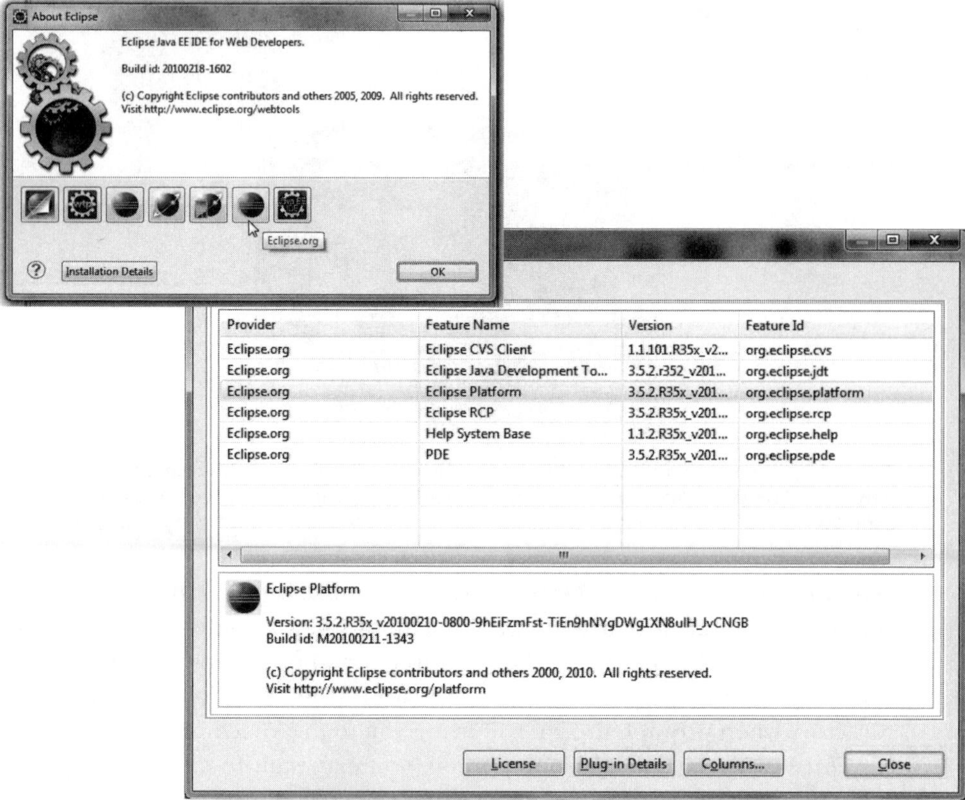

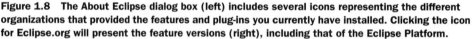

Figure 1.8 The About Eclipse dialog box (left) includes several icons representing the different organizations that provided the features and plug-ins you currently have installed. Clicking the icon for Eclipse.org will present the feature versions (right), including that of the Eclipse Platform.

of Eclipse, or the version of any installed plug-in, you choose Help > About on the menu bar. On the About screen there will be several buttons, as shown in figure 1.8. You'll want to click the button that has the tooltip "Eclipse.org." Clicking this will bring up the versions of the individual features. The feature version you're interested in is the Eclipse Platform.

Once you've determined the version of Eclipse you're running and the URL of the update site for your version, you can install the Google Plugin. In Eclipse click Help > Install New Software. This brings up the Install dialog, as shown in figure 1.9.

In the Install dialog you can click the Add button, which will bring up the Add Site dialog. In this dialog you should supply "Google Eclipse Plugin" for the Name field and the update site URL for the Location field. Click OK when you're finished.

This should bring you back to the Install dialog, which will now provide a list of plug-ins that you can install, as shown in figure 1.10.

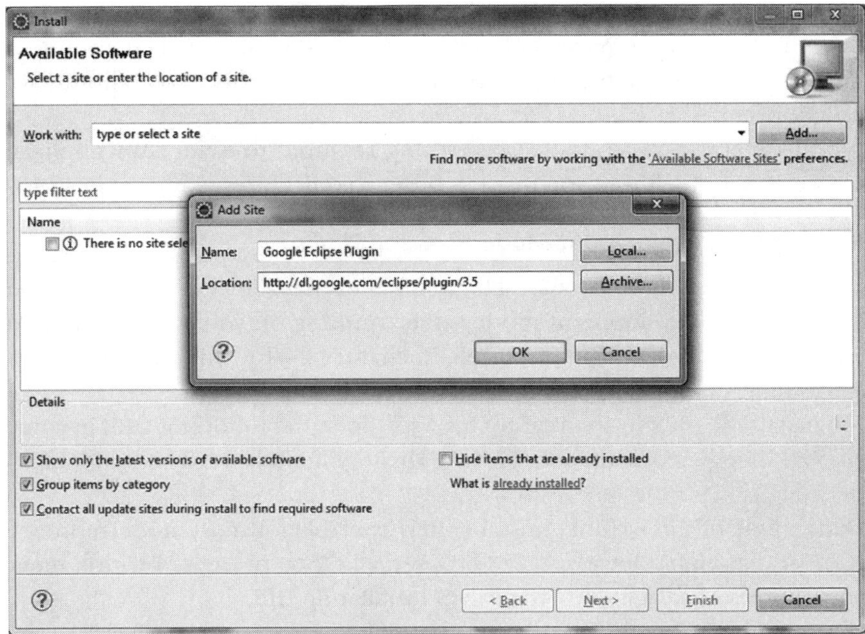

Figure 1.9 The Eclipse Add Site dialog is used to add a new URL to Eclipse where plug-ins can be downloaded. The Add Site dialog is displayed by clicking the Add button in the Install dialog, which is shown in the background.

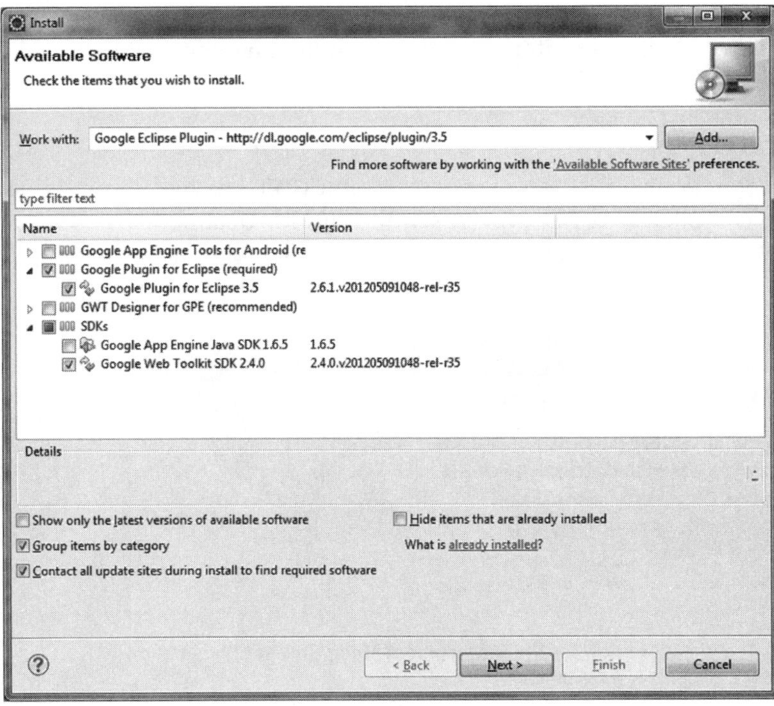

Figure 1.10 Once you add the update site for the Google Plugin for Eclipse, it will present you with a list of software available for installation.

You'll want to select the options for the Google Plugin for Eclipse and the Google Web Toolkit SDK; then click Next. Follow the instructions provided to continue the process. Once you complete the process, it will ask you to restart Eclipse to finish the installation.

At this point you've installed everything required to write GWT applications, but you have one tool left that you need in order to quickly test your application.

1.3.4 Installing the Development Mode Browser Plugin

The Development Mode Browser Plugin is a tool that allows your web browser to communicate with a development mode server running on your workstation. We'll show you how to launch development mode in chapter 2—for this chapter we'll only show you how to install the plug-in.

To install the plug-in for a target browser, open the following URL in your browser: http://gwt.google.com/missing-plugin/MissingPlugin.html. This will look like figure 1.11.

At the time of this writing, this plug-in is available for most modern browsers. If the plug-in isn't available for a specific browser, you'll be presented with a message indicating where you navigate to the plug-in installation URL.

Before moving on we should point out that if you ever try to view your application as it's running in development mode, you'll be presented with this same installation dialog.

At this point you've finished with the setup of your environment. You have Eclipse, the GWT SDK, the Google Plugin for Eclipse, and the Development Mode Browser Plug-in installed. Let's recap everything we covered in this chapter and discuss where we go from here.

1.4 Summary

In this chapter we provided an overview of what GWT has to offer, ranging from an optimizing compiler, to a rich widget set, to tools for dealing with popular data formats like JSON and XML, to communicating with the server and managing history.

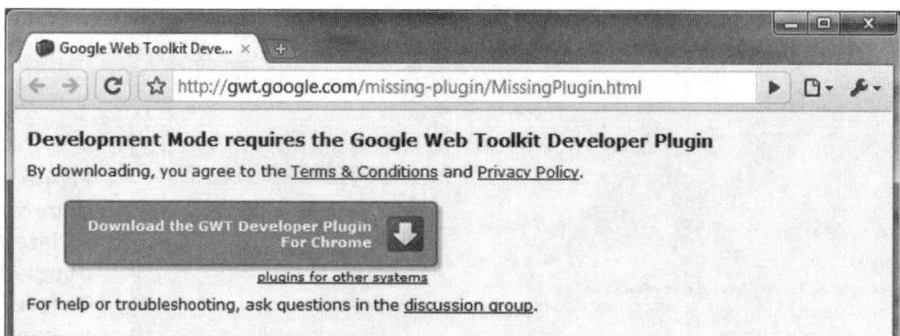

Figure 1.11 The dialog window for the Development Mode Browser Plugin allows you to install the plug-in for your browser.

Tools are great, but the takeaway we want you to have from this chapter is that GWT is more than a tool for writing JavaScript applications in Java. GWT is a platform with which you can build extraordinary, complex applications that run in the browser without any proprietary plug-ins.

But this isn't anything new. The truth of the matter is that browsers have had support for Dynamic HTML and making remote calls for a decade, yet we see few large browser-based applications outside of those coming from Microsoft, Google, and Yahoo!. The reason is that writing large applications in JavaScript is difficult and complex. This is the primary reason for the adoption of GWT.

Developers who write desktop applications have for a long time had great tool support. They have had the ability to design layouts using a visual designer, support for working with databases, and structural tools like those that facilitate dependency injection. GWT might not provide all of this quite yet, but it's a major step forward for the web developer.

GWT is currently limited by the limits of JavaScript in the browser, and if you haven't been watching, HTML5 is adding loads of new tools to facilitate richer JavaScript applications. Many browsers now support the new canvas tag for bitmap drawing, some support built-in databases, some support offline JavaScript application caching, and some even support dragging files right into the browser for file uploads. If you aren't a Gmail user (or didn't notice), you can now drag files into the browser in order to attach them to an email, as long as you're using a browser that supports that functionality.

At the time of this writing, GWT provides support for some of these new HTML5 features (offline storage, canvas, audio, video), and you can expect additional support to be added in the future. And that's another feature of GWT: a dedicated development team that continually advances the product to match advances in the web. This makes GWT a good bet for the future. And given that GWT is also open source with the extremely liberal Apache 2 license, it's an even better bet.

We don't mean to sound like cheerleaders, but GWT excites us as web developers and is why we wrote this book. RAH, RAH, GWT!

Now that you have a good understanding of what GWT provides and a development environment that you can use to develop GWT applications, we can proceed to building GWT applications. In chapter 2 you'll immediately put your development environment to work by creating a GWT application and walking through what a GWT project looks like.

2 Building a GWT application: saying “Hello World!”

This chapter covers

- Understanding GWT terminology
- Using the Google Plugin for Eclipse
- Running an application in development mode
- Compiling an application for production
- Exploring common debugging techniques

Following directly from chapter 1, we’ll now put the development tools and plug-ins you installed to use. In the next two chapters you’ll create and run the GWT application shown in the mock-up in figure 2.1.

Figure 2.1 shows a fairly simple application with a logo, a tabbed panel with some content, a search button, and a slide-in feedback tab. Although simple, it’s typical of a common web application, and it will allow you to see the use of widgets, panels, events, styling, adding items to the browser page, and managing history (clicking the browser’s Back and Forward buttons) in action. Don’t worry if those terms mean nothing to you now; by the end of chapter 3 it will all be second nature.

We’ll also show how a typical GWT application is developed in two steps:

1. Use some tools to create a basic framework GWT application.
2. Enhance the framework GWT application to become the application you want.

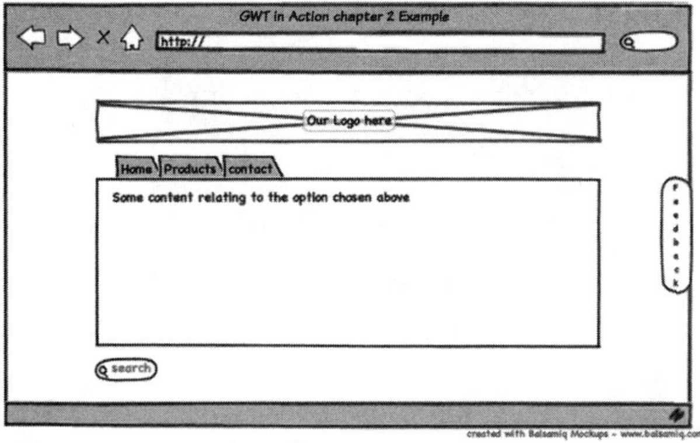

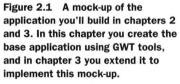

Figure 2.1 A mock-up of the application you'll build in chapters 2 and 3. In this chapter you create the base application using GWT tools, and in chapter 3 you extend it to implement this mock-up.

This chapter covers step 1, and we'll go through the process of creating a simple `HelloWorld` application using some of the wizards from the Google Plugin for Eclipse (GPE). The resulting application is the simplest GWT application that can be built that places some text on a web page. You'll use this to explore the wizards, understand some GWT terminology, get familiar with application code layout and the files involved, and learn how to run and debug the application in Eclipse as well as compile it to JavaScript—the basics of GWT development.

Chapter 3 covers step 2, but rather than take the steps together we'll present a brand-new application, `BasicProject`, and examine the changes that allow it to have the functionality of figure 2.1. `BasicProject` will allow us to examine functionality such as web page (DOM) manipulation, widgets and panels, event handling, history management, and styling—typical techniques in a nontrivial GWT application.

Unusually, we'll hold off discussing client/server interaction until chapters 7, 8, 9, and 12—because GWT gives you a number of approaches and we want to demonstrate these useful client-side techniques, such as client bundles and declarative UI (UiBinder) first.

You could download the results of this chapter from our book's download site, but we recommend instead that you take the steps with us to get some hands-on experience in creating a basic GWT application. The example is available for download in case you decide to experiment with what we're doing along the way and you want a reference to refer to.

When you look at the code you'll create, you may think this simple hello world example contains a lot of overhead—after all, you can do the same in JavaScript with a few lines of code. This is true, but GWT is designed to support pushing the boundary of web applications and user experience, as you'll see from chapter 4 onward. This quality in GWT makes the overhead fade into insignificance because of the benefits of simpler team development, industrial-strength concepts, and reduced and simplified maintenance.

> **Places to get help**
>
> If you do run into problems, don't forget you have a number of places where you can go for help:
>
> The GWT Discussion Group:
>
> http://mng.bz/3a44
>
> The GWT Issue List (to see if someone else is having a similar issue, or if a solution exists):
>
> http://mng.bz/8Kyj
>
> The *GWT in Action* forum:
>
> www.manning-sandbox.com/forum.jspa?forumID=659
>
> If you're a little more technical or interested in what the future holds for GWT, we also recommend the GWT Contributor's Group: http://mng.bz/2BW1

One exercise you might like to do is to take your results from this chapter and expand them to have the functionality of `BasicProject` or whatever functionality you wish by adding your own widgets, panels, or event handling, or altering the styling.

It's almost time to get into the action and create your first GWT application, but before you do that we want to briefly discuss what we mean by a GWT application—it will be good to know what it is from a user's and developer's perspective—and the different ways you can create one (and why we're going to use the Google Plugin for Eclipse).

2.1 What's a GWT application?

We'll try to describe a typical GWT application. We'll highlight the key aspects in this chapter and then expand on them throughout the book. To do this, we'll consider the application from the user's view next; later we'll cover it from the developer's perspective.

2.1.1 Seeing the user's view

The user runs your application by requesting its start web page (which is usually an HTML page but could be a JSP, or a PHP, or whatever). Figure 2.2 shows what happens when a user requests a GWT application's web page.

First, the user enters the URL of your application, which triggers the browser to request the application's HTML file. The HTML downloads a specifically named nocache.js file—the so-called *bootstrap file*. The bootstrap code determines which specific permutation of your application in JavaScript is required and then requests it. When the permutation is loaded, the bootstrap calls the compiled `onModuleLoad` method from the `EntryPoint` and the application starts.

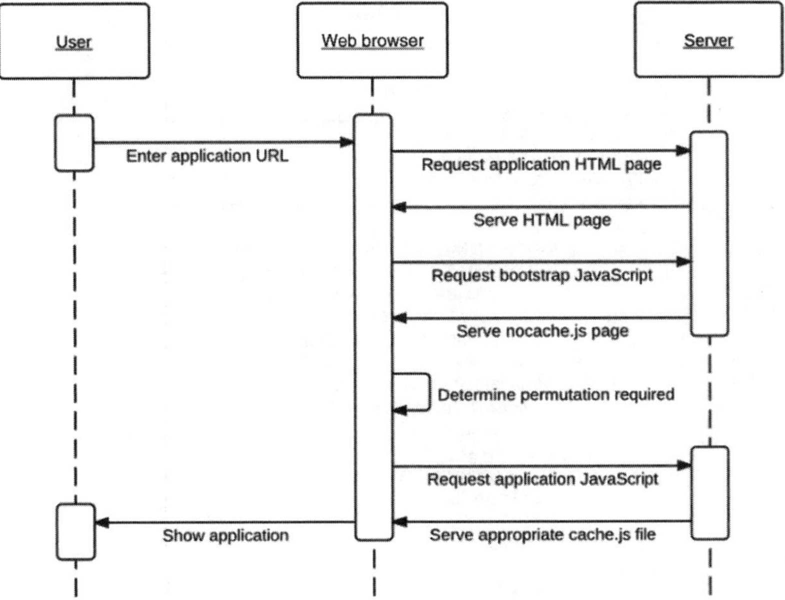

Figure 2.2 A sequence diagram showing a user request to start a GWT application

This is the typical case. You could alter the bootstrapping slightly by applying different linkers (which we'll briefly consider in section 2.8.1), but we'll assume in this book that the applications are sticking to the plain-vanilla approach described.

It's good to know this, and we'll come back to it later, particularly when we talk about deferred binding, but you're probably more interested in the developer's view at this point.

2.1.2 *Examining the developer's view*

A typical GWT application consists of client-side code written in Java and server-side code written in any language you like. One option for the server side is to use Java code and link to the client via GWT-RPC; other options include using GWT's Request-Factory approach, or have normal Java servlets, or PHP code, or you choose. As you'll see, GWT is remarkably flexible.

In your IDE the code of a complete application is split into two parts, as shown in figure 2.3:

- The uncompiled part of the application (your Java code).
- The deployable part of the application, created using web technologies such as Cascading Style Sheets, HTML, servlets, and when appropriate, your compiled application in JavaScript, all in a Java-compliant web archive that you can drop into a server for deployment. You can also keep any non-Java aspects of your server code in this part, such as PHP code.

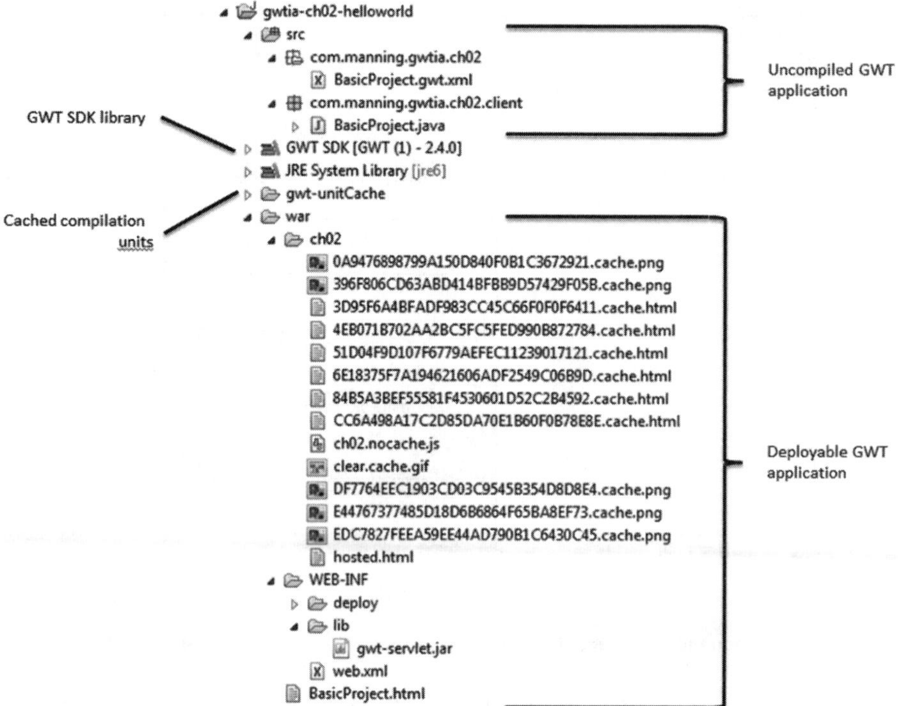

Figure 2.3 The structure of a GWT application as you'd see it in Eclipse project view. We're mainly interested in the uncompiled and deployable GWT application parts in this chapter.

The Java code is compiled to JavaScript and moved to the *deployable part* during compilation. (In figure 2.3 you can see the compiled code in the deployable part as the strangely named .cache.html files.)

Because the deployable part is a Java-compliant web archive (.war) file, it's already packaged and ready to be deployed to your favorite web container—could it be simpler?

Both of these parts are important to your application at different points in their life, and it's good that you know about that now. But we think it's better for you to get some practice under your belt before diving into the theory, so let's park this discussion for now and return to it at the end of the chapter.

If we're agreed on parking the theory, let's walk through the different modes in which you can run your application: development and web. (If we're not in agreement, you can shift to the more theoretical parts in section 2.6 and then come back here.)

2.1.3 Understanding development vs. web mode

Currently, you can run your application in two modes: development and web.

> **NOTE** Where is hosted mode? You might see references in other (older) sources to GWT's hosted mode. It has been replaced with the massively more flexible development mode.

Let's look at these in turn, starting with development mode.

DEVELOPMENT MODE

You use development mode when you're developing your code. In this mode you're running the Java code you've written—via a development mode browser plug-in—in the browser of your choice. GWT translates your Java code into the necessary JavaScript on the fly.

> **DEFINITION** *Development mode*—Running client Java code in the browser (interpreted by a development mode plug-in) and server code on a GWT-provided development server.

Development mode is quite useful. Not only can you quickly check your code in your browser of choice, but you can also run your code in debug mode in your IDE through development mode and step through it as if it was a normal Java program, as shown in figure 2.4.

Development mode starts up two servers. The first is called the *code server* and is the one that the GWT browser plug-in communicates with to enable, among other things, debugging of your application in your IDE while it's running in the browser. The other server is a typical JEE server that runs your servlets and provides your resources in development mode. You'll see later, in table 2.1, that you can alter how, and if, these servers start, giving you some flexibility in development.

It's possible that in the future this mode will become known as "classic" dev mode because there's a new toy emerging: super dev mode.

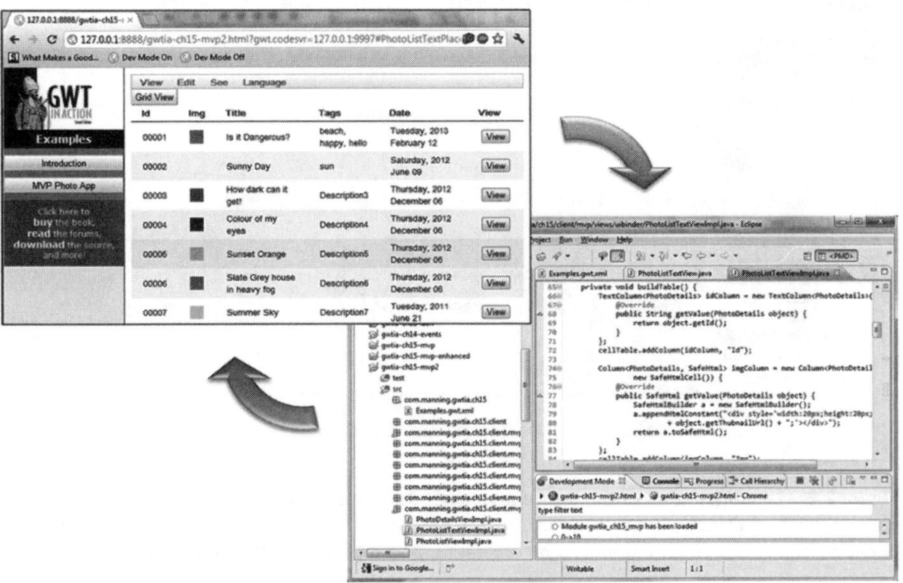

Figure 2.4 Development mode in action showing the round trip between browser, browser plug-in, Java code server, and Java code

SUPER DEV MODE

In the future you can expect to be able to use super dev mode, where you can debug your Java code running directly in the browser, doing away with the need for the current plug-in. The compiler producing source maps[1] and the browsers understanding them enables this.

GWT 2.5 starts down this path, but the functionality is limited to Chrome and Firefox, because at the time of this writing the other browsers don't support source maps, and it's highly experimental—it's subject to change and takes a lot of digging around and patience to use. You can see it running in figure 2.5, and we'll update the book's website on how to use it as it becomes more stable.

We mention this mode because it's sure to cause a buzz and we want to be able to show you where it will fit in the future (and it certainly looks interesting, as you can see from figure 2.5). This figure shows chapter 15's MVP example running in super dev mode inside of Chrome. The interesting part is in Chrome's web developer tool that we've fired up at the bottom of the page. There you can see the Java code of the example's Welcome view; if you have good eyesight, you'll see that we're at a breakpoint in the code. All this can be seen and controlled from directly within the browser.

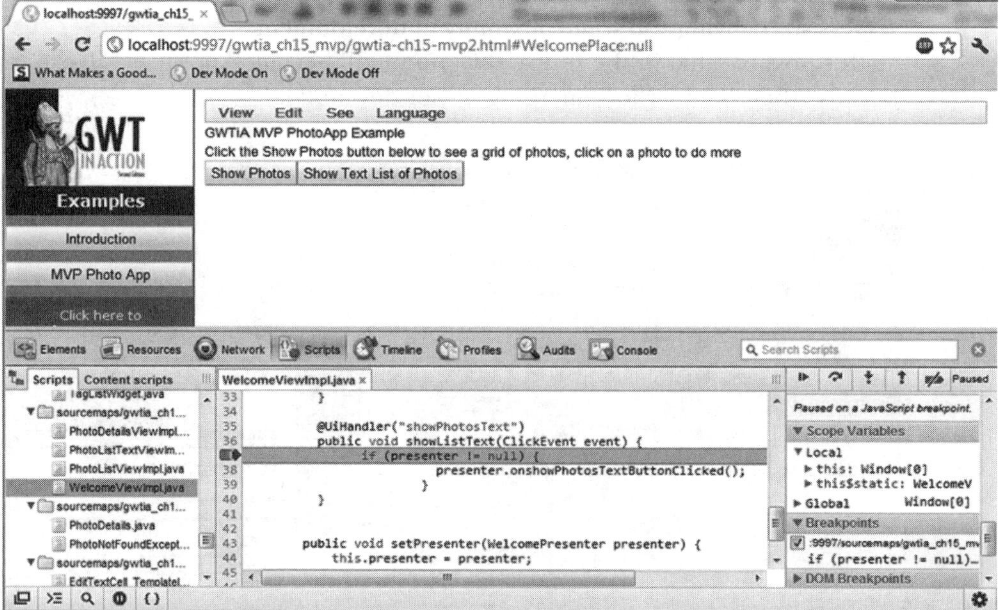

Figure 2.5 Looking ahead to the future and super dev mode. Starting in GWT 2.5 you'll be able to debug your application directly in the browser. At the moment it's experimental, but you should expect this to become stable over time, expand to all browsers, and replace the Development Mode Browser Plugin.

1 Overview of source maps: http://mng.bz/JENs.

WEB (PRODUCTION) MODE

You're in web mode when you've compiled your application and have deployed it to a web server of your choice. In this mode, you don't need the browser plug-in or a development server, and your code is pure HTML, JavaScript, and CSS (plus any server-side technology you've chosen to use, which would include any GWT-RPC you've developed).

> **DEFINITION** *Web mode*—Running a compiled GWT application that consists of only HTML, JavaScript, and CSS, and server code on a server of your choice.

It usually takes more effort to test your application in web mode because you have to wait for the compilation process to finish before running. Then if you find an error, you have to start the whole cycle again. That's why we have development mode.

You're ready to start building an application. The first step is to decide how to do it. Remember, you have to get a structure similar to that shown in figure 2.3. Let's look at the options.

2.2 Examining the options for building an application

The structure of a GWT project is slightly more complicated than that of a normal application. It's not massively complicated, but enough subtleties exist that trying to build it by hand is likely to lead to errors and frustration.

It's therefore quite useful to have an automated way of building a simple application that you then enhance. You can create an application, automatically or manually, in several ways:

- Using Google Plugin for Eclipse (GPE) wizard
- Using GWT command-line tools
- By hand

You already know that our preference is the GPE wizard. It's easy to use and creates the simplest structure possible, which you then enhance to implement your functionality. The GPE doesn't only provide wizards for creating applications; it also has a host of supporting functions to make your development smoother, as you'll see in the rest of this book. But it requires that you use Eclipse as your IDE for the GPE approach to work.

If you aren't using Eclipse as your IDE, or you don't like the idea of using the wizards (why ever not?), you could use the GWT command-line tools. GWT comes with two command-line tools:

- `webAppCreator`—For creating web application structure
- `i18nCreator`—For creating internationalization interfaces from existing property files

The problem with the `webAppCreator` command-line tool, and GPE if you forget to stop it, is that it produces a relatively complicated default client/server application. Although that's useful to show off what you can do with GWT, it's not so useful to you when it comes to examining what is a GWT application. Nor is it useful when you want to have only a framework application to enhance, because you have to remove a lot of code and configuration first. This gets confusing when you get errors—is it your code, or parts of configuration from that unavoidable application that you forgot to remove, or did you remove the wrong thing?

On the upside, the `webAppCreator` command-line tool creates an Ant build file with various useful targets, such as for compiling, running development mode, and running any JUnit tests all outside an IDE, although we'd go with common best practice and say that using an IDE is going to help you. The application resulting from the command-line tool can also be imported into your choice of IDE. We won't cover the command-line tools in this book, but they're amply covered in the online GWT documentation.[2]

If the GPE and the command-line tools aren't your thing, you could try to create a GWT application by hand. The issue here is that you must remember to do everything, do it correctly, and make sure all interconnections and links are there. One mistake and you'll likely spend loads of time trying to fix issues that should never have popped up, instead of developing your application.

Because we assume that you're using Eclipse as your IDE and that you agree the GPE wizards will be helpful, you're ready to start creating `HelloWorld`. We'll introduce terminology and concepts as we go, and then after you've finished creating we'll recap some of the key points and troublesome areas.

2.3 Creating the HelloWorld application with the GPE

Figure 2.6 shows the Eclipse toolbar when you have the Google Plugin for Eclipse (GPE) installed (you may have additional buttons if you've installed other items, such as GWT Designer).

To avoid some potential confusion as we move forward in this chapter over what tool we're using where, we'll use the following:

- GPE to create a new project and add necessary aspects
- Eclipse Run/Debug buttons to launch development mode

The first thing to do is to get the GPE wizards to create the web application structure.

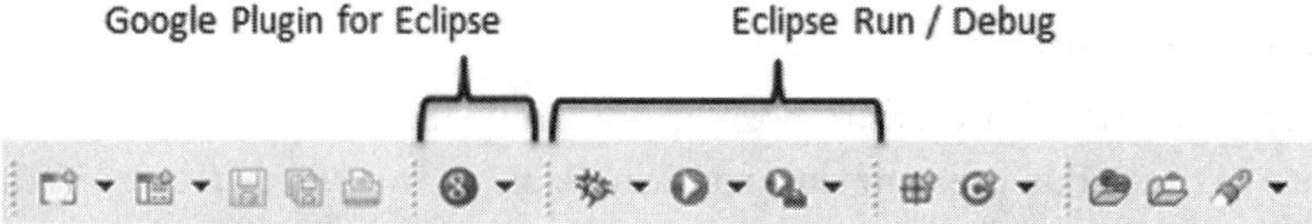

Figure 2.6 The Eclipse toolbar, showing the buttons relating to the Google Plugin for Eclipse (left) after it's installed, and the standard Eclipse Run/Debug functions (right)

---

[2] GWT command-line tools information: http://mng.bz/2hoi.

2.3.1 Creating a web application

To start creating your new application, click the arrow next to the Google Plugin for Eclipse button shown in figure 2.6 to reveal the drop-down menu shown in figure 2.7.

Figure 2.7 The tools available within the Google Plugin for Eclipse (GPE) drop-down menu

The drop-down menu contains a number of tools, some directly related to GWT and some indirectly. Three tools that are directly related to GWT are highlighted in figure 2.7:

- New Web Application Project
- GWT Compile Project
- Profile Using Speed Tracer

We'll concern ourselves with the first and second wizards in this chapter and leave the Profile Using Speed Tracer tool to our optimization chapter (chapter 19).

To create a new GWT application, click the New Web Application Project button, which will bring up the New Web Application Project wizard. You'll need to complete three pages of this wizard to create your application. You can see the completed first page of the wizard in figure 2.8. (Google may have made changes to the wizard since this writing, but the concepts should be the same.)

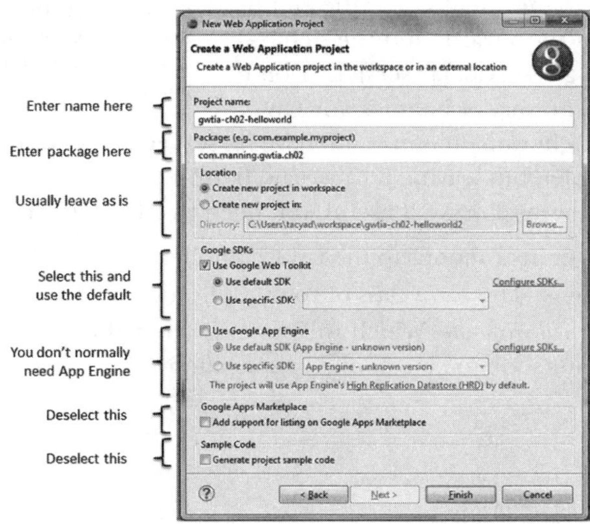

Figure 2.8 The GPE New Web Application Project Wizard—fill in the project and package name, and deselect Use Google App Engine and Generate Project Sample Code (your versions of GWT and Google App Engine are likely to be the same or later than those shown here).

All you need to do is enter a project and a root Java package name. We've chosen `gwtia-ch02-helloworld` as the project's name and the Java package name `com.manning.gwtia.ch02`. As with all Java applications, you need to store your classes within a package hierarchy. The package name can be anything you choose or restricted to the naming conventions of your development group; if you want some advice on package naming, you could check out the relevant Java tutorial.[3]

If you have several GWT SDK versions installed on your machine, now is the time to select the one you wish to work with—you'll leave it as is in this example. Also deselect Use Google App Engine because you don't want support for it in the application (the plug-in provides, among other things, support for real-time validation that code is compatible with Google App Engine and enhancement of JDO classes).

Also deselect Generate Project Sample Code because you'll create the application yourself. Leaving this selected means the wizard would produce the default client/server application code that we mentioned earlier and you'd end up tying yourself in knots trying to delete bits to get a basis to move forward. (The example is good if you want to see a whole prebuilt client/server application, and you may want to do that at some point, but for now leave the box unchecked.)

Once you click the Finish button, you've created the basic project structure, and you should see something like figure 2.9.

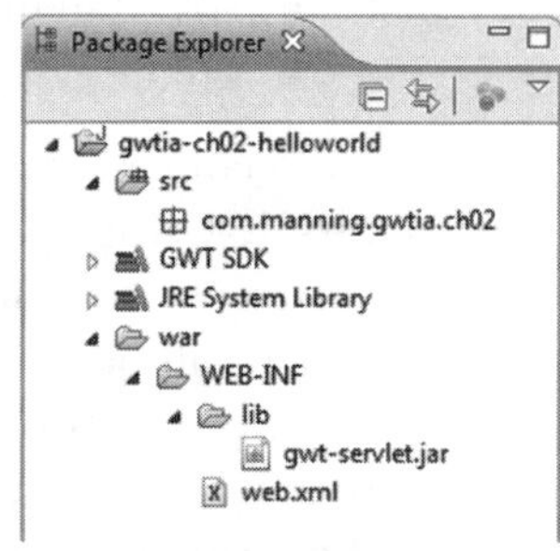

Figure 2.9 Project structure and contents after creation in Eclipse using the GPE's New Web Application Project Wizard

If you find that you now have more classes and packages in the src folder, you probably neglected to stop the wizard from creating its sample application. If this happens you should delete the project and start again.

So what do you have? The project contains two folders: an src folder, which is where your GWT Java code will sit, and the war folder, which is where the deployable application sits. At this point, the client side is the empty Java package you named in the wizard, and the deployable part contains only the gwt-servlet.jar servlet. (Don't worry about this for now. The servlet handles any GWT-RPC communication you might implement; you'll have no server side in our example, so you could delete this servlet, but leaving it causes no harm.)

To take what you have now and make it useful, you need to create the following:

- *A GWT module*—A set of instructions to the GWT compiler
- *A Java* `EntryPoint` *class*—The *main* class of your application
- *An HTML file the user will request*—Which will, among other things, request the bootstrap code for your soon-to-be compiled application

---

3 Java package-naming tutorial: http://mng.bz/maoh.

You can create all three using GPE wizards by opening the File menu and selecting New and then Other. You'll get a list of relevant wizards under the Google Web Toolkit folder (see figure 2.10).

The ClientBundle and UiBinder wizards are topics for later chapters, but the middle three are of interest right now. You don't have to run these three wizards in any strict order, but we find it easier to start with the Module wizard, because it's the unit of a GWT application.

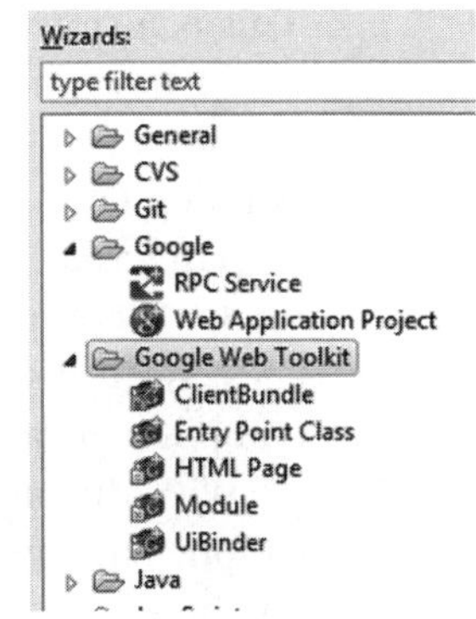

Figure 2.10 Under the Google Web Toolkit folder in Eclipse are the other GPE wizards that are available to help build GWT applications (more wizards are likely to become available over time).

2.3.2 Defining a GWT module

Highlight the `com.manning.gwtia.ch02` package in the Eclipse package/Project Explorer, and start the Module wizard through the File > New > Other menu option. You'll get a dialog box similar to that shown in figure 2.11.

Because we highlighted the package before starting the wizard, it automatically filled in the Source Folder and Package fields. If you highlighted the wrong package name before launching the widget or didn't select one, you can change it now through the Browse button.

A GWT module gives instructions to the GWT compiler. These instructions are fairly varied, but you must at least once tell the GWT compiler that you're inheriting all of the instructions in the `com.google.gwt.user.User` module. All GWT applications need to inherit this `User` module because it contains the basic GWT compiler rules for any GWT application. We'll come back to these rules later.

All you need to do in the wizard is enter the module name you want (`HelloWorld`) and click Finish. The wizard creates the module file in the package you indicated, and it's an XML file that will be called HelloWorld.gwt.xml. It looks like the following:

```
<module>
    <inherits name="com.google.gwt.user.User" />
    <source path="client"/>
</module>
```

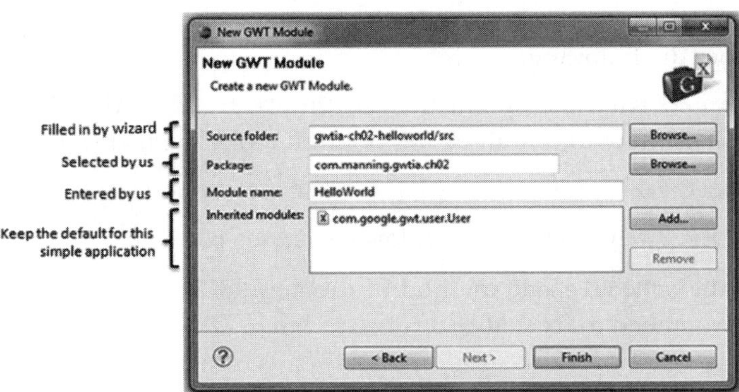

Figure 2.11 The GPE Module wizard. You should type in the module name and make sure the source folder and package are what you want.

This is a simple application with only one module; a more complicated application could have more modules. In section 2.5.2 we'll discuss this in a little more detail together with module naming and how to tell the difference and the relationship between GWT modules and Java packages.

The created module file, for now, tells GWT to inherit the `User` module and that the GWT compiler should compile code found in the `client` package and its subpackages. We'll discuss the specific reasons for needing to tell the GWT compiler what to compile (or rather, what not to compile) in section 2.6.3.

With the module in place you've told the GWT compiler how to handle your application, but you haven't provided any code for the application yet. You need to create an entry point.

2.3.3 Adding an entry point

An application's entry point is a Java class that contains the `onModuleLoad` method. You can think of this method as equivalent to the `main` method of a normal Java program and in a class that extends the `EntryPoint` interface. You need to tell the GWT compiler the name of that class through an entry in a module.

> **How many entry points?**
>
> Typically, a GWT application will have only one `EntryPoint`—you only have one way to start your application.
>
> If you define multiple `EntryPoints`, then they *all* execute, in the order in which they're defined in the module file(s), when your application starts.
>
> Sometimes developers forget that a GWT application isn't a set of pages and they create a module/class per "page" and create multiple `EntryPoints`, hoping only the relevant one will start—but GWT doesn't work that way.

Luckily, you can do all that in one go using the Entry Point Class wizard. It's contextually aware, so if you run it after highlighting the src folder in the project, you'll see some data filled in; if you run it when the project is selected, other data is filled in. The end point you want to get to is shown in figure 2.12.

The wizard does the following:

- It adds the necessary entry-point item to the `HelloWorld` module, telling the GWT compiler where to find the entry point. It looks like this:

  ```
  <entry-point class="com.manning.gwtia.ch02.client.HelloWorld"/>
  ```

- It creates a `HelloWorld` Java class under the `client` package.

At the moment, the `onModuleLoad` method in the new `HelloWorld` class is an empty implementation; you need to fix that.

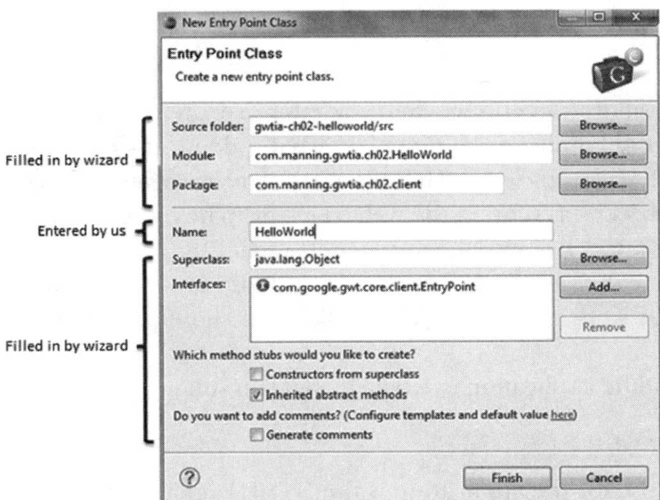

Figure 2.12 The Entry Point Class GPE wizard. Enter the class name that will be the entry point, and check that the rest of the data is what you want.

IMPLEMENTING SOME FUNCTIONALITY

As we've mentioned, the `onModuleLoad` method is the first thing executed when your application starts. It's in here that you'd normally create the application's user interface and start reacting to users' interactions. A simple application will probably do that directly in the method; more complicated applications will, like any sensible application, have functionality divided across many class files, encapsulating functionality in a well-designed manner.

Open the recently created HelloWorld.java file in Eclipse, and replace the `onModuleLoad` method with the code shown in ❷ in listing 2.1 (note that because you use the `RootPanel` and `Label` GWT user interface components in this new version of `onModuleLoad`, you need to import them into the class using the `import` statements at ❶ in listing 2.1. You can do that by either right-clicking the errors shown against the `onModuleLoad` method and selecting Fix Imports or directly typing them at the top of the `HelloWorld` class. Or you can copy all of the code in listing 2.1 into HelloWorld.java.

Listing 2.1 The entry point of the basic `HelloWorld` framework application

```
package com.manning.gwtia.ch02.client;

import com.google.gwt.core.client.EntryPoint;
import com.google.gwt.user.client.ui.Label;
import com.google.gwt.user.client.ui.RootPanel;

public class HelloWorld implements EntryPoint {

   @Override
   public void onModuleLoad(){
      Label theGreeting = new Label("Hello World!");
```

❶ Added import statements

❷ Creating new widget

```
        RootPanel.get().add(theGreeting);
    }
}
```

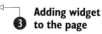

❸ Adding widget to the page

Now the entry point will do something when you later execute the application—without wanting to jump too far ahead, we'll explain what it does. At ❷ you create a new widget—a `Label`—that holds the text "Hello World!" The `RootPanel`, in ❸, is a GWT panel that can be seen as representing the web page (or to be more exact, the body of the application's HTML). By getting the panel (`RootPanel.get()`) and adding (`add(...)`) the `Label` created in ❷, the entry point will display "Hello World!" on the application's web page when executed. (We'll talk more about panels and widgets in chapter 3.)

We've talked about the application's web page, but you still need to create the page.

2.3.4 *Providing the web page*

The final wizard you use for the application is the HTML Page wizard, as shown in figure 2.13. You need to fill in the filename of the web page. You don't have to follow any naming conventions here, and you'll call it a fairly obvious HelloWorld.html. You should leave Support for Browser History checked in the wizard (which results in an iFrame being inserted into the resulting HTML page) because most applications are likely to need history support. We'll cover history in the next chapter, but it's always good to include support for it from the start.

Clicking Finish means the wizard creates the HelloWorld.html file in the war directory, which should be the same as what you see in listing 2.2 (be careful to check that the wizard has created the link to the nocache.js properly, and if for some reason you can't get this wizard to work, you can manually create the file yourself with the contents of listing 2.2).

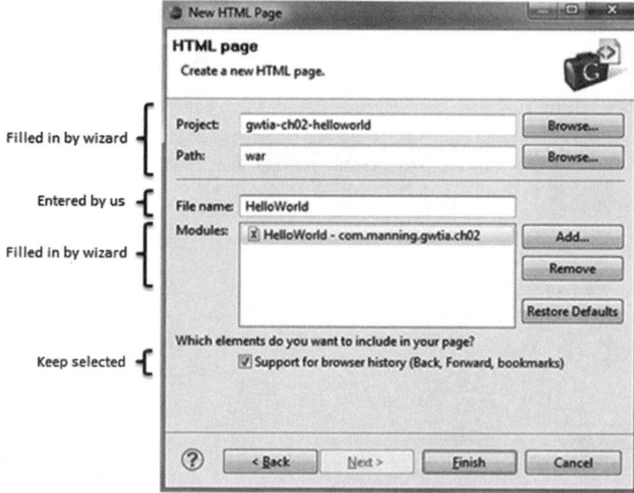

Figure 2.13 The HTML Page GPE wizard. You should enter the filename, and we recommend you keep the Support for Browser History check box selected.

Listing 2.2 Simple HTML page for the GWT application

```
<!doctype html>                                                  ❶ Indicates standards mode
<html>
   <head>
      <meta http-equiv="content-type" content="text/html; charset=UTF-8">
      <script language="javascript"                            ❷ Bootstrap application
         src="com.manning.gwtia.ch02.HelloWorld/com.manning.gwtia.ch02.
         ➥ HelloWorld.nocache.js">
      </script>
   </head>
  <body>                                                         ❸ The RootPanel
    <iframe src="javascript:''" id="__gwt_historyFrame"
            tabIndex='-1'
            style="position:absolute;width:0;height:0;border:0">
   </iframe>                                                     ❹ Supports history in IE
  </body>
</html>
```

BEWARE Some versions of Google Plugin for Eclipse do not create the HTML file correctly. Make sure the `<script>` tag is as shown in ❷ in listing 2.2.

The web page `doctype` indicates the application will run in standards mode, which means that the browser will adhere to W3C standards ❶. It also contains the bootstrap code for the application ❷ and has an iFrame ❹ that allows GWT to support browser Back/Forward buttons in IE (we'll look at this, known as *history*, in section 3.7). Your GWT application will see the HTML body element as the `RootPanel` that you used in the entry point to add a `Label` with some text.

> **Please note**
>
> You aren't restricted to HTML for the application's web page. You could use a JSP, a PHP, or whatever new technology comes out in the future. Doing so is useful if you need to create dynamic content in the page on the server side before sending it to the user.
>
> As long as the link to the bootstrap code is included in the page, your GWT application will work (don't forget to include the iFrame as well if your application is managing history and you think your user is possibly using IE).

OK, that was a lot of information; let's take a moment to recap.

2.3.5 Recapping the magic

If you take a moment to think through what you've done in the wizards, you'll notice you created

- An HTML page for the application. Importantly, this page had four key aspects:
  - A body element that can be accessed in your Java code through a `RootPanel.get()` call
  - An iFrame that will be used to support browser history management

  - A script tag that's used to download the bootstrap code, which will download the compiled-to-JavaScript version of the GWT application and start it
  - A doctype indicating the browser should treat the application in standards mode
- A Java class file that
  - Implemented the `EntryPoint` interface
  - Implemented the `onModuleLoad` method—the compiled-to-JavaScript version that is called to start the application
  - Created a `Label` widget with some text and added it to the `RootPanel`
- A GWT module that tells the GWT compiler
  - To inherit all of the rules in the `User` module
  - To compile all the code in, and under, the `client` Java package and not other packages
  - Which class implements the `EntryPoint` interface, so it knows where to find the start of the application to insert into the bootstrapping code
- A GWT application/project that holds all of these in the appropriate structure

The most interesting thing you can do now is run the application, and you can do that in either development mode or in web mode. We'll start with development mode.

2.4 Running HelloWorld in development mode

Development mode is where you'll spend most of your time. Once you've used development mode for a while, it's easy to forget how magical it is. In this mode your application is running in a browser linked back to your Java code in your IDE by the Development Mode Browser Plugin we discussed in chapter 1. The benefit, beyond using the browser of your choice, is that you don't need to keep going through compilation cycles in order to check your application.

Even better, if you're using an IDE with a debugger, you can link your running application to it. You can add break points in Eclipse, and when you reach that part of the code while using the browser, Eclipse's debugger kicks in. Then you can inspect variables and step over or into code—all the normal things you can do in a debugger, for a web application running in a browser. That's real development power.

The downside to development mode is that it can sometimes be a little slow (though this is a minor issue, in our experience, compared to the benefits). Also, when you're working with a new version of a browser, there's often a need for a new version of the browser plug-in—those two aren't always in sync, so you have to be careful about when you update your browser (it's safest to not have automatic updates enabled). These two issues are some of the problems that the future super dev mode will remove. But, as we said earlier, as of GWT 2.5 super dev mode is still highly experimental, so we limit ourselves to talking about the usual development mode (and only mention super dev mode in passing).

Figure 2.14 shows the results of running the newly created GWT application in development mode. OK, we didn't say it was going to be the most exciting application.

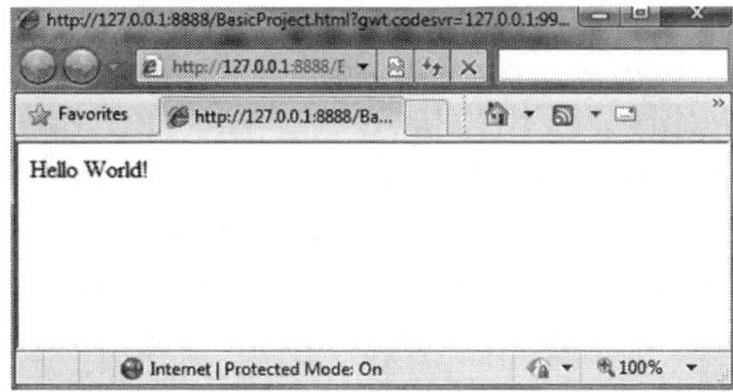

Figure 2.14 The result of running the `HelloWorld` application created using the GPE wizards

But it has enough for us to explore some key concepts of GWT before you add in some complexity.

2.4.1 Starting development mode in Eclipse

To start development mode, all you do is select the project in Eclipse's Package Explorer, click the Run button in the Eclipse toolbar, and navigate down to Run As > Web Application (see figure 2.15).

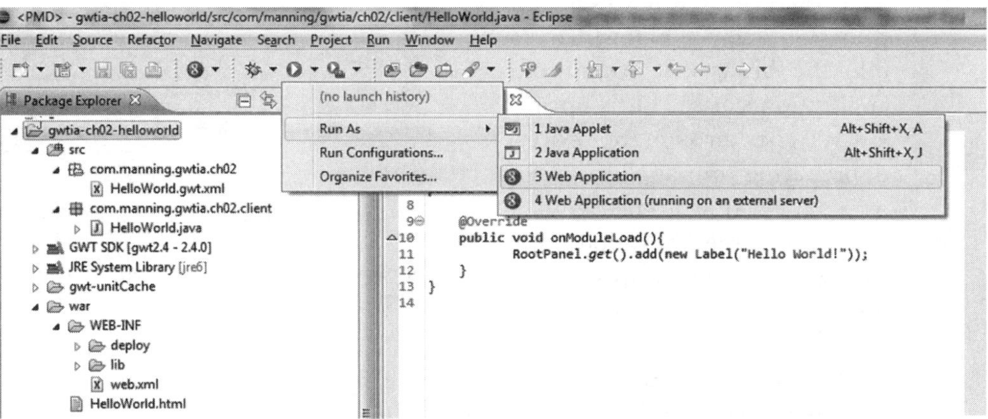

Figure 2.15 Running the project in development mode through the Eclipse Run button (highlight the project in Package Explorer, click the Play button, and choose Run As > Web Application)

If you have only one HTML page in your project, as we do, then GWT will assume that's the page you want to load when the user arrives at your application (projects with several HTML pages will trigger GWT to ask which page is the startup URL). After a while, you'll notice a new view window open inside Eclipse, with a URL in it (usually at the bottom of the screen). You can see part of this view in figure 2.16.

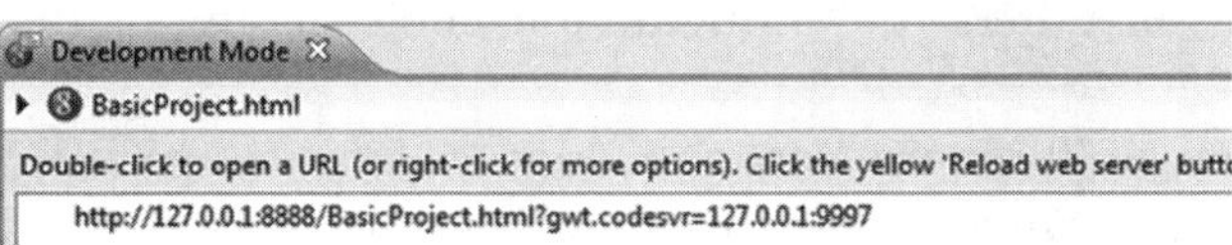

Figure 2.16 In development mode the Eclipse view window shows the project's URL. You can then enter the URL into a browser of your choice as long as it supports the Development Mode Browser Plugin.

Development mode is now running, but you won't see your application yet. To see your application, you need to fire up your favorite supported browser: IE, Firefox, Safari, or Chrome. When your browser is running, go back to Eclipse, copy the URL you see in the development mode view window, paste it into your browser, and press Enter.

If you're running development mode for the first time in the browser you chose, you may be missing the necessary Development Mode Browser Plugin. See section 1.3 for how to install it, or click the Download button shown in the browser window.

Assuming the browser plug-in is in place, it will connect back to the development mode server and your application will start. Figure 2.17 shows the development mode window in Eclipse, and that the Safari GWT plug-in has connected and the module has been loaded.

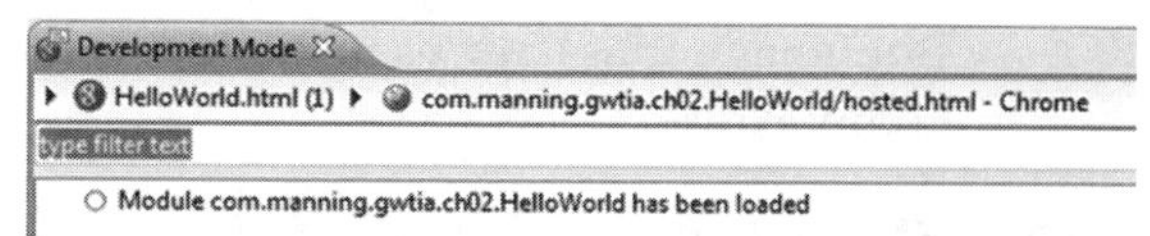

Figure 2.17 Development mode view window in Eclipse once the Safari browser has connected. You can connect more browsers, and each gets its own entry in the development mode Eclipse view window.

It might take a few moments from the time you enter the URL into the browser to when your application starts. This is normal as GWT goes through the process of preparing your application for use. Once the preparation is over, you'll see the application running in your browser. For now, it shows the "Hello World!" text, as shown in figure 2.18.

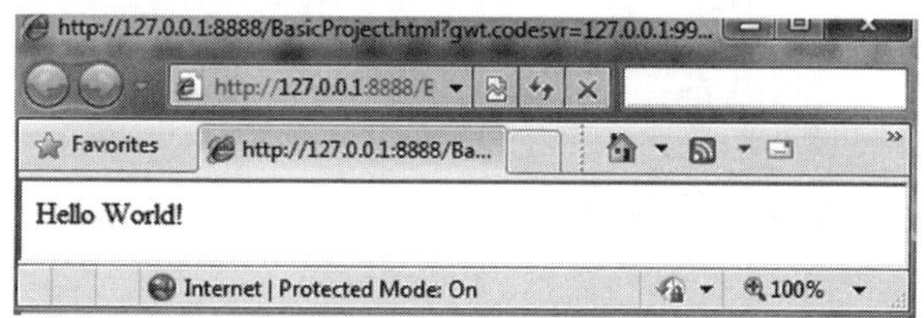

Figure 2.18 Running the `HelloWorld` application in a browser

If startup produces any errors, they'll appear in the console view window of Eclipse, though you shouldn't have any at this point.

When you started development mode at the beginning of this section, you started it using its default set of functionality. In the next section we'll show how you can change some of that by passing in some parameters.

2.4.2 Passing parameters to development mode

Starting development mode through Eclipse's Run As button fires it up using a default set of parameters. If, instead of selecting Run As, you select Run Configuration, you'll see the dialog box shown in figure 2.19, where we've already selected the Arguments tab (in some versions of Eclipse these options are at the same level in the menu, as in figure 2.15; in others the configuration choice is under the Run As menu).

In the Arguments tab you'll see two sections: Program Arguments and VM Arguments. You can use the VM Arguments section to pass any normal Java VM arguments.

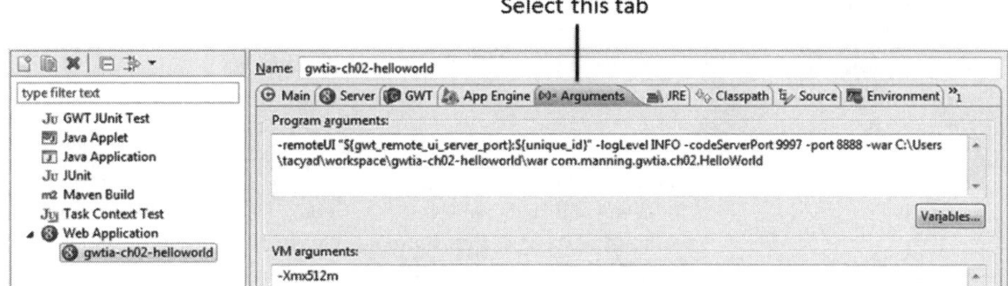

Figure 2.19 Using the Run Configuration option to set both development mode and Java VM configurations for your application

The example we have sets stack size to 512 MB as well as a couple of Mac-specific parameters.

The Program Arguments area allows you to set GWT-specific parameters. Assuming you've already run the project once, the following is what's in the standard setup:

```
-remoteUI "${gwt_remote_ui_server_port}:${unique_id}"
-startupUrl HelloWorld.html
-logLevel INFO
-codeServerPort 9997
-port 8888
-war /Users/adam/workspace/HelloWorld/war
com.manning.gwtia.ch02.HelloWorld
```

If you haven't run the project yet, then the `-startupUrl` parameter won't be there.

Our example tells development mode that it will be using a remote user interface. Next, it informs development mode what HTML page to serve when the browser plug-in connects. Development mode has logging capabilities, and the next parameter sets logging to the INFO level.

The next two parameters are associated with the development mode server. Parameter `codeServerPort` sets the port with which the browser plug-in will communicate. You see it in play in the URL you used to launch development mode, highlighted in bold as follows:

```
http://127.0.0.1:8888/HelloWorld.html?gwt.codesvr=127.0.0.1:9997
```

The `port` parameter sets the port number on which the development mode server will listen (access to any server-side GWT code you'll have would be found here). Typically you'd only change these ports if your development machine is already using them for something else. If you're running server-side code on a different server, then use the `server` parameter.

The `war` parameter is the location of the web archive (`WAR`) in which your application sits. Again, we'll cover that in more detail in the next section. Finally, you need to tell development mode the class file where the `EntryPoint` can be found.

The GPE wizards added all this information for you as you used them. If you're doing it by hand, you'll need to get this correct in order for things to work.

Table 2.1 defines the parameters you can use.

Table 2.1 Arguments that can be passed to GWT development mode

Argument	Description
`-logLevel levelVal`	The level of logging detail to provide. The `levelVal` can be one of the following: ERROR, WARN, INFO, TRACE, DEBUG, SPAM, or ALL. It works similar to Log4J in that there's a hierarchy (in the order shown previously). By setting the level to WARN, you won't see INFO or TRACE messages, for example.
`-logDir dir`	Sends the logging to the directory dir as well as to the normal screen location.
`-workDir path`	The directory that the compiler uses for storing its internal working files. It must be writable, and it defaults to the system's temporary directory. Usually, you won't have a case for changing this, unless the system's temporary directory isn't writable in your setup.
`-gen path`	The directory where the compiler will store all code created by generators. You'll use this in chapter 17 to see the code your generators are creating for debug purposes.
`-noserver`	Prevents the embedded development mode web server from starting. You might do this if you have no server-side code (note that this isn't the code server). If you're providing the server-side code on another server, then see the `-server` parameter.
`-port num`	Gives the port number for the embedded development mode server. You could change it if you need to deal with firewalls in development environments.
`-whitelist`	A comma-separated list of regular expression URLs that the user is allowed to browse to (within development mode).
`-blacklist`	A comma-separated list of regular expression URLs that the user is blocked from browsing to (within development mode).
`-bindAddress addr`	Changes the address for the code and embedded web server. It defaults to 127.0.0.1.
`-codeServerPort num`	The TCP port number, `num`, for the code server. It defaults to 9997.
`-server serv`	By providing a value here, you specify that a different embedded server is to run. The server must implement `ServletContainerLauncher`. You also need to take account of any cross-site issues you may run into.
`-startupUrl url`	Automatically launches the URL defined. This is the start page of your application.
`-war dir`	The directory, dir, to which the web archive of compilation will be sent. By default, this is the war directory in your project.
`-extra dir`	The directory into which extra files, not intended for compilation, will be placed. You'll use this in chapter 13 on internationalization, where you want to get hold of a file the compiler produces.

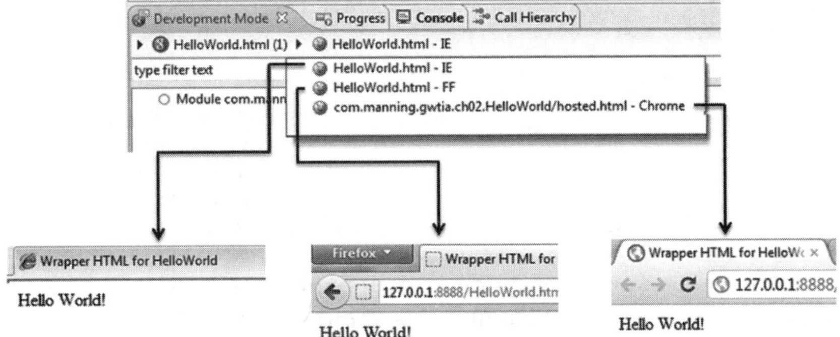

Figure 2.20 Development mode running in three different browsers at the same time, through Eclipse

In development mode you can quickly test to see if your application is doing what you want. You can set debug points in your Java code, and when the application gets there, you're taken back to your IDE to step through your Java code line by line. You can run the application in several browsers at once to quickly check that you have no browser issues; see figure 2.20. Development mode is truly powerful in cutting down your development and debugging time.

Although unlikely, it could be the case that something has gone wrong and you don't see the text on the screen. Let's see what you can do if the application isn't working as you expect.

2.5 Finding out where it went wrong

It's unlikely that `HelloWorld` has gone wrong, because it's such a simple application, but once you step beyond that simple world, things can happen. We think it's useful to check out briefly where you can look if something is going wrong, and the first place is usually the Java code in your IDE.

2.5.1 Checking the code in the IDE for errors

It should be quickly obvious if there's a syntactical problem with your Java code, it will be flagged in the IDE, usually with a red marking. In Eclipse you get a red X next to the lines in error, and in the explorer view a red X appears next to classes and packages where those errors are, as you can see in figure 2.21.

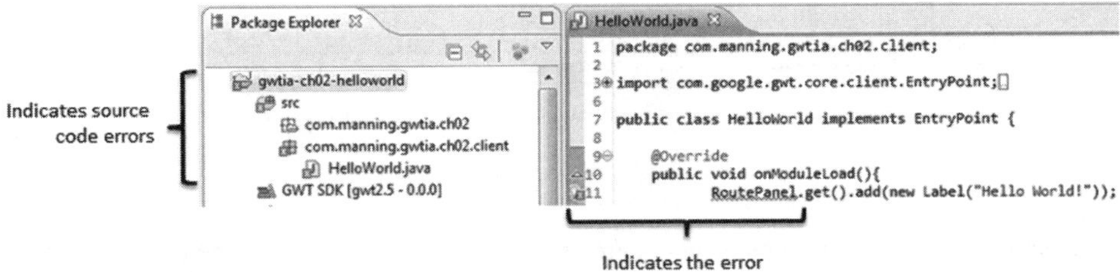

Figure 2.21 Java syntax errors highlighted by the IDE, waiting for us to fix them

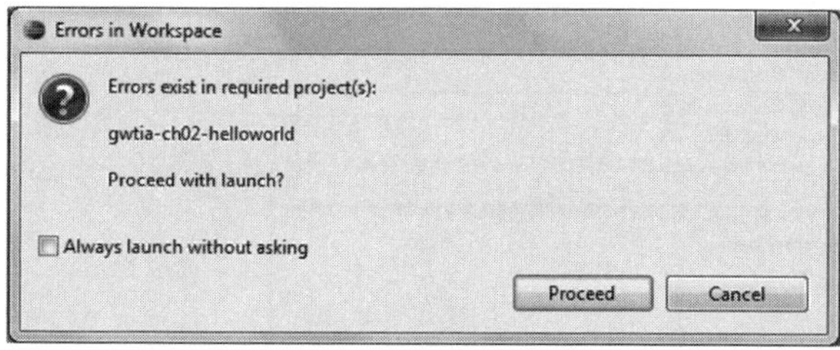

Figure 2.22 You'll see this error if you try to launch development mode when you have Java syntax errors in your application. It's not usually sensible to proceed until they're fixed.

Additionally, if you try to run dev mode without fixing these types of errors or noticing that you have them, you'll get the dialog box shown in figure 2.22.

In both these cases it's a matter of going back to the source code and fixing the underlying Java error, which is most likely a spelling issue, or you've forgotten to import a class that you're using, or there's a missing semicolon at the end of a line, and so on.

If you manage to launch dev mode without a problem, then the next place to look for errors is in the output of dev mode.

2.5.2 *Looking at development mode output*

The next place to look for issues is in the dev mode output. If you're using Eclipse with the Google plug-in, then you'll see that at the bottom of the IDE, as shown in figure 2.23.

The error you can see in figure 2.23 is because we forgot to include the `User` module in the application's module file (or rather, in this case, we deleted it in order to get the error). You might see in figure 2.23 that dev mode is complaining about the `Core` module being missing. We could fix this by adding it, but then we'll get a message saying that another module is missing and then another. The solution is to inherit the `User` module in our application because that inherits several other modules necessary for a GWT application to run smoothly.

Assuming there are no errors in dev mode output, you could check the console output to see if anything has gone wrong there.

2.5.3 *Reading the console output*

GWT dev mode runs its own web server, unless you've told it not to by using the `-noserver` flag or told it another system is running the server using the `-server` flag

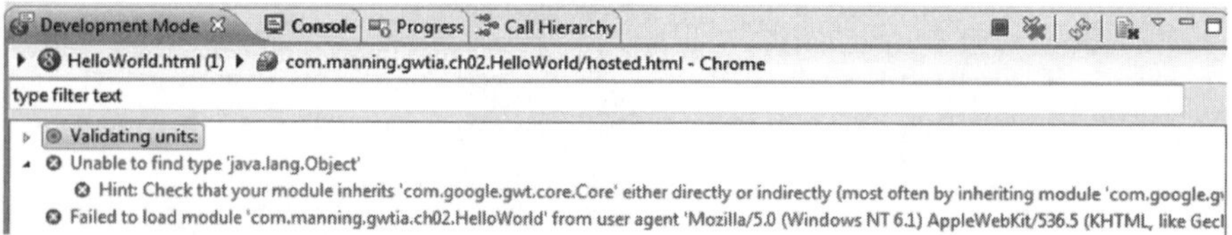

Figure 2.23 Development mode errors are usually shown on the development mode output, which is in the Eclipse window if you're using Eclipse with the GPE, or it could be in your standard output if you launched development mode from the console.

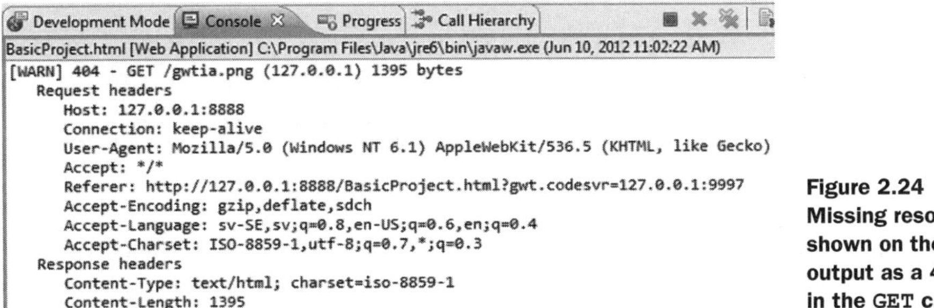

Figure 2.24 Missing resource issue, shown on the console output as a 404 warning in the `GET` call

(remember from table 2.1?). Output from the built-in web server goes to the standard console. This is different from the development mode output, but in the Eclipse interface it usually sits right next door.

Typical errors you'll see here relate to missing resources. For example, let's say we expect to show an image called gwtia.png, and it's missing; then we'd see output similar to figure 2.24. To resolve these types of errors you need to make sure resources are in the expected place and named correctly.

But it's not only syntax and missing resources that can mess up your application. Sometimes you have the logic incorrect or have misunderstood how the DOM manipulation is happening. In that situation, we need to dig a little deeper into debugging.

2.5.4 Debugging in Eclipse

Figure 2.25 Firing up a GWT application in Eclipse to debug it

The great benefit of dev mode is the ability to debug your Java code while it's running as interpreted JavaScript in the browser. It's simple to do in Eclipse. Instead of using the Run As menu that you saw in figure 2.15, you'd use the Debug As menu item located right next to it, as shown in figure 2.25.

You launch the application in exactly the same way as running it; that is, a URL appears in the launch window, you open that, and your application starts the same as before. Back in Eclipse you can set breakpoints on lines of code where you want to dig deeper into what's happening. You do that by double-clicking next to the line of code you want to stop at, and a breakpoint symbol will appear (see figure 2.26).

HelloWorld.java

```
package com.manning.gwtia.ch02.client;

import com.google.gwt.core.client.EntryPoint;

public class HelloWorld implements EntryPoint {

    @Override
    public void onModuleLoad(){
        Label theGreeting = new Label("Hello World!");
        RootPanel.get().add(theGreeting);
    }
}
```

Figure 2.26 A breakpoint inserted into the `HelloWorld` application. This will trigger the debugger to kick in if you run dev mode through the Debug As menu option rather than the Run As option.

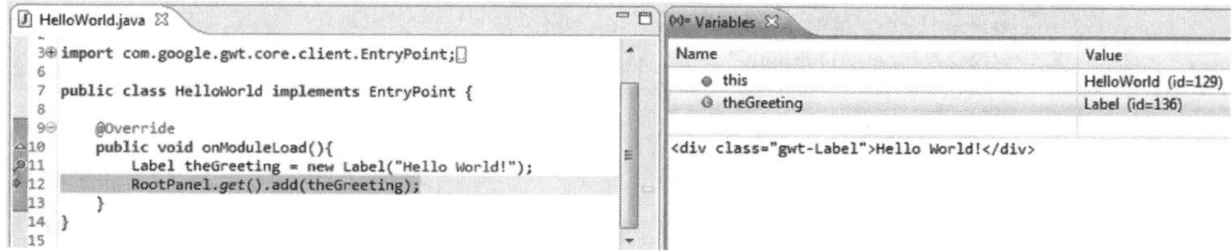

Figure 2.27 Debugging in action. We've stepped over line 11 and the variable `theGreeting` has been created. We can inspect it and see that it's a `div` element with our text in it.

With a breakpoint set, if you refresh the application in the web browser, the IDE debugger kicks in, allowing you to step into code execution and watch variable values and so on. It's a great way to check that things are happening in your code and in the order you expect.

Looking at figure 2.27 you can see that the breakpoint was hit at line 11; we ran that line, which created the `theGreeting` variable.

In the variable inspection part of the debugger, you can select that variable and see what value it has. You can see in figure 2.27 that it has the value `<div class="gwt-Label">Hello World!</div>`. This is a hint that GWT Java widgets are DOM elements (we'll come back to this more in chapter 4).

You can couple debugging in your IDE to using the browser's development tools, and you'll get visibility as to what's happening.

2.5.5 Inspecting using browser development/inspection tools

Some browsers come with a comprehensive set of development tools built in or that you can add in. Chrome has a great built-in set (so does Safari, but it doesn't have a development mode plug-in, so that's more applicable to debugging in web mode). For Firefox there's Firebug (http://getfirebug.com/), and IE has, for example, the F12 Developer Tools[4] (or Firebug Lite).

If you fire up your favorite inspector, you can see what has happened in the DOM, check that the right scripts have been downloaded, and so on.

Figure 2.28 shows the Chrome development web tools (accessed through the wrench at the top right of Chrome) in action. We've selected the Elements tab in the tool, and you can see the whole active web page on the left side.

Inspecting the DOM elements, you can see our label inserted (the `div` element you saw in figure 2.27). Highlighting the label in the tool shows on the right side what styles it has.

Coupling the Java debugger with a web development/inspection tool is a powerful way to debug those awkward issues you can't find otherwise. You get to step through your code line by line and see the impact on the DOM in real time.

---

[4] IE F12 Developer Tools: http://mng.bz/6Fe4.

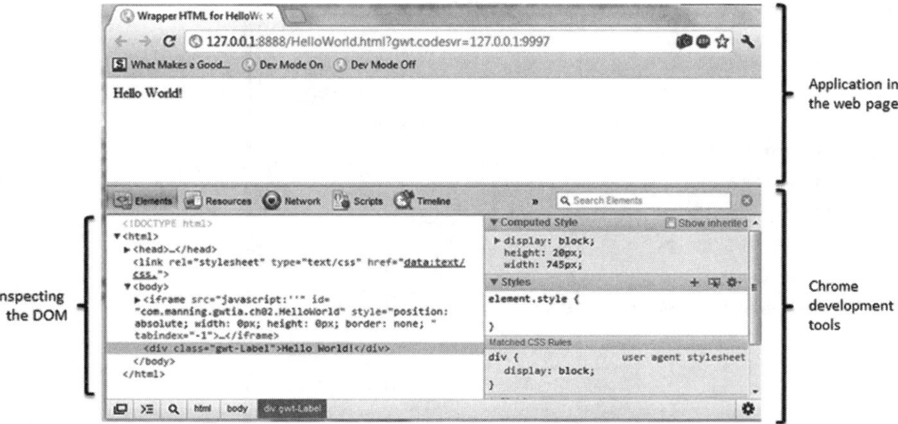

Figure 2.28 The Chrome development tools in action on the simple `HelloWorld` application

Once you're happy that your application is working as you want it—usually when you're ready to deploy it for real web testing and production—it's time to turn the client side from Java into JavaScript. With the GPE it's as simple as clicking a button.

2.6 Compiling HelloWorld for web mode

In this short section, we'll look at how to compile an application for real-world use: that is, make it into a complete package that can be deployed to a web server for users to access. We'll do that in Eclipse as well as look at what parameters can be passed to the GWT compiler.

> **TIP** Want to get efficient JavaScript? From GWT 2.5 you can get GWT to use Google's Closure[5] Compiler to extract as much efficiency as possible in the compiled JavaScript of your application. Pass the `-XenableClosureCompiler` flag to the compiler.

Ready to compile? Then let's do it.

2.6.1 Running the GWT compiler from Eclipse

To run the GWT compiler from Eclipse you select the GWT Compile Project menu option from the Google Plugin for Eclipse's drop-down menu (as shown in figure 2.29).

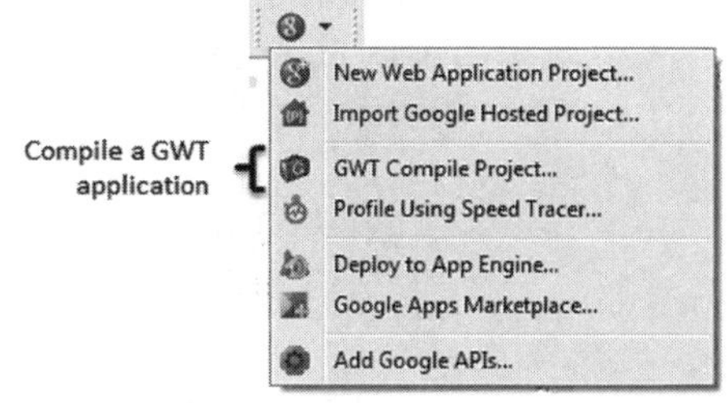

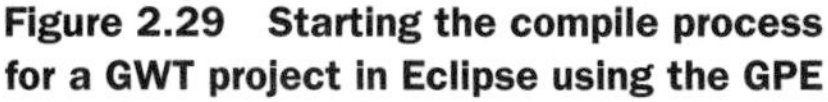
Figure 2.29 Starting the compile process for a GWT project in Eclipse using the GPE

5 Closure compiler: https://developers.google.com/closure/compiler/.

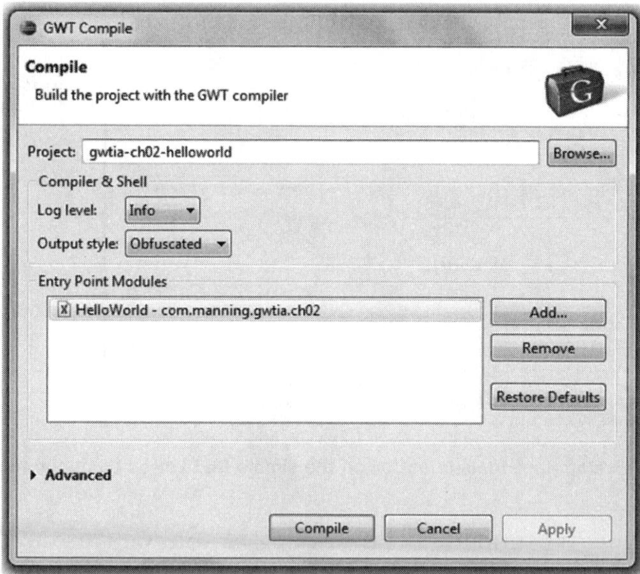

Figure 2.30 Compiling `HelloWorld` using Google Plugin for Eclipse. Check that the information is correct, and click the Compile button to start compilation.

This opens the dialog box shown in figure 2.30.

The GWT Compile dialog shows the project it will compile, the level of logging it will output, and the output style. By default, the GWT compiler will output JavaScript code in Obfuscated style; following is a quick sample from compiling this chapter's project as Obfuscated:

```
function Pb(a,b){a.length>=b&&a.splice(0,b);return a}
function hi(a,b){var c;c=di(a,b);if(c==-1){throw new Yl}gi(a,c)}
function Tk(a){if(a.b>=a.c.c){throw new Yl}return ml(a.c,a.b++)}
function ni(a){if(a.b>=a.c.c){throw new Yl}return a.c.b[++a.b]}
```

This is next to impossible for humans to read and get a sense of what's happening, but it's highly compacted into the smallest size possible. That's good, because the smaller the download size, the quicker your application will start, and 99.9999% of the time you should have no interest in reading the outputted JavaScript. But it's not so great that 0.0001% of the time when all your other error-resolution and debugging techniques still haven't found the cause of an issue and you want to read the compiler output. If you change the output style to Pretty, then the output code is much more readable:

```
function gwtOnLoad(errFn, modName, modBase, softPermutationId){
  $moduleName = modName;
  $moduleBase = modBase;
  if (errFn)
    try {
      $entry(init)();
    }
     catch (e) {
```

```
        errFn(modName);
      }
    else {
      $entry(init)();
    }
}
```

Setting the output style to Detailed provides even more information in the JavaScript file, such as fully qualified function names that include the package and class they came from. We'll leave that to you to experiment with if you want.

You can also add/remove entry points to/from your application and indicate which one should be used. For now, leave this as it is, because the example application has only one entry point.

If you click the Compile button, then your client-side code will be compiled into the war folder inside the HelloWorld folder, along with any Java server-side classes being moved to the WEB-INF classes folder (you don't have any in this example). Assuming you haven't found any compilation errors, your complete application is now almost ready for deployment to your test or production servers and should look similar to figure 2.31.

We say "almost ready" because there's one final step you might like to do: tell the web server what file to serve up as the welcome page to the application.

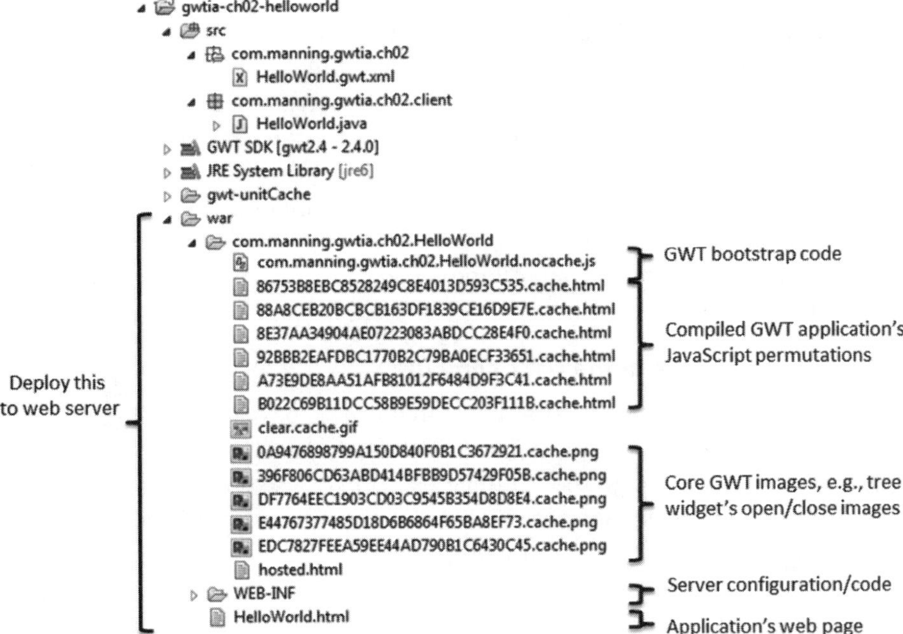

Figure 2.31 The result of compiling this chapter's example application into JavaScript held within a web archive format that's almost ready for deployment to your server (you might optionally want to indicate a welcome page for the application before deploying)

2.6.2 Welcoming the user

Because you're dealing with a web archive here, you can tell your server which page to serve up as the default. You need to add an entry into the deployment descriptor[6] (web.xml) file stored under the WEB-INF folder. The GPE has already created that file for you, and the following listing shows it together with an entry for the welcome.

Listing 2.3 Default web.xml file with an entry added for your welcome page

```
<?xml version="1.0" encoding="utf-8"?>
<web-app xmlns:xsi="http://www.w3.org/2001/XMLSchema-instance"
xmlns="http://java.sun.com/xml/ns/javaee"
xmlns:web="http://java.sun.com/xml/ns/javaee/web-app_2_5.xsd"
xsi:schemaLocation="http://java.sun.com/xml/ns/javaee
http://java.sun.com/xml/ns/javaee/web-app_2_5.xsd" version="2.5">
   <!-- TODO: Add <servlet> tags for each servlet here. -->        ❶ Servlet definitions
   <!-- TODO: Add <servlet-mapping> tags for each <servlet> here. -->
   <welcome-file-list>
      <welcome-file>HelloWorld.html</welcome-file>                 ❷ Welcome page
   </welcome-file-list>
</web-app>
```

You'll see in the chapters on server-side code what you'd put into listing 2.3 at ❶ if you had server code, but because you don't, you can either leave in the `TODO` comments or delete them. ❷ is the interesting part for us. You've added the application's HTML page to the descriptor, so that the user can write the prettier http://www.myapp.com rather than http://www.myapp.com/HelloWorld.html. Because you're still most likely running in dev mode, adding ❶ to web.xml means you can write http://127.0.0.1:8888/?gwt.codesvr=127.0.0.1:9997 in the browser to start the application (note that you still need the ? before the `url` parameter) instead of the longer http://127.0.0.1:8888/HelloWorld.html?gwt.codesvr=127.0.0.1:9997.

How you deploy the WAR to the server is dependent on which server you're using, so we won't cover that.

As you could for development mode, you can pass a number of parameters pass to the compiler.

2.6.3 Passing parameters to the GWT compiler

Table 2.2 shows some of the parameters that can be passed to the compiler (the others we defined in table 2.1: `-logLevel`, `-workDir`, `-gen`, `-war`, `-extra`). You pass most of these parameters through the Advanced section of the dialog shown in figure 2.30 by typing them in with any associated value. Two parameters can be set directly in the dialog box itself: the log level and the output style.

---

[6] web.xml: http://en.wikipedia.org/wiki/Web.xml.

Table 2.2 Arguments that can be passed to the GWT compiler

Argument	Description
`-style styleVal`	The style that the created JavaScript will have. The `styleVal` can be one of OBF[USCATED], PRETTY, or DETAILED. OBF is used for production because it produces the smallest code; but it's not easily readable, so for debugging you may prefer PRETTY, or to get the compiler to show all information in the output, try DETAILED.
`-ea`	Makes the compiled code include asserts from the source.
`-validateOnly`	Validates all source code but doesn't compile it.
`-draftCompile`	Compiles the code in a faster but not so optimized manner.
`-compileReport`	Use this argument, and the compiler will produce a Story of Your Compile report. This is useful to understand what decisions the compiler made; you'll see this again in chapter 18.
`-localWorkers num`	The number of local worker threads to use in compilation.
`-soyc`	Enables the production of the Story of Your Code report (see chapter 19 on optimization).
`-strict`	Succeeds with compilation only if all input files have no errors.

Let's also review a number of other options that are somewhat experimental at the time of writing. Table 2.3 lists them.

Table 2.3 Experimental arguments that can be passed to the GWT compiler

Argument	Description
`-XdisableAggressiveOptimization`	Disables the aggressive optimization the compiler performs.
`-XdisableClassMetadata`	Disables some `java.lang.Class` methods. This can reduce compiled file sizes.
`-XdisableCastChecking`	Disables runtime checking of cast operations. This can reduce compiled file sizes.
`-XenableClosureCompiler`	From GWT 2.5 onward, there's the option Use the Closure Compiler on GWT Output—this should create smaller JavaScript output.
`-XfragmentMerge`	Enables the GWT 2.5 fragment merge code splitter (as opposed to the pre-GWT 2.5 standard one—see the optimization chapter for details).
`-XdisableRunAsync`	Disables the ability to code split.
`-XdisableSoycHtml`	Disables the production of HTML from the Story of Your Code report, leaving only the XML output.

Table 2.3 Experimental arguments that can be passed to the GWT compiler *(continued)*

Argument	Description
`-XdisableUpdateCheck`	Disables the update check for a new version of GWT at compilation time.
`-XsoycDetailed`	Enables extra detailed information to be produced for the Story of Your Code report.
`-XcompilerMetrics`	From GWT 2.5, compiler metrics aren't emitted by default for the Compile report; this flag turns them on.

That's it; you now have a basic application that you can use as the basis for any application. In the next chapter we'll present the results of doing that in the form of the `BasicProject` application, which gives the functionality of figure 2.1.

You could take the output you now have and play with different widgets and panels (see the `com.google.gwt.user.client.ui` package of GWT for different types if you want to get hacking, or look through chapter 4 for some more guidance).

Looking to generate source maps?

GWT doesn't have a compiler flag to generate source maps yet. Instead, you need to add the following to a GWT module that your application uses:

```
<set-property name="compiler.useSourceMaps" value="true">
```

You may have noticed that we introduced a lot of terminology when we went through the wizards, such as `EntryPoint` and module. These might be new to you, or you might be wondering what the difference is between concepts that seem close, such as Java packages and GWT modules. Let's spend a few minutes trying to clarify these areas of potential confusion, starting with perhaps the most easily confused: GWT modules and Java packages.

2.7 Understanding modules vs. packages

Every GWT application/project will contain Java packages and GWT modules. You're probably fairly familiar with Java packages; they're a way of encapsulating related Java classes and/or functionality together under a single namespace.

DEFINITION *Java package*—Encapsulates related Java classes and functionality under a single namespace. They're useful, among other reasons, for the separation of logical units of code.

The application you'll create shortly will have a package called `com.manning.gwtia.ch02.client`, with a single Java class file.

GWT overlays a parallel module structure in the source code, which is invisible and inconsequential to the Java compiler but is visible and important to the GWT compiler.

DEFINITION *GWT module*—Encapsulates units of GWT configurations (paths, properties, deferred binding, and so on) on the source code of your application. They're defined in an XML module file and stored in the Java package hierarchy. They're useful, among other reasons, for the separation of logical chunks of functional instructions to the GWT compiler.

A module is defined by an XML format file that gives instructions to the GWT compiler. These instructions tell the compiler, among other things, where to find source Java files to compile into JavaScript, where the application's entry point is, and how to handle generators and deferred bindings (these are techniques GWT relies on to minimize code you need to write and handle such things as browser differences; we discuss them in detail in chapters 16 and 17), and they can define a number of properties (such as what locales are used in internationalization; see chapter 11) or what other modules need to be inherited.

Modules are defined in a *.gwt.xml files, which we'll call module files. Let's take a moment to look a little more at a module file.

2.7.1 What's in a GWT module?

Listing 2.4 shows a relatively complicated example of a module file (more complicated than the simple one in `HelloWorld`).

Listing 2.4 A more complicated GWT module file

```
<module>
  <inherits name='com.google.gwt.user.User'/>
  <inherits name='com.google.gwt.i18n.I18N'/>
  <inherits name='com.google.gwt.user.theme.standard.Standard' />
  <inherits name="com.google.gwt.logging.Logging" />
  <inherits name="com.google.web.bindery.requestfactory.RequestFactory" />

  <entry-point
         class='com.manning.gwtia.ch02.client.HelloWorld'/>
  <source path='client'/>

  <define-property name="dev.mode" values="debug,prod"/>
  <property-provider name="dev.mode"
                     generator="com.gwtia.ch17.DMPropProvGenerator"/>


  <extend-property name='locale' values='en_US, en_GB, fi, is, sv, ar'/>
  <set-property-fallback name='locale' value='en_US'/>
  <set-property name="gwt.logging.logLevel" value="ALL" />
  <set-property name="gwt.logging.enabled" value="FALSE"/>
```

```
  <extend-configuration-property
        name="compiler.splitpoint.initial.sequence"
        value="com.manning.gwtia.ch19.client.car.CarGateway" />
  <set-configuration-property name="CssResource.style"
                              value="stable-notype"/>

  <replace-with class="com.manning.gwtia.ch17.client.devmode.Type_Debug">
    <when-type-is class="com.manning.gwtia.ch17.client.devmode.Type"/>
      <when-property-is name="dev.mode" value="debug"/>
  </replace-with>

  <generate-with
         class="com.manning.gwtia.ch18.rebind.WidgetDebugGenerator">
    <all>
      <when-type-assignable class="com.google.gwt.user.client.ui.Widget"/>
        <none>
          <when-type-assignable
                       class="com.google.gwt.uibinder.client.UiBinder"/>
          <when-type-assignable
                   class="com.google.gwt.logging.client.LoggingPopup"/>

        </none>
    </all>
  </generate-with>
</module>
```

Listing 2.4 contains a number of `inherit` instructions telling the compiler to find, and use, the rules in those inherited modules in another module in the first line. Inheritance in this case means that the GWT compiler will apply all the instructions it finds in the inherited module as well as those written in this module. For some entries GWT treats inherited rules as additions; you can have multiple inherits and more inherits in the inherited module. But other entries, particularly when setting properties, are hierarchical; a later entry will replace an earlier one. We'll note these in the relevant chapters.

The rest of this module file plays around with a number of properties and configuration properties, extending and setting them. These will all drive different behaviors in how the compiler operates. For example, the extending of the `locale` property tells the GWT compiler it needs to create a number of outputs for different locales (UK English, American English, Swedish, and so on).

Instructions such as `replace-with` and `generate-with` are powerful. The first tells the compiler to replace a certain type with another type when certain conditions are met; this is how GWT handles differences with browser implementations (more on this in chapter 17). Giving the GWT compiler a `generate-with` tag tells it that when it sees a particular type, it needs to automatically start creating code based on a generator class. Think of that—the GWT compiler can automatically create parts of your program for you.

We'll introduce the items that can be found in a module file when we need them as we go through the book.

The module file is always named after the related module. When you run the GWT tools in a moment, you'll create the `HelloWorld` module, and that will be defined in the HelloWorld.gwt.xml module file. It's stored within the Java package structure, and although a module can be placed anywhere, it's strongly recommended to place it in the root package, where it's most applicable.

For a simple application with only one module, that means the module file is found in the root Java package (`com.manning.gwtia.ch02` in our example). Other, more complicated applications may have more than one module. But before we discuss how many you should have, we'll have a little discussion on the benefits of a module.

2.7.2 What are the benefits of modules?

The benefit of a GWT module is that it allows you to group together necessary instructions for the GWT compiler at the lowest level possible in your code tree, enabling reuse.

Say you have a math library that you'll use in your application, so you add it to your project. At first glance there's little benefit in creating a GWT module for it, because there are unlikely to be any GWT compiler-specific instructions for it.

But maybe this is a legacy math library that's shared with other applications. Because of that, its namespace is `com.myco.math` rather than `com.myco.client.math`. You'll see later that the GWT compiler works, by default, on code under `client`, so your math library won't currently be visible to the GWT compiler. That can be fixed by putting a `<source path="math"/>` instruction in a GWT module.

It could also be the case that the library needs to implement a math function a different way for IE6 than for other browsers. You'll see later in chapter 17 that you can use deferred binding to manage this by using a `<replace-with>` instruction in a module file.

You could put both of these instructions into the application's main module file, but that would hinder you if you wanted to use the math library in another application (because you'd have to remember to copy both instructions into that new application's module file).

The simpler solution is to put a GWT module file in `com.myco.math`, say Math.gwt.xml, which contains only those two GWT compiler instructions necessary to use the math library. You'd then inherit that module in your existing application's module, via an `<inherits name="com.myco.math.Math"/>` instruction, to make it all visible.

> **TIP** Sharing GWT code? You must remember to include the source code in any .jar file you create because the GWT compiler works from Java source code.

When it comes to sharing or reusing this module, you export the source files from the `com.myco.math` package, together with subpackages and the module file, as a .jar file. Then you make sure the .jar file is on the new application's class path, to make the Java compiler happy, and inherit the `Math` module in the new application's module file, to make the GWT compiler happy.

Inheriting a module?

When sharing GWT code across applications, you need to remember that in addition to putting the new code on your classpath, you must inherit the appropriate module (through an `<inherit>` tag) in your new application's module file.

Failure to do so will result in GWT throwing a "did you forget to inherit a module?" error.

The act of inheriting the module makes the instructions visible to the GWT compiler of the new application. Unfortunately, inheriting isn't automatic. The author of the module needs to tell others what module to inherit for things to work.

If you don't inherit the correct module, the GWT compiler will throw a "did you forget to inherit a module?" error. You can even get this error in standard GWT if you use functionality outside the standard aspects, for example, client bundles. An efficient way to manage resources, which is discussed in chapter 5, requires you to explicitly inherit the `Resources` module (we'll cover these as and when needed).

Now that we've looked at the benefits, you probably have the question "How many modules should I have?" in your mind.

2.7.3 How many modules should you have?

You could have one module for your whole application, or at the other end of the scale, you *could* have a module per Java class. In practice, the number of modules you'll have will be a design decision based on how decoupled you wish to make logical GWT units of the code and how much reuse you expect in the future.

Our chapter examples are, we like to think, a good example. Let's take chapter 11's example about three different ways of supporting languages in your user interface. Like

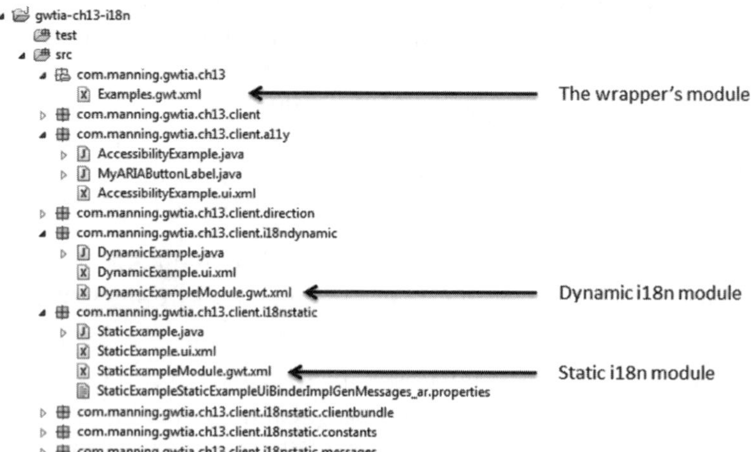

Figure 2.32 Chapter 11's module setup: one module for the wrapper application and one module for each of the distinct examples. This allows a nice separation of concerns, which means each example's module file shows only those module instructions necessary for it to work.

most of the chapter examples, it consists of a wrapper application that allows the user to select one of a number of examples. The wrapper is treated as one module and each example as another; see figure 2.32.

The benefit in such a setup is that each module describes only what it needs and no more. You can therefore quickly see what inherits and properties, for example, you need for a particular functionality.

The wrapper's module file, Examples.gwt.xml, is shown in the next listing.

Listing 2.5 An example of a module inheriting other modules

```
<module rename-to="gwtia_ch13_i18n">
   <inherits name='com.google.gwt.user.User' />
   <inherits name='com.google.gwt.user.theme.standard.Standard' />
   <inherits name="com.google.gwt.resources.Resources" />
   <inherits name=
     "com.manning.gwtia.ch13.client.i18nstatic.StaticExampleModule" />
   <inherits name=
     "com.manning.gwtia.ch13.client.i18ndynamic.DynamicExampleModule" />
   <entry-point class='com.manning.gwtia.ch13.client.Examples' />
   <source path='client' />
</module>
```

❶ Inheriting the static example's module

❷ Inheriting the dynamic example's module

In listing 2.5 you can see that inheriting is merely a case of using the `<inherits>` tag and providing the fully qualified name of the module ❶ and ❷ (package structure, for example, `com.manning.gwtia.ch13.client.i18nstatic`, plus module name, for example, `StaticExampleModule`).

The module holds the entry point definition, so GWT knows where to find the "main" function, and it inherits GWT's browser history management functionality. It also inherits the three example module files; otherwise they'd be orphaned (meaning the GWT compiler may miss important information, and compilation will fail).

Each of the individual example modules contains only the GWT instructions it needs. For example, the StaticExampleModule.gwt.xml module file contains only the necessary instructions to tell the GWT compiler that we'll be using static internationalization. This means inheriting the `I18N` module, extending the `locale` property (defined in the `I18N` module) with the locales we're using, and setting a fallback locale.

As an interesting exercise, you can investigate the module structure GWT employs by looking at the `User` module defined in `com.google.gwt.user`, which is inherited by all GWT applications, and following all the inherits that are in there.

In this book we'll introduce the various instructions the module file can contain as and when they're needed (for example, in the chapters on internationalization, generators, deferred binding, and so on).

We hope modules now make a little more sense, and we hope that as you look at the example code in this book they become even clearer. With the knowledge of modules under your belt, we should dig into the *uncompiled* part of application a little more to see what structures and restrictions we need to consider.

2.8 Digging deeper into the uncompiled application

In the uncompiled part of the project sits the Java code for your application and any GWT module definitions, both client and server side (if you're using GWT-RPC or RequestFactory). You should stick to certain conventions for folder structure as well as Java package structure. Also noteworthy are some (sensible when you think about it) restrictions on the Java constructs you can use on the client side, as well as some Java classes GWT expects to see, as we'll cover next.

2.8.1 Folder structure convention

Typically, a GWT application structure has four folders: src, lib, bin, and test. The content of your test cases is usually found in the test folder. Because you aren't including any other Java/GWT libraries in the example here, you won't have a lib directory, but if you were, then you'd probably put them in here.

The src directory is where you'll put all of your Java source code, and sometimes Eclipse or another IDE will show the bin folder. The bin folder isn't relevant to GWT, but IDEs typically create it and store IDE-compiled versions of your Java source code there (the normal class files that aren't used by GWT).

Within the src folder, you'll find your project's Java package structure, along with its GWT modules.

2.8.2 Package structure convention

You're free to use any Java package structure you want, but there are some conventions GWT expects:

- Code you want the GWT compiler to compile to JavaScript should go under the `client` package.
- GWT RPC code for the server (see chapter 7) should go under the `server` package.
- Code that's shared between server and client should sit in a `shared` package.
- Code used for generators (see chapter 17) typically sits in a `rebind` package.

These are all "should" conventions, and GWT offers the flexibility to use different packages if you want through definitions in module files.

If you want GWT to compile code in a package other than the default `client` package, say `some_other_package`, use a `<sourcepath="some_other_package">` entry in one of your module files.

Have code to compile outside the client package?

Sometimes you may wish to store your code in a package other than `client`. That's possible with GWT by providing a `<source>` directive in your module file. For example,

```
<source path="shared"/>
```

> ***(continued)***
>
> would tell the GWT compiler that the package `com.manning.gwtia.ch02.shared` and its subpackages also contain code it should compile into JavaScript.
>
> We'll come to this point here a few times with GWT. Because something is visible to the Java compiler (that is, you've imported it using an `import` statement) doesn't mean it's visible to the GWT compiler. The `source` directive may be required.
>
> Similarly, if you're using code in another module, make sure it's inherited in your module definition; otherwise you'll get a "did you forget to inherit a module?" error in development mode/compilation.

The src directory holds your application's Java files, but there are some restrictions on what parts of Java you can use, which we'll explore next.

2.8.3 *What parts of Java can you use in GWT?*

Everything that's in a source package for GWT will be compiled to JavaScript. By default that means the `client` package, but you can add other packages, as you've seen.

Any code that's compiled to JavaScript needs to be written in the subset of Java that GWT understands. This restriction is common sense if you take a moment to think it through: you can only use those parts of Java that make sense in a browser context (for example, currently most of the file aspects of `java.io` aren't available because browsers can't, pre-HTML5, access the filesystem).

It's easy to forget this restriction when you're working in a Java environment only, and you'll be reminded at compile time only if you've used something you can't.

> **What Java can you use on the client side?**
>
> Check out the GWT JRE emulation document, which tells you what Java packages and classes you can use in your client-side code:
>
> http://mng.bz/V0xm
>
> As a rule, if a browser can't perform some functionality, it won't be available in the GWT JRE.

Outside of code that's to be compiled to JavaScript, you can use any Java you want. One particularly important Java class that each application will have at least one of (and usually only one) is the `EntryPoint`, which we covered back in section 2.3.3.

Up until now, we've talked mainly about the client-side part of your application, the bit your user sees on the screen. In preparation for the section on deployed applications, let's take a sneak peek at the server side of a GWT application, which might reside in the uncompiled application part or the deployable part, depending on your choice of server code.

2.8.4 The server side

The `server` package is, by convention, where the Java code you wish to execute on the server is stored in the project. Because the package is normally not included in any `<source>` directives in module files, it will never be compiled to JavaScript, and therefore you have no restrictions on what Java constructs you use.

Java code in the `server` package of the undeployed application will be compiled into class files and moved by the GWT compiler into the classes directory in the deployable part of the project automatically—one less thing for you to worry about. In chapter 7 we'll look at introducing server-side code to applications using GWT's RPC approach, and in chapter 8 we'll look at the newer `RequestFactory`.

But if you have non-GWT-RPC/`RequestFactory` code, for example, other servlets or server-side code in another language, you can store it directly in the deployable application part of your code package, and that's what we'll look at next.

2.9 Reviewing the deployable application part of a GWT application

The web archive (war) is where the application you'll deploy to your production server resides. It's a standard Java Enterprise Edition[7] (JEE) web archive, which means your compiled GWT application is standards compliant (and if you're familiar with wars you can expect it to behave in line with your expectations).

Before you compile your application for the first time, this folder holds only the static resources of the project, for example, the application's HTML file and perhaps CSS files, images, and any non-GWT-RPC server-side code.

After compilation, the resulting JavaScript files for the client side are placed in the web archive and then any GWT-RPC server-side code is moved into the classes directory for you. You have to manually put any .jar files your server-side code relies on in the lib directory. GPE has already put the gwt-servlet.jar used by GWT-RPC code (see chapter 7) in this lib directory; you can safely delete this if you aren't using GWT-RPC.

What's with the funny filenames?

You'll have noticed in the deployable part of the application some strange filenames, such as 524C229849DD7888D1BBAB1A1C867FB5.cache.html. These are the JavaScript implementations of your application that the compiler creates and names. Within the bootstrap code of your application (also created by the compiler), the correct file will be requested.

By naming these files using an MD5 hashing algorithm, GWT ensures two things:

1. The browser can cache the file with no confusion. The next time you run the application, the startup is even faster.

---

7 Java Enterprise Edition: http://mng.bz/815h.

> ***(continued)***
>
> 2. If you recompile, then the bootstrap code will force the browser to load the new version of your application (because it will be asking for a new filename). The next time you run the application, you'll get the latest version.
>
> It's as simple as that.

Finally, in the war is a web.xml file. This file is also JEE standard and contains a set of directions for the web server. It should list the URL of any server-side code and in which package the server can find the Java code to run for that URL. This is a standard servlet-mapping definition, and it's something else we'll cover in chapter 7. As you've seen, you can also include a welcome file list in this file.

If you're thinking this sounds familiar, then yes, it should. GWT has taken many leaps and bounds to make the deployable application as standard as possible. If you have a modern application server, then deploying a GWT application should be as simple as deploying any other web application.

There's one more trick that can change the output of the GWT application for your needs: linkers.

2.9.1 *Harnessing different linkers*

The previous description of a GWT application's deployable part is the default view; it can be altered. Perhaps you want only a single script output or you want to use the application in a cross-site manner (in a different URL). In those and other cases, you can use GWT's linkers to help.

GWT's compilation is in two parts: Java to JavaScript and then linking and packaging. The default linker is the `com.google.gwt.core.linker.IFrameLinker` and is responsible for the default output you saw previously.

If you look in GWT's `Core` module and those it references, you'll see several linkers defined:

- `IFrameLinker`—This is the default linker and creates the bootstrapping process already described, loading the GWT application into an iFrame (it's named `std`).
- `SingleScriptLinker`—This produces a single script output where all code is in the nocache.js output (it's named `sso`).
- `XSLinker`—For use when you need a cross-site-compatible bootstrap sequence (named `xs`).
- `CrossSiteIframeLinker`—This uses an iFrame to hold the code, with a script tag being responsible to download it for use when you need a cross-site-compatible output.
- `DirectInstallLinker`—This is another cross-site-compatible approach. According to the documentation, this adds a script tag to the iFrame rather than downloading as a `String` and then inserting into the iFrame.

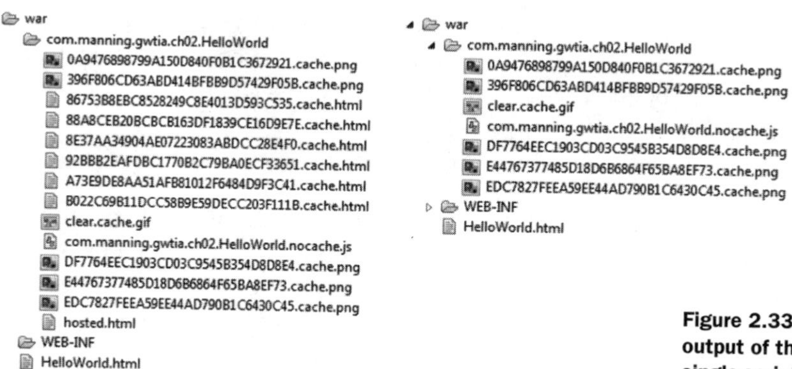

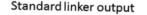

Figure 2.33 Comparison of output of the standard versus single-script linkers

We mention these so you know you have some options, and we won't explore them further. Most of the time the standard linker is what you need, so there's no need to fiddle. If you do find you need to use a different linker—maybe you're creating code that will be embedded into another person's site—then you can change the linker by adding it into your module definition. For example, to use the single-script linker you'd add

```
<add-linker name="sso" />
```

Doing so would change the output of the compiler, as shown in figure 2.33.

The difference shown in figure 2.33 is that the single-script linker has put all the JavaScript code into one file (com.manning.gwtia.ch02.HelloWorld.nocache.js—what a mouthful!), whereas in the standard output that file contains only the bootstrap code, which then selects the most appropriate cache.html file.

We won't cover linkers more in this book; as we said, most of the time you never need to think of them. But if you feel an urge to understand a little more, then you can find an interesting session[8] at Google IO in 2010 that talked about them (though it might be getting a little out of date).

We're at the end of the first part of building a GWT application. Before we summarize, we suggest that you play with the code and get a good feeling for all the concepts we've looked at. To that end, we'll introduce a brief section suggesting some things you might want to do to enhance your understanding.

2.10 Building on your understanding

Now that we've built a first application together, we suggest you spend a little time playing with what we've discussed before moving on. For example, you might try the following:

- Get comfortable with running development mode.

  Try running this chapter's simple application in several different browsers.

---

8 Google IO session on linkers: http://mng.bz/5An6.

- Get comfortable with compiling.

  Try the different output styles and see the differences.
- If you're brave and eager to get ahead, try adding some different widgets and panels to the `RootPanel`.

  We'll discuss these more in the next chapter, but you can find a list of widgets online.[9] For example, you could write the following in the `onModuleLoad` method:

```
RootPanel.get().add(new Label("Hello World"));
RootPanel.get().add(new Button("Click Me!"));
SimplePanel testPanel = new SimplePanel();
testPanel.add(new Label("A label in a panel"));
RootPanel.get().add(testPanel);
```

- Try running the chapter's example in debug mode and set breakpoints in the `onModuleLoad` method.

  If you've changed that method to the code we showed, you'll have plenty of places to put the breakpoint.
- Use a `rename-to` attribute in the module file to make your code's URL more manageable.

  For example, change the first real line of the module file to the following and then see how to get your application running again:

```
<module rename-to="ch02">
```

  Hint: try clearing your browser cache, running your application in development mode, and then refreshing the code tree in Eclipse. Check the path shown for the bootstrap code in your HTML file (❷ in listing 2.2).

  Answer: see the sidebar in section 3.2.
- If you're eager to see a client/server application now, run the GPE New Web Application wizard you saw in figure 2.4.

  Use a different project name to avoid having problems in Eclipse, but don't turn off the generation of the sample application. You'll get a complete and more complicated GWT application to examine and play with.

2.11 Summary

You've reached the end of this chapter, and we expect you to be in possession of a simple GWT project that displays "Hello World!" on the screen. Not an earth-shattering application, but it has been useful. In this application we accomplished the following:

- Introduced some of the terminology used in GWT
- Showed how to use the GPE plug-in wizards to create a `HelloWorld` project
- Used Eclipse to run the project in development mode

---

9 List of GWT widgets: http://mng.bz/C6p1.

- Examined the files produced and how they fit together to form an application
- Used the GPE to compile the application for deployment
- Looked at various ways you could find out where something has gone wrong in the application

Our hope is that this chapter has helped you become comfortable with how to create, run, and debug a GWT application, and you know what the structure of it looks like and how it's compiled. These are the steps you'll follow for every GWT application you create, and we can't overstate the importance of the benefits of development mode and the full debugging capabilities of an IDE. As your applications get bigger, you'll surely be happy this mode exists.

The next step is to take the structure you created and enhance some of the files to get to a more complicated application, and that leads us nicely into chapter 3.

3 Building a GWT application: enhancing HelloWorld

This chapter covers

- Enhancing chapter 2's output for the real world
- Using widgets, panels, and layout panels, and handling events
- Manipulating the Document Object Model (DOM)
- Managing history in a GWT application

In the last chapter, we went through the steps to generate a basic GWT application using the Google Plugin for Eclipse (GPE). The result was the framework of an application with a simple entry point whose `onModuleLoad` method displayed the text "Hello World!" on the browser page. It wasn't the most exciting of applications, but it allowed us to examine the structure of a GWT application as well as run it in development mode and compile it for web mode—the basics of GWT development, we called it.

We hope you're comfortable with those steps now, so it's time to take the next step—enhancing the basic framework to provide the functionality you want. You could add more HTML content to the application's web page; enhance the Java code to use more widgets, panels, and handle events; manage a user clicking Forward and

Back browser buttons; and apply styling to make the application look beautiful—we called these the typical techniques used in a nontrivial GWT application.

We'll be up front here: Rather than walk through the steps to do some of these typical techniques, we'll look at a new `BasicProject` and explore how to implement those techniques. The way to get the most out of this chapter is to download the chapter's examples and start playing with the code. `BasicProject` was built using the process in chapter 2 and then physically enhanced to implement the mock-up in figure 2.1 as figure 3.11 near the end of this chapter.

This chapter's main example, called `gwtia-ch03-basicproject`, contains `BasicProject`, which you can import into Eclipse without getting any conflicts or confusion. Along the way, we'll also discuss the `gwtia-ch03-historyhelper` project, which helps you explore GWT's approach to history in a simple and isolated manner.

Now that you're back from getting and importing the examples, the first thing we should do is recap what you're trying to build and what it shows you about GWT.

3.1 Reexamining the example application

Figure 3.1 highlights how you'll be implementing the mock-up. You'll use GWT widgets and panels to insert a logo as an `Image` widget into a predefined location in the application's HTML file, via a panel called `RootPanel`. That logo could be put in the HTML file directly, but we want to show a principle of GWT, and this is a simple way to do that.

You'll construct the tab area using a couple of GWT panels. The GWT `TabLayoutPanel` lets you look at three GWT concepts. You'll see GWT manipulating the Document Object Model (DOM) by extracting content from an HTML page and placing it in `HTMLPanels`, which are in turn used in the tab panel. Building this component, you'll see how widgets and panels are added to each other.

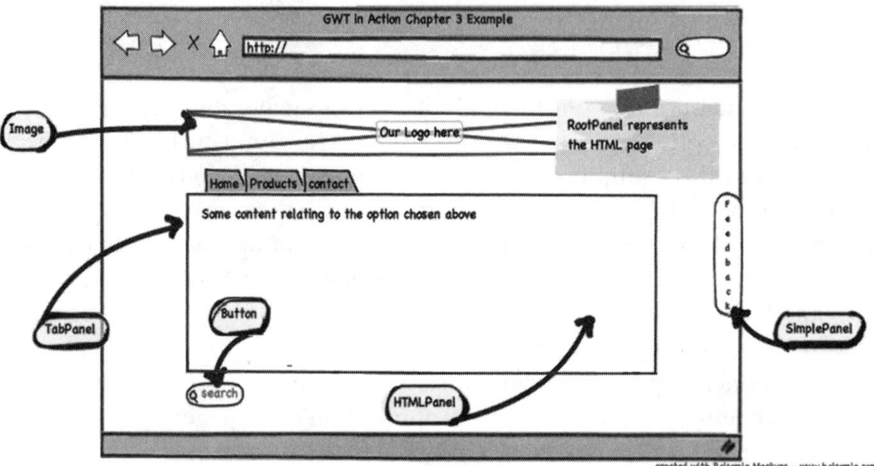

Figure 3.1 Mock-up of chapter 3's main example application showing the layout in the browser window and which widgets and panels you'll use

In addition, we'll explore GWT history with this tab panel. Each click on a tab will change the content. If you then click the browser's Back or Forward button you'll change to the expected tab content automatically. As well as seeing history in action in the `gwtia-ch03-basicproject` project, you'll see a more isolated use of GWT history in the `gwtia-ch03-historyhelper` project.

On the right side of the application is a *feedback* tab, something that's becoming as common on websites nowadays as the "How is my driving?" stickers on commercial vehicles. Our application will explore how you can use some simple event handling and CSS styling to pop this panel in and out as the mouse is moved over it.

GWT can also wrap existing components in your HTML page—useful if you want to introduce GWT into a legacy application. Down on the bottom of the application is a Search button, which you'll define in the HTML page and wrap into the application to pop up a text box where a search term can be entered.

The last thing you'll do in the application is apply some Cascading Style Sheet styles to the panels and widgets. You'll do that in three ways: programmatically, by giving a widget a style name, and by using one of the provided GWT themes. These styles will give the application the final touches so it resembles our mock-up.

Out in the real world your GWT applications will be applying a more complicated version of some or all of these techniques together with some client/server interaction. You might bolster your design and development and support your maintenance team by applying the industrial-strength techniques we cover later in this book, but it will still be an application that applies the previously mentioned techniques.

In this chapter we'll look into the `BasicProject` code and see how the items we've discussed are realized. Our aim is for you to understand how to get to figure 3.11 later in this chapter. As you read through this chapter, we ask that you take the example as something that allows us to show off various GWT techniques rather than wonder why we haven't done it in an easier and more sensible way.

We don't want it to look like we're pulling a rabbit out of a hat and present chapter 3's code and expect you to be impressed, so let's quickly discuss the enhancements we made to go from the framework of step 1 to the implementation of figure 3.11.

3.1.1 Enhancements

Table 3.1 lists the key enhancements we've made to the output of step 1 in chapter 2 to get to the final implementation of this chapter's application.

Table 3.1 Changes made to the similar output of chapter 2 to get to this chapter's project

Chapter 2 object	Chapter 3 changes
Overall	We created a project in the same way we did in chapter 2, except we called it `BasicProject` instead of `HelloWorld` so it wouldn't cause confusion.
HelloWorld.html versus BasicProject.html	We added content to the HTML file inside named `div` sections that will be used as the content for the Home, Products, and Contact tabs in the application.

Table 3.1 Changes made to the similar output of chapter 2 to get to this chapter's project *(continued)*

Chapter 2 object	Chapter 3 changes
HelloWorld.java versus BasicProject.java	We updated the `onModuleLoad` method so that it first calls a method to set up the UI for the application (`setUpGUI`) and then starts the GWT history-handling functionality. We added methods to support setting up the UI and handling events, as well as how to handle history. The history handling uses an enumeration to keep things consistent, but it might be a little confusing if you aren't familiar with Java enumerations—don't worry, when we get to the section describing history, we have a simplified example you can download to see how it works using only constants.
HelloWorld.css versus BasicProject.css	We added some style definitions so that the application looks prettier than having text on a screen and positions our feedback tab.
HelloWorld.gwt.xml versus BasicProject.gwt.xml	We added an inherit directive that directs the standard theme for GWT UI components to be included in the application—this makes the application look prettier than only text on the screen and saves us from having to add a lot of style definitions to the BasicProject.css. We added two other, commented-out theme inherits (they're there in case you want to play with them).

All of these changes will be covered in this chapter, sometimes in an obviously named section, sometimes spread out a little more where it makes the flow easier (unless explicitly mentioned otherwise, our future discussion is going to be about the `gwtia-ch03-basicproject` project).

3.2 Updating the HTML

Every GWT application has at least, and 99% of the time only, one HTML page. It can contain anything you could normally have in an HTML file: images, hyperlinks, `div` objects, other JavaScript code, plain text, and so on. This is great for flexibility because it means you can incrementally GWT-ify an existing web page/application, adding GWT where needed. You can gradually swap out functionality for GWT implementations or, as you'll do here, put content in the page that the GWT application can use. Equally, the HTML file could contain no content; that is, it could be a blank page on which your GWT application will create everything.

As we noted in chapter 2, the file must contain a link to your GWT application's bootstrap JavaScript code. Bootstrap code? This is the nocache.js script produced by the compiler that will determine which permutation of your code to request and then start the application when loaded. For our application this script is called basicproject.nocache.js, and you can find it in the basicproject folder of the web archive once the application is compiled or you've run development mode at least once.

If you've used any of the GWT-creation tools, including GPE, then this link has already been created for you in the HTML file. If you're incrementally adding GWT to an existing web application, then you'll need to add this link yourself.

Be careful

If you change or add a `rename-to` tag in your main module definition, you'll need to make sure the bootstrap code in your HTML points to the right place. For example, if you have the following for your `MyApp` module

```
<module rename-to="look_here" />
```

it would mean that your HTML needs to link to the bootstrap code, as follows:

```
<script language="javascript"
       src="look_here/look_here.nocache.js">
```

Listing 3.1 shows the HTML file of `BasicProject` with the mandatory bootstrap code, a link to some optional styling, an iFrame to support history management (needed for Internet Explorer), and some content.

Listing 3.1 The HTML file

```
<!doctype html>
<html>
  <head>
    <meta http-equiv="content-type" content="text/html; charset=UTF-8">
    <link type="text/css" rel="stylesheet" href="BasicProject.css">
    <title></title>
    <script type="text/javascript" language="javascript"
            src="basicproject/basicproject.nocache.js"></script>
  </head>
  <body>
    <iframe src="javascript:''" id="__gwt_historyFrame" tabIndex='-1'
         style="position:absolute;width:0;height:0;border:0">
    </iframe>

    <div id="logo"></div>
    <div id="home">Welcome to the application!</div>
    <div id="products">Here are some of our top products...</div>
    <div id="contact">
       You can contact us at
           <a href="mailto:a@a.com">1 Rudolf Street, The North Pole</a>
    </div>
    <button type="button" id="search">Search</button>
  </body>
</html>
```

❶ Declaring a doctype
❷ Linking a stylesheet
❸ Bootstrapping the GWT application
❹ Managing history in IE 6/7
❺ Creating placeholder for the logo
❻ Providing content for the tabs
❼ Defining an HTML button to be wrapped in the application

The application's HTML file looks like (and is) a standard HTML file: ❶, ❷, ❸, and ❹ are the result of the creation tools; ❺, ❻, and ❼ are standard HTML content we've added ourselves for this specific application.

You indicate the application will run in the browser's so-called standards mode[1] by declaring a `doctype` ❶. This isn't necessary, because most of GWT will currently work in "quirks" mode (except the layout panels we'll discuss shortly), but because we're looking to the future, let's start off in the right direction (GWT might drop support for "quirks" mode in the future as browsers converge on standards). Putting the browser in standards mode also has some impact on the way you use panels, as you'll see in section 3.4.2.

The application bootstrapping code is at ❸, followed by two optional parts. First, there's a link to a stylesheet ❷. You don't need styling, but your application will look much better for it. Section 3.8 looks at styling in more detail. Second, there's an iFrame ❹, needed to support GWT's approach to history management in Internet Explorer (you'll see more about this in section 3.7). Like the link to bootstrap code, this item is added automatically by the creation tools. If you aren't using history support in your application, you could delete this entry.

This is all you need in an HTML file for a GWT application. But you'll add some additional content because you're expecting this application to do the following:

- Insert things in defined areas of the existing page.

  For example, you'll add an image to the `logo div` ❺.
- Use existing components of the page.

  You'll wrap the `search` button ❼ and use it in the application.
- Pull in content.

  The `home`, `products`, and `contact divs` ❻ all hold content that you wish to delete from the HTML page and use directly within the tabs we'll show.

If you're sharp eyed, you may have noticed you give the `divs` and `Button` objects in the list an `id` as you declare them in the HTML page. It's that `id` that you'll use later in the enhanced Java code to get access to them.

3.3 Enhancing the code

Here's `BasicProject`'s `EntryPoint` class (the class that's identified to have the `onLoad` method that's called when the application loads in the user's web browser):

```
public class BasicProject implements EntryPoint {        ❶ Implementing EntryPoint

  public void onModuleLoad() {                           ❷ Providing the entry point
    setUpGui();
    startHistoryHandling();
    setUpEventHandling();
  }
}
```

It implements the `EntryPoint` interface ❶ and the `onModuleLoad` method ❷ as you'd expect. Unlike `HelloWorld`'s entry point, where you added a `Label` to the `RootPanel`,

[1] Information about various browser modes is available at www.quirksmode.org/css/quirksmode.html.

BasicProject's method calls two helper methods defined in the same class to set up the user interface and start GWT's history handling. You can put any valid Java code in the onModuleLoad method; our preference is to keep it clean and simple and use helper methods.

Setting up the GUI is achieved by the helper method shown in the following listing.

Listing 3.2 Setting up BasicProject's GUI

```
private void setUpGui() {
  buildTabContent();
  wrapExistingSearchButton();
  insertLogo();
  createFeedbackTab();
  styleTabPanelUsingUIObject();
  styleButtonUsingDOM();
  RootPanel.get().add(feedback);
  RootPanel logoSlot = RootPanel.get("logo");
  if (logoSlot!=null)logoSlot.add(logo);
  RootPanel contentSlot = RootPanel.get("content");
  if (contentSlot!=null) contentSlot.add(content);
}
```

❶ Creating content

❷ Programmatically styling content

❸ Adding content to page

In listing 3.2's method you call several methods ❶ that help you create content either by inserting the logo image or wrapping the Search button in the HTML page, as you'll see in section 3.4, or scraping out the content for the tabs that we'll look at in section 3.5.

A lot of the content is styled via plain CSS or a GWT theme, but you can also choose to apply styles using methods in the widget's underlying UIObject class or through GWT's DOM class ❷. You'll see how all this is done in section 3.8.

The rest of the method is concerned with manipulating the browser DOM (web page), inserting GUI components onto the page ❸. For now you'll build the user interface directly in your code because it's the simplest way to get across the points in this chapter. But from chapter 6 you'll use the UiBinder approach—GWT's approach to declarative user interface definition. There's no right or wrong way here, but after using UiBinder in chapter 6, we hope you'll find it the best way.

Let's take a look at how to create user interfaces with widgets, panels, and events.

3.4 Creating your user interface

When you display some text to the user, provide a button for them to click, or animate a dialog box giving some information, you're using a widget. When you want to display widgets in some form of structure, then you're most likely going to be using a panel.

DEFINITIONS A *widget* is a component of your web application with which the user may interact. A *panel* is a widget that can hold one or more other widgets in a specific visual/functional structure.

`HelloWorld`'s entry point gave perhaps the simplest example. It created a `Label` widget that's able to hold some text and added it to a panel called `RootPanel` (that represents the web page).

Widgets and panels have some subtle differences between them, so we'll look at them in separate sections—the first on widgets, the second on panels, and a third on a relatively new type of panel called a *layout panel*.

In this chapter you'll programmatically build the interface; you'll create widgets and panels in code and use Java methods on panels to add the widgets. In any real application you'll probably use a declarative approach; UiBinder, which is introduced in chapter 5, allows for separation of concerns between functionality and presentation. But to fully understand the magic behind UiBinder we feel it's necessary to look at the programmatic way first—what you learn won't be lost if you use UiBinder—and our next section starts our journey, looking at widgets.

3.4.1 Presenting widgets

As you saw at the start of this section, widgets are the components that are used to interact with the user: buttons, labels, and so on. GWT has widgets that represent standard HTML/DOM objects such as images and buttons, and widgets that represent more abstract concepts, such as trees or menu bars. There's even a set of data-presentation widgets, discussed in chapter 10, that give an efficient view of large data sets. Luckily we don't need to differentiate between the types; they're all widgets and they're created and used in exactly the same way.

We'd particularly recommend running the GWT Showcase of Features that comes with the GWT download (or can be accessed online[2]) to get a good view of the types of

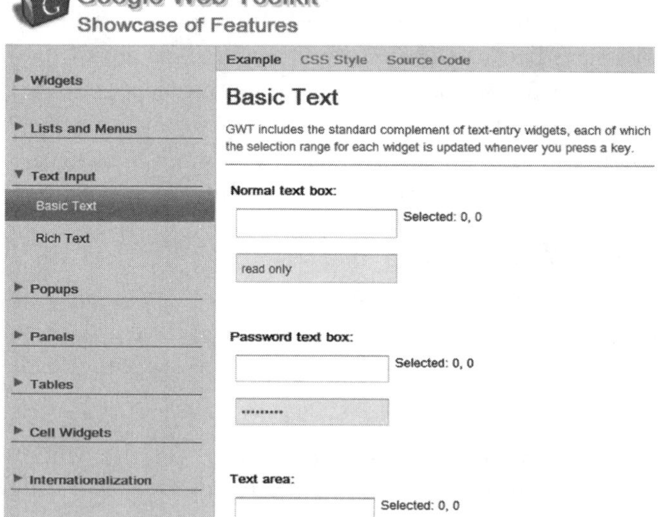

Figure 3.2 A screenshot of GWT's Showcase of Features

[2] The GWT Showcase can be found online at http://gwt.google.com/samples/Showcase/Showcase.html.

widgets that GWT provides—see figure 3.2 for an example. You can also find third-party libraries that provide even more widgets or fancier versions of the standard ones; let's not worry about those for now because we want to concentrate on widgets in general.

In the rest of this section we'll look at the two ways that widgets can be created, as well as how they fit into a particular object hierarchy.

CREATING WIDGETS

The example application's `setUpGui` method in the `EntryPoint` class creates GWT widgets in a couple of ways. It wraps existing widgets, as you'll see in a moment, and it creates widgets from scratch; for example, the logo image is created and inserted into the browser in the `insertLogo` method in a manner similar to this:

```
String LOGO_IMAGE_NAME= "gwtia.png";
Image logo = new Image(GWT.getModuleBaseURL()+"../" + LOGO_IMAGE_NAME);
```

In the Java code, you create a Java object of the type `Image` and pass the location of the image resource into the constructor. The `GWT.getModuleBaseURL` method returns the path to your web application, onto which the image filename, stored as a constant for future maintainability, is appended to give the full path, showing the logo as in figure 3.3.

You may be wondering why you go up a directory first to find the image file. The GWT-generated code goes into the BasicProject folder in the war; the image, though, is directly under the war, one folder up from our code. You keep the source image at that level to ensure it's not overwritten by GWT during compilation. You can place it anywhere in the war file that suits you as long as you link correctly.

Behind the scenes, widgets have a dual existence. In your Java code they're pure Java objects, and in the browser they're DOM elements. The Java `Image` object previously shown becomes the following DOM object when you're running your application (where xxxxxxx is the path to the JavaScript code of the application):

```
<image src="xxxxxxxxx/../gwtia.png">
```

Do you need to know this? Most of the time you don't, because GWT handles all this for you. But remembering this fact will help you understand why you sometimes can't do things you want to do, or think you should be able to do—the DOM restricts you.

A good example of DOM restrictions is the standard `FileUpload` widget. It's common to hear people ask why you can't set the default text of this widget to a specific filename. You can't do this because the GWT `FileUpload` widget is implemented by

Figure 3.3 The application's logo created as a GWT `Image` widget

the DOM `FileUpload` element—and the DOM stops you from programmatically selecting a filename for good security reasons.

> **NOTE** Always remember that your Java code gets compiled to JavaScript that manipulates the browser DOM. Although GWT can support you in pushing the boundaries of Ajax applications, it can't break the rules of the DOM.

You can also wrap HTML elements that already exist on the web page. This method is particularly useful if you want to incrementally add GWT to your page. You might already have a button that when clicked starts some functionality, and you're moving that functionality into GWT. You can wrap that existing button in your application, and when it's clicked, your new GWT functionality starts.

To wrap an existing element, you use the closest widget's static `wrap` method. Not all widgets support this approach, so you need to check the API. When a widget allows this, it also checks to see that the element you're trying to wrap is of the DOM element it normally represents.

The `Button` widget allows you to wrap an existing `BUTTON` element. In `BasicProject` the existing Search button in the application's HTML page is wrapped in the `wrapExistingSearchButton` method as follows:

```
Button search = Button.wrap(DOM.getElementById("search"));
```

You need to pass the `wrap` method the relevant DOM element, and you'll find that through the `DOM.getElementById` method, passing in the `id` of the element you're trying to find. You might remember in listing 3.2 that you defined the button in the HTML page to have an `id` of `search`—this is the value you use here.

It's worth noting that wrap methods don't exist for all widgets, and they don't wrap any existing event handling on the DOM element—so you'll need to add event handling yourself in your GWT application. Also, if the wrapped element is removed from the DOM, you need to watch for that and call the `RootPanel.detachNow` method to ensure no memory leaks are introduced (this is covered more in chapter 4).

WIDGET HIERARCHY

A benefit of the Java/DOM dual view of widgets is that on the Java side they live within a hierarchy, giving predictable behavior through inheritance. You can find the standard GWT widgets in the `com.google.gwt.user.client.ui` package, and the first few levels of the hierarchy are shown in figure 3.4.

Figure 3.4 First three layers of the GWT widget hierarchy starting with `UIObject` descending to, for example, `Tree`

Every widget is a subclass of UIObject, which provides methods for setting a widget's size (for example, setWidth, setHeight, SetSize, and SetPixelSize), getting its size and position (for example, getWidth and getAbsoluteLeft), and setting its visibility (setVisible).

Widget is a subclass of UIObject and extends the functionality by adding the ability to deal with attaching and detaching widgets to/from the browser DOM and hooking into the GWT event system. By managing these two aspects, GWT removes the chance of memory leaks that can often sneak into Ajax applications when manipulating the DOM directly. If you're interested in the mechanics of attaching/detaching widgets, we cover the topic in more detail in chapter 4.

Next in the widget hierarchy you'll find some real widgets, such as FileUpload, Image, and Tree. You may be wondering where widgets for button, text box, radio button, and so on are. These are all hiding under the FocusWidget class, along with some GWT additional widgets such as PushButton, ToggleButton, RichTextArea, and others.

Two subclasses of Widget deserve a little more explanation: Composite and Panel. Composite widgets are widgets typically made from two or more other widgets that you wish to treat as a single widget. You'll probably spend a large part of your development time creating these types of widgets because they'll form the valuable and reusable components of your application. We'll look at how to create Composite widgets in chapter 4, but GWT provides some as standard. These include, among others, CaptionPanel (a panel that has a caption), DatePicker (for picking dates), and TabPanel.

Panels, from a Java perspective, are a subset of Widget, but they have some special properties that earn them a section all their own.

3.4.2 Organizing layout with Panels

A Panel is a special case of Widget: it can hold one or more other widgets (which themselves might be panels holding other widgets, or panels that hold other widgets or panels that hold other widgets or panels, that hold...well, you get the gist). So panels give you a way of organizing the presentational structure of other panels and widgets. To do that, a Panel introduces the add and remove methods to the basic Widget class.

The way the add method is implemented gives a panel its specific functionality. For example, the add method in a SimplePanel allows only one widget to be added, throwing an exception if you attempt to add a second widget, whereas a VerticalPanel allows one or more widgets to be added, appearing in a visual vertical list that grows downward with each new added widget; by contrast, any number of widgets can be added to a DeckPanel but only one is visible at a particular time.

Panels are also constrained by their underlying DOM implementation—panels have the same dual Java/DOM existence as normal widgets—remember they're a special type of widget. Typically div- and Table-based panels, such as SimplePanel and VerticalPanel, are used for structuring internals of more complicated widgets, for example, the composite widgets we'll look at in chapter 4. For application structure, it's preferable to use layout panels, such as DockLayoutPanel and TabLayoutPanel, which are based on box model dimension constraints. Doing that, you let the browser do the hard work of rendering and layout, making these panels super-fast—but this means you have to put the browser into its standards-compliant mode (more about this and layout widgets in general in chapter 4).

> **Using your browser's standards mode?**
>
> If you're using the standards mode of browsers, you should consider using layout panels for a number of different panels to avoid some layout gremlins.
>
> For `DockPanel` use `DockLayoutPanel`, for `SplitPanel` use `SplitLayoutPanel`, and for `StackPanel` use `StackLayoutPanel`.
>
> For `VerticalPanel` use `FlowPanel`, which by default breaks each new item onto the next line.
>
> For `HorizontalPanel` use `FlowPanel` and set the CSS `float` property to `left` on all added widgets (to suppress the behavior of `FlowPanel` previously described for `VerticalPanel`).
>
> Standards mode means a browser will render DOM and so on, adhering to W3C and IETF standards; some browsers allow a "quirks" mode for backward compatibility for cases where they may have implemented rendering slightly differently.

As we did for widgets, let's look at how to create panels. We'll also give you a flavor of the panel types that GWT provides.

CREATING A PANEL

In the `BasicProject` example you use five panels, `TabLayoutPanel`, `HTMLPanel`, `FocusPanel`, `VerticalPanel`, and `RootPanel`, in the following ways:

- A `TabLayoutPanel` is used for structuring the main display of the application.

  We could have used a `TabPanel` instead because it's functionally equivalent, but we want to harness the flexibility and speed of layout panels for the application structure.
- The example's feedback object on the right of the screen (see figure 3.2) will be a `VerticalPanel` holding two label widgets.
- The `VerticalPanel` will be wrapped in a `FocusPanel`, which listens to all mouse events because `VerticalPanel` doesn't allow that directly.

  The application will listen for *mouse over* and *mouse out* events—you grow the panel when the mouse is over it and shrink it when the mouse moves out of it.
- You extract the HTML content of `BasicProject`'s HTML page's `div`s with `id`s `home`, `product`, and `contact` into `HTMLPanel`s (panels that hold HTML content).
- You place all three `HTMLPanel`s into a `TabLayoutPanel` (a panel that shows a number of tabs and one of its enclosed panels depending on which tab button is selected).
- You use the `RootPanel` to place all these panels on the browser page.

The tabs are built up as shown in listing 3.3 (from the `BasicProject`'s `buildTabContent` method; `getContent` is another helper method, and we'll look at that when we consider manipulating the page a little later in this chapter).

Listing 3.3 Creating part of the panel structure for the chapter example

```
static final int DECK_HOME = 0;
HTMLPanel homePanel;
HTMLPanel productsPanel;
HTMLPanel contactPanel;
TabLayoutPanel content

private void buildTabContent(){
   homePanel = new HTMLPanel(getContent("home"));
   productsPanel = new HTMLPanel(getContent("product"));     ❶ Creating HTMLPanels
   contactPanel = new HTMLPanel(getContent("contact"));
                                                              ❷ Creating TabPanel
   content = new TabLayoutPanel(20, Unit.PX);

   content.add(homePanel, "home");                            ❸ Adding content
   content.add(productsPanel, "products");                       to TabPanel
   content.add(contactPanel, "contacts");

   content.selectTab(DECK_HOME);                              Which TabPanel
}                                                           ❹ content to show first
```

Figure 3.5 shows the tab panel created from the code in listing 3.3, and the code creates new HTML panels from content already in the HTML ❶, creates a new `TabLayoutPanel` ❷, and then adds the content created in ❶ to that new panel ❸. Finally, it selects the Home tab ❹. (If you look at the downloaded code you'll see that the hardcoded strings in listing 3.3, for example, "home," are replaced with a more flexible approach, but we used the hardcoded strings for brevity.)

When you add a widget to a panel, different things happen depending on whether you're thinking about the Java or DOM world. In the Java world, the panel contains a variable to represent the widget(s) it holds, and the widget is added to that variable if the rules of the panel are followed (it's in Java that `SimplePanel` is restricted to having

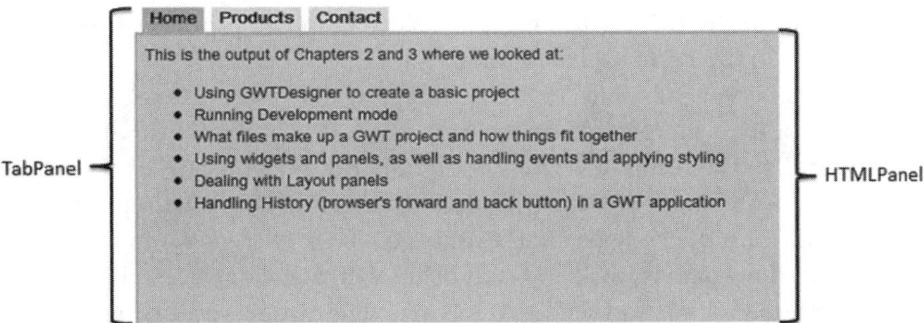

Figure 3.5 A GWT `TabPanel` whose content is made up of several `HTMLPanels`—one per tab

only one widget). Over in the DOM world, the DOM is manipulated so that the widget is inserted into the appropriate DOM structure. Table 3.2 shows the two views when adding a `Button` to a `SimplePanel` and then adding that panel to the `RootPanel`.

Table 3.2 Comparing Java code to DOM when building up a simple panel with a button added to it and adding the panel to the HTML page

Java code	DOM representation
`SimplePanel holder = new SimplePanel();`	`<div></div>`
`Button stop = new Button("Stop");`	<button type="button"> Stop </button>
`holder.add(stop)`	<div> <button type="button"> Stop </button> </div>

`RootPanel.get().add(holder)`	<html>
	  <head>
	    :
	  </head>
	  <body>
	    :
	    <div>
	      <button type="button">
	        Stop
	      </button>
	    </div>
	    :
	  </body>
	</html>

The `SimplePanel` is represented by a `div` element in the DOM and a `Button` as a `button` DOM element. When we add the button to the panel, we're setting a private field in the Java representation of the `SimplePanel` to be the Java representation of the `Button`. Over in the DOM world we're physically inserting the DOM representation of the button into the DOM representation of the simple panel.

In the final row of table 3.2 we're inserting the `SimplePanel` onto the browser page. In Java it's a simple call to the `get` method of the `RootPanel` and adding the `SimplePanel` to the result. Over on the right-hand side you can see that this Java code translates to some more DOM manipulation, inserting the DOM representation of the `SimplePanel` into the `body` of the HTML page.

So, that's how panels work and differ slightly from widgets. In chapter 4 we'll peek under the hood a little and see how GWT manages widgets and panels in more detail, but for now we'll continue by considering what types of panels GWT provides.

TYPES OF PANELS

GWT provides many types of panels, and, as with widgets, GWT's Showcase is a good place to get familiar with them—anything we write in this book would soon be out of date with new panels being added all the time. Instead of discussing the Java hierarchy of panels, as we did with widgets, it's better to think of a panel as sitting in one of five buckets:

- Simple panels that can take only one widget
- Split panels that contain two widgets on either side of a splitter bar that can be dragged by the mouse
- Table-based panels—`Grid` and `FlexTable`; other table-based panels are known as cell panels under the complex panel category (these cell panels shouldn't be confused with the `cell` widgets discussed in chapter 10, easy as it is to do)
- So-called complex panels
- Layout panels

Within the class of simple panels you'll find `FocusPanel` (which can handle all browser focus events), `FormPanel` (for standard HTML forms), `PopupPanel`, and `ScrollPanel`. All work as you'd expect, although you should take care with `Scroll-Panel` to explicitly set its size. (If you don't, it will expand to the size of the widget you add, and no scroll bars will appear.)

The simple panel class also includes `LazyPanel` and `DecoratorPanel`. `LazyPanel` defers some of its computation until it's required, which might be useful if you're looking to speed up your application. `DecoratorPanel` is GWT's way of adding nice rounded corners to widgets.

Split panels allow you to add two widgets, one on either side of a splitter bar that you can drag—a horizontal one and a vertical one come for free.

You'd use the table-based `Grid` panel if you know the dimensions of the panel aren't going to change once you've created it. On the other hand, you can use a `FlexTable` when the dimensions might change after creation (with `FlexTable` you can add as many new rows and columns as you want).

Complex panels cover `AbsolutePanel` (where the x/y position of widgets within the panel can be explicitly set), `DeckPanel` (which acts as a deck of cards showing only one widget at a time), `FlowPanel` (where widgets should flow in the direction of the locale,[3] though you need to remember what you're putting in here—adding a `Label` widget won't flow as you expect, because `Label` is implemented by a `div` element, which will force a new line unless you get funky with some CSS and set the `float` property to left—try using GWT 2.0's new `InlineLabel` instead), `HTMLPanel` (holds HTML content), `StackPanel`, and a set of cell-based (table) panels such as `VerticalPanel`, `HorizontalPanel`, and `DockPanel`.

[3] For example, left to right for English or right to left for Arabic.

Some panels have animation built into them. Panels and widgets that implement the `HasAnimation` interface, such as `Tree`, `SuggestBox`, `PopupPanel`, `MenuBar`, `DisclosurePanel`, and `DeckPanel`, can be set to animate as changes are made to them, for example, opening a tree branch. If you're running this chapter's main example, you'll see the pop-up, which appears when you click the Search button, animate into view. It does this because you call `setAnimationEnabled(true)` when you create it, and the GWT designers had built this animation into the panel.

The final bucket of panels we mention are `Layout` panels. These provide some powerful layout functionality and are driven by style constraints—all you need to know about that for now is that it makes them blisteringly fast. In older versions of GWT we had `DockPanel`, `TabPanel`, `HorizontalSplitPanel`, and `StackPanel`. The latest versions of GWT still have those but also provide `Layout` panel equivalents, such as `DockLayoutPanel`, `TabLayoutPanel`, `SplitLayoutPanel`, and `StackLayoutPanel`. As we've mentioned, `Layout` panels are best suited to the outer structure of your application, and we'll look at them in some more detail in section 4.6, whereas the older-style non-layout versions are more often used for structuring a widget's internals (but see the sidebar "Using your browser's standards mode?" to see some suggestions on using non-layout panels when using the browser's standards mode).

Once you've created widgets and panels, you need to add them to the browser DOM; otherwise, your user will never be able to see or use them. That's done, as you'll see next, by manipulating the page.

3.5 Manipulating the page

You can manipulate the browser page in one of two ways. The preferred way is to treat it as a panel—where GWT looks after you a lot—or via the DOM directly—the Wild West approach. We'll look at both of these in this section, starting with the preferred approach.

3.5.1 Using the RootPanel/RootLayoutPanel

Manipulating the browser page to show your widgets is surprisingly easy, and you already know how to do that. The HTML page is generally treated as a panel—the `RootPanel`—and you use that panel's `add` method.

DEFINITION The `RootPanel` provides access to the underlying HTML page.

You can't create a `RootPanel` in your code; rather you get access to it by calling `RootPanel`'s static `get` method. Accessing the whole HTML page is achieved by calling

```
RootPanel.get()
```

You use that approach to place the feedback link in the `BasicProject` onto the page:

```
RootPanel.get().add(feedback)
```

`RootPanel` is a subclass of `AbsolutePanel`, which allows you to give absolute coordinates for the widget, so you could write `add(feedback, 400,200)` to place the feedback panel in an absolute position if you wanted to. But in BasicProject we decide to position the panel using CSS styling, as you'll see later, so you use the add method without parameters.

The first time you call the get method in RootPanel it links your application into the window-closing event of the browser. This allows GWT to clean up and remove widgets and events from the DOM before the browser window closes—one way GWT works hard in the background to prevent memory leaks and problems for you.

You can also use RootPanel to access defined segments in the HTML by supplying a String that matches the id attribute—remember you want to place a logo image into a specifically defined slot in the HTML and you defined that location by giving a div element an id; back in listing 3.1 we had:

```
<div id="logo"></div>
```

To access that part of the HTML and insert the logo, you pass in the element's id to the get method and check to see if the result isn't equal to null (if GWT can't find the element, then the RootPanel.get(element) method will return a null):

```
Image logo = new Image(GWT.getModuleBaseUrl+"../logo.png");
RootPanel logoSlot = RootPanel.get("logo");
if (logoSlot!=null)
  logoSlot.add(logo);
```

What is the RootLayoutPanel?

If you're using a layout panel (which needs to know about its container resizing so it can resize itself), then you should add it to the browser page using RootLayoutPanel rather than RootPanel (if you don't, then it won't get resize events).

It's not possible to wrap parts of the page with a RootLayoutPanel, so a RootLayoutPanel("someElement") call isn't available.

If you look at the setUpGui method in the BasicProject application, then you'll see you use both techniques of RootPanel to get the widgets and panels onto the page.

The second but less-preferred way of manipulating the page is directly via the DOM.

3.5.2 *Manipulating the DOM directly*

Most if not 99% of the time you'll have no need to directly manipulate the DOM; you can do what you need using widgets and panels. This means you can generally live in a fairly protected world and let GWT worry about most issues you might encounter.

Sometimes, though, you might need more control over the DOM, and GWT doesn't restrict you from doing this or force you to do it in only one way. In BasicProject you wish to take content from the HTML page and use it in the tabs of the TabPanel (you'll also have to delete that content from the HTML page so it's not shown twice). You can do all that only through direct DOM manipulation.

Listing 3.4 shows the `getContent` method you define in BasicProject.java to do these tasks, and it makes use of the both the `getElementId` and `getInnerHTML` methods from GWT's `DOM` class in the `com.google.gwt.user.client` package.

Listing 3.4 Accessing the DOM directly

```
private String getContent(String id) {
  String toReturn = "";
  Element element = DOM.getElementById(id);                    // 1 Getting the Element
  if (element!=null){
     toReturn = DOM.getInnerHTML(element);                     // 2 Getting the Element content
     DOM.setInnerText(element, "");                            // 3 Clearing the existing Element
     SafeHtml sfHtml = SimpleHtmlSanitizer.sanitizeHtml(toReturn);  // 4 Protecting against XSS attack
     toReturn = sfHtml.asString();
  } else {
     toReturn = "Unable to find "+id+" content in HTML page";
  }
}
```

This `DOM` class contains many methods, and you use only three in listing 3.4. To get the text from the HTML page, you first find the `Element` that contains it ❶—remember way back in listing 3.1 you gave the `div`s in the HTML `id`s specifically for this situation; it's those `id`s that you now use.

Assuming that you've found the right `Element`, for example, the `Element` for `id` `contact`,

```
<div id="contact">
   You can contact us at
      <a href="mailto:a@a.com">1 Rudolf Street, The North Pole</a>
</div>
```

you get its inner HTML ❷, which happens to be

```
You can contact us at
   <a href="mailto:a@a.com">1 Rudolf Street, The North Pole</a>
```

Now that you have the inner HTML of the `Element`, you should clear the `Element` to prevent it from still being visible. That's done in ❸ by setting the DOM element's text to the blank string, giving you the following on the HTML page:

```
<div id="contact"></div>
```

You may have noticed that you return an object of type `SafeHtml` from the `getContent` method rather than a `String` ❹. That's to try to protect your application against attacks such as cross-site scripting and is one part of GWT's approach to help secure applications—we'll come back to this at the end of the chapter.

Now you should be able to read the `setUpGui` method and the methods it calls of the application and understand what's going on with creating all the widgets and panels and getting them onto the browser page. Take some time to become comfortable with panels, widgets, and adding them to the page, and when you come back we'll look at how to react to the user doing something in the application.

3.6 Handling events

You now have the widgets on the screen in `BasicProject`, the layout is (nicely) structured via the various panels you're using, and you're displaying it to the user. What happens next is the user will start clicking things, typing, and generally trying to interact; a call to the server might return with data, or the browser might even be closing. Dealing with all these interactions is the process of handling events.

> **DEFINITION** An *event* is an indication that something has happened. If your application is interested in a particular event, then you need to attach a relevant handler to the widget that fires the event.

We'll look at the following in this short section:

- What events are
- How to handle events
- How to prevent the browser from handling events itself—useful if you want to stop text selection or image dragging

In chapter 14 we'll go into events in a lot more detail, including how to preview, cancel, and prevent them, as well as look at how to create your own events (which you might want to do for various reasons, including if you're implementing an `EventBus`-style architecture). For now, we'll define what events are and how to handle them.

3.6.1 What are events?

When we think of an event in GWT, we're thinking about an indication that something has happened. Conceptually, GWT contains two types of events: browser (also known as native) and logical events. A native event is one that's raised by the browser. It might come from the DOM indicating that someone has clicked a button or that an image has loaded. Or it might come from the browser when someone tries to close the browser window or resize it, or when an Ajax call to the server returns, or something else that the browser handles.

Logical events are those that mean something specific to a widget or application. For example, when you change tabs in a `TabPanel`, a `SelectionEvent` is raised by GWT.

Both types of event are treated the same in GWT, and that's through event handlers.

3.6.2 Handling events

Both native and logical events are handled in GWT by an event handler added to the object that could receive the event.

> **Event listener vs. event handler**
>
> GWT 2 uses an event handler model, for example, `ClickHandler`. You may see legacy code using an old event listener model, for example, `ClickListener`; that model is deprecated, and you should move the code to the handler model.
>
> The handler model gives greater flexibility to access details about the event.

The next listing shows how to handle a click event on the example application's Search button by attaching a click handler to the button.

Listing 3.5 Adding a ClickHandler to a Button

```
public void setUpGUI(){
   ...
   search = Button.wrap("search");
   ...
}

public void setUpEventHandling(){
   ...
   search.addClickHandler(
      new ClickHandler(){
         public void onClick(ClickEvent event) {
            final PopupPanel searchRequest = new PopupPanel();
            ...
         }
   });
   ...
}
```

❶ Adding a handler
❷ Defining the handler
❸ Reacting to the event

Handling events follows the same, simple pattern in GWT. You add a specific event handler to the object that will receive the event. That handler will include an `onEvent` method specific to the event—`onClick` in the case of `ClickHandler`—which takes as its parameter the Java representation of the event.

This event object often has various methods that allow you to retrieve information about the event. For example, the `MouseWheelEvent` object has `isNorth/isSouth` methods allowing you to know which way the mouse wheel was spun and a `getDeltaY` method to know how far it was spun. Logical events have similar useful methods; the `SelectionEvent` has a `getSelectedItem` method so you can tell what item was selected.

In listing 3.5 you attach a `ClickHandler` ❷ through the `addClickHandler` method ❶ on a `Button`. The required `onClick` method ❸ handles a `ClickEvent`, though that event object doesn't have any other methods, so you only know a click has happened (if you're interested in which mouse button was clicked, you should use `MouseDown-Handler` instead).

Native events are all raised by the browser and trapped by GWT for you—click a button, and GWT intercepts the DOM click event, creates the GWT `ClickEvent`, and fires it at all the click handlers attached to that button.

In listing 3.5 you added a click handler to the button as an anonymous class—a fairly common approach in Java, meaning you defined it locally as an expression. You can quite easily take a named approach if you want, such as shown here:

```
class ButtonClickHandler implements ClickHandler{
   public onClick(ClickEvent event){...]
}
clicker = new ButtonClickHandler();
```

```
Button search = new Button("search");
search.addClickHandler(clicker);
```

To remove an event handler, regardless of whether it's an anonymous or named class, you need access to its `HandlerRegistration`. And you only get that when you add the handler to the widget, so if you know you'll need it later, you need to slightly amend your code to save it, as follows:

```
HandlerRegistration clickHandlerRegistration = search.addClickHandler(...);
```

Having saved the reference to the `HandlerRegistration`, you can use it later to remove the handler:

```
clickHandlerRegistration.removeHandler();
```

The restrictions on what handlers can be added to a particular widget are usually driven by the underlying DOM element for native events or common sense for logical events. The widget's Javadoc, or your IDE's code-completion functionality, will let you see what events a widget or panel can handle.

Need to handle mouse or key events on a widget that doesn't support that?

Wrap the widget in a `FocusPanel` and add the event handlers to that panel. The event will bubble up to the `FocusPanel` to be handled there (the way GWT manages events hides the differences for you from how IE traditionally bubbles events differently to other browsers).

To the user it looks like the event is being handled by the widget.

The `BasicProject` example uses this approach on the feedback tab—it places it in a `FocusPanel` in order to manage mouse-over and mouse-out events.

With the ability to handle events, the application becomes more useful. But you may also have times when too many events are being handled. Have you ever held the mouse button down and dragged the mouse over your browser screen? All the DOM elements underneath the mouse were highlighted—which would ruin any drag-and-drop functionality you might have been building. You need a way to prevent the default browser action on events.

3.6.3 *Preventing the browser from handling events for you*

Have you ever dragged an image from a web page to the browser location bar? The browser loaded the image as the only item on the page. This is a default browser action that you can prevent, along with others. To do this, you override a widget's `onBrowserEvent` method, called by GWT as part of its event-handling process, and tell it to prevent any default event action. Listing 3.6 shows this for the logo `Image` of this chapter's example.

Listing 3.6 Preventing default browser event handling behavior

```
logo = new Image(GWT.getModuleBaseURL() + "../" + LOGO_IMAGE_NAME){
   public void onBrowserEvent(Event evt){
      evt.preventDefault();
      super.onBrowserEvent(evt);
   }
};
```

❶ Preventing default action

❷ Playing nicely

When you create the `Image` object for the `BasicProject`'s logo, you override its `onBrowserEvent` method (which every widget inherits from the base `Widget` class). To prevent the browser from running its standard functionality, you call the `preventDefault` method on the `evt` parameter ❶. To play nicely with the GWT event-handling system, you must call the `super.onBrowserEvent` method ❷; otherwise, you wouldn't be able to handle the event later in your own code if you wanted to.

Try running the `BasicProject` application and dragging the logo to the browser location bar—nothing will happen. If you comment out the `preventDefault` call in the BasicProject.java code (in the `insertLogo` method), you can then try dragging the logo to the location bar. The behavior will be different.

Now you're at another milestone in your development; you might want to take some time to play with events in the example code. Add a few more widgets, and put some relevant event handlers on them. Often it's easiest to check out the Javadoc[4] to find out what events a widget will handle. Figure 3.6 shows part of the Javadoc entry for `Label`.

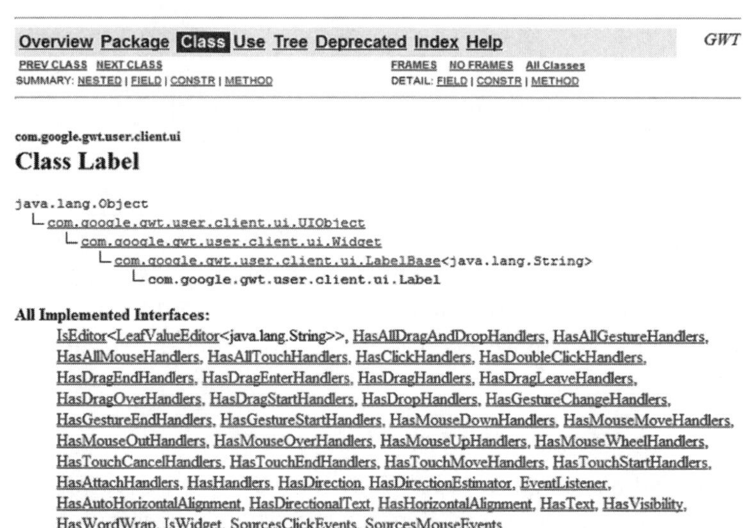

Figure 3.6 Javadoc of `Label` showing all of the event-handling interfaces that it implements—all the events you can handle for a `Label`

[4] For example, the Javadoc for the Label widget is http://mng.bz/0WzH.

Looking at figure 3.6 you can generally quickly translate any of the `HasXXXXXHandlers` interfaces into writing:

```
Label testLabel = new Label("Some text");
testLabel.addXXXXXHandler(new XXXXXHandler(){
   public onXXXXX(XXXXXEvent evt){
      Window.alert("XXXXX happened");
   }
});
```

As we mentioned, we go into events in a lot more detail in chapter 14, so when you've finished exploring events yourself, we'll jump to our next topic, which is covering a specific logical event that can cause Ajax applications problems—history management.

3.7 Managing history

History in an Ajax application is a series of states. In a normal website, clicking the Forward or Back button takes you to a new page; in an Ajax application, you should move between already visited states. For the chapter example, the state will be whichever of the tabs is shown.

GWT harnesses the event structure that we covered in the last section to support telling your application that the history (state) has changed. You can handle these change events by setting up an appropriate event handler and reacting to it, which is what we'll look into in this section.

3.7.1 Handling history in GWT

Ajax applications can employ many techniques to manage history, each more successful in one browser than in another. Some use an iFrame, some react to changes in the URL, others have a timer that checks to see if the URL has changed, and more still use HTML 5's `onhashchange` event. JavaScript libraries, such as DOJO or JQuery, can manage history and hide the various implementation details from you, and GWT is no exception.[5]

If you run a GWT application that manages history, you'll see tokens appearing in the hash part of the URL. Try running the `BasicProject` application and clicking the tabs for Home, Products, and Contact, and look at the URL; it will look something like the following, depending on the tab selected:

http://*www.somename.se/*Historyexample.html#Home

http://*www.somename.se/*Historyexample.html#Products

http://*www.somename.se/*Historyexample.html#Contact

DEFINITION A *history token* is the hash part of a URL (the text from the # symbol). For example, in the following URL, http://www.manning.com/index .html#books, the token is books.

[5] If you're interested in how history is implemented in GWT (as of GWT 2.1), IE8 uses HTML5's `onhashchange` event, IE6/7 uses an iFrame, and Mozilla/Opera/Safari are based on a timer checking for hash changes on the URL.

Changing the hash part in a URL is the only change that can happen that doesn't make the browser request a new page from the server (in a normal HTML page, the hash part of a URL is used to jump to an anchor link within the page). In the GWT world, we refer to the hash part of the URL as the history token.

That's the theory; now let's look at how to handle history in GWT in practice.

3.7.2 Implementing history management in your application

To implement history management in a GWT application, you need to do the following:

1. Add a `ValueChangeHandler` to the `History` object; this is the same principle as adding a `ClickHandler` to a `Button` object.
2. When a notable state change happens, you need to add a new history item to the `History` object using `History.newItem(token)`; this will update the browser's URL with a new history token.
3. Implement the `ValueChangeHandler`'s `onValueChange` method to change your application's state based on a presented history token in the URL.

In the `BasicProject` example, history tokens represents which tab content is visible, so it makes sense to use token values: `home`, `products`, and `contact`.

> **I can't get history working in IE6/7**
>
> If you're using GWT history support, you must have an iFrame in your application's HTML page with an `id` of `__gwt_historyFrame` to support IE6/7 (it's usually hidden from view by specifying its style as `position:absolute;width:0;height:0;border:0`).
>
> This is usually added by the creation tools, but you may have deleted it, or perhaps you're adding GWT to an existing application and so have to add this manually.

In order to examine history without having a lot of other distracting code around, let's look at the `historyhelper` example, in particular the class `com.manning.gwtia.ch03.client.history.HistoryExample`. This example is similar to `BasicProject` but has only the code relating to history management in it (and that code is

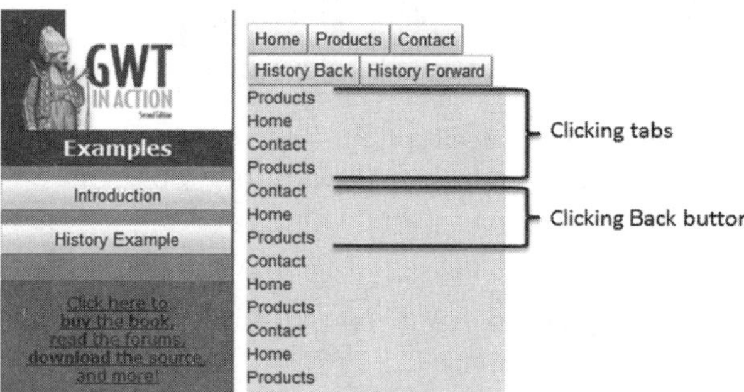

Figure 3.7 The `HistoryExample` helper application in action—the first four labels are from starting the application and clicking the Products, Home, Contact, and then Products buttons in that order. The next three labels are from clicking the Back button three times; notice that the order is the reverse for these three labels, as you would expect going backward through history.

simplified, for example, defining the tokens as String constants rather than as part of an enumeration as in BasicProject). Figure 3.7 shows the helper application HistoryExample in action.

State is changed in the application by clicking one of the buttons. Click the Products button, and the application reacts by creating a new history token via the History .newItem method, with the PRODUCT String constant as the parameter.

History is treated as a logical event in GWT. By adding a ValueChangeHandler to GWT's static History object, GWT will call the handler's onValueChange method when the token changes in the URL. The token can be changed either by the application creating new tokens or the user typing in a new URL (or more likely the user clicking Back/Forward in the browser or arriving at a bookmark).

In HistoryExample a simple setUpHistoryManagement method is called from the constructor:

```
public class HistoryExample extends Composite
                              implements ValueChangeHandler<String>{
   :
  public void setUpHistoryManagement(){
      History.addValueChangeHandler(this);
      History.fireCurrentHistoryState();
   }
   :
```

Usually the EntryPoint class will implement the ValueChangeHandler interface for the whole application, and so it will implement the onValueChange method (although in the helper-apps example, it's the example composite that implements the necessary interface).

After adding the ValueChangeHandler handler to GWT's History object, you directly call the fireCurrentHistoryState method. This allows the application to react to any token already present on the URL when the application starts—this will be the case if, for example, the user has bookmarked your application at a particular history point and is returning.

Here's the implementation of onValueChange that's used in the helper-apps project:

```
public void onValueChange(ValueChangeEvent<String> event){
   String token = null;
   if (event.getValue()!=null) token = event.getValue().trim();
   if ((token==null)||(token.equals("")) showHomePage();
   else if (token.equals(PRODUCTS)) showProducts();
   else if (token.equals(CONTACT)) showContact();
   else showHomePage();
}
```

The first thing to do is use event.getValue to find out the new token (you trim it to remove any hidden white spaces). If there's no token, then you change the state of the application to show the home page; otherwise, if the token matches one of the constants, you show the appropriate page.

Showing the page in the helper application means adding a label to the screen. In a real application it would do more—for the BasicProject example, it changes the tab to the relevant content.

> **Have you run out of history?**
>
> Not many things are more annoying than clicking the Back button one too many times and being unexpectedly thrown out of an application. To prevent that from happening, you could add a ClosingHandler such as the following:
>
> ```
> Window.addWindowClosingHandler(new ClosingHandler(){
>    public void onWindowClosing(ClosingEvent event) {
>       event.setMessage("Ran out of history.  Now leaving application, is
>              that OK?");
>    }
> });
> ```
>
> Now the user gets a warning message from the browser before the application exits.

The history token is simple, merely a reference to the page you want to see. You could envision it encoding more information. For example, a future products page could show many different type of products, perhaps 10 at a time. You could encode the history token to say which subpage of products to show—products 1–10 could have the token products, and products 21–30 could have the token products?page=3. Showing the right state requires a little parsing of the token, but that's not impossible.

You can also fire history backward and forward programmatically. In the history-helper project, clicking the History Back button is the same as clicking the browser's Back button. It's as simple as writing the following in the History Back button's ClickHandler:

```
History.back();
```

With GWT's approach to history, your imagination (well, that and Internet Explorer's max URL length of 2,038 characters) is your only limit.

From GWT 2.1, the concept of *places* was introduced. Places can, in some sense, be seen as History plus and automate some of the encoding we previously discussed; we won't worry about it for now because History is more than adequate for our needs here (we'll cover Places in detail in chapter 15 on MVP).

All of the functionality for BasicProject is now in place. The only thing left is to make it look pretty and get some of the components in the right place. You do that with styling.

3.8 Styling components

You can style widgets in the following five ways:

- Programmatically, such as saying button.setWidth("100px"); in your code

- Low level via the DOM, by writing in your code `button.getElement().getStyle().setWidth(100);`
- By using Cascading Style Sheets, which means placing a definition in your CSS file `.gwt-button{width:100px;}`
- By inheriting one of GWT'S built-in themes in your module definition
- By using an expression language

The latter point on expression language we'll leave until chapter 6's discussion on GWT's UiBinder (declarative user interface design). We'll use the rest of this chapter to look at the other.

If you had no styling then the `BasicProject` application would look as uninspiring as figure 3.8. (You'll probably also see this view for a few seconds when first running in development mode because GWT is busy preparing itself but has already served the HTML.)

It's not difficult to see that figure 3.8 is a long way from our mock-up. But you can fix it with some simple styling, starting with the first of our techniques.

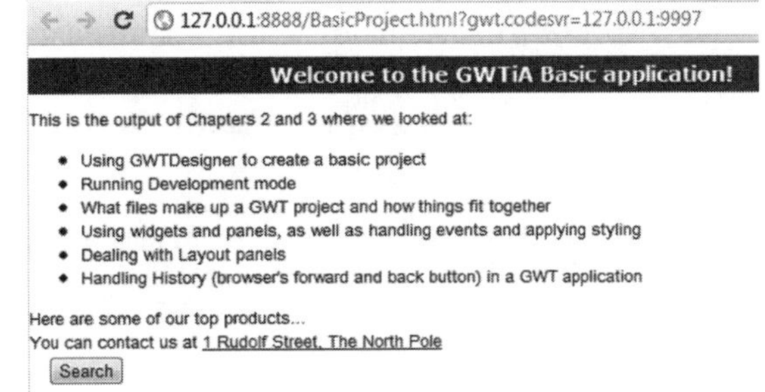

Figure 3.8 The unstyled chapter 3 `BasicProject` example looking less than appealing—but you'll fix that with some CSS styling.

3.8.1 *Programmatic styling*

All widgets can be styled using methods they inherit from `UIObject` (such as `setWidth` and `setSize`). To set the size of `HTMLPanels` and the `TabLayoutPanel` within `BasicProject`'s tab panel, you use the `setHeight` method, for example:

```
home.setHeight("400px");
```

You can look at the `styleTabPanelUsingUIObject` method to see the rest of the definition.

Most often you'd use programmatic styling if you have to dynamically change values as a reaction to something in your application, such as animating the size of a widget.

An issue with this approach is that if you need to change values, you have to recompile and distribute your code, and `UIObject` provides only a few methods for this. Wider access is given through the DOM, as you'll see next.

3.8.2 *Low-level styling*

If you need fine-grain control over styling in your code, for example, in DOM-based animation, then you can access style attributes using the `getStyle` method on a widget's element. You can set generic properties using the `setProperty` method or specific properties such as `setOpacity`. You use both methods to style the Search button in `BasicProject` (see the `styleButtonUsingDOM` method):

```
search.getElement().getStyle().setProperty("border", "2px solid");
search.getElement().getStyle().setOpacity(0.5);
```

One benefit of using the DOM class methods, such as `setOpacity`, is that you don't have to care how the browser does it (which incidentally is differently for IE6/7 compared with FireFox, Opera, IE8, and others). GWT takes care of that for you.

If you use the generic approach, remember that the property must be given in `camelCase`, that is, the CSS `background-color` must be written as `backgroundColor` (development mode will remind you about this with an assertion error). Note that this prevents you from using browser-specific CSS extensions because they include a hyphen in their names.

Figure 3.9 shows the before and after images of the button styling for `BasicProject`.

Figure 3.9 Styling a regular HTML button (left) in GWT and using Cascading Style Sheets (right)

You might see legacy code using the `DOM.setStyleAttribute` method to set style through the DOM. It's better to use the `Element` approach given here because it's more efficiently compiled.

Setting style in code is useful in certain circumstances, but like all good web design, it's often better to do it through Cascading Style Sheets to provide flexibility. This is easily supported by GWT.

3.8.3 *Cascading Style Sheets*

Most widgets have a style name associated with them when they're created. For example, an image has the style name `gwt-Image` associated with it. The Javadoc of GWT shows you what style names are associated with each widget by default.

> **TIP** How do you style a widget using CSS? Check out the Javadoc for the widget class, which will tell you the style names attached to various component parts of the widget/panel. For example, a `Button` has the standard style name `.gwt-Button`.

If you give a definition for the widget's default style name in a linked CSS file, then all widgets of that type will use that style. In `BasicProject` you put a simple border around the logo `Image` by adding the following to BasicProject.css:

```
.gwt-Image{
   width: 80%;
   height: 60px;
   margin: 25px;
   border: 1px black solid;
}
```

Often you don't want all widgets of the same type to have the same style. That's solved by using the `setStyleName` method on a widget to give an individual name to a widget. You use this approach for the feedback panel in `BasicProject`, by using

```
feedback.setStyleName("feedback");
```

and then refer to this name in the stylesheet (note the dot at the start of the definition):

```
.feedback{
   color: white;
   height: 150px;
   position: absolute;
   right: 0%;
   top: 35%;
}
```

You can use the methods `addStyleName` and `removeStyleName` to add styles to and remove them from a widget. For the feedback tab you want it to have a different style when the mouse is over it than when it's not. That's achieved by putting a `MouseOverHandler` on the panel to add a style called "active" and a `MouseOutHandler` that removes that active style and replaces it with a "normal" style. Both styles are defined in the stylesheet.

GWT has a mechanism for applying optimization techniques even to CSS—a `CssResource`. We'll look at that in chapter 5 and see how it supports runtime substitution, conditionals, minification, selector merging, and other things.

It would be a pain to have to create a stylesheet component for every widget you use. Luckily, GWT comes with three built-in themes you can select from.

3.8.4 GWT themes

In the module file you can tell GWT to use a particular theme for CSS styling. This saves you from having to define stylesheet entries for every widget you're using; you can see the results of the standard theme in figure 3.10.

You can choose from four themes out of the box. For the example application we've put them all in the module file, but we commented out two of them. If you want to change themes in the example, comment out the existing one and uncomment the one you wish to try:

```
<inherits name='com.google.gwt.user.theme.standard.Standard'/>
<!-- inherits name='com.google.gwt.user.theme.chrome.Chrome'/ -->
<!-- inherits name='com.google.gwt.user.theme.dark.Dark'/ -->
<!-- inherits name='com.google.gwt.user.theme.clean.Clean'/ -->
```

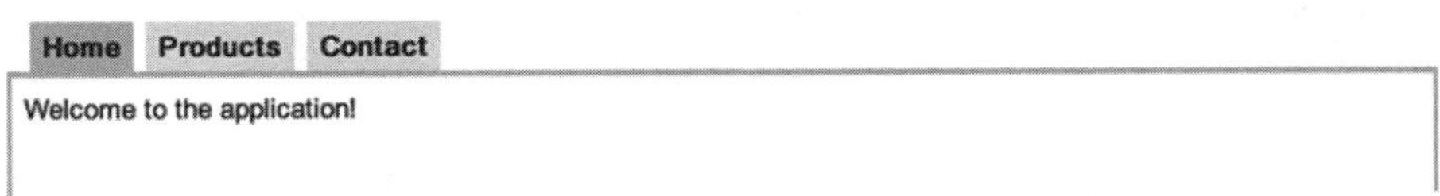

Figure 3.10 The result of using a GWT theme on the `TabLayoutPanel`

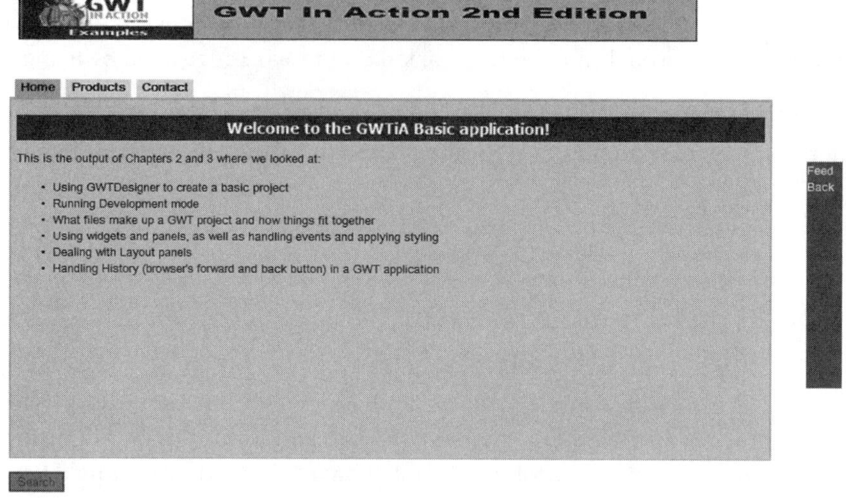

Figure 3.11 Final styled application showing all widgets, panels, pulled-in content, and styling in place—compare it with figure 3.8 to see how far we've come.

You could generate your own themes—the simplest approach is to copy an existing one and adapt as needed.[6]

When you apply all the approaches we've been talking about in this chapter, you get the `BasicProject` example to look like figure 3.11.

We touched on it a little earlier, but now let's briefly review how GWT helps you protect your application.

3.9 Securing your application

You may have noticed that this book doesn't have a specific chapter on security. We'd rather leave this extensive and rapidly changing topic to the experts, but we can't write a book on web applications without touching on how GWT can help secure your application.

If you read GWT's "Security for GWT Applications,"[7] you'll see that it summarizes four vectors of attack to which the GWT team feels GWT applications are vulnerable:

- JavaScript on your host page that's unrelated to GWT
- Code you write that sets `innerHTML` on GWT widget objects
- Using the JSON API to parse untrusted strings (which ultimately calls the JavaScript `eval` function)
- JSNI code that does something unsafe

---

[6] An alternative is to use an online theme generator, such as the one found at http://gwt-theme-generator.appspot.com/.

[7] "Security for GWT Applications": http://mng.bz/pq07.

For JavaScript on your host page that's unrelated to GWT, such as a third-party library you're using, you have to make sure you trust that third-party code to do nothing dangerous to your application—maybe an OK assumption for well-known libraries.

This chapter's example is a good demonstration of the second point—using innerHTML. Although not explicitly constrained to DOM manipulation, it's always wise to consider if you need to make safe any HTML you're handling to minimize against cross-site scripting (XSS) attacks.

GWT provides a SafeHtml object that allows you to sanitize text against cross-site scripting attacks. In BasicProject, you use that to sanitize the content you pull out of the HTML and put into content tabs. You might feel safe in BasicProject, because you control the HTML file that's manipulated, but it's better to be safe than sorry and guard against anyone sitting in the middle or hacking your HTML file.

At ❹ back in listing 3.4 you take the precaution of using SafeHtml on your extracted content:

```
SafeHtml sfHtml = SimpleHtmlSanitizer.sanitizeHtml(toReturn);
```

The impact of using SimpleHtmlSanitizer is to stop the contact in the HTML from being a live URL, as you can see in figure 3.12—sometimes safety can get in the way of functionality.

As you go through the chapters you'll see time and again that GWT allows you to guard against attacks—although you have to proactively use the techniques available to you:

- Chapter 4 talks about using SafeHTML, SafeHtmlBuilder, SafeHtmlUtils, SimpleHtmlSanitizer, and SafeHtmlTemplates—all of which you can use when creating new widgets to protect against hack attacks.
- Chapter 4 also looks at UriUtils to ensure a URI is safe; it also notes that you can use SafeStylesBuilder and SafeStylesUtils to help protect against attacks contained within any injected stylesheets.
- Chapter 10 looks at how you can use SafeHtmlTemplates to create new cell widgets.
- Chapter 13 looks at how to use SafeHtml in internationalization messages to help protect against attacks. In the example it's possible to inject a malicious image tag that runs some JavaScript (fires up an alert box)—a simple example of what and how to protect against.

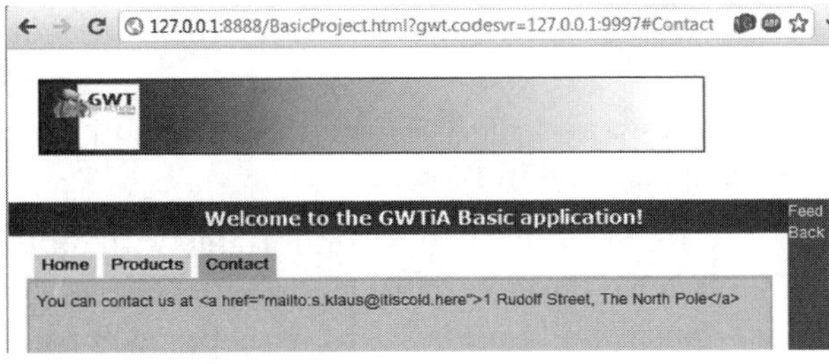

Figure 3.12 The result of using the SafeHTML object on the manipulated HTML in BasicProject—note that the mailto URL of the contact has been sanitized to plain text and is no longer an active URL (to not use the SafeHTML approach, comment out the two lines of code in the example).

Unfortunately, XSS isn't the only attack you need to be careful about. Your server-side communication may (will?) need protecting against cross-site request forgery (often referred to as XSRF or CSRF):

- Using `RequestBuilder` (chapter 12) you can set a custom header in the request (using the `setHeader` method) to contain the value of a cookie originally set by the server. On the server side you can compare the value of the cookie sent in the request to the copy of the cookie in the header—if they don't match, then you're being attacked.
- You can also protect RequestFactory (chapter 8) in a similar way by extending the `DefaultRequestTransport` object to include a custom header.
- In chapter 7 we look in detail at how to use GWT's `XsrfProtectedService-Servlet` instead of `RemoteServiceServlet` to gain access to GWT's built-in XSRF protection for GWT-RPC.

We've arrived at the end of this chapter with an application resembling the mock-up from the start—figure 3.1 (and it would probably look even prettier if we were designers and not developers).

3.10 Building on your understanding

In chapter 2 we gave a couple of suggestions on how you could build on what we'd covered to that point. We'll do the same for this chapter because it can be useful, although we're sure by now you probably have lots of ideas yourself. To follow are our suggestions:

- Add some more named items in the HTML file (for example, `div`s or `SPAN`s or a `TD` in a `TABLE`), and in the code find them and add some widgets of your choice.
- Add some more content to the HTML like the contact/products content, pull it into a new tab in the tab panel, and link it into the history handling.
- Add some content into the HTML and use the DOM methods to retrieve it in the application, put it into a `Label`, put that `Label` into a `DialogBox`, and then enable animation on the `DialogBox` and show it on the screen (hint: check out the online Javadocs to see how to use `DialogBox`).
- Change the theme used in the application (hint: look in the application's module file).
- Add a `ClickHandler` to the application's green sidebar that displays a JavaScript alert (hints: remember that you had to wrap the sidebar in the `FocusPanel` to handle events, and you can find the alert in the `com.google.gwt.user.client.Window` package).
- Turn off the `SafeHtml` handling, and see the result on the tab panel content (hint: look at the `getContent` method in BasicProject.java).

We're sure you can think of more things to do to get comfortable with all these concepts. In the rest of this book we'll delve into the more complicated aspects of GWT—the techniques that will help you push the boundaries of web applications. We won't explicitly have this type of "building on your understanding" section in those chapters, but if you're like us, we know you'll be taking the examples and fiddling, extending, and learning more yourself.

3.11 Summary

This has been quite a hike through GWT, and you should now have an understanding of the key parts of the client side. You've seen how to use widgets and panels and how to add those to the browser page. We covered layout panels, which we're sure will become a larger part of GWT going forward, particularly as we head to a world where standards mode in browsers is more common. We looked at wiring up events so that the user can interact with your application, and we showed how to handle the user clicking the Forward and Back buttons on the browser and getting expected behavior.

We were a little over the top with the use of various techniques in our discussion. Typically, a GWT application won't use every one of the approaches to styling or creating widgets. We've done so in the example application, but that's to make a point of showing the flexibility of GWT.

We've created the `BasicProject` and `historyhelper` applications as downloads so you can extend and play with them to your heart's content to get a better understanding of the fundamentals.

We're ready to move into the next section of the book and start taking the next steps with GWT. That includes creating new widgets, talking to the server, using GWT's declarative UiBinder approach, internationalization, and more. If you're wondering about how to interact with a server, you could check out chapter 7, which covers GWT-RPC, and chapter 10, which looks at classic Ajax interactions and forms.

The real journey starts in the next part with the GWT aspects that will take your application to the next steps.

Part 2

Next steps

Where part 1 gives you the basics of GWT and enough knowledge to play around and gain understanding of GWT applications and their lifecycle, part 2 takes the next step, diving into the details of typical functionalities you'd use in real-world applications.

We cover client-side aspects such as creating new widgets, the Editor framework, data presentation widgets, as well as efficiency aspects such as using client bundles and how to make your application as widely available as possible using internationalization, localization, and accessibility. Most importantly, we emphasize declarative UI development with UiBinder, giving you that long-needed separation of functionality, UI layout, and styling.

This part also covers a plethora of tools for communicating with the server. These include the general-purpose GWT-RPC, the model-focused RequestFactory, the Ajax-style RequestBuilder, and HtmlForm.

In addition, we look at the JavaScript Native Interface aspect of GWT, which we recommend you use in limited places to interface directly to JavaScript. The section looks first at why not to use this approach and then identifies four areas where it makes sense to use it and how to do so.

Our intention with the chapters in this section is that you read them as you need them—there's no need to follow the order in which they're provided. But we certainly recommend you get comfortable with UiBinder because the examples in that chapter and onward use it and we believe it's the best way for UI design.

4 Creating your own widgets

This chapter covers

- Understanding widgets and their lifecycles
- Creating new types of widgets, composite widgets, and panels
- Using layout panels

After you've spent some time using and styling the standard widgets GWT provides you, perhaps as you were exploring and extending the example in chapter 3, you may start having a number of questions, such as

- Why isn't this "thingy" provided as a widget?
- Why can't widget X do this little extra thing?
- How can I treat a group of widgets that I use regularly as only one widget?

Fear not; the answers to these questions and more are the topic of this chapter. Once you move past any nontrivial application, treating a group of widgets as one new reusable widget is where you'll spend most of your time—these are known in GWT as `Composite` widgets.

In this chapter we'll look at how you can create new widgets. We'll start with the approach that you'll use the least often—creating a widget directly from a DOM element. It's the least-used approach because GWT provides a lot of widgets already, but it does give us the best way of talking through the things you need to think of when looking at the two other approaches we consider: extending an existing widget to give the functionality you need (saves you time and effort) or creating a `Composite`, as we mentioned.

Another area of importance to your application is layout, which is done via panels (a special subset of widgets). Your overall application layout is most likely to use a layout panel (for example, `DockLayoutPanel`), whereas individual `Composite` widgets are more likely to use table-based layouts (for example, `VerticalPanel`).

Before we get quite technical and dig into the lifecycle of widgets (and panels) at the end of this chapter, we'll stop and look at how to apply animation to widgets. For fun you'll build a highlight effect that progressively changes the background color of a widget from white to yellow. Then it's time to look at lifecycles—what happens when you create, add, remove, and destroy a widget. By doing so you'll see what's going on, where you can hook into these processes, if needed, and how GWT protects you from memory leaks.

As ever, we've included sample code for this chapter, and you can get it from the book's download site; the project you'll be interested in is `gwtia-ch04-widgets`. Within this, you'll find the `GWTiACanvas` widget, which you'll create from scratch; the `ReportSizeLabel` widget, which you'll extend from the existing `InlineLabel` widget; and a `DataField` widget, which is an example of a `Composite`. We also include the `HighlightEffect` animation and four layout panel examples.

We'll start the chapter by answering the question that's most likely on your lips—what is a widget?

4.1 What is a widget, again?

In chapter 3 we introduced widgets and panels. We said that a widget is something the user interacts with, and a panel is a widget that gives the user interface structure.

We'll refine that definition a little and say that a widget is a chunk of user interface that we wish to handle in our application code as a single unit. Look again at the mock-up of our chapter 3 example shown in figure 4.1.

Some widgets in figure 4.1 map directly to DOM elements. `Button` and `Image` are perfect examples—they wrap to DOM `button` and `image` elements. This is true for some panels as well—`SimplePanel`, `FlowPanel`, and `HTMLPanel` are DOM `div` elements. All of these are perfect to think of as a self-contained unit of the user interface.

> **DEFINITION** The *DOM* is the Document Object Model—an interface to the content and structure of your HTML page. You may well have come across it when writing JavaScript code. In GWT, you'll mainly access it via GWT Java methods, and you'll let GWT handle all the browser differences for you.

Other widgets are composed of two or more widgets; `TabPanel` in the mock-up is an example of this. It's made up of a `TabBar` and a `DeckPanel`. Unless you dug into the

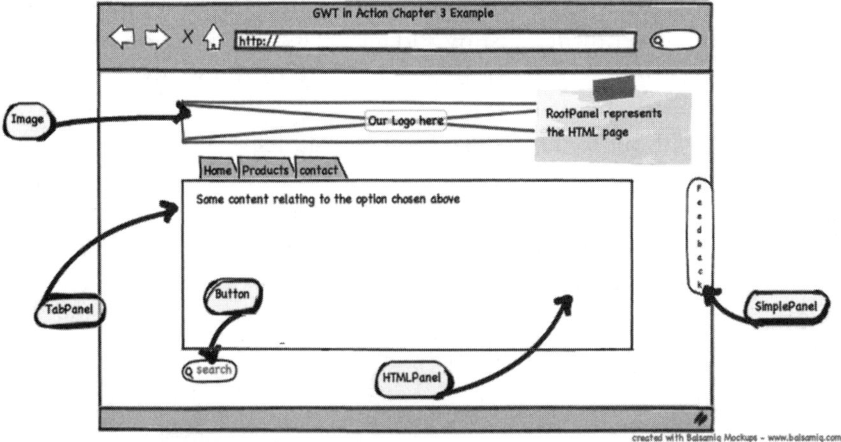

Figure 4.1 Mockup of chapter 3's main example application showing the layout in the browser window

code of `TabPanel` you'd never know this (or need to know this). The composite of the two widgets is the self-contained unit of user interface—a widget in its own right. `Composite` widgets can themselves be made up of other `Composite` widgets and so on.

Figure 4.2 shows some widgets; on the left are some bound directly to DOM elements, and on the right are some that are more conceptual, such as trees and push buttons.

A widget can be a direct representation of a DOM element or a more conceptual item built out of other widgets (and so on). At all times, though, it's a self-contained unit of the user interface.

How do you build widgets? Luckily, most of the direct DOM widgets are already built, and each new release of GWT brings more. For example, version 2.3 started to reflect capabilities of modern browsers with its `Canvas` widget. There might be a DOM element that you need that isn't wrapped; in that case you can wrap it yourself, as you'll see in the next section.

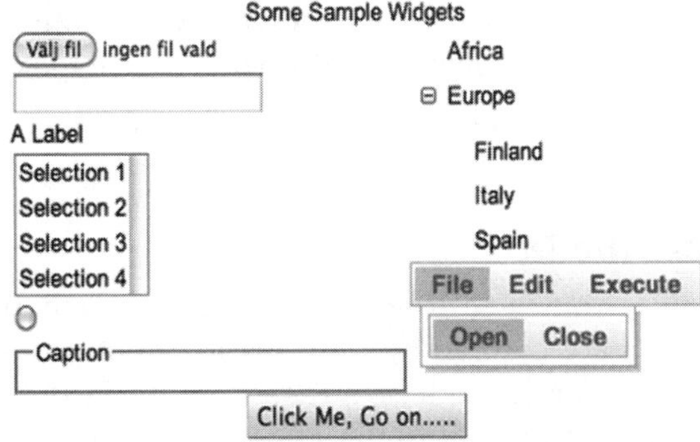

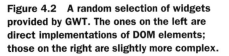

Figure 4.2 A random selection of widgets provided by GWT. The ones on the left are direct implementations of DOM elements; those on the right are slightly more complex.

Maybe there's an existing widget that does most of what you want but isn't quite right. In this case, you can extend the existing widget's class and override the functionality. You'll do that in section 4.3 to get the `InlineLabel` to report its size as soon as it's added to the DOM.

Overwhelmingly, though, in our experience, you'll spend most of your time with widgets creating your own `Composite` widgets as you break down your user interface into self-contained units at a level where you wish to manage them.

It wasn't so necessary to build composites for the toy example in chapter 3, but it will be for any real-world application. You'll need your Twitter widget, your Facebook feed widget, your log-in widget, and so on. Some of them you might be able to get from widget libraries, but most you'll be building.

Widget efficiency

We have a couple of tips for you on increasing the efficiency of your application when it comes to user interface components.

If you don't need a user interface component to react to events, then create it as a simple HTML item in your HTML page (or as HTML components in UiBinder—see chapter 6). This way it isn't managed by your application, saving effort. For example, the logo in the example application would be better defined as an `<img>` tag directly in the HTML (if it wasn't for the fact that we want to show how to insert a widget into a named area of the page).

Use layout versions of panels where you can, for example, `DockLayoutPanel` instead of `Dockpanel`—these delegate layout calculations to the browser.

Use cell-based versions of widgets where you can, for example, `CellTree` instead of `Tree`—the cell-based widgets are much more efficient to use (see chapter 10).

But before we get to `Composite` widgets, let's look at the three techniques for building new non-`Composite` widgets:

- Creating a new widget from the DOM
- Extending an existing widget
- Extending an existing panel (remember, they're a subset of widget, but you probably want to create a composite rather than extend a panel—we'll look at why)

The principles you'll learn here will help you understand how to extend existing widgets and build composites.

4.2 Creating a new widget from the DOM

It should be a rare occasion where you need to create a widget directly from the DOM—because most DOM elements are covered by GWT already, and each new version of GWT increases the coverage. For example, GWT 2.2 brought in the `InlineLabel` to wrap the `span` element, and GWT 2.3 wraps the `canvas` element.

The only time you need to think of doing this is when GWT hasn't done it for you. But the fact that GWT now provides a Canvas widget could have changed this chapter (com.google.gwt.canvas.client.Canvas). When we started writing, we'd written this section to show how to provide a DOM element that was missing. But let's stick with our version here, because it's useful to see how to start building a widget, and you can compare and contrast it with GWT's own version if you wish.

What we'll do in the next few sections is introduce the concept of the Canvas widget, show the code that you use to create it (and also optionally wrap an existing canvas DOM element). We'll investigate what GWT interfaces we want our new widget to implement, so it declares what GWT functionality it implements as well as how it will handle events. So, let's introduce the new widget.

4.2.1 Introducing the GWTiACanvas widget

A canvas element in HTML allows you to draw objects and bitmaps on the browser screen. Figure 4.3 shows an example of our Canvas widget in action drawing a square on the screen.

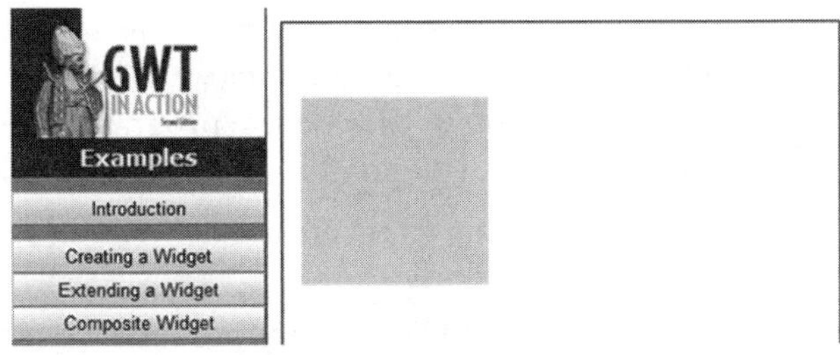

Figure 4.3 Canvas widget in action displayed in the Creating a Widget example. The widget is bordered by a thin solid line, and the green rectangle is drawn onto the canvas.

To keep our page count down, you'll create the bare bones of a supported Canvas widget; you won't include any error checking and we'll assume you're using a canvas-aware browser, such as Chrome, Firefox, Safari, IE9, or Opera[1] (if you're not, then you'll see an error when this example runs). GWT's own Canvas widget is much more robust, but we want to focus on the essentials. You can find the full code for our widget in the GWTiACanvas.java file in the package com.manning.gwtia.ch04.client.create_new_widget; the following listing shows the notable parts we'll discuss further.

Listing 4.1 Example Canvas widget code focusing on the various ways to create it

```
public class Canvas extends Widget {                          ◁ ❶ Extending the Widget class

   public Canvas() {                                          ❷ Creating a new widget
      Element element = Document.get().createElement("canvas");
       setUpWidget(element);
   }

   protected Canvas(Element element) {                        ◁ ❸ Private constructor
```

1 Browser support of the Canvas element: http://en.wikipedia.org/wiki/Canvas_element#Support.

```
        assert element.getTagName().equalsIgnoreCase("canvas");
        setUpWidget(element);
    }

    public static Canvas wrap(Element element) {                    ❹ Wrapping an existing canvas element
        assert Document.get().getBody().isOrHasChild(element);
        assert element.getTagName().equalsIgnoreCase("canvas");
        Canvas canvas = new Canvas(element);
        canvas.onAttach();
        RootPanel.detachOnWindowClose(canvas);
        canvas.context = canvas.getCanvasContext(element);
        return canvas;
    }
}
```

Every widget will extend the `Widget` class, and so you do that at ❶. The `Widget` class provides basics for a widget, such as a variable for the DOM element to be held in; methods inherited from `UIObject` to set width, height, visibility, and so on; and the lifecycle-management methods we discussed earlier.

It's common to provide the programmer with three approaches to create your new widget, though you don't have to if they don't make sense:

- Create the DOM element directly ❷, that is, `Document.get().createElement("canvas")`.
- Use the DOM element created elsewhere in the programmer's code ❸, but double-check that it's a `canvas` DOM element before using it.
- Wrap an appropriate DOM element that already exists in the application's HTML page ❹.

  There's much more work to do in this case because you have to call lifecycle functions yourself, such as the `onAttach` method (see section 4.7) and crucially the `RootPanel.detachOnWindowClose` to tell GWT that when the application window closes, it also needs to clean up this widget to prevent memory leaks.

Once it's created, via whichever method, you can use it like any other widget. Creating the square in figure 4.3 in a browser that supports canvas uses the following code:

```
GWTiACanvas c = new GWTiACanvas();
c.setPixelSize(400, 400);
RootPanel.get().add(c);
c.fillStyle("rgb(80,255,80)");
c.fillRect(10, 20, 100, 50);
```

This code creates a new `GWTiACanvas` widget instance, sets its size, adds it to the `RootPanel`, and then uses two specific methods you defined in the widget to set the fill style and draw the rectangle.

If you had the following HTML in the body of your application's HTML file

```
<canvas id="demo-canvas" width="400" height="400"></canvas>
```

you could use the `wrap` method to create the widget. You'll get the same result as figure 4.3 using the following code:

```
GWTiACanvas c =
    GWTiACanvas.wrap(RootPanel.get("demo-canvas").getElement());
c.fillStyle("rgb(80,255,80)");
c.fillRect(10, 20, 100, 50);
```

The other methods in our widget, for example, `fillStyle` and `getCanvasContext`, provide ways of interacting with the widget to draw things on the canvas. We won't go into them in this chapter, but you may notice they're written in a strange way. They're defined as JavaScript Native Interface (JSNI) methods, and this is because you have to use JavaScript to talk to the canvas. Most widgets won't need to do this. We'll cover JSNI in chapter 11.

The widget is effectively complete. You could extend it further to implement other canvas functionality and perhaps use some deferred binding (see chapter 17) to cope with Internet Explorer 7 and 8's lack of canvas implementation.

We should look at two other things in order to make the widget feel more rounded and GWT-like: what functionality the widget should declare it implements, and how events are handled.

4.2.2 *Indicating functionality*

A widget can implement a number of Java interfaces to tell the world it has certain functionality. You don't need to make your widget implement any of these interfaces, but it does help to adhere to the GWT style.

In chapter 14 you'll see a number of these interfaces that are related to event handling, but there are others, for example, the `HasText` interface. That interface indicates that the widget has some text and that you can expect to be able to call the `setText` method to change that text and the `getText` method to retrieve the text value.

> **TIP** Some users may have difficulty using your widgets if you don't think about making them accessible. We have some tips in section 13.9 of chapter 13 on this, including alternative styling, keyboard shortcuts, and using ARIA roles and states (for use with screen readers).

When you create a new widget, you should consider what interfaces the widget should implement. Some of these are shown in table 4.1, along with an indication of which package they're in to help you find others you may need to consider.

Table 4.1 An overview of some of the interfaces a widget can use to indicate functionality

Interface name	Description

`HasDirection`	This widget can alter the document directionality of its element (for example, write text in a right-to-left manner). The interface can be found in `com.google.gwt.i18n.client`, and these methods must be implemented:
	`void setDirection(Direction direction);`
	`Direction getDirection();`

Table 4.1 An overview of some of the interfaces a widget can use to indicate functionality *(continued)*

Interface name	Description

`HasVertical-Alignment`	This widget can be aligned vertically. The interface, like the next few, can be found in `com.google.gwt.user.client.ui`, and these methods must be implemented:
	`VerticalAlignmentConstant getVerticalAlignment();`
	`void setVerticalAlignment(VerticalAlignmentConstant align);`

`HasAlignment`	This widget can be aligned both vertically and horizontally (a shorthand way of saying the widget implements `HasVerticalAlignment` and `HasHorizontalAlignment` interfaces).

`HasText`	This widget has text that can be set or retrieved using the following methods:
	`String getText();`
	`void setText(String text);`
	For widgets that hold a value rather than only text, look at the `HasValue<T>` interface.

`HasWidgets`	This widget can hold other widgets; that is, it's a panel. It must provide the following:
	`void add(Widget w);`
	`void clear();`
	`boolean remove(Widget w);`
	`Iterator<Widget> iterator();`

`HasClickHandlers`	This widget has click handlers associated with it. Like all interfaces associated with events, it can be found in `com.google.gwt.event.dom.client`. It requires the implementation of `HandlerRegistration addClickHandler(ClickHandler handler);` Remember that in chapter 3 you saw that events are removed using the `HandlerRegistration`'s `remove` method, so you don't need a `removeClickHandler` method in this interface.

For our `Canvas` widget, we don't have any non-event-specific GWT interfaces we want to implement, but widgets you build may have such interfaces. What about events? We'll look at those next.

4.2.3 Hooking up events

We looked briefly at events in chapter 3, saying that they're an indication that something has happened and that we typically handle them via dedicated event handlers. In chapter 14 we'll look at the detailed mechanism of this, but for now we're only concerned with the "what" and not the detailed "how." We'll split the discussion into two parts: handling the event internal to the widget and handling it external to the widget.

HANDLING EVENTS INTERNAL TO THE WIDGET

If you're going to handle events internally to a widget, you need to do two things: sink the event, and manage when it's raised.

Sinking an event means that you indicate what events the widget will handle internally. It's simple to do; in the `Canvas` widget you'll manage the click event and say that by writing

```
sinkEvents(Event.ONCLICK);
```

Having sunk the event, you need to handle it, and you do that by overriding the widget's `onBrowserEvent` method:

```
public void onBrowserEvent(Event evt){
  super.onBrowserEvent(evt);
  switch(evt.getTypeInt()){
    case Event.ONCLICK:
       Window.alert("You clicked me!");
       break;
  }
}
```

Here you switch on the `Integer` value of the event, and if it happens to be the click event you sunk, then you pop up an alert.

As well as handling events internal to the widget, you might like to allow external users of the widget to know that events have happened.

HANDLING EVENTS EXTERNAL TO THE WIDGET

Not all widgets will expose all events that can happen on them (despite the fact that at the DOM level you hook any event happening on the DOM element into the GWT event-handling system, as you saw in the `onAttach` method). To make it clear what handlers a widget will handle and externally expose, you say the widget implements the appropriate `HasXXXXXHandler` interface (such as `HasMouseOverHandler`). This requires the widget to provide an `addXXXXXHandler` method (such as `addMouseOverHandler`) that calls the widget's inherited `addDOMHandler` method (another of the methods available to you from the `Widget` class your widget extends).

To show this in practice, let's add the ability to handle mouse-over events to the `Canvas` widget.

Listing 4.2 Adding `MouseOver` event handling to the `GWTiACanvas` widget

```
public class Canvas extends Widget
                    implements HasMouseOverHandler {      <-- 1 Creating a new Widget

   public HandlerRegistration                              <-- 2 Adding a MouseHandler
              addMouseOverHandler(MouseOverHandler handler){
     return
       this.addDomHandler(handler, MouseOverEvent.getType());   <-- 3 Wrapping an existing canvas element
   }

}
```

In listing 4.2 you tell the world that your widget implements the `HasMouseOverHandler` interface ❶, and so you expect to find an `addMouseOverHandler` method, which you do

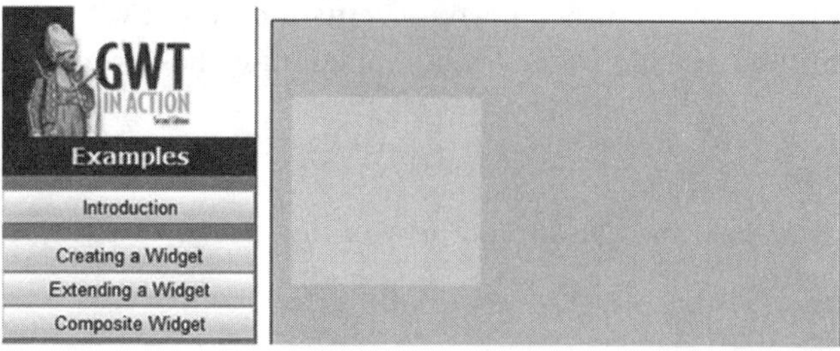

Figure 4.4 Result of moving the mouse over the updated canvas widget. Compared to figure 4.3, this has a colored background (light blue if you run the example; light gray if you're reading the printed book).

at ❷. That method adds the handler to the GWT's event-handling system for this widget, and you're good to go (the details of these concepts are in chapter 14).

Now you can add an event handler to change the background color of the widget when the mouse goes over it by adding a `MouseOverHandler`:

```
GWTiACanvas c = new GWTiACanvas();
RootPanel.get().add(c);
c.addMouseOverHandler(new MouseOverHandler(){
   public void onMouseOver(MouseOverEvent event){
      c.getElement().getStyle().setBackgroundColor("lightblue");
   }
});
```

When the mouse goes over the widget now, you get the result shown in figure 4.4.

The event system does allow you to cheat and not adhere to the defined interfaces—you can add a `ClickHandler` quite simply by writing directly to the `addDomHandler` method:

```
theCanvas.addDomHandler(new ClickHandler(){
   @Override
   public void onClick(ClickEvent event) {
      Window.alert("Clicked!");
   }}, ClickEvent.getType());
```

But somehow that feels unclean.

That's all we'll discuss about creating new widgets from the DOM. The pattern will become fairly clear: create the widget, indicate what someone can expect from the functionality via interfaces, and handle any required events via handlers.

Our example is relatively benign, but you should be aware of the underlying HTML nature of widgets and so you need to think about protection.

4.2.4 Getting secure by using SafeHTML, SafeUri, and SafeStyles

You should always be conscious that underpinning widgets is HTML—and this means you're always open to hack attacks via cross-site scripting (XSS). GWT provides mechanisms to help protect you against these:

- *DOM level*—Try to use the `setInnerText()` method on DOM elements rather than `setInnerHtml()`.

- *Widget level*—Use one of the following:
  - `SafeHtml` versions of widget methods where possible, for example, instead of `HTML.setHTML(String s)` use `HTML.setHTML(SafeHtml s)`
  - `SafeHtmlBuilder` class to build up safe HTML strings in your code
  - `SafeHtmlUtils` class methods, such as `fromString` and `fromTrustedSource` to conveniently turn `Strings` into `SafeHtml`
  - `SimpleHtmlSanitizer` to sanitize a `String` but allow a restricted set of HTML markup through unescaped
  - `SafeHtmlTemplates` to sanitize `Strings` in a template manner

When building a new widget you must consider using these mechanisms to minimize the risk to users of the widget.

To use the text in a `SafeHtml` object, you need to call its `asString` method. That should be done as late as possible—just before it's inserted on the screen by the widget. If the widget is a `Composite`, then you should pass the `SafeHtml` object to any children that need it and let them call the `asString` method as late as possible.

The example for this chapter contains an area where you can play with the various approaches we discussed, as shown in figure 4.5. We'll come back to `SafeHtml-Templates` in chapter 10 when we look at how you create data presentation (`cell`) widgets. And if you're using internationalization (i18n) messages in your widgets, be sure to check out chapter 13's overview of using `SafeHtml` in i18n.

You can use the `UriUtils` class to manage URIs and ensure they're safe through its `fromString` method that will return a `SafeUri` object. Similarly, if you're allowing styling (CSS) to be entered from an external source, you'll want to protect against that

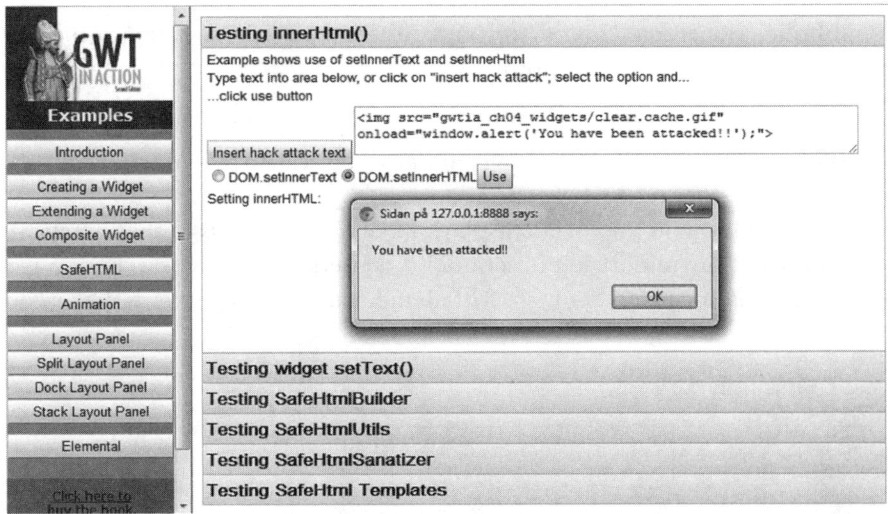

Figure 4.5 Using the `SafeHtml` part of the chapter's example to understand the various techniques and implementations in order to protect your user

having XSS attack code within it (for example, attacks using expressions in IE or HTC/XBL behavior issues). You can use `SafeStylesBuilder` and `SafeStylesUtils`.

As we mentioned, creating widgets from the DOM isn't expected to be common, and you should always check to see if GWT has a built-in widget for doing what you want before starting. Sometimes, GWT has a widget that almost does what you want but not quite. In that case, why not extend and override functionality (as we look at next)?

4.3 Extending an existing widget

GWT is Java, so creating a new widget that's based on an existing widget is merely a case of subclassing that existing widget and overriding and adding the methods you need. For example, GWT's own `Canvas` widget extends `FocusWidget` and adds all the canvas functionality it needs. The benefit in doing that is that `FocusPanel` is a simple `div` element that holds one widget but also already provides code for all the `MouseHandler` handlers.

We'll show you how to create a new label-type widget that reports its dimensions once it's attached to the DOM—the `ReportSizeLabel` widget—by extending the existing `InlineLabel` widget. To get there, we'll take the next two sections to introduce it, and as in the previous approach, we'll show what interfaces it should implement to make it feel like a full GWT widget. Because we're extending an existing widget, we also need to think about what functionality the existing widget has that we don't want in the extended widget. In our example, we'll pretend that for some reason `ReportSizeLabel` shouldn't handle mouse clicks and show how to prevent that.

Let's jump straight into our first example and say hello to the `ReportSizeLabel` widget.

4.3.1 Introducing the ReportSizeLabel widget

You'll build a label that reports to you its dimensions when added to the application, that is, when executing the following code:

```
RootPanel.get().add(new ReportSizeLabel("What's my Size?"));
```

You should expect to see something similar to figure 4.6 (see the Extending a Widget example).

Why would you do this? Well, displaying data in an alert isn't that practical in a real-world app, but the underlying functionality is useful if you are, say, building an animation library that needs to know sizes of elements and the like when they're added.

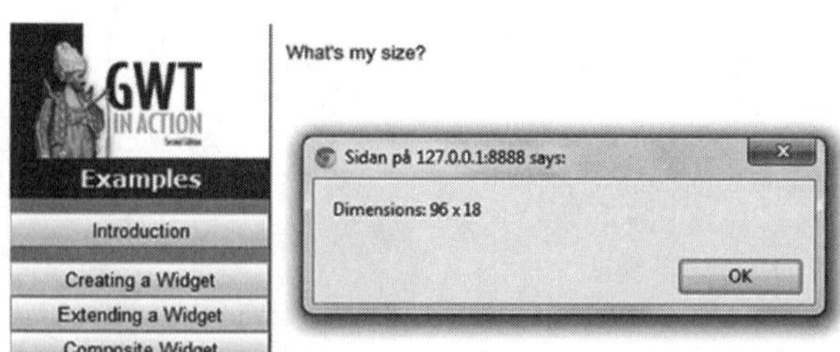

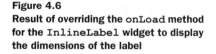

Figure 4.6 Result of overriding the `onLoad` method for the `InlineLabel` widget to display the dimensions of the label

To build the widget you extend GWT's `InlineLabel` widget—because you want the widget to behave the same—and you'll override the widget's inherited `onLoad` method. See the following listing.

Listing 4.3 Extending an existing widget to create the `ReportSizeLabel`

```
public class ReportSizeLabel extends InlineLabel{      <-- (1) Extending an existing widget

   public ReportSizeLabel(String value){
      super(value);
   }

   public void onLoad(){                                    (2) Overriding a method
      Window.alert("Dimensions: " +
                   this.getOffsetWidth() +
                   " x " + this.getOffsetHeight());
   }
}
```

`ReportSizeLabel` extends `InlineLabel` (1), and in (2) you override the `onLoad` method to create an alert onscreen to display the widget's dimensions.

You'll see in section 4.8 that the `onLoad` method is part of the widget's lifecycle and is called by GWT after the DOM element for the widget is attached to the DOM. That means you know when you'll get a valid set of dimensions when calling `getOffsetWidth` and `getOffsetHeight`. If you tried to get the size another way or before GWT called the `onLoad` method, then it wouldn't be clear what you'd get.

That's the new widget fully defined in terms of functionality. Simple, don't you think? Next, we'll consider what functionality we wish to tell the world the widget exposes.

4.3.2 *Indicating functionality*

When creating a brand-new widget from the DOM, as you did in section 4.2, we had to consider what interfaces it should implement (see section 4.2.2). When we're extending an existing widget, we have to consider two things:

- Are there interfaces in addition to the parent's to indicate and implement?
- Does it continue to make sense to implement the parent's interfaces?

Subclasses of a widget will often add to the inherited functionality. So most of the time we just need to decide if there are additional interfaces to declare, add them to the definition, and implement the required methods. For example, if we wanted to handle additional event types, then we'd follow the process given in section 4.2.3.

If you're in the situation where the new widget has to restrict the functionality of the parent, then you can't just take an interface away. Instead, you have to override the appropriate methods to provide an empty implementation, but it's also useful to let the developer know they've tried something unsupported, perhaps via raising an exception.

Let's pretend that for some reason ReportSizeLabel shouldn't handle mouse clicks. We know it does by default because we can look at its class hierarchy and examine what those classes implement. In Eclipse you can see this hierarchy by selecting the class and pressing the F4 button (or using the context menu and selecting Class Hierarchy). The result for the ReportSizeLabel widget is shown in figure 4.7.

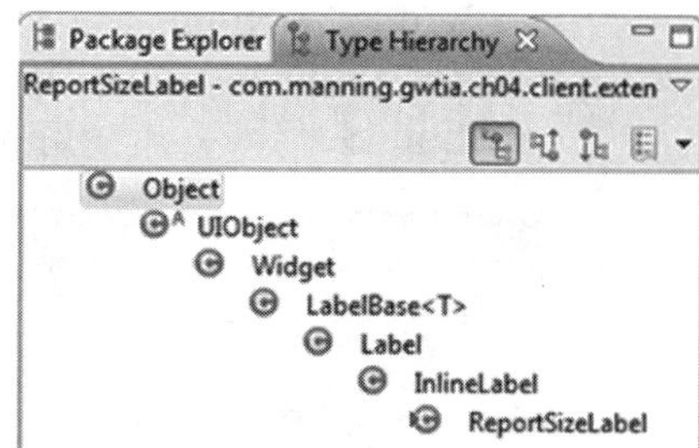

Figure 4.7 Class hierarchy of ReportSizeLabel in Eclipse showing that it inherits from InlineLabel and Label

If you were to look at the definition of Label, then you'd see that one of the interfaces it implements is HasClickHandlers, which requires the widget to implement the addClickHandler method. Because there isn't a mechanism in Java to take this away, you must override the addClickHandler method in the ReportSizeLabel widget to prevent clicks from being handled. The next listing shows the addClickHandler method in the new widget.

Listing 4.4 Suppressing functionality of an existing widget

```
public HandlerRegistration addClickHandler(ClickHandler handler){
   GWT.log("",
           new Exception("Cannot add ClickHandler " +
                         "to ReportSizeLabel"));
   return null;
}
```

If you try to add a ClickHandler to the widget, you'll get an exception raised in development mode, and no handler will be added—see figure 4.8. The application continues to execute anyway.

Because panels are widgets, we can extend them too, but there's a subtlety to take into account.

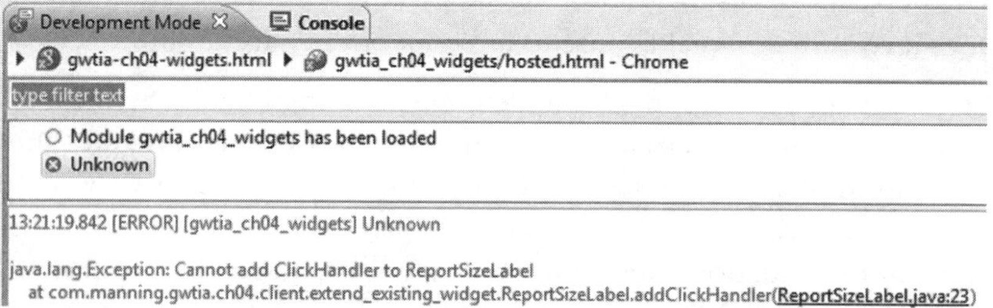

Figure 4.8 The expected development mode error that occurs when you try to add a ClickHandler to the ResizeLabel—this happens because we set it up that way in listing 4.4.

4.4 Extending a panel

Panels are a subclass of widgets. This means you can use the same technique to extend panels as you've seen for widgets. But we need to make a distinction between widgets and panels: panels have a set of methods that allow you to add and remove other widgets. If you extend a panel, then your new widget inherits those panel-specific methods.

> **Should you be extending a panel?**
>
> You should only extend a panel if you want the result to look, feel, and act like a panel. This might sound obvious, but extending a panel means a developer can easily add new widgets to it by calling the `add(Widget w)` method.
>
> If you're trying to create a new widget that's really a panel holding a determined set of other widgets, then you should create a `Composite` widget (see section 4.5).

In a short while you'll build a question-and-answer widget (see figure 4.12). If you were to build it by extending a panel, then you'd allow developers access to its `add` method. Allowing that means the developers can add anything they want to the previously well-crafted panel (see figure 4.9 where we added a `FileUpload`, `CheckBox`, and `Button` to the panel).

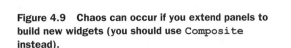

Figure 4.9 Chaos can occur if you extend panels to build new widgets (you should use `Composite` instead).

Sometimes this behavior is what you want, and you really do want to extend a panel to create a new panel. For example, let's say you want to create a vertical panel that can hold only four items, and if you try to add more than four widgets, the new widgets are added to the top and you lose the bottom widgets.

Figure 4.10 shows the result of adding six buttons to such a panel (after the fourth is added, Button 5 is added to the top, and then Button 6 on top of it—Buttons 3 and 4 are lost).

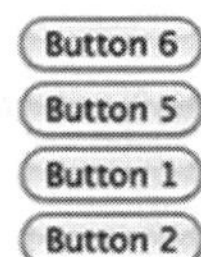

Figure 4.10 Adding six buttons to our newly created `BoundedVerticalPanel`

We call this panel `BoundedVerticalPanel`, and although we don't provide it in the downloads, listing 4.5 shows its definition (we used it to create figure 4.10).

Listing 4.5 Extending an existing panel to create the `BoundedVerticalPanel`

```
public class WrappedVerticalPanel extends VerticalPanel{        ❶ Extending VerticalPanel

   int bound = 1;

   private WrappedVerticalPanel() {
      super();
   }
```

```
    public WrappedVerticalPanel(int bound){
        super();
        this.bound = bound;
    }

    public void add(Widget w){                    ❷ Overriding the add method
        if (this.getWidgetCount() < bound)        ❸ Checking how many widgets on the panel
            super.add(w);
        else {
            this.remove(bound);
            super.insert(w,0);
        }
    }
}
```

Extending a panel uses the same approach as for any widget; you subclass as in ❶ of listing 4.5. For `WrappedVerticalPanel` you extend `VerticalPanel` (a panel that uses a HTML table as its backing structure—each row being a new TR element) and override the `add` method ❷ to provide the wrapping functionality you want.

To implement this cyclic functionality, you check to see if the number of widgets already held by the panel is less than the bound ❸. If it is, then you add the widget as a normal `VerticalPanel` by calling the parent's `add` method via `super.add(w)`. If there are more widgets than the bound, then you do two things: call the parent's `insert` method to place the new widget at the top (that is to say with index = 0), and call the parent's `remove` method to remove the last widget (the widget with index = bound).

Quite often, you'll want to use a panel to hold together a number of widgets and to treat that structure as a new widget. It's tempting to extend a panel to do that, but you then allow a user of your new widget to add other widgets and perhaps remove your existing ones. The right approach to prevent that and encapsulate your structure as a new widget is to create a `Composite` widget.

4.5 Creating a composite

`Composite` widgets are just what they sound like—a composite of widgets acting together as if they're one. The internal structure of a composite is usually hidden from the outside world, and you typically can't add or remove components unless you build it to be explicitly hidden—a composite is essentially a façade.

You may have already used a composite without knowing about it. `TabPanel`, which we used in the last chapter's example, is composed of two separate widgets. There's a `TabBar` that contains the tabs you click and a `DeckPanel` that holds the contents (see figure 4.11). When

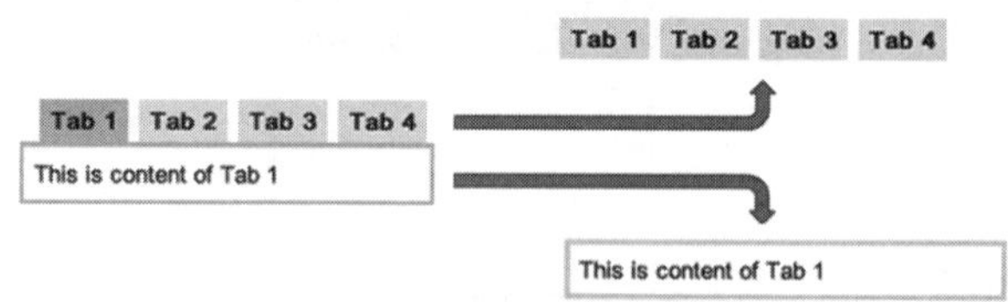

Figure 4.11 `TabPanel` exploded into its two component parts—a `TabBar` and a `DeckPanel`

you click one of the tabs in the TabBar, you want the appropriate widget in the DeckPanel to be displayed. TabPanel was made as a composite so that these two widgets could be combined and the user doesn't have to worry about the internal working of making the correct panel appear when a tab is clicked.

In this section, you'll build your own composite from scratch that acts as a question and answer–type widget. We'll make it a simple example but one that gives us enough complexity to be useful. It will have a Label for the question part and a TextBox for the answer.

> **Composite is a façade**
>
> A Composite widget acts as a façade to the component widgets it holds.
>
> You can filter out the functionality of component parts by not implementing them in the Composite; vice versa, to get to component part's functionality you need to pass it through the Composite to the component.

We'll look at how to put it together, and like the other two approaches, you'll see how to use interfaces to make it feel like a real GWT widget. Only this time we might also need to think about which component part we need to delegate event handling and interface implementations to. Along the way, we'll also look briefly at GWT's direction capability, that is, how to display text in the correct direction—left to right or right to left depending on the locale.

This is all much easier to see by looking at the example, so let's get going.

4.5.1 Introducing the DataField question/answer widget

It's quite common that an application will at some point require a question and answer widget, something like that shown in figure 4.12. It would be great to have a widget with which you can create this type of question, such as

```
DataField questionOne =
    new DataField("What type of Swallow (African or European)?");
```

and later in the program retrieve the answer the user has typed in:

```
String answerOne = questionOne.getText();
```

You won't find such a widget in the basic GWT classes. You could extend a FlowPanel that holds a Label and a TextBox. That would work, but conceptually you'd have a panel, so someone could add new widgets to it directly—which as we discussed in section 4.3.3 is probably not what you want. Also, getText is a known method on widgets

What type of Swallow (African or European)? Errr....

Figure 4.12 Displaying a Composite of Label and TextBox

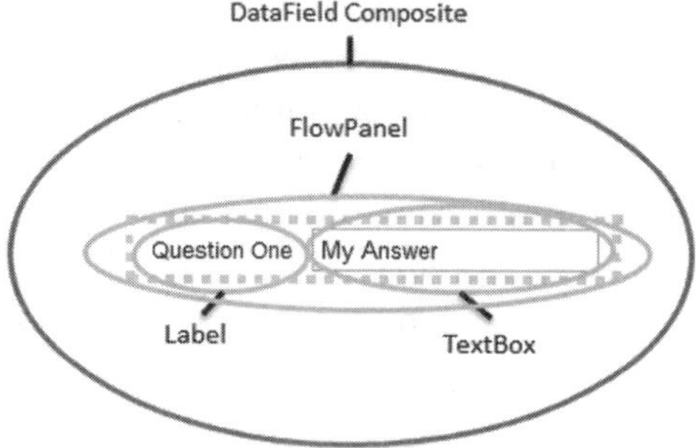

Figure 4.13 The `DataField` composite as built from its constituent parts. An external user can't see the internals unless they're exposed, usually via delegation, through the outer layer.

applicable to both `Label` and `TextBox`—we'll discuss in section 4.5.2 which one we want it to apply it to here and why we have it and don't, say, implement a `getAnswer` method. We want to treat it just like the `TabPanel` is treated—as a single widget, as shown in figure 4.13.

The idea is that a user of `DataField` doesn't need to know, and indeed should not know, that it's made up of a `FlowPanel`, a `Label`, and a `TextBox`. They're just interested in creating a `DataField`, setting the question, and retrieving an answer. The way to do that is to create a `Composite` widget, such as the one in the following listing.

Listing 4.6 Creating a simple `Composite`

```
public class DataField extends Composite{                      ❶ Extending Composite

   protected FlowPanel panel;
   protected InlineLabel theQuestion;
   protected TextBox theAnswer;

   public DataField(String question){
      theQuestion = new InLineLabel(question);
      theAnswer = new TextBox();                                ❷ Creating widget structure
      panel = new FlowPanel();
      buildDisplay();

      initWidget(panel);                                        ❸ Calling the required initialization method

      this.getElement().getStyle().
           setProperty("border", "solid lightblue 2px");        ❹ Treating the composite as a unit
   }

   protected void buildDisplay(){
      panel.add(theQuestion);
      panel.add(theAnswer);
   }
}
```

A `Composite` widget must do two essential things:

- Extend the `Composite` class (or `ResizeComposite` class if it contains a layout panel).
- Call the `initWidget` method, passing in as a parameter the widget that acts as the parent.

The DataField composite does both these things—extends the Composite class, at ❶, and calls initWidget, at ❸ (the widget's structure is built in ❷).

Are you using a layout panel as the basis to your composite?

If so, you should extend ResizeComposite instead of Composite. This ensures that resize requests are passed to the container panel of your composite. Note that if you try to call the initWidget method of a ResizeComposite without a layout widget, then you'll get an assertion error.

NOTE The initWidget method of Composite or ResizeComposite must be called once and only once. That must happen before the widget is added to your application (and before any external classes make calls to methods). If you forget, you'll get an error at runtime.

To finalize the creation of your composite and GWT to understand it, you need to call the initWidget method with the panel that acts as your composite's container. You have to do this before the widget is added to any panel, so in practice this means you should call initWidget in the constructor before doing anything with it, as you do at ❸. If you try to make any external calls to the composite's methods before initWidget is invoked, you'll also get runtime errors.

Now that you've called the initWidget method, you can treat your construction as a widget in its own right. The first thing we did was to make it look pretty for our screenshot by setting up a border using some CSS styling at ❹. The thing to note here is that we're applying this style to the composite, and, as you can see from figure 4.6, the border is indeed applied to the composed label and text box.

Now you can use the composite as you would any widget and create many instances of it if you wish:

```
DataField q2 = new DataField("What is the ultimate answer?");
DataField q3 = new DataField("Why does 1+1 = 2?");
```

As with any other widget you may create, you should look to see if it should indicate its functionality and what events it will handle. Unlike the other two ways of creating a widget, Composites need to be quite explicit here because they act as a façade to underlying widgets. We'll explain that in the next two sections.

4.5.2 Indicating functionality

In section 4.2 we talked about the GWT interfaces that a widget could declare it will implement to let people know what they can do with the widget. When it comes to a Composite widget, you have to decide two things:

- What interfaces from the constituent widgets of the composite should be visible through the façade
- What additional interfaces the composite should implement

When you extend an existing widget, the new widget inherits the interfaces and functionality of the parent (see section 4.3). When you create a composite, however, this inheritance doesn't happen—not even from the panel used as the container.

For example, the `DataField` composite contains a `TextBox`, a `Label`, and a `FlowPanel`, but you can't call `addClickHandler` (from `Label`) or `getText` (from `TextBox` and `Label`) on the composite without doing a little more work.

The first step is to decide which interfaces from the components you wish to expose at the composite level. Once they're known, you make the composite implement them, add the required methods into the composite, but delegate the functionality to the component.

To simplify things in our example, we'll decide that the only interface from the components your composite should implement is `HasText`. This is because we know we want to be able to get the answer, and it makes sense to use the `HasText` interface's `getText` method for this. The definition of the composite now becomes

```
public class DataField extends Composite implements HasText{...}
```

and you should implement the `getText` method in the composite. At this point we hit a little conceptual problem. Both widgets that are in the composite—`Label` and `TextBox`—implement `HasText`. So which one do you delegate to? The answer is the one that makes sense for the widget. Because you want `getText` to retrieve the answer, then for this widget you delegate to the `TextBox`, shown as follows:

```
public String getText(){
   theAnswer.getText();
}
```

The second aspect is to consider what additional interfaces make sense for this composite widget. Because you're adding an answer box to a question, you could wonder how this will be displayed in countries that have right-to-left text. In this case, you'd like the `TextBox` before the `Label`.

You can implement the `HasDirection` interface to support bidirectional applications. This means you have to provide `getDirection` and `setDirection` methods. Listing 4.7 shows the updated example with `HasText` and `HasDirection` interfaces implemented in the composite.

Listing 4.7 Snippet of `DataField` `Composite` showing setting and getting values

```
public class DataField extends Composite
                       implements HasText, HasDirection {      ❶ Implementing interfaces

   protected Direction dir = Direction.DEFAULT;                ❷ Setting the initial direction

   public DataField(String question){
      :
      buildDisplay();
      initWidget(panel);
   }
```

```
    public buildDisplay(){
       thePanel.clear();
       theQuestion.setDirection(dir);
       theAnswer.setDirection(dir);
       if(dir.equals(Direction.RTL)){
          panel.add(theAnswer);
          panel.add(theQuestion);
       } else {
          panel.add(theQuestion);
          panel.add(theAnswer);
       }
    }

    public void setDirection(Direction dir){
       this.direction = dir;
       buildDisplay();
    }
}
```

❸ **Updating display based on direction**

❹ **Implementing HasDirection interface method**

`Label` itself supports bidirectional text, so you could argue that we're still implementing the interface of a component but as we restructure the widget. The changes we've made to the widget are to add `HasText` and `HasDirection` as interfaces ❶ and to implement the required getter and setter methods ❹.

Because you now have a direction ❷, the method to build the display takes that into account. If the direction is right to left, then the code in ❸ puts the `TextBox` before the `Label`; otherwise, it puts the `Label` before the `TextBox`. Figure 4.14 shows this in action for the following code:

```
DataField questionLTR = new DataField("Question One ");
DataField questionRTL = new DataField("سؤال واحد");
questionRTL.setDirection(Direction.RTL);
RootPanel.get().add(questionLTR);
RootPanel.get().add(questionRTL);
```

Figure 4.14 Two of the `DataField Composite` widgets, with the second set to be displayed right to left and using Arabic

The same is true for event handling; either the composite handles the event or it delegates to one of its component parts. In our example the composite handles mouse-over events and the `TextBox` is delegated to handles value-change events, as shown in the next listing.

Listing 4.8 Event handling in the `DataField Composite` widget

```
public class DataField extends Composite
                              implements HasText, HasDirection,
                              HasMouseOverHandlers,
                              HasValueChangeHandlers<String> {

    public HandlerRegistration
```

❶ **Implement interfaces**

```
            addMouseOverHandler(MouseOverHandler handler){
        return addDomHandler(handler, MouseOverEvent.getType());
    }

    public HandlerRegistration
            addValueChangeHandler(ValueChangeHandler<String> handler){
        return theAnswer.addValueChangeHandler(handler);
    }
}
```

2 Handle MouseOver events itself

3 Delegate handling ValueChange events

You indicate that the `Composite` widget will implement the appropriate `HasMouseOver` and `HasValueChange` interfaces **1**. At **2**, you use the normal code to indicate that this widget will handle mouse-over events, and you delegate handling of change-value events to the `TextBox` in **3**.

That's three ways to create new widgets in GWT. It's our experience that most of your widget-creation time will be spent creating or reusing `Composite` widgets, and those `Composite` widgets will be made up of panels with widgets inside them.

If composites provide the micro structure of your application, then the macro structure is provided by the way you add them and other components to the `RootPanel` or `RootLayoutPanel`.

`LayoutPanels` are relatively new in GWT and are flexible, quick-layout widgets. Let's look at them in a little more detail.

4.6 Using layout panels

When constructing the container of your `Composite` widget, you'll need to consider which panel is best. Quite often that will be a `div`-based panel such as `FlowPanel` or a `table`-based one such as `VerticalPanel` or the more complicated `DockPanel`.

Using tables to provide structure may feel rather old school if you're coming from a design or HTML background. And it is, but we're talking about using them for the structure of discrete widgets. When it comes to application layout, it's better to use GWT's `LayoutPanels` that provide predictable layout, harnessing the browser layout engine to make them as blisteringly fast as possible (though you could use `LayoutPanel`'s internal widgets structure if you want).

Layout panels

These panels give predictable layout in a browser's standards mode. They're based on style constraints (for example, left, top, right, bottom, width, height) rather than tables, and they're typically used for application layout.

They only work in the browser's standards mode; that is, you must have the following declaration at the top of your HTML page for them to work:

```
<!DOCTYPE html>
```

The basic `LayoutPanel` provides great flexibility on positioning and dimensions of its children. You add your widgets to the panel and then set constraints for those child widgets. These constraints could be a left position, a width, a height, or a combination of those. Let's look at a few types of layout panels.

4.6.1 Types of layout panels

To examine layout panels in a little more detail, let's look at the second chunk of examples provided in this chapter's example. Figure 4.15 shows four layout panels that we've used in this chapter's layout panel examples. It includes four out of six standard layouts created using layout panels:

- The basic `LayoutPanel`, which is the most flexible but perhaps the hardest to use.

  It allows you to lay out your structure any way you wish. In the next section you'll see how we created the layout for figure 4.15.
- A `SplitLayoutPanel` is much more flexible than the standard `SplitPanel` (which allows for only two widgets).

  You can see in figure 4.15 that you can put splits anywhere—try the example, and you can drag all the sliders to resize everything.

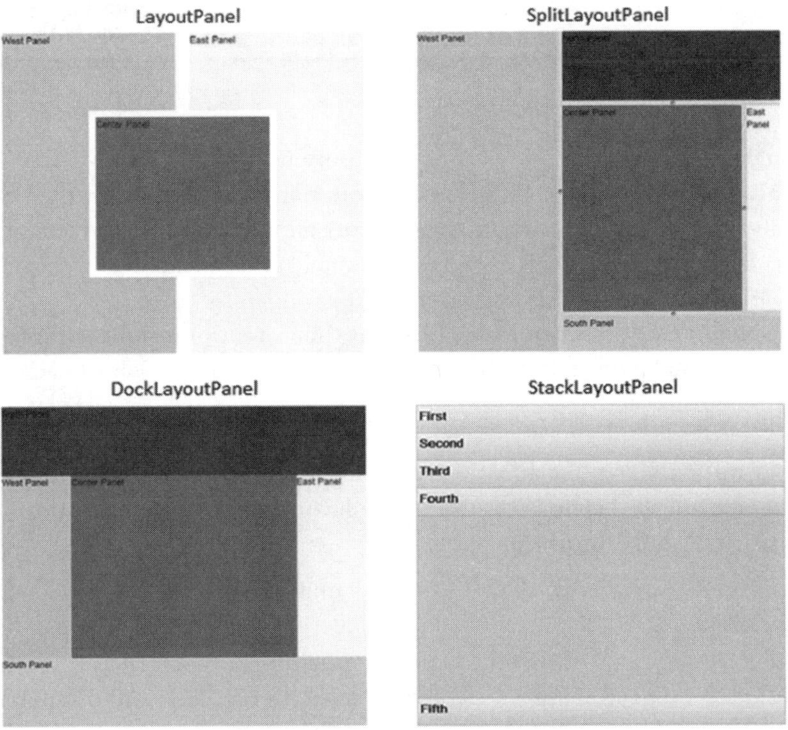

Figure 4.15 The different types of layout panel (excluding `TabLayoutPanel`, which you saw in chapter 3)

- The `DockLayoutPanel` acts the same as the `DockPanel` in that you have north, south, west, east, and center components.

  Depending on the order in which you add them to the panel, you get different structures. In figure 4.15 we added them in the order north, south, west, and east to get the north and south to fill the entire width. The center panel is always added last and expands to fill the remaining space.
- `StackLayoutPanel` provides a standard stacked view of headers with one visible child widget. Clicking a header changes the visible widget.
- `TabLayoutPanel`, not shown in figure 4.15 because we used it in chapter 3, is the layout equivalent of `TabPanel`.
- `DeckLayoutPanel`, again not shown in figure 4.15, is the layout equivalent of `DeckPanel`. It show only one of its widgets at a time, like a deck of cards.

Beyond these direct layout panels, there are a number of other panels and widgets that exhibit a similar need to know if they been resized[2] (that is, they implement the `RequiresResize` interface), as shown in figure 4.16.

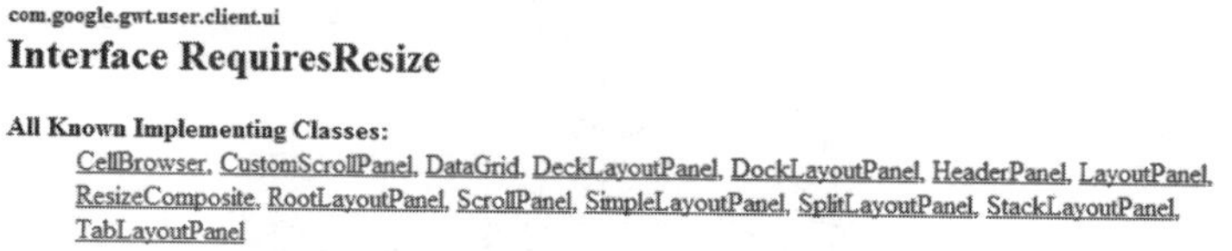

com.google.gwt.user.client.ui
Interface RequiresResize

All Known Implementing Classes:
CellBrowser, CustomScrollPanel, DataGrid, DeckLayoutPanel, DockLayoutPanel, HeaderPanel, LayoutPanel, ResizeComposite, RootLayoutPanel, ScrollPanel, SimpleLayoutPanel, SplitLayoutPanel, StackLayoutPanel, TabLayoutPanel

Figure 4.16 The GWT GUI components that are `LayoutPanels`, or act in a similar manner

We'd like to further point out one of those components shown in figure 4.16: `SimpleLayoutPanel`. We've mentioned before that layout panels are best suited to the overall structure of your application; `SimpleLayoutPanel` allows you to use layout panels at a lower level. Its single child will be a layout panel, and it manages resizes for you (rather like `ResizeComposite` does for `Composite` widgets).

The one challenge with layout panels is that their creation is a little more complicated than for normal panels, but it's not so difficult once you get your head around it.

4.6.2 Creating layout panels

You create layout panels in broadly the same way as any other panel—you create the appropriate Java object. During creation some layout panels require you to indicate, in their constructor, what units they'll be using:

- `LayoutPanel`—There's no need to specify units in the constructor, for example, `LayoutPanel p = new LayoutPanel();`.
- `DockLayoutPanel`—You need to specify units in the constructor, for example, `DockLayoutPanel d = new DockLayoutPanel(Units.PCT);` to use percentages.

---

2 GWT GUI components that are layout panels or act in a similar manner: http://mng.bz/1n5q.

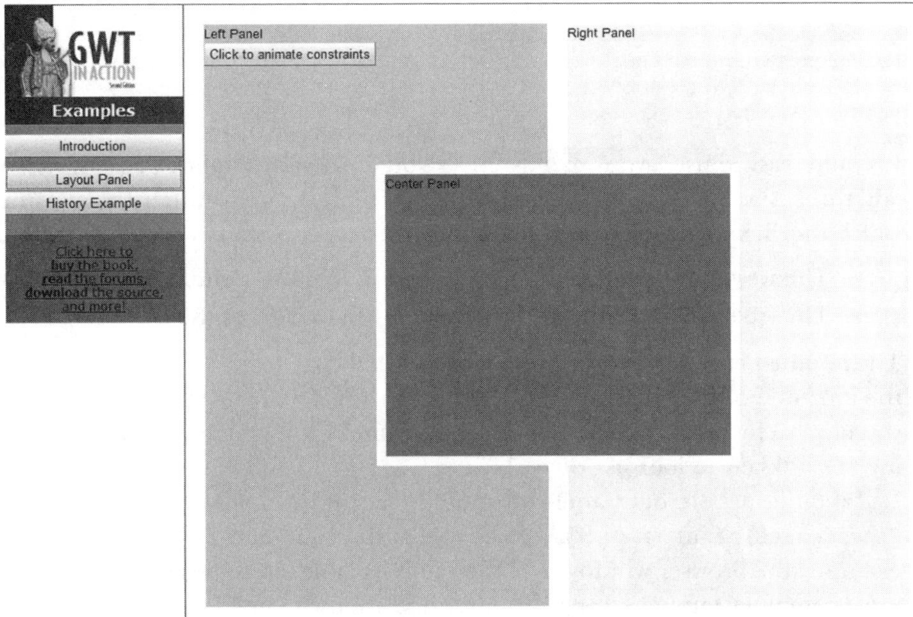

Figure 4.17 The result of `LayoutPanel` constraints to position three panels on the browser. There's a west panel on the left, an east panel on the right, and a center one in the middle—you'll soon change those positions.

- `SplitLayoutPanel`—Automatically uses pixel units and can't be changed.
- `StackLayoutPanel`—You need to specify units in the constructor, for example, `StackLayoutPanel s = new StackLayoutPanel(Units.EM);`.
- `TabLayoutPanel`—You need to specify units in the constructor, as well as the height of the tab, for example, `TabLayoutPanel t = new TabLayoutPanel (130, Units.PX);` for tab bars of 130 pixels.

The example creates the layout shown in figure 4.17 using a `LayoutPanel` panel.

We'll now look at how layout panels are created to show how figure 4.17 was created, how to animate them (try clicking the button in the Layout Panel part of `helper-app`), and what using standards mode means to your design.

The layout is created with the following code.

Listing 4.9 Creating a `LayoutPanel` in GWT

```
SimplePanel west = new SimplePanel();
SimplePanel east = new SimplePanel();
SimplePanel middle = new SimplePanel();

LayoutPanel holder = new LayoutPanel();
holder.add(west);
holder.add(east);
holder.add(middle);
```

❶ Creating LayoutPanel/adding content

```
holder.setWidgetLeftWidth(west, 0, Unit.PCT, 50, Unit.PCT);
holder.setWidgetRightWidth(east, 0, Unit.PCT, 50, Unit.PCT);
holder.setWidgetLeftRight(middle, 25, Unit.PCT, 25, Unit.PCT);
holder.setWidgetTopBottom(middle, 25, Unit.PCT, 25, Unit.PCT);
holder.forceLayout();
```

❷ **Setting constraints**

❸ **Forcing the layout**

It's quite easy to use layout panels. In ❶ you create an instance of a `LayoutPanel` and add three `SimplePanels` to it. You have to set their sizes (or rather the constraints into which they'll expand), and you do that in ❷. The constraints are set as follows:

- The west panel's left width should be 0% to 50% of the page.
- The east panel's right width should be 0% to 50% of the page.

The middle panel's left and right edges should be set to 25% in from the browser, and the top and bottom edges should also be set to 25% in from the browser edge. Finally, you have to force the dimensioning of the panel ❸; if you don't force the dimensioning, it's unlikely to look as you wish.

When using a layout panel you should place it in a container that implements the `ProvidesResize` interface. This ensures that the container listens to any resizes of, for example, the browser window and then tells its children to resize. If you choose not to use a container implementing this interface, then you need to explicitly set the size of the panel programmatically.

In practical terms this means the following:

- When adding a layout panel directly to the page, you should use `RootLayoutPanel` rather than `RootPanel`.
- When using a layout panel as the container of a `Composite` widget, then you should use the `ResizeComposite` class instead of `Composite`, so that resize requests from outside the composite get routed correctly to your container.
- When adding a layout panel to a part of the page, for example, a named `div`, then you need to wrap it in a `SimpleLayoutPanel` first to ensure resizes are directed through.

Potential LayoutPanel gotchas

You can't use `setVisibiity(false)` to set the visibility of a widget in a layout panel. Instead, you have to set the visibility of the container holding the widget—this is an implementation detail—by doing the following:

```
UIObject.setVisible(panel.getWidgetContainerElement(child), false);
```

Putting a layout panel in a panel implemented using tables or frames means you need to explicitly set its width and height style properties to 100%.

You must call `forceLayout` on layout panels to get them to your initially set up dimensions onscreen (except for `TabLayoutPanel`, which is a composite rather than a panel and so calls this method for you when added).

In the chapter's example code, although we used a layout panel as the container in a `ResizeComposite`, we placed it in a panel (the example framework) that doesn't implement the `ProvidesResize` interface—and so we needed to set the size of the widget to 100% for it to show.

One nifty thing that you can do with layout panels is to set up new constraints, and they'll come into existence once `forceLayout` is called again. This gets more interesting if we reword that to say "layout panels can automatically animate and/or morph between old and new constraints with one line of code."

4.6.3 Animating layout panels

Those layout panels that implement the `AnimatedLayout` interface, such as `SplitLayoutPanel`, `DockLayoutPanel`, and `LayoutPanel`, can animate between original and new constraints. You set the new constraints and call the `animate` method with a duration value. If we start with figure 4.17 from the `helper-app` project, we can set new dimensions to get to figure 4.18.

Comparing figure 4.18 to figure 4.17 you can see that the middle panel has moved to the right (and grown), the east panel to the left, and the west panel to the center (as well as shrinking). You can set the center panel to move to the right by saying

```
holder.setWidgetTopHeight(center, 0, Unit.PCT, 100, Unit.PCT);
holder.setWidgetRightWidth(center, 0, Unit.PCT, 50, Unit.PCT);
```

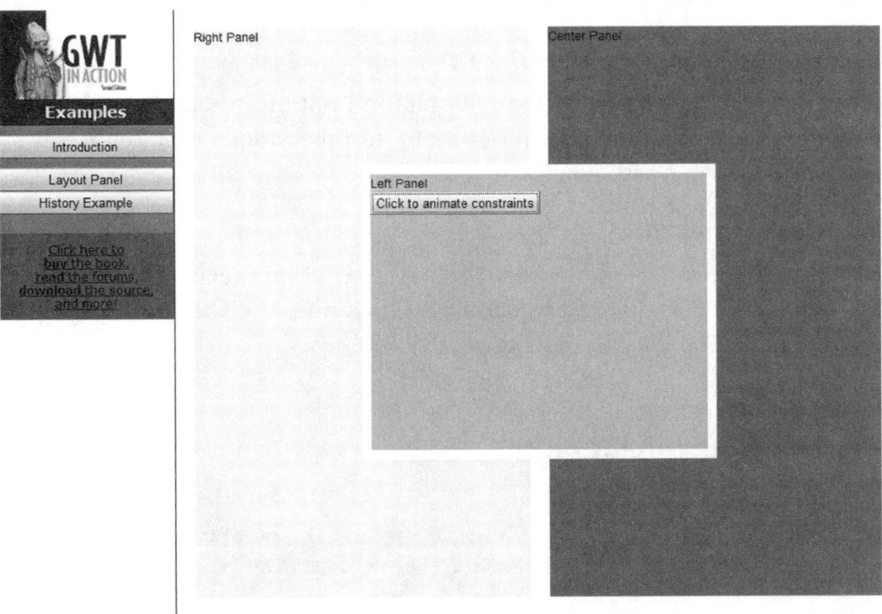

Figure 4.18 `LayoutPanel` after animation of constraints. The result is that the west panel has moved to the center and shrunk, the east panel has moved to the left, and the previous center panel has grown and moved to the right.

Here you set the height of the panel to be between 0% and 100% and its right width to be 0% to 50%. To move the east panel left, you set its left width (it used to have a right width):

```
holder.setWidgetLeftWidth(right, 0, Unit.PCT, 50, Unit.PCT);
```

Moving the west panel to the center means updating its dimensions to the ones the center panel previously had:

```
holder.setWidgetLeftRight(left, 25, Unit.PCT, 25, Unit.PCT);
holder.setWidgetTopBottom(left, 25, Unit.PCT, 25, Unit.PCT);
```

You also change the `zIndex` of the west panel—its depth on the screen—otherwise, it won't appear on top when it moves. Because it was added to the panel first, it has the lowest `zIndex`, so it will be half hidden by the east panel when it moves and the east panel moves left:

```
left.getElement().getStyle().setZIndex(zIndexCount++);
```

After setting these new constraints, a simple call to `forceLayout` will change to the new constraints immediately. To animate from existing constraints in figure 4.17 to their new ones in figure 4.18 within 500 milliseconds, you call:

```
holder.animate(500);
```

Layout panels aren't the only widgets that have animation or can have animation applied to them. GWT provides a predictable animation framework.

4.7 Applying animation to widgets

As you've seen, layout panels have animation built into them, but can you apply animation to other widgets? It turns out that yes, some widgets do already have it built in, and others we can build ourselves.

4.7.1 Widgets that animate

GWT components that implement the `HasAnimation` interface have animation capabilities built in. The simplest way to find which ones do is to look at the Javadoc[3]—at the time of writing it looks like figure 4.19.

com.google.gwt.user.client.ui

Interface HasAnimation

All Known Implementing Classes:

CellBrowser, CellTree, DeckPanel, DecoratedPopupPanel, DecoratedTabPanel, DialogBox, DisclosurePanel, LoggingPopup, MenuBar, PopupPanel, SuggestBox, SuggestBox.DefaultSuggestionDisplay, TabPanel, Tree

Figure 4.19 The widgets that, at the time of this writing, have built-in animation capabilities

[3] `HasAnimation` Javadoc showing which widgets have animation built in: http://mng.bz/fvkE.

You saw the PopupPanel animation in action in chapter 3's search functionality. By calling the panel's setAnimationEnabled method with the value true, the panel grew into view. For those widgets that don't have animation, or if you want to build a different type of animation, there's the Animation class.

4.7.2 Building your own animation

Let's say you want to build a simple animation that highlights a widget; it changes the widget's background color from whatever it currently is to yellow. You can use the com.google.gwt.animation.client.Animation class to drive the change. It gives you the ability to make updates based on a progression over time (and is typically what the widgets in the previous section are using).

Animation in GWT is built on a progression between values 0.0 and 1.0 within a defined time slot with successive calls to an onUpdate method as the animation runs. Because the browser is single threaded, you can't have a guaranteed frame rate, such as 50 frames a second, but you can be reasonably confident that, say for a 2-second animation, the value of progress passed to the onUpdate method is as follows:

- 0.0 at 0 seconds
- 1.0 at 2 seconds
- Somewhere between 0.0 and 1.0 when the time is between 0 and 2 seconds

To create your own animation you simply extend the Animation class and implement the onUpdate method. In the chapter's example we implement a simplified version of highlight that assumes the starting background color is white and the ending color is yellow, because that avoids lots of juggling of the colors and transparencies. The following listing shows the heart of the Highlight animation.

Listing 4.10 Creating an animation to morph between two different colors

```
protected void onUpdate(double progress) {
   double factor2 = progress;
   double factor1 = 1 - factor2;
   curr[R] = (int) Math.floor(start[R] * factor1 + end[R] * factor2);
   curr[G] = (int) Math.floor(start[G] * factor1 + end[G] * factor2);
   curr[B] = (int) Math.floor(start[B] * factor1 + end[B] * factor2);
   colour = "rgb(" + curr[R] + "," + curr[G] + "," + curr[B] + ")";
   elementToAnimate.getStyle().setBackgroundColor(colour);
}
```

❶ Calculate new RGB color

❷ Set background color

All we're saying in listing 4.10 is that whatever the value of progress, you calculate ❶ where on a sliding scale of values you'd be for that progress for each of the red, green, and blue components of a color. If progress is at 0, then you have the start color rgb(255,255,255); if progress is 1, then you have the end color, and in between you have an in-between value. The final step of onUpdate is to make the change ❷; here you manipulate the background CSS style of the DOM element that represents the widget you're animating, as shown in figure 4.20.

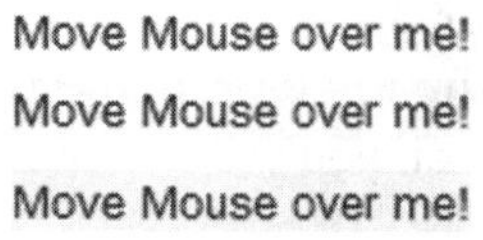

Move Mouse over me!

Move Mouse over me!

Move Mouse over me!

Figure 4.20 The `Highlight` animation in action showing the change to the background color of a widget progressively over the length of the animation

The animation is started by calling one of the `run` methods in the underlying `Animation` class, the simplest taking only the length of animation time in milliseconds as its parameter. We do that in the example, calling it from within a mouse-over event handler placed on the `InlineLabel`:

```
highlightEffect.run(5000);
```

As with a lot of things in GWT, animation is limited only by your imagination.

Before we leave the topic of widgets, we should look at the lifecycle they follow—we've already briefly hinted at this when we extended the `InlineLabel` earlier. Now it's time to see what we were talking about.

4.8 Exploring the lifecycle of a widget

From a developer's perspective, using a widget is easy. You create the widget and *add* it to your application via a panel. When you're finished with the widget, you *remove* it from the panel (or remove the panel), and you're done.

In the background, GWT is working hard on your behalf to link the Java view of the widget to the browser DOM's view of the widget, to protect you from introducing memory leaks and circular references, and to clean up after you. All that makes your code less likely to mess up your users' experience. GWT has a lifecycle for a widget, and we show that in figure 4.21.

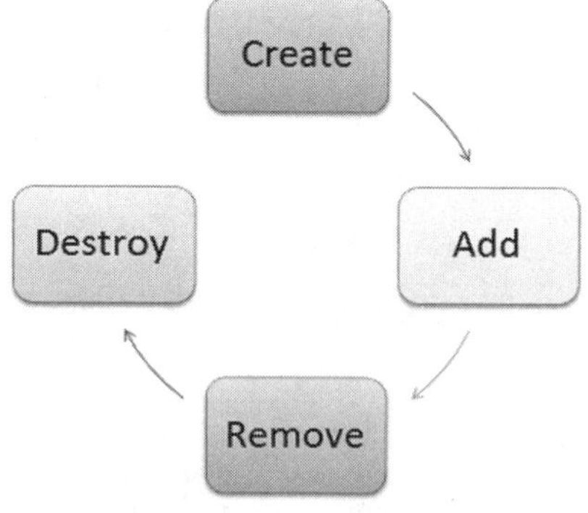

Figure 4.21 The lifecycle stages of a GWT widget

Sometimes it's useful to hook into GWT's widget lifecycle—you may want to know the size of a widget once it's attached in order to perform some animation on it later or to do something as the widget is removed from the DOM.

Just as there is a Java view and a DOM view of widgets, so there is a Java distinction and a DOM distinction in the lifecycle. In GWT Java we'll talk about adding and removing widgets, but in the DOM we'll refer to attaching and detaching; it's useful to keep that distinction in mind.

Let's start our walkthrough of the lifecycle by looking at creating a widget.

4.8.1 Creating a widget

Widgets are created in your application by using the Java `new` construct. Want a new `Button` widget? Write the following:

```
Button myShinyButton = new Button("Shiny!");
```

In the background GWT will be creating the appropriate DOM structure for this widget—in this case it creates a DOM BUTTON element:

```
<BUTTON type="BUTTON">Shiny!</BUTTON>
```

But you won't see the widget on your application until you add it—which is what we'll look at next.

4.8.2 Adding a widget

Adding a widget is achieved in your Java code by the following ways:

- Adding it directly to the `RootPanel/RootLayoutPanel`, for example, `RootPanel.get().add(new Button())`
- Adding a widget to the `RootPanel/RootLayoutPanel` in which your widget is added, for example, a `VerticalPanel` that has the widget within it (`Rootpanel.get().add(new VerticalPanel.add(new Button()))`)
- Adding a widget that includes a widget that includes your widget, `Rootpanel.get().add(new DeckPanel.add(new VerticalPanel.add(new Button())))`
- And so on—you get the picture?

When you call `RootPanel.get().add(w)` for a widget `w`, GWT ends up calling the `add` method in `ComplexPanel` (of which `RootPanel` is a subclass). This is defined as the following:

```
protected void add(Widget child, Element container) {
   child.removeFromParent();                              // ❶ Remove widget from anywhere else
   getChildren().add(child);                              // ❷ Logically add the widget
   DOM.appendChild(container, child.getElement());        // ❸ Physically add the widget
   adopt(child);                                          // ❹ Adopt the widget
}
```

GWT will first ensure that the widget being added is removed from any panel (parent) it might already have ❶. A widget can't have more than one parent—you can't have the same button in two different panels, for example. Next, ❷ the widget is logically added to the `RootPanel`'s collection of widgets (the Java view), and in ❸ it's added to the DOM (the DOM view).

Finally, the `RootPanel` adopts ❹ the widget. The parent's `adopt` method calls the widget's `setParent` method. If the parent isn't currently attached to the DOM, then GWT stops processing because there's nothing more to be done. If it's attached to the DOM, then `setParent` makes a call to the widget's `onAttach` method.

The `RootPanel` is always attached to the DOM, and because you're adding a widget to that, let's look at a simplified version of its `onAttach` method.

Listing 4.11 Attaching a widget

```
protected void onAttach() {
  if (isAttached()) throw new IllegalStateException("Cannot attach");
   attached = true;
```

```
    DOM.setEventListener(getElement(), this);        ❶ Plug widget into event system
    doAttachChildren();                              ❷ Attach widget's children
    onLoad();
    AttachEvent.fire(this, true);                    ❸ Declare widget is loaded
}
```

The code in listing 4.11 first checks that the widget you're trying to attach isn't already attached, but if it is, it throws an exception—you can't attach to the DOM a widget that's already attached elsewhere. Usually the widget won't be already attached, particularly if you're coming through the panel's `add` method, because the first thing that it does is detach the widget if it's already attached, but GWT is playing safe here with this check. Assuming the widget isn't attached elsewhere, the `attached` variable is set to `true` to indicate it's now attached.

❶ is an example of where GWT protects you against memory leaks. GWT imposes its own event-managing subsystem on widgets, and here it's hooking the widget into that for any event that may be raised. Whether a widget handles a particular event or not, and how it handles an event, is the subject of chapter 14. Having a single event handler for everything simplifies event handling, leading to a reduced potential for memory leaks.

The widget next attempts to attach any children it may have ❷. For a widget that isn't a panel, the `doAttachChildren` method is usually empty because there should be no children; for a panel, `doAttachChildren` is usually a case of calling the children's `onAttach` methods, which may recur further if those children have children.

When `doAttachChildren` completes, the widget, and any contained widgets in the case of a panel, can be thought of as being attached to the browser's DOM. Now you can handle that attachment in your Java code.

HANDLING WIDGET ATTACHMENT

It's tempting, if you need to do something once the widget is attached, to override the `onAttach` method. You shouldn't. If the underlying approach is changed in the future, you risk your application being unstable.

Instead, `onAttach` provides two ways of indicating the widget is fully attached:

- It calls the widget's `onLoad` method.

  By default this is normally empty, and you can safely override this to provide your needed functionality.
- An `AttachEvent` is fired.

  Add an `AttachEventHandler` to the widget to handle this event (check the value of `AttachEvent.isAttached()` to distinguish between attach and detach events).

GWT's distinction between Java and DOM allows you to create user interface structures that aren't yet attached to the DOM. As soon as you add it to the DOM, GWT cascades up through the structure, attaching children to parents and event handlers to DOM elements.

The reverse process happens when you remove a widget from the application.

4.8.3 Removing a widget

You can remove a widget from the application in one of two ways. Either you do it explicitly via a call to a panel's `remove` method, or it's done implicitly by GWT when the browser deletes your application because you've navigated elsewhere.

In both cases, you can only remove a widget from its direct parent, and if you remove a widget, all of its child widgets are also removed. When you navigate away from your application, one of the last things GWT does is call `remove` on all widgets added to the `RootPanel/RootLayoutPanel`; hence everything—DOM and event handling—gets cleaned up nicely.

Let's look at removing the button you previously added to the `RootPanel`. You could call `RootPanel.get().remove(button)`, which results in a call to `remove(button)` in the `ComplexPanel` class (of which `RootPanel` is a subclass). We hope you won't be too surprised to see this method looks like the opposite and reverse of `onAttach`. To follow is a simplified version of it:

```
public boolean remove(Widget w) {
  if (w.getParent() != this) { return false; }       // 1 Check that this is the parent
  try {
     orphan(w);                                      // 2 Orphan the widget
  } finally {
     Element elem = w.getElement();
     DOM.removeChild(DOM.getParent(elem), elem);     // 3 Physically detach the widget
     getChildren().remove(w);                        // 4 Logically detach the widget
  }
  return true;
}
```

When you request to remove a widget, GWT checks that the panel is the parent of the widget you wish to remove ❶. If so, then you orphan the widget ❷, physically remove it from the DOM view ❸, and logically remove it from the panel's Java view ❹.

Similar to the `adopt` method you use when adding the widget, the `orphan` method calls the widget's `setParent` method. This time it sets the parent to `null`, which invokes the widget's `onDetach` method. Listing 4.12 shows a simplified version of `onDetach`. Again, the `onDetach` method is the opposite and reverse of `onAttach`, which you saw in the previous section (compare listing 4.12 with listing 4.11).

Listing 4.12 Detaching a widget

```
protected void onDetach() {
  if (!isAttached()) throw new IllegalStateException("Unable to Detach");
   try {
      onUnload();                         // 1 Declare widget is unloaded
      AttachEvent.fire(this, false);
   } finally {
      try {
         doDetachChildren();              // 2 Detach widget's children
      } finally {
```

```
            DOM.setEventListener(getElement(), null);
            attached = false;
        }
    }
}
```

❸ **Unplug widget from event system**

If you look at the onDetach method, you can see that GWT first checks that the widget you wish to remove is attached. Assuming it is, then you do the reverse process of what happened when attaching.

GWT first tries to indicate to you as a programmer that the widget is unloaded—we'll come back to that in a second. Then GWT tries to detach any children the widget may have ❷. As with attaching, it's usually only panels that will have an implementation of doDetachChildren. Finally, GWT unplugs the widget from the event-handling system ❸ to stop handling any events and by doing so remove any memory leak issues.

The Java try/finally structure in the code is there to ensure that the widget cleans up after itself, regardless of errors in the code you've written in onUnload or any raised while trying to remove child widgets.

HANDLING WIDGET DETACHMENT

Remember that when we added a widget, we said we shouldn't override the onAttach method? The same thing is true when removing the widget—we shouldn't overload the onDetach method (❶ in listing 4.12).

Instead, onDetach provides two ways of indicating the widget is about to be detached from the DOM:

- It calls the widget's onUnload method.

  By default this is normally empty, and you can safely override this to provide your needed functionality.
- An AttachEvent is fired.

  You add an AttachEventHandler to the widget to handle this event (check that the value of AttachEvent.isAttached() equals false to know that this is a detach event).

Note the subtlety here: When attaching, you're notified once the attachment to DOM is fully completed; when detaching, you're notified before the detachment from DOM is done.

If the widget is detached, then the last step in the lifecycle is for it to potentially be destroyed.

4.8.4 Destroying a widget

Once you've removed a widget, you're in the land of potential garbage collection. Luckily GWT handles most problematic aspects affecting garbage collection for you, the largest being event handlers hogging memory once widgets are removed. That's not an issue in GWT, because the removal process we described takes the event handler out of the browser's concern.

When you're finished with a widget you can set its reference to `null`, if you prefer, to indicate to the garbage collector it will definitely not be used in the future.

Before we close this chapter, let's look a little into the future, with Elemental.

4.9 Getting Elemental, my dear Watson!

GWT 2.5, the latest release at the time of writing, brings with it a new API called Elemental.

> **NOTE** Don't forget to explicitly add the gwt-elemental.jar file to your classpath because it's not included in the standard gwt-user.jar of GWT.

This API is intended to bind as closely as possible to HTML5 and melt away during compilation (leave no overhead). It comes without a lot of the protection of normal GWT but should give access to modern browser functions as quickly as they and GWT are updated. Let's take a quick look at it now so you're at least aware of it.

4.9.1 Examining Elemental

Table 4.1 shows how you'd add a button that reacts to clicks to a simple panel, which is itself added to the HTML page. The left column presents the functionality in the normal GWT way; the right column uses classes from the new-to-GWT 2.5 Elemental classes.

Table 4.2 Comparison of standard GWT and Elemental approaches to create simple functionality

	GWT proper	Elemental in GWT (experimental and APIs are subject to change)

1	`Button b = new Button();`
	
	`b.setText("Some Text");`
		`ButtonElement b = getDocument()`
		`                    .createButtonElement();`
		`b.setInnerHTML("Some Text");`

2	`FlowPanel p = new FlowPanel();`	`DivElement p = getDocument()` `                    .createDivElement();`
3	`b.getStyle().setColor("red");`	`b.getStyle().setColor("red");`

4	`p.add(b)`
	`RootPanel.get().add(p);`
		`p.appendChild(b)`
		`getDocument().getBody()`
		`                  .appendChild(p);`

We hope you can see that an Elemental approach requires you to know much more about browsers and the JavaScript approach of coding. For example, on line 2 you use a `DivElement` in Elemental rather than the `FlowPanel` in GWT; in line 1 as well as having to know to create a `ButtonElement` you have to use the `setInnerHTML` method to set the button label. (And see how you've lost the direct access to `SafeHTML`? Although because you have access to normal GWT, you can use, say, `SafeHtmlBuilder` to create the text first before putting it into the `setInnerHtml` method—you just need to remember to use it.)

You have to append children rather than adding (line 4); and event handling, although similar, is less safe in the Elemental approach (you don't get automatic access to the memory leak protection that GWT proper provides).

So why aren't we using Elemental for everything in GWT? Well, it brings some challenges.

4.9.2 Understanding the challenge

If you use Elemental at the moment, you should be aware of a few challenges:

- It's experimental (in GWT 2.5).

  That means it's likely to change in future releases, so if you start using it, you'll need to be prepared to keep updating and changing your application with each update.
- You aren't protected from browser changes.

  Because the API is automatically built from IDL specifications, if those specs change, the API changes and your application may break until you fix it.
- You don't get GWT's protection against memory leaks.

  For example, you're having to manage event handler registration and removal.
- It's not currently available for all browsers.

  At the time of writing it's available for only Safari and Chrome, and if it was more widely available it wouldn't necessarily act the same way across all browsers. Because you're coding directly to the browser implementation, GWT has no control over consistency. Certainly it won't be maintainable in older browsers currently supported by GWT.

With those challenges, you might be wondering what the benefits are of using Elemental.

4.9.3 Noting the benefit

The main benefit to Elemental is speed to market of new browser features in GWT applications. Because the API is automatically generated from the browser developer's interface description language documents, you don't need to wait for the GWT developers to create the necessary GWT APIs—just wait for the next GWT (or live off the trunk if you're living life dangerously).

Elemental isn't only for widgets; you can use it for all HTML5 aspects that aren't yet in GWT. For example, you won't find in GWT 2.5 proper classes for understanding the state of the battery (`BatteryManager`), the HTML 5 File API, speech-recognition events, scalable vector graphics or WebGL APIs, local workers, or web sockets, yet you can get access to them through Elemental library. As we said, though, even if you can access them in Elemental, it doesn't mean they're supported in all browsers.

Our advice? Keep an eye on Elemental because it will undoubtedly be a powerful thing in GWT, but for now it needs to find its place in the overall GWT technology. We suggest you shy away from using it unless you absolutely need some functionality GWT doesn't yet provide and you can live with a limited user base (because the functionality you want to use has restricted browser support).

4.10 Summary

This chapter looked at three different ways to create new widgets. The first was creating a widget from scratch to represent a DOM element, although we mentioned that it's unlikely you'll have to do this because GWT already provides widgets for most DOM elements.

We had a useful discussion on the process of attaching and detaching widgets from the DOM and what GWT does for you to protect against memory leaks. Throughout the rest of the chapter we returned to those points a few times because it was useful to override the `onLoad` method when a widget had completed loading.

Next, we looked at how you can take a widget that almost does what you want and extend it to create what you need. In this case, you made an `InlineLabel` report its dimensions when it was added to the DOM. You knew you could do that because we'd discussed that there were a couple of hooks into the process of attaching and detaching widgets in the first section of the chapter.

Finally, we moved on to looking at `Composite` widgets. In this approach you built a simple question and answer widget and learned how to implement functionality in the widget or delegate to the components.

You've created widgets in a direct programmatic manner up until now. There's an alternative way of building user interfaces—a declarative way—which in GWT is achieved by using UiBinder, and that will be covered in chapter 6.

Before we get to that chapter, we'll look at how you can efficiently bundle resources together (images, text, and others) using a resource bundle—which you'll then use in the declarative approach.

5 Using client bundles

> ***This chapter covers***
> - Examining `ClientBundle`s and `DataResource`s
> - Creating and using text and image resources
> - Dealing efficiently with styling problems using CSS resources

In this chapter we'll take a look at how access to images, binary documents, text files, stylesheets, and other static resources GWT uses can be optimized at compile time through the use of the `ClientBundle`.

Typically, a web application will request each needed resource individually, making no attempt to bundle similar resources and requiring a new connection for each. Where load times are concerned, connection count is the enemy. Each connection requires a nontrivial amount of time to set up, so anything that you can do to reduce the number of connections required will help reduce an application's load time. Think of it this way: if you were moving cross-country, would you drive each of your belongings individually, making hundreds of trips? Or would you carefully pack everything into a single truck and make the trip once? You could think of each of these cross-country trips as making a connection, and it's pretty obvious that packing everything into a moving truck is more efficient. You can think of `ClientBundle` as GWT's moving truck, but this moving truck knows a few tricks.

One technique used by `ClientBundle` to reduce connection count is resource embedding. This means adding the text or bytes of the resource to the main application payload.

Besides connection count, the total number of bytes also has an effect on load time. If you can reduce the total number of bytes transferred, your page will take less time to load. In some cases, `ClientBundle` will try to combine and compress similar resources to reduce the byte count, something akin to putting a closetful of sweaters into a vacuum storage bag before loading them onto the truck. For instance, images referenced as `ImageResources` may be combined into a single image strip, which simultaneously reduces the total number of bytes transferred as well as the number of requests required.

Another trick that GWT uses to reduce load times is caching. The idea with caching is to avoid transferring any bytes at all. If the content is already at its destination, there's no point in loading a copy onto the truck. You don't even need the truck. GWT uses the cache.*xxx* extension to indicate that the browser can cache (save) certain files indefinitely. When a browser encounters one of these files and sees that it's already in its cache, it will use the copy it already has rather than creating a connection and requesting a new copy.

In this chapter, we'll explore all of the techniques used by `ClientBundle` to optimize resource delivery. We'll start with the `DataResource` to learn the basics of using `ClientBundle` resources, and you'll see `ClientBundle`'s use of both caching and embedding. We'll then move on to the text resource types, where we'll introduce you to resource bundling. Next, we'll look at `ImageResource`, which uses all of the previously mentioned optimization techniques, but we'll take some time to learn how to control `ClientBundle`'s use of these optimizations. Finally, we'll explore `CssResource`, which adds minification, obfuscation, and selector merging to the optimization techniques used by `ClientBundle`.

`CssResource` is unique in that it's the only resource type that adds extra features to the underlying resource. You'll learn to use CSS constants to declare reusable values in a central location, runtime evaluation to set attribute values when the resource is injected, and conditional sections to create CSS blocks that are chosen based on values determined either during compilation or upon resource injection.

Let's begin learning about `ClientBundles` by exploring an example using the most basic resource type, the `DataResource`.

5.1 Client bundle basics using DataResources

The `ClientBundle` is an interface that defines methods to access any resources that you choose to load it with. For this example you'll be loading a `ClientBundle` with `DataResources`, but the interface could easily define methods for any combination of resources that you'd like.

You use the resource type DataResource to bundle arbitrary file types. For instance, a DataResource could be an icon, or a PDF, or a Zip archive. As such, there's no good way to extend GWT to optimize its inclusion in a ClientBundle, so it sticks to some basic noninvasive embedding or caching techniques that don't require knowledge of the specific file type.

5.1.1 DataResource

Most any static data that you'd like to access via URL can be a DataResource. It's primarily concerned with improving the cacheability of the data, without considering much else. Over time this results in something akin to grabbing an identical item from your local store rather than moving the original cross-country.

GWT uses one of two techniques to provide deterministic caching for a DataResource. The first and most common method is to copy the file into the module's output directory, giving it a strongly cacheable filename. This filename is constructed the same way as all of GWT's cacheable files: a 32-character hash, followed by ".cache.", and finally, the file's original extension (jpg, for instance). As long as the web server is configured to add the correct cache-control headers for *.cache.* files, the browser will cache the file indefinitely.

The second technique is used only for smaller files and only on browsers that support data URIs. This method involves converting the bytes of the file to Base64, building a URL that looks something like data:[content-type];base64,[Base64 Data],[1] and embedding it into the module's JavaScript payload. Because Base64 increases the byte count of the encoded data by about one-third, connection count is reduced at the expense of bytes transferred. In many cases, the additional bytes will be less expensive, with regard to load time, than the extra connection would have been. But if many resources are being added to the payload as data URIs, the initial load time of the application might be increased. We don't subscribe to any hard-and-fast rules here. A few inlined data objects aren't likely to cause any noticeable issues, but dozens that aren't necessarily going to be used all the time may. Disabling inlining is one way to defer the loading of the DataResource until it's needed (code splitting is another option but is more of an advanced topic, covered in chapter 19).

In this case, you could tell the GWT compiler to not be so helpful and stick to using the cacheable filename technique. You'd accomplish this by setting the ClientBundle.enableInlining deferred binding property to false in a module file associated with the application, by adding the following line:

```
<set-property name="ClientBundle.enableInlining"
              value="false"/>
```

ClientBundle.enableInlining is a deferred binding property that will affect the whole project and will prevent GWT from creating any data URLs from any resources defined in any ClientBundle. This means that not only would DataResource be

1 "Data URI scheme," Wikipedia, The Free Encyclopedia, http://en.wikipedia.org/wiki/Data_URI_scheme.

affected but also any other resources that might be bundled as data URLs, like `Image-Resource`.

> **NOTE** GWT uses the deferred binding technique to create code implementations at compile time. One technique for controlling the code created is via deferred binding properties, as you've seen. Deferred binding is discussed in depth in chapter 17.

If you'd prefer to not disable inlining for the whole project, `DataResource` includes the `@DoNotEmbed` annotation that allows you to disable inlining on a case-by-case basis. You could add `@DoNotEmbed` to the `DataResource`'s accessor method. A technique for disabling inlining on a bundle-by-bundle basis is described later in section 5.3.3 of this chapter.

In addition, the configuration property, `ClientBundle.enableRenaming`, can be set to `false` to prevent GWT from creating cacheable filenames. Disabling cacheable filenames would defeat the whole purpose of a `DataResource`, but we mention it anyway because it could be useful while debugging, and we'll use it later to demonstrate another feature of `ClientBundle`. To disable renaming, add the following to a module file in your application:

```
<set-configuration-property name="ClientBundle.enableRenaming "value="false"/>
```

Notice that `ClientBundle.enableRenaming` is a configuration property (see chapter 18) rather than a deferred binding property (chapter 17); therefore it uses the `<set-configuration-property>` element rather than the `<set-property>` element. Again, this property affects the entire project and disables cacheable filenames for other resource types as well.

Finally, the `@MimeType` annotation allows you to specify the mime type for resources that are likely to be included as data URIs.

Next, we'll move on to adding some `DataResources` to a `ClientBundle`.

5.1.2 A simple ClientBundle

Now that you know a little bit about how GWT optimizes resource delivery, let's take a look at a `ClientBundle` that contains some `DataResources` and then discuss what GWT does with them. Much of what you'll see with `DataResource` applies directly to the other resources as well, so keep that in mind as we discuss this simplest of the resource types; an example of this is shown in the following listing.

Listing 5.1 `ClientBundle` containing `DataResources`

```
public interface DataResources extends ClientBundle {

  DataResources IMPL =
    (DataResources) GWT.create(DataResources.class);
```

❶ Interface extends ClientBundle

❷ Convenience field to hold bundle implementation

```
    @Source("resources/BigPhoto.jpg")
    DataResource bigPhoto();

    @DoNotEmbed
    @Source("resources/Document.pdf")
    DataResource document();

    @MimeType("image/png")
    @Source("resources/slashdot.png")
    DataResource slashdot();
}
```

❸ Annotation references the resource file
❹ Large photograph that's nonembeddable
❺ Internationalized document
❻ Declare the mime type as image/png
❼ Small icon that can be embedded

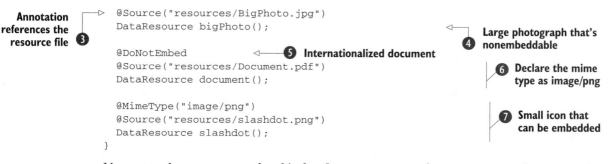

No matter how many or what kinds of resources you plan to use, you always start by defining an interface that extends `ClientBundle` ❶. The `DataResources` interface will become your moving truck for delivering the resources you decide to load it with.

You don't ever have to concern yourself with implementing this interface because GWT will create a browser-appropriate implementation at compile time, but you'll need to get an instance of your bundle somehow. If you're working with widgets in pure Java, you'd have to use `GWT.create()` to get an instance. For this reason, we've added a convenience field to our interface ❷ where this instance can be easily accessed. If you're using `UiBinder`, then including a `<ui:with>` element will give you an instance of the bundle for use with UiBinder templates.

With the formalities out of the way, you can move on to loading the `ClientBundle` with some resources. You use the `@Source` annotation ❸ to indicate the file that will be represented by the resource. GWT expects the filename in the annotation to be located relative to the interface source file, so you need to place the resources in a subdirectory and prepend the filename with the directory (resources/BigPhoto.jpg, for instance). This is what we do in this chapter's example, as you can see in figure 5.1.

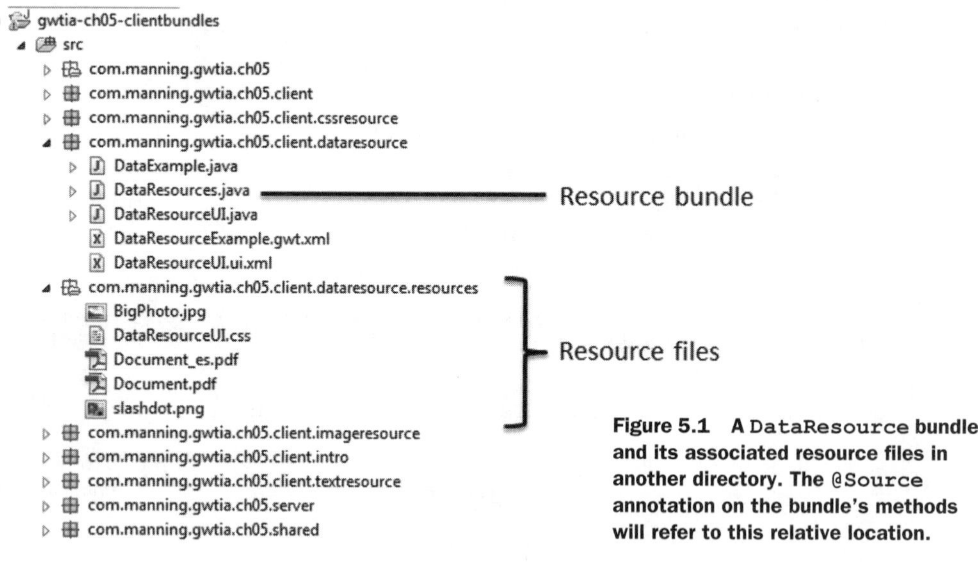

Figure 5.1 A `DataResource` bundle and its associated resource files in another directory. The `@Source` annotation on the bundle's methods will refer to this relative location.

The `DataResource` is defined in the `dataresource` package, and as shown in listing 5.1, the resources are in the resources folder located relative to the package. You don't need to manually copy resources or manually place them in the compiled part of the application—the compiler will do this for you (and the compiler will push the bundled resource there for you).

@Source annotations

You use the `@Source` annotation to associate a `ClientBundle` resource with the file it represents. Resource types that have default file extensions defined can omit the annotation if the `Resource` accessor method and the filename (sans extension) are identical.

`TextResource` and `ExternalTextResource` define .txt as the default extension. `ImageResource` defines .png, .jpg, .gif, and .bmp as default extension types. `CssResource` defines .css as the default extension. But you must always use `@Source` annotations with `DataResource` because it doesn't define any default extension types.

You must always use `@Source` annotation if the resource filename doesn't match the `Resource` method name. There's no harm in always including the annotation even when the filename and method name match.

The first `DataResource` is BigPhoto.jpg ❹. Although BigPhoto could be added as an `ImageResource`, large and infrequently displayed images might be added as a `DataResource` instead. The second ❺ is an internationalized PDF document that's large enough that it shouldn't be inlined, but you include the `@DoNotEmbed` annotation ❻ to be sure. And the final resource you define ❼ is an icon that's small enough that GWT will turn it into a data URL on the browsers that support it. You also declare the mime type for this resource as `image/png`. This icon would probably be more appropriate as an `ImageResource`, but we include it here for demonstration purposes.

The BigPhoto and slashdot resources are straightforward. The `DataResource` for each is generated and the file is either copied to the output directory or inlined in the JavaScript payload. The document resource, however, is more interesting. By using `ClientBundle` to access this resource, you get internationalization for free.

NOTE Internationalization (i18n) allows the application to serve documents to the user in their native language. Internationalization is discussed in depth in chapter 13.

All you have to do is include the various translations of the document in your source directory. In this case we have Document.pdf (our English version) and Document _es.pdf (a Spanish translation), both located in the resource directory under our DataResources.java file (see figure 5.1). Then all you have to do is tell GWT which locales you've included by extending the `locale` deferred binding property in your module file:

```
<extend-property name='locale' values='es'/>
```

Notice that we extended the locale property to include only the es value. Because our default version happens to be English, we don't need to include the en locale. Any locale that isn't es gets the default version, so declaring an extra locale without having specialized (translated) resources would do nothing more than cause extra permutations to be generated at compile time. That's all there is to it. We've just internationalized our document. Whenever an application reports the es locale, it will automatically get the Spanish version; all others will get the English version. See chapter 13 for more information on internationalization.

5.1.3 Creating ClientBundles using the Google Plugin for Eclipse

The Google Plugin for Eclipse (GPE) can automatically generate most of the code you saw in listing 5.1. Select New > ClientBundle from the File menu in Eclipse or from the contextual menu in the package explorer. The resulting dialog allows you to give your ClientBundle a name and choose the resources that you'd like to add to the bundle, as in figure 5.2.

When you've named the resource bundle and added/edited the resources, the plug-in automatically creates the ClientBundle interface, and if any CSS files were selected, it will also create the CssResource interfaces (described in section 5.3 of this chapter) based on the class names defined in the stylesheet.

The interfaces created by GPE can be used directly or fine-tuned by adding additional annotations to accessor methods.

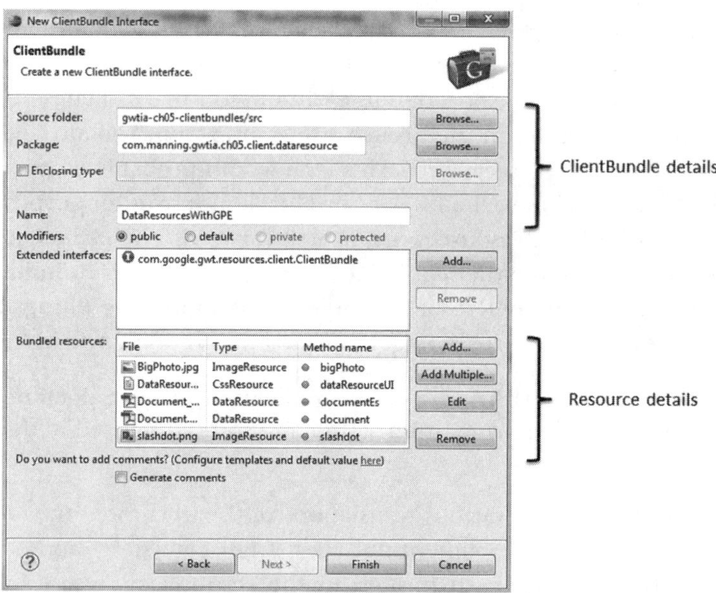

Figure 5.2 Using the GPE to create ClientBundles. When you add a resource in the Bundled Resources section, the GPE picks what it feels are the most appropriate resource type and method names. You can change those by selecting the resource and clicking the Edit button.

Regardless of whether you created the bundle by hand or through the plug-in, the next step is to use it.

5.1.4 Using ClientBundles in an application

Now that you've created a `ClientBundle`, you can build a simple application that demonstrates how you might use your `DataResources`. In this simple demonstration, you'll create a grid that will have a row to hold each of your resources. Each row will display the name of the resource, followed by the URL generated by GWT, and finally, a simple example of how to use the `DataResource` in an application.

When we load the resulting application in Safari, we get a page that looks like figure 5.3. The next listing shows the code you'll use to create figure 5.3.

Listing 5.2 Partial code showing how data resources are added to a `Grid` widget

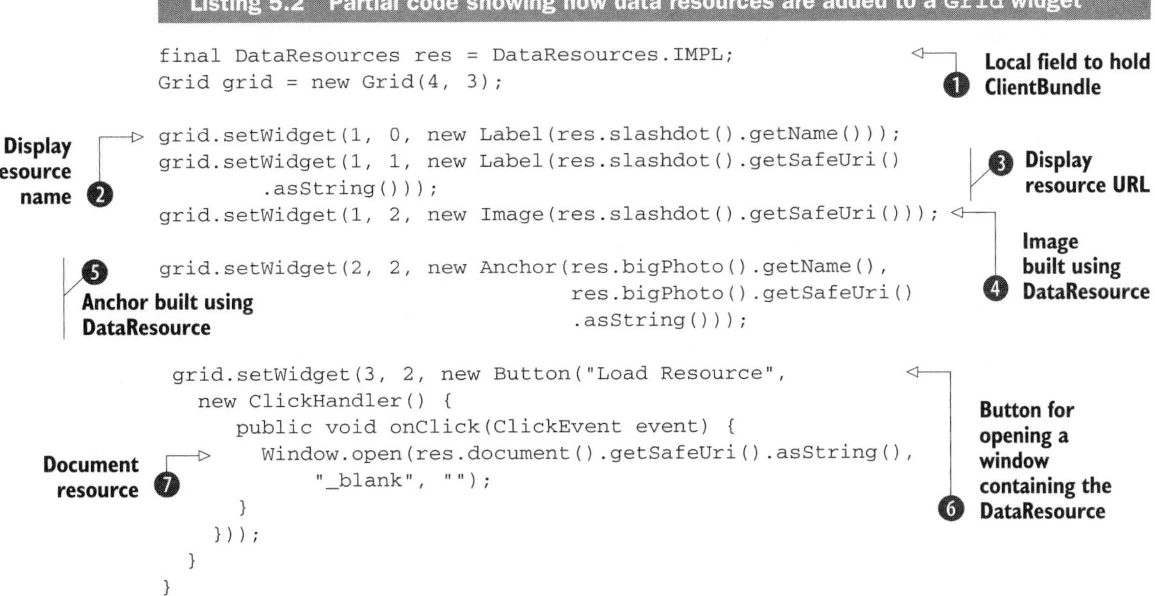

```
final DataResources res = DataResources.IMPL;
Grid grid = new Grid(4, 3);

grid.setWidget(1, 0, new Label(res.slashdot().getName()));
grid.setWidget(1, 1, new Label(res.slashdot().getSafeUri()
        .asString()));
grid.setWidget(1, 2, new Image(res.slashdot().getSafeUri()));

grid.setWidget(2, 2, new Anchor(res.bigPhoto().getName(),
                                res.bigPhoto().getSafeUri()
                                .asString()));

  grid.setWidget(3, 2, new Button("Load Resource",
    new ClickHandler() {
       public void onClick(ClickEvent event) {
         Window.open(res.document().getSafeUri().asString(),
             "_blank", "");
       }
    }));
  }
}
```


First, you create a local variable to hold a reference to the `ClientBundle` ❶ so that instead of using `DataResources.IMPL` everywhere, you can use the smaller `res`

http://localhost/DataResourceDemo.html

Name	URL	Example
slashdot	data:image/png;base64,iVBORw0KGgoAAAANSUhEUgAAAQAAAAEACAYAAABccq	
bigPhoto	http://localhost/DataResource/AFD97D9B575A9D19EDEA7225D57DF35F.cache.jpg	bigPhoto
document	http://localhost/DataResource/8EFEA9599781C83DDF2C1ADA6C4DD473.cache.pdf	Load Resource

Figure 5.3 `DataResource` URLs displayed in Safari

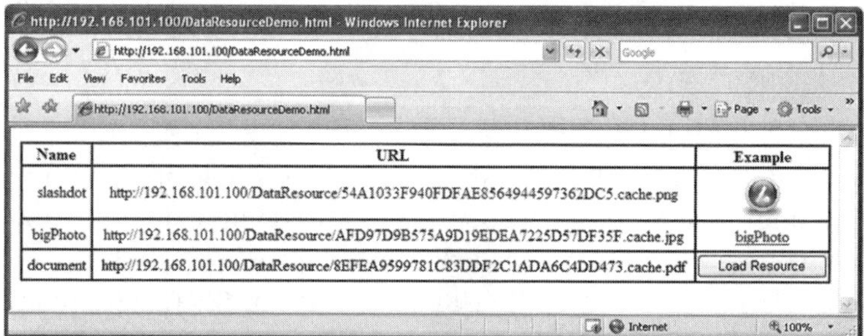

Figure 5.4 Internet Explorer doesn't support data URLs.

reference. In the first column of the second row of some `Grid` widget defined somewhere in the code you add a `Label` using the name of the slashdot resource ❷. Similarly, you display a string representation of the `DataResource`'s `SafeUri` ❸ in the second column so you can see the URL to see what, if anything, has happened to it.

The third column of your `Grid` is where you finally demonstrate how an `Image` would be created from the `DataResource` ❹. It's simply a case of getting the `SafeUri` from the bundle and passing it to an `Image` widget.

Similarly, you add an `Anchor` widget in the next row of the grid ❺ that would load the BigPhoto image from a `DataResource` when selected.

The last row of the example in listing 5.2 contains a button that will load the `DataResource` in a new window when it's clicked. ❻ creates such a `Button` widget, and by adding a `ClickHandler` to it, you can fire up the resource in a new window ❼.

One thing to note is that the underlying implementation of `DataResource` is constrained by the browser being targeted. For example, back in figure 5.1 you saw the result for Safari, and you can see that both the BigPhoto and document resources have been given cacheable URLs, whereas the slashdot resource has been converted to a data URL. But data URLs aren't supported on all browser platforms. By loading the application in Internet Explorer, as shown in figure 5.4, you can see that the slashdot resource uses a cacheable filename rather than a data URL (compare the second column in figure 5.4 with that in figure 5.1).

What isn't obvious, because of the cacheable filename, is which version of the document resource is being delivered. This is where you can use the `ClientBundle.enableRenaming` property that we mentioned earlier. If you disable renaming, as shown in figure 5.5, you can plainly see that the default Document.pdf URL is used.

http://localhost/DataResourceDemo.html

Name	URL	Example
slashdot	data:image/png;base64,iVBORw0KGgoAAAANSUhEUgAAAQAAAAEACAYAAABccqh	
bigPhoto	http://localhost/DataResource/BigPhoto.jpg	bigPhoto
document	http://localhost/DataResource/Document.pdf	Load Resource

Figure 5.5 `DataResources` displayed with renaming disabled

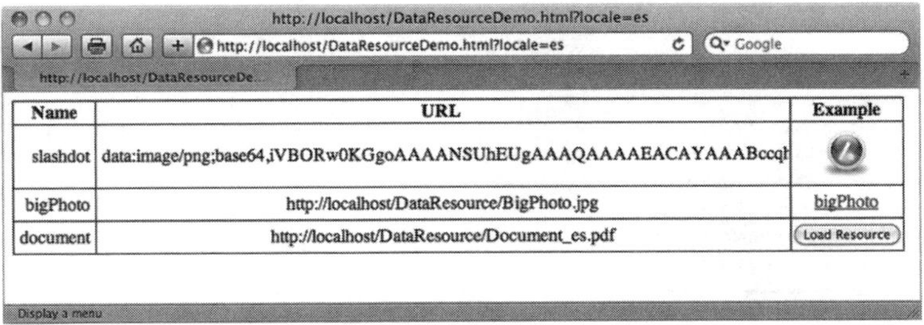

Figure 5.6 `ClientBundle.enableRenaming` disabled

But if you declare the es locale, as in figure 5.6, the `DataResource` will supply the URL for the Spanish version.

The `DataResource` is the most basic of the resource types, but it has demonstrated some of the core concepts of the `ClientBundle`. It has shown you how GWT can convert a resource into a data URL so that it can be delivered with the main JavaScript payload. When that isn't possible, GWT rewrites the filename so that it can be identified by the web server as indefinitely cacheable. Finally, you've seen that GWT will automatically supply appropriately internationalized versions of your resource if you've defined them correctly.

Now that you've learned the basics of `ClientBundle`, we can look at more resource types, starting with the two different text resource types.

5.2 Text resource types

Static text resources can be added to a `ClientBundle` in one of two ways:

- `TextResource`—Embedded in the JavaScript payload during compilation and can be used directly in Java code
- `ExternalTextResource`—Bundled together into a separate cacheable file, which is loaded asynchronously and stored in memory as soon as the first `ExternalTextResource` is requested

The difference between the two is therefore which techniques the compiler use to optimize delivery to the application. Let's start by looking at a simple `TextResource`.

5.2.1 TextResource

The `TextResource` optimizes access to text files by embedding them into the JavaScript payload. This reduces the connection count as well as guarantees cacheability.

Much like the `DataResource`, creating a method annotated with the `@Source` annotation adds a text resource to the `ClientBundle` interface:

```
public interface Resources extends ClientBundle {
  Resources IMPL = (Resources) GWT.create(Resources.class);

  @Source("text.txt")
  TextResource text();
}
```

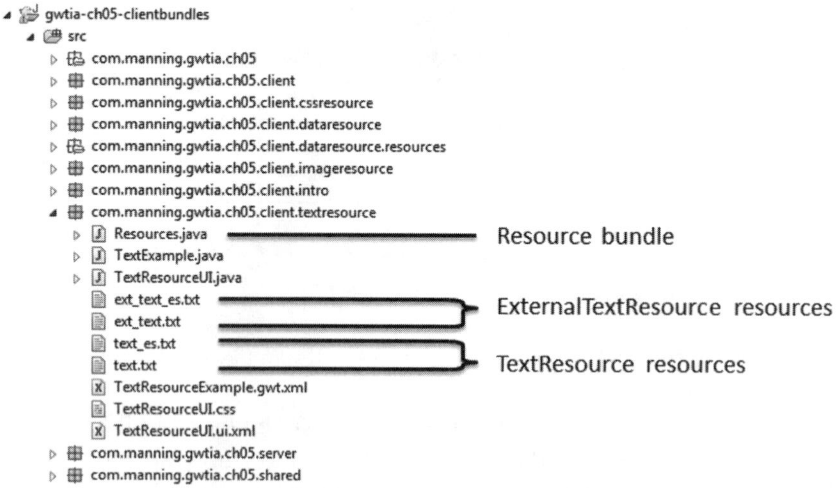

Figure 5.7 Internationalized `TextResource` and `ExternalTextResource` files (not compared to the previous example; we have the resources at the same level as the `ClientBundle` definition, so the `@Source` definition is simple)

A `TextResource` is automatically internationalized using the same method as `DataResource`. Just add extra files for each region with the appropriate locale suffix. So, if you were supporting both English and Spanish again, you'd have a text.txt file and a text_es.txt file; see figure 5.7.

To use the `TextResource`, you call its `getText` method. This will give you the appropriate internationalized text:

```
Label l = new Label(Resources.IMPL.text().getText());
```

From within a UiBinder you'd call the `getText` method as follows:

```
<g:Label text="{res.text.getText}" />
```

NOTE Although the `TextResource` gives you a way to internationalize static text resources, we'll describe more efficient methods in chapter 13.

Each `TextResource` is embedded in the JavaScript payload. This adds additional bytes to the initial download. In cases where you might not want to incur the expense of additional bytes in the initial payload, or if you'd prefer to load static text asynchronously at runtime, you could use `ExternalTextResource` and still get the benefits of `TextResource`.

5.2.2 *ExternalTextResource*

`ExternalTextResources` referenced in a `ClientBundle` are grouped into a single file at compile time and given a strong cacheable filename. This whole bundle is loaded asynchronously once the first `ExternalTextResource` is requested from the bundle.

ExternalTextResources are defined in the ClientBundle interface similarly to a TextResource:

```
@Source("ext_text.txt")
ExternalTextResource extText();
```

But because of the asynchronous nature of the resources loading, instead of using a simple getText method, you'll have to use a ResourceCallback to get to the text of the resource. The example class ends up looking like listing 5.3.

NOTE The code example in this chapter uses a UiBinder layout that will be described fully in chapter 6. But you'll see in listing 5.3 that the business logic we use to access the resource is a normal Java approach.

Listing 5.3 ExternalTextResource example

```
  try {
    res.extText().getText(                                  // 1 Getting the external text
        new ResourceCallback<TextResource>() {              // 2 Creating ResourceCallback definition
      public void onSuccess(TextResource resource) {
        etextLabel.setText(resource.getText());             // 3 Handling success
      }
      public void onError(ResourceException e) {
        Window.alert(                                       // 4 Handling error
            "Failed to retrieve ExternalTextResource:\n"
            + e.getMessage());
      }
    });
     } catch (ResourceException e) {
    Window.alert(                                           // 5 Handling failure
        "Failed to retrieve ExternalTextResource:\n"
        + e.getMessage());
   }
 }
}
```

When trying to access your ExternalTextResource ❶, you'll have to use a ResourceCallback ❷. In this example, you aren't doing anything complicated in the callback, so you create it as an anonymous inner class and provide implementations of the onSuccess and onError methods it requires.

The first time any ExternalTextResource is accessed from this ClientBundle, GWT will perform an XML HTTP Request (XHR), which will fetch all of the ExternalTextResources as a single file. Upon receiving the response, GWT will separate the individual text resources and store them in memory. If all has gone according to plan, GWT will call the onSuccess method of your ResourceCallback ❸, supplying a TextResource containing your text. At this point, you can call getText just as you'd do with any other TextResource.

Because the first request for an ExternalTextResource gets all of the ExternalTextResources and stores them in memory in one fell swoop, subsequent calls requesting any ExternalTextResource from your ClientBundle will supply the resource stored in memory to the Resource callback without need for another request.

But the initial XHR is a possible failure point, so you need to handle a couple of different failure modes. First, you'll have to wrap your ExternalTextResource.getText method call in a try/catch to handle the possibility of the XHR failing altogether. You could end up in the catch clause ❺, for instance, if your generated text resource file wasn't deployed with the application, or if the server suddenly became unreachable, or if any of a host of other issues happened that would prevent a successful HTTP response.

A second failure mode would be if GWT didn't format the file returned from the server as expected and the file couldn't be successfully parsed into individual TextResources. In that case, the onError ❹ method of the ResourceCallback would be invoked. In either case, the ResourceException will contain information indicating why the resource couldn't be produced.

Further optimizing ExternalTextResource

The asynchronous nature of ExternalTextResource allows you to choose an appropriate time to load the resources. You don't have to wait for the last second before you need the resource to request the first resource. You could proactively call the getText method after the application loads but before you need an ExternalTextResource.

Remember that the first call to getText loads all of the ExternalTextResources and caches them in memory, so if you preload the resource by calling getText, even if you don't do anything with the resource in the onSuccess method, all of the ExternalTextResources in the client bundle will now be cached, and successive calls to getText won't require a round-trip to the server. And, because the getText method is asynchronous, it can be called anytime without stalling the application. For instance, you could preload the ExternalTextResources in the onModuleLoad method or maybe when you need a particular panel that's likely to use the resources.

ExternalTextResource begins to delve into some of the more advanced capabilities of ClientBundle, such as combining multiple files into a single resource and compressing the total bytes of the bundled file, but the ImageResource will give ClientBundle a workout.

5.3 ImageResource

Rather than using images directly in your GWT applications, you can add the images to a ClientBundle as ImageResources. You can use these ImageResources anywhere in an application that the source image would be used; but when they're added to the ClientBundle as ImageResources, the GWT compiler is given a chance to optimize their delivery to the application.

ClientBundle uses all of the tricks you've seen previously to optimize the delivery of ImageResource, plus more. Small images may be embedded in the JavaScript payload; multiple images may be combined into a single, more efficient, image strip file; and animated images may be given cacheable filenames. ClientBundle will decide the best technique to use at compile time and handle all of the details for you.

First, we'll take a look at internationalization of ImageResource and how it can handle right-to-left languages. Then we'll demonstrate how to use ImageResource in an application. Finally, we'll look at some of the techniques you can use to control the optimizations used by ClientBundle.

5.3.1 *Internationalizing image resources*

ImageResource can be internationalized the same way the other resources were—you add additional files with the proper locale suffix. But ImageResource employs one additional trick when it comes to internationalization. You can use the @ImageOptions annotation to indicate that a particular ImageResource should be mirrored when displayed in a right-to-left language (languages such as Arabic are read from right to left; therefore it makes sense that certain images are also orientated this way). This is demonstrated in the DefaultImages ClientBundle from GWT's DisclosurePanel. Here is a small extract:

```
interface DefaultImages extends ClientBundle {
    @ImageOptions(flipRtl = true)
    ImageResource disclosurePanelClosed();
}
```

❶ Mirror the image horizontally for RTL locales

❷ Define method to get image resource

You use the @ImageOptions annotation ❶ with flipRtl = true to indicate that the disclosurePanelClosed image should be mirrored for RTL locales. This image is a right-pointing triangle in a left-to-right language, such as English, and is placed on the left of the panel's title. In a right-to-left language, it makes more sense for the image to be a left-pointing triangle on the right side of the title. Traditionally, you'd have to do all this yourself. No additional file needs to be supplied in GWT because GWT will automatically create the mirrored image automatically at compile time if flipRtl is set to true.

You also may have noted in the previous code listing that this ClientBundle didn't include @Source annotations ❷. This is because, in the absence of a @Source annotation on an ImageResource, GWT will search for an image file with a name that matches the method name and has an extension of .png, .gif, .jpg, or .bmp (in that order; for example, if there are logo.png and logo.gif in the resource folder, logo.gif would be ignored).

5.3.2 *Using ImageResource in an application*

You'll now use ImageResource to build a simple icon rotator widget that will cycle through images. You start by defining the ImageRotator that will do the work, as the following listing shows.

Listing 5.4 Image rotator (for brevity the normal null reference checking is omitted)

```
public class ImageRotator extends Composite {
   static final int DURATION = 1000;

   private Image icon;
   private int iconIndex = 0;
   private ImageResource[] icons;

public ImageRotator(ImageResource[] images) {
   icons = images;
   icon = new Image(icons[iconIndex]);
   initWidget(icon);

   Scheduler.get().scheduleFixedPeriod(
       new RepeatingCommand() {
          public boolean execute() {
             if (++iconIndex >= icons.length) {
                iconIndex = 0;
             }
             icon.setResource(icons[iconIndex]);
             return true;
          }
      }, DURATION);
}
}
```

❶ Array of ImageResources
❷ Set first image
❸ Scheduler to rotate images
❹ RepeatingCommand to handle the rotation
❺ Change image resource
❻ Return true to keep rotating

The example in listing 5.4 will cycle through an array of `ImageResource` resources ❶ passed in to the constructor. To create an image from an `ImageResource`, you can instantiate the image by supplying the desired `ImageResource` rather than a URL ❷. Later you can change which icon is displayed by calling the `setResource` method on `Image` ❺ to display a different `ImageResource`.

To generate the rotations you schedule ❸ a `RepeatingCommand` ❹ to cycle through the `ImageResource` array provided at instantiation. Each invocation of the `execute` method changes the image resource set in the icon ❺ and returns `true` ❻ so that the `RepeatingCommand` will continue to be scheduled. The `images` array allows the `ImageRotator` to be reused with any array of `ImageResources` you want to supply it with, but for now, you'll build a client bundle with a bunch of social media icons. We expect you'll see that this is created in the rather familiar way now.

Listing 5.5 `ClientBundle` containing social media icons

```
public interface Resources extends ClientBundle {

Resources IMPL = (Resources) GWT.create(Resources.class);

  ImageResource blogger();
  ImageResource delicious();
  ImageResource digg();
  ImageResource facebook();
  ImageResource google();
  ImageResource mail();
  ImageResource reddit();
```

```
  ImageResource slashdot();
  ImageResource twitter();
  ImageResource yahoo();
}
```

Each method in this `ClientBundle` has a corresponding .png file in the Java package with the same name, so no `@Source` annotations are required.

Passing the images to the widget is a case of creating the array and then passing that to the widget constructor:

```
ImageResource[] icons = new ImageResource[] {
   Resources.IMPL.blogger(),
   Resources.IMPL.delicious(),
   Resources.IMPL.digg(),
   Resources.IMPL.facebook(),
   Resources.IMPL.google(),
   Resources.IMPL.mail(),
   Resources.IMPL.reddit(),
   Resources.IMPL.slashdot(),
   Resources.IMPL.twitter(),
   Resources.IMPL.yahoo()
}
```

Overall, a relatively simple example, but it does demonstrate a couple of different techniques GWT uses to prepare the image resources. First, you'll notice a *.cache.png file in the output (war) directory that's a single image strip containing all 10 of our social media icons, as shown in figure 5.8.

Figure 5.8 Image strip containing all the `ImageResources` in the `ClientBundle`

This image strip is 132 KB. By comparison, individually, the images have a sum total of 391 KB. This means that for the browsers that use the image strip, not only do they save nine requests, but they also reduce the total number of bytes transferred by 259 KB.

But because these icons are all under the 64 KB threshold for inlining, most browsers will embed all of the icons in the JavaScript payload as data URIs. In many cases that's fine, because the added few bytes from the Base64 encoding are outweighed by not requiring an extra connection to fetch the resource. But, as you could imagine, if you had dozens or even hundreds of icons, you could grow your JavaScript payload to undesirable levels.

5.3.3 *Controlling ImageResource optimizations*

In a case where you have many resources in a single `ClientBundle` being inlined, you could certainly set the `ClientBundle.enableInlining` property to `false` to disable the inlining, but that would disable the inlining of all resources in every bundle compiled in the entire project.

If you want finer control over which `ClientBundles` are allowed to be inlined, you could use deferred binding to specify the generator to use.

NOTE We discuss deferred binding in chapter 17 and generators in chapter 18.

GWT usually uses one of two different generators to create the link between the `ClientBundle` interface and the resources you provide: a static one and an inline one. Normally GWT will choose between those at compile time, based on which browser platform it's generating code for and whether the `ClientBundle.enableInlining` property is set.

You could create a deferred binding rule that says if the client bundle is of a specific user-defined type, then it should always use the static generator. This isn't as complicated as it sounds. Let's start by defining an interface that you'll use to trigger the use of the static approach (more technically, setting the GWT compiler to use the `StaticClientBundleGenerator`):

```
public interface StaticClientBundle extends ClientBundle {}
```

If you extend this interface instead of a normal `ClientBundle`, then you can also write a rebinding rule telling the GWT compiler that when it sees a class extending `StaticClientBundle`, it should ignore the normal rules it has and follow the rule in listing 5.6 (defined in the example code in ImageResourceExample.gwt.xml in the `imageresource` package).

Listing 5.6 Module file that prevents inlining via deferred binding

```
<module>
   <generate-with
      class="c.g.g.resources.rebind.context.StaticClientBundleGenerator">
      <when-type-assignable
         class="c.m.g.ch05.client.imageresource.StaticClientBundle" />
   </generate-with>
</module>
```

Generator to use ❶

When compiling this type ❷

This rule tells the GWT compiler to use the `StaticClientBundleGenerator` ❶ any time it encounters the `StaticClientBundle` interface ❷. To use the rule in the example, you only need to change which interface the `ClientBundle` extends:

```
public interface Resources extends StaticClientBundle {
  Resources IMPL = (Resources) GWT.create(Resources.class);

  ImageResource blogger();
}
```

We've replaced `ClientBundle` with `StaticClientBundle`, but the rest of the bundle ❷ remains unchanged from what you saw earlier. Because GWT handles the implementation details of the resources in a `ClientBundle`, you don't need to do anything else differently when using these `ImageResources`. You've guaranteed that none of the resources in this bundle will be inlined; but resources in other bundles will still be inlined where appropriate.

The previous method prevents *all* resources in a particular bundle from being inlined. If instead you prefer to exclude a single `ImageResource` from being inlined, you could add the `@ImageOptions(preventInlining=true)` annotation to the `ImageResource`'s accessor method in the `ClientBundle`. The annotation also prevents the `ImageResource` from being bundled with other `ImageResources` in the `ClientBundle`, so its use is most appropriate for large, infrequently used images where the overhead to construct the connection is less significant compared to file size than it would be when fetching a small icon.

Now that you've seen a rather simple use for `ImageResource`, we can move on to `CssResource`. `CssResource` provides all of the optimization techniques that you've already seen in the other resource types, but it also adds new features to our otherwise static stylesheets. We can even use the image and data resources defined in a `ClientBundle` in our `CssResources`.

5.4 *CssResource*

Cascading Style Sheets (CSS) work fine for styling HTML, but when it comes to styling dynamic applications, CSS begins to show its limitations. Have you ever wished you could define constants or put conditional sections in your CSS? How about making method calls from CSS or defining values at runtime (runtime substitution)? `CssResource` gives you all of these features and more. It also adds optimization and obfuscation to make the CSS as efficient as possible.

Like the other resources, you define a method in our `ClientBundle` to return an instance of your `CssResource` and use a `@Source` annotation if necessary to point to the CSS file.

Unlike the other resource types you've already seen, you can't use `CssResource` directly. The `CssResource` interface will have to be extended to define accessor methods for the class names defined in the CSS file. If your CSS file defines any constants that you'd like to access programmatically, the `CssResource` interface will need to define accessor methods for them as well.

> **NOTE** The Google Plugin for Eclipse (GPE) will create the required interface, extending `CssResource` automatically for you when you include a CSS file, while you create a new `ClientBundle` via GPE.

A `CssResource` consists of two parts: an interface that extends `CssResource` and the CSS file itself. When you create the CSS file, it likely will end up embellished with "annotations" (at-rules) and functions to add some of the previously mentioned features to the `CssResource`, for example:

- Constants
- Runtime evaluations
- Conditionals
- Other `ClientBundle` resources

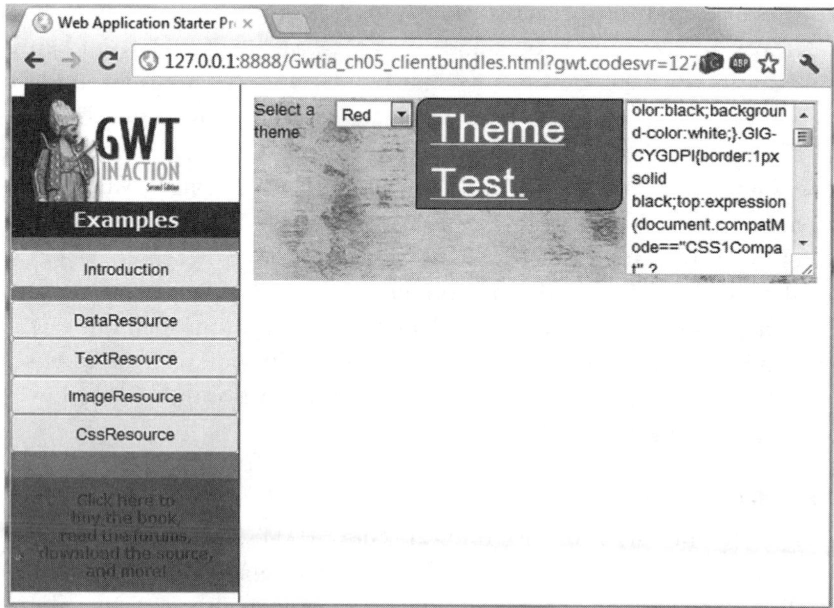

Figure 5.9 Using various aspects of `CssResource` in a `ClientBundle` to "theme" a GWT application

Although these embellishments are performed with valid CSS syntax and shouldn't prevent the file from being parsed by a non-GWT CSS parser, a `CssResource` CSS file will probably not work well in its uncompiled form. The example for this chapter shows this in action, when "theming" a simple GWT application, as shown in figure 5.9.

We'll start by examining the various optimizations that are applied to CSS files used as `CssResources`. We'll then look at the features that `CssResource` adds on top of bare CSS. And finally, we'll demonstrate how to use other resources from the `ClientBundle` in your `CssResource` stylesheets.

5.4.1 Optimizations

`CssResource`, like other `ClientBundle` resource types, attempts to minimize size and optimize the files that GWT uses. First, the compiler will minimize the individual CSS files by removing comments, empty selectors, and unneeded whitespace. GWT will then try to merge rules within each file that have identical selector names. It will also attempt to merge selectors within each file whose properties are identical. For instance, a section of a CSS file that looks like the following

```
.one {
    color: white;
}
.one {
    background-color: black;
}
```

```
.two {
    color: white;
    background-color: black;
}
```

could be merged by the GWT compiler to look like this:

```
.one, .two {
  color : white;
  background-color : black;
}
```

> **CSS resource merging**
>
> When merging selectors and properties, GWT is careful to not perform any reordering that would change the rendering of the page.
>
> CSS class name selectors aren't usually as simple as our example, and it's possible that multiple CSS files could define class names that conflict with one another. GWT's solution is to first obfuscate the CSS classes within each file, giving each a three-character name. Then it prepends that class with a hash derived from the CSS file. This technique results in generally shorter class names, given that class names commonly take a form like `gwt-StackPanelItem-below-selected`. This obfuscation also all but guarantees that naming collisions will be nonexistent throughout the compiled resource.

Once you apply minimization and selector obfuscation, the generated CSS would look something like this:

```
GK5UV03BFI,.GK5UV03BII{color:white;background-color:black;}
```

You'd then add the optimized CSS to the main JavaScript payload in much the same way a `TextResource` would be. The obfuscation makes it impossible to use the class names defined in CSS directly in UiBinder or Java source files. But all is not lost: the obfuscated class names are made available through methods declared in your interface that extends `CssResource`:

```
public interface MyCss extends CssResource {
    String one();      // Would return the selector GK5UV03BFI
    String two();      // Would return the selector GK5UV03BII
}
```

Because a CSS class name is unusable without an accessor method in the `CssResource` interface, GWT will complain at compile time about class names that don't have accessors defined. This behavior isn't always desirable, particularly while transitioning legacy code to `CssResource`. GWT provides two ways to allow legacy code to coexist with newer code using `CssResource`. First, to disable obfuscation and accessor method requirements on a class-by-class basis, apply the `@external` at-rule to the CSS, as shown in the next listing.

Listing 5.7 More complicated CSS file

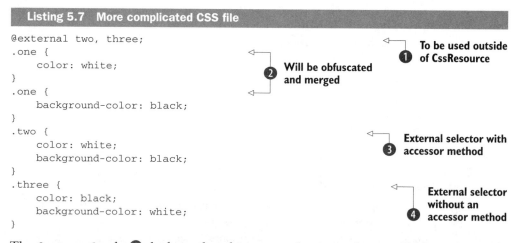

```
@external two, three;                                    ❶ To be used outside of CssResource
.one {
    color: white;                                        ❷ Will be obfuscated and merged
}
.one {
    background-color: black;
}
.two {                                                   ❸ External selector with accessor method
    color: white;
    background-color: black;
}
.three {                                                 ❹ External selector without an accessor method
    color: black;
    background-color: white;
}
```

The `@external` rule ❶ declares that the `.two` and `.three` classes will be used outside of `CssResource`. The `.one` class selectors ❷ will be merged and obfuscated as previously described. The `.two` ❸ still merges with `.one`, but the class name remains unobfuscated, and the interface method `.two()` will return `two`. Finally, `.three` ❹ won't be obfuscated, and because the interface has no accessor method, there's no way to use this selector from the `CssResource`; but it will still be usable from legacy code.

Although the `@external` rule is an effective way to mix legacy and `CssResource` code, it can become cumbersome with large CSS files that are being transitioned. Rather than adding all legacy selectors to the `@external` rule, the `@CssResource.NotStrict` annotation could be added to the `css()` method of the `ClientBundle`:

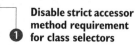

```
public interface Resources extends ClientBundle {
  Resources IMPL = GWT.create(Resources.class);
  @Source("main.css")
  @CssResource.NotStrict                          ❶ Disable strict accessor method requirement for class selectors
  MyCss css();
}
```

The `NotStrict` annotation ❶ has the effect of adding every selector name without an accessor method to an `@external` rule. Unfortunately, `NotStrict` is more of an either/or solution. The selectors with accessor methods will be obfuscated, whereas the ones without will remain unmolested. Therefore, it will still be necessary to use an `@external` rule for any selectors that are used by both legacy code and `CssResource`.

CSS optimization is just one benefit of using `CssResource`. Next, we'll look at a feature of `CssResource` that adds a level of convenience to CSS: constants.

5.4.2 Constants

Constants can be defined in one place in CSS and then used throughout the entire file. You could use constants to define colors, sizes, or any value that you plan to use in multiple places in a CSS file. To define a constant in a CSS file, you use the `@def` at-rule, shown in the following:

```
@def DARK_COLOR #000000;
@def NORMAL_BORDER_STYLE solid;
@def NORMAL_BORDER_SIZE 2px;
```

Then, later in the CSS, those constants could be used in the following way:

```
table, th, td
{
    border: NORMAL_BORDER_SIZE NORMAL_BORDER_STYLE DARK_COLOR;
}
```

If you use the same uppercase naming convention you'd use for static final class members, the constants will be easier to spot in your CSS later, and the names will be easier to distinguish from CSS class selectors in your `CssResource` interface. Also, it helps avoid naming collisions with class selectors that may have a similar name.

If you must use an `@def` identifier that's named the same as a selector, you will have to annotate the `CssResource` method accessing the class name. For instance, the following shows a collision between a constant name and a class name:

```
@def someBorder solid;
.someBorder {
    border: 1px someBorder black;
}
```

To gain access to the `.someBorder` class, you'd have to use the `@ClassName` annotation in your `CssResource` interface, as in the following:

```
public interface Basic extends CssResource {
  String someBorder();                    ❶
  @ClassName("someBorder")
  String someBorderClass();               ❷
}
```

❶ **Method to access the value of the someBorder @def**

❷ **Annotation required to access class with same name as an @def**

The `someBorder()` method ❶ will return the value of the `someBorder` constant. But to prevent a compile error complaining of a shadowed CSS class name, another method must be declared to access the class selector ❷. The `@ClassName` annotation is used to identify which selector the method should return. Again, this entire situation could be avoided by using uppercase naming for constants, as the following shows:

```
@def SOME_BORDER solid;

.someBorder {
    border: 1px SOME_BORDER black;
}
```

This would prevent naming collisions in your `CssResource` interface:

```
public interface Basic extends CssResource {
  String SOME_BORDER();      <- Uppercase naming denotes a constant
  String someBorder();       <- CamelCase naming for class accessor names
}
```

This convention makes an obvious differentiation between which methods refer to CSS constants and which are class selectors.

The @def annotation is handy for placing commonly used CSS values in a central location, but so far we're still working with a rather static CSS file. The next feature will allow you to begin making your CSS more dynamic.

5.4.3 Runtime evaluation

The @eval at-rule is similar to the @def at-rule except its value is evaluated at runtime. This allows CSS to obtain values from static class methods when the stylesheet is injected. It also allows certain aspects of the CSS to be dictated by user preferences or client requirements, without the need to recompile the application. Like the @def rule, the @eval rule takes two parameters. The first is the variable name that will be used elsewhere in the CSS. The second, rather than the value used in @def, is a static method that's to be called. Because the method invocation is a single parameter of the @eval rule, it's necessary to avoid adding spaces; otherwise, the compiler will discard everything after the space, thinking that they're additional parameters.

You might create a "theme" class that contains a static method for supplying values on injection, as shown in the following listing.

Listing 5.8 Theme class used to provide runtime property values

```
public class Theme {
    private static HashMap<String, String> props;
    public static void setProperties(HashMap<String, String> props) {
        Theme.props = props;
    }
    public static String getProperty(String prop, String def) {
        String value = def;
        if (null != props && null != prop) {
            if (props.containsKey(prop)) {
                value = props.get(prop);
            }
        }
        return value;
    }
}
```

❶ Static method to call from @eval rule

The static getProperty() method ❶ takes both a property name and a default value. The default allows you to at least supply a value from within the CSS even if the implementation doesn't include a value for a specific property.

You could then use this class along with the @eval rule in your CSS, as shown in the next listing.

Listing 5.9 CSS file using the @eval at-rule

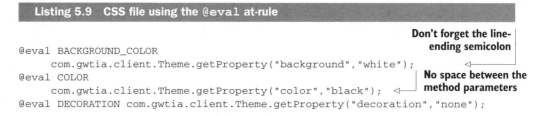

```
@eval BACKGROUND_COLOR
     com.gwtia.client.Theme.getProperty("background","white");
@eval COLOR
     com.gwtia.client.Theme.getProperty("color","black");
@eval DECORATION com.gwtia.client.Theme.getProperty("decoration","none");
```

Don't forget the line-ending semicolon

No space between the method parameters

```
@eval FONT_SIZE com.gwtia. client.Theme.getProperty("fontsize","medium");
.themedLabel {
    background-color: BACKGROUND_COLOR;
    color: COLOR;
    text-decoration: DECORATION;
    font-size: FONT_SIZE;
}
```

❶ Defined names used as values

You'll use the defined `@eval` variables in the CSS ❶ in much the same way you used the `@def` variables. Note that the difference is that `@eval` variables can't have accessor methods in the `CssResource` interface.

The `value()` function is a close cousin of `@eval`, but rather than calling static methods, it's used to call no-argument methods on other resources in the bundle. This is useful, for instance, to get the height or width of an `ImageResource`. The `value()` function, shown in the following code, can be used directly in the CSS as a property value or as the value expression of an `@def` rule:

```
@def IMAGE_WIDTH value("image.getWidth", "px");

.example {
    width: IMAGE_WIDTH;
    height: value("image.getHeight", "px");
}
```

Used as the value of a constant

Used directly as a property value

Occasionally, legacy CSS may contain nonstandard property values that look to the GWT compiler like `CssResource` features, causing GWT compile errors. Luckily, `CssResource` includes a function that you can use to hide these values from the GWT compiler.

5.4.4 Nonstandard CSS values

Because the `@eval` and `value()` features of `CssResource` require the GWT compiler to parse functions, there's an additional feature, the `literal()` function, that can be used to protect non-`CssResource` methods that might be needed in the CSS. For instance, Internet Explorer 6 and earlier don't contain a `max-width:` property, so it's often simulated via an `expression()` value:

```
div {
  width: expression(document.body.clientWidth > 500
                    ? "500px" : "auto");
}
```

IE 6 500 px maximum width expression

But the Internet Explorer value function `expression()` will cause the GWT compiler to throw an error. To use an expression like this in a `CssResource`, it would have to be fed to the `literal()` function as a string literal, escaping any backslashes or double quotes:

```
div {
  width: literal("expression(document.body.clientWidth > 500
                           ? \"500px\" : \"auto\")");
}
```

Because nonstandard property values like this expression are browser specific, it would also help to limit their inclusion to the CSS supplied to that particular browser type. For that you'd use a conditional section.

5.4.5 Conditional sections

The `@if`, `@elif`, and `@else` at-rules are used to create conditional sections of CSS. These rules allow sections of CSS to be selected either at compile time or at runtime depending on the conditions used. The conditions themselves can be based on deferred binding properties. In this case the rule will be evaluated at compile time, and only the appropriate condition will be output into the appropriate permutation. Or the condition can use static method calls, like `@eval` rules, allowing the rule to be evaluated on injection.

The rules take on one of two forms depending on whether they use deferred binding properties or method expressions. The first form, using deferred binding properties, uses the at-rule followed by the property and then a space-separated list of values (for example, the rule `@if user.agent ie6 ie8` covers IE 6 and IE 8 browsers; a more complex example is shown in the following listing).

Listing 5.10 CSS containing conditional sections

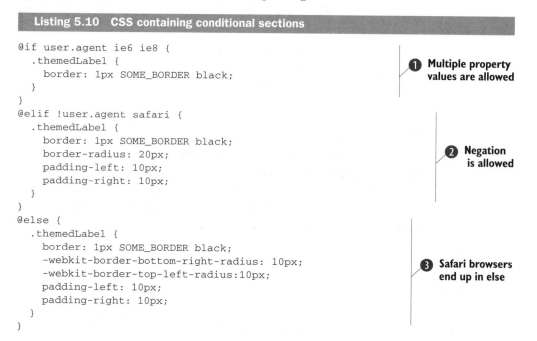

```
@if user.agent ie6 ie8 {
  .themedLabel {
    border: 1px SOME_BORDER black;
  }
}
@elif !user.agent safari {
  .themedLabel {
    border: 1px SOME_BORDER black;
    border-radius: 20px;
    padding-left: 10px;
    padding-right: 10px;
  }
}
@else {
  .themedLabel {
    border: 1px SOME_BORDER black;
    -webkit-border-bottom-right-radius: 10px;
    -webkit-border-top-left-radius:10px;
    padding-left: 10px;
    padding-right: 10px;
  }
}
```

❶ Multiple property values are allowed

❷ Negation is allowed

❸ Safari browsers end up in else

In listing 5.10, you first define some CSS for older Internet Explorer browsers ❶. The `@elif` clause ❷ defines CSS with fancier borders for all non-WebKit (called Safari in GWT) browsers. And finally, the `@else` clause ❸ defines CSS with WebKit-specific properties. These CSS sections will be chosen at compile time and will participate in the optimizations explained earlier.

The second form uses an expression enclosed in parentheses in a way more familiar to Java developers:

```
@if (com.gwtia.client.Theme.isUseBoldFonts()) {        <-- ❶ Expression evaluated on injection
    .themedLabel {
     font-weight: bold;
    }
}
```

When the CSS is injected, the expression in this example ❶ will be evaluated and the decision on whether or not to include the section will be made. Because expression evaluation doesn't happen until runtime, these sections of CSS aren't candidates for selector merging, though the CSS class names will still be obfuscated.

Conditional sections can be nested to any depth, and they can contain anything that would be a top-level CSS rule.

5.4.6 Using other resources in CSS

`DataResources` and `ImageResources` defined in your `ClientBundle` can both be used from within your CSS. `DataResouces` can be used anywhere you might reference binary data via a URL, for instance, a custom cursor or a special font. `ImageResources` can be used anywhere in CSS where you'd use an image, for instance, borders or background images.

First, you'd need to define a client bundle that contains not only your `CssResource` but also the other resources that you plan to use in the CSS, as shown in the next listing.

Listing 5.11 `ClientBundle` with multiple types of resources

```
public interface Resources extends ClientBundle {

    Resources IMPL = GWT.create(Resources.class);

    @Source("basic.css")                         Accessor method for
    Basic basic();                               the CssResource

    @Source("Unavailable.cur")                   Accessor method for
    DataResource unavailable();                  the DataResource

    @Source("brushed-metal-002951-light-gray.jpg")     ❶ ImageResource configured
    @ImageOptions(repeatStyle = RepeatStyle.Both)        to tile horizontally and
    ImageResource brushedMetal();                        vertically
}
```

`ImageResource` defines the `repeatStyle` attribute for its `@ImageOptions` annotation. This attribute is used to control image tiling when the image is used in CSS. Valid values are `RepeatStyle.None`, `RepeatStyle.Horizontal`, `RepeatStyle.Vertical`, and `RepeatStyle.Both`. Our example defines an image that will be tiled in both directions ❶.

You'll use each type of resource somewhat differently. DataResources can be accessed by using a @url at-rule to define a constant containing the DataResource's URL.

A DataResource in a ClientBundle can be used in the CSS via the @url rule. The @url rule is composed of three parts: @url is the first part, a constant name is the second, and the third part is the accessor method name of the DataResource:

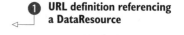

```
@url NO unavailable;                    <-- 1 URL definition referencing a DataResource

.noCursor {                             2 Use of DataResource as a cursor
  cursor: NO, pointer;
}
```

In the example, you first define an @url constant ❶ with the name NO. This constant will be populated with the URL (possibly a data URL) to the DataResource obtained by calling the unavailable() method of the ClientBundle. Later in the CSS file, you can use that @url as a value for a CSS property (❷).

You can take advantage of ImageResources in your client bundle in the CSS by a combination of the @sprite at-rule and the gwt-image CSS property:

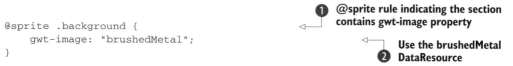

```
@sprite .background {                   <-- 1 @sprite rule indicating the section contains gwt-image property
    gwt-image: "brushedMetal";          <-- 2 Use the brushedMetal DataResource
}
```

The @sprite at-rule tells the GWT compiler to look for the gwt-image property inside the associated block. The gwt-image property is then expanded at compile time to include a background-image property, possibly with a data URL, as well as any clipping and size properties that you may need to properly display the image. Unfortunately, this technique isn't supported in Internet Explorer 6 and earlier, so image sprites won't be rendered properly on those browser platforms.

CssResource, at first glance, optimizes delivery of CSS files to your application. But you've also seen that CssResource adds constants, runtime evaluation, and conditional sections that add value over static CSS files. And finally, you saw how you could reuse any ImageResources or DataResources that were defined in the ClientBundle.

5.5 Summary

We've shown you how ClientBundle allows you to organize all of the static resources you may need for a component into a nice, neat package that's considerably more efficient than if the resources were loaded using traditional methods. We've also covered how you can optimize data, text, and images.

You also saw that DataResource allows arbitrary binary documents to be packaged into the ClientBundle, where their cacheability is improved via the use of a hashed URL, or by incorporating the file into the JavaScript payload as a data URL.

Next, we showed you how to use `TextResource` to both add static text resources to the JavaScript payload and load them asynchronously. Both techniques reduced connection count and improved cacheability of the resources.

With the last of the simple resources, `ImageResource`, you saw how images are collected into a single image strip and given a cacheable URL, improving both connection count and cacheability.

Then we introduced you to `CssResource`. This resource, like the other simple resources, helps improve the efficiency of the stylesheet via caching but also adds features to further improve performance and convenience of the stylesheet while allowing the CSS to be more dynamic.

You learned how to further optimize the CSS using both selector merging and class name obfuscation. These features reduce the overall file size while preventing class name collisions that can occur when using multiple CSS files. Next, you learned to use constants to centrally locate property values in a CSS file. This is convenient for making changes that propagate to the entire file. We also covered runtime evaluation to set property values when the CSS is injected, allowing for nonstructural theming of the application. We demonstrated how to use the `literal()` function to protect nonstandard CSS property values from the GWT compiler. We also showed how you could add conditional sections to the CSS that allow for structural changes to the stylesheet both at compile time and at injection. This allows you to have CSS that's specific to particular browsers or locales. Finally, you learned how to include other resources from the `ClientBundle` in your CSS files.

In all, you learned that `ClientBundle` adds both optimization and convenience to all types of static resources that you might need in a project. In the next chapter, you'll learn how to lay out GWT user interfaces in a declarative XML markup style rather than plowing through pure Java code.

6 Interface design with UiBinder

This chapter covers

- Creating templates using markup instead of Java code
- Binding templates to Java
- Handling events
- Adding style to templates

Let's face facts: programmers aren't usually good designers. It all comes down to specialization. Whereas some of us specialize in application development, others specialize in making those applications look great.

When you look at traditional web frameworks, there's always some sort of template tool that bridges the gap between developer and designer. The most common of these for Java frameworks is Java Server Pages (JSP), which allows you to mix the HTML a designer develops with data a developer provides. UiBinder is GWT's designer-developer bridge, allowing you to design your interface in an HTML-like file instead of in your Java code.

And like many other template tools, it's more than just a bridge; it also offers functionality to developers to increase productivity and reduce the amount of Java code they need to write. Let's look at some of what you can expect to see in this chapter:

- Mix HTML and widget declarations in a single XML template.
- Bind widget declarations to variables in your code.
- Bind widget events to methods (no more anonymous classes).
- Write less Java code.

In this chapter you'll build the most common of widgets with UiBinder, the login form. It's something every web developer has built at least a few of, so the idioms will be familiar. Let's get right into it and see how UiBinder can simplify widget development. First stop, linking the designer's HTML to your code.

6.1 Binding the designer's HTML to Java code

As you might have guessed by its name, UiBinder will *bind* a template to the Java code. This is accomplished by markup in the template and annotations in the Java source. Because you're going to build a login form, let's start by looking at listing 6.1, which contains some basic HTML code that you might use for a login form.

Listing 6.1 A basic HTML login form

```
<!DOCTYPE HTML>
<html>
<head>
  <!-- head stuff omitted -->
</head>
<body>
<div class="container">
  <div class="content">
    <h1>S-Mart Login</h1>
    <div class="form-divider"></div>
    <form action="" method="post" id="login-form">
    <ul>
    <li><label>Email</label></li>
    <li><input type="text" /></li>
    <li><label>Password</label></li>
    <li><input type="password" /></li>
    <li><input type="submit" value="Login" class="login-submit" /></li>
    </ul>
    </form>
  </div>
</div>
</body>
</html>
```

Perhaps this isn't quite the basic example we promised, because we use <li> elements for the form structure, but that's for a reason. Designers sing to a different tune than we developers.

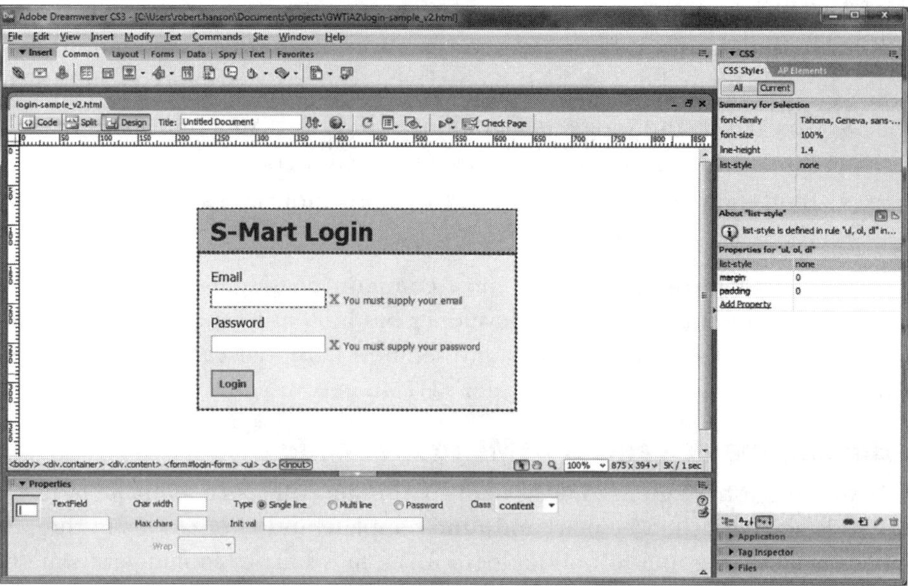

Figure 6.1 This is our login form within Adobe's Dreamweaver editing environment. To the designer the page has design and CSS styling, and prior to UiBinder this wouldn't translate easily to widgets.

For commercial public-facing web applications it's fairly common for a designer to be employed to develop the front-end code, and a programmer employed to connect it to the company databases. This division makes a lot of sense because it's rare to find a person who does both jobs extremely well, but it also has its difficulties.

In our world using HTML tables is an easy way to create a layout on the page, but this goes against the popular design thinking of the past few years. Designers use CSS for layout, not tables. To them it provides flexibility and accessibility, but for us it presents some challenges. Figure 6.1 shows our login dialog in Adobe Dreamweaver, a popular tool that web designers use.

The good news is that UiBinder shines when it comes to taking the designer's work and converting it into widgets that you can use in an application.

But before we proceed, a word of warning. This section is very looong! That isn't to say that it's difficult to understand; it's that we have a lot of details we want to cover. As you're reading this section it's possible that you might miss some key fact that causes a little confusion, but don't worry. In the final subsection, "Making sense of it all," we take a step back from the fine details and show you how everything we covered combines to make the whole work. This will allow you to get your bearings and reorient yourself before we move into the later sections and explore the full UiBinder feature set.

With that out of the way, let's begin the work of converting the raw HTML to a widget by creating the template file.

6.1.1 Creating the UiBinder XML template from HTML

In planning, we decided to turn the designer's code into a subclass of `PopupPanel`, and we decided to name the widget `LoginDialogBox`. By default the UiBinder template, which is an XML file, needs to have the same name as the Java class that will use it, so we created a template file named LoginDialogBox.ui.xml.

We created this template file using the designer's work as a base. The following listing provides the contents of this file, complete with UiBinder-specific markup.

Listing 6.2 The designer's HTML source with UiBinder markup

```
<!DOCTYPE ui:UiBinder SYSTEM
    "http://dl.google.com/gwt/DTD/xhtml.ent">
<ui:UiBinder xmlns:ui="urn:ui:com.google.gwt.uibinder"
    xmlns:g="urn:import:com.google.gwt.user.client.ui">

  <g:HTMLPanel>
  <div class="container">
    <div class="content">
      <h1>S-Mart Login</h1>
      <div class="form-divider"></div>
      <div id="login-form">
      <ul>
        <li><label>Email</label></li>
        <li><g:TextBox /></li>
        <li><label>Password</label></li>
        <li><g:TextBox /></li>
        <li><g:Button text="Login" styleName="login-submit" /></li>
      </ul>
      </div>
    </div>
  </div>
  </g:HTMLPanel>

</ui:UiBinder>
```

As you can see, the HTML is intact, but let's review the differences. For now we'll ignore the CSS that the designer provided, and we'll concentrate on the HTML that you'll use to display the widget. But even with postponing a discussion of style, we have a lot to cover here, so we'll need to spend the remainder of this section discussing this example.

To make this example easier to follow, we'll provide code snippets from the full example as they're discussed. We begin the discussion with how UiBinder handles HTML entities.

HANDLING HTML ENTITIES

Because this is an XML file and not an HTML file, we need to deal with some restrictions. The first of these is that XML understands only a few named entities, whereas HTML understands a lot.

> **What's an entity?**
>
> If you've done HTML work in the past but don't know what an entity is, you've likely already seen them. An entity begins with an ampersand (`&`), ends with a semicolon (`;`), and has a name or number in between. Some examples of named entities include `"`, which is the entity for a double quote, and `©`, which is an entity for a copyright symbol.
>
> You'll usually use an entity when you want to use a symbol or a restricted character in the web page. A good example of this is the less-than symbol (`<`), which confuses the parser because it looks like the beginning of a tag, so to use it as part of the text in the page, you'd use the entity `<` instead.

In order to allow the use of the standard HTML entities, you need to import them. You accomplish this by adding the `DOCTYPE` statement as the first line of the XML file:

```
<!DOCTYPE ui:UiBinder SYSTEM
  "http://dl.google.com/gwt/DTD/xhtml.ent">
```

This will allow you to use HTML entities in the file without getting XML-related errors. As you can see, a URL is provided as part of the `DOCTYPE`. Although GWT won't download this file, your editor may if it understands XML.

The next step is add the UiBinder-specific tags and to replace some of the HTML code with GWT widgets.

USING UIBINDER TAGS AND WIDGETS IN THE TEMPLATE

When you use UiBinder you'll need to place all of the HTML content within a `<ui:UiBinder>` element. You'll do this by adding `<ui:UiBinder>` to the top of the template, just under the `DOCTYPE` declaration, and `</ui:UiBinder>` at the end of the template:

```
<!DOCTYPE ui:UiBinder SYSTEM "http://dl.google.com/gwt/DTD/xhtml.ent">
<ui:UiBinder xmlns:ui="urn:ui:com.google.gwt.uibinder"
        xmlns:g="urn:import:com.google.gwt.user.client.ui">
  <!--the rest of the designers code -->
</ui:UiBinder>
```

In the `<ui:UiBinder>` element two XML namespaces are declared: `urn:ui:com.google.gwt.uibinder` and `urn:import:com.google.gwt.user.client.ui`. These have been given the prefixes `ui` and `g`, respectively. The first namespace (prefix `ui`) will be used in every UiBinder XML file, whereas the second namespace (prefix `g`) points to a Java package that has widgets that we intend to use in this file. In this case we're declaring that we want to use widgets from the Java package `com.google.gwt.user.client.ui`. The format of this namespace is `urn:import:` plus that Java package name.

Understanding XML namespaces

An XML namespace is a way of associating a collection of XML elements to a name, and the name is a URI. With UiBinder you can use a collection of tags in the document, like `<UiBinder>` and `<style>`. The namespace for these elements is `urn:ui:com.google.gwt.uibinder`. But when you're adding standard GWT widgets like `<HTMLPanel>` and `<Button>` to the XML document, they're part of the namespace named `urn:import:com.google.gwt.user.client.ui`. In order to mix these in a single XML document, the XML parser needs to be able to tell the two sets of tags apart. You do this by declaring each namespace, giving it a prefix, and including the prefix when using a tag (for example, `<g:HTMLPanel>`).

Next, you wrap the HTML contents with `<g:HTMLPanel>`. The `g` is the namespace prefix, followed by the class name of the widget:

```
<!DOCTYPE ui:UiBinder SYSTEM "http://dl.google.com/gwt/DTD/xhtml.ent">
<ui:UiBinder xmlns:ui="urn:ui:com.google.gwt.uibinder"
        xmlns:g="urn:import:com.google.gwt.user.client.ui">
  <g:HTMLPanel>
    <!--the rest of the designers code -->
  </g:HTMLPanel>
</ui:UiBinder>
```

When using UiBinder to help you create your widgets, you need to understand that the template isn't your widget. Instead, it represents a widget or an HTML element that your widget can use when it's initialized. It's like in the old song, "the leg bone is connected to the hip bone." In this case the UiBinder template is connected to your Java class.

As we stated earlier, our intention is to build a subclass of `PopupPanel`, which allows you to add a single widget to it. Because that's our intention, the template must return a `Widget` object and not an `Element` object. Because we wrapped the contents in an `HTMLPanel`, when we write our Java code to use this template it will provide us with this `HTMLPanel` that we can use to initialize our `PopupPanel`.

The reason we chose to use `HTMLPanel`, as opposed to some other GWT panel (for example, `FlowPanel`) is that `HTMLPanel` may contain both widgets and HTML elements. Because we want to make as few changes as possible to the designer's work, `HTMLPanel` is a logical choice and will usually be the right choice for many projects.

Going back to the original example, we need to make a few minor changes. First, because we're going to handle this login within the GWT application and not submit it to a form, we removed the `<form>` HTML element and replaced it with a `<div>`. We did this because the designer has an `id` attribute on the form, so the element likely has some CSS attached to it, and we don't want to anger the designer by losing any styling:

```
<form action="" method="post" id="login-form"> <!-- old -->
<div id="login-form">                          <!-- new -->
```

Next, we replace the email input box with `<g:TextBox/>`, which is a `TextBox` widget, and the password input with another `<g: TextBox/>`. We could've used `PasswordTextBox` for the password widget, but using `TextBox` will allow us to include more features of UiBinder in this example widget:

```
<li><label>Email</label></li>
<li><g:TextBox /></li>
<li><label>Password</label></li>
<li><g: TextBox /></li>
```

It should be no surprise by now that we replace the Submit button with `<g:Button/>`, a `Button` widget. But this one is a little different than the others, which brings us to dealing with widget properties.

SETTING WIDGET PROPERTIES WITH UIBINDER

The original HTML for the Submit button had a `class` attribute on it, setting the CSS class used to style the HTML element. But this doesn't work when we replace it with a GWT `Button` widget. Specifically, you can only set an attribute on a widget when it has a setter for a property. In this case the `Button` widget doesn't have a "class" property, but it does have a `setStyleName()` method:

```
<li><g:Button text="Login" styleName="login-submit" /></li>
```

By setting the `styleName` attribute, we're effectively calling `setStyleName()` on the `Button` widget. This is how UiBinder allows you to set properties on widgets defined within the template. Notice that the attribute name dropped the "get" portion of the method name. This is because UiBinder used JavaBean semantics (getters and setters) when setting properties via attributes.

> **Special style name attributes**
>
> In GWT all widgets have an `addStyleName()` method, but because this method name doesn't follow the bean-naming conventions, you wouldn't normally be able to access this method from within the template. To work around this, GWT provides two special widget attributes: `addStyleNames` and `addStyleDependentNames`. Note that both of these attributes end with an `s` to differentiate them from the `UIObject` methods `addStyleName()` and `addStyleDependentName()`. They behave differently as well. They allow you to pass in multiple style names separated by spaces, so that you can add them all at once, for example, `addStyleNames="styleOne styleTwo"`.

As you can see, the changes we made were minimal, and they don't prevent the designers from updating their CSS. And it's likely that even if designers needed to update the HTML code, they could understand this UiBinder file.

Before we continue with the example, we need to break away for a moment and discuss a topic that we glossed over, and that's the finer points of working with panels, the XML template file.

6.1.2 Working with panels

In the example we used HTMLPanel as the root of the UiBinder template. As you may recall, the reason for doing this was that we can freely mix HTML and widgets within the panel. This makes converting our designer-delivered HTML into a widget fairly easy, but it won't always be the right fit for every project.

When it comes to panels outside of HTMLPanel, most of them fall into one of two categories: panels where widgets added to the panel in sequential order are displayed in that same order, and panels where you specify the "side" where the widget will appear. The first category includes most panels in GWT, including commonly used panels like VerticalPanel, FlowPanel, and StackPanel.

The following listing provides a simple example of this, where we also do some embedding of panels. The root widget is a StackPanel, with two other panels embedded within.

Listing 6.3 Example of structuring widgets and panels

```
<ui:UiBinder xmlns:ui="urn:ui:com.google.gwt.uibinder"
    xmlns:g="urn:import:com.google.gwt.user.client.ui">

<g:StackPanel>
  <g:HorizontalPanel>
    <g:HTML>One</g:HTML>
    <g:HTML>Two</g:HTML>
    <g:HTML>Three</g:HTML>
  </g:HorizontalPanel>

  <g:VerticalPanel>
    <g:HTML>One</g:HTML>
    <g:HTML>Two</g:HTML>
    <g:HTML>Three</g:HTML>
  </g:VerticalPanel>
</g:StackPanel>

</ui:UiBinder>
```

This same technique can also be applied to HorizontalSplitPanel and VerticalSplitPanel, but you can only have at most two nested widgets because these panels have only two sides:

```
<g:HorizontalSplitPanel>
    <g:HTML>One</g:HTML>
    <g:HTML>Two</g:HTML>
</g:HorizontalSplitPanel>
```

Another class of panels allows you to pin a widget to a specific side of the panel. We're talking about panels like DockPanel and SplitLayoutPanel. For these UiBinder supplies a set of tags used to denote the direction and size of each panel. The next listing shows the XML template that defines a SplitLayoutPanel containing three panels.

Listing 6.4 Demonstration of using directional tags

```
<ui:UiBinder xmlns:ui="urn:ui:com.google.gwt.uibinder"
    xmlns:g="urn:import:com.google.gwt.user.client.ui">

  <g:SplitLayoutPanel>
    <g:north size="100">
      <g:HTML>One</g:HTML>
    </g:north>
    <g:center>
      <g:HTML>Two</g:HTML>
    </g:center>
    <g:east size="100">
       <g:HTML>Three</g:HTML>
    </g:east>
  </g:SplitLayoutPanel>
</ui:UiBinder>
```

In the example we use directional tags like `<g:north>` and `<g:center>` to specify to which side each widget should be pinned. UiBinder provides tags for north, south, east, west, and center. You can also use the `size` attribute to specify the size of each section as a number of pixels.

Some panels that support pinning also support specifying the unit of measurement, for example, if you want to specify "em" instead of "px," like `DockLayoutPanel`.

> **Units of measurement**
>
> Let's look at the various types of measurements when it comes to layout: pixels, picas, ems, inches, and many others. Some widgets that allow pinning let you specify the width of each panel using something other than pixels. One such panel is the `DockLayoutPanel`. The Java class `com.google.gwt.dom.client.Style.Unit` provides a list of units of measurement constants.

But other panels also don't fit into either of these cases or have custom situations. For these you should consult the latest documentation for that widget to see how you can use them with UiBinder. A good example of this is the `DisclosurePanel`, which provides some custom tags for you to use. In this example we use the `<g:header>` tag to specify the header value for the panel, in addition to some other widget for the content area:

```
<g:DisclosurePanel>
  <g:header>Header</g:header>
  <g:HTML>Content</g:HTML>
</g:DisclosurePanel>
```

OK, that was a bit of a detour, but it's time to get back to the example. At the point where we left off we'd converted the designer's work into a UiBinder XML template file. Now we continue by defining the Java class that will use this file to render our `LoginDialogBox`.

6.1.3 Binding the UiBinder XML template to the Java code

As we mentioned in the last section, by default the XML template and the Java class need to share the same name. In addition to this, both the XML template and the Java class need to be in the same package. As we did in the last section, let's begin with a code example. The following listing presents the minimum amount of code to bind the template to its widget class.

Listing 6.5 Minimum code required to bind to the template

```
import com.google.gwt.core.client.GWT;
import com.google.gwt.uibinder.client.UiBinder;
import com.google.gwt.user.client.ui.*;

public class LoginDialogBox extends PopupPanel {

  interface MyBinder extends UiBinder<Widget, LoginDialogBox>{}      ❶ Define marker interface

  private static MyBinder uiBinder = GWT.create(MyBinder.class);     ❷ Create implementation

  public LoginDialogBox() {
    setStyleName("");
    add(uiBinder.createAndBindUi(this));                             ❸ Initialize
  }
}
```

The first thing to note is that this class is complete and functional. Well, perhaps not completely functional because we don't add any login code yet, but it will display the login form if you create an instance of this widget.

You must follow three steps to bind the Java class to the XML template. The first is to create an interface that extends the `UiBinder` interface ❶, which we arbitrarily named `MyBinder` here. It might look odd to create an inner interface within a class, but this interface is only referenced within this class, so doing this reduces the number of Java files in the project. The key part of the interface declaration is the type parameters that we specify for UiBinder (the two types within the angle brackets).

The first type parameter is the root type that we used in the XML template. As you might recall, we used `HTMLPanel` to wrap all of the HTML code in the template. We could use `HTMLPanel` as our first type parameter, but because `HTMLPanel` is a subclass of `Widget` we can use that as well, which is what we do in this section.

The second type parameter is the class that we want to bind the XML template to. In this case we want to bind it to the `LoginDialogBox`, which is the class we're creating now.

Next, we need to create an instance of `MyBinder` calling `GWT.create()` ❷. The object returned from `GWT.create()` is a Java class that's generated by the GWT compiler at compile time. In this case the GWT compiler will generate a class based on the contents of our XML template and the class to which we want to bind it.

And finally, we use the binder object created by `GWT.create()` to get hold of the root widget that we defined in the XML file so that we can initialize our class ❸. We do this by calling `uiBinder.createAndBindUi(this)` in our constructor.

How did GWT.create() know how to do that?

When you use UiBinder you pass an interface to `GWT.create()` that extends the `UiBinder` interface, and that's the key. `GWT.create()` will inspect the interface passed to it and will notice that the interface extends `UiBinder`, so it will use the `UiBinderGenerator` to generate the Java class that will be returned. The `UiBinderGenerator` in turn inspects the interface definition and takes note of the type parameters used in the declaration of the `UiBinder` interface. The first type parameter determines the return type, and the second is the Java class to bind to, which also by default is the same name as the XML template. For more information on how this works behind the scenes, take a look at chapters 17 and 18, where we discuss deferred binding and generators.

At this point we now have a working widget that we can instantiate and display. We still have a bit to do in order to add some functionality to the widget, and we didn't address the styling yet, but it does work. Instantiating and showing the dialog box at this point will look like what you see in figure 6.2.

It doesn't look pretty yet because we didn't address the CSS that the designer sent with the HTML code. We'll get to this soon, but let's finish binding the widget by tying the inputs to variables in our class.

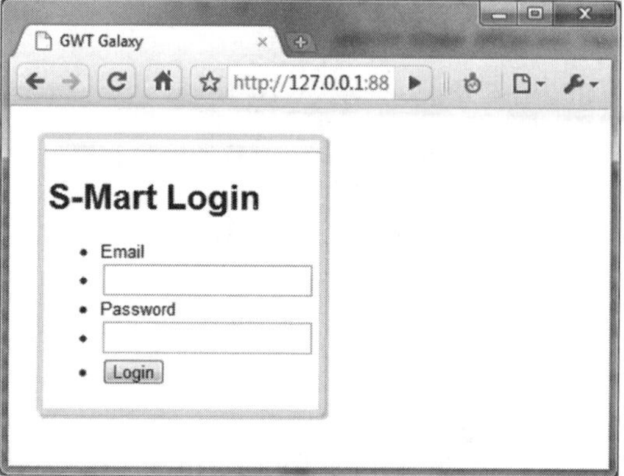

Figure 6.2 The `LoginDialogBox` being displayed in the browser. At this point we haven't applied the designer's CSS, so it lacks style.

6.1.4 Binding XML template elements to Java variables

UiBinder makes binding Java variables to the widgets we defined in the template extremely simple. All you need to do is give the widget in the template a field name and then use an annotation in the Java code to bind the two together.

BINDING TEMPLATE DECLARATIONS TO CLASS FIELDS

Let's start with the template side of things. Listing 6.6 presents a slightly enhanced version of the template from listing 6.2. This listing adds some <div> and <span> elements where validation error messages will appear. But you can ignore that for your purposes right now, in order to focus on the binding.

Listing 6.6 Adding field names to the `LoginDialogBox`

```
<ui:UiBinder xmlns:ui='urn:ui:com.google.gwt.uibinder'
    xmlns:g="urn:import:com.google.gwt.user.client.ui">
```

```
<g:HTMLPanel>
    ...
    <li><label>Email</label></li>
    <li><g:TextBox ui:field="txtEmail"/>
      <div ui:field="eEmailError">
        <span>X</span>
        <span ui:field="eEmailErrorText">Email error</span>
      </div>
    </li>
    <li><label>Password</label></li>
    <li><g:TextBox ui:field="txtPassword"/>
      <div ui:field="ePassError">
        <span>X</span>
        <span ui:field="ePassErrorText">Password error</span>
      </div>
    </li>
    <li><g:Button ui:field="btnLogin" text="Login"/></li>
   ...
</g:HTMLPanel>

</ui:UiBinder>
```

Provided field names

If you look at the two `TextBox` widgets, the `Button` widget, as well as some of the new `<div>` and `<span>` elements, you can see that we've added the `ui:field` attribute.

Using the `ui:field` attribute is a way to provide a field name for those widgets and elements. Likely you can see where we're going with this, which is that by providing field names to these tags, the binder will bind them to variables in your Java class. But before you make any changes to your Java code, we'll note one important thing: the code *still* runs, meaning that even though you specify a `ui:field` attribute in the template, it doesn't mean that you must tie it to a field. So feel free to use `ui:field` liberally; it won't break anything. Now let's look at the next listing and see the Java code that ties this together.

Listing 6.7 Example of using `@UiField` to bind fields

```
import com.google.gwt.core.client.GWT;
import com.google.gwt.dom.client.*;
import com.google.gwt.uibinder.client.*;
import com.google.gwt.user.client.ui.*;

public class LoginDialogBox extends PopupPanel {
  interface MyBinder extends UiBinder<Widget, LoginDialogBox> {}
  private static MyBinder binder = GWT.create(MyBinder.class);

  @UiField Button btnLogin;
  @UiField TextBox txtEmail;

  @UiField SpanElement eEmailErrorText;
  @UiField SpanElement ePassErrorText;
  @UiField Element eEmailError;
  @UiField Element ePassError;
```

❶ **Define bound widgets**

❷ **Define bound elements**

```
  @UiField(provided = true) TextBox txtPassword;        ❸ Disable autoconstruction

  public LoginDialogBox() {
    setStyleName("");
    txtPassword = new PasswordTextBox();                ❹ Construct "provided" widget
    add(binder.createAndBindUi(this));
  }
}
```

In order to link to widgets in the XML template to the code, you use the `@UiField` annotation ❶. Notice that you use the default package visibility for this variable. You do this because UiBinder isn't able to set fields that are private, but anything other than private will do. Using `@UiField` on a widget like this implies that UiBinder will instantiate this widget for you and then set your variable with the results.

For the next set of fields in the example you use `@UiField` in the same way, but these are elements, not widgets ❷. UiBinder can bind elements as well as it can bind widgets. The available element classes are found in GWT's `com.google.gwt.dom.client` package.

If this is undesirable, you can tell the binder that you'll provide the widget instance, which is what you do for the `txtPassword` field ❸, where you pass an attribute to `@UiField` of `provided=true`. When you do this you're indicating that you'll set `txtPassword` with a value, which must be done prior to calling `binder.createAndBindUi()`, as in this example ❹. If you recall, you declared the `txtPassword` field as being a `TextBox`, but because you're providing the widget instance you can use `TextBox` or any subclass of `TextBox`.

The great thing about this is that it opens up the possibility of creating a template that has one or more `<g:Widget/>` elements that can be determined and inserted at runtime. This flexibility will be valuable in some situations.

Now let's take another path and discuss some additional UiBinder annotations that may be useful depending on your project.

USING @UIFACTORY AND @UICONSTRUCTOR

In the previous section you saw how you could use `@UiField(provided=true)` to instantiate a `PasswordTextBox` widget yourself instead of delegating that task to the binder. An alternative to this would be to use `@UiFactory` to create a factory method. The concept of a factory method is well known, so let's look at some code:

```
@UiFactory
Button createLoginButton () {
  Button button = new Button();
  button.setTitle("Submit the login form");
  return button;
}
```

The binder will use this method to instantiate any `Button` widgets that have been declared in the template. The key information here is the return value, because the method name isn't important.

You could use `@UiField(provided=true)` for this same purpose, but let's imagine that you had a dozen `Button` widgets in the template, and you want them all instantiated the same way. In that case creating a factory method makes more sense.

Now let's look at construction. Let's suppose that you've created a widget, and you expect your widget to be used in some other template file. Now let's suppose that your widget requires a constructor argument. A good example of this is the `RadioButton` widget that comes with GWT. It requires a constructor argument, which is the group name that the button belongs to.

Because `RadioButton` requires a constructor argument, UiBinder wouldn't normally be able to instantiate it. This is where `@UiConstructor` fits in. Following is the constructor of the `RadioButton` widget that comes with GWT:

```
@UiConstructor
public RadioButton(String name) {
  ...
}
```

This informs UiBinder that it should use this constructor and that the `name` attribute should be passed to the constructor. So your template code would look like the following:

```
<g:RadioButton name="bestActor">Bruce Campbell</g:RadioButton>
<g:RadioButton name="bestActor">Timothy Hutton</g:RadioButton>
<g:RadioButton name="bestActor">Robert Redford</g:RadioButton>
```

As you can see, some overlap exists between `@UiConstructor`, `@UiFactory`, and `@UiField(provided=true)`. Use whichever method better fits your specific needs.

Getting back to our example application, if you followed along with the example you now have the start of a dialog box, but it's likely that you didn't mentally connect all of the dots quite yet. That's what we want to do now by reviewing what we've covered and explaining how it all connects together.

6.1.5 Making sense of it all

Let's start from the top. You have two files you need to deal with when using UiBinder: the XML template and the Java class to which it will be bound. At the core of UiBinder is some generator class that will take the XML template and turn it into a bunch of Java code that will plug into your Java class. The key to understanding UiBinder is in understanding how the code generator knows what to do.

We start with the three things you need to do in your Java code to create the binder class and get the root element so that you can initialize your widget:

1. Create an interface that extends `UiBinder`.
2. Call `GWT.create()` to create a concrete class that implements the interface.
3. Call `createAndBindUI(this)` to get the root element or widget.

In order to make sense of this, let's start at the end and go up the list. In step 3 you call `createAndBindUi()`, passing a reference to `this`. But why do you need to pass a reference to your widget? The reason is that calling `createAndBindUi()` will bind the widgets that were defined in the template to the fields that were annotated with `@UiField` in your class. If you didn't pass `this` and instead passed a reference to some other object, it would have bound the widgets to that object instead. You'll likely never have a reason to pass anything other than `this`, but the possibility of doing so is available if a need presents itself.

Going up the stack to step 2, you use `GWT.create()` to create an instance of `UiBinder`. This is what kicks off the code generator that will write the custom code to generate the UI you defined in the template and bind it to your class. But the questions you need to ask are, how does the generator know what to do? How does it know where the XML file is? And how does it know what Java class the UI will ultimately be bound to?

If you didn't have the "aha" moment yet, this is where it all comes together. The generator knows how to do this because of the interface you defined in step 1. If you recall, you needed to provide two type parameters in the interface declaration of your `MyBinder` interface:

```
interface MyBinder extends UiBinder<Widget, LoginDialogBox> {}
```

The first is the class that `createAndBindUi()` should return, which in this case is a `Widget`. Although this is useful, this isn't the important bit of information. For that you need to look at the second type parameter you passed, which is the name of your widget class. This is how the generator knows what class the template is ultimately bound to. At code-generation time the generator will then scan your class for annotations like `@UiField`, `@UiFactory`, and `@UiConstructor` so that it can generate the appropriate code for the `createAndBindUi()` method.

But this doesn't explain how the generator knows the name of the template file. For this the code generator relies on convention. It makes the assumption that the template file has the same name as the Java class. We hope you can see how it all fits together now. By specifying a type parameter of `Foo` in the interface declaration, the code generator will look for a Java source file named Foo.java and an XML file named Foo.ui.xml. It then scans both in order to know what code to generate.

You can override this convention by placing the annotation `@UiTemplate` on the interface definition. The annotation takes one parameter: the name of the XML template file to use. This would allow you to share the same XML template with multiple Java classes or use multiple templates for the same class:

```
@UiTemplate("SomeTemplate.ui.xml")
interface MyBinder extends UiBinder<Widget, LoginDialogBox> {}
```

One thing to remember in this example is that "SomeTemplate.ui.xml" must still reside in the same directory as the Java class referencing it. Note that it's also possible to specify a *forward* relative path like "templates/SomeTemplate.ui.xml," but you can't use an absolute path or a path that traverses to parent directories.

We've covered quite a bit up to this point, but we have a lot more where that came from. The next logical step is to write the event handling that will drive your `LoginFormDialogBox`.

6.2 Handling events with UiBinder

Event handling in Java is ugly, and when writing an event handler Java provides limited options. You could create a new class to handle the event, possibly have your class implement the method, or write a nasty-looking anonymous class. With the first option you wind up with a ton of classes in your project. With the second you're limited to handling one of each event type (that is, one `onClick()` method). And the third is why Ruby developers snicker when they look at Java code. To give you a visual of what we're referring to, take a look at this example. The following shows a simple `ClickHandler` that will display an alert that says "Hello" when the `myButton` widget is clicked:

```
Button myButton = new Button("Click Me");
myButton.addClickHandler(new ClickHandler()
{
    @Override
    public void onClick (ClickEvent event)
    {
        Window.alert("Hello");
    }
});
```

If you've been working with Java for any length of time, you might say "That's not too horrible." If you're one of those people, then perhaps you've gotten used to it. But let's take a step back to understand that this is hard to read, which in turn makes your code harder to maintain.

Let's try to forget Java's ugly side for a moment and look at how UiBinder can clean this up for you. You already have the ability to bind your fields to the widgets in the template via `@UiField`, so let's see how you can bind events, too. Building on the `LoginFormDialogBox` example, let's add a `ClickHandler` to the class for the `btnLogin` field (a `Button`) so that you can trigger processing of the login form:

```
@UiHandler("btnLogin")
void submitLoginForm (ClickEvent event) {
  if (validateEmail() && validatePassword()) {
    Window.alert("Logging in...");
  }
}
```

Now this is a major improvement over the last example, and it does the same thing. Let's discuss the few things you need to know to create event methods. First, when you create the method it can't be private, and it must return `void`. In most cases, package visibility, which you use here, is sufficient. Second, you need to add the `@UiHandler` annotation, using the field name as the sole argument. This is how you inform UiBinder which widget the event should be bound to. And third, the method must take a single parameter, and that parameter is the event type you want to receive. This is how UiBinder can determine what event type you want this method to handle, and in this case you specify `ClickEvent`.

To reiterate, the three steps are as follows:

1. Create a nonprivate method that returns `void`.
2. Add the `@UiHandler` annotation and specify the field name.
3. Specify as a parameter the event type that you want to handle.

When handling an event in this way, the event object you specify as the parameter to your method must be a subclass of `GwtEvent`. Currently, more than 30 subclasses of `GwtEvent` exist, including `ValueChangeEvent`, `ScrollEvent`, `MouseMoveEvent`, and `ClickEvent`.

> **NOTE** You can handle multiple events with a single handler by passing multiple field names in the `@UiHandler` annotation, for example, `@UiHandler ({"field1", "field2"})`.

When trying to determine what events a widget exposes, it may not be completely clear. If it isn't obvious what events a widget supports (for example, a `Button` supports `ClickEvent`), you should first consult the Javadocs. The method, if there is one, will have a method name in the format `addSomethingHandler`, where the `Something` is what it's handling (for example, `Click`, `Scroll`, `MouseMove`). In most cases you can assume that an `addSomethingHandler` will mean the event type is `SomethingEvent`, but that isn't always the case. For example, the `DatePicker` widget has this method:

```
addValueChangeHandler(ValueChangeHandler<java.util.Date> handler)
```

You might assume that this means you could specify an event type of `ValueChangeEvent` for your handler, but this isn't the case because of the generics involved. This method takes a handler of type `ValueChangeHandler<java.util.Date>`. `ValueChangeHandler` is a generic interface, which in this case has been specified to handle `Date` objects. Taking this into account means that your handler method should look like the following:

```
@UiHandler("datePicker")
void handleNewDate (ValueChangeEvent<java.util.Date> event)
{
  Window.alert(datePicker.getHighlightedDate().toString());
}
```

So where does that leave you? That leaves you with most everything you need to know about UiBinder outside of styling. But before we discuss styling, we have some prerequisite information you need to know about. Therefore we introduce to you the UiBinder expression language.

6.3 Introducing the UiBinder expression language

As with any template technology, UiBinder wouldn't be complete without an expression language (EL) to allow you to write simple expressions within the template. And because much of the content in the second half of the chapter relies on the UiBinder EL, you need to understand how it works.

In UiBinder the EL is referenced in the documentation as "field references," but that name isn't clear or descriptive, so we'll instead refer to it as the UiBinder EL, or EL.

The UiBinder EL doesn't provide language constructs like `if/else` or loops. It allows you to execute methods on template fields and use that result to set attributes of elements within the template. With that in mind, the UiBinder EL provides the following features:

- You can execute methods only on a declared field.
- You can only use EL to set element attributes in the template.
- The method must take no arguments.
- The method must return a value that's the correct type for the attribute you're attempting to set.
- You may call methods on the result of the method (for example, `field.methodOne.methodTwo`).
- An EL statement is delimited by curly braces, `{}`.
- EL doesn't use JavaBean semantics, so use `field.getText` and not `field.text`.

The rules are fairly simple, and so let's see them in action:

```
<g:Label text="{messages.greetings.hello}" />
<g:Button text="Hello {person.getName}" />
<div class="{style.bold} {style.tall}">S-Mart</div>
```

The first example sets the `text` attribute to the result of `messages.greetings().hello()`, which accepts a `String` value. The second example concatenates the text "Hello" with the output of `person.getName()`. And the third example sets the CSS class of the `<div>` element to the output of `style.bold()` and `style.tall()`. This shows that you can use the EL with not only widgets but HTML elements as well.

But where do these objects come from? You already saw how to give a field name to a widget declared in the template. For example, you could create a `<g:Button>` and then use the EL to call its methods, like the following:

```
<g:Button ui:field="myButton" text="Click Me!" />
<g:Label text="{myButton.getText}" />
```

You'll set the label to use the same text as the button. This works because the button has provided a field name (that is, `myButton`) and because the `<g:Label>` appears after the `<g:Button>` in the template. The "code" in the template is executed in the same way you execute your Java code, from top to bottom. So when the label is created, the button text must already be set. If you, for example, reversed the order of the elements, the label would be blank.

Besides being able to access methods on widgets declared in the template, you can create references to external objects. This is accomplished by using the `<ui:with>` element, as follows:

```
<ui:with field="person" type="com.manning.gwtia.ch6.client.Person" />
<g:HTMLPanel>
  <g:Label text="Hello {person.getName}" />
</g:HTMLPanel>
```

Using `<ui:with>` is similar to declaring a widget in the template. First of all, you aren't required to add anything to your Java code. By default UiBinder will create a new instance of the referenced object and use that, as it does for widgets. But you'll usually want to have the object injected into your Java class, and this is done in the same way as with widget declarations, by using `@UiField`. And as with widgets, you can specify that the object will be provided. For example, you might use this code with the previous example:

```
public class MyWidget extends Composite {

  @UiField(provided = true) Person person;

  public MyWidget () {
      person = new Person();
      person.setName("David Oliver");

      ...other code omitted...
  }
}
```

In this example you construct the `Person` instance, but it could easily be passed in as a constructor argument for your widget. Or you could use `@UiFactory`, as follows:

```
public class MyWidget extends Composite {

  @UiField Person person;

  @UiFactory
  public Person getPerson () {
      Person person = new Person();
      person.setName("Kathryn Grace");
      return person;
  }

  ...other code omitted...
}
```

As the previous example shows, you use `@UiFactory` in the same way you did in section 6.1.4 when you were working with widgets. In this case you create the `Person` object from scratch, but it could have come from anywhere. Perhaps this widget is part of an address book application, in which case the information might be stored in an array of a hundred other addresses, or maybe it will be fetched from the server.

This is handy when you have a `ClientBundle`, which we introduced in chapter 5, and want to use its values in the template. Perhaps you have a `ClientBundle` that looks like the following listing.

Listing 6.8 `MyBundle`—an example `ClientBundle`

```
import com.google.gwt.core.client.GWT;
import com.google.gwt.resources.client.*;

public interface MyBundle extends ClientBundle {
```

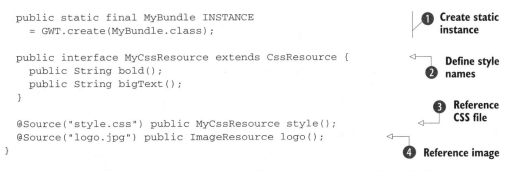

```
  public static final MyBundle INSTANCE
    = GWT.create(MyBundle.class);

  public interface MyCssResource extends CssResource {
    public String bold();
    public String bigText();
  }

  @Source("style.css") public MyCssResource style();
  @Source("logo.jpg") public ImageResource logo();
}
```

❶ Create static instance

❷ Define style names

❸ Reference CSS file

❹ Reference image

All of this was covered in chapter 5, so we'll keep the explanation of this code to a minimum. You'll create a new interface `MyBundle` that extends `ClientBundle`. It includes a static `INSTANCE` field ❶ so that you can use this bundle in multiple classes with only a single instance. You then define a `MyCssResource` interface ❷ that extends `CssResource`. `MyCssResource` defines two methods; each of these will need to match a CSS class name found in an external CSS file. Next, you define a `style()` method ❸, using the `@Source` annotation to map your `MyCssResource` interface to the external file we mentioned. And finally you add a `logo()` method ❹, which will reference logo.jpg, as noted by the `@Source` annotation. If you use `ClientBundles`, this should all look familiar.

Once you've coded the `ClientBundle`, you have only two additional steps to take. Let's start by providing a `@UiFactory` in your widget class:

```
public class MyWidget extends Composite {

  ...other code omitted...

  @UiFactory
  public MyBundle createTheBundle () {
    MyBundle.INSTANCE.style().ensureInjected();
    return MyBundle.INSTANCE;
  }
}
```

In the previous example you create a `@UiFactory` that will be called when you bind to your template. Prior to returning the instance, you call `ensureInjected()` on the `CssResource` to make sure that the external CSS file has been loaded. The last step is to reference your bundle in the UiBinder template:

```
<ui:with type="com.gwtia.ch06.client.MyBundle" field="myBundle" />

<g:HTMLPanel>
    <g:Image resource="{myBundle.logo}" />
    <div class="{myBundle.style.bigText}">Welcome!</div>
</g:HTMLPanel>
```

Here you use `<ui:with>` to create a new field `myBundle`, which in turn will call the factory method you defined with `@UiFactory`. Then you use `{myBundle.logo}` as the resource for the `Image` widget and use `{myBundle.style.bigText}` to style the `<div>`.

The <ui:with> tag must be at the top of the template, outside any widget or HTML declarations. In this example, had you placed the <ui:with> tag inside the <g:HTMLPanel>, it would have thrown an exception at compile time.

One thing worth pointing out is that building the CssResource can be time consuming. In the example you had only two styles, but what if you had 20? What if you had 100? Fortunately, UiBinder can help you out there too.

6.4 Applying style with UiBinder

If you've been following along with the example, at this point you've created an XML template, created a Java class for your widget, and used UiBinder to tie the two together. Along the way we purposely avoided discussing CSS styling, which we'll talk about now.

At the beginning, our designer delivered some CSS code with the HTML, and we need to decide how to handle this. We could include an HTML <link> in the web page hosting our application and have it point to the CSS file as follows:

```
<link href="/css/LoginDialogBox.css" rel="stylesheet" type="text/css" />
```

This will work, but you can do better. Ideally, you'd have this stylesheet code available to you as a CssResource. This would give you syntax validation, conditional statements, CSS modularization, selector obfuscation to avoid name clashes, and everything else we discussed in chapter 5 when we covered using CssResources.

But all of these features come at a cost. You'd need to write a ton of code in order to create the ClientBundle and CssResource. Specifically, if the stylesheet contains a few dozen CSS classes, you'd end up having to define a few dozen methods in your CssResource. But why should it be so hard?

6.4.1 Using <ui:style> to generate a CssResource

UiBinder provides a <ui:style> element that can save you a tremendous amount of effort if you want to use a CssResource in your project. In listing 6.9 you'll use the <ui:style> element to generate a CssResource and use UiBinder EL to access the methods of the CssResource.

Listing 6.9 Using <ui:style> in a UiBinder template

```
<ui:UiBinder xmlns:ui='urn:ui:com.google.gwt.uibinder'
    xmlns:g="urn:import:com.google.gwt.user.client.ui">

<ui:style field="style" src="LoginDialogBox.css" />        ❶ Autocreate a CssResource

<g:HTMLPanel>
<div class="{style.container}">                            ❷ Style by class
  <div class="{style.content}">
    <h1>S-Mart Login</h1>                                  ❸ Style by element
    <div class="{style.form-divider}"></div>
    <div id="login-form">
    <ul>
      ...most of the form contents omitted...
      <li>
```

```
        <g:Button ui:field="btnLogin" text="Login"
           styleName="{style.login-submit}" />          <-- Style using dashed name (4)
      </li>
    </ul>
    </div>
    <div class="{style.form-divider}"></div>
  </div>
</div>
</g:HTMLPanel>

</ui:UiBinder>
```

So what's happening in the previous listing? The focus of listing 6.9 is the addition of the `<ui:style>` element ❶, which does a bit of "magic" for you. At compile time it will cause a `ClientBundle` and `CssResource` to be generated automatically from the CSS file. In addition you use the `field` attribute to declare that the `CssResource` should be bound to the field named `style`. Strictly speaking, this wasn't necessary because `style` is the default field name if you don't include the `field` attribute for a `<ui:style>` tag, but we included it in order to increase the clarity of the example.

Now that the `CssResource` is a field, you can use the EL to reference those styles in the template. You do this on the opening `<div>` ❷, where you set the `class` attribute to `{style.container}`. Again, `style` is a reference to the `CssResource`, and `container` is a method defined in that class, which returns the obfuscated CSS class name used by the `CssResource`.

Remember that only CSS class selector names will be included in the `CssResource`. Although we haven't shown the real CSS code, the designer added styling to the `<h1>` tag as well the ID `"login-form"` ❸. Because these aren't CSS class selectors, there won't be methods for them in your `CssResource`. But rest assured, the stylesheet declarations for these will still be loaded, so you won't lose any styling.

One additional nuance to using `<ui:style>` with EL is that you can use a dash in the method name even though you can't normally do this with the EL. For instance, when you set the style for the button in the example ❹, you use the EL `{style .login-submit}`. This only works when the `CssResource` is created by `<ui:style>` and wouldn't work if you'd created the `CssResource` manually. In addition, you could use a CamelCase version of this name and remove the dashes, `{style.loginSubmit}`. Either of these will work but again only when using `<ui:style>`, because it's not a general feature of the EL.

> **<ui:style> CSS gotchas!**
>
> When you're working with `<ui:style>` you must remember that this isn't vanilla CSS code. Ordinarily CSS code is parsed by the browser, but in this case it will be initially parsed by GWT at compile time. That means that some features of CSS may not function, for example, the use of the CSS `@import()` directive, and the parser may choke if you try to place an HTML tag in a CSS comment.

In addition to including an external file, you can include the styles inline, as you did with the HTML style tag. It's important, though, that you give this `<ui:style>` its own unique field name because each style block will create its own `CssResource` and is its own field.

For the `LoginDialogBox` example you'll need to alter some styling on the fly. This includes changing the border of the `TextBox` fields to indicate a good or bad value, and you'll need to hide or show error messages accordingly based on the validation results:

```
<ui:style field="myStyle">
  .hidden      { visibility: hidden;          }
  .borderEmpty { border: 3px #999999 solid; }
  .borderOk    { border: 3px green solid;    }
  .borderError { border: 3px red solid;      }
</ui:style>
```

You define four style classes to accomplish this. The `hidden` style will be used to hide the error message `<div>` when there's no error. The `borderEmpty` will provide the initial border on the `TextBox` fields in your form. And `borderOk` and `borderError` will be used to indicate the validity of the field. Figure 6.3 shows the completed `LoginDialogBox` to give you a sense of how you can use these styles once you've completed the client-side validation.

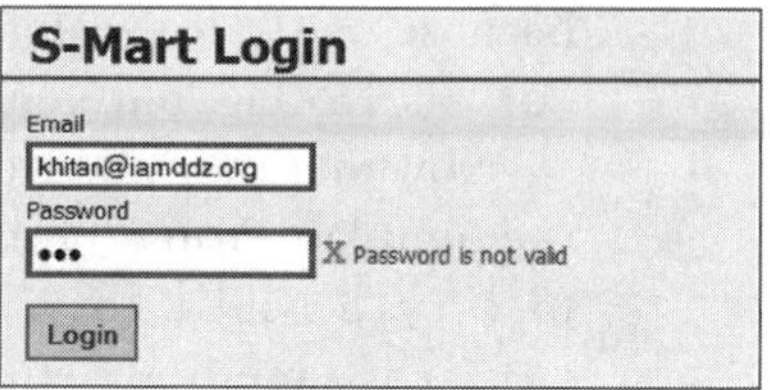

Figure 6.3 The `LoginDialogBox` client-side validation in action. The Email field has a green border indicating a valid email, and the Password box has a red border to indicate that it failed the validation test. These are controlled by applying the styles `borderOk` and `borderError` as required.

As we mentioned, the presence of this `<ui:style>` tag will trigger the creation of a `CssResource`, and as the example shows, you used the `field` attribute to specify the field name of `myStyle`. But in order to add or remove the hidden style from a `UIObject` you need to perform some additional steps, which we'll look at next.

6.4.2 *Accessing a generated CssResource in your widget*

Once you've added a `<ui:style>` to your UiBinder template, you have three additional steps to take in order to gain access to the methods of the underlying `CssResource`:

1. Create an interface to declare the methods to which you need access.
2. Use the `type` attribute of `ui:field` to specify the field name used in the class.
3. Use `@UiField` to bind the field to the Java class so that you can use it.

Nothing too major, so let's get started with creating the interface. The purpose of doing this has more to do with Java than anything else. Java is a static language, meaning you can only use methods the compiler knows about. The problem is that the `CssResource` is generated when the application is compiled to JavaScript, so you can't use it at design time. The solution is to create an interface and write your code to that interface.

Looking again at the `<ui:style>` block you added to the `LoginDialogBox` template, you see that you'll need to access all four style classes in your Java widget code:

```
<ui:style field="myStyle">
  .hidden      { visibility: hidden;         }
  .borderEmpty { border: 3px #999999 solid; }
  .borderOk    { border: 3px green solid;    }
  .borderError { border: 3px red solid;      }
</ui:style>
```

The `<ui:style>` block contains four styles, so when UiBinder generates the `CssResource`, it will create four methods: `hidden()`, `borderEmpty()`, `borderOk()`, and `borderError()`. As we mentioned, you need to create an interface for this if you want to be able to access these methods within your code. And because this interface will only be used within your widget class, you'll nest it inside your `LoginDialogBox` so that you can keep everything together:

```
public class LoginDialogBox extends PopupPanel {
  interface MyStyle extends CssResource {
    String hidden();
    String borderEmpty();
    String borderOk();
    String borderError();
  }  ...the rest of our widget code...
}
```

The return value of `CssResource` methods is always a `String`, which will be the obfuscated name that has been generated during the `CssResource` creation. One thing to note, which doesn't apply to this example, is that if the `<ui:style>` element has multiple CSS style classes, the underlying `CssResource` will have a method defined for every one of them, but when you define your interface, you need only include those to which you require programmatic access.

> **NOTE** Although our example uses `MyStyle` for the `CssResource` interface name and `myStyle` for the `@UiField` name, you're not required to give them the same name. But in most cases it will make sense to name them the same so that it's easier to understand the connection when reading the source code.

The second step, as outlined, is to inform the code generator that the `CssResource` should implement your interface. Following is the updated `<ui:field>` block in the template, which now includes that information:

```
<ui:style field="myStyle"
 type="com.gwtia.ch06.client.LoginDialogBox.MyStyle">
  .hidden      { visibility: hidden;         }
  .borderEmpty { border: 3px #999999 solid; }
  .borderOk    { border: 3px green solid;    }
  .borderError { border: 3px red solid;      }
</ui:style>
```

As the previous example shows, the `type` attribute to `<ui:field>` is used to inform the code generator of the name of your interface, so that the generated `CssResource` can implement it.

The last step in the process is to bind the field to your class using `@UiField`. You declare its type as `MyStyle` (the interface you created) and name the variable `myStyle` (the field name you specified):

```
@UiField MyStyle myStyle;
```

You now have access to the CSS class name in your application. Building on our `LoginDialogBox` you can now add a host of handler methods to perform your client-side validation of the form, as shown next.

Listing 6.10 Rounding out the `LoginDialogBox` with handlers to control styles

```
private void setBorderStyle(TextBox textBox, String styleName) {      ❶ Change border
  textBox.removeStyleName(myStyle.borderOk());
  textBox.removeStyleName(myStyle.borderError());
  textBox.removeStyleName(myStyle.borderEmpty());
  textBox.addStyleName(styleName);
}

private boolean validateEmail() {
  return txtEmail.getText().matches("[^\\s@]+\\@[^\\s@]+");
}

private boolean validatePassword() {
  return txtPassword.getText().length() >= 6;
}

                                                                      ❷ Handle focus
@UiHandler("txtEmail")
void emailHasFocus (FocusEvent event) {
  eEmailError.addClassName(myStyle.hidden());
  setBorderStyle(txtEmail, myStyle.borderOk());
}
                                                                      ❸ Handle blur
@UiHandler("txtEmail")
void emailBlur (BlurEvent event) {
  if (validateEmail()) {
    eEmailError.addClassName(myStyle.hidden());
    setBorderStyle(txtEmail, myStyle.borderOk());
  }
  else {
    eEmailErrorText.setInnerHTML("Email is not valid");
    eEmailError.removeClassName(myStyle.hidden());
    setBorderStyle(txtEmail, myStyle.borderError());
  }
}

@UiHandler("txtPassword")
void passwordHasFocus (FocusEvent event) {
  ePassError.addClassName(myStyle.hidden());
```

```
  setBorderStyle(txtPassword, myStyle.borderOk());
}

@UiHandler("txtPassword")
void passwordBlur (BlurEvent event) {
  if (validatePassword()) {
    ePassError.addClassName(myStyle.hidden());
    setBorderStyle(txtPassword, myStyle.borderOk());
  }
  else {
    ePassErrorText.setInnerHTML("Password is not valid");
    ePassError.removeClassName(myStyle.hidden());
    setBorderStyle(txtPassword, myStyle.borderError());
  }
}

@UiHandler("btnLogin")                                    <-- 4 Handle click
void submitLoginForm (ClickEvent event)
{
  if (validateEmail() && validatePassword()) {
    Window.alert("Logging in...");
  }
}
```

If you've been following along with the `LoginDialogBox` example, this code completes the project. It defines six handlers and three utility methods. Of the three utility methods, `validateEmail` and `validatePassword` do what you would expect, so we won't discuss them here. The third, `setBorderStyle()` ❶, makes use of your newly added `myStyle` field. It takes a `TextBox` and style name as inputs, removing all border styles from the `TextBox` before adding the supplied style name.

The `setBorderStyle()` method is referenced in your event handlers, like `emailHasFocus()` ❷, which is called when the `txtEmail` field has focus. It hides the error message for the email `TextBox` and then uses `setBorderStyle()` to set the current border to `myStyle.borderOk()`.

A second handler for the `txtEmail` is the `emailBlur()` method ❸, which is called when the blur event is received (that is, loses focus). This validates the field as soon as the user moves the focus to another element in the form and updates its border and error message accordingly. This sort of instant feedback is useful to the user, allowing them to be notified of the error as soon as possible.

The next two methods include focus and blur handlers for the `txtPassword` field, which work like the ones you saw for `txtEmail`. These are followed up by `submitLoginForm()`, a handler for handling click events for the login button ❹.

If you've worked with GWT prior to the inclusion of UiBinder, you'll see that this code is much more elegant and readable than it would be without UiBinder. That's what UiBinder is all about.

We covered quite a bit in this chapter, so it's understandable that you might not remember exactly how to define the UiBinder subinterface or the XML namespace that was used in the UiBinder template. In this next section we'll review the UiBinder features that the Google Plugin for Eclipse (GPE) provides.

6.5 Using the Eclipse plug-in with UiBinder

Although UiBinder is simple to use, you'll likely have some trouble remembering all of the steps at first, and this is yet another reason to use GPE if you aren't already doing so. To create a new UiBinder template and Java class in your GWT application project, click File > New and select UiBinder from the menu, which will bring up the New UiBinder dialog box that you see in figure 6.4.

One of the options in the dialog box is to create the user interface (UI) based on HTML or GWT widgets. If you select GWT Widgets, as we've done in figure 6.4, the sample template will use `<g:HTMLPanel>` as the root widget, as we did for our `LoginDialogBox`. In addition, the sample Java code will extend `Composite`, but you can alter this as needed.

The other option is to create the UI based on HTML. When you choose this option the root UI element in the template will be an HTML `<div>` element, and the generated Java class will extend `UIObject`. This demonstrates that you can use UiBinder with not only widgets but plain-old HTML as well.

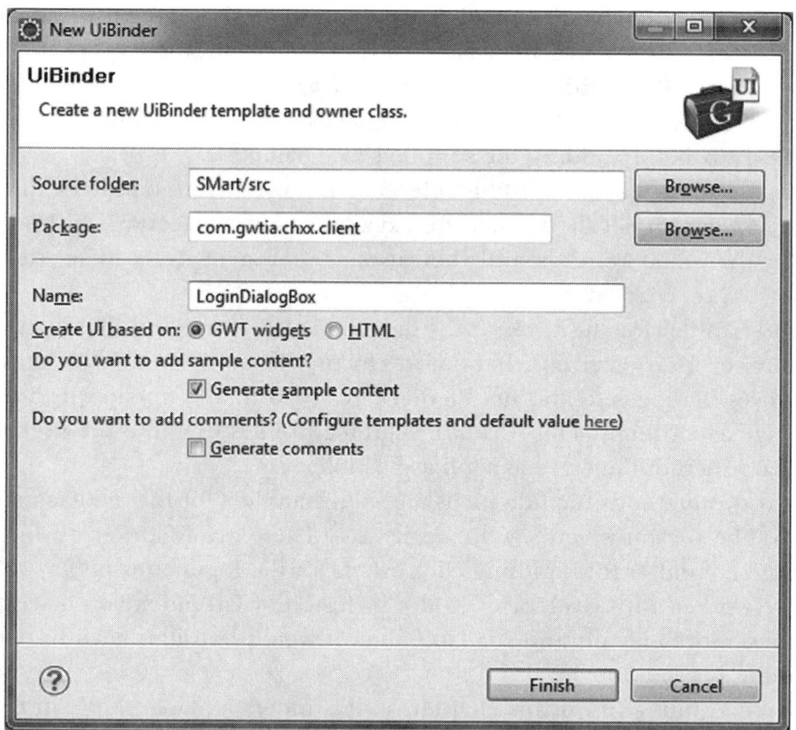

Figure 6.4 The New UiBinder dialog box lets you specify several options, including basing your interface on widgets or HTML.

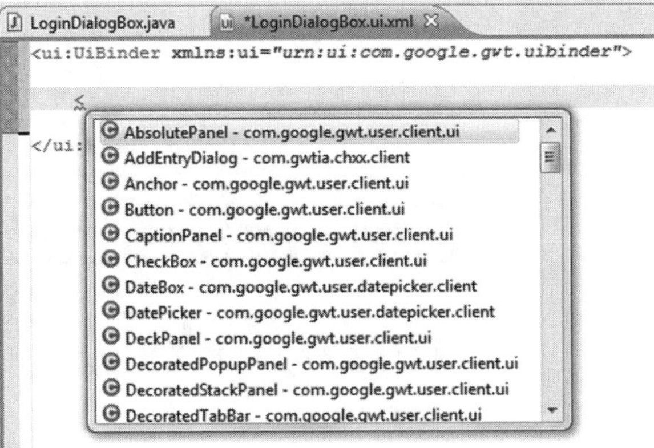

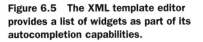

Figure 6.5 The XML template editor provides a list of widgets as part of its autocompletion capabilities.

In addition, the Eclipse plug-in will flag errors if things don't match up, such as if the template file is named incorrectly or if you reference a widget in the template that doesn't exist. It also offers autocomplete when working with the template. Figure 6.5 shows an example of this, where typing < will provide you with a list of widgets, and selecting one of those widgets will automatically include the proper namespace in the root element if it isn't already declared.

At the time of this writing GPE feels a little kludgy in some areas, but it's still extremely useful. The fact that it can flag common errors and provides autocompletion will save you time during development, and we expect that the functions of the plug-in will feel more solid as the tool matures.

And with that, this concludes our coverage of UiBinder.

6.6 Summary

In this chapter we took you from the designer's HTML code to a functional widget. Not only is our `LoginDialogBox` functional, but it's also user friendly, and user friendliness is the key to building a great application. What UiBinder did for you was to make this straightforward and fairly simple to do by allowing you to bind the designer's HTML code to your Java code with a minimal amount of work. In this chapter, you used annotations to bind widgets and stylesheet resources to variables and bind events to methods. And all it took was a few annotations.

At this point in the book you've learned how to control the browser to do your bidding. Your interfaces are super-interactive and work in all of the popular browsers. But in order to become a master developer of rich internet applications, that isn't enough. Now you need to look past the browser and understand how your client-side applications can communicate with the server.

Looking ahead, we've included three chapters that provide this knowledge. The first of these is coming up next, and it's called "Communicating with GWT-RPC."

7 Communicating with GWT-RPC

This chapter covers

- Using GWT-RPC to make remote calls
- Debugging communication between client and server
- Protecting against XSRF attacks

At this point in the book you've learned the basics of creating a GWT application, allowing you to do some great stuff in the browser. The next step will be learning to communicate with the outside world. GWT offers several tools for this, including HTML forms (chapter 12), `RequestBuilder` (chapter 12), `RequestFactory` (chapter 8), and GWT-RPC. HTML forms are exactly as the name implies, and `RequestBuilder` is your typical Ajax solution. But the next two, `RequestFactory` and GWT-RPC, are special in the sense that they allow you to send Java objects between the client and server, as opposed to JSON,[1] XML, or whatever other program you can dream up.

[1] JSON stands for JavaScript Object Notation. Learn more at http://json.org.

In this chapter we discuss GWT-RPC, or GWT Remote Procedure Call, which allows you to call Java methods on the server, passing and receiving back Java objects and primitives. You'll find this to be a convenient solution for general-purpose RPC calls when you're already running Java on the server.

Before we get into the specifics, we believe it's pertinent to explain how we structured this chapter, because we approach this topic differently than you may find in other books and tutorials. We start with a non-GWT implementation of a method and slowly transform it into a GWT-RPC call. This will allow us to start on familiar ground before we move into the specifics of GWT-RPC.

> **How to read this chapter**
>
> We devised this chapter to be used as both a tutorial and a reference. The chapter follows a single example from start to end, but GWT-RPC has lots of features, many of which won't apply to the development of the example application. We've grouped those features we didn't use in our example with related features.
>
> If you're reading through this chapter as a tutorial, you'll end up with both a working application and an understanding of other features that will be applicable in certain situations. If you're instead looking for a reference, you can skip to any section in this chapter and expect it to be a complete reference.

With an understanding of the method we want to execute, we then look at how we can make the method's input and output types compatible with GWT serialization. Once this is complete, we'll implement the server side of the equation followed by the client and then follow up with how to add some cross-site request forgery (XSRF) protection to your RPC calls.

If you plan on developing the example project as you read through this chapter, we strongly recommend using the Google Plugin for Eclipse (GPE), which we introduced in chapter 2. It includes several features that will help you along the way and warn you of potential mistakes.

Before we dive into the tutorial, we begin with a broad overview of GWT-RPC and provide a few diagrams to give you an idea of the big picture.

7.1 Surveying GWT-RPC

As they say, the devil is in the details, and this holds true for GWT-RPC. But before we get to those, we want to provide a broad overview of how GWT-RPC works and the classes involved. This includes surveying the parts of GWT-RPC that are provided and the parts you'll need to write.

The parts that you'll need to write include your server-side business logic, the service interface, and potentially custom data objects that will hold the data that's passed between the client and server. The provided parts include everything else, namely the code that glues the client and the server together. Much of this glue code is generated at compile time and is unseen by the developer.

At its core GWT-RPC is a way to have the GWT code on the client make an asynchronous call to Java code on the server. Although asynchronous calls have become more and more common, we still wanted to provide a few paragraphs to explain what they are and why we use them, so that's where we begin.

7.1.1 Understanding asynchronous behavior

If you've ever bought something online, you've participated in asynchronous behavior. The first step is to go to an online store like Amazon and purchase something, perhaps the latest edition of *GWT in Action*. The second step is to wait for it to arrive. But until it arrives, you don't sit out at the mailbox; you do other things. And when it does arrive, then you deal with it. That's asynchronous behavior.

That's how GWT-RPC and Ajax work. If you haven't used Ajax before, particularly if you've only done procedural programming, this feels a bit strange, but it's absolutely necessary. The unfortunate truth is that JavaScript is single-threaded. So if you performed a synchronous call, meaning you blocked execution until the RPC call returned, the browser wouldn't be able to handle other events, like mouse clicks. The browser will appear to have locked up, and that wouldn't be a user-friendly interface.

With this in mind, let's move on to looking at the classes involved when using GWT-RPC to see how this fits into the puzzle.

7.1.2 Defining the GWT-RPC classes, interfaces, and annotations

In order to help you understand all of the working parts of GWT, we present two tables, followed by a diagram to help you visualize how the parts fit together. The first table provides a list of GWT's classes, interfaces, and annotations that you'll use each time you write a new GWT-RPC service. The second table lists the classes and interfaces that you'll need to write yourself.

For each table we provide a short description of each item and point to the section in this chapter where you can get the details. The goal is to provide you with not only a brief overview but also a quick reference of where to get more information.

Let's begin with the GWT classes in table 7.1.

Table 7.1 Classes, interfaces, and annotations you'll use when creating a GWT-RPC service

GWT class	Explanation
`com.google.gwt.user.server.rpc` `RemoteServiceServlet`	This is a specialized servlet that your implementation class on the server will extend. It provides serialization, deserialization, and auto-dispatching services. We cover the details in section 7.5.
`com.google.gwt.user.client.rpc` `RemoteService`	This is a marker interface with no methods that will need to be implemented. Your implementation of this class will serve as the contract the client and the server will use for communication. We work through the details of this in section 7.5.

Table 7.1 Classes, interfaces, and annotations you'll use when creating a GWT-RPC service *(continued)*

GWT class	Explanation
`com.google.gwt.user.client.rpc` `ServiceDefTarget`	This is an interface that will be implemented by your client-side service implementation. You won't implement this yourself; it will be implemented by the GWT-generated client-side service implementation. We discuss this more in section 7.6.
`com.google.gwt.user.client.rpc` `@RemoteServiceRelativePath`	This annotation is used when creating the service interface and specifies the URL to the server where the service is implemented. We discuss the details in section 7.5.
`com.google.gwt.user.client.rpc` `IsSerializable`	This is a marker interface to indicate that the class is serializable. This marker would be placed on classes that you pass between the client and server. In section 7.4 we explain how this works and its compatibility with Java's `java.io.Serializable` interface.

If you read through the table, you'll notice that we hinted at the fact that GWT will generate some code for you. This is the key to how GWT-RPC works. At compile time GWT will inspect your service interface and generate the code required to make the calls to the server. This includes generating the serialization and deserialization code required to handle the Java objects passed between the client and server.

> **DEFINITION** *Serialization* is the act of taking an object graph (for example, a Java object instance) and converting it into a binary or textual data, allowing it to be transported to another computer or stored on disk. *Deserialization* is the reverse, where you read the serialized data and convert it back into a Java object. The serialized Java objects are often binary data, but in some cases, like with GWT-RPC, the serialized data is (semi) readable text.

This is all made possible by GWT's deferred binding, which allows a code generator to inspect your Java code and generate additional Java code prior to all of the code being compiled to JavaScript. In order to use GWT-RPC you don't need to understand how deferred binding and generators work, but if you're curious, it's covered in chapter 19.

Let's look at the code you need to write, which table 7.2 summarizes.

Table 7.2 The classes and interfaces you need to create when using GWT-RPC

Construct	Explanation
Servlet implementation	You'll create a servlet that extends `RemoteServiceServlet` and implements your service interface. This will be the server-side implementation for your service. We cover the details in section 7.5.
Service interface	The service interface will define the remote methods that may be called from the client, and your servlet will implement this interface. See section 7.5 for more information.

Table 7.2 The classes and interfaces you need to create when using GWT-RPC *(continued)*

Construct	Explanation
Asynchronous interface	This interface is a copy of your service interface but has modified method signatures in order to allow for asynchronous communication. This is covered in section 7.6.
Data transfer objects	Any data objects that you pass between the client and server will need to be created and will need to be tagged with the `IsSerializable` interface. This is covered in detail in section 7.4.

This list of code you need to write isn't daunting, but it's perhaps more than you expected. In particular, the asynchronous interface is an added piece of code you need to create because of the asynchronous requirement when communicating from the web browser.

The last thing we want to look at is a diagram of how all of these parts fit together to help you visualize how the system works, shown in figure 7.1. You can see how the client-side code uses the asynchronous interface, whereas the server-side code uses the regular service interface. If there's anything tricky about GWT-RPC it's the asynchronous behavior, because it not only adds one additional interface to create but also changes the way you'd normally code the client portion of the application.

As you can see in figure 7.1, you'll be writing code for both the client and server, so you need to understand how to lay out your packages properly in order for this to work.

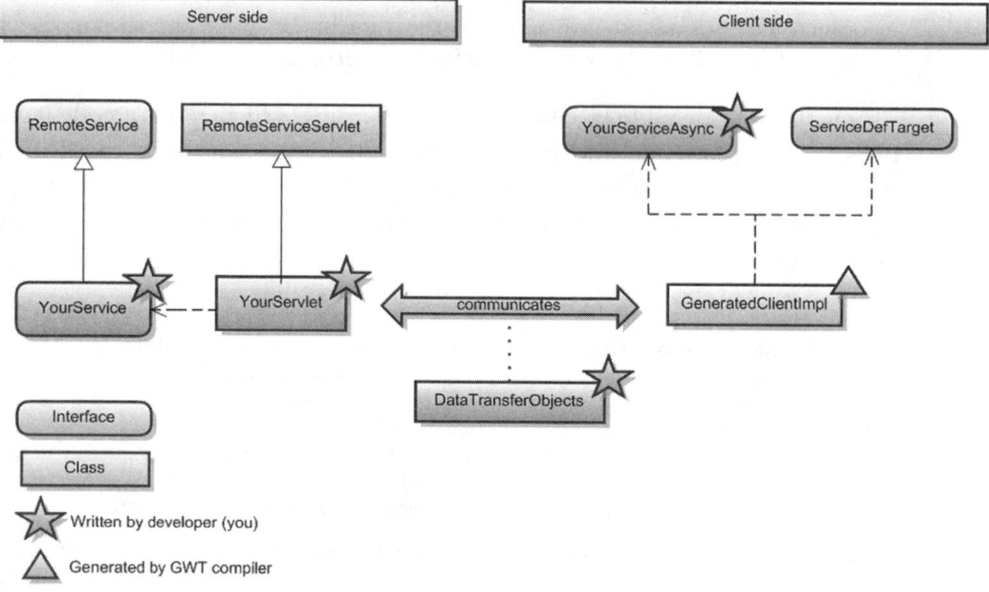

Figure 7.1 An overview of the GWT-RPC landscape

7.1.3 Understanding GWT-RPC package structure

As you learned earlier, you can't use any library in your GWT project because of the restrictions of the GWT compiler (compiles from source, limited JRE, and so on). So the question is, how can we mix server-side and client-side code in the same project, where the client-side code meets the GWT compiler requirements and the server-side code doesn't? And in the case of GWT-RPC we also have data objects that are used by both the client and the server.

Ultimately, the answer is simple. When you create your GWT project, using whatever means, you'll have created a client package. You've seen this throughout the book. This package should be used for both client-side and shared code. This works because although the GWT compiler compiles only the client package code into JavaScript, the Java compiler compiles all of the code, both client and server code, into Java bytecode. Therefore, the server-side code can make use of every class in your project.

So where does the server-side code go? The answer is, anywhere your client-side code isn't. Typically, if you have a package named `org.foo.project.client` for the client-side code, then you'd create `org.foo.project.server` for the server-side code. But again, the only real requirement is that the client-side code is segregated into its own package structure.

If you're using GPE, you'll see that it creates three packages for you: one for client, one for server, and one for shared. You can see this in figure 7.2.

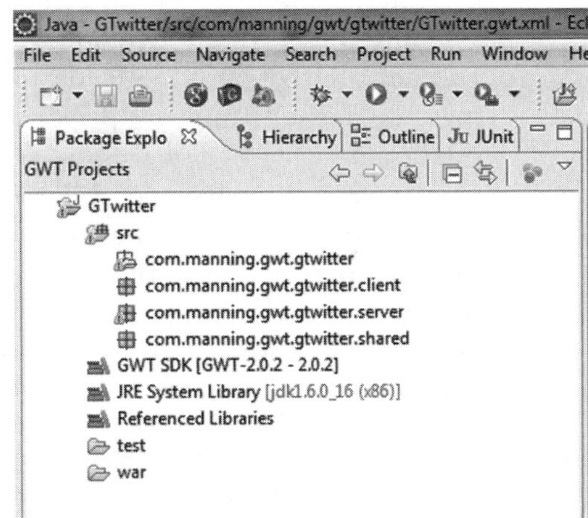

Figure 7.2 The default package structure that's created when you use GPE includes client, server, and shared packages.

Looking at the figure, you may have noticed that this seems to break the rule in that the shared code isn't inside the client package. The way this works is that the plug-in alters the default source package to include both client and shared. This is achieved by adding the shared package as a source code package in the module configuration that the GWT compiler should compile. For example, here's a snippet of module configuration that was generated by the Google plug-in:

```
<!-- Specify the paths for translatable code-->
<source path='client'/>
<source path='shared'/>
```

As you read through this chapter we use the package hierarchy created by GPE, so throughout the chapter we'll use the client package for client-only code and the shared package for code used by both the client and server.

Now that you have a broad overview of GWT-RPC, let's write some code. In the sections that follow we show you how to create a simple Twitter client that has a lot of the same challenges you can expect when using GWT-RPC.

7.2 Learning GWT-RPC with Twitter

In selecting an example to demonstrate GWT-RPC, we settled on the idea of a simple Twitter client. Twitter, once the secret of techies, has gone mainstream, with celebrities and companies using it to keep their fans informed. So Twitter seemed like a good choice because GWT is a tool for the modern web application, and social media is a cornerstone of that class of application.

> **NOTE** If you want to follow along and run the example project, you should create a new GWT project with the name `GTwitter` and a base package of `com.gwtia.ch07`. Or you can download the project source code and follow the provided instructions.

The Twitter client that we'll build in sections 7.3 through 7.6 is named GTwitter. It's a simple client that will only display the latest tweets for a specific Twitter user. The GWT application will send the request to Twitter via our web server, so the client won't be communicating with Twitter directly. This offers some advantages over a client-only solution in that we can extend the server code over time to also return content from Facebook, Orkut, and RSS feeds, to name a few. On top of that we can also add caching if we desire to improve performance, something that you can't do in a client-only solution.

GTwitter will make use of Twitter4J,[2] an open source Java library for interacting with the Twitter API. You'll need to download Twitter4J if you wish to follow along with the example. The examples in this chapter use version 2.1.1 of Twitter4J and only require the use of twitter4j-core-2.1.1.jar. If you wish to use a newer version of the Twitter4J API, you may be required to make some changes to the examples in order to match any changes made to the API.

> **Including the Twitter4J library in your project**
>
> In order to develop and run the GTwitter example, you'll need to download the Twitter4J jar file and add it to the /war/WEB-INF/lib/ directory of your project, as well as add it to the classpath of your IDE. You'd also do this for any other jar file that you need to include on the server side of your application. This is different from libraries used to create the client side, which don't need to be placed in /war/WEB-INF/lib/ or even be deployed with the application to the server.

We'll develop the GTwitter client over the next few sections. This includes looking at model considerations in section 7.4, developing the server component in section 7.5,

---

[2] Twitter4J can be downloaded from http://twitter4j.org.

and writing the client portion in section 7.6. But first we begin by looking at an example of a non-GWT Twitter4J call from a Java application. This will be a good way to see what issues and limitations come to play when using GWT-RPC.

7.3 Fetching data from Twitter the non-GWT way

With the Twitter4J library in your classpath, you need a few lines of code to fetch a feed and display the results. Take a look at the following listing, and then we'll explain it.

Listing 7.1 A non-GWT version of fetching a Twitter feed using Twitter4J

```
package com.gwtia.ch07.server;

import twitter4j.*;

public class TwitterServiceImpl
{
  public static void main(String[] args) throws Exception
  {
    TwitterServiceImpl impl = new TwitterServiceImpl();
    ResponseList<Status> resList = impl.getUserTimeline("ianchesnut");

    for (Status status : resList) {
      System.out.println(status.getCreatedAt()
        + ": " + status.getText());
    }
  }

  public ResponseList<Status> getUserTimeline (String screenName)
    throws TwitterException
  {
    Twitter twitter = new TwitterFactory().getInstance();
    return twitter.getUserTimeline(screenName);
  }
}
```

❶ Fetch a user's feed

❷ Print feed contents

❸ Helper method

As you can see, fetching data from Twitter doesn't require a lot of code when you use the Twitter4J library. Still, we'll explain what's going on before we point out the issues you'll face when trying to port this to GWT-RPC.

❶ In the `main` method you create a new instance of the class and then call the `getUserTimeline()` method, passing the Twitter screen name of the user you want tweets for. This is essentially what the GWT-RPC client-side code will look like.

The part that isn't GWT-compatible is the fact that this is a synchronous call, meaning that your code waits until the method returns the `ResponseList`. As you saw in section 7.1, GWT-RPC solves this by using asynchronous calls, which will alter the way you call the service.

❷ Next, you iterate over the results returned from the call. Note that the `ResponseList` object that you're iterating over and the `Status` objects in the list are classes from the Twitter4J library. These classes aren't GWT-compatible either, because GWT requires the Java source code in order to compile it to JavaScript.

This is one of the more common issues you'll run into with GWT-RPC, and the solution is to make use of data transfer objects (DTO).[3] What this means is that you need to have your own versions of `ResponseList` and `Status` that are GWT-RPC-compatible (the DTOs), and copy the data into these.

> **DEFINITION** A *data transfer object* is a design pattern used for transferring data between different applications. A DTO is characterized by not having any behavior, meaning it doesn't "do" anything; it stores data. DTOs are often used when it's not possible to transfer your business or data access objects. In the case of GTwitter, the Twitter4J objects can't be serialized by GWT, so you'd want to create DTO objects that are serializable in order to transfer the data to the client browser.

❸ The last part of the code example is the part that will run on the server. Here you use the Twitter4J API to fetch the status data and return it to the caller. The best thing about this is that this runs on your server, so you don't need to make any changes.

You'll have to do a little extra work here, like copying the `ResponseList` into the GWT-RPC-compatible DTO that we mentioned. And this is exactly where we'll start. In this next section we'll define the requirements of the objects returned from a GWT-RPC call, as well as discuss some common issues like trying to use JPA entities as DTOs.

7.4 Defining a GWT-RPC-compatible model

When deciding on the data types to pass between the client and server, the most important concern is to make sure that the data types can be serialized by GWT. Table 7.3 provides a list of these types.

Table 7.3 Data types that can be serialized for GWT, not including types with custom serializers

Java type	Explanation
Primitive	Includes `byte`, `char`, `short`, `int`, `long`, `float`, `double`, and `boolean`.
Java enum	Enumeration constants are serialized by name only; any other field values won't be carried over.
Array	Must be an array of other serializable types.
Serializable user defined	A class that implements the `IsSerializable` or `Serializable` marker interface, along with a no-arg constructor and serializable fields.

You may have noticed that this list is missing quite a few basic types, like `java.util.Date` and `java.lang.Integer`. In GWT these are handled by creating custom serializers, and GWT ships with a bunch of them. We'll discuss how to create your own custom serializer soon, but for now table 7.4 provides a list of Java types for

---

[3] For more information on data transfer objects, refer to its Wikipedia page at http://en.wikipedia.org/wiki/Value_object.

which GWT provides custom serializers. For reference, these serializers are found under the subpackages of `com.google.gwt.user.client.rpc.core` in the gwt-user.jar file.

Table 7.4 Java classes for which that GWT provides custom serializers out of the box

Package	Classes
`java.lang`	`Boolean`, `Byte`, `Character`, `Double`, `Float`, `Integer`, `Long`, `Short`, `String`
`java.sql`	`Date`, `Time`, `Timestamp`
`java.util`	`ArrayList`, `Collection`, `Date`, `HashMap`, `HashSet`, `IdentityHashMap`, `LinkedHashMap`, `LinkedList`, `Map`, `TreeMap`, `TreeSet`, `Vector`

As you can see, GWT either provides built-in serialization for your data or gives you a way to build your own serializer. There's a good amount of information to cover here, so let's start by looking at using `Serializable` and `IsSerializable`, which directly relate to our example.

7.4.1 Using the Serializable and IsSerializable interfaces

GWT provides two marker interfaces for identifying classes that can be serialized. The first is Java's own `java.io.Serializable`, and the second is `com.google.gwt.user.client.rpc.IsSerializable`. A marker interface has no methods that need to be implemented and acts as a marker to let other classes know that certain semantics apply. The semantics in this case are those required for the class to be serializable by GWT. By implementing either of these interfaces you're agreeing that the class meets the following requirements:

- All nonfinal and nontransient fields must in turn be serializable by GWT.
- The class must have a zero-arg constructor.

If you've used `java.io.Serializable` before, you might have noticed that this isn't at all compatible with Java's definition of a serializable class. It's provided merely as a convenience for developers who wish to reuse their database entities that already implement this interface. In GWT the semantics of the two interfaces are exactly the same. In general you should use `IsSerializable` because it's more correct.

IsSerializable vs. Serializable

When GWT was first released, the designers felt that because GWT couldn't comply with the semantics of Java's own `Serializable` interface, they should create a GWT-specific `IsSerializable` interface. This caused some pain for developers who wanted to pass their database entities directly to the browser via GWT. After quite a bit of discussion, the GWT community opted to allow the use of `Serializable` as the equivalent of `IsSerializable` because the benefit was deemed greater than the possible semantic confusion that it might cause.

Let's take this information and apply it to the GTwitter client. As you might recall, the Twitter4J library returned a `ResponseList<Status>`, essentially a list of `Status` objects. To make the return objects more generic so that they can be used for other types of values, our model will consist of a list of `FeedData`. The `FeedData` class is presented in the next listing.

Listing 7.2 GTwitter serializable model object

```
package com.gwtia.ch07.shared;

import java.util.Date;
import com.google.gwt.user.client.rpc.IsSerializable;

public class FeedData implements IsSerializable
{
  private Date createdAt;
  private String text;

  public FeedData() {}

  public FeedData(Date createdAt, String text) {
    this.createdAt = createdAt;
    this.text = text;
  }

  public Date getCreatedAt() {
    return createdAt;
  }

  public String getText() {
    return text;
  }
}
```

In listing 7.2 the only GWT-specific remnant is that the bean implements `IsSerializable` and the package in which the class resides. Specifically, the class is in the shared package, which will be one of the packages compiled by the GWT compiler, assuming you're using the default-generated module configuration for the project. Strictly speaking, you can place your DTO classes in any package that your client-side application uses. See chapter 2 for how to configure your project and alter the `<source>` packages.

Implementing `IsSerializable` will cover many use cases but not all. In some cases you may want to use the same classes as your JPA or JDO entities, and we'll look at some special rules regarding their use.

7.4.2 Special considerations when using JPA/JDO model objects as DTOs

If you plan on using the Java Persistence API (JPA) or Java Data Objects (JDO) and want to use the same entity objects as DTOs that will transfer data between server and client, you have two issues to consider. First is that GWT's `IsSerializable` interface is no longer desirable, and `java.io.Serializable` should be used instead. As mentioned previously there are no semantic differences from GWT's point of view, but your persistence mechanism will require it.

The second and more important issue is how GWT handles enhanced persisted classes. Some persistence mechanisms work by enhancing either the source code or bytecode of the class prior to deploying it to a server. A good example of this is the JDO support for Google App Engine (GAE), which will use the Data Nucleus to enhance your bytecode prior to deploying it to the server. We'll provide an example of this in chapter 12 when we discuss using GWT with GAE.

When a class is enhanced, additional static or instance fields are added to the class. These won't be present in the source code that GWT compiles, which means that compiled client-side code and the server-side code for these same classes will differ. One of the enhancements in GWT 2.0 is the ability to handle this situation, but be warned that it may not work with all persistence tools.

GWT will consider a class as being enhanced if one or more of the following are true:

- For JPA, the class is annotated with `javax.persistence.Entity`.
- For JDO, the class is annotated with `java.jdo.annotations.PersistenceCapable` with the attribute `detachable=true`.
- The GWT module file includes the fully qualified class name in the `rpc.enhancedClasses` configuration property.

GWT handles these classes differently. When sending these classes from the server to the client, it will use Java serialization to serialize the added fields but won't deserialize them on the client side. This means the client won't be able to access this persistence engine–specific data. If you send the same object back to the server, this data will be deserialized on receipt so that it can be used by the persistence engine.

In order to do this work, GWT makes some assumptions about the data entity. It assumes that the object is in a detached state. This means that changes to the fields of the object don't affect persistent storage. Furthermore, GWT will also assume that all nonstatic and nontransient fields are serializable.

In general, if you fall into this use case, you'll need to experiment a little to see if GWT-RPC works with your persistence tool or if some tweaking is required. If some research is necessary, we suggest starting with the archives of the GWT General Discussion mailing list[4] and perhaps even using it to get help from others who've already trod the same ground.

But what if your serialization needs are more complex, and you need to customize how the serializer works? GWT provides a mechanism for that as well.

7.4.3 Developing custom serializers

In some cases GWT developers have had a need to customize the process of serializing their data objects. This is usually a last resort, used when GWT can't automatically handle this for you. Some of the common reasons for this include the following:

- The default serialization causes performance issues for a complex object.

---

[4] The GWT general discussion list is found at http://groups.google.com/group/google-web-toolkit.

- The class that needs to be serialized doesn't implement `IsSerializable` or `Serializable`.
- The class that needs to be serialized doesn't have a zero-argument constructor.

When you do need to create your own custom serializer, as you will for the Twitter example, GWT makes this a relatively easy task. For the purposes of example we'll use the DTO that we created for the GTwitter client, which would be serializable by GWT, but then make some changes so it isn't—and so you need to create a custom serializer, as shown in the following listing.

Listing 7.3 An unserializable GTwitter DTO

```
package com.gwtia.ch07.shared;

import java.util.Date;

public class BadFeedData
{
  private Date createdAt;
  private String text;

  public BadFeedData(Date createdAt) {
    this.createdAt = createdAt;
  }

  public Date getCreatedAt() {
    return createdAt;
  }

  public String getText() {
    return text;
  }

  public void setText(String text) {
    this.text = text;
  }
}
```

In listing 7.3 you take the GTwitter DTO and remove the `IsSerializable` interface and the no-arg constructor, making it GWT-incompatible. In addition you add one argument to the constructor so that you can fully exercise the capabilities of a custom serializer. Now let's look at how to create a custom serializer for the modified DTO.

A custom serializer is a class that you'll place in the same package as the DTO, with specific requirements for naming the class. You don't have any classes to extend or any interfaces to implement. Before we codify the rules, let's see what the custom serializer for this class looks like.

Listing 7.4 A custom serializer for the `BadDataFeed` DTO

```
package com.gwtia.ch07.shared;

import java.util.Date;
import com.google.gwt.user.client.rpc.*;
```

```
public class BadFeedData_CustomFieldSerializer                    ❶ Special class name
{
  public static void serialize(SerializationStreamWriter ssw,
      BadFeedData instance) throws SerializationException {
    ssw.writeObject(instance.getCreatedAt());                     ❷ Send instance
    ssw.writeString(instance.getText());                            properties to stream
  }

  public static BadFeedData instantiate(SerializationStreamReader ssr)
      throws SerializationException {
    return new BadFeedData((Date) ssr.readObject());              ❸ Instantiate new
  }                                                                 instance from stream

  public static void deserialize(SerializationStreamReader ssr,
      BadFeedData instance) throws SerializationException {
    instance.setText(ssr.readString());                           ❹ Set properties
  }                                                                 from stream
}
```

The first thing to note is that the class name is the name of the DTO plus the postfix `_CustomFieldSerializer` ❶. This scheme is the unfortunate side effect of Java 1.4. GWT was initially released without support for Java 5 language features like generics. Because of this, custom serializers make use of this naming rule.

Getting into the body of the class, you'll need to write three methods. The first is the `serialize()` method ❷. The method takes a writer and an instance and writes the properties of the instance to the writer. The writer allows you to write Java primitives, `String`s, and `Object` types. `Object` types are then serialized by their own serializer. For example, in our serializer we write a `java.util.Date` instance to the stream, and because GWT ships with its own customer serializer for `Date`, that serializer will be called in order to convert the object to a primitive value.

The order in which you write the values to the stream is important, because when you deserialize you need to read the values in the same order. In this case the DTO doesn't have a zero-arg constructor, so you need to provide an `instantiate()` method ❸. This method takes a reader and uses it to create and return a new object instance. If you had a zero-arg constructor you wouldn't need to provide this method at all, and GWT would handle creating a new instance for you. But you don't have one, so you need to handle this. When you serialize the object, you write the value of the `createdAt` field first, and that's because you need it for the constructor. Note that you call `readObject()` on the reader. Because the writer would in turn use the `Date` custom serializer to write the `Date` value, that same serializer is used to read the `Date` value.

Finally, you need to provide a `deserialize()` method ❹. The `instantiate()` method has already created the object you'll return and set the `Date` value; now you need to read in any remaining values and use them in the setters of the instance. In this case, that means you need to read the text and set the value in the instance.

As with the DTO itself, the custom serializer is shared code, used by both the server and the client. Because of this you're limited to the parts of the JRE that can be compiled to JavaScript, as you are with any GWT client code.

So now that we've explained it, let's boil this down to a simple list that you can use as a reference when you need to create your own customer serializer:

- The serializer must be in the same package as the object it serializes/deserializes.
- The name is the name of the DTO plus `_CustomFieldSerializer`.
- The required serialize method has a signature of `public static void serialize(SerializationStreamWriter ssw, T instance)`.
- The required deserialize method has a signature of `public static void deserialize(SerializationStreamReader ssr, T instance)`.
- The optional instantiate method has a signature of `public static T instantiate(SerializationStreamReader ssr)`.
- All methods may rethrow `SerializationException`.

As you've seen, depending on your project needs, your GWT-compatible model can be either extremely easy or quite complex. Fortunately, this is likely the most complex of the GWT-RPC topics, and things will fall into place from here on out.

So with that we move to the server side of the equation, which is perhaps the easiest because it's familiar territory for Java web developers.

7.5 Building and deploying the server side

In section 7.4 we defined a GWT-compatible model for our GTwitter client. Now we want to look at coding the server side of the equation and deploying it to a servlet container.

GWT makes developing the server-side code easy. The first rule is that this is the server, so anything goes. You're not limited to what the GWT compiler can accept, because your server-side code isn't processed by the GWT compiler. You can use all of your favorite Java libraries and aren't limited to specific classes in the JRE as you are with your client-side code. If you felt a bit overwhelmed by all of the rules of GWT-compatible serialized objects, this section will be a nice break.

This section assumes some familiarity with servlet containers, what a servlet is, and how to deploy an application to a servlet container. If you're unfamiliar with servlet containers, we suggest going through the process of downloading Apache Tomcat[5] and walking through some of the introductory material before continuing.

Three topics need to be addressed when writing and deploying server-side code: writing the servlet, deploying the servlet, and handling exceptions. Because the GTwitter example throws an exception, we start with handling exceptions and show how to make an exception GWT-compatible.

---

[5] Apache Tomcat downloads and documentation are available at http://tomcat.apache.org/.

7.5.1 Handling exceptions

Besides sending Java objects to and from the client, GWT supports having the server throw exceptions that are handled on the client. This is handled by enforcing the same methods we covered in section 7.4 when discussing how to make a GWT-compatible DTO. And an exception instance, from GWT's point of view, is merely another object that needs to be transported between the client and server.

To make this easier, you may use any of the exceptions provided by GWT's JRE Emulation Library without having to do anything else. These include `Throwable`, `Exception`, `IllegalArgumentException`, `NullPointerException`, and `NumberFormatException`, to name a few. In addition, because these already implement `Serializable`, you can create a subclass of these without having to do any additional work. But as you saw with DTO handling, there may be cases where you need to create a custom serializer. Again, custom serialization for exceptions is no different than handling DTOs; all the same rules apply.

Getting back to the GTwitter example, when we look at the non-GWT-compatible version we see that the Twitter4J library will throw `TwitterException` if it should fail to load the feed data for the specified user. This exception isn't part of the GWT Emulation Library and is therefore incompatible with GWT. To handle this, you can create your own `GTwitterException` and use it instead.

Listing 7.5 An application-specific exception for the GTwitter service

```
package com.gwtia.ch07.shared;

public class GTwitterException extends Exception {
    public GTwitterException() { }

    public GTwitterException(String reason) {
        super(reason);
    }
}
```

The `GTwitterException` is about as basic as they come. You extend `Exception` and provide some constructors. Because you extend `Exception`, which in turn implements `java.io.Serializable`, you meet that requirement. In addition to that, you provide a no-arg constructor to meet the remaining requirement.

As you saw with the DTO, this class lives in a package that will be compiled to JavaScript by the GWT compiler. This is because you'll be using this class on both the client and server side of the application.

Now that you have a GWT-compatible DTO and exception, let's define the service interface that will need to be implemented on the server.

7.5.2 Defining the service interface

Although creating the service interface isn't as complicated as dealing with GWT-compatible DTOs, you still have a few GWT specifics you need to deal with.

The easiest way to explain how this works is to start with a code example and then provide an explanation. The following listing shows the service for the GTwitter application.

Listing 7.6 The server-side interface for the GTwitter application

```
package com.gwtia.ch07.shared;                                              ❶ Shared package

import java.util.ArrayList;
import com.google.gwt.user.client.rpc.RemoteService;
import com.google.gwt.user.client.rpc.RemoteServiceRelativePath;         ❷ Provide the servlet path

@RemoteServiceRelativePath("service")
public interface TwitterService
    extends RemoteService                                                   ❸ Extend RemoteService
{
    public ArrayList<FeedData> getUserTimeline(String screenName)          ❹ Define the service methods
        throws GTwitterException;

}
```

This code is devilishly simple, but there's quite a bit to it. Let's explore each of part of listing 7.6.

❶ Like the DTO, the service is used by both the client side and the server side. So this class must reside in a directory that will be compiled to JavaScript by the GWT compiler.

❷ When GWT compiles the code to JavaScript and turns the service into an Ajax call, it needs to know the location of the servlet on the server. The `@RemoteServiceRelativePath` annotation allows you to do this. The value, `"service"` in this case, is appended to the result of `GWT.getModuleBaseURL()`. The URL that this translates to depends on where you deploy the compiled GWT code on your server. Most of the time this will make sense, but there are always exceptions. Because of this, this annotation is optional and can be specified when you write the client-side code. We'll look at that more in section 7.6, but for now it suits our purposes to use the annotation.

❸ Your service needs to extend `RemoteService`. This is another one of those marker interfaces, as you saw earlier when we looked at `IsSerializable`, and it doesn't require you to implement any additional methods. The purpose of this interface is to trigger the generation of the code by the GWT compiler that will do the real work of allowing you to (somewhat) transparently call your server-side service. If you want to know more about how compile-time code generation is triggered in GWT, you should read about deferred binding, covered in chapter 19.

Why does Eclipse show "Missing asynchronous interface"?

If you're developing the application using GPE, Eclipse will report the error "Missing asynchronous interface TwitterServiceAsync." The reason is that the plug-in is anticipating that you also need to create a client-side asynchronous interface. We create this interface in section 7.6. If you're coding along with the example, you can ignore this error for now.

❹ You need to define the server-side service that you'll implement. No additional rules apply here other than what we already defined. Specifically, all of the parameters, return types, and exceptions need to be compatible with GWT serialization. The GWT compiler will inspect this method during code-generation time in order to know what type serializers must be included in the resulting JavaScript output.

For this same reason it's important to be as specific as possible when specifying the types, because this will result in code bloat. For example, specifying that this method throws `Exception`, as opposed to `GTwitterException`, requires the generated code to include every available `Exception` type. So instead of only `GTwitterException`, the compiled code would include closer to 30 exception types and the code to serialize all of them.

> **NOTE** Be as specific as possible when specifying the types. Using `java.util.List` instead of `java.util.ArrayList` will force the compiler to include every `List` implementation in the JavaScript output, which results in larger files that the browser will need to download. So be specific with your types.

The flip side of that coin is that if your code were to throw a `NullPointerException`, it wouldn't be serialized and sent to the client as such. Instead it would be returned as a generic failure. So be as specific as possible, but be sure to include every exception that you'd want sent to the client.

> **NOTE** When compiling GWT code to JavaScript, you can use the -gen <DIR> switch to tell the compiler to output the generated Java code to the specified directory. This will include generated field serializers, type serializers, and RPC proxy code. Besides this being a way to get a handle on what's being generated, it's also a great way to learn about the inner workings of GWT-RPC.

Now that we've defined the service, we can write the server-side servlet that will act as an implementation of our service.

7.5.3 Writing the servlet

When using GWT-RPC, the server-side code takes the form of a servlet, although it doesn't look much like one. For many of us, using Spring, Struts, or other servlets may be a relic of the past, because our favorite framework provides an abstraction above the basic servlet. GWT-RPC is the same, and although it's a servlet, it doesn't resemble one.

Let's start the conversation as we've done before, presenting the code up front followed by a detailed explanation. The next listing presents our GTwitter servlet implementation.

Listing 7.7 The server-side implementation of the GTwitter client

```
package com.gwtia.ch07.server;

import java.util.ArrayList;
import twitter4j.*;
import com.google.gwt.user.server.rpc.RemoteServiceServlet;
```

```
import com.gwtia.ch07.shared.*;

public class TwitterServiceImpl
  extends RemoteServiceServlet implements TwitterService
{

  public ArrayList<FeedData> getUserTimeline (String screenName)
    throws GTwitterException
  {

    ArrayList<FeedData> result = new ArrayList<FeedData>();
    Twitter twitter = new TwitterFactory().getInstance();

    try {
      ResponseList<Status> responses
        = twitter.getUserTimeline(screenName);

      for (Status status : responses) {
        result.add(
          new FeedData(status.getCreatedAt(), status.getText()));
      }
    }
    catch (TwitterException e) {
      throw new GTwitterException(e.getMessage());
    }

    return result;
  }
}
```

❷ Defines superclass and service interface

❸ Create Twitter instance

❹ Fetch timeline

❺ Copies data into a GWT-RPC-compatible DTO

❻ Rethrows as GWT-RPC-compatible exception

Listing 7.7 is a little longer than the original non-GWT version of this code that we provided in section 7.3, so let's look at what's going on.

❶ This class lives in the server package of your project. Specifically, the rule is that this class can live in any package *not* compiled to JavaScript by the GWT compiler. The reason is that server-side GWT-RPC code uses classes outside of the JRE Emulation Library and therefore is unable to be compiled to JavaScript.

❷ When you define the class, you need to extend `RemoteServiceServlet`. This is the GWT servlet that handles the incoming request from the client, deserializes the incoming data, and executes your method. In addition, you implement the `TwitterService` interface that you created in the previous section. The `RemoteServiceServlet` uses reflection to read your interface definition so that it knows what methods may be called remotely, meaning that it won't allow calls to methods not defined in your interface.

The code you use to get the tweets from Twitter is the same as it was in the non-GWT version of the code. You use the Twitter4J library's `Twitterfactory` to create a `Twitter` session ❸ and then call `getUserTimeline()` to fetch the tweets for that user ❹.

❺ Once you have the list of `Status` objects, you need to convert them to a GWT-compatible DTO. In this case you copy them into the `FeedData` objects defined in section 7.4. The need to copy data, particularly complex data, is one of the major complaints with GWT-RPC. One popular remedy for this is to use Dozer,[6] a library that provides the tools to copy data between objects of different types. If you find a need to copy complex data structures, you may want to consider using Dozer.

❻ When you're using the Twitter4J library, it will throw a `TwitterException` if it's unable to fetch the requested data. This could occur in your application if someone requested tweets for a screen name that doesn't exist. Here you convert the `TwitterException` into your `GTwitterException`. Recalling the earlier discussion on serialization, you need to do this because `TwitterException` isn't serializable by GWT, and you therefore can't pass this exception back to the client. Your exception, on the other hand, is serializable by GWT and is defined in your service interface, so exceptions of this type will be sent to the client.

And there you have it, a GWT-RPC servlet. As you can see, the fact that you're using GWT or a servlet is hidden rather well. You can even test our method without a servlet container at all. Listing 7.8 provides some test code that you can add to your GWT servlet so that you can also run it as an application.

Listing 7.8 Test code to verify the functionality of the GTwitter server

```
public static void main(String[] args) throws Exception
{
  TwitterService impl = new TwitterServiceImpl();
  ArrayList<FeedData> resList = impl.getUserTimeline("ianchesnut");

  for (FeedData status : resList) {
      System.out.println(status.getCreatedAt() + " " + status.getText());
  }
}
```

Executing this code will result in output similar to what you see here, which shows several tweets displayed along with the date and time they were posted:

```
Sat Mar 21 21:39:43 EDT 2009 Super test
Sat Mar 21 21:13:22 EDT 2009 test already
Sat Mar 21 21:12:48 EDT 2009 Test again
```

This is basic output, but it shows that our code works. That's good enough for us right now until we develop the client side of our application. So now that we have our servlet, we'll want to deploy it to a servlet container.

7.5.4 Deploying the servlet

As noted throughout this book, when you create a new GWT project, it creates a war directory at the top level of the project. This is your web root, where the files destined to be deployed are stored. Within this directory is a WEB-INF folder that contains the servlet deployment descriptor file web.xml.

---

6 Dozer is available at http://dozer.sourceforge.net/.

To configure the servlet, open this file, war/WEB-INF/web.xml, and add the servlet configuration. The following listing shows the full web.xml after making our changes.

Listing 7.9 Servlet deployment descriptor for the GTwitter application

```
<?xml version="1.0" encoding="UTF-8"?>
<!DOCTYPE web-app
    PUBLIC "-//Sun Microsystems, Inc.//DTD Web Application 2.3//EN"
    "http://java.sun.com/dtd/web-app_2_3.dtd">

<web-app>
  <servlet>
    <servlet-name>twitterServlet</servlet-name>
    <servlet-class>
      com.gwtia.ch07.server.TwitterServiceImpl
    </servlet-class>
  </servlet>                                                   ❶ Define servlet

  <servlet-mapping>
    <servlet-name>twitterServlet</servlet-name>
    <url-pattern>/GTwitter/service</url-pattern>
  </servlet-mapping>                                           ❷ Define mapping

  <welcome-file-list>
    <welcome-file>GTwitter.html</welcome-file>
  </welcome-file-list>                                         ❸ Define the welcome file
</web-app>
```

If you're following along, and you used the Eclipse plug-in or command-line tool to create the basic app structure, you'll see that you stripped out the example servlet configuration and are left with only what you need for this project. What's left are three important sections, so we'll explain each.

❶ The `<servlet>` element is used to register a servlet with the servlet container. Here you give the servlet an arbitrary name with the `<servlet-name>` element, in this case `twitterServlet`, and provide the full package and class name of the servlet in the `<servlet-class>` element.

❷ Next, you need to map the registered servlet to a URL, and that's where the `<servlet-mapping>` comes into play. Here you specify the same `<servlet-name>` that you used in the `<servlet>` element. This is what ties this mapping to that servlet. In addition, you use `<url-pattern>` to specify the path to the servlet. The URL that you specify is relative to the servlet context, or the root of the project. The path is the directory where the project is deployed plus the name you specified in the `@RemoteServiceRelativePath` annotation in the service interface. In this case the GWT application is deployed to /gtwitter, and the path used in the annotation was service, which gives you the resulting path shown in listing 7.9.

❸ The last item in your web.xml is a pointer to the welcome file. If configuring servlets is new to you, this is the file that's served if the user navigates to / on the application. It's the default page when none is defined.

TIP The most common cause for a non-working GWT-RPC service is when the URL pattern defined in the mapping doesn't match the URL used by the client application. In section 7.7 we show you how to verify the URL used by the client when we discuss how to debug remote calls.

With the servlet written and registered in the servlet descriptor, we can move on to coding the client to call the service.

7.6 Writing the client

We're almost at the end—only two steps left. As you might expect, we need to write the code that calls the server and receives the result. As we explained earlier, a GWT-RPC call is made asynchronously. And you may have noticed that the service interface that we created for the server side won't work for an asynchronous call. The reason is that it doesn't allow for a callback, meaning that there's no way to handle the result that's returned at some time after the call is made. We need to start by creating one last interface, which will allow for a callback.

7.6.1 Defining the asynchronous interface

The asynchronous interface is the interface that the client side is coded to. It's a mirror image of the service interface you already defined, assuming that the mirror you use is one of those funhouse mirrors. Specifically, it's an altered version of the service interface, altered in a specific way. The next listing contains the code for this interface.

Listing 7.10 Asynchronous interface used by the client side of the GTwitter application

```
package com.gwtia.ch07.shared;

import java.util.ArrayList;
import com.google.gwt.user.client.rpc.AsyncCallback;

public interface TwitterServiceAsync                    ❶ Interface name
{
  void getUserTimeline(String screenName,               ❷ Returns void
      AsyncCallback<ArrayList<FeedData>> callback);     ❸ Add AsyncCallback
}
```

This looks a lot like the service interface, but with two differences. The first is the name of the interface. The asynchronous interface uses the same name as the service interface plus `Async` ❶. So the `TwitterService` service interface will have a `TwitterServiceAsync` asynchronous interface. This interface must also reside in the same package as the service interface.

Second is the method definition. All methods in the asynchronous interface must return `void` ❷ and have an additional `AsyncCallback` parameter added ❸. The `AsyncCallback` uses generics, so you'll need to specify the return type here. If the return type of the method is `void`, you'll specify `java.lang.Void`.

Of interest here is that this method doesn't declare any exceptions. That's because the handling of the server side is taken care of by the `AsyncCallback`. We'll look at the

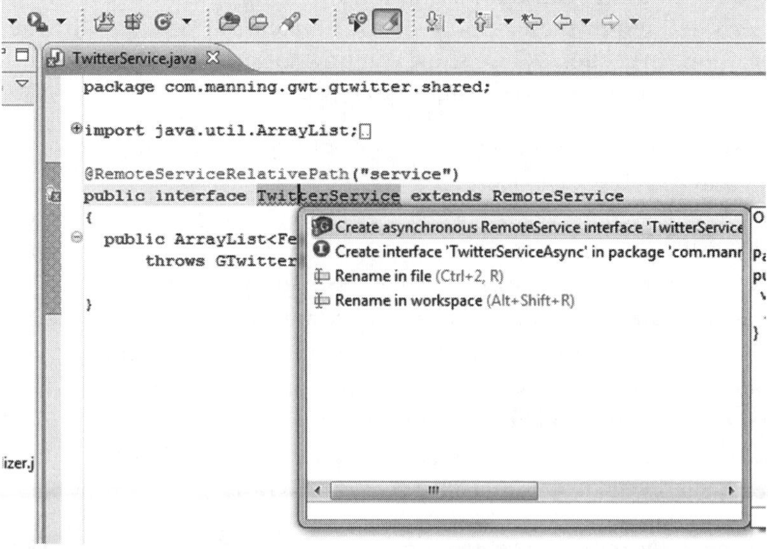

Figure 7.3 Using the quick-fix menu in Eclipse can save you typing by creating the asynchronous interface for you.

callback code shortly, but for now let's recap the set of steps to create the asynchronous interface:

1. Copy the service to a new file with the same name plus Async (for example, Foo to FooAsync).
2. Add an `AsyncCallback` parameter to each method, as the last parameter, using the method's return type as the generic's type (for example, `AsyncCallback<Foo>`).
3. Change the return type of all methods to `void`.
4. Remove any exceptions declared on methods in the service interface.

If you're using GPE, you can use an autofix function to create this interface for you and save yourself some typing as well as reduce the possibility of introducing a bug. Eclipse provides several ways to do this. One way is to open the service interface `TwitterService`, click the interface name, and press Ctrl+1 (one, not L). This will open the quick-fix menu. Select the first option, Create Asynchronous RemoteService Interface 'TwitterServiceAsync', as shown in figure 7.3.

At this point we've created everything except the client-side code that will make the call. Let's look at that now.

7.6.2 Making the call to the server

For simplicity's sake, we'll build an overly simple client in order to show off how to call a GWT-RPC service. Figure 7.4 shows what the final application looks like in the browser.

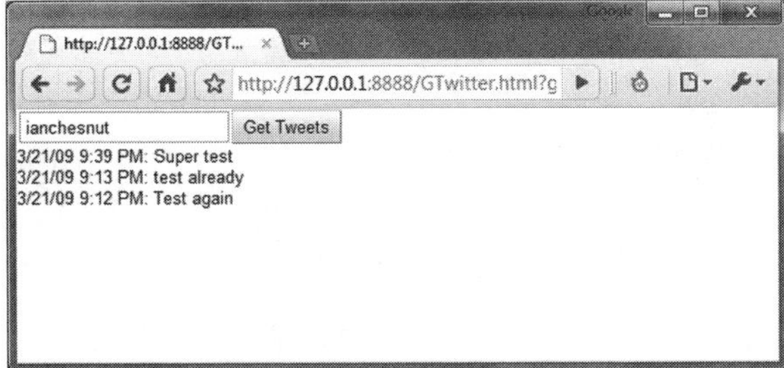

Figure 7.4 The finished GTwitter application running in the Google Chrome browser

As you can see, it's basic. It includes a `TextBox` for input, a `Button` for activation, and a `VerticalPanel` for output. The next listing shows the start of the application.

Listing 7.11 Basic structure for the GTwitter application's `EntryPoint`

```
package com.gwtia.ch07.client;

import java.util.ArrayList;

... imports omitted for brevity ...

public class GTwitter implements EntryPoint {
  private TextBox txtScreenName = new TextBox();
  private Button btnGetTweets = new Button("Get Tweets");
  private VerticalPanel tweetPanel = new VerticalPanel();

  public void onModuleLoad() {
    RootPanel.get().add(txtScreenName);
    RootPanel.get().add(btnGetTweets);
    RootPanel.get().add(tweetPanel);

    // final AsyncCallback<ArrayList<FeedData>>
    //  updateTweetPanelCallback = ...

    // btnGetTweets.addClickHandler(new ClickHandler() { ... }
  }
}
```

This is a basic application, and the purpose is to explore GWT-RPC, so we won't provide any further explanation here. You need to add two things to complete the application, as noted by the commented lines in listing 7.11. First, you need to create an implementation of `AsyncCallback` that will receive the result from the server, and second, you need to add a `ClickHandler` to the `Button` to trigger the server call.

We'll tackle the `AsyncCallback` first. The following listing shows the code for this; it's added to the body of the `onModuleLoad` on the `EntryPoint`.

Listing 7.12 The `AsyncCallback` that will receive the GTwitter data from the server

```
final AsyncCallback<ArrayList<FeedData>> updateTweetPanelCallback
  = new AsyncCallback<ArrayList<FeedData>>() {
```

Anonymous AsyncCallback declaration ❶

```
  public void onFailure(Throwable e) {                          Handles
    Window.alert("Error: " + e.getMessage());                ❷ exceptions
  }

  public void onSuccess(ArrayList<FeedData> results) {       Handles receipt
    tweetPanel.clear();                                    ❸ of result data
    for (FeedData status : results) {
      PredefinedFormat fmt = PredefinedFormat.TIME_SHORT;
      String dateStr =
        DateTimeFormat.getFormat(fmt).format(status.getCreatedAt());

      tweetPanel.add(new Label(dateStr + ": " + status.getText()));
    }
  }
};
```

As you saw when we developed the asynchronous interface, all calls to the server require an `AsyncCallback` parameter, typed to the data type being returned from the server. Let's walk through listing 7.12 and examine the details.

❶ In this example you create the callback as an anonymous class. You could create a separate class for this, but an anonymous class works well for the purposes of this example. You also declare the variable as `final`, which isn't a requirement of GWT; it's a requirement of Java because of how you use this variable in the `ClickHandler` code that we'll look at soon. Notice that the type of your `AsyncCallback` matches the last parameter of the `getUserTimeline()` of the asynchronous interface.

❷ You need to implement two methods for the callback, the first of which is `onFailure`. This method will be called if the server throws a checked exception (in this case the `GTwitterException`), or if any number of other errors occur, for example, if the target service is unavailable. In our code we show the error in an alert box.

❸ The second method you need to implement is `onSuccess`, which will receive the results from the server on a successful call. Notice that the parameter type is keyed on the type you used in the `AsyncCallback` declaration, in this case `ArrayList<FeedData>`. When you receive the callback, you clear the `VerticalPanel` used to display the results and fill it with the results from the server.

Now that you've defined the handler for the response, you can make the call to the server in the `ClickHandler` of your application's action button, as shown in the next listing.

Listing 7.13 Calling the GTwitter service from within a button `ClickHandler`

```
btnGetTweets.addClickHandler(new ClickHandler() {              Create the async ❶
                                                                implementation
  public void onClick(ClickEvent event) {
    TwitterServiceAsync service = GWT.create(TwitterService.class);

    service.getUserTimeline(txtScreenName.getText(),          ❷ Call the remote
        updateTweetPanelCallback);                               method
  }
});
```

In your handler, which is attached to your action button, you trigger the call to the server. Some explanation of what's going on here is in order.

❶ First, you create an instance of the `TwitterServiceAsync` interface by calling `GWT.create()`, passing the service interface class object as the parameter. The implementation returned is the class that will handle the serialization of the parameters, the call to the server, and the deserialization of the result.

Under the hood this is all driven by GWT's deferred-binding feature. Specifically there's a deferred binding that triggers code generation when the class passed to `GWT.create()` extends the `RemoteService` interface. When this is encountered by the GWT compiler, it kicks off a code generator that generates the asynchronous interface implementation as well as the serialization and deserialization classes to handle the calls defined in the interface. Although you don't need to understand deferred binding to use GWT-RPC, it does help with understanding how this works. Deferred binding is covered in chapter 19.

❷ You then make the call to `getUserTimeline`, passing your callback object as the second parameter, which starts a chain of events that will result in a call to the `onError` or `onSuccess` method of the `AsyncCallback`.

One thing to note is that the service returned by `GWT.create()` also implements `ServiceDefTarget`. This interface is used to alter how the generated service works, including setting the URL of the service. For example, here is an altered version of the server call that we already presented.

Listing 7.14 Calling the server service with an explicit server URL

```
import com.google.gwt.user.client.rpc.ServiceDefTarget;
...
TwitterServiceAsync service = GWT.create(TwitterService.class);
((ServiceDefTarget) service).setServiceEntryPoint(GWT.getModuleBaseURL()
  + "service");

service.getUserTimeline(txtScreenName.getText(),
    updateTweetPanelCallback);
}
```

The only thing new here is that you cast the service to `ServiceDefTarget` and call the `setServiceEntryPoint` method, passing the URL to the servlet that will handle the request. This can be used instead of, or to override, the `@RemoteServiceRelativePath` annotation that we put in our service in section 7.5.

In addition, you can also use this interface to specify a custom `RequestBuilder`, a lower-level API used to make the call to the server. This allows you to make changes to how requests are made, including setting custom header values and credentials. We'll discuss `RequestBuilder` in chapter 12.

If you've been following along, you now have a finished application. It's time to launch it and take it for a test drive. We expect that everything went well and it works out of the box, but if not, this next section is for you.

7.7 Debugging GWT-RPC

There are a lot of ways to debug your GWT application. Speed Tracer,[7] a plug-in for Chrome, can provide you information on the headers sent between client and server as well as execution times. Wireshark,[8] an open source packet sniffer, will show you all of the network traffic, allowing you to inspect interaction RPC calls over the network. Eclipse can execute your application in debug mode, allowing you to step through the application line by line.

All of them are great at what they do, but Firebug, a Firefox add-on, possibly provides the most benefit for debugging GWT-RPC calls. You can learn about and download Firebug from http://getfirebug.com/.

The Firebug website has a great video to introduce you to the tool, but this isn't a book about Firebug, so we'll only cover the bits of Firebug that apply to GWT-RPC. Figure 7.5 shows Firefox with the Firebug panel opened.

With regard to accessing network resources, Firebug will show you the URLs accessed by your browser. This is useful if you want to verify that your client-side code is hitting the correct URL on the server.

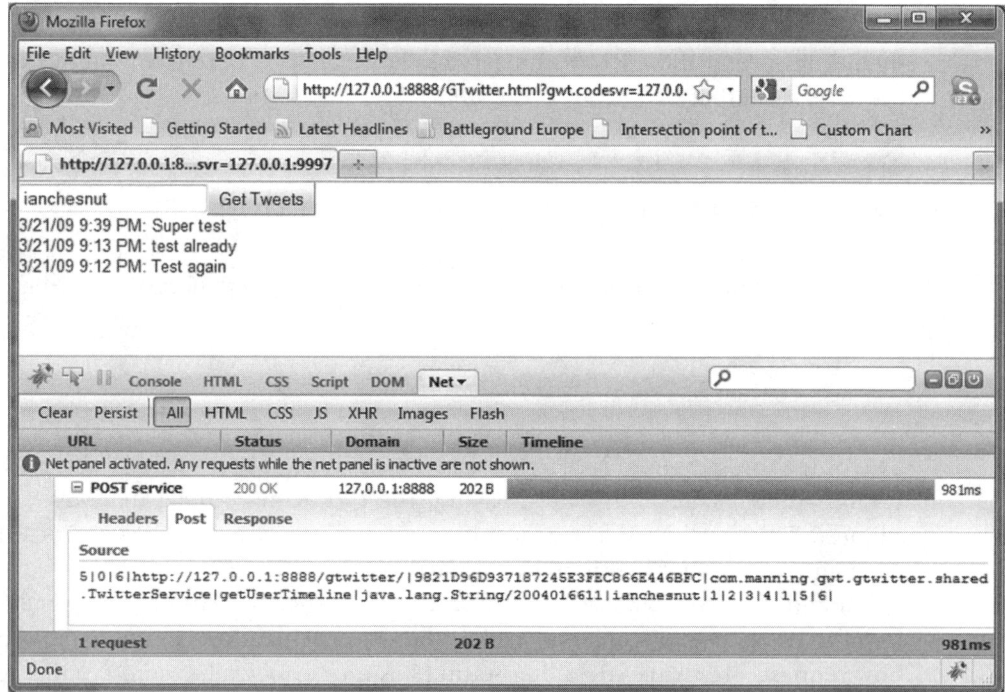

Figure 7.5 The finished GTwitter application as it runs in Firefox, with the Firebug panel opened

---

7 Speed Tracer can be found at http://code.google.com/webtoolkit/speedtracer/.

8 Wireshark is available at www.wireshark.org/.

When browsing a single request from the browser, you can then view the request/response headers and the content passed. Assuming the service URL is correct and hit the server, the most useful information is the contents of the request and reply. It's important to understand that the format of the serialization of GWT is unpublished and changes from time to time, but it's still fairly human readable. For example, it's easy to pick out the method name that was called by the client and the general contents of the reply.

So if you need to ask the question, "Am I hitting the right URL?," "Am I passing the data I think I am to the server?," or "Is the server sending me what I think it is?," then Firebug is a good tool for the job.

Next up is something that we don't talk too much about in this book, and that's security. We've opted to not make this a book about security because it's a deep topic, one that we hope you'll explore thoroughly, but in this case GWT provides some explicit support that's worth sharing.

7.8 Securing GWT-RPC against XSRF attacks

XSRF (or CSRF) is short for cross-site request forgery, and it's an attack that could allow an attacker access to your web mail, your social networking account, or even your bank account. If you haven't come across this term before, we suggest that you do some additional research, but let's see if we can describe it briefly.

7.8.1 Understanding XSRF attacks

To help you better understand how an XSRF attack works, let's examine a hypothetical situation. Pretend you're a high-ranking executive for company X-Ray Alpha Delta, and you're logged in to the top-secret extranet application doing some product research. Once you log in to the top-secret application, it keeps track of who you are by giving you a web cookie. Using cookies as a way of handling user sessions is a common tool used by most secured web applications.

As you're working on the top-secret extranet, you receive an email prompting you to review some competitor content on the internet. You click the link and start reading the page, which seems to be a legitimate news site. Unknown to you, the "news" site is running JavaScript in your browser and is making requests against your top-secret extranet.

This is possible because your browser automatically passes your session ID contained in a cookie to the top-secret extranet server, even though the JavaScript calling the server originated from the "news" site. Now understand that this isn't a bug in your browser; it's the way browsers work. The XSRF attack is taking advantage of how browsers work, which is why this type of attack is so problematic.

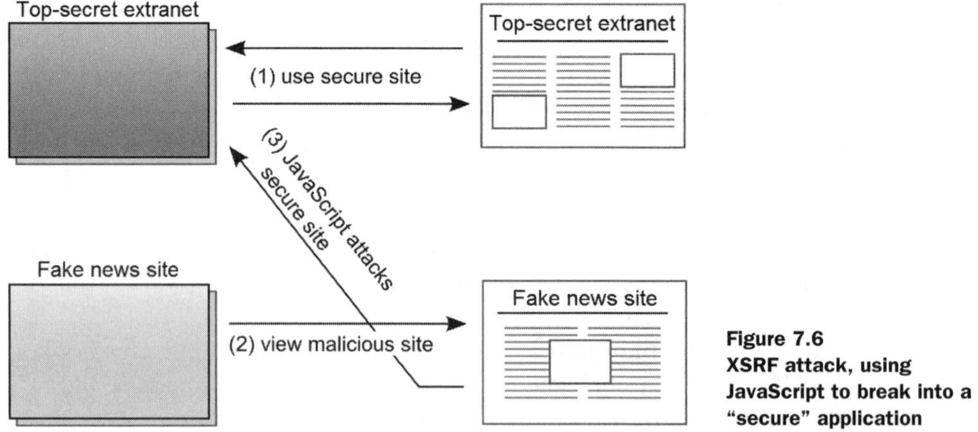

Figure 7.6 XSRF attack, using JavaScript to break into a "secure" application

Figure 7.6 shows the order of events in such an attack, allowing the malicious JavaScript access to the "protected" site.

The one advantage that you do have is that the attacker is making blind calls to the server. The attacker can trigger a call to a secured web page but won't be able to read the result. So an attacker couldn't use an XSRF attack to read an email on your web mail site, but it could call a method on the server that the attacker knows will change your password.

It's the fact that these attacks are blind that allows us to prevent them.

7.8.2 Adding XSRF protection to your RPC calls

Because XSRF takes advantage of your browser automatically sending your session ID to the server, you can't rely on that alone. What you need is a second key, but one that your browser won't automatically send.

The mechanism that GWT-RPC can be enabled to use is to make an additional call to the server to get a second secret key and then have your normal server calls pass this extra key in the request. Now it's true that someone could trigger a XSRF attack to call the server service that creates the secret key, but as we said earlier an attacker can't read the result of the call, so they won't be able to gain access to this key.

> **Warning: this code won't work!**
>
> GWT-RPC's XSRF protection requires that the browser have the ability to pass a cookie value to the server, and for real protection this needs to be tied somehow to the application authentication. In almost all Java deployment scenarios, this cookie name is JSESSIONID. In a typical application, the JSESSIONID cookie value allows the application server to tie the user to a Java `HttpSession` in memory, which in turn has the user's authentication information. A problem, however, is that when you run the example code in Eclipse without any login mechanism, the Jetty server doesn't create

(continued)

an HttpSession or pass a JSESSIONID to the server. To counter this, our example code in the source download includes a ForceSessionCreationFilter that will make sure that a JSESSIONID is issued to the client browser. Please review the source code download for details on how we did this.

To implement the protection, you have to make changes to three parts, and all of the changes are relatively minor. In the sections that follow we'll show you how to implement the change on the server, on the service interface, and in the call you make to the server.

ENABLING XSRF PROTECTION ON THE SERVER

Enabling XSRF protection on the server side is as simple as swapping out RemoteServiceServlet and replacing it with XsrfProtectedServiceServlet. Back in section 7.5.3 you might recall that we implemented the class TwitterServiceImpl, which is the server-side servlet that's the target of GWT-RPC calls from the client. In the example we had that class extend RemoteServiceServlet, which provides the glue that connects incoming GWT-RPC calls to our class. The class XsrfProtectedServiceServlet is a drop-in replacement for RemoteServiceServlet, so all you need to do is change the class declaration, as shown in the following listing.

Listing 7.15 The GTwitter server-side implementation, now supporting XSRF protection

```
package com.manning.gwtia.ch07.server;

import com.google.gwt.user.server.rpc.XsrfProtectedServiceServlet;
...other imports omitted...

public class TwitterServiceImpl extends XsrfProtectedServiceServlet
    implements TwitterService
{
  ...implementation omitted...
}
```

As you can see, it's that simple; have your server-side code extend XsrfProtectedServiceServlet, and you're finished with this class.

But you do need to make some changes to the deployment descriptor. The next listing provides an updated version of our project's web.xml file, annotated to show the new additions.

Listing 7.16 An updated web.xml with additions for supporting XSRF protection

```
<?xml version="1.0" encoding="UTF-8"?>
<!DOCTYPE web-app
    PUBLIC "-//Sun Microsystems, Inc.//DTD Web Application 2.3//EN"
    "http://java.sun.com/dtd/web-app_2_3.dtd">
<web-app>
```

```
<context-param>
  <param-name>gwt.xsrf.session_cookie_name</param-name>
  <param-value>JSESSIONID</param-value>
</context-param>

<servlet>
  <servlet-name>twitterServlet</servlet-name>
  <servlet-class>
    com.manning.gwtia.ch07.server.TwitterServiceImpl
  </servlet-class>
</servlet>

<servlet>
  <servlet-name>xsrf</servlet-name>
  <servlet-class>
    com.google.gwt.user.server.rpc.XsrfTokenServiceServlet
  </servlet-class>
</servlet>

<servlet-mapping>
  <servlet-name>twitterServlet</servlet-name>
  <url-pattern>/gwtia_ch07_gwtrpc/service</url-pattern>
</servlet-mapping>

<servlet-mapping>
  <servlet-name>xsrf</servlet-name>
  <url-pattern>/gwtia_ch07_gwtrpc/xsrf</url-pattern>
</servlet-mapping>
</web-app>
```

1 Specify session cookie name

2 Add XSRF token service

3 Map XSRF service

The first thing you must add to the web descriptor is the name of the cookie that holds the key to the user's authentication information on the server 1. In most cases this will be JSESSIONID, which is the standard for Java servlet containers.

To understand how this works, let's connect the dots. Let's assume that you use Spring Security to serve all of your services on the server. Spring Security does this by using a servlet filter that analyzes each URL that the browser is requesting, determining what the user does and doesn't have access to. Spring Security, like most Java applications, stores the authentication information in the in-memory `HttpSession` instance for that user. And the servlet container (such as Jetty or Tomcat) associates the `HttpSession` with the individual request.

Running that in the reverse order, that means the browser sends a JSESSIONID cookie value to the server, which then uses that as a key that allows it to associate the request with an `HttpSession`, which in turn is used by Spring Security to ensure the user is allowed to access the requested resource. Simple, right?

The next thing you need to do is configure the `XsrfTokenServiceServlet` 2 using the `<servlet>` tag and map it to some path 3 using a `<servlet-mapping>`. The `XsrfTokenServiceServlet` is a GWT-RPC service that will allow you to request a token from the server. More on that in a bit. All you need to know at this point is that you've installed the service and mapped it to the path /gwtia_ch07_gwtrpc/xsrf.

At this point you can run your application and it should work fine, but realize that you haven't protected anything yet. You need to do that on the service interface.

ENABLING XSRF PROTECTION ON THE SERVICE INTERFACE

In our GTwitter example we created an interface called `TwitterService`, which extended the `RemoteService` interface. You can force XSRF in two ways; the first is to secure individual methods by using annotations, and the second is to require XSRF protection for all methods by changing the interface that your service extends. The second way is the easiest and in many cases is the right thing to do, so we'll visit that one first.

The following listing presents an updated version of `TwitterService`, which now forces XSRF protection on all methods.

Listing 7.17 An updated `TwitterService` with XSRF protection

```
package com.manning.gwtia.ch07.shared;

import com.google.gwt.user.client.rpc.XsrfProtectedService;
...other imports omitted...

@RemoteServiceRelativePath("service")
public interface TwitterService extends XsrfProtectedService
{
  ...implementation omitted...
}
```

The change in the previous listing, as with the server implementation, is subtle. The only change made to the interface is to change the interface that you extend. Where the version without XSRF protection implements `RemoteService`, it now implements `XsrfProtectedService`. By having your service interface extend `XsrfProtected-Service`, you're now requiring that all method calls include a token, which acts as a key. If the token passed along with the server call is valid, the server will accept it; if it's invalid, it's rejected.

Before we show you how the tokens work, let's first concentrate on what we have here. As we mentioned, all methods are now secured, but what if for some reason XSRF protection is enforced only for some methods while leaving others unsecured? For that you can use method-level annotations.

For those rare occasions when you need to protect only some of the methods in your interface, you can extend `XsrfProtectedService` and turn off protection on individual methods by using the annotation `@NoXsrfProtect`. Alternatively, you can go the opposite way and have your service interface extend `RemoteService`, which provides no protection, and then mark methods that should be protected with `@XsrfProtect`.

Now that the methods are protected, you'll find that the GTwitter application no longer works. Each GWT-RPC request will come back with the error message "Invalid RPC token (XSRF token missing)." If you get this, it means that your methods are now secured. Next, let's look at how to change the GWT-RPC call from the client side.

ADDING XSRF PROTECTION IN YOUR CLIENT-SIDE RPC CALLS

XSRF protection changes how you make calls from the server. Where you were making only a single call, you now need to make two. The first call to the server is to fetch a token. The default implementation takes the cookie value passed to the server and creates an MD5 hash from it, returning the result to the client. The client then uses this token as a key for calling the target GWT-RPC method.

The next listing shows the changes to the client-side call from our GTwitter application. Following the listing we discuss what's going on in the code.

Listing 7.18 Updated GTwitter client using XSRF token to unlock the service method

```
XsrfTokenServiceAsync xsrf = GWT.create(XsrfTokenService.class);     ❶ Create token service

((ServiceDefTarget)xsrf).setServiceEntryPoint(
    GWT.getModuleBaseURL() + "xsrf");

xsrf.getNewXsrfToken(new AsyncCallback<XsrfToken>() {               ❷ Call token service

  public void onSuccess (XsrfToken token)
  {
    TwitterServiceAsync service = GWT.create(TwitterService.class);
    ((HasRpcToken) service).setRpcToken(token);                      ❸ Set token

    service.getUserTimeline(
       txtScreenName.getText(), updateTweetPanelCallback);
  }

  public void onFailure (Throwable caught)
  {
    try {
      throw caught;
    }
    catch (RpcTokenException e) {
      Window.alert("Error: " + e.getMessage());
    }
    catch (Throwable e) {
      Window.alert("Error: " + e.getMessage());
    }
  }
});
```

For brevity, listing 7.18 includes only the code that's changed. If you want to review the rest of the class, you should refer back to section 7.6.2. Listing 7.18 should look familiar, because it's a GWT-RPC call. What's different is that you nest the original call inside the `onSuccess()` method. That's useful to understand, but let's talk specifics.

In order to get a token, you use `GWT.create()` to get a service for `XsrfTokenService` ❶ and set the end point, which in this case is the module base URL plus /xsrf. This matches the mapping that you added to the web.xml for the `XsrfTokenServiceServlet`.

You then use the service to call the method `getNewXsrfToken()` ❷. The purpose of this method is to call the server, which will then return a token to the client.

In the `onSuccess()` method of the callback, you use the token as a parameter to `setRpcToken()` on your `TwitterService` method call ❸. The `setRpcToken()` method is made available by casting the `TwitterService` asynchronous implementation to `HasRpcToken`. You then call your service method as usual, but now it will include the token that will be used like a key to unlock the service.

At this point we want to point out that this code only works if your browser passes a JSESSIONID cookie to the server, which is then turned into the token. If you see errors on the server saying "Session cookie is not set or empty," go back to the beginning of section 7.8.2 and review the sidebar titled "Warning: this code won't work!"

As an alternative for the purposes of testing, you could also add this code snippet to your application, which generates a random value and sets the JSESSIONID cookie:

```
if (Cookies.getCookie("JSESSIONID") == null)
  Cookies.setCookie("JSESSIONID", Double.toString(Math.random()));
```

This isn't ideal to have in production code, because it's better to be able to tie the session ID to the user's authentication, but it works great for testing this example. For more information on GWT and security, we recommend that you visit the security section of the online documents for GWT. It's fairly comprehensive and goes beyond what we discuss in this book.

With that, we need to wrap up our tour of GWT-RPC. So let's review what we covered in this chapter.

7.9 Summary

In the last few dozen pages we showed you everything you need to know about GWT-RPC, but it was a long journey. You might be asking how this helps you simplify your GWT applications over other remoting methods. We could take a mother's approach and say that you should take your medicine because it's good for you. But we're all big boys and girls now and can make our own decisions.

The biggest benefit of using GWT is that you can use Java objects throughout, sharing data objects on both the client and server and reducing the code you need to write because all the serialization is handled for you. But you will pay a price for less code, and it's in complexity. In order for GWT to generate the serialization code for you, it needs you to provide enough information so that it can do its job. This could be as simple as tacking on the `IsSerializable` interface to your DTOs, or it could require you to create custom serializers.

As programmers we know that the best way to deal with complexity is practice. The more you practice, the easier it gets, and over time it becomes habitual, requiring little thought to accomplish. We never said that GWT-RPC is the right solution for every problem. That's an architectural decision that you'll need to make on each and every project.

Getting beyond the reasons for using GWT-RPC, in this chapter we reviewed the four components of GWT-RPC that you need to build yourself: the model, the servlet, the service interface, and the asynchronous service interface. We provided tips on debugging and showed you how to handle serialization of JPA and JDO entities, how to deploy to your GWT-RPC servlet, how to lay out your project, and much more.

Next, we'll look at another tool in GWT's repertoire for managing entities: RequestFactory.

8 Using RequestFactory

This chapter covers

- Creating RequestFactory-compatible domain objects
- Generating, editing, and deleting domain objects
- Handling errors using Java's Bean Validation framework

GWT provides several ways for your data to communicate between the client and server. In chapter 7 we explored GWT-RPC, which as you saw is a great general-purpose tool that allows you to transport a Java object between client and server. In this chapter we move to a relative of GWT-RPC named RequestFactory. And this raises the question, how is RequestFactory different than GWT-RPC?

GWT-RPC was designed to be a generic service-based mechanism, whereas RequestFactory was designed to work specifically with data objects, which are usually database-persisted objects. So although you can use GWT-RPC with the database, certain aspects of it can make it a difficult fit for your project. Key features of RequestFactory include the following:

- No shared domain classes, facilitating easier integration with existing projects
- No servlet to write, and easier integration with dependency injection containers
- Only data diffs are communicated, providing improved performance

By "no shared domain" we mean that the domain classes live only on the server and aren't accessed directly by code running in the browser. On the client side you instead use proxy classes, which GWT generates at compile time based on an interface contract.

When you fetch data from the server, RequestFactory copies the data into the proxy instance, and when you save a proxy, RequestFactory copies it back to the server-side model. Because you aren't sharing classes, you have almost no restrictions on your server-side classes. In contrast, with GWT-RPC you use your domain objects on both the client and server sides, so you can use GWT-compatible code and it must be serializable.

With RequestFactory you don't need to write a servlet because it already provides one, whereas with GWT-RPC you have to provide one. The provided servlet knows how to turn a request from the client into a service call on the server. But there's a contract, and you'll need to create an interface to define the service methods that are available, much as you did with GWT-RPC.

When we say that only data diffs are communicated, we mean that RequestFactory is only able to send updated properties instead of the entire object. It does this by making use of a data object version number, where it only needs to transport the entire object if the version number has changed. With GWT-RPC the entire object is always transported, which makes RequestFactory more efficient.

> **NOTE** A common source of confusion when learning about RequestFactory is the fact that there are two RequestFactorys. The first is the RequestFactory framework, which consists of various Java interfaces, Java classes, and a code generator. The second is `RequestFactory`, the interface. `RequestFactory` the interface is part of the RequestFactory framework. Confusing for sure, so we'll try to make it clear which one we're referring to throughout the chapter.

You can deploy RequestFactory in two different ways, and we'll cover both in this chapter. The first requires less coding, which we refer to as the "simple way," but it requires that your server-side domain classes follow some rules. In particular you'll need to add your service code along with some RequestFactory-specific methods in your domain classes. For some this is a deal breaker and is way too invasive, which is when you'll want to use the second way.

The second way, which we refer to as the "long way," allows you to move your service methods and RequestFactory-required methods into external classes called `ServiceLocator` and `Locator`. This way requires a little extra coding, but it allows you to completely separate GWT infrastructure code from your domain class.

This chapter opens with an overview of the architecture, followed by the "simple way" of doing things. In this section we'll also apply JSR-303, Bean Validation, using annotations on the server to validate fields on the client.

Once you have an understanding of RequestFactory basics, we'll move on to creating locators so that our model classes have no idea that they're being passed to a GWT client (the "long way").

For our example in this chapter we'll show you how to create the tooling required to pass contact information, as you'd find in an address book, to and from the server. An address book application isn't all that glamorous, but it's a great learning tool. Fred Sauer, the creator of several popular GWT libraries (such as gwt-dnd), told us that when he wants to learn a new language or tool he'll use it to build an address book.

We won't create a fancy interface, though, only the bare minimum. We could spend an entire book on crafting the perfect address book interface, but that isn't our focus. So instead, we'll create an address book without the interface, meaning we'll create an interface that allows us to send data between the client and server with only a few buttons and a debug window. This will allow us to spend the maximum time on the tool.

But first, we need to explain a topic that has to do with setting up annotation processing with your development environment and build tools.

8.1 Enabling annotation processing

As of GWT 2.4, RequestFactory relies on the execution of a Java annotation processor. Annotation processors can be considered code generators that are part of Java (not GWT). In this case GWT requires the generation of some additional server-side classes that are used in conjunction with the RequestFactory servlet to service RPC requests.

So, what does this mean to you? It means that in any project where you use RequestFactory you must allow annotation processing to occur. In Eclipse this means turning on annotation processing and pointing it to a specific jar file, and in Maven it means a slight configuration change. When the RequestFactory annotation processor hasn't been run, you can expect to see an error like the following at runtime:

```
java.lang.RuntimeException: The RequestFactory ValidationTool must be run
```

Or you might see an error message like the following

```
com.google.web.bindery.event.shared.UmbrellaException
...
```

at com.google.web.bindery.requestfactory.shared.Receiver.onFailure.

In this section we cover how to enable annotation processing when compiling your server-side classes using plain old javac, how to turn on annotation processing in Eclipse, and what configuration changes are required in your Maven build file. If you're using other build tools or run into issues, we recommend you take a look at the GWT wiki page that provides details on the RequestFactory annotation processor. This page is located at http://mng.bz/475m.

8.1.1 Enabling RequestFactory annotation processing with javac

Annotation processing is built into Java 6 and higher and is triggered automatically when a specific configuration file is found in the classpath. In this case all you need to do is include the requestfactory-apt.jar file found in your GWT distribution in addition to any other dependencies required for your application.

This jar file contains the configuration file along with the Java classes that will be called on to generate the additional server-side source files. These new source files will then be included in the compiled output.

Next, let's look at how to enable annotation processing in Eclipse.

8.1.2 Enabling RequestFactory annotation processing in Eclipse

When you create a new GWT project in Eclipse, annotation processing is turned off by default. In order to turn on annotation processing for a project, you need to open the project properties dialog (*not the Eclipse global properties dialog*). You do this by right-clicking the project name in Eclipse and selecting Properties. From there you'll want to navigate to the Annotation Processing properties page and turn processing on, as shown in figure 8.1.

You turn on annotation processing by checking Enable Project Specific Settings and Enable Annotation Processing. The location of the generated source directory defaults to .apt_generated, but you can change this if there's a need. Once you've turned on annotation processing, you'll also need to point to the requestfactory-apt.jar file. You can do this on the Factory Path properties page, which is nested under the Annotation Processing page in the project properties dialog. This is shown in figure 8.2.

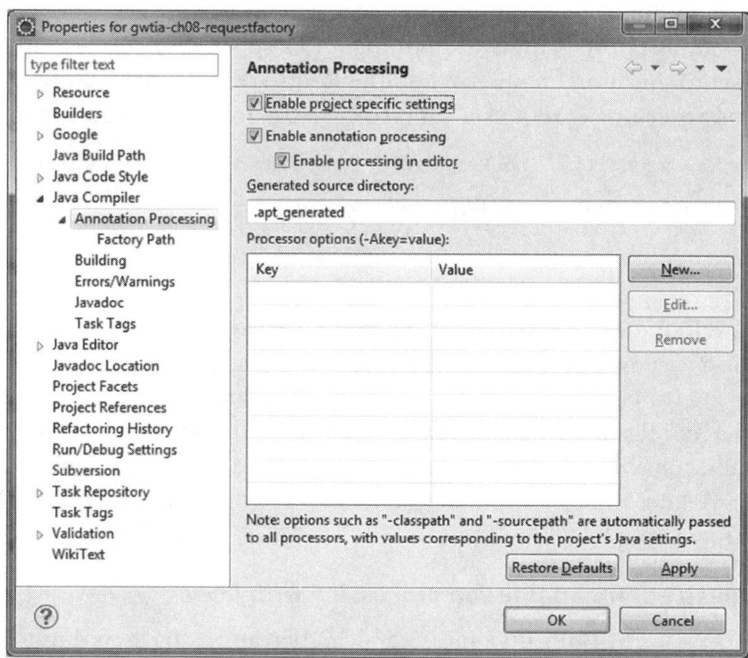

Figure 8.1 In order to set up Eclipse for a project making use of RequestFactory, you need to navigate to the Annotation Processing page of the project properties and turn on processing.

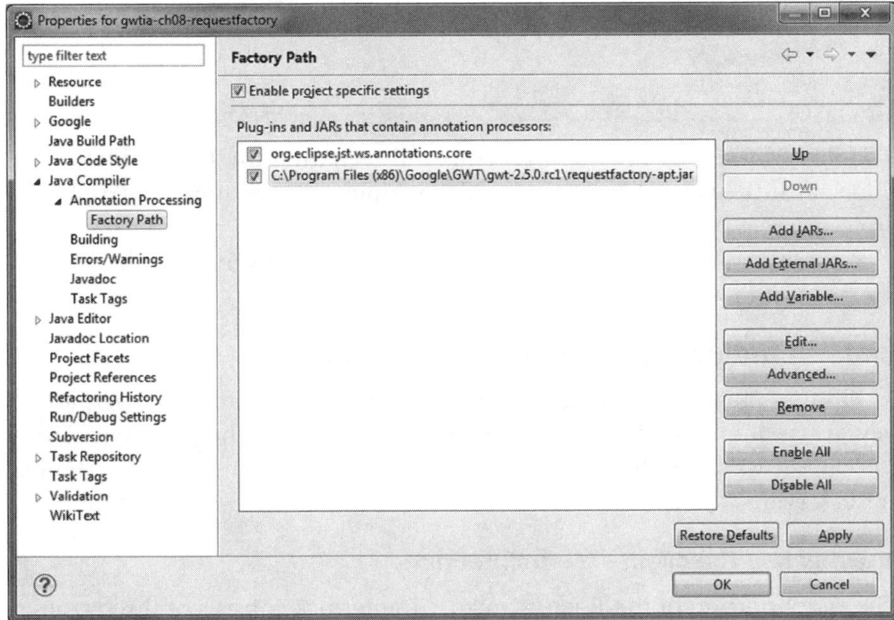

Figure 8.2 The second step in setting up the annotation processor is to add requestfactory-apt.jar to the factory path.

The requestfactory-apt.jar file is included in the GWT distribution. If you installed GWT via the Google Plugin for Eclipse, you'll need to download the full GWT distribution, in which you'll find requestfactory-apt.jar. With annotation processing turned on, you should now be able to run the examples in Eclipse without any issues.

Last, we want to look at how this changes your Maven configuration.

8.1.3 Enabling RequestFactory annotation processing in Maven

Enabling the RequestFactory annotation processor with Maven is the same as how you enable it when you use javac, but you need to include the appropriate jar file in the classpath of the build.

The following POM snippet shows how to do this, by adding requestfactory-apt.jar as a dependency of the compiler plug-in:

```
<plugin>
  <artifactId>maven-compiler-plugin</artifactId>
    <version>2.5.1</version>
    <configuration>
        <source>1.6</source>
        <target>1.6</target>
    </configuration>
    <dependencies>
        <dependency>
            <groupId>com.google.web.bindery</groupId>
```

```
            <artifactId>requestfactory-apt</artifactId>
            <version>2.5.0.rc1</version>
        </dependency>
    </dependencies>
</plugin>
```

If you're a Maven user, we also recommend reviewing the DynaTableRf example that comes with the GWT distribution. This provides a full example POM file for a Maven project that makes use of RequestFactory.

Now that you have Eclipse set up, let's discuss the overall architecture of RequestFactory before we move into writing the code.

8.2 Understanding RequestFactory architecture

As with GWT-RPC, using RequestFactory requires quite a few moving parts. So before we start coding the individual components, we'll look at the picture as a whole so that you can see where each part fits. We'll start on the client side first and then take a look at the server.

8.2.1 Investigating the client-side architecture

The client portion of the RequestFactory framework consists of three types of objects: the `RequestFactory` interface implementation, the `RequestContext` implementation, and entity proxy implementations. These classes and their relationship are shown in figure 8.3.

Let's take this one object at a time so that you can understand how the whole thing works. The `RequestFactory` in the diagram is a generated class that implements the `RequestFactory` interface. The purpose of this class is to create new `RequestContext` instances.

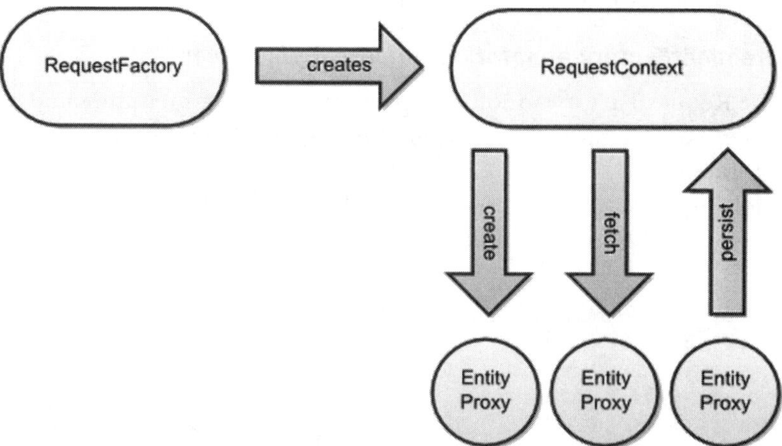

Figure 8.3 On the client side, the `RequestFactory` is used to create a context, which in turn is used to create, fetch, and store entity proxies.

The RequestContext allows you work with entities, including making server-side calls and creating new entity instances. With the RequestContext you'll queue up one or more actions and then trigger them. Triggering the actions is referred to as *firing*, and once fired, the context instance can't be reused.

The entity proxies are the data objects you'll create, fetch, and manipulate with the help of the RequestContext. These are client-side versions of your server-side entities. Part of the RequestFactory framework is a servlet that will copy data between the server-side entities and client-side proxies.

Suppose you were building an address book application; your client-side code might look like this:

```
context = factory.createPersonContext();
contactProxy = context.create();
contactProxy.setName("Barbara");
context.persist().using(contactProxy);
context.fire();
```

You use the factory to create the context and then use the context to create a new entity instance. You can then set the properties on the entity and then use the context to call the server-side persist() service. All of these instructions are loaded into the context until fire() is called, which fires the instructions to the server for processing.

One thing to note is that you won't be creating these classes. All you need to do is create the interfaces for the factory, context, and entities. The GWT compiler will handle the rest, generating these classes at compile time. This reduces the amount of code that you'll need to write.

So if that seems simple enough to understand, let's look at how to implement RequestFactory on the server.

8.2.2 Investigating the server-side architecture

On the server you'll have, as you expect, some sort of service class that does *stuff* and entities that the service class works with. Usually the service will manipulate the contents of a database with methods that are named similar to fetch(), update(), persist(), and delete().

You can create this service in two different ways. The first is to implement the service in the entity class, and the second is to implement the service externally. We acknowledge that it may be unpopular to implement your service methods in the entity, but doing so simplifies things for the RequestFactory servlet. And these savings are passed along to you, the customer, in the guise of less coding. In this chapter we'll often refer to implementing the service methods in the entity as the "simple way."

For the rest of you who can't live with that, it's still possible to implement your service outside the entity, at the cost of a little additional coding. In this chapter we refer to this as the "long way." The long way is popular with users of DI containers like Spring. We provide an example of how you can integrate RequestFactory with Spring as part of discussion on the long way.

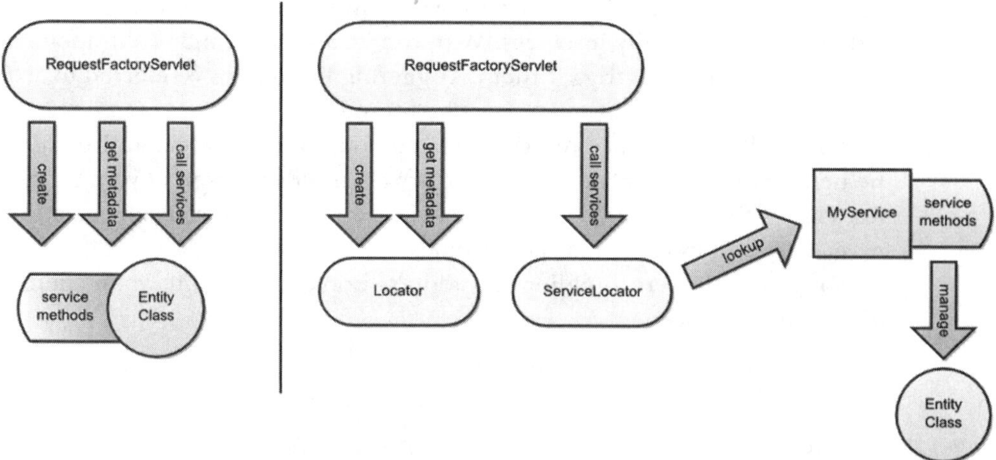

Figure 8.4 You can implement the server side of RequestFactory in one of two ways. The first requires that you implement certain methods along with service methods in your entity; the second allows you to completely decouple these methods from your entity.

Figure 8.4 provides a visual overview of these two options. In the simple way (left side of figure 8.4) the service methods are contained in the entity. Along with that, you must adhere to a few rules. Your entity must provide a no-arg constructor, a `getId()` method, a `getVersion()` method, and a fetch-by-id method. As long as you can live with those rules, the simple way might be a match for your project.

For everyone else, the long way will be a more workable solution. The long way (right side of figure 8.4) requires you to create a `Locator`. The `Locator` is used by the `RequestFactoryServlet` in lieu of the rules we discussed for the simple way. The `Locator` knows how to construct a new entity instance, how to get the ID and the version, and how to fetch an instance by the ID.

The second thing you need is a `ServiceLocator`, which is responsible for returning a service instance to the `RequestFactoryServlet`. The implementation of your `ServiceLocator` is completely project-dependant, but if you're using Spring (or similar container), you'll return the Spring-managed bean instance.

And finally you have your service and the entities it will operate on.

In both the simple and long ways the client side shares *no* interfaces, but some rules apply. Your service methods must have the same names as those defined in the `RequestContext` interface on the client side. And your entities must have getters and setters with the same names as those defined in the client-side entity proxy interfaces.

The lack of tight coupling (that is, a shared interface) is designed to allow for easy integration. You need to be careful, though, when refactoring your code, because changing a method name on either the client or server can cause the whole mechanism to break.

Now we want to start coding, but before we can begin we need to explain our example project and create a simple interface.

8.3 Understanding the example project in this chapter

We believe it's important for us to provide working yet simple examples to help teach the subject matter, and at times this can be challenging. This chapter in particular was a bit of a challenge because RequestFactory was designed for working with the database, but we didn't want to add that sort of complexity.

What we came up with for this chapter is an address book application but without the user interface or database. To replace the interface we developed a simple test interface that allows you to persist, delete, and update at the touch of a button. And to replace the database we use a `ConcurrentHashMap`.

This will allow us to focus on using RequestFactory without dealing with all of the interface and database details. The interface we created looks like what you see in figure 8.5.

The interface uses UiBinder, and each button is tied to a handler that performs some action using RequestFactory. In this chapter we'll provide the code examples for each of the eight button handlers, but we won't provide all of the UiBinder code. For that you can download the examples from the Manning website.[1]

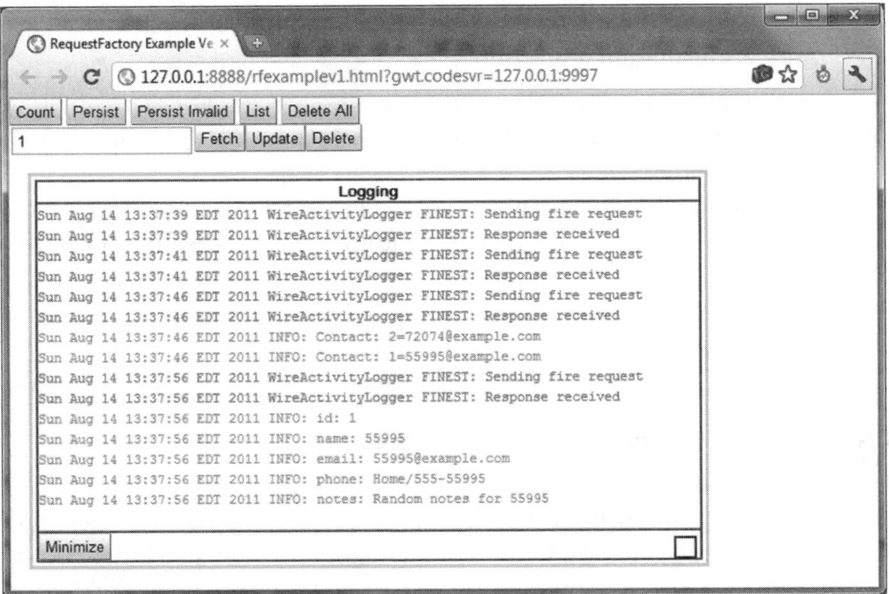

Figure 8.5 The example project interface; it takes nothing more than a click to activate the interface, with a logging console for output.

---

1 You can download the example code from www.manning.com/tacy/.

For the project "database" we've created a class named `CEM` (Contact Entity Manager). `CEM` has four methods: `persist()`, `delete()`, `fetch()`, and `list()`. The purpose of the `CEM` class is to act like a persistence mechanism but without the persisting. In a real project you'd replace `CEM` with the entity-management framework of your choosing (JPA, JDO, and the like) or use JDBC calls.

We strongly recommend that you do download and try the example application. Using RequestFactory is complex, and the example application will be a valuable tool in understanding everything RequestFactory has to offer.

Now let's get right into some coding, starting with the simple way of implementing RequestFactory.

8.3.1 *Enabling RequestFactory the simple way*

The title of this section might imply that RequestFactory is simple, but that probably isn't the case. What the title means by "simple" is that we'll take the most direct route to enabling communication with the least amount of code.

In order to enable RequestFactory, you'll need to do the following:

1. Create proxy interfaces that map to your server-side domain classes.
2. Create a factory interface for creating server requests.
3. Add service methods to your `Contact` domain class.
4. Add the `RequestFactoryServlet` to your deployment descriptor.
5. Write code to initiate requests and handle responses.
6. Add JavaBean validation (optional).

We'll cover the first four of these in this section. For the last two, initiating requests and validation, these topics are large enough to warrant their own section and are explained in section 8.4.

A good portion of the plumbing consists of interfaces that will be consumed by the compiler and used to generate the code required to plug everything together. As with UiBinder and GWT-RPC, this is performed through code generation. Because of the complexity of understanding how code generation works in GWT, this has its own chapter—chapter 18.

Getting back on topic, the first step is to create interfaces for our domain classes.

8.3.2 *Creating proxy interfaces for the domain classes*

First, you must understand what we're trying to accomplish. With GWT-RPC we used a shared domain to allow both the client and server to use the same classes, but with RequestFactory it's different. With RequestFactory the domain classes belong solely to the server, which begs the question, what do we use on the client side? The answer is a proxy.

DEFINING A PROXY INTERFACE

The way it works is that when the server sends data to the client, the object on the server is converted to JSON and sent to the client, and then code on the client side remaps the JSON data back to a Java object. Now your job is to create the interface for the client-side Java object, and GWT will automatically generate a class that implements our interface and the code that copies the JSON data to that Java object.

Take a minute for that to sink in. It's similar to using GWT-RPC with a data transfer object (DTO), as we discussed in chapter 7, except that GWT will autogenerate a lot of the code for you. For our example application, listing 8.1 presents the `ContactProxy` class, which lives in the client package of the project and maps to a server-side class named `Contact`.

Listing 8.1 `ContactProxy`, a proxy interface for the server-side `Contact` class

```
package com.manning.gwtia.ch08.client;

import java.util.List;
import com.google.web.bindery.requestfactory.shared.EntityProxy;
import com.google.web.bindery.requestfactory.shared.ProxyFor;
import com.google.web.bindery.requestfactory.shared.ValueProxy;
import com.manning.gwtia.ch08.server.Contact;
import com.manning.gwtia.ch08.server.Contact.Phone;

@ProxyFor(value = Contact.class)                                    ❶ ProxyFor annotation
public interface ContactProxy extends EntityProxy                   ❷ Extends EntityProxy
{
  Long getId ();                                                     ❸ Missing setter allowed

  String getName ();
  void setName (String text);

  String getEmail ();
  void setEmail (String text);

  List<PhoneProxy> getPhones ();
  void setPhones (List<PhoneProxy> phones);

  String getNotes ();
  void setNotes (String text);

  @ProxyFor(Phone.class)
  public interface PhoneProxy extends ValueProxy                     ❹ Extends ValueProxy
  {
    String getType ();
    void setType (String type);
    String getNumber ();
    void setNumber (String number);
  }
}
```

The proxy interface mirrors all of the getters and setters of the server-side domain class but without the method bodies, meaning that if in your proxy you define a `getName()` method, the server-side class must also have a `getName()` method.

It's important that the method signatures match the server-side code, and if you change the server-side implementation, you'll also need to update the interface.

Besides that, we have a few things to point out in the example, the first being the `@ProxyFor` annotation ❶. This annotation is used to reference the server-side class. Note when you look at the `import` statements that the `Contact` class is a server-side class only and isn't compiled to JavaScript. And as you know, you can't directly reference a server-side class in your client code, but you can reference the server-side class in an annotation.

The second important bit is that the proxy interface needs to extend `EntityProxy` ❷. The only new method that this parent interface introduces is `stableId()`, which returns an ID value (specifically a `EntityProxyId<?>`) that's unique across all of your domain classes. Think of it as an ID value that takes into account both the numeric ID and class name of the instance. This could prove useful for certain applications.

In looking at the methods, notice that you don't have a `setId()`, only a `getId()` ❸. The server-side `Contact` does have a `setId()` method, but your proxy doesn't need to include all of the methods that exist in the server-side class. If your server-side class is somewhat large, you could even split it up on the client side and have multiple proxy classes for the same server-side class. You'd do this by having two or more interfaces, both referencing the same server-side class in the `@ProxyFor` annotation and each defining a different subset of the server-side methods.

Now when you look at `PhoneProxy` ❹, you can see that the interface extends `ValueProxy` instead of `EntityProxy`. The difference is that the server-side class for an `EntityProxy` has an ID and version, whereas the server-side class for the `ValueProxy` does not. We'll talk more about the specific requirements of `EntityProxy` versus `ValueProxy` in section 8.3.3 when we add service methods to the domain class.

One thing we should talk about is the allowable parameter and return types that you can use in your interface, also known as *transportable types*.

DEFINING TRANSPORTABLE TYPES

As with GWT-RPC, you have restrictions on the data types that you can send between client and server. In table 8.1 we list the allowable types.

Table 8.1 List of transportable types you can use with RequestFactory

Type name	Description
Primitive	Java primitive types: `int`, `long`, `double`, and so on
Boxed primitive	`Integer`, `Long`, `Double`, and so on
`Set<T>` or `List<T>`	`Set` and `List`, where `T` is a transportable type, for example, `List<Integer>`
Other Java types	`BigInteger`, `BigDecimal`, `Date`, and enums
`EntityProxy`	A different proxy that extends `EntityProxy` in your project
`ValueProxy`	A different proxy that extends `ValueProxy` in your project

This list is current as of GWT version 2.5 and is limited compared to GWT-RPC, but it's likely that this list will be expanded in future versions.

The next step for us is to create the factory interface that will be used to generate new server requests.

8.3.3 Developing the factory interface

The factory interface is used to create a request context, which is then used to make a call to the server. The request context instances are also interfaces, which define the service methods available on the server. The work you need to perform is to create the interfaces, and using that information GWT will generate the classes that implement them at compile time.

Defining the factory is simple, and it's much easier to show via a code example than it is to explain, so for that we present Factory.java.

Listing 8.2 `Factory` interface used to create new request instances

```
package com.manning.gwtia.ch08.client;

import java.util.List;
import com.google.web.bindery.requestfactory.shared.InstanceRequest;
import com.google.web.bindery.requestfactory.shared.Request;
import com.google.web.bindery.requestfactory.shared.RequestContext;
import com.google.web.bindery.requestfactory.shared.RequestFactory;
import com.google.web.bindery.requestfactory.shared.Service;
import com.manning.gwtia.ch08.server.Contact;


public interface Factory extends RequestFactory                  ❶ Factory definition
{
  ContactRequest createContactRequest ();


  @Service(value = Contact.class)                                ❷ Request definition
  public interface ContactRequest extends RequestContext
  {
    Request<Integer> count ();
    Request<ContactProxy> find (Long id);                        ❸ Static request method
    Request<List<ContactProxy>> findAllContacts ();

    InstanceRequest<ContactProxy, Void> persist ();              ❹ Instance request method
    InstanceRequest<ContactProxy, Void> remove ();
  }
}
```

There's a lot to see here, so we're going to take it one line at a time. We begin with the definition of the `Factory` interface ❶. We liked the idea of calling it `Factory` instead of `ContactFactory` because you can have the same factory interface serve up request contexts for any number of services. And that's what the factory is doing; it's creating service-request contexts, which are ultimately backed by a server-side service.

The interface must extend the `RequestFactory` interface, which is partially a marker interface in that it's a signal to the GWT compiler for how to generate the code that will implement your interface.

Within the interface you'll define one method per server-side service class. Each method must take no parameters and returns an interface that extends `RequestContext`. In our example project we have only one server-side service, and we've defined that service as the interface `ContactRequest` ❷.

We chose to embed the request context interface within the factory interface to reduce the number of files in the project, but there's no requirement to do so. The requirements are that it must extend `RequestContext` and be annotated with `@Service`. The `@Service` annotation points to the server-side service class, which in this case is also the server-side domain class. The server-side service doesn't have to be the same class as the domain object, and we'll look at how you can separate it in section 8.5 when we show the "longer" way to use `RequestFactory`.

In this interface you define the service methods that will be available on the server-side service class. Requests come in two types, the first being those that return `Request` instances ❸.

In the "short" form of using `RequestFactory`, all methods that return `Request` are static methods on the service class. Furthermore, the static methods have a return type that matches the generics on the `Request`. So the method `count()` returns a `Request<Integer>`, and this implies that on the server there's a static method `count()` that returns an `Integer`.

The reason you return a `Request` and not an `Integer` is that server calls are made asynchronously, and the `Request` instance will allow for that. When you make a call to `count` in your code it will look something like this:

```
factory.createContactRequest().count().fire(callback)
```

The factory is used to create a request context, which then allows you to call `count()`. Calling `count` doesn't call the server; instead, it returns a request that you need to call `fire()` on to make the server-side call. When you call `fire()` you pass a callback, and it's that callback that receives the result from the server. We'll show plenty of examples of how to use this as we begin to implement the methods in our `TestPanel`.

Also worth noting is that the `Request` methods that do return contact objects return the client-side `ContactProxy` interface as opposed to the server-side `Contact` class. When using `RequestFactory`, the proxy on the client side is synonymous for the domain class on the server. So our method `find()` in the example returns `Request<ContactProxy>` translated to a return type of `Contact` on the server.

The second type of method that you can define in this interface returns an `InstanceRequest` ❹. These differ from the first in that the server-side methods are instance methods, not static methods. The generics of the `InstanceRequest` have two parameters; the first is the proxy class being acted on (that is, the client-side domain class), and the second is the return value of the server-side method.

On the server side, calling the `persist()` method is the equivalent of calling `object.persist()`, but from the client side you'll make the call like the following:

```
factory.createContactRequest().persist().using(object).fire(callback)
```

You can see that using `InstanceRequest` is like using `Request` with the addition of the `using()` call to specify the object instance to act on.

Now that we have the client-side service interface completed, we need to visit the server side and create the matching methods that will ultimately be called.

8.3.4 Using the domain class as the service

Ultimately, when using RequestFactory you'll want to send objects between the client and server, and the orchestrator conducting the process is the RequestFactory servlet. In order to do its work this servlet needs to be able to determine certain bits of information about your classes, or more specifically classes that are backed by a client-side `EntityProxy`.

Let's spell that out, because it's important. When creating your client-side proxy interfaces you can create interfaces that extend `EntityProxy` *or* `ValueProxy`. This section applies only to the server-side counterparts of `EntityProxy` proxies. For `ValueProxy` no additional requirements are needed other than what we've already explained.

In this section we'll describe one of two ways for you to provide the servlet with the information it needs, starting with what we like to refer to as the "simple" way. The simple way of using RequestFactory is to use the domain class as the service. In order to do this you need to adhere to two sets of rules.

The first is that the RequestFactory servlet needs to be able to locate specific information about an object instance, and it does this via a `Locator`. By default, the domain class is also the `Locator`. Through the `Locator`, the RequestFactory servlet can fetch things like the ID of a domain object, the version, and an instance from the data store using the ID.

The second set of rules revolves around the methods we defined in the client-side `RequestContext`. Specifically, the RequestFactory servlet needs to be able to locate the service methods, and this is done through a `ServiceLocator`. The `ServiceLocator` is used to return the class that contains the server-side service methods. In the simple way, the `ServiceLocator` is prewired into the RequestFactory servlet (which means you don't need to do anything), and this default `ServiceLocator` will tell the servlet to use the domain class as the service class. So all you need to do is implement the server-side methods in the domain class.

We've thought of a lot of reasons why you wouldn't want to put your `Locator` and service methods in the domain class, and we'll look at these later in section 8.5 when we show you how to write your own `Locator` and `ServiceLocator`. But for now we'll use the domain class for these, and we begin with the `Locator` rules.

ADDING LOCATOR METHODS TO THE DOMAIN CLASS

Unless you make a point of creating your own `Locator` class (covered in section 8.5.1), you'll need to add several methods to your domain class. Table 8.2 lists the requirements for this.

Table 8.2 List of requirements for implementing `Locator` methods in the domain class

Requirement	Description
No-arg constructor	A no-arg constructor to be used for creating new instances.
Static `find` method	A static `find` method in the form `findXxxxx`, where `Xxxxx` is your domain class, and which takes an ID as the parameter. For example, if the domain class is `Contact`, then the `find` method is `findContact(id)`. Returns `null` if no entity with the requested ID exists.
`getId()`	Instance method that returns the ID of the entity. The return value must be a *transportable type* (see table 8.1 in section 8.3.1).
`getVersion()`	Instance method that returns the version of the entity as a `java.lang.Integer`.

When we apply these rules to the `Contact` class of our example project, we come up with what you see in the following listing.

Listing 8.3 Application of the `Locator` rules on the example `Contact` class

```
package com.manning.gwtia.ch08.server;

import java.util.List;

public class Contact {
  private Long id;
  private Integer version;
  private String name;
  private String email;
  private List<Phone> phone;
  private String notes;


  public Contact () { }                                  ❶ No-arg constructor

  public static Contact findContact (Long id) {          ❷ Find method
    return CEM.fetch(id);
  }

  public Long getId () {                                 ❸ Get ID
    return id;
  }

  public Integer getVersion () {                         ❹ Get version
    return version;
  }
```

```
  ...omitted getters/setters...

  public static class Phone {
    private String type;
    private String number;

    ...omitted getters/setters...
  }
}
```

In listing 8.3 we omitted the getters and setters so that you can focus on what's important. The first important thing is that you don't have to do anything to the static inner class `Phone`, because on the client side it's represented by a `ValueProxy`. The `Contact` class, though, is represented by an `EntityProxy` and has the four rules applied to it.

The first is the no-arg constructor ❶, which could have been omitted in this case because in Java any class without a constructor will by default inherit a no-arg constructor. Next is the `find` method ❷, whose name is based on the name of the class, which in this case is `findContact()`. In `findContact()` you have a single line of code that returns the entity form of our fake data store (`CEM`), which would in a real project be replaced with a call to Hibernate, JPA, or whatever persistence tool you use. The `findContact()` method must return `null` if there's no entity for the specified ID.

This is followed by `getId()` ❸ and `getVersion()` ❹. As noted in table 8.2, `getId()` can return any transportable type, whereas `getVersion()` must return `Integer`. The ID type returned by `getId()` must match the parameter of `findContact()`.

After adding the `Locator` methods, you need to add the service methods.

ADDING SERVICE METHODS TO THE DOMAIN CLASS

Adding service methods to the domain class is fairly intuitive. For each method defined in the client-side `RequestContext`, you must have a matching method in the domain class (unless you use a `ServiceLocator`; see section 8.5.2).

For each method in the `RequestContext` that returns a `Request` value, you'll have a static method on the server; and for each method returning `InstanceRequest`, you'll have an instance method. The only other requirement is that all parameters and return values must be a valid transportable type (see table 8.1 in section 8.3.1).

The next listing shows our same `Contact` class again, but with all of the code omitted except our added service methods.

Listing 8.4 The `Contact` example class with service methods added

```
package com.manning.gwtia.ch08.server;

import java.util.List;

public class Contact
{
  ...fields omitted...

  public static Integer count() { return CEM.list().size(); }
```

```
  public static List<Contact> findAllContacts() { return CEM.list(); };

  public static Contact find (Long id) { return CEM.fetch(id); }

  public void persist() { CEM.persist(this); }

  public void remove() { CEM.delete(this.getId()); }

  ...other methods omitted...
}
```

You can see that the three static methods and two instance methods correspond to the three methods from our `RequestContext` interface from section 8.3.2. And again you make use of our in-memory persistence class (`CEM`) to fetch/store the `Contact` objects.

When creating your service, a common source of errors is in mismatches between the client-side `RequestContext` methods and the server-side implementations. So be sure to make sure that all parameter types match and that the service method is correctly static (or not).

At this point we have the entire infrastructure in place to start using RequestFactory, except for one piece. We still need to configure the RequestFactory servlet.

8.3.5 Adding the RequestFactory servlet to the web.xml

The engine that makes the whole thing go is the RequestFactory servlet. By default the client-side code makes the assumption that the servlet is available at the URL `GWT.getHostPageBaseURL() + "gwtRequest"`. It's possible to change it, which we explain in section 8.4.1 when we get to the client side, but for now we'll use the default.

In order to activate this servlet, you need to add both the servlet and a URL mapping in the web descriptor of your project (/war/WEB-INF/web.xml). Listing 8.5 shows the full web descriptor of the sample project with the servlet and mapping.

Listing 8.5 Web descriptor including the RequestFactory servlet

```
<web-app>

  <servlet>
    <servlet-name>requestFactoryServlet</servlet-name>
    <servlet-class>
      com.google.web.bindery.requestfactory.server.RequestFactoryServlet
    </servlet-class>
  </servlet>

  <servlet-mapping>
    <servlet-name>requestFactoryServlet</servlet-name>
    <url-pattern>/gwtRequest</url-pattern>
  </servlet-mapping>

</web-app>
```

The RequestFactory servlet will use reflection to inspect your classes based on the requests it receives, so no additional setup is required.

Once this is in place, you have all of the components to use RequestFactory in your application (we admit that there are quite a few things). In the next section we shift our focus to the client side and start using RequestFactory to make calls to the server.

8.4 Making calls to the server

Once you have all of the components in place (which can be a bit of a project), making calls to the server is fairly simple. But before we begin, because this section is somewhat long, we want to explain how the section has been laid out. In the first subsection we initialize the factory and make a simple call to the server to get the count of persisted objects. This is followed by an examination of calling instance methods (as opposed to static methods), followed by persisting, fetching, and finally editing objects. We then round out the discussion by explaining how you can use JSR-303, Bean Validation, to provide client-side validation.

> **NOTE** For the client-side code you'll need to add the following `<inherits>` element to your module configuration file:
>
> ```
> <inherits name="com.google.web.bindery.requestfactory.RequestFactory" />
> ```

We begin the exploration by creating a new instance of the RequestFactory and making a simple call to the server.

8.4.1 Initializing RequestFactory and making a simple call to the server

As noted before, our downloadable example provides a `TestPanel` that's laid out with the use of UiBinder and contains buttons to trigger commands to be sent to the server. In listing 8.6 we provide you part of this class, which includes the constructor that will initialize the RequestFactory, along with our first button handler.

Listing 8.6 Calling `count()` on the server using RequestFactory

```
package com.manning.gwtia.ch08.client;

import com.google.gwt.event.dom.client.ClickEvent;
import com.google.web.bindery.event.shared.SimpleEventBus;
import com.google.web.bindery.requestfactory.shared.Receiver;
import com.manning.gwtia.ch08.client.Factory.ContactRequest;
...

public class TestPanel extends Composite {
  ...

  Factory factory;

  public TestPanel () {
    factory = GWT.create(Factory.class);                    ❶ Instantiate factory
    factory.initialize(new SimpleEventBus());               ❷ Initialize factory
    initWidget(uiBinder.createAndBindUi(this));
  }
```

```
  @UiHandler("btnCount")
  public void count (ClickEvent event) {
    Receiver<Integer> rec = new Receiver<Integer>() {        ❸ Implement receiver
      public void onSuccess (Integer count) {
        log.info(count.toString());
      }
    };

    factory.createContactRequest()                           ❹ Call server
      .count()
      .fire(rec);
  }
}
```

In the constructor you initialize the factory, which is a two-step process. The first is to use `GWT.create()` to create the factory ❶, and then you need to initialize the factory with an event bus ❷. The event bus is a communication pipeline that RequestFactory uses to communicate requests between components. Typically you won't care about the traffic that passes across this bus, and we don't cover that here, but know that it's there if your project demands it.

> **NOTE** When initializing the factory, you may also pass a second `RequestTransport` parameter. By default the `RequestTransport` used is the `DefaultRequestTransport` class, and that class is configured to use a default server URL of `GWT.getHostPageBaseURL() + "gwtRequest"`. There will be times when this isn't appropriate, or perhaps you have to add custom headers to each server request. In cases where you only need to change the URL, you can do that by creating an instance of `DefaultRequestTransport` on your own and calling `setRequestUrl()`. If you need more control, you can look at either extending `DefaultRequestTransport` or creating your own `RequestTransport` from scratch.

The `SimpleEventBus` is exactly what its name implies, simple. GWT ships with a couple of other event buses, and you could make your own if the need should arise. We discuss using event buses in chapter 14.

Once the factory is initialized, you can go ahead and use it in your application. In the example you define a method `count()` and bind it to the example interface using `@UiHandler` (UiBinder is covered in chapter 6), and in this method you make your first RequestFactory call.

Because the server-side count method returns a value, you need to create a `Receiver` in order to capture it ❸. You use generics to specify the type returned, which in this case is `Integer`. The `Receiver` handles not only return values but server errors and validation errors as well. We look at those a little later in this section.

You then use the `Receiver` in your call to the server ❹. The call to the server consists of using the factory to create a new request context, using that context to specify the command details, followed by a call to `fire()`. The `fire()` method takes an optional `Receiver`, which you specify here, and this method is what triggers the call to the server. Everything else prior to the `fire()` call is setup.

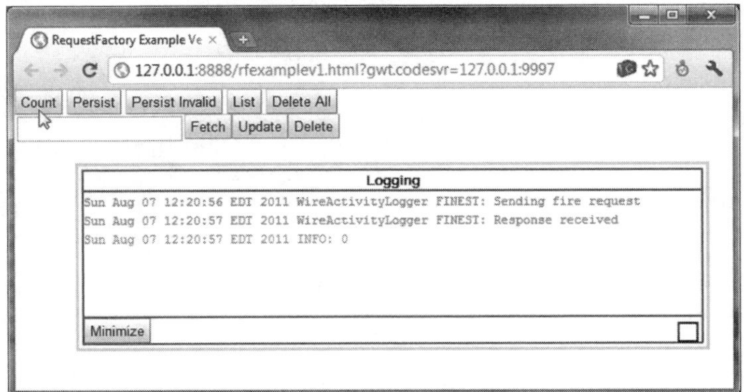

Figure 8.6 Clicking the Count button in the interface triggers a call to the server, the output of which can be seen in the Logging panel of the example application.

The RequestFactory syntax was designed so that you could chain commands together when setting up the call to the server, as you've done in this snippet. This allows you to write less code that's also easier to read.

In the case of this method, once `fire()` is called the request is sent to the RequestFactory servlet on the server, which carries out the command and returns the result to the client. Once received, the result is passed to your `Receiver` so that you can act on it. In this case you log the result, and if you're using the example application, the result will appear in the pop-up Logging window, like what you see in figure 8.6.

So that explains how you can send a request to the server and get back a simple value, but ultimately you want to be able to create domain objects on the client and send them back to the server to be persisted.

8.4.2 Creating and persisting using instance methods

If you recall from section 8.3.2, we defined a `persist()` method in the context interface, and that method returned an `InstanceRequest`. Targeting a method that returns `InstanceRequest` is slightly different than targeting one that returns `Request`, as `count()` did in the previous section. In this section we'll target the `persist()` method in our example, which also requires us to construct a new contact object instance.

We begin with the example in listing 8.7, which adds to our `TestPanel` example interface by adding a new handler. The purpose of the method is to create a new contact instance, populate it with random data, and send it to the server to be persisted.

Listing 8.7 Constructing a new domain instance and persisting it

```
package com.manning.gwtia.ch08.client;

import java.util.Arrays;
import com.manning.gwtia.ch08.client.Factory.ContactRequest;
import com.manning.gwtia.ch08.client.ContactProxy.PhoneProxy;
...

public class TestPanel extends Composite {
  ...
```

```
  @UiHandler("btnPersist")
  public void persist (ClickEvent event) {
    String rand = "" + (int) (Math.random() * 99999);

    ContactRequest context = factory.createContactRequest();        ← 1 Create context

    PhoneProxy phone = context.create(PhoneProxy.class);            ← 2 Construct PhoneProxy
    phone.setType("Home");
    phone.setNumber("555-" + rand);

    ContactProxy contact = context.create(ContactProxy.class);      ← 3 Construct ContactProxy
    contact.setEmail(rand + "@example.com");
    contact.setName(rand);
    contact.setPhones(Arrays.asList(phone));
    contact.setNotes("Random notes for " + rand);

    context.persist()                                               ← 4 Persist to server
      .using(contact)
      .fire();
  }
}
```

As you did in the handler from the previous section, you begin by creating a new context ❶, which will be used to prepare and fire off your request. Using this context you can create a `PhoneProxy` ❷ with a call to `context.create()`. You must always create the domain proxy instance with the same context that will be used to send it to the server.

After populating the phone object with some random data, you create a `ContactProxy` ❸ instance using the same context with another call to `context.create()`. Again you populate it with some random data for testing.

Once all of your objects are ready to go, you use the context to call the `persist()` method on the server ❹. Now this is where you'll see the distinction between `Request` and `InstanceRequest` objects. When you call `context.persist()` an `InstanceRequest` is returned (as specified in our context interface), which has a method `using()`. Because the `persist()` method on the server is an instance method (as opposed to static), you use `using()` to inform the RequestFactory servlet what instance to call `persist` on. In this case you want to call `persist()` on the newly constructed contact instance.

When you call `fire()` the request is sent to the server and is replayed. The RequestFactory servlet creates a new Phone instance and a new Contact instance, sets the values, and then calls `persist()` on the Contact instance.

The results of the call are sent back to the client, but because you didn't pass a `Receiver` to the `fire()` call, the results are ignored. By not using a `Receiver`, as you did in the previous section, you're saying you'll assume the call succeeded and you don't care if it didn't. This is usually the wrong thing to do, but there may be occasions where this makes sense.

If you're running the `TestPanel` example, you should be able to click the Persist button a few times and then click the Count button to see that you have Contact instances on the server. Now that you have some server-side objects, let's fetch them from the server.

8.4.3 Fetching persisted objects from the server

In this section we'll look at the `List` and `Fetch` functions from the `TestPanel` example. The first retrieves all of the Contact instances from the server, and the second fetches only a single instance. When fetching a contact from the server, embedded objects aren't attached to the result, so we'll explore how to tell the server to include them as well.

Let's begin with calling the `List` function shown in the next listing, which is similar to when we implemented the `count()` method.

Listing 8.8 Fetching a list of Contact entities from the server

```
package com.manning.gwtia.ch08.client;

import com.google.web.bindery.requestfactory.shared.Receiver;
import com.manning.gwtia.ch08.client.Factory.ContactRequest;
import com.manning.gwtia.ch08.client.ContactProxy.PhoneProxy;
...

public class TestPanel extends Composite {
  ...

  @UiHandler("btnList")
  public void list (ClickEvent event) {
    Receiver<List<ContactProxy>> rec;

    rec = new Receiver<List<ContactProxy>>() {                    ❶ Create Receiver
      public void onSuccess (List<ContactProxy> contacts) {
        for (ContactProxy c : contacts)
          log.info("Contact: " + c.getId() + "=" + c.getEmail());
      }

      public void onFailure (ServerFailure error) {             ❷ Handle errors
        Window.alert(error.getMessage());
      }
    };

    factory.createContactRequest()                              ❸ Execute call
      .findAllContacts()
      .fire(rec);
  }
}
```

Listing 8.8 is similar to the `count()` example, where you create a `Receiver` ❶ and then create a context to call the server-side method ❸, which in this case is `findAllContacts()`.

What's new here is that you're receiving a list of `ContactProxy` instances instead of a simple `Integer`. When we developed the server-side code for this instance in section 8.3.3, the `findAllContacts()` method returned a list of `Contact`, not `ContactProxy`.

This ties into the idea that RequestFactory keeps your client-side proxy separate from the server-side entity.

In addition, you're supplying an `onFailure()` method to handle errors ❷. Unlike GWT-RPC where you're required to supply an error handler, it's optional when using RequestFactory. Arguably it's a good idea to always include it, but there may be some cases where errors don't matter.

Now let's look at listing 8.9, where you use the server-side `find()` method to retrieve only a single instance. The twist is that you also want to receive the embedded `Phone` objects.

Listing 8.9 Fetching a single Contact with embedded `Phone` objects

```
@UiField TextBox txtInput;

...

@UiHandler("btnFetch")
public void fetch (ClickEvent event) {
  Receiver<ContactProxy> rec = new Receiver<ContactProxy>() {
    public void onSuccess (ContactProxy contact) {
      log.info("id: " + contact.getId());
      log.info("name: " + contact.getName());
      log.info("email: " + contact.getEmail());

      if (contact.getPhones() != null) {
        for (PhoneProxy p : contact.getPhones())
          log.info("phone: " + p.getType()
            + "/" + p.getNumber());
      }
      else {
        log.info("phone: null");
      }

      log.info("notes: " + contact.getNotes());
    }
  };

  factory.createContactRequest()
    .find(((Long) Long.parseLong(txtInput.getText())))
    .with("phones")
    .fire(rec);
}
```

❶ Show results

❷ Force population

In listing 8.9 you're fetching a single contact, and in the `Receiver` you log the properties of the embedded `PhoneProxy` objects ❶. By default RequestFactory won't populate embedded objects, so `contact.getPhones()` will always return `null` unless you instruct RequestFactory to behave differently.

This is done by calling `with()` on the request context prior to calling `fire()` ❷. In this example you call `with("phones")`, which will cause the RequestFactory servlet to also include the values for any embedded objects in the `phones` property of the contact.

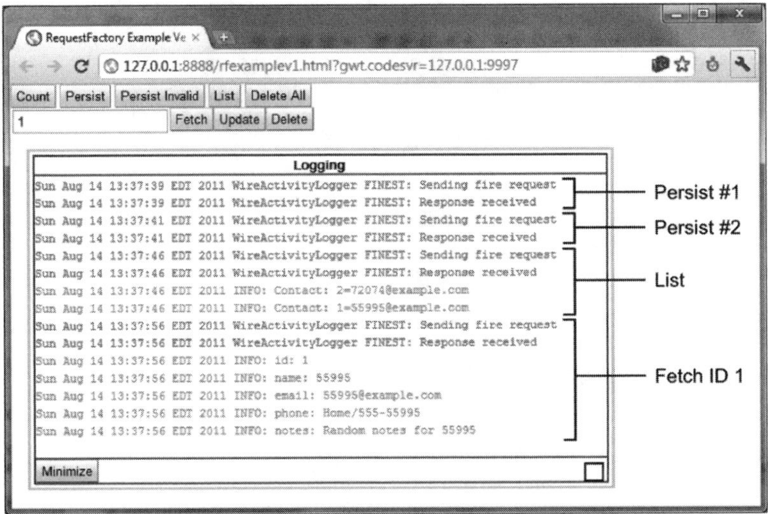

Figure 8.7 Logging output for our example application, which shows off the functions for Persist, List, and Fetch

If you need to have RequestFactory return embedded objects for more than one property, you'll call `with()` with multiple values, for example `with("foo", "bar", "baz")`.

When you run the example application, click the Persist button a few times followed by clicking the List and Fetch (with a specified ID) buttons, and you'll see the messages shown in figure 8.7.

Now that you can persist and fetch objects, let's discuss how to edit and update them.

8.4.4 Editing domain objects and updating them on the server

Editing a server object is a little more than updating the contents and persisting it. In this section we'll implement the Update, Delete, and Delete All buttons on our example interface.

Let's jump right into it with the following listing, which adds `update` and `delete` methods to the example `TestPanel` class.

Listing 8.10 Implementing `update` and `delete` handlers in the `TestPanel` example

```
@UiField TextBox txtInput;

...

private Long txtInputAsLong () {                              ❶ Utility method
  return (Long) Long.parseLong(txtInput.getText());
}

@UiHandler("btnUpdate")
public void update (ClickEvent event) {
```

```
  Receiver<ContactProxy> rec = new Receiver<ContactProxy>() {
    public void onSuccess (ContactProxy contact) {
      ContactRequest ctx = factory.createContactRequest();
      ContactProxy editableContact = ctx.edit(contact);
      editableContact.setNotes("Last updated " + new Date());
      ctx.persist().using(editableContact).fire();
    }
  };

  factory.createContactRequest()
    .find(txtInputAsLong()).fire(rec);
}

@UiHandler("btnDelete")
public void delete (ClickEvent event) {

  Receiver<ContactProxy> rec = new Receiver<ContactProxy>() {
    public void onSuccess (ContactProxy contact) {
      ContactRequest ctx = factory.createContactRequest();
      ContactProxy editableContact = ctx.edit(contact);
      ctx.remove().using(editableContact).fire();
    }
  };

  factory.createContactRequest()
    .find(txtInputAsLong()).fire(rec);
}
```

❷ Create context

❸ Create editable proxy

❹ Create context

❺ Create editable proxy

The `update` and `delete` methods share a similar pattern. In both you need to fetch a specific contact from the server and then alter the object by either updating or deleting it. So in both methods you create a `Receiver` to receive the result of the fetch and fire off a `find()` call to the server. When you call `find()` you need to pass the ID of the record to retrieve, and for that you're getting the value from the `TextBox` in our test interface. The code example includes the utility method `txtInputAsLong()` ❶ to fetch the value from the `TextBox` so that you aren't repeating code.

Within the `Receiver` you create a new context ❷ ❹. Remember that you can't use the same context that you used to fetch the context from the server, because once you call `fire()` you can't reuse the context. You create a new one to use to send the change back to the server.

Next, you need to make the contact received before you can make changes to it. The way it works is that the `ContactProxy` received from the server can't be altered in any way, and if you try to do so, an exception will be thrown. So what you need to do is use the context to create an editable version of the contact. This is done by calling `ctx.edit(obj)` ❸ ❺, where `obj` is the object that you want to edit. The `edit()` method returns an editable copy of the object, which can be altered or deleted.

Now that you have a copy of the contact that can be edited, your `update` handler alters the notes field and persists the change, whereas the `delete` handler uses the editable contact in a `delete` call to the server.

Next let's look at how to implement the `deleteAll` handler.

Listing 8.11 Implementing the `deleteAll` handler in the `TestPanel` example

```
@UiHandler("btnDeleteAll")
public void deleteAll (ClickEvent event) {

  Receiver<List<ContactProxy>> rec;
  rec = new Receiver<List<ContactProxy>>() {
    public void onSuccess (List<ContactProxy> contacts) {
      ContactRequest ctx = factory.createContactRequest();    ❶ Create context
      for (ContactProxy contact : contacts) {
        ctx.remove().using(ctx.edit(contact));                ❷ Edit and remove
      }
      ctx.fire();                                             ❸ Send changes to server
    }
  };

  factory.createContactRequest()
    .findAllContacts().fire(rec);
}
```

The example in listing 8.11 isn't too different from ones you've seen before. You create a `Receiver` and then fire off a call to `findAllContacts()`. This in turn activates your `Receiver`, passing a list of all server-side contacts as the parameter.

As in listing 8.10, you create a new context ❶ that you'll use to issue the `remove()` command to the server, but then you do something slightly different. Here you loop through each contact and call `remove()` on the editable version of the contact ❷. The difference here is that you're adding multiple `remove()` calls to the context, instead of doing a single `remove` prior to calling `fire()`. RequestFactory allows you to send multiple changes to the server in a single `fire()` call ❸, which is much faster than sending one change to the server at a time. In this method, when you call `fire()`, you're sending all of the `remove` requests in one message to the server.

So that covers everything you need to create a CRUD[2] application, but one thing we haven't discussed is how RequestFactory helps you handle errors and validation.

8.4.5 *Error handling and validation*

When sending a request from the client to the server, there's always a need for error handling. For example, if the request to the server times out or outright fails, your application would want to be aware of that. When you look at GWT as a whole, all of the RPC tools include error handling, and RequestFactory is no exception. But in addition, RequestFactory provides a server-side validation mechanism built in, and instead of reinventing the wheel, it makes use of JSR-303, Bean Validation.[3]

---

[2] CRUD is an acronym for create, retrieve, update, delete, which are the basic operations you'd perform on a database.

[3] JSR-303 is a specification of the Java Community Process that you can find at http://jcp.org/en/jsr/detail?id=303.

If the Bean Validation specification is new to you, you'll be happy to know that it's easy to use. Instead of adding a bunch of validation code, you annotate the fields on your server-side domain class with annotations like `@NotNull` and `@Size(min=3,max=10)`. A JSR-303 validation engine then uses these annotations to validate the contents of the object. With RequestFactory failing validation, this means that the errors are sent back to your client application so that you can present them to the user.

Besides adding server-side annotations and adding some client code to handle validation errors, you also need to include a JSR-303 implementation in your project and register a validation provider. In this section we'll handle the setup first, which is to register a provider; then we'll provide examples of both the server-side and client-side code for handling communication and validation errors.

REGISTERING THE JSR-303 VALIDATOR

The Bean Validation specification (JSR-303) contains several open source implementations, including Hibernate Validator and Apache Bean Validation. At the time of this writing the Apache project is still in incubation, so we've opted to go with Hibernate Validator, found at www.hibernate.org/subprojects/validator.html. The downloadable example code for this book includes the bare minimum jar files required for using Hibernate Validator for our example application, but in practice you'll want to get the full distribution from the Hibernate Validator site.

As we mentioned, besides adding other jar files to the project, you need to register a validation provider. In practice, if you're using JPA or Hibernate in your project, this will likely already be done for you. But because our example makes use of a fake datastore, you need to do this manually. The following servlet does this.

Listing 8.12 A servlet for registering the Hibernate Validator provider

```
package com.manning.gwtia.ch08.shared.server;

import javax.servlet.ServletException;
import javax.servlet.http.HttpServlet;
import javax.validation.Validation;

import org.hibernate.validator.HibernateValidator;

@SuppressWarnings("serial")
public class BootstrapValidationServlet extends HttpServlet
{
  @Override
  public void init () throws ServletException {
    super.init();
    Validation.byProvider(HibernateValidator.class).configure();
  }
}
```

In listing 8.12 you use the `init()` method of the servlet to register the validation provider. You place this class in a shared package, but it can be deployed to any server-side package. You then need to add a reference to the deployment descriptor (web.xml) to load this class on startup:

```
<web-app>
  <servlet>
    <servlet-name>init</servlet-name>
    <servlet-class>
    com.manning.gwtia.ch08.shared.server.BootstrapValidationServlet
    </servlet-class>
    <load-on-startup>1</load-on-startup>
  </servlet>
  ...
</web-app>
```

This will cause the `BootstrapValidationServlet` to be initialized when the web application is started, which in turn registers the validation provider. With the setup out of the way, we can now go back to the heart of the matter, which is to add error handling to the example application, starting with the server.

ADDING JSR-303 VALIDATION ANNOTATIONS

The first step in adding validation is to add JSR-303 annotations to the server-side domain class. Some of these annotations include `@Null`, `@NotNull`, `@Min`, `@Max`, `@Size`, `@Pattern`, and many more. For a full list you should refer to the JSR-303 documentation. In the next listing we've updated our example `Contact` class to make use of two of them.

Listing 8.13 An updated `Contact` example making use of JSR-303 annotations

```
package com.manning.gwtia.ch08.server;

import java.util.List;
import javax.validation.constraints.Pattern;
import javax.validation.constraints.Size;

public class Contact
{
  private Long id;
  private Integer version;
  private List<Phone> phone;

  @Size(min = 2, max = 20) private String name;          ❶ Validate String length
  @Size(max = 100) private String notes;

  @Pattern(regexp = "[^@\\s]+@[^@\\s]+",                  ❷ Validate against pattern
    message = "email address is not valid")
  private String email;
  ...
}
```

Listing 8.13 limits the valid lengths of both the `name` and `notes` fields ❶. In the case of `name`, you expect a name of at least 2 characters but no more than 20, and this is enforced by using `@Size(min=2,max=20)`. This would refuse a single letter and really long names. If you were persisting this to a real database, the `max` value would likely be the maximum length of the field in the database. For notes we've decided to allow up to 100 characters using `@Size(max=100)`. By not specifying a `min` value for the size of the notes, you're saying that the minimum is zero.

For email you want to do a little more and ensure that it looks like an email address ❷. If you're a fan of regular expressions (and who isn't?), using the `@Pattern` annotation is a great way to ensure valid data. Our regular expression isn't comprehensive but is good enough to protect users from common data-entry errors. To spell it out, the pattern ensures that the part of the address before and after the `@` sign doesn't contain spaces or other `@` signs. So `foo@bar` will pass validation, but `foo@@bar` and `f o o@bar` won't.

For the email `@Pattern` validation you also provide a `message` parameter, which is the error message that will be used when validation of that field fails. For all of the validation annotations there's a default message that's built from the annotation parameters. In this case the default message would be "must match '[^@\s]+@[^@\s]+'", which isn't all that user friendly.

Now that the annotations are in place, we move back to the client-side code where we'll handle failures.

ADDING ERROR HANDLING ON THE CLIENT

As you've seen in the previous sections, you use a `Receiver` to capture the value returned from the server. The `Receiver`, though, has two additional handler methods that you aren't required to implement by default but are there when you want to override the default behavior of quietly failing. There two handler methods are `onFailure()` and `onConstraintViolation()`. The next listing provides the code behind the Persist Invalid button in our test interface, which overrides these two `Receiver` methods.

Listing 8.14 An example of handling errors in the `Receiver`

```
package com.manning.gwtia.ch08.client;

...

public class TestPanel extends Composite
{
  ...

  @UiHandler("btnPersistInvalid")
  public void persistInvalid (ClickEvent event) {

    ContactRequest context = factory.createContactRequest();

    ContactProxy contact = context.create(ContactProxy.class);

    contact.setEmail("invalid email");
    contact.setName("");

    String notes = "";
    for (int i = 0; i < 20; i++) { notes += "too-long"; }
    contact.setNotes(notes);
```

❶ Provide invalid data

```
    Receiver<Void> receiver = new Receiver<Void>() {
      public void onSuccess (Void response) {
        log.info("We passed validation");
      }

      public void onConstraintViolation(
        Set<ConstraintViolation<?>> violations) {
          for (ConstraintViolation<?> err : violations)
            log.info(err.getPropertyPath() + " : " + err.getMessage());
      }

      public void onFailure (ServerFailure error) {
        log.info("Server failure: " + error.getMessage());
      }
    };

    context.persist()
      .using(contact)
      .fire(receiver);
  }
}
```

❷ Handle validation errors

❸ Handle server errors

In listing 8.14 you attempt to persist a `Contact` to the server, much like you've done in previous examples, but this time you're populating it with invalid data ❶. You use an invalid string as the email address, provide a zero-length name, and provide a notes string that goes well beyond the 100-character limit.

By default the `Receiver` will ignore errors and silently fail, so in order to get validation error messages sent from the server, you need to implement the `onConstraintViolation()` method in the `Receiver` ❷. The `onConstraintViolation()` method is passed a `Set` of `ConstraintViolation<?>` objects, each of which provides the details of a single validation error. In this case you loop through the errors and log them. When you log them you include both the property path and the message. The property path is the name of the field, which in this case will be "email," "name," and "notes." The message is the error message, which is either the default JSR-303 message or one that you explicitly provide in the server-side annotation.

In addition you implement the `onFailure()` method, which receives a `ServerFailure` object as the parameter ❸. The `onFailure()` method will be called when something goes wrong with the call to the server, for instance, if the server returns a 500 error or if the call to the server times out. Again, you log the message on the client side.

When you run the example application with this code and click the Persist Invalid button in the interface, the output in the logging window will look like what you see in figure 8.8.

By now you should have a good handle on how to use RequestFactory in your applications, but there's one last thing to cover. In the beginning of this chapter we implemented the server-side methods in the domain object, and we mentioned that you can move these methods out of the domain object and into a custom `Locator` and `ServiceLocator`. We'll look at that next.

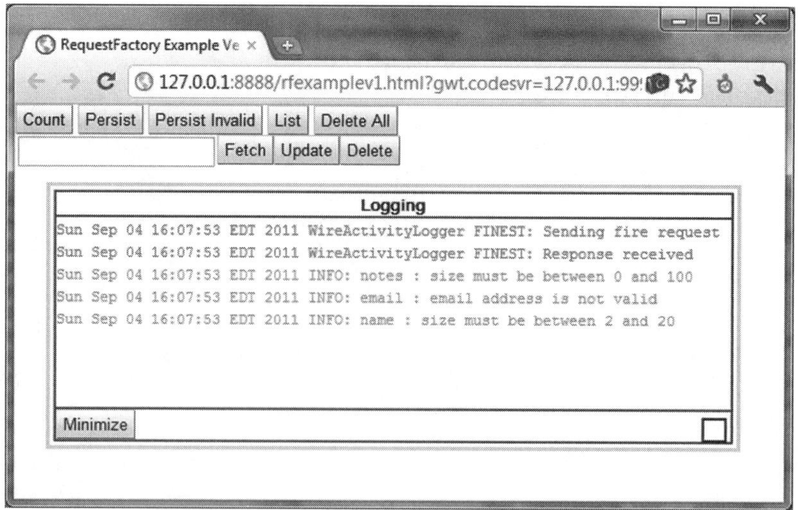

Figure 8.8 Clicking the Persist Invalid button activates our handler code, sending invalid data to the server to be persisted. The server in turn returns validation errors that we display in the Logging dialog.

8.5 Using custom Locators and ServiceLocators (the "long way")

Let's recap some important points before we move forward. First, in section 8.3.3 we provided a list of the Contact `Locator` methods that had to be contained within your domain class. These were a no-arg constructor, a static `findContact(id)` method, a `getId()` method, and a `getVersion()` method. In addition we also created several service methods to the domain class that implemented our server-side functionality. These service methods include `count()`, `persist()`, and `remove()`. In this section we'll move both sets of methods out of our domain class.

You may have a lot of valid reasons for wanting to do this. Perhaps your class can't have a no-arg constructor, perhaps you don't have a version field, or perhaps you don't believe your service methods should be mixed in with your domain model. In the case of our example code, we want to play the role of the purist and keep our server-side domain model free of any methods that tie us to GWT.

In this section we'll tackle one set of methods at a time, starting with the `Locator` methods, and then we'll move on to the service methods.

8.5.1 Creating a custom Locator

The `Locator` is a tool used by the `RequestFactoryServlet` to find persisted objects, create new objects, and determine their ID and version. In the previous sections you did this by adding a no-arg constructor to your domain class along with `findContact()`, `getId()`, and `getVersion()` methods. In this section you'll remove those and replace them with an implementation of the abstract Locator class, which is shown next.

Listing 8.15 Locator implementation for the example Contact domain class

```
package com.manning.gwtia.ch08.server;

import com.google.web.bindery.requestfactory.shared.Locator;

public class ContactLocator extends Locator<Contact, Long> {        ❶ Extends Locator

    @Override
    public Class<Contact> getDomainType () {                          ❷ Type discovery
        return Contact.class;
    }

    @Override
    public Class<Long> getIdType () {
        return Long.class;
    }

    @Override
    public Contact create (Class<? extends Contact> clazz) {         ❸ Locator functions
        return new Contact();
    }

    @Override
    public Contact find (Class<? extends Contact> clazz, Long id) {
        return CEM.fetch(id);
    }

    @Override
    public Long getId (Contact contact) {
        return contact.getId();
    }

    @Override
    public Object getVersion (Contact contact) {
        return contact.getVersion();
    }
}
```

The Locator class makes use of generics, as shown by how you extend it ❶. Locator takes two generic parameters; the first is the type of your domain class, and the second is the type of the ID. In this case the class is of type Contact, and the ID is of type Long. You can use all of these types in all of the method signatures of the methods you need to provide.

The first two methods that you need to provide have to do with type discovery ❷. These two methods are getDomainType() and getIdType(). You return the Class object for each of these types, which are the same ones used in the generics parameters.

This is followed by the four methods that replace the Locator functions that you'd placed in your domain class ❸. These methods are create(), find(), getId(), and getVersion(), and they do what you'd expect. Because you now have control over these implementations, you might be able to see where this would be useful. For example, if your domain class didn't have a no-arg constructor, you could have used the create() method to create a new instance with the appropriate constructor args. Another example is where your domain class has a last-updated value instead of a version number. The getVersion() method returns an object, so you'll be able to return a date object.

For the methods getId() and getVersion(), you should return null if the object has not yet been persisted. And for find() you'll return null if there's no persisted object with the specified identifier.

Now, creating a custom Locator doesn't mean that the RequestFactoryServlet will use it; you need to tell the RequestFactoryServlet to use it. For that you go back to your client-side proxy, the ContactProxy. Here you alter the @ProxyFor annotation to set the class of your custom Locator:

```
@ProxyFor(value = Contact.class, locator = ContactLocator.class)
public interface ContactProxy extends EntityProxy {
  ...
}
```

In the code snippet you can see that the value parameter still refers to the server-side Contact class, but now you've added a locator parameter to refer to the custom Locator. With this in place you can now remove the Locator methods from the domain class that you added in section 8.3.3, assuming you don't need them for anything else. Specifically, in this case you still need the getId() and getVersion() methods on the Contact class because you use them elsewhere. The findContact() method, though, was only there because it was required for use with RequestFactory, so you can remove that one.

That covers the Locator methods, but now we need to address the service methods.

8.5.2 Creating a custom ServiceLocator

A ServiceLocator does what its name implies: it locates a service. By default, as you've seen in earlier sections, our domain class was our service class. In this section we'll construct a new service class named ContactService, and we'll implement the service methods there. We'll then make changes to the application to allow RequestFactory to discover our new service class.

Using an external service has three parts: (1) develop a service class, (2) create a ServiceLocator implementation that allows RequestFactory to find the service, and (3) update the @Service annotation on the client-side RequestContext to inform RequestFactory of the ServiceLocator.

IMPLEMENTING A SERVICE CLASS EXTERNAL TO THE DOMAIN CLASS

To start the discussion on how the external service class differs from the implementation of the service methods in the domain class, we present the following listing, a service class named `ContactService`.

Listing 8.16 A service implementation for managing `Contact` instances

```
package com.manning.gwtia.ch08.server;

import java.util.List;

public class ContactService {
  public Integer count() { return CEM.list().size(); }
  public Contact find(Long id) { return CEM.fetch(id); }
  public List<Contact> findAllContacts() { return CEM.list(); };

public void persist(Contact c) { CEM.persist(c); }
  public void remove(Contact c) { CEM.delete(c.getId()); }
}
```

The methods in the service are almost the same as what we implemented in the domain class in section 8.3.3. When we implemented the service methods in the domain class we used static methods for `count()`, `findAllContacts()`, and `find()`, but now those are instance methods. All methods in your service implementation should be instance methods.

The other change is that `persist()` and `remove()`, which were instance methods when we implemented them in the domain class, now take a `Contact` instance as a parameter. This makes sense because when we implemented this in the domain class we could use this to refer to the `Contact` class, but now we need a handle to the instance passed to us.

The next step is to create the `ServiceLocator` implementation.

CREATING THE SERVICELOCATOR

The purpose of the `ServiceLocator` is to allow the `RequestFactoryServlet` to find the service class that contains methods defined in the client-side `RequestContext`. When you call `find()` on the client side, the `RequestFactoryServlet` uses the `ServiceLocator` to fetch a `ContactService` instance and calls `find()` on it. The result is then passed back to the client.

The next listing presents the `ContactServiceLocator`, which we follow with a discussion.

Listing 8.17 A `ServiceLocator` implementation for getting the `ContactService`

```
package com.manning.gwtia.ch08.server;

import com.google.web.bindery.requestfactory.shared.ServiceLocator;
```

```
public class ContactServiceLocator implements ServiceLocator
{
  private static ContactService serviceInstance;

  @Override
  public Object getInstance (Class<?> clazz) {             ❶ Fetch service
    return ContactServiceLocator.getServiceInstance();
  }

  private static ContactService getServiceInstance () {    ❷ Initialize and fetch
    if (serviceInstance == null)
      serviceInstance = new ContactService();
    return serviceInstance;
  }
}
```

The implementation will extend the `ServiceLocator` interface, which defines a single method `getInstance()` ❶. The `getInstance()` method returns the service instance. In our example project we created a static method `getServiceInstance()` ❷, which creates a new instance of the `ContactService` and stores it in a static field for reuse the next time it's asked for.

In practice, your `getInstance()` might do a little more than create a new service instance. For example, if you use Spring, you'll want to go into the Spring container and fetch the service bean. Here's an example of what that might look like:

```
public Object getInstance (Class<?> clazz) {
  HttpServletRequest request =
    RequestFactoryServlet.getThreadLocalRequest();
  ServletContext servletCtx = request.getSession().getServletContext();
  ApplicationContext springCtx =
    WebApplicationContextUtils.getWebApplicationContext(servletCtx);
  return springCtx.getBean(ContactService.class);
}
```

This isn't a book on Spring,[4] so we don't want to get into too much detail here, but a simple walkthrough may be valuable for Spring users. What we're doing is grabbing the request in order to get to the `ServletContext` instance. With the `ServletContext` in hand, we can use the `WebApplicationContextUtils`, a Spring utility class, to get a handle on the Spring context. Once we have that, we can make a call using one of the many forms of `getBean()` to get the managed service instance.

The reason for having to do all of this work is that the `ServiceLocator` will be instantiated by the `RequestFactoryServlet` and not your Spring (or any other) container. You need to first get a handle on the container before you can get the bean.

You now have the `ServiceLocator`, so the last step is to tell the `RequestFactoryServlet` to use it.

---

[4] For a book on Spring, we recommend *Spring in Action*, third edition, by Craig Walls (Manning 2011): www.manning.com/walls4/.

HOOKING IN THE SERVICELOCATOR

In order to hook in our newly created `ServiceLocator`, we go back to the client side and revisit the `Factory` class that we created in section 8.3.2. The following listing shows the `Factory` class again, with a minor change.

Listing 8.18 Revisiting the client-side `Factory` to hook in the custom `ServiceLocator`

```
package com.manning.gwtia.ch08.client;

import ...

public interface Factory extends RequestFactory {
  ContactRequest createContactRequest ();


  @Service(value = ContactService.class,
      locator = ContactServiceLocator.class)
  public interface ContactRequest extends RequestContext {
      Request<Integer> count();
      Request<ContactProxy> find(Long id);
      Request<List<ContactProxy>> findAllContacts();
      Request<Void> persist(ContactProxy contact);
      Request<Void> remove(ContactProxy contact);
  }
}
```

❶ **ServiceLocator defined**

The difference here is the addition of the `locator` parameter on the `@Service` annotation ❶. Here you're telling the `RequestFactoryServlet` to use `ContactServiceLocator` to locate the server-side service instead of the default, which is to use the class defined by the value parameter.

One source of confusion is the difference between the `Locator` and `ServiceLocator` and how to point to them. The `Locator` is a collection of methods used to help the `RequestFactoryServlet` construct new instances and determine the ID of an instance, as well as the version. The `Locator` allows the `RequestFactoryServlet` to work. You can define a custom `Locator` implementation in the `@ProxyFor` annotation of the client-side proxy class.

The `ServiceLocator`, on the other hand, provides the `RequestFactoryServlet` with the server-side class that implements the service methods that you defined on the client side. These service methods are defined by you, and the `RequestFactoryServlet` converts client-side calls to server-side calls on the service. You define a custom `ServiceLocator` in the `@Service` annotation that's on the `RequestContext` interface.

There have been questions as to why both a `Locator` and a `ServiceLocator` exist, because that implies that you need to have two server-side classes to perform these functions; but that isn't the case. In our example we provided two server-side classes, but in most implementations it will make sense to implement both the `Locator` and `ServiceLocator` in the same class.

8.6 Summary

We covered a lot in this chapter and carefully explained each point. We believe the thorough explanation and the working example we provided are warranted given the newness and importance of RequestFactory. The importance is that RequestFactory is the first RPC tool provided with GWT that allows you to communicate using Java objects without tying the client and server code together.

In previous versions of GWT the only comparable RPC tool was GWT-RPC, but because of how it works it was difficult sometimes to integrate with both server-side persistence frameworks and Dependency Injection (DI) containers like the Spring Framework. Workarounds were always found, but they weren't clean solutions, like those RequestFactory provides.

In addition, RequestFactory is also integrated with the Editor framework, a tool for syncing a set of form fields with a Java data object. And because the Editor framework includes a RequestFactory driver, you can sync form fields almost directly between a client-side form and the database on your server. We look at that in the next chapter.

9 The Editor framework

This chapter covers

- Introducing the Editor framework
- Moving data from objects using editors and drivers
- Using adapters that provide reusable editor logic

In the previous chapter you learned how to store and transfer data from beans residing on the server side to a client. In this chapter we'll take a closer look at how you can plug this data into form fields on the client side through the use of the Editor framework, which saves you writing a bunch of code for copying data from widgets to bean objects.

The Editor framework is perhaps best explained with an example. Suppose you have a form with 10 `TextBox` fields, and when the user clicks Submit, you want to copy this data to a Java object that you can then send to the server for processing. If you think about this, the code is somewhat cumbersome. You need to write the code that copies the value of each `TextBox` into the JavaBean, which means a minimum of 10 lines of code. Now, what about when you want to allow the user to fetch that same JavaBean from the server and edit those values? You just added 10 additional lines of code.

The Editor framework is meant to perform this work for you by automatically mapping bean fields to, usually, UI elements. It does this by using a driver, known as `SimpleBeanEditorDriver`, to take defined values from your UI, known as the editor, and synchronize them with a local (on the client) JavaBean.

Additionally, the Editor framework includes a special driver, `RequestFactory-EditorDriver`, which allows you to synchronize with a JavaBean held on the server via RequestFactory communication. This driver automatically generates the necessary code required for the round trip between client and server, assuming your RPC tool of choice is RequestFactory. These GWT objects provide an effective technique to instantly visualize data from Java bean objects straight to the user, with a minimum amount of user-written code. The other main thing in the framework is adapters. GWT provides classes that conform to the Editor framework and give general reusable logic. This means that occasionally you could use adapters for editing domain objects instead of defining your own editors.

In this chapter we begin with an overview of each of the components of the framework starting with the editors, have a quick look at drivers, give an introduction to the editor subinterfaces, and finally show you how to use adapters. Along the way we'll look at everything you need to know in order to handle edge cases like embedded editors (objects of objects). So let's jump right into the discussion starting with editors.

9.1 Framework and editor overview

What is the Editor framework? The Editor framework is a set of classes that structures the transport of data from any bean-like object to a user interface (UI). Let's look at the several objects typically involved in using editors:

- *Domain object*—The JavaBean that has a number of properties that hold data and represent a real-life entity. This could, in other sources, be called the backing object to an editor, or the supported object. In this book we'll call it the domain object.
- *Editor*—An object that supports the editing of zero or more properties of the domain object. Typically, it contains a number of fields known as subeditors—they implement the `Editor` interface. These subeditors are usually either widgets (GWT widgets implement the `Editor` interface) or other user-declared editors.
- `Editor` subinterfaces—The framework provides several subinterfaces of `Editor`, giving specific additional functionality.
- *Driver*—This is responsible for traversing the editor and either moving data from the subeditors to the domain object (when flushing) or from the domain object to the editor (when editing).
- *Adapters*—These objects provide several prebuilt behaviors for the Editor framework such as lists of domain objects and their associated editors or widgets of `HasText` and `TakesValue` type.

A common workflow in a client is to display data from some domain object graph and update the object graph with user input. By using the Editor framework, you reduce the need for unnecessary classes and monotonous copying of data for this common scenario. You'll only need to construct two types of classes—editors and domain objects—and GWT will automatically generate all the necessary boilerplate code to move data between these objects.

The collaboration between these objects is as follows: the editor updates the domain object with data, and the domain object propagates data back to the editor. This cooperation is done by a driver that has two main operations called *flush* and *edit*. The framework provides two different drivers to choose from, the `RequestFactory-EditorDriver` and the `SimpleBeanEditorDriver`. You can create your own driver if you wish, but that's a little beyond the scope of this book. We're going to talk more about drivers later in this chapter. The *flush* operation is used to update the domain object from an editor (for example, store data), and the *edit* is used to propagate the data from a domain object to the editor (for example, display data).

Figure 9.1 depicts the major interaction between the three participating components in the Editor framework. You can see that the editor *flushes* user input through the driver into the domain object and that the domain object *edits* the editor object with its property values, once again through a driver.

The simplest way to define an editor is to construct a Java object that implements one of the editor types, like the editable widgets provided by GWT (for example, `TextBox`). There's a hierarchy of editor interfaces to choose from: `Editor` itself and several subinterfaces, each suitable for different occasions. You'll get more familiar with the different types in section 9.3.

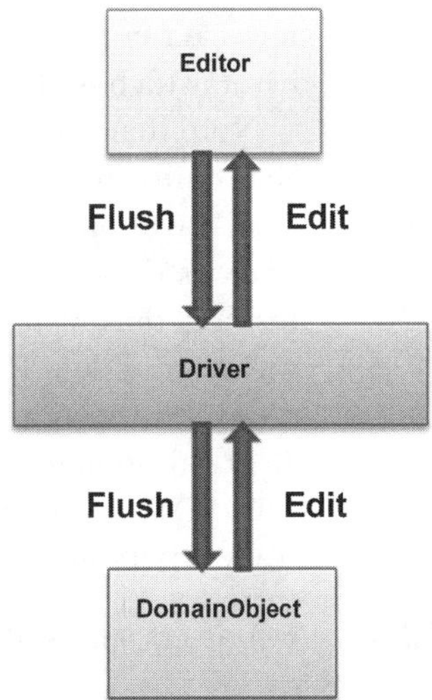

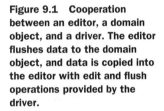

Figure 9.1 Cooperation between an editor, a domain object, and a driver. The editor flushes data to the domain object, and data is copied into the editor with edit and flush operations provided by the driver.

Because the main purpose of editors is to integrate a UI with domain objects, most widgets are already of the editor type. This means that you need two main objects in your client UI views: a widget of the type `Editor` and a domain object. The binding between them is done automatically by one of the two top-level drivers, `RequestFactoryEditorDriver` or `SimpleBeanEditorDriver`, provided by the framework.

Widgets acting as editors could be bound to both local and remote domain objects. The benefit of editors is that you get an automatic presentation of domain object values on forms with only a pair of classes, regardless of whether they reside on a server or on a client. Let's look briefly at both of those cases.

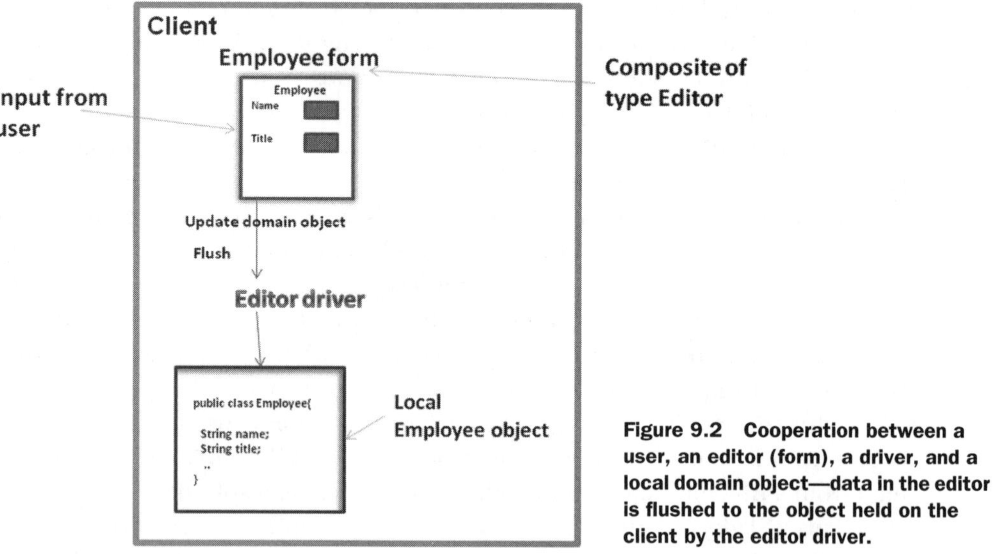

Figure 9.2 Cooperation between a user, an editor (form), a driver, and a local domain object—data in the editor is flushed to the object held on the client by the editor driver.

9.1.1 Local domain object

Figure 9.2 displays how user input is transferred to a local domain object. It depicts how data entered in a UI is automatically moved to the domain object through the driver, which is an instance of `SimpleBeanEditorDriver`.

Note that the Employee form is a `Composite` that implements an `Editor` interface. That editor indicates which subeditors in the `Composite` (in this case the two `TextBoxes`) are mapped to properties in the local employee domain object. The editor driver is defined as an instance of `SimpleBeanEditorDriver` and is responsible for flushing data from the Employee form to the Employee local domain object and transferring data from the domain object to the editor. You'll see exactly how this is achieved in section 9.4.

Local domain objects are useful for temporary storage, and may be in the future with HTML 5 storage APIs. More commonly, your domain object will be on the server to allow persistence long after the application has been closed.

9.1.2 Remote domain objects

As a more efficient way to use remote domain objects, you should use the driver that works with the RequestFactory framework: `RequestFactoryEditorDriver`. We'll cover the driver in depth in section 9.5.

When you're working on a remote domain object and choose `RequestFactory` for client/server communication, the editors work on a proxy object rather than the domain object itself. Figure 9.3 illustrates the same flow as figure 9.2, with the difference being that the domain object is a remote object residing on a server. The driver returns a `RequestContext` object part of the RequestFactory framework, which you could use to fire changes to the server.

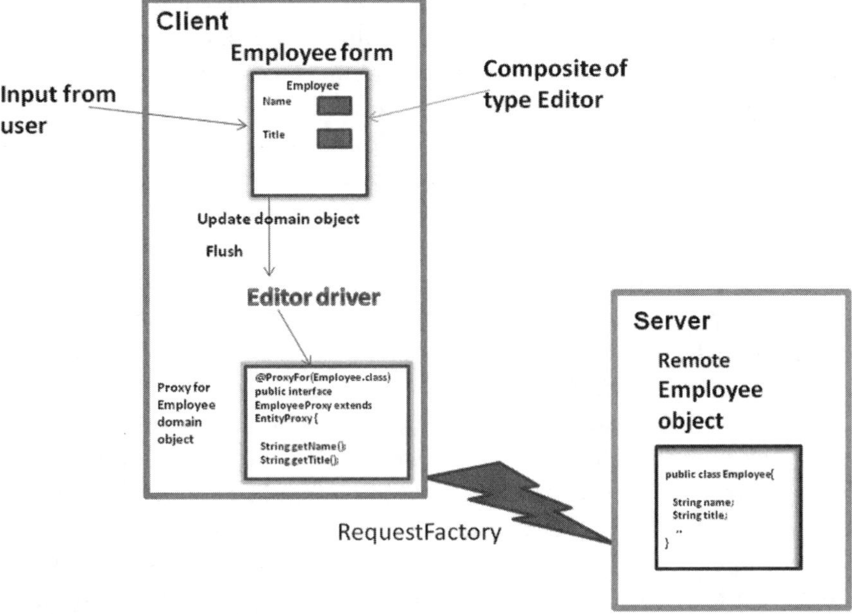

Figure 9.3 Cooperation between a user, an editor (form), a driver, and a remote domain object. Data in the editor is flushed to the proxy object held in the client by the Editor driver and is subsequently automatically transferred to the server domain object.

As it stands now, if you're not using RequestFactory to move data to the server, for example, if your server side is written in PHP, then you'll either have to build your own driver or use a local domain object and write the code to update the server side yourself.

In this section you got acquainted with the Editor framework. You saw the basics of the framework—the domain object and editor, linked together by a driver—and we mentioned briefly subeditor interfaces and adapters. Keep them in mind when we go deeper into the details later.

Some handy examples attached to this chapter are supplied to increase your comprehension of this framework. The sample code has been put together to give you a quick start to implement the most common workflows regarding fetching and visualizing data. We hope that after looking into the sample code, you'll get a good idea where the framework is applicable.

9.2 Examining the chapter's examples

Five different examples are built in this chapter's sample code to help you understand how editors could be used in realistic scenarios. The most common workflows in system development are CRUD transactions. Editors play a significant role in these common operations. The examples are chosen to show that editors are one piece of the big picture and that in cooperation with other objects from other GWT basics they become extremely useful.

The first two examples are constructed to give sample code for local interaction between UI and domain objects. The other three give sample code for interaction between UI and remote domain objects using more complex editor types and show how to employ adapters instead of defining your own editors.

In this chapter we're going to use Employee example objects to show how you could use the same domain object in simple situations where it exists locally as well as in more complex situations where the same object resides on the server side. We'll start with displaying the domain object in simple widgets and proceed to constructing widgets of a more complicated nature. In our Employee example we're going to refer to the five examples in the sample code, and we'll use snippets of code you can find in the sample code. Figure 9.4 shows the launch menu and the introduction page for the sample code accompanying this chapter.

The first example, Employees, is a widget that adds and edits an `Employee` object with two fields name and title. It's a simple example with interaction between a UI (in this case a form) as the editor with data residing in a local `Employee` domain object. The `SimpleBeanEditorDriver` maintains the editor/bean relationship.

The second example, Phone Book, is a composite widget consisting of two editors; the widget manipulates two domain objects, one for employee data and one for keeping phone number data. The interaction between the two editors and the domain objects is also done with the `SimpleBeanEditorDriver`.

The third example uses the `Contact` domain object from the previous chapter with the `RequestFactoryEditorDriver`. The `Contact` domain object is a remote object.

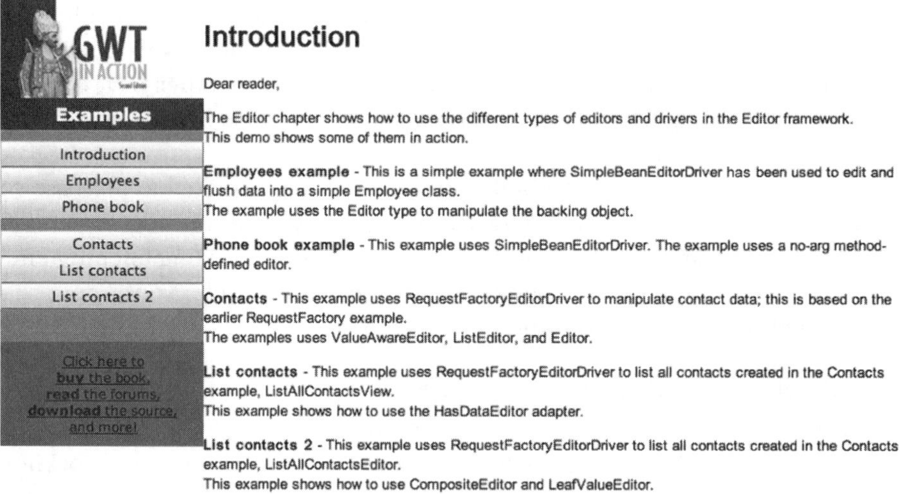

Figure 9.4 Menu and introduction page of the sample code showing the five examples to which we'll refer

The UI provides widgets to perform CRUD operations on `Contact` objects residing on a server. The RequestFactory example from chapter 8 has been slightly modified for this example. Additional code to handle a list of phone numbers is added to show how to use the Editor framework for CRUD operations performed on lists of objects residing on the server. In this example we've constructed composite widgets consisting of various complex editors.

The fourth example lists all inserted contacts. The list widget uses adapters in the UI instead of editors. It shows that in some cases you can skip editors and use already-defined adapters.

The fifth example also lists all inserted contacts; the difference from the fourth example is that a `CompositeEditor` is used with a `LeafValueEditor` for each list row. The purpose is to show how to use different editors and subeditor interfaces to cover more complex situations.

Now you have a good view of what to expect in the sample code. It's time to go forward and examine the different editor types using the `Employee` example objects in different situations.

9.3 Editor types

We mentioned earlier that editors are Java objects conforming to the editor contract. In order for a Java object to be an editor, it has to implement either the `Editor` interface or one of the Editor subinterfaces. We emphasized earlier that the purpose of editors is to reduce the amount of code required for moving data from a domain object to the UI and back to the domain object. Most editors are therefore widgets, but they don't have to be. You're free to define "headless" editors, that is, without any UI, changing the state of properties where editing of a domain object is programmatically done.

Besides implementing one of the editor types, an editor has to specify zero or more fields in its body. These fields have a correlation to the properties in the domain object the editor supports.

By implementing the `Editor` interface, you signal to the framework that all fields in this particular class should be treated as subeditors. An editor could choose to provide access to its fields, but it could also prevent access to them. In order to hide fields from the framework, you use the `@Ignore` annotation. What happens in that case is that the framework won't treat the field as a subeditor (and so it won't try to flush or edit the content). There are a variety of editor interfaces to use that reside in a hierarchy of interfaces, as you can see in figure 9.5.

At the top level of figure 9.5 you find the base `Editor` interface, with all subinterfaces extending the base `Editor`. Which one you use depends on the nature of your editor and the complexity needed. The base `Editor` is for simpler use; if you need more complex behavior, you could use one of the subinterfaces (we'll cover these subinterfaces in section 9.6).

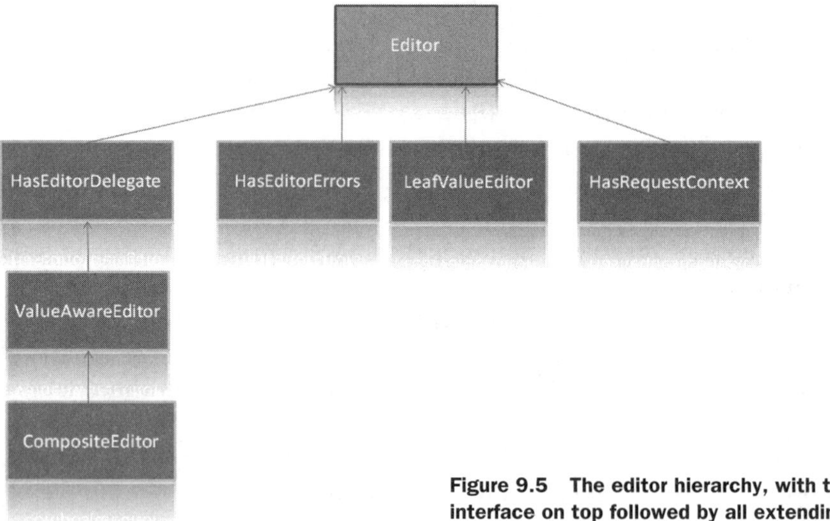

Figure 9.5 The editor hierarchy, with the base `Editor` interface on top followed by all extending subinterfaces

When you declare an editor, you have to specify the domain object that it will edit in the generic type parameter marker. To follow is the basic `Editor` interface; note that `T` specifies the object the editor should edit:

```
public interface Editor<T>{}
```

`T` could be a simple bean object, in the case of a local domain object, or an `EntityProxy` when dealing with a remote domain object.

This was a short introduction to editor types. Now you know enough to build your first simple editor, which you'll do in the next section. You'll start by editing a local domain object; later on in this chapter you'll see how to edit remote domain objects.

9.4 Constructing your first editor

In this section, we're going to implement a simple editor that could receive input from a user and send that input to a domain object. You can find the full source code for this in com.manning.gwtia.ch09.client.widgets.

Let's consider the steps you have to perform when you define an editor. First, as you saw at the end of the last section, you have to specify the domain object that it will edit. Because editors could support both local and remote domain objects, you must decide if the object supported by the editor will be an ordinary bean or an `EntityProxy`.

Once you've declared the domain object and the proxy if required, you can build the editor. The fastest way to construct an object of the type `editor` is to implement the base `Editor` interface. The base `Editor` interface doesn't require implementation of any particular behavior. It's enough to declare which properties of the domain object your editor will *edit*.

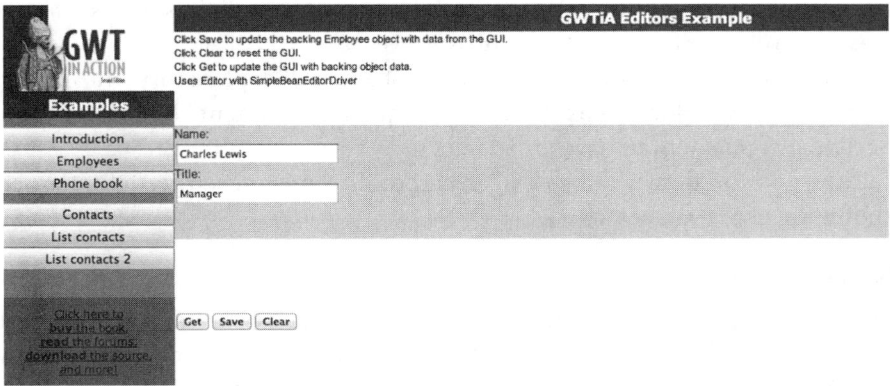

Figure 9.6 The UI for your first editor. It displays the name and title of an employee.

Your first editor will support a local domain object. The UI will be simple, as you can see in figure 9.6. The user can either click the Get button to edit data already in the local domain object or type in new information and flush it to the local domain object by clicking the Save button (they can also reset the GUI by clicking the Clear button).

In this example's case, we want no particular actions to be performed, such as validation, when a user changes values—we'll use a subeditor later to see how functionality such as this might be done.

Let's start our construction of the editor by performing the first step: defining the domain object.

9.4.1 Defining the local domain object

The editor should edit an `Employee` bean class that contains properties. The `Employee` class is a classic JavaBean, and we define it in the following.

Listing 9.1 Definition of `Employee` domain object

```
public class Employee {
   private Long id;
   private String name;
   private String title;
   public Long getId(){return id;}
   public String getName(){return name;}
   public String getTitle(){return title;}
   public void setId(Long id){this.id=id;}
   public void setName(String name){this.name=name;}
   public void setTitle(String title){this.title=title;}
}
```

You can see that this JavaBean has three fields (properties): `id`, `name`, and `title`, as well as the expected six getter/setter methods. Be aware that you have to provide getters/setters for all properties whose values will be transported between the UI and the domain object. Because this bean will reside on the client side, as a local domain object, there's no need to define a proxy class.

The name and title properties are probably self-explanatory; the id property is something we've added to explain a technique in a moment (but it's not uncommon for state management to have an id field).

Now that the domain object is specified, we can proceed to define an editor for editing the Employee bean.

9.4.2 Defining the editor

With the Employee bean created, you need to create the editor. We'll break this into two steps, looking first at how the editor is declared and second at what's in the editor body. We'll also show how to use the editor; remember, we're talking for now about a local domain object.

DECLARING THE EDITOR

The Editor class can be defined initially as

```
public class EmployeeEditor implements Editor<Employee>{
}
```

This definition meets the requirements; we've said that it implements the Editor interface as parameterized by the domain object Employee.

But we haven't defined a GUI component yet—this could be defined as a headless editor, but that's not what we want. We know that our name and title GUI elements will be held within a UI panel, so let's make that the editor. In this case, that frame will be Composite, so you initially define our editor as

```
public class EmployeeEditor extends Composite implements Editor<Employee>{
}
```

We'll continue with our construction of an editor by exploring the different types of body declaration.

CONSTRUCTING THE EDITOR CLASS BODY

You can use three different techniques to define subeditors in the editor body. These are exact name, path definition, and no-arg. There's also a way to inform the framework if a property should be ignored, and that's to use the @Ignore annotation. You don't have to declare all domain object properties in your editor; you're free to declare the ones that you're interested in.

In the following listing we complete the editor definition using the syntax for exact name, path declaration, and @Ignore.

Listing 9.2 The editor body with exact name, path, and @Ignore annotation

```
public class EmployeeEditor extends Composite implements Editor<Employee>{
   TextBox name;                                        <-- 1 Exact name definition

   @Path(value = "title")                               <-- 2 Path definition
```

```
    TextBox employeeTitle;
    @Ignore                                         <-- ❸ Ignore this property
    Label id;

    public EmployeeEditor(){

    }
}
```

What you usually have to do in an editor is specify exactly the same property names that the domain object has. ❶ shows this in action by providing a nonprivate instance field with the exact same name as the property it's supposed to edit in the domain object. GWT will infer that `name` in the editor declaration and map to the `name` object defined in the bean.

As we've discussed, most editors consist of subeditors, and because most GWT widgets conform to the editor contract, you can use them in your editor declaration. In our example, we can declare properties of the type `TextBox` to match user input. These widgets are automatically going to display values from the domain object, and if a user enters values in the `TextBox`, the changes will be *flushed* to the domain object when we programmatically request it.

There could be reasons for not using the exact name in the bean for the edited objects. For instance, if you want your editor to reference a property in the domain object, which in turn is part of another class, or if you want to use an alias for a property in the editor, you could use the `@Path` annotation ❷. This annotation is used to define an alias for a property in the domain object. In the annotation you have to specify the path to the referenced property.

You're free to use whatever name you think is suitable for the particular editor, but in the `@Path` annotation you have to give the exact name in order to give the framework information to make the proper data binding.

In our example you can see that we define `employeeTitle` in the editor, but that doesn't exist in the bean. To fix that, you use the `@Path` annotation ❷ to tell GWT that `employeeTitle` in the editor can be found as `title` in the `Employee` bean.

You may want the Editor framework to not work on certain properties. To achieve that, you declare the property as usual in the editor but annotate it with `@Ignore`. You do this in ❸ because you don't want the field `id` to be flushed or edited by the editor driver.

Our example used widgets as subeditors, but remember, you could use other editors you've defined as subeditors. It's easy to imagine a more complicated case where you've defined four separate editors that you need to combine—in that case, you define a new editor that has the four individual editors as subeditors.

The one type of editor definition we haven't used in our example is the no-arg method declaration. This type is useful if you want to build a composite of editors. It lets you define more complex editor structures. You could reuse editors to build new combinations of widgets. For instance, suppose you have a `PhoneNumberEditor` that's

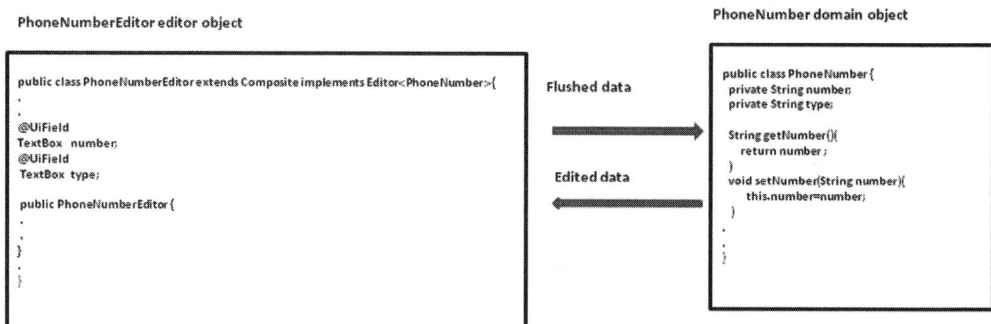

Figure 9.7 A `PhoneNumberEditor` coupled with a `PhoneNumber` domain object

coupled with a `PhoneNumber` domain object. Figure 9.7 shows an editor coupled with a domain object.

You can reuse the `PhoneNumberEditor` with the Employee editor to build a phone book widget where you can enter both employee data and phone number data. This new editor will be a composite editor consisting of an `EmployeeEditor` and a `PhoneNumberEditor`. In figure 9.8 you can see the UI of a simple phone book.

New combinations of editors could be defined with the no-arg method declaration. You'd define an interface extending the editor type. And in this interface you'd specify no-arg methods with names that match the properties of the domain object. In our case we have to define a `PhoneBook` domain object that will be coupled with the `PhoneBookEditor`:

```
public class PhoneBook {
private Employee employee;
private PhoneNumber phoneNumber;
```

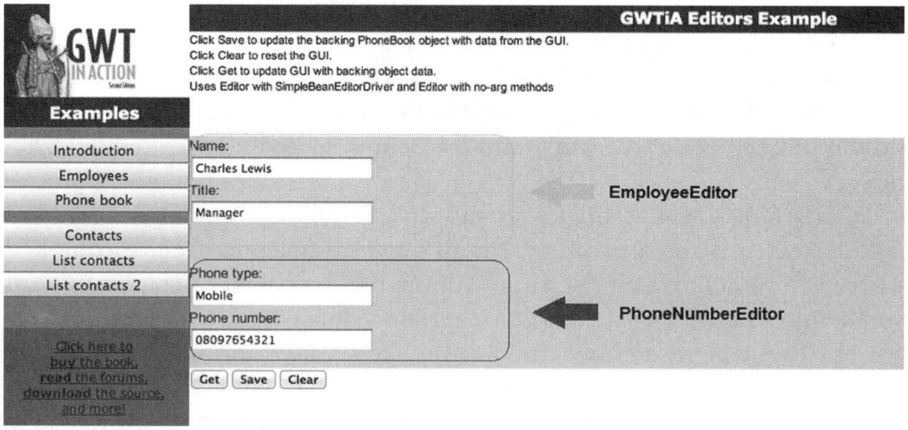

Figure 9.8 A simple phone book with employee fields from the `EmployeeEditor` and phone number fields from the `PhoneNumberEditor`

```
public Employee getEmployee() {
return employee;
}
public void setEmployee(Employee employee) {
   this.employee = employee;
}
public PhoneNumber getPhoneNumber(){
   return phoneNumber;
}
public void setPhone(PhoneNumber phoneNumber) {
   this.phoneNumber = phoneNumber;
}

}
```

`PhoneBookEditor` is an interface with a no-arg method property declaration. First, you have to define the interface, parameterized with the domain object it should be paired with:

```
public interface PhoneBookEditor extends Editor<PhoneBook>{
   EmployeeEditor employee();
   PhoneNumberEditor phoneNumber();
}
```

You could construct a hierarchy by implementing this interface consisting of two editors in a single `Editor` class:

```
public class PhoneBookView extends Composite implements PhoneBookEditor{

    @UiField
    EmployeeEditor employeeEditor;
    @UiField
    PhoneNumberEditor phoneNumberEditor;

    public PhoneBookView() {
      .
      .

    }

    @ Override
    public EmployeeEditor employee() {
           return employeeEditor;
    }

    @ Override
    public PhoneNumberEditor phoneNumber() {
           return phoneNumberEditor;
    }
.
.
}
```

The Phone Book example in this chapter's sample code is a no-arg method–defined editor.

USING THE EDITOR IN THE GUI

Our editor is a widget, so we create and use it in the GUI as we would any other widget. We're missing the code to create the component, and we'd usually put that in the constructor—either to create programmatically the `TextBox`es and add them or to invoke UiBinder functionality on a template that does that. For simplicity here, let's complete the editor from listing 9.2.

Listing 9.3 The finalized `EmployeeEditor`

```
public class EmployeeEditor extends Composite implements Editor<Employee>{
   private static EmployeeEditorUiBinder uiBinder = GWT
.create(EmployeeEditorUiBinder.class);

interface EmployeeEditorUiBinder extends UiBinder<Widget, EmployeeEditor> {
}

   @UiField
   TextBox name;

   @UiField
   @Path(value = "title")
   TextBox employeeTitle;

   @Ignore
   Label id;

   public EmployeeEditor() {
    initWidget(uiBinder.createAndBindUi(this));
   }

   public void resetValues() {
    name.setValue("");
    employeeTitle.setValue("");

   }
}
```

Now we can create our widget/editor as any normal widget and display it on the UI. Our EmployeeEditor.ui.xml will look like the following:

```
<!DOCTYPE ui:UiBinder SYSTEM "http://dl.google.com/gwt/DTD/xhtml.ent">
<ui:UiBinder xmlns:ui="urn:ui:com.google.gwt.uibinder"
xmlns:g="urn:import:com.google.gwt.user.client.ui"
xmlns:u="urn:import:com.google.gwt.editor.ui.client">
<ui:style src="../common.css"/>
<g:HTMLPanel>
    <g:FlowPanel addStyleNames="{style.flowpanel}" height="123px">
           <g:FlowPanel>
               <g:Label addStyleNames="{style.label}">Name:</g:Label>
               <g:TextBox ui:field="name" textAlignment="ALIGN_LEFT"
                 visibleLength="30" maxLength="30"></g:TextBox>
           </g:FlowPanel>
           <g:FlowPanel height="62px">
                <g:Label addStyleNames="{style.label}">Title:</g:Label>
```

```
                <g:TextBox ui:field="employeeTitle"
                   textAlignment="ALIGN_LEFT" visibleLength="30"
                   maxLength="30"></g:TextBox>
            </g:FlowPanel>
    </g:FlowPanel>
</g:HTMLPanel>
</ui:UiBinder>
```

This section has given the simplest possible way to construct an editor. We declared a class that implemented the base `Editor` interface. As you saw, the base interface doesn't require any method implementations. We defined a local domain object, and in the editor declaration we specified which domain object our editor is supporting. You've also learned how to declare the editor properties, and that could be done in different ways. Which one to use depends on the circumstances. Properties have also to conform to the Editor framework, and if you want the framework to ignore properties in your editor, you could use the `@Ignore` annotation.

We've now gone through the main activities required to develop a class of the editor type. Let's move on to drivers and to constructing objects of a more-complex editor type.

9.5 Binding an editor with drivers

The piece of code that performs the magic behind the editing and flushing of data is the driver. Drivers are essential in the process of editing beans.

In that process the driver needs to know how to bind data. It tries to find a hint of how to relate the properties of a domain object and the editor together. That clue comes from the way you choose to declare your editor's properties. You've seen that editors are nested and could present a whole object hierarchy graph, but you only have to bind the driver on the top-level editor.

The driver descends into everything that it identifies as an editable property in the editor. Every editable property, as we mentioned before, has to be of the editor type. So if the property isn't annotated with `@Ignore` in the editor, the driver will try to find a corresponding property in the domain object. In the following pages you'll see how to use our previously defined editor and domain object with both drivers. There's a slight variation in the syntax required in order to initialize and declare the *edit* and *flush* instructions between the two drivers. Otherwise, the piece of code needed for gluing the two objects together is similar for both drivers. Here we'll start out with the `SimpleBeanEditorDriver` and end with the `RequestFactoryEditor-Driver`.

NOTE In the editor, you aren't allowed to declare properties private in order for the driver to detect properties that are subeditors. The `Editor` driver generator will build a representation of the editor's tree using reflection: any nonprivate field or nonprivate no-arg method whose (return) type is an editor will be seen as a subeditor. This doesn't apply to `@Ignore`-annotated properties.

When we declared our domain object we found out that we could declare it as a remote or local object, and depending on that we had to choose an appropriate driver. As you know, the framework already provides two different types of drivers. These two top-level drivers are `SimpleBeanEditorDriver` and `RequestFactoryEditorDriver`.

`SimpleBeanEditorDriver` can be used with any bean-like object such as our `Employee` bean. `RequestFactoryEditorDriver` is designed to integrate with RequestFactory. This driver type requires a `RequestContext` in order to automatically call `RequestContext.edit()` on any `EntityProxy` instances that are encountered.

Both types of drivers bind an editor with an `EditorDelegate`. The `EditorDelegate` object provides framework-related services to the editor. Normally the delegate object isn't available to the editor. But you could access the delegate object by making the editor implement the `HasEditorDelegate` interface or one of the interfaces extending `HasEditorDelegate` (we'll talk more about the editor interfaces in section 9.6). Following are the services that the delegate object provides:

- `getPath()`—This could be used to access the current path of the editor within an editor hierarchy.
- `recordError()`—This could be used by the editor to report input validation errors to its parent editors and eventually to the driver. `RecordError` will produce an `EditorError` object. Data can be attached to the generated `EditorError` by using the `userData` parameter. This error will be reported to the nearest super-editor that implements the `HasEditorErrors` interface. We'll talk about this type of editor later on.
- `subscribe()`—You could make your editor subscribe to receive notifications if any external updates occur in its domain object. Unfortunately, `SimpleBeanEditorDriver` doesn't provide support for update subscriptions. The `EditorDelegate` provided from this driver has a no-operation implementation of the `EditorDelegate.subscribe` method. This means that you can't subscribe to notifications when a domain object is updated. The call to `subscribe()` will return `null`. `RequestFactoryEditorDriver` supports subscriptions. In that case it's possible for an editor to receive `EntityProxy` changes. If the editor is of the type `ValueAwareEditor`, it's meant to receive `EntityProxy` updates in its `onPropertyChange` method (but as of GWT 2.4 it appears that isn't currently working because updates are passed to the `setValue()` method). Otherwise, if you use a `ValueAwareEditor` with `SimpleBeanEditorDriver`, changes on a domain object will be passed to the `setValue()` method.

Let's move on to complete the workflow between your first editor and a domain object.

9.5.1 EmployeeEditor with SimpleBeanEditorDriver

Now we can add code to perform a complete data flow cycle that includes our editor and domain object. What's left is to declare a view class containing an Employee form with two fields, `name` and `title`. The form will be our `EmployeeEditor`. The view contains three buttons to trigger flushing, editing, and clearing of the UI fields. The user could flush entered values to the domain object by clicking the Save button. They could clear the fields by clicking the Clear button and finally update the form with the current values of the domain object. This is a simple example to show the flow between the editor and the domain object. The view uses a driver that will do the binding between our `EmployeeEditor` and the `Employee` domain object. In this case `SimpleBeanEditorDriver` is our candidate driver because our domain object is a local domain object (residing on the client). In the following listing you can see how the view creates and initializes the participating objects.

Listing 9.4 View using editor, local domain object, and `SimpleBeanEditorDriver`

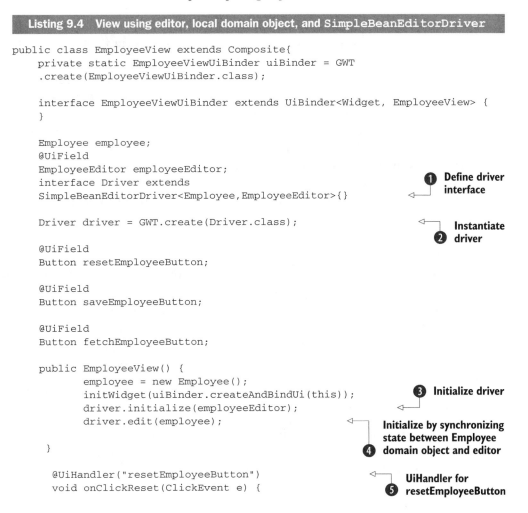

```
public class EmployeeView extends Composite{
    private static EmployeeViewUiBinder uiBinder = GWT
    .create(EmployeeViewUiBinder.class);

    interface EmployeeViewUiBinder extends UiBinder<Widget, EmployeeView> {
    }

    Employee employee;
    @UiField
    EmployeeEditor employeeEditor;
    interface Driver extends
    SimpleBeanEditorDriver<Employee,EmployeeEditor>{}          ❶ Define driver interface

    Driver driver = GWT.create(Driver.class);                  ❷ Instantiate driver

    @UiField
    Button resetEmployeeButton;

    @UiField
    Button saveEmployeeButton;

    @UiField
    Button fetchEmployeeButton;

    public EmployeeView() {
           employee = new Employee();
           initWidget(uiBinder.createAndBindUi(this));
           driver.initialize(employeeEditor);                  ❸ Initialize driver
           driver.edit(employee);                              ❹ Initialize by synchronizing state between Employee domain object and editor

     }

      @UiHandler("resetEmployeeButton")
      void onClickReset(ClickEvent e) {                        ❺ UiHandler for resetEmployeeButton
```

```
        employeeEditor.resetValues();
    }

    @UiHandler("saveEmployeeButton")                    ❻ UiHandler for
    void onClickSave(ClickEvent e) {                       saveEmployeeButton
        driver.flush();                                  ❼ Flush operation
        if (driver.hasErrors()) {
            Window.alert("There are errors!");

        }
    }

    @UiHandler("fetchEmployeeButton")                   ❽ UiHandler for
    void onClickGet(ClickEvent e) {                        fetchEmployeeButton
        driver.edit(employee);                           ❾ Edit operation

    }
}
```

In the class body you have to define the driver type and the pair of editor and domain objects. The driver type has to be an interface because GWT will provide the implementation itself.

In the SimpleBeanEditorDriver interface definition ❶ you declare the component it's supposed to edit and the editor that should be bound to the specific component. In this example the driver will edit Employee using an EmployeeEditor.

You have to instantiate the driver ❷ by using the GWT's deferred-binding system; you'll see more details in chapter 17. But for now all you need to know is what you have to write it in order to create a driver.

In your view you initialize the driver ❸ with the editor in the class constructor. You initialize your driver with EmployeeEditor, which is part of this widget. Finally, you initialize your editor ❹ with the current editor status by calling the driver's edit operation.

You also defined UIHandlers to handle button presses as follows:

- The resetEmployeeButton will be triggered when user clicks this button ❺. This triggers clearing of the form fields.
- The saveEmployeeButton ❻ flushes ❼ values from the UI to the Employee domain object.
- The fetchEmployeeButton ❽ will trigger an edit operation ❾ to propagate values from the Employee domain object to the editor.

TIP Be sure to perform driver.edit(model) after initialization to sync the state between the editor and the domain object before the user edits any fields.

Our first view with automatic flow of data between editor and domain object is completed; you can find the EmployeeView implementation in this chapter's first example code (see the package com.manning.gwtia.ch09.client).

What would the same view in this example look like if we used a remote domain object?

9.5.2 EmployeeEditor with RequestFactoryEditorDriver

`RequestFactoryEditorDriver` is designed to join the RequestFactory with the Editor framework. If you use the `RequestFactoryEditorDriver`, you can't reuse the domain object in the editor; instead, you need a proxy object of the `EntityProxy` subtype. This is because the domain object remains on the server, yet you need to access something in the client—the proxy (the driver will make sure that changes in the UI are reflected on the proxy). This driver is a little more complicated to use than `SimpleBeanEditorDriver`. It needs a `RequestContext` object for performing an edit on any `EntityProxy` instance and also a `RequestFactory` to create a `RequestContext` instance. That wasn't necessary with the `SimpleBeanEditorDriver`.

In order to use our original `EmployeeEditor` with `RequestFactoryEditorDriver`, you have to define a proxy object that references a remote `Employee` object. You also have to change the declaration of the `EmployeeEditor` in listing 9.3 to act on the proxy object and not on the domain object. Using this type of driver makes it easier to connect the GUI on the client side to server-side logic.

Let's now define an `EmployeeProxy` class that will reside on the client side of the application (that is, it will sit within the subpackage of the client package). We're using the same `Employee` class from listing 9.1, with the difference being that it now resides on the server side. The `EmployeeProxy` must extend the type `EntityProxy`. `EntityProxy`, `RequestContext`, and `RequestFactory` are part of the RequestFactory framework; for more details on how these objects interact, see chapter 8. Listing 9.5 isn't included in the sample code—we only use it in this chapter to make it clear how you could use a proxy with a domain object. In the sample code you'll instead find `PhoneProxy` and `ContactProxy`.

Listing 9.5 An `EntityProxy` for the `Employee` domain object in listing 9.1

```
@ProxyFor(value = Employee.class)
public interface EmployeeProxy extends EntityProxy {
   Long getId ();
   void setId (Long id);

   String getName ();
   void setName (String name);

   String getTitle ();
   void setTitle (String title);
}
```

❶ Define the domain object this object is proxy for

❷ Extend type EntityProxy

In the `EmployeeProxy` definition in listing 9.5, you extend the `EntityProxy` class, as we already said ❷. You also annotate the class ❶ with the `@ProxyFor` annotation, which takes the name of the class this is a proxy for.

In order to use EmployeeEditor with the EmployeeProxy, you must alter the declaration in listing 9.3 slightly. The following listing shows what you have to change in order to let the EmployeeEditor handle an EmployeeProxy object.

Listing 9.6 Alter the EmployeeEditor class type to handle EmployeeProxy

```
Public class EmployeeEditor extends Composite implements
Editor<EmployeeProxy>                                    ← ❶ Define the EmployeeEditor type
{
...
}
```

The EmployeeEditor is declared to be a type that acts on the EmployeeProxy object ❶.

Now you can use the Editor and proxy objects with the RequestFactoryEditor-Driver to propagate changes from the UI to the proxy and all the way to the domain object on the server by using RequestContext and RequestFactory. In order to accomplish this round-trip you have to connect instances of RequestContext, RequestFactory, and Editor to each other by instantiating and initializing the driver with an editor and a RequestFactory. You use the RequestFactory to create a RequestContext object. The RequestContext object is used to create a proxy object. The editor then has to be initialized with current status with an edit operation using the driver and the created proxy. In listing 9.7 you can see how the EmployeeView is updated to connect to a remote domain object. If you want a full example of how to use an editor, a remote domain object, and RequestFactoryEditorDriver, see the Contacts example in the sample code for this chapter (package com.manning.gwtia.client.widget).

Listing 9.7 EmployeeView connecting to remote domain object

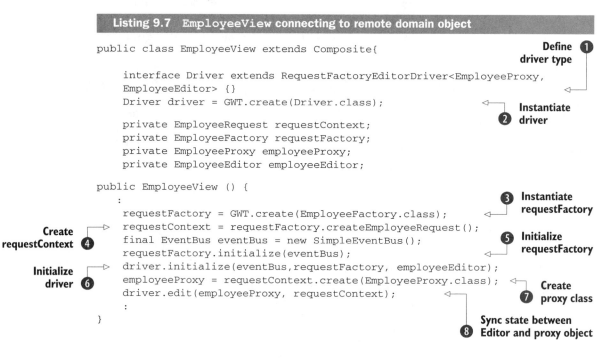

```
public class EmployeeView extends Composite{

    interface Driver extends RequestFactoryEditorDriver<EmployeeProxy,
    EmployeeEditor> {}                                   ← ❶ Define driver type
    Driver driver = GWT.create(Driver.class);            ← ❷ Instantiate driver

    private EmployeeRequest requestContext;
    private EmployeeFactory requestFactory;
    private EmployeeProxy employeeProxy;
    private EmployeeEditor employeeEditor;

public EmployeeView () {
    :
    requestFactory = GWT.create(EmployeeFactory.class);  ← ❸ Instantiate requestFactory
    requestContext = requestFactory.createEmployeeRequest();  ← ❹ Create requestContext
    final EventBus eventBus = new SimpleEventBus();
    requestFactory.initialize(eventBus);                 ← ❺ Initialize requestFactory
    driver.initialize(eventBus,requestFactory, employeeEditor);  ← ❻ Initialize driver
    employeeProxy = requestContext.create(EmployeeProxy.class);  ← ❼ Create proxy class
    driver.edit(employeeProxy, requestContext);          ← ❽ Sync state between Editor and proxy object
    :
}
```

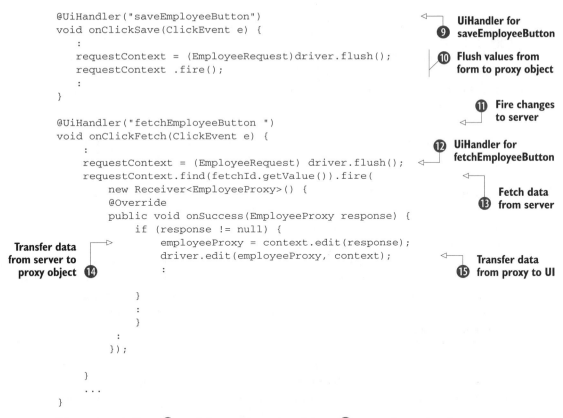

```
@UiHandler("saveEmployeeButton")
void onClickSave(ClickEvent e) {
   :
   requestContext = (EmployeeRequest)driver.flush();
   requestContext .fire();
   :
}

@UiHandler("fetchEmployeeButton ")
void onClickFetch(ClickEvent e) {
    :
    requestContext = (EmployeeRequest) driver.flush();
    requestContext.find(fetchId.getValue()).fire(
        new Receiver<EmployeeProxy>() {
        @Override
        public void onSuccess(EmployeeProxy response) {
            if (response != null) {
                employeeProxy = context.edit(response);
                driver.edit(employeeProxy, context);
                :

            }
            :
            }
      :
        });

    }
    ...
}
```

❾ UiHandler for saveEmployeeButton
❿ Flush values from form to proxy object
⓫ Fire changes to server
⓬ UiHandler for fetchEmployeeButton
⓭ Fetch data from server
⓮ Transfer data from server to proxy object
⓯ Transfer data from proxy to UI

First, you define ❶ and instantiate the driver ❷, exactly as the former example—though you use `RequestFactoryEditorDriver` instead of `SimpleBeanEditorDriver`.

In order to create a proxy and send data back and forth from the UI to the proxy object, you need a `RequestFactory` object and a `RequestContext`. You have to instantiate a `RequestFactory` object first by using GWT's deferred binding system ❸. You proceed by using the `RequestFactory` object to create a `RequestContext` ❹ object. The `RequestFactory` object has to be initialized ❺ with an `EventBus`. The `EventBus` object is used by the RequestFactory to post events whenever it detects changes on proxies. For more details on how this works, read about the Request-Factory in chapter 8.

In the view constructor you have to prepare for editing and flushing operations by initializing the driver. The initialization of the driver is done slightly differently here compared to the procedure for the local domain approach. The driver has to be initialized ❻ with an `EventBus` for subscription services, with an editor, as well as with a `RequestFactory`, which gives access to the remote domain object. Finally, you have to sync the status between the editor and the remote domain object. In the `edit` operation of this driver you pass an `EntityProxy` and a `RequestContext`, so prior to the `edit` operation you have to create the `EmployeeProxy` ❼ using our `RequestContext`. The `RequestContext` is used to provide the changes back and forth between the editor and the server-side domain object. You then perform synchronization between the editor and the `EntityProxy` object ❽.

Not so simple! But you only have to write all this once, and then it's up and running. Who knows, future updates to editors may even implement this boilerplate code. Or you could use the approaches shown in chapter 16 on dependency injection to automatically inject these dependencies.

You define your logic for saving values from the form to the `EntityProxy` and prepare for a possible update of the domain object residing on the server. For example, when the user clicks the Save button ❾, you flush the values from the `EmployeeEditor` to the `EmployeeProxy` ❿. After this, you could perform the transfer of these values to the domain object residing on the server by calling `fire` on the `RequestContext` ⓫ The Contacts example in this chapter's sample code shows how you could combine the Editor and RequestFactory frameworks to communicate with the server and do more complex CRUD operations.

You now define the logic for transferring values from an `EntityProxy` to the form. When the user clicks the Get button, you edit the form with values from the server domain object into the `EntityProxy` ⓬, in this case the employee ID for the employee the user wants to fetch from the server. Before the `edit` operation you can transfer the values from a server-side domain object to the `EntityProxy` using the RequestFactory framework and perform `requestContext.find(fetchId.getValue()()).fire` ⓭ and transfer when the data arrives from the server to the `EntityProxy` using `RequestContext.edit` ⓮; for more details on how to do that, see chapter 8 or see the Contacts example in this chapter's sample code. You perform an `edit` operation to move values from the `EmployeeProxy` that you previously got from the server-side domain object into the form ⓯ using the `RequestFactoryEditorDriver`.

You've learned how to construct a view with an `Editor` object that manipulates properties on a domain object that could reside locally on the client side but also remotely on a server. You've used two different drivers. You used `SimpleBeanEditorDriver` to edit the local object and `RequestFactoryEditorDriver` to edit the remote object.

The editor that you've used for both types of domain objects is of the basic type. There may be cases where an editor with a more complex behavior is desirable, such as for handling an unknown number of subeditors of the same type. In the next section we'll investigate the editor subinterfaces and how to accomplish more advanced editor behavior.

9.6 Editor subinterfaces

Earlier you learned how to use the Editor framework in the fastest possible way. We used the base editor interface that was suitable for our purpose, which was to build a simple editor.

Now it's time to talk about the available subinterfaces that you saw back in figure 9.5. These subinterfaces are useful in situations where more editor logic is needed than the basics—for example, you might want to handle a list of objects or have an editor where its behavior depends on other changes somewhere in the editor hierarchy.

You could use one or several of the subinterfaces to construct enhanced behavior. Which ones to pick depend on the type of behavior the particular editor needs to implement. Once you know how your editor should act, you could choose from the editors mentioned in this section. In summary, the subinterfaces do the following:

- `HasEditorDelegate`—Provides the `Editor` with its peer `EditorDelegate`. This allows the `Editor` to get its path, record errors, or subscribe to domain or `EntityProxy` object changes.
- `HasEditorErrors`—Implementing this interface indicates that the editor wants the ability to get a list of constraint violations, possibly for display to the user.
- `LeafValueEditor`—Sometimes you want to use editors that the framework should not descend into, where you're interested in performing some logic of your own instead of the general framework logic. Then you could use `LeafValueEditor`, which is most useful when defining editors that are immutable.
- `ValueAwareEditor`—In cases where you want the editor to conduct some logic after user updates have been flushed to the domain/proxy object, you could use `ValueAwareEditor`, for example, if you need to update other objects that depend on the same changes.
- `HasRequestContext`—Editors that implement this interface and use the `RequestFactoryEditorDriver` are provided with the `RequestContext` associated with the current editing session.
- `CompositeEditor`—If you want to handle an unknown number of editors of the same type at once, you could use `CompositeEditor`. Maybe you'll have an interface that has questions added dynamically to it, each question widget being its own editor—in this case, you'd make the widget that the questions are added to implement the `CompositeEditor` subinterface.

You've already seen in section 9.3 that subeditors could be parameterized to operate on both beans residing locally on the client or proxy objects for beans kept on a server. In our examples in this section we assume that we act on a local `Employee` domain object defined in listing 9.1 except for the `HasRequestContext`, where we use the proxy object `EmployeeProxy` from listing 9.3, because `HasRequestContext` is useful only with remote domain objects. If we were supposed to work with the remote `Employee` domain object, then we'd have parameterized our editors with `EmployeeProxy`. Now, let's go on and find out more details about the available subinterfaces.

9.6.1 Accessing the backing framework services

All editors have an `EditorDelegate` object that binds the editor with the backing framework services. In general, that delegate object isn't accessible to the editor, but by implementing the `HasEditorDelegate editor` type you tell GWT that it should call the setDelegate method. In the next listing you can see how EmployeeEditor would look if it was of the type HasEditorDelegate and operated on the Employee domain object.

Listing 9.8 EmployeeEditor of type HasEditorDelegate

```
public class EmployeeEditor implements HasEditorDelegate<Employee> {
    :
    @UiField
    TextBox name;

    @UiField
    @Path(value = "title")
    TextBox employeeTitle;

    @UiField
    @Ignore
    Label id;
    private EditorDelegate employeeDelegate;

    public EmployeeEditor(){
    :
    }

    public void setDelegate (EditorDelegate delegate){
       employeeDelegate = delegate;
    }
}
```

❶ Implement HasEditorDelegate interface

❷ Provide method setDelegate

You changed your former editor declaration from listing 9.3 from implementing the Editor type to implementing the HasEditorDelegate type ❶.

In order to conform to this interface, you have to give an implementation of the setDelegate ❷ method. This setDelegate is called by the editor's driver with the purpose of providing the attached delegate object and is called before any value initialization is performed. In your new EmployeeEditor class you keep a local delegate object, which you set when the driver calls the setDelegate method. Now you can use this instance to access services provided by the framework at some other point in the code.

An editor of the HasEditorDelegate type can access backing framework services, but it's quite simple in its behavior. Coming up next is the HasEditorErrors type. This editor type is valuable if you want to take care of constraint violations on edited data and give an appropriate error message to the end user.

9.6.2 Editors with error handling

Editors can be defined to provide an automatic error handling by implementing the HasEditorErrors type. This type has the ability to act on errors and gives the possibility of notifying the end user with a proper error message. The subinterface HasEditorErrors indicates that the editor expects a notification from the editor driver when errors are raised on a value. You could let your top editor in the hierarchy implement this interface to provide some general error handling whenever a subeditor reports any errors.

You can see an example of how to use this interface in the Contacts example in this chapter's sample code, but for now, the next listing shows how an `EmployeeEditor` would look if it was of the `HasEditorErrors` type and operated on the `Employee` domain object.

Listing 9.9 `EmployeeEditor` Implementing `HasEditorErrors`

```
public class EmployeeEditor implements HasEditorErrors<Employee> {    ❶ Implement interface
     :
    @UiField
    TextBox name;
    @UiField
    @Path(value = "title")
    TextBox employeeTitle;

    @Ignore
    Label id;

    public EmployeeEditor(){
    }

    public void showErrors(List<EditorError> errors) {    ❷ Provide method showErrors
        for(EditorError e:errors){
            log.info(e.getMessage());
            e.setConsumed(true);    ❸ Consume the error
        }
    }
}
```

You change the `EmployeeEditor` ❶ to be of the type `HasEditorErrors`. This type of editor has to provide a `showErrors` method ❷. Whenever a `ConstraintViolation` has occurred, the `EditorDriver` calls the `showErrors` method with a list of unconsumed errors reported by subeditors. You can loop through those errors, as you do in ❷, and take some action, such as logging them.

After digesting errors, the editor should mark that the errors have been consumed by calling `EditorError.setConsumed()` ❸ to avoid the error being propagated farther up in the editor hierarchy.

We proceed to another uncomplicated type to implement, the `LeafValueEditor` type.

9.6.3 Editing immutable objects or read-only editors

Editors that are going to support domain objects that consist of immutable properties can be of the `LeafValueEditor` type. By implementing this editor type, you indicate to the framework that the editor supports immutable values. The consequence is that the Editor framework won't descend into the subeditors. It's suitable for read-only editors and immutable domain objects where you want to perform some logic whenever changes occur higher up in the editor hierarchy.

Listing 9.10 shows an editor of the `LeafValueEditor` type. You can see an example of how to use a `LeafValueEditor` in the fourth example in this chapter's sample code (the second of the List Contacts examples).

Listing 9.10 Implementing `LeafValueEditor`

```
public class EmployeeEditor implements LeafValueEditor<Employee> {     ❶ Implement interface
   :
   @UiField
   TextBox name;

   @UiField
   @Path(value = "title")
   TextBox employeeTitle;

   @Ignore
   Label id;

   private Employee employee;

   public EmployeeEditor(){
     :

   }

   public Employee getValue() {                                        ❷ Provide method getValue
       return this.employee;
   }

   @Override
   public void setValue( Employee employee) {                          ❸ Provide method setValue
       this.employee = employee;
   }
}
```

You convert `EmployeeEditor` to be of the type `LeafValueEditor` ❶. The interface `LeafValueEditor` imposes the implementation of two methods: `setValue` and `getValue`.

The `setValue` and `getValue` methods could be used for accessing and modifying the domain/proxy object manually. The framework calls both methods. The `getValue` method ❷ is called after flushing an editor's state to the edited domain/proxy object. The method `setValue` ❸ is called after an `edit` operation. It provides the domain/proxy object instance that's bound to this particular editor. If some of the values have to be updated when changes happen somewhere in the editor hierarchy, you could add the code to update the properties in these two methods.

This type is practical for objects you don't want the driver to descend into. For example, this is suitable for editors where the output is read only. It gives the developer the chance to control the editor logic as desirable.

The editors you've seen up until now are quite elementary and provide basic behavior. In cases where you'd like to add more customized behavior to the editor, you should implement the `ValueAwareEditor` subinterface.

9.6.4 Building customized editor behavior

In cases where you'd like to add more customized behavior to the editor, implement the `ValueAwareEditor` subinterface. It indicates that this particular editor behavior is affected when its properties are edited and changed. If you use this type of editor with a `RequestFactoryEditorDriver` object, you get the possibility of changing behavior when updates occur on the domain/proxy object.

If you use this type of editor with `RequestFactoryEditorDriver`, you could use the `EditorDelegate` object to subscribe to external changes on the proxy instance. Changes in the proxy object could be reported in the `onPropertyChange` method (but as of GWT 2.4 it appears that it isn't working, because updates are passed to the `setValue` method). Otherwise, if you use `SimpleBeanEditorDriver`, the updated domain object will be passed into the `setValue` method. In listing 9.11 you can see `EmployeeEditor` of the `ValueAwareEditor` type. In the second List Contacts example in this chapter's sample code, you can see a real implementation of a `ValueAwareEditor`.

Listing 9.11 `EmployeeEditor` implementing `ValueAwareEditor`

```
public class EmployeeEditor implements ValueAwareEditor<Employee> {    // 1 Implement interface
:
@UiField
TextBox name;
@UiField
@Path(value = "title")
TextBox employeeTitle;

@Ignore
Label id;

private EditorDelegate employeeDelegate;
private Employee employee;
private HandlerRegistration subscription;

public EmployeeEditor(){
:
}
@Override
public void setDelegate (EditorDelegate delegate){    // 2 Provide method setDelegate
    employeeDelegate = delegate;
    subscription = delegate.subscribe();    // 3 Subscribe for changes
}
@Override
public void setValue(Employee employee){    // 4 Provide setValue
    this.employee= employee;
```

```
}
@Override
public void flush(){                                              ❺ Provide method flush
    this.employee.setName(this.employee.getName().toUpperCase());
    this.employee.setTitle(this.employee.getTitle().toUpperCase());
}
@Override
public void onPropertyChange(String...paths){                    ❻ Property onPropertyChange
//No-op
}

}
```

In listing 9.11 you change the `EmployeeEditor` example to be a `ValueAwareEditor` ❶. This type of editor has to provide three methods that belong to `ValueAwareEditor` interface and one that this editor inherits from the `HasDelegateEditor` interface.

The framework calls all methods. It inherits the method `setDelegate` ❷ from `HasDelegateEditor`; the `EditorDriver` calls this method to give access to the delegate object connected to this editor. In order for the class to get notifications, the subscribe method ❸ has to be called on the delegate object.

The method `setValue` ❹ is called when the editor's values are set. The framework passes the object this editor is responsible for editing. Here you could add initialization of any affected subeditors or other objects that aren't defined in the specific editor to be accessible by the Editor framework.

The method `flush` ❺ is called when the editor cycle is finished, in a depth-first manner. You could put any logic in this method that you'd like to perform after flushing, for example, as you do here to always transform the name and title to uppercase, or you can add validity checks on your data and report errors by using the delegate object.

If you have code that you want to execute when some property in the underlying proxy object is changed, you could put that logic into the `onPropertyChange` ❻ method. The framework notifies this editor that one or more values have been changed. Not all backing services support property-based notifications; for example, `SimpleBeanEditorDriver` doesn't. If your delegate doesn't support this, you could put your logic in the `setValue` method instead.

This type is useful because it gives you more control when the user updates the editor properties. Until now we've assumed that we always have to handle one domain/proxy object. But what about handling multiple objects of the same type? A technique to handle lists of objects is to implement the `CompositeEditor` interface.

9.6.5 Handling subeditors of the same type

The type `CompositeEditor` helps you to deal with lists of an unknown number of domain/proxy objects. The subinterface `CompositeEditor` indicates that this editor is composed of an unknown number of subeditors all of the same type. This type handles a chain of subeditors with domain/proxy objects. New subeditors could be added, updated, or deleted at runtime. All editors and domain/proxy objects should be of the same type.

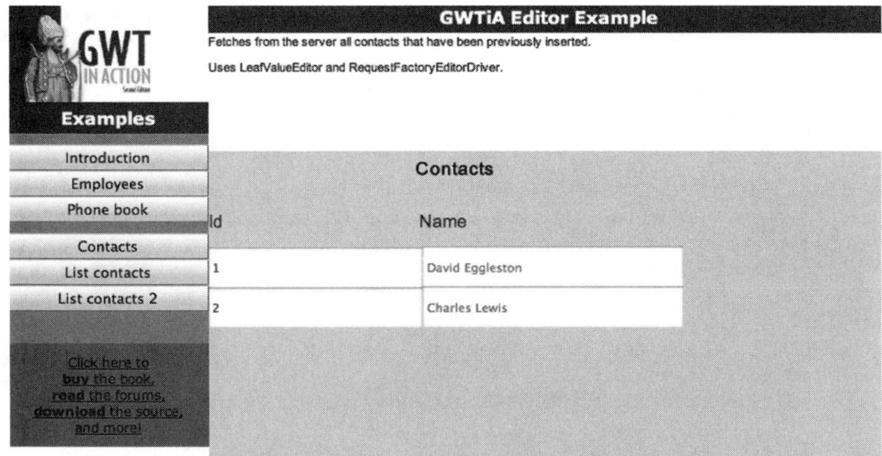

Figure 9.9 The `CompositeEditor` displaying a list of contacts

> **NOTE** You still have to define an editor that's going to support a single domain or `EntityProxy` object and use that type in the list.

The `CompositeEditor` type is a subeditor to the `ValueAwareEditor`. That means in order to conform to `CompositeEditor`, you have to provide the methods that are part of the `ValueAwareEditor` interface and three additional methods that are part of the `CompositeEditor`:

- `createEditorForTraversal`
- `setEditorChain`
- `getPathElement`

Listing 9.12 shows how to define a `CompositeEditor`. This code uses a list of `Employee` domain objects, where each individual object is of type `Employee` and an `EmployeeEditor` supports every single `Employee` domain object. In the second List Contacts example in figure 9.9 and in this chapter's sample code you can see an additional example of implementation of a `CompositeEditor`.

We'll stick with `EmployeeEditor` in the text (you should be able to see the same principles in action in listing 9.12).

Listing 9.12 `EmployeeEditor` implementing `CompositeEditor`

```
public class ListEmployeeEditor extends Composite implements
     CompositeEditor<List<Employee>,Employee,EmployeeEditor>{

private CompositeEditor.EditorChain<Employee, EmployeeEditor>
    editorChain;

private EditorDelegate<List<Employee>> listEmployeeDelegate;

private List<EmployeeEditor> editorList;
```

Implement interface CompositeEditor ❶

```
@Override
public EmployeeEditor createEditorForTraversal () {          ❷ Provide method createEditorForTraversal
    EmployeeEditor employeeEditor= new EmployeeEditor();
    return employeeEditor;
}

@Override
public void setEditorChain (CompositeEditor.EditorChain<Employee,
    EmployeeEditor> chain) {                                  ❸ Provide method setEditorChain
    editorChain= chain;
}
@Override
public void setValue(List<Employee> employees) {             ❹ Provide method setValue
    if (editorList==null){
        editorList=new ArrayList<EmployeeEditor>();
    }else{
        //reset subeditors list
        for(EmployeeEditor subEditor:editorList){
            editorChain.detach(subEditor);
        }
        editorList.clear();
    }
     for (Employee e : employees){
        EmployeeEditor editor= new EmployeeEditor();
        editorChain.attach(e,editor);
    }
}
@Override                                                      ❺ Provide method setDelegate
public void setDelegate (EditorDelegate<List<Employee>> delegate) {
    listEmployeeDelegate = delegate;
}
@Override
public String getPathElement (EmployeeEditor subEditor) {    ❻ Provide method getPathElement
    return "["+editorList.indexOf(subeditor)+"]";
}
@Override
public void flush(){                                           ❼ Provide method flush
    :

}
@Override
public void onPropertyChange(String...paths){                 ❽ Provide method onPropertyChange
    :
}

...
}
```

When you declare a `CompositeEditor` you have to define the type parameters for the domain/proxy object to be edited and the editor type that will edit the component.

You change the example to be an editor of the `CompositeEditor` type ❶. The class `ListEmployeeEditor` will edit a list of domain objects, `List<Employee>`, using its sub-editors of the type `EmployeeEditor`. The `ListEmployeeEditor` contains an unknown number of `Employee` objects. Each `Employee` object is bound to an `EmployeeEditor`.

The method createEditorForTraversal ❷ should return a subeditor of the same type, in this case EmployeeEditor. This editor will handle a single domain object in the list. The framework uses this method to create new subeditors to attach to the chain of the list.

The method setEditorChain ❸ gives you the possibility of acquiring the chain so that you can attach and detach instances of objects to and from the chain at runtime. In the setEditorChain method you copy the editorChain object into a local copy in order to attach and detach EmployeeEditor objects to the editor hierarchy. You declare a local variable of type CompositeEditor.EditorChain, which you set in this method.

You could use the editorChain to attach new EmployeeEditors in your setValue method ❹. The driver calls this method when a domain Employee object is set by its attached EmployeeEditor.

You create a copy of the delegate object this editor is coupled with in the setDelegate method ❺. This object could be used to record errors.

The framework calls the method getPathElement ❻ every time you attach a new subeditor. You could return the path element for the attached object. CompositeEditor handles indexable data structures such as List, so you could use this method to return an index for the attached object.

As you saw in section 9.6.4 when we talked about the ValueAwareEditor, the method flush ❼ is called when the editor cycle is finished, and the method onPropertyChange ❽ is called if some property in the underlying object is changed.

If you use RequestFactoryEditorDriver and want access to the RequestContext associated with the current editing session, you could implement the HasRequestContext interface.

9.7 Accessing the RequestContext

Editors that are used with a RequestFactoryEditorDriver can be provided the RequestContext currently used in the edit session by implementing the interface HasRequestContext. The benefit is that you don't have to pass the RequestContext to the subeditors manually. Instead, the RequestFactoryEditorDriver calls the setRequestContext method that you provided by implementing the HasRequestContext interface and passes the RequestContext used in the edit operation. You can then use the RequestContext to create new proxy classes or check if changes have been done to the proxies that are mutable under this context. Listing 9.13 shows sample code of how to define a HasRequestEditor. In this code we define the EmployeeEditor to be of the type HasRequestContext and act on EmployeeProxy.

Listing 9.13 EmployeeEditor implementing HasRequestContext

```
public class EmployeeEditor implements HasRequestContext<EmployeeProxy> {   ❶ Implement interface
:
@UiField
TextBox name;
```

```
@UiField
@Path(value = "title")
TextBox employeeTitle;

@Ignore
Label id;

RequestContext context;

public EmployeeEditor(){
:
}
@Override
public void setRequestContext(RequestContext context){     <-- ❷ Provide method setRequestContext
    this.context = context;
}

}
```

Here you change the example to be an editor of the `HasRequestContext<EmployeeProxy>` type ❶.

When you declare a `HasRequestContext` you have to define the `type` parameter for the proxy object for the domain object to be edited. Here you use the `EmployeeProxy` defined in listing 9.5; you're using the proxy object because this works only with the `RequestFactoryEditorDriver`.

The `RequestFactoryEditorDriver`, which passes the `RequestContext` associated with an edit operation, calls the method `setRequestContext` ❷.

In this section we've created simple editors but also more advanced ones that could be useful in real-life scenarios. The framework provides types for simple processing of data but also for more complex conditions. These subinterfaces could be combined to build sophisticated widget behavior. You could structure your editor to access backing framework services and add error handling. You can customize behavior depending on user input. You can also manage immutable domain objects or operate on multiple objects of the same type.

Before we jump into adapters as our final topic, we'll cover one alternate way to construct editors: by using the `IsEditor` type.

9.8 Alternate way to construct an editor

In situations where you have a view that you don't want to be an editor, but you want this class to be part of an editor structure, you can use the `IsEditor` type. This is useful, for example, if you want to build a composition of central source code logic that's going to appear more than once. You could define a reusable editor, and by implementing the `IsEditor` interface, any object could participate in the same hierarchy as the reusable editor without your having to write code to adapt to the Editor framework, and you avoid duplication of code. In the following listing you can see a widget implementing the `IsEditor` interface.

Listing 9.14 View of type `Composite` participating in an editor hierarchy

```
public class CompanyListEditor
extends Composite
implements IsEditor<ListEditor<Employee,EmployeeEditor>> {      ❶ Participating object Implements the IsEditor interface

public ListEditor<Employee, EmployeeEditor> controller =
ListEditor.of(new EmployeeEditorSource());      ❷ Create reusable editor

public ListEditor<Employee, EmployeeEditor> asEditor() {      ❸ Implementation of asEditor method

   return controller;
}

void onAddButtonClicked() {      ❹ Use reusable editor to manipulate list of employees
   controller.getList().add(new Employee());
}

void onClearButtonClicked() {
   controller.getList().clear();
}
}
```

In our example the view `CompanyListEditor` reuses the `ListEditor` behavior. It lists `Employee` domain objects (`Employee` could be exchanged with `EmployeeProxy` for remote domain objects) using related `EmployeeEditor` objects. You want the framework to be able to descend into each object in the entire list of domain objects. You want your `CompanyListEditor` class to conform to the Editor framework. The reason why you want this view to be part of the framework is to have an automatic flow of data between the domain objects and the related editors. Instead of creating a complex class to do this, you reuse an object called `ListEditor`, which handles a list of objects as one. The `ListEditor` class is an adapter and is provided by the framework. This class gives lots of useful editor behavior. You therefore declare the `CompanyListEditor` class as a `Composite`, which behaves as a `ListEditor`. The object to be reused, `ListEditor`, implements the `Editor` interface ❶ as usual. The participating object, `CompanyListEditor`, incorporates this reusable editor by implementing the `IsEditor` interface. `CompanyListEditor` becomes an editor without having to implement all the methods in the incorporated editor. This gives you the possibility of creating composite logic.

A new instance of `ListEditor` is created by calling the `of()` method ❷; the instance is backed by an `EditorSource`. An `EditorSource` is capable of creating and destroying instances of editors. This type is used by editors that operate on ordered data, such as `ListEditor`.

In order for an object to reuse editor behavior, it has to implement the `IsEditor` interface and implement the `asEditor` method ❸. This method should return an instance of the incorporated reusable editor. The method `asEditor` returns a

ListEditor that's encapsulated in the CompanyListEditor. This ListEditor will act as a coeditor to the CompanyListEditor.

The methods onAddButtonClicked and onClearButtonClicked show ❹ how you can access the list of domain objects from the ListEditor functionality. You can manipulate the list by inserting and deleting domain objects. The result is that CompanyListEditor acts as a ListEditor and edits and flushes domain objects automatically whenever changes occur.

> **NOTE** The type Editor<T> could be changed to the equivalent type definition IsEditor<Editor<T>>. It's legal for a class to be typed with both Editor and IsEditor.

You know how to build editors at this point; you've built simple and advanced editors and also seen an alternative quick way to conform to the Editor framework.

In the next section you'll see that the framework provides mechanisms to increase reuse of editor logic. These classes are called *adapters* and are available to facilitate reusing generic editor logic.

9.9 Adapters

The framework provides adapter classes in order to adapt logic to the Editor framework. Adapters provide generic logic and reduce the amount of code needed, for instance, when displaying and manipulating a set of objects or individual objects. Each adapter provides an implementation for one or several editors and can be used to adapt widgets to the Editor interface without writing any specific code.

A number of adapters are available. For instance, if you want to adapt any list of objects to the Editor framework, you can use the HasDataEditor class, which implements CompositeEditor, Editor, LeafValueEditor, HasEditorDelegate, and ValueAwareEditor. This class adapts a list of objects to conform to all editors without you having to provide any source code yourself.

Another useful adapter for handling many objects is ListEditor, which you'll see in action in the next section; this adapter keeps a list of the same type of domain/proxy objects in sync with a list of subeditors. ListEditor implements the CompositeEditor, Editor, HasEditorDelegate, and ValueAwareEditor interfaces. The following adapter classes, HasDataEditor, TakesValueEditor, and ValueBoxEditor, manage single objects and implement the LeafValueEditor.

What mostly characterizes an adapter is that it provides an of() method in order to provide an instance of the particular adapter.

In this section we're going to show some basic information about the available adapters, how to create them, and where they're useful.

9.9.1 Editing a range of domain objects

The HasDataEditor adapter helps you to edit a range of domain/proxy objects. This adapter uses a view of the HasData type like CellList and CellTable widgets to

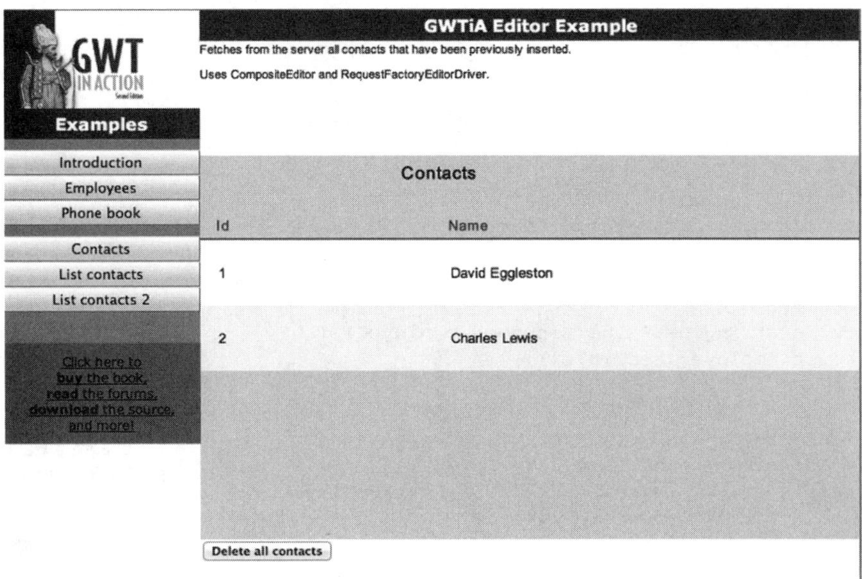

Figure 9.10 A widget that uses `HasDataEditor` adapter to list a set of contacts residing on the server

display the list of domain/proxy object values. You parameterize the `HasData` view with the domain/proxy object type you want to edit. The Contacts examples in this chapter's sample code uses this type of adapter to display the lists of contacts. In figure 9.10 you can see the UI for that example.

Now we're going to use our `Employee` objects. Our plan is to show an `EmployeeListWidget` with a list of `Employee` objects (for remote domain objects, we use `EmployeeProxy`). We want an automatic update of the domain `Employee` object whenever a user enters a new value in a cell. Also, we want changes in the domain objects to be smoothly propagated back to the UI.

We won't use a `CellTable` to display the name and title of all the employees. We won't define our own editor code; instead we'll use a `HasDataEditor` adapter, which lets us implement most editors. Listing 9.15 shows how it can be done. In the Contacts example in this chapter's sample code you can see another example of how to use a `HasDataEditor` adapter.

Listing 9.15 List of employees edited by a `HasDataEditor`

```
public class EmployeeListWidget extends Composite[

HasDataEditor<Employee> hasDataEditor;                        ❶ Declare editor

public EmployeeListWidget () {                                ❷ Declare a CellTable for
initWidget(uiBinder.createAndBindUi(this));                     the list of Employee
                                                                domain objects
CellTable<Employee> table = new CellTable<Employee>();
```

```
table.setKeyboardSelectionPolicy(KeyboardSelectionPolicy.ENABLED);
TextColumn<Employee> nameColumn = new TextColumn<Employee>(){       ❸ Instantiate a text column to show name

   @Override
      public String getValue(Employee employee) {
      return employee.getName();
   }
   };
table.addColumn(nameColumn, "Name");

TextColumn<Employee> titleColumn = new TextColumn<Employee>() {
   @Override
   public String getValue(Employee employee) {                      Instantiate a text column to show title ❹
   return employee.getTitle();
   }
   };
hasDataEditor = HasDataEditor.of(table);                            ❺ Create a HasDataEditor backed by a CellTable
table.addColumn(nameColumn, "Title");
List<Employee> employees = new ArrayList<Employee>();
hasDataEditor.setValue(employees);                                  ❻ Initialize adapter
}
...
}
```

In listing 9.15 you declare a `HasDataEditor` object where `Employee` is the domain object ❶. It will keep a range of data of the type `Employee` where the `Employee` domain object is the type of data you want to edit.

Now you define a `CellTable`, which will contain your list of `Employee` domain objects ❷. (If you want to know a bit more about `Cell` widgets, you can find them described in chapter 10.) In this widget you'll display two columns: name and title. You create a text column to display the name. In the `getValue()` method of the `TextColumn` body, required by the `CellWidget` specification, you return the employee name ❸.

You also have to create a text column to display the title. In the `getValue()` method of the `TextColumn` body, you return the employee title ❹.

You have to instantiate the `HasDataEditor` adapter and declare it to be backed by your `CellTable` ❺. Finally, you initialize the adapter with a list of domain objects ❻.

The `HasDataEditor` provides complex `ListEditor` functionality because it implements all of the following `Editor` interfaces: `CompositeEditor`, `LeafValueEditor`, `Editor`, `ValueAwareEditor`, and `HasEditorDelegate`. This means that you can add in the functionality you saw in the section on subinterfaces if you want.

In the next section you'll find yet another way to handle multiple objects.

9.9.2 *Adapting a list of objects with associated editors*

We talked about `ListEditor` in the previous example. You can see that a list of objects could be edited with the adapter `ListEditor`, which keeps your domain/proxy objects in sync with their associated editors. `ListEditors` have to be backed by an `EditorSource` object whose purpose is to create subeditors. The Contacts example in this

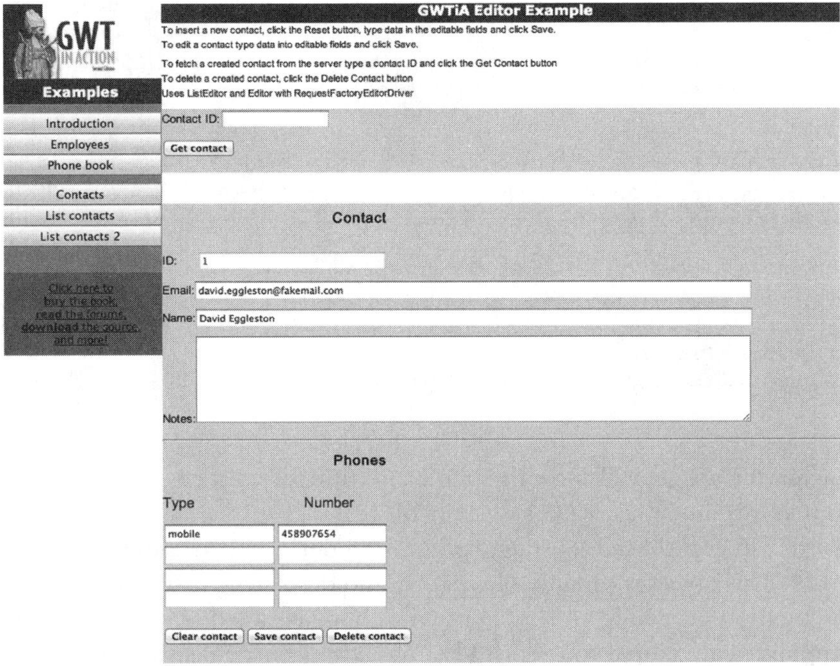

Figure 9.11 The Contacts example displaying a contact with a list of phone numbers. The `PhoneListWidget` uses `ListEditor`.

chapter's sample code uses this type of adapter to display a list of phone numbers belonging to a contact object. In figure 9.11 you can see the UI for that example.

This `EditorSource` adapter implements the following `Editor` interfaces: `CompositeEditor`, `Editor`, `HasEditorDelegate`, and `ValueAwareEditor`. We modify our example widget from listing 9.15 to use a `ListEditor` instead of a `HasDataEditor`.

In the next listing you can see how you could use a `ListEditor` to display a list of `Employee` objects (for remote domain objects we'd have used `EmployeeProxy`).

Listing 9.16 List of employees edited by a `ListEditor`

```
public class EmployeeListWidget extends Composite{
private class EmployeeEditorSource extends                    ❶ Declare EditorSource
EditorSource<EmployeeEditor> {
@Override                                                     ❷ Used by the ListEditor to
public EmployeeEditor create(int index) {                        create instances of editors
   EmployeeEditor editor = new EmployeeEditor(eventBus,factory,request);

        editor.setValue(employee);
   container.insert(editor, index);

   return editor;
}
```

```
@Override
public void dispose(EmployeeEditor subEditor) {
        subEditor.removeFromParent();
}

@Override
public void setIndex(EmployeeEditor editor, int index) {
         container.insert(editor, index);
}

ListEditor<Employee, EmployeeEditor> editor;

public EmployeeListWidget() {
   editor = ListEditor.of(new PhoneEditorSource ());
}
}
```

❸ Used by the ListEditor to remove employees from the list

❹ Used by the ListEditor to set index on list rows

❺ Create a ListEditor that uses PhoneEditorSource

Once again the widget will show the name and title for a list of employees. The difference is that this time it uses a `ListEditor` object.

In order to control the UI state, you have to declare a class that extends `EditorSource` ❶. This object is capable of creating and destroying instances of editors.

The method `create` in the `EditorSource` body is called by the `ListEditor` when new employees are added to the list ❷. The `ListEditor` calls the method `remove` ❸ when employees are removed from the list.

The method `setIndex` is called by the `ListEditor` to set the index on list rows ❹. Finally, you create a `ListEditor` that uses `PhoneEditorSource` ❺.

Now you know how to manage lists of objects of the same type. Let's proceed and examine how you can use the adapters for simpler situations where you have only one item to handle.

9.9.3 Adapters for single-domain objects

When a type being edited has an optional field that may be nullified or reassigned as part of the editing process, you can choose to use `OptionalFieldEditor`. This editor implements `LeafValueEditor`, `Editor`, `ValueAwareEditor`, and `HasDataEditor`:

```
private OptionalFieldEditor<Employee, EmployeeEditor>  fieldEditor;

fieldEditor=OptionalFieldEditor.of(new EmployeeEditor());
```

The editors are mainly used to wire UI widgets with domain objects; this requires that the subeditors be widgets, but if you want to use an editor for keeping hidden values or null values, you can use a `SimpleEditor`. This class provides a trivial implementation of an editor that could be used for beans that could have null values or that will be hidden and won't be displayed on the UI.

For instance, if in our `Employee` domain object we want to edit a value that's going to be hidden (not visible in the UI), we declare a property in our `EmployeeEditor` and keep some value there. The framework won't care about this property but will still propagate the value back and forth to the domain object automatically:

```
SimpleEditor<String> hiddenValue;

public EmployeeEditor() {
initWidget(uiBinder.createAndBindUi(this));
hiddenValue = SimpleEditor.of("hidden");

}
```

Objects of the `HasText` type like `Button` or `Label` conform to the `Editor` interface with the `HasTextEditor` adapter. `HasText` objects contain text.

`HasTextEditor` implements `Editor` and `LeafValueEditor`:

```
HasTextEditor nameLabel;
Label labelName;

public EmployeeEditor() {
   initWidget(uiBinder.createAndBindUi(this));
   nameLabel = HasTextEditor.of(labelName);
}
```

In cases where you'd like to use objects that implement the `TakesValue` interface like `DateBox` or `CheckBox`, you can use the `TakesValueEditor` to adapt to the Editor framework. This adapter implements the `Editor` and `LeafValueEditor` interfaces:

```
@UIField
TextBox name;
TakesValueEditor<String> nameEditor;

public EmployeeEditor() {
   initWidget(uiBinder.createAndBindUi(this));
   nameEditor = TakesValueEditor.of(name);
}
```

Text-based widgets that extend the `ValueBoxBase` abstract class like `TextBox` and `TextArea` can be used with the `ValueBoxEditor` adapter to adjust to the Editor framework. This adapter class implements `Editor` and `LeafValueEditor`. The editor parses the string value of the widget; if a parse exception occurs, the exception will be reported via an `EditorError`:

```
@UiField
TextBox boxName;
ValueBoxEditor<String> name;

public EmployeeEditor() {
   initWidget(uiBinder.createAndBindUi(this));
   name = ValueBoxEditor.of(boxName);
}
```

The last adapter mentioned is used for text-based widgets with error messages.

This class can be used to display `leaf` widgets with an error message. The adapter implements the following interfaces: `Editor` and `HasEditorErrors`. This adapter combines a `ValueBoxBase` widget as a `TextBox` with a `Label` to show any errors that occur during parsing the `ValueBoxBased` widget:

```
@UiField
ValueBoxEditorDecorator<String> title;

<u:ValueBoxEditorDecorator ui:field="title">
<u:valuebox>
<g:TextBox/>
</u:valuebox>
</u:ValueBoxEditorDecorator>
```

In the Employees example in this chapter's sample code, you can see how to use `ValueBoxEditorDecorator` and `ValueBoxEditor` as subeditors.

Adapters are useful in situations where you don't need specific logic for your editors. These ready-to-use classes implement one or many `Editor` interfaces and give a variety of logic. They contribute to more efficient coding once you know where and how you can use them.

9.10 Summary

The Editor framework cuts programming time. It automates copying operations from some backing objects all the way to the user.

Different types of editors exist that would be suitable for all kinds of situations. The framework provides all sorts of adapters for reusing editor logic and reduces the need for defining your own editors.

The combination of the RequestFactory framework and Editor framework gives you a powerful tool for moving data from remote objects on a server all the way to a widget that presents the data to the end user.

We hope you found out how useful the Editor framework is for building widgets quickly without any boilerplate code to move data between the UI and a domain object graph. In the next chapter we'll talk about data-presentation widgets. Yet another way to build a UI efficiently, these objects provide a useful technique to let the user easily navigate through large data sets.

10 Data-presentation (cell) widgets

This chapter covers

- Defining data-presentation widgets and data cells
- Creating new cell types
- Using the data-presentation widgets
- Sorting, paging, and retrieving data
- Generating custom-cell table builders

Until this point, we've been building applications using regular UI widgets. This is fine for many tasks, but they're not ideal for rendering large data sets. They're somewhat heavyweight objects that take time to instantiate, as well as occupy memory. Modern web browsers can generally render a page containing dozens or even hundreds of widgets almost instantaneously, but if we try to draw a data set that's made up of thousands of widgets, we could well encounter a perceptible delay while the data is rendered, or worse, receive a slow script warning (SSW).

We could handle this delay through the use of an incremental `RepeatingCommand` to draw a few results at a time, which occasionally returns control to the

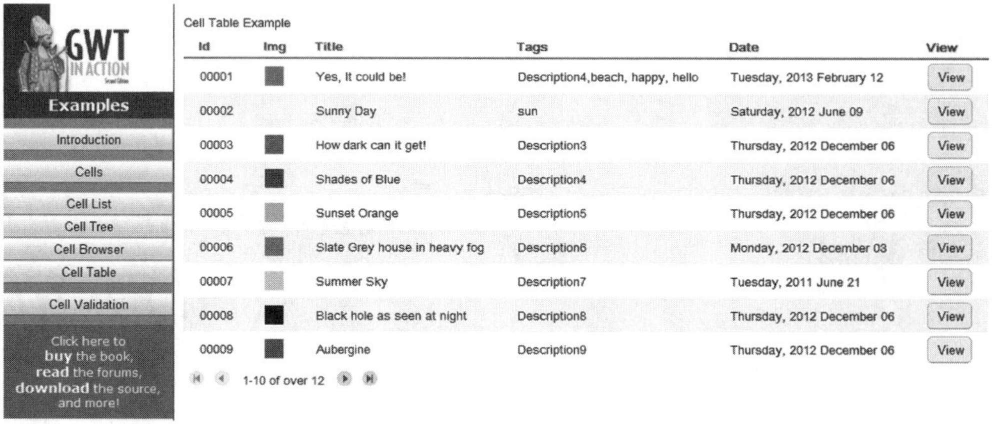

Figure 10.1 Example of cell widget in action showing a `CellTable` of data together with ability to page through data

browser to prevent a slow script warning (older versions of GWT used `IncrementalCommand`). That's an applicable approach if we're performing a lot of computation in any particular step, but for drawing large data on the screen we now use cell widgets; an example is shown in figure 10.1.

GWT provides 16 different types of cells such as `TextCell`, `EditTextCell`, `ImageCell`, and `DateCell`, and in addition, we can create our own custom cells. Each cell type is a rubber stamp of HTML allowing quick creation and manipulation into the DOM.

Cells can't survive on their own and need to be used within a cell widget, which provides the necessary context and other management aspects. GWT 2.5 contains six cell widgets: `CellWidget`, `CellList`, `CellTree`, `CellBrowser`, `CellTable`, and `DataGrid`.

Unlike UI widgets, cell widgets are lightweight, perform at a high level, and are designed to render large data sets efficiently. The cell widget's efficiency is derived from the cells that it uses to directly render data as HTML.

Cell widgets are backed by data coming from local or remote sources (using `DataProviders`). When a cell widget needs to display data on a page, it hands that data to specific cells that then produce the necessary HTML for the cell widget.

Beyond providing the data to cells, cell widgets typically support data paging, sorting, item-selection models, updating of data, as well as data validation.

There's a lot to cover, and no better place to start than with what are the types of cells.

10.1 Understanding cells

The cell is the basic building block of a cell widget. Each cell is typed so that it knows exactly what kind of data it's going to be expected to render. You can think of cells as being the rubber stamps that act on the DOM.

DEFINITION Cells are HTML rubber stamps that act directly on the DOM. GWT provides 16 types, and they need to sit within a cell widget to be functional.

Besides rendering HTML for a cell widget, a cell can declare that it plans to handle particular browser events, giving it a chance to perform complex behavior like displaying a date picker or changing to an editable state or asking a delegate to perform some task. This allows cell data to have complex user interaction like a full-blown widget, without needing separate code for each data item rendered (therefore making cells more efficient).

A cell is created with an associated type parameter that defines its underlying data type. For example, a cell that displays a `String` will be defined as `Cell<String>`, or you can use your own object, as you'll see later for creating `Cell<PhotoDetails>`.

Some convenience classes are provided by GWT to (sometimes) help make things clearer: `TextCell` can be used instead of `Cell<String>`, `ImageCell` instead of `Cell<Image>`, `SafeHtmlCell` for `Cell<SafeHtml>`, and so on. We'll leave it to your coding standard to define which versions to use in your case.

As we've mentioned, GWT supplies a number of cells, and you can see them in the hierarchy shown in figure 10.2. (note that the cells don't sit in the usual user interface package, they're over in the `com.google.gwt.cell.client` package).

Rather than looking at cells based on this hierarchy, we feel they're best thought of as falling into one of three groups:

- Display cells that render only the data provided
- Editable cells that give a user the opportunity to change the value shown by the cell
- Action cells that trigger an action of some sort

Let's look at some of the cells in each of these categories, and then afterward we'll explore how we might create a custom cell if none of the supplied cells are sufficient.

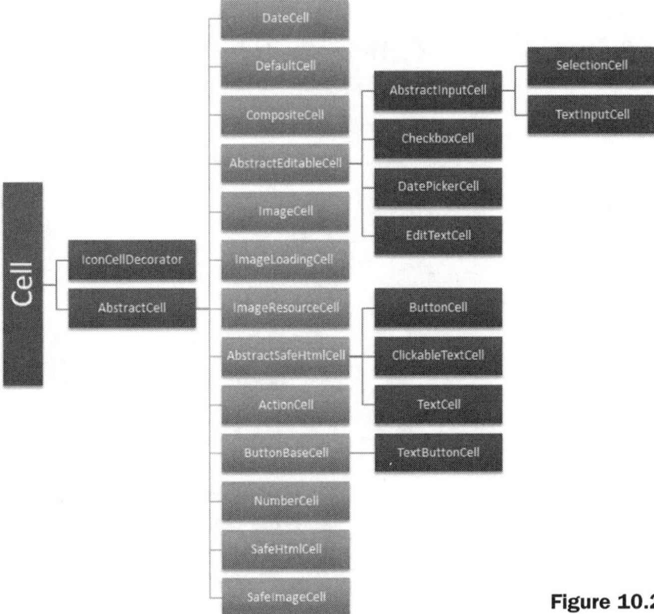

Figure 10.2 Hierarchy of cells (in GWT 2.5)

10.1.1 Looking at display cells

Display cells are those cells that can be used to present some data to the user—some text or an image or whatever you can think of. You can't do anything else with these cells such as react to clicks or make changes to the data.

In the chapter's example (`celltypes.CellTypesExample`) we use a `CellWidget` to act as the container of the cell—remember we said earlier that a cell can't live without being inside a cell widget; `CellWidget` is the simplest of cell widgets and allows only one cell to be within it. Here's how you create the `TextCell` in its `CellWidget`:

```
Cell<String> cell = new TextCell();                                    ❶ Creating the cell
CellWidget<String> cellWidget = new CellWidget<String>(cell);          ❷ Creating the CellWidget
cellWidget.setValue("Some Static Text");                               ❸ Setting the cell value
```

The first thing you do is create the cell you're interested in ❶. In this case it's the `TextCell` object. We've not made a mistake here by declaring the variable to be of type `Cell<String>` but using the `TextCell` constructor. Doing it this way reminds you that `TextCell` is a convenience class for `Cell<String>` and that the underlying type is a `String`.

In ❷ you create the `CellWidget` widget, which must be parameterized with the same type as the cell it holds, which means in this case that the `type` parameter is `String`. If you look in the example code you'll see that the other cell examples use `type` parameters such as `Number` for `NumberCell`, `Date` for `DateCell` and so on.

Now you can set the value of the cell—but you do that through the `CellWidget` because it holds the context of the cell. A simple call to the `CellWidget`'s `setValue` method is all you need. It's possible to do it on the cell itself, but then you'll need to get the context and row—so it's best to do it through the widget.

Figure 10.3 shows more of the display type widgets this chapter's example covers, and table 10.1 contains a summary of these types of cells.

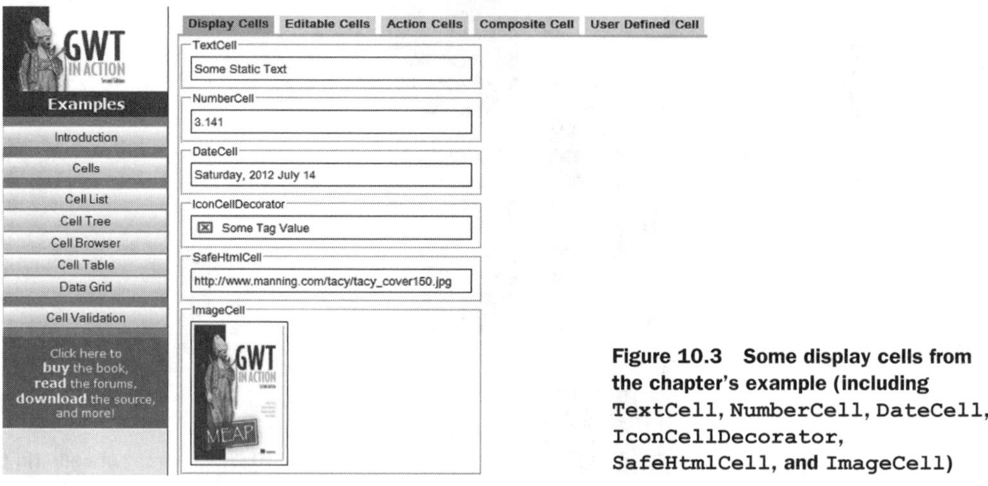

Figure 10.3 Some display cells from the chapter's example (including `TextCell`, `NumberCell`, `DateCell`, `IconCellDecorator`, `SafeHtmlCell`, and `ImageCell`)

Table 10.1 The different types of display cells

Cell	Type	Overview
TextCell	Cell<String>	Displays simple text.
NumberCell	Cell<Number>	Can render any of the Java numerical wrapper types. If a com.google.gwt.i18n.client.NumberFormat is provided in the constructor, then that's used to format the display (for example, supplying NumberFormat.getPercentFormat() would show numbers as a percent; by default the number is shown in decimal format).
DateCell	Cell<Date>	Displays dates as a string. A DateTimeFormat can be provided in the constructor to alter how the date is displayed (for example, DateTimeFormat.getFormat(PredefinedFormat.DATE_SHORT) would display dates in short format; by default the format is long). Additionally, a TimeZone can be provided in the constructor.
ImageCell	Cell<String>	Assumes the String passed to it is the URL of an image. The String is sanitized before use, but no attempt is made to ensure the URL is pointing to a valid image or if it's a URI.
ImageLoadingCell	Cell<String>	Like ImageCell, but displays some loading HTML (by default an animated image) while waiting for the real image to load. If loading is successful, the loaded image replaces the loading HTML; otherwise some error HTML is displayed. It's possible to provide alternate ImageLoadingCell.Renderers in the constructor for the loading, error, and image display.
ImageResourceCell	Cell<ImageResource>	Like ImageCell but takes data from an ImageResource instead of a String.
SafeImageCell	Cell<SafeUri>	Like ImageCell but takes data from a SafeUri object instead of a String.
SafeHtmlCell	Cell<SafeHtml>	Displays the contents of a SafeHtml object.
IconCellDecorator		Wraps another cell and allows an icon to be displayed (in our example we display a delete icon next to a TextCell).

Each cell has a default render method that's responsible for rendering the cell content in HTML. For example, to follow is the render method for the ImageCell:

```
public void render(Context context, String value, SafeHtmlBuilder sb) {
   if (value != null) {
      // The template will sanitize the URI.
      sb.append(template.img(value));
   }
}
```

This method appends the results of a `SafeHtmlTemplate` (`template`), which creates an `img` tag, to the contents of a `SafeHtmlBuilder` passed in as a parameter (this comes from the cell widget in which the cell is sitting).

All these `SafeHtml` types are one of GWT's ways of protecting your application from hacking attacks. You may remember we discussed them briefly in chapter 4 on widgets, and we'll look a little more at `SafeHtml` templates in this chapter when we create our own cells. For now, we can briefly look at the template used in `ImageCell`:

```
interface Template extends SafeHtmlTemplates {
   @Template("<img src=\"{0}\"/>")
SafeHtml img(String url);
}
```

When the template's `img` method is called, the parameter is inserted into the contents of the `@Template` annotation at the placeholder `{0}`, giving us a standard HTML `img` tag that then goes into the cell widget for our display.

Now that you've seen how the simpler display cells work, let's turn up the complexity a little and look at the group of edit cells.

10.1.2 Updating edit cells

Edit cells allow the user to update their initial value. Figure 10.4 shows the `DatePickerCell` in action, which, unlike the data-display `DateCell`, allows the date to be updated. If the user clicks it, a `DatePicker` widget appears to help the user change the value.

An edit cell is created in the same manner as you saw for display cells; for example, the following creates an `EditTextCell`:

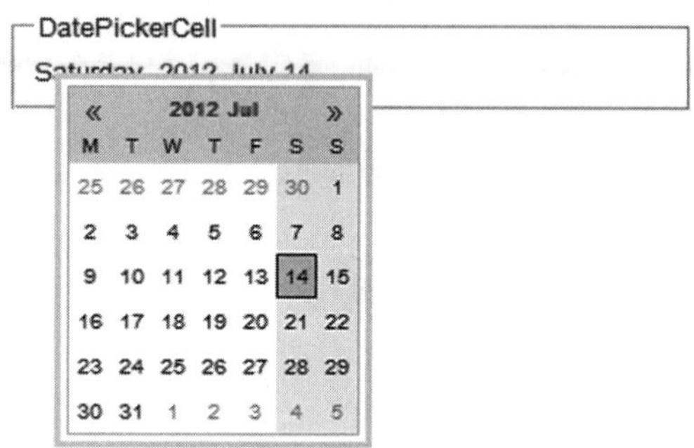

Figure 10.4 The `DatePickerCell` (an example of edit cells) in use

```
Cell<String> cell = new EditTextCell();
CellWidget<String> cellWidget = new CellWidget<String>(cell);
cellWidget.setValue("Some Editable Text - click me to edit!");
```

You can also add a handler to the cell widget that handles updates on the cell. The approach is different depending on the cell widget. For `CellWidget` that means adding a `ValueChangeHandler` handler (you'll see later the approaches for other cell widgets):

```
cellWidget.addValueChangeHandler(new ValueChangeHandler<String>(){
   @Override
   public void onValueChange(ValueChangeEvent<String> event) {
      Window.alert("Changed EditTextCell value to: "+event.getValue());
   }
});
```

Now when the user changes the value of the `EditTextCell`, a `ValueChangeEvent` is raised and is handled by the handler (and in this case an alert is shown to the user).

Table 10.2 contains the details of the edit group of cell widgets.

Table 10.2 The various GWT edit cells

Cell	Type	Overview
`EditTextCell`	`Cell<String>`	A cell that displays simple text, which when clicked turns into an input field.
`TextInputCell`	`Cell<String>`	A cell that's an input field.
`CheckboxCell`	`Cell<Boolean>`	A check box.
`SelectionCell`	`Cell<String>`	A cell that's a drop-down box of strings, one of which can be selected. The data is provided as one of the concrete implementations of Java's `List` object.
`DatePickerCell`	`Cell<Date>`	A cell that displays a date and that, when clicked, shows a GWT `DatePicker` object. A `DateTimeFormat` can be provided in the constructor to alter how the date is displayed (for example, `DateTimeFormat.getFormat (PredefinedFormat.DATE_SHORT)` would display dates in short format; by default the format is long).

Edit cells typically override the `isEditing` method to indicate the state of editing the cell is currently in. They also have the interesting property that they separate model and view data—in short, this means the value the cell holds in its model (real value) may be different than the value shown on the screen—that is, you can have pending updates.

MANAGING PENDING UPDATES

When a user changes the value in an edit cell, the change is visible on the screen (the view) straight away; but the value held in the cell (the model) isn't changed until you "commit" the change—perhaps by calling the cell's `commit` method if it has one—or it's cleared—through calling the `clearViewData` method. This is useful in cases where the cell is re-rendered (such as refreshing), because the pending value is shown rather than refreshing to the old value.

Cells that have this capability are subclasses of `AbstractEditableCell`. And it can be a common approach to keep a list of these cells so that a general commit can be made on all data when appropriate.

The final group of cell widgets are those that react to some form of action—a button click, perhaps.

10.1.3 Reacting with action cells

Action cells don't allow the user to change the data value directly, but they do allow a trigger of an action of some sort, such as buttons or clickable text (shown in figure 10.5).

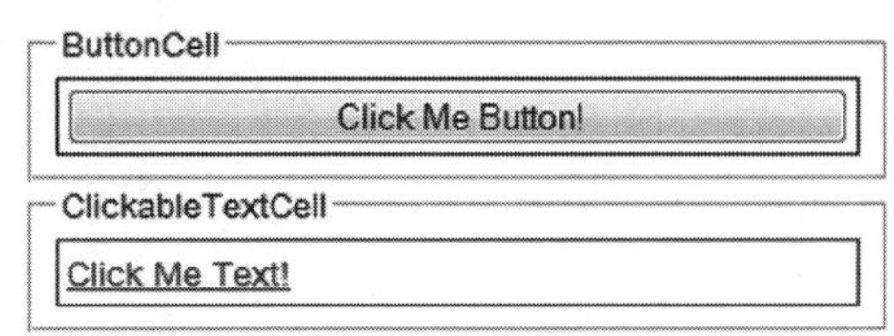

Figure 10.5 Two of the action cells being displayed in this chapter's example

Unfortunately, not all action cells work well in the simple `CellWidget`. You have to add a click handler manually through the widget's standard `addHandler` method for the `button`, `clickable text`, and `button text` cells (see chapter 14 for a discussion on event handling in widgets and the `addHandler` method). This problem doesn't exist for these cells in other cell widgets or for the `ActionCell` in any cell. For the `ActionCell` you need to provide a `Delegate` instance whose `execute` method is called when the cell is clicked. In the example we have the following:

```
Cell<String> cell = new ActionCell<String>("", new Delegate<String>(){
   @Override
   public void execute(String object) {
      Window.alert("Action cell has been Clicked!");
   }
});
```

The types of action cell are listed in table 10.3.

Table 10.3 The various GWT action cells

Cell	Type	Overview
`ButtonCell`	`Cell<String>`	A cell that represents a standard HTML button. When it's clicked, or the Enter key is pressed when it has focus, the associated `ValueUpdater` is called.
`ClickableTextCell`	`Cell<String>`	A cell that has simple text that handles mouse clicks (you can make it look like an HTML anchor by using CSS). Like `ButtonCell`, the `ValueUpdater` is called upon a mouse click or a key press.
`ButtonTextCell`	`Cell<String>`	A cell that acts like a button but is rendered as pure HTML using the Appearance pattern. (GWT documentation hints that this is the way most widgets will go in the future, but that has not happened yet.[a])
`ActionCell`	`Cell<C>`	A generic `Cell<C>` that forwards its value object to an `ActionCell.Delegate<C>` when it's clicked. This cell renders as a button. Both the button label and the `Delegate` implementation are supplied at cell instantiation.

a. CellBackedWidgets and the Appearance pattern: http://mng.bz/9oi1.

We've now covered the three groups of cells. We can display data, get the user editing data, and also react to clicks the user makes. All the cells are low-level DOM manipulation, which makes them extremely fast.

Can you use GWT widgets inside a cell?

The lightweight approach of cells isn't geared up for including GWT widgets within a cell.

There is a way if you absolutely must,[a] but the widget probably won't work, and you'll be going against the reasons you're using cell widgets in the first place.

a. http://mng.bz/C6y1.

When using cell widgets you'll perhaps come across the case where the provided cells aren't quite what you need. For such cases we'll look at creating custom cells.

10.2 Creating custom cells

Creating your own custom cell is something you'll need to do if you want to go beyond the standard set of cells. As you saw in chapter 4 on UI widgets, you can create custom cells in a couple of ways:

- Create a composite of existing cells.
- Create a cell from scratch.

In this section we'll build a simple cell that will display `title`, `date`, and `largeUrl` fields from an underlying `PhotoDetails` object. The title and date will be text cells, and the other field will drive the display of an image (a block of color for this example's purpose). Let's take a quick look at how we'd achieve that in a composite cell, and then we'll move on to creating it from scratch.

10.2.1 Composite

Composite cells display a number of cells together within a `span` element. This means that generally the component cells will be displayed in left-to-right manner in the order in which they're added, as shown in figure 10.6.

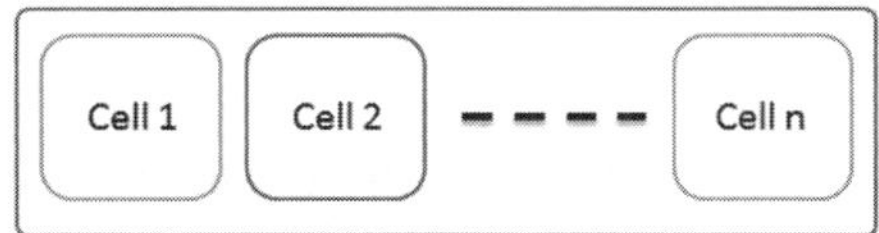

Figure 10.6 The general principle behind a composite cell, showing the left-right layout that happens

If any of the cells internally use a block-level element, such as `div`, then they'll be displayed vertically—which may or may not be useful. It's possible to override the composite cell's renderer to lay out component cells as required (but in our opinion, you're probably better off creating the cell from scratch).

Okay, so let's start building a composite—we warn you in advance that it's full of spaghetti typing that will seem obvious after seeing an example but may appear somewhat of a nightmare on first reading.

First off, you create an `ArrayList` of `HasCell<T,C>` objects, which will be the list of component cells to be passed to the composite cell's constructor. `T` relates to the underlying data object—`PhotoDetails` in this case—and `C` relates to the type of `Cell` values. If all the cell values in the composite are the same, for example, `Strings`, you can substitute that type here (though in this case maybe the `CellList` widget is more appropriate for you). Let's assume you have different cell types—it's best to define them as follows:

```
ArrayList<HasCell<PhotoDetails, ?>> cells =
new ArrayList<HasCell<PhotoDetails, ?>>();
```

Then you add the cells in order in which you wish them to be displayed; the following listing shows how to add a cell that will display the title text.

Listing 10.1 Adding one cell to the list of cells that will be in the CompositeCell

```
cells.add(new HasCell<PhotoDetails, String>() {          // 1 Adding a new cell

   private TextCell cell = new TextCell();                // 2 Private copy of cell

   @Override
   public Cell<String> getCell() {                        // 3 Returning the cell
      return cell;
   }

   @Override
   public FieldUpdater<PhotoDetails, String> getFieldUpdater() {
      return null;
   }

   @Override
   public String getValue(PhotoDetails object) {          // 4 Returning the rendered cell
      return (object == null) ? "" : object.getTitle();
   }
});
```

You create a new instance of the `HasCell` interface that's tightly typed now to indicate that the underlying data object is `PhotoDetails` and the display type is `String` ❶. Inside the definition at ❷ you create the `Cell`—a `TextCell` for this example—which the required `getCell` method ❸ will return (remember from table 10.1 that the `TextCell` type is the same as `Cell<String>`).

The method of interest is `getValue` ❹. This returns the value that will be displayed in the cell. Because you type this `HasCell` instance with `PhotoDetails` and `String`, the parameter to this method is of type `PhotoDetails` and the return is `String`. It's necessary to guard against the value being null, so that's why there's the little check here.

Other cells are added to the `ArrayList` in the order in which you wish them to be displayed in the composite. In our example (defined in the `addCells` method within `UserDefinedCellFactory.java`) there's a `SafeHtml` cell for the image and another `TextCell` for the date, to be different.

Defining the composite is a case of supplying the just-created list of cells to the `CompositeCell` constructor and appropriate type parameter:

```
CompositeCell<PhotoDetails> compCell =
                        new CompositeCell<PhotoDetails>(cells);
```

You can use the composite cell in the same way as any other cell, and it displays as shown in figure 10.7.

Figure 10.7 The standard layout of CompositeCell, showing the horizontal nature driven by the surrounding SPAN element

As you can see in figure 10.7, the three cells we've used in the composite have come out horizontally as expected. If this isn't what you want, then you have to start changing the CompositeCell's renderer.

ALTERING HOW COMPOSITECELL LAYS OUT CELLS

Let's say you want your cells in the composite cell to be laid out differently for simplicity: vertically. The first thing you could do is change the HTML used for the image to be a block element. That would force the three cells to be vertical in this case, but that isn't the general solution!

Generally, to solve this layout problem you override the render methods of the CompositeCell. Following is part of the definition you can find in the VerticalCompositeCell class (in the celltypes.custom package):

```
@Override
public void render(Context context, PhotoDetails value, SafeHtmlBuilder sb)
{
   sb.appendHtmlConstant("<table><tbody>");
   super.render(context, value, sb);
   sb.appendHtmlConstant("</tbody></table>");
}
```

From this segment you can see that you're building the structure around a table, which gives you the vertical layout needed.

The alternative to CompositeCell is to build the cell from first principles, and we'll cover the ways to do that.

10.2.2 *From first principles*

If you want a little more control over the layout of a custom cell, and in our opinion an easier process than composite cells give you, then you can build a new cell from scratch by extending AbstractCell.

> **Don't forget**
>
> Never implement the Cell interface yourself, always use AbstractCell.
>
> GWT documentation states that the Cell interface may change in the future but that AbstractCell always provides a stable implementation of Cell.

Extending AbstractCell means you need to do two things:

- Implement the render method (that draws the cell), that is, implement the following method:

  ```
  public void render(Context context,
                     PhotoDetails value,
                     SafeHtmlBuilder sb)
  ```

  Note the type of the value parameter: this always matches the type of the cell's underlying data object, so in our example it's PhotoDetails.

- Potentially handle events on the cell, that is, implement the following method:

```
public void onBrowserEvent(Context context,
                           Element parent,
                           PhotoDetails value,
                           NativeEvent event,
                           ValueUpdater<String> valueUpdater)
```

Figure 10.8 shows the three ways that you can render a cell widget yourself, by using

- The `SafeHtmlBuilder` passed to the cell's `render` method by the `CellWidget`
- A `SafeHtmlTemplate` to build the HTML that's then inserted into `SafeHtmlBuilder`
- UiBinder (possible from GWT 2.5 onward)

The cell itself will comprise the following HTML:

```
<table>
   <tr>
      <td rowspan=2 bgcolor=color_of_photo> </td>
      <td>Wonderful Sunset</td>
   </tr>
   <tr>
      <td>Taken: 15/01/2012</td>
   </tr>
</table>
```

The text in bold and italic will come from a `PhotoDetails` object—specifically the title (Wonderful Sunset) and date (15/01/2012) fields. The background color of the first cell will come from the `PhotoDetails largeUrl` field (in a real implementation that would be a URL to an image, but in our case we commandeer it to be a color so that later examples can have many instances without us having to have many images).

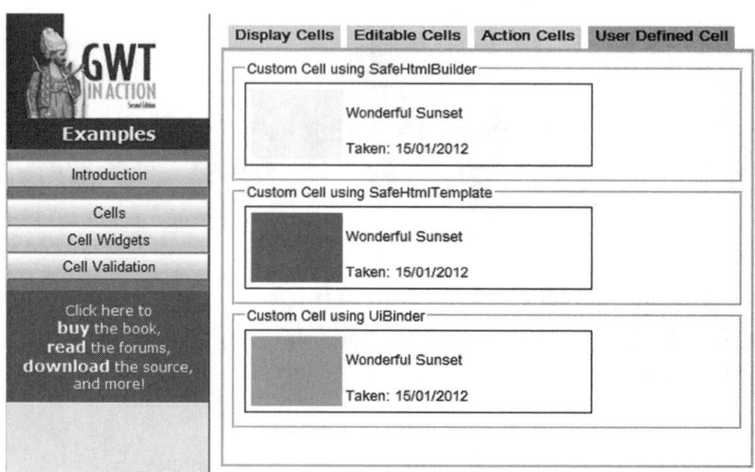

Figure 10.8 Examining all three user-defined cells showing a photo's image, title, and date taken (they were built using `SafeHtmlBuilder`, using `SafeHtmlTemplate`, and declaratively using UiBinder)

Let's look at all three different ways of rendering that HTML table, starting with writing directly to the `SafeHtmlBuilder` argument of the `render` method.

RENDERING VIA SAFEHTMLBUILDER

The `render` method is called by the cell widget that the cell will be sitting in. That cell widget provides a number of things, for example, the `Context`, which we'll look at in more detail later, and a `SafeHtmlBuilder` class, both of which are passed to the cell's `render` method.

You can think of the `SafeHtmlBuilder` instance as a writing stream to the browser that helps protect against XSS (cross-site scripting) attacks by escaping input where necessary.

To build our cell, we'll append the necessary HTML to it in the cell's `render` method. If we were using a cell widget that has more than one cell, then the updated `SafeHtmlBuilder` instance would get passed to the next cell by the cell widget so that that cell could draw itself and so on. The next listing shows how to write the `render` method using this type of approach.

Listing 10.2 Using a `SafeHtmlBuilder` to draw the custom cell for `PhotoDetails`

```
@Override
public void render(com.google.gwt.cell.client.Cell.Context context,
                PhotoDetails value, SafeHtmlBuilder sb) {
if(value!=null){                                          ❶ Is value to render non-null?
   sb.appendHtmlConstant("<table>");
   sb.appendHtmlConstant("<tr height=40px>");
   sb.appendHtmlConstant("<td width=80px rowspan=2
                  bgcolor=\""+value.getLargeUrl()+"\"> </td>");   ❷ Append HTML constants
   sb.appendHtmlConstant("<td>");
   sb.appendEscaped(value.getTitle());                    ❸ Append escaped text
   sb.appendHtmlConstant("</td>");
   sb.appendHtmlConstant("</tr>");
   sb.appendHtmlConstant("<tr>");
   sb.appendHtmlConstant("<td>Taken: ");
   sb.appendEscaped(CalendarFactory.getDisplayFormatter()
                                   .format(value.getDate()));
   sb.appendHtmlConstant("</td>");
   sb.appendHtmlConstant("</tr>");
   sb.appendHtmlConstant("</table>");
}
}
```

The first thing to do in any version of the render method is check if the value to be rendered is not `null` ❶. Because the `render` method can be called on instantiation, it might get a `null` object, so you exit in this case.

Assuming the data is not `null`, you use various `append` methods in the `SafeHtmlBuilder` class to add the necessary HTML for the cell. You can use `appendHtmlConstant` to put unescaped values onto the builder, as in ❷. But to use that method you must have HTML that's fully determined before runtime and is a complete tag. That's why we had to write ❷ the way we did; the following wouldn't be a valid alternative:

```
sb.appendHtmlConstant("<td width=80px rowspan=2 bgcolor=\"");
sb.appendHtmlConstant(value.getLargeUrl());
sb.appendHtmlConstant("\"> </td>");
```

That's because the `<td>` tag in the first line is `<td` and isn't completed by the > until the third line. When you're running in development mode (or web mode with assertions turned on), these rules for `appendHtmlConstant` are enforced. In web mode without assertions turned on, they're not compiled in for efficiency.

Where you want to be doubly sure that no XSS attacks are let in, you can use the `appendEscaped` method, as in ❸. You do that there because the data in the `PhotoDetails` object might come from somewhere over which you have no control (and so someone could sneak an attack in). By using `appendEscaped` you neutralize that possibility because all HTML aspects, including any sneaked-in JavaScript, are escaped.

We hope you can see by inspection of listing 10.2 that it builds up the necessary HTML for this cell widget that then is displayed in figure 10.8.

We said earlier though that cells are rather like rubber stamps, which would imply that a template approach might be a neater way, and indeed you can use `SafeHtmlTemplates`.

RENDERING HTML VIA SAFEHTMLTEMPLATES

`SafeHtmlTemplates` is an interface whose method declaration(s) contain an annotation describing the HTML they should produce. A key aspect of this template is that it can contain placeholders for arguments of the method declaration.

This is probably easier to see with an example, so let's take a quick look at the following listing which shows the interesting parts of this approach.

Listing 10.3 Building the `PhotoDetails` custom cell using a `SafeHtmlTemplates`

```
public class PhotoCellWithTemplate extends AbstractCell<PhotoDetails> {

  interface Template extends SafeHtmlTemplates {                  ❶ Extending SafeHtmlTemplates
    @Template("<table>"+                                          ❷ Defining a template
                "<tr height=40px>"+
                  "<td width=80px rowspan=2 bgcolor=\"{1}\"/>"+
                    "  "+
                  "</td>"+
                  "<td>{0}</td>"+                                 ❸ Indicating placeholders
                "</tr>"+
                "<tr>"+
                  "<td>Taken: {2}</td>"+
                "</tr>"+
              "</table>")
    SafeHtml photo(String title, String Image, String date);      ❹ Method declaration for template
  }

  @Override
  public void render(com.google.gwt.cell.client.Cell.Context context,
                     PhotoDetails value, SafeHtmlBuilder sb) {
```

```
      if(value!=null){
         sb.append(template.photo(value.getTitle(),
                                  value.getLargeUrl(),
                                  CalendarFactory.getDisplayFormatter()
                                           format(value.getDate()));
      }
   }
}
```

❺ Using template with data

Now you're starting to see more what we mean by rubber stamping. You have a template interface ❶ with a single method ❹ (there could be more). Associated with the method is a `Template` annotation ❷ that declaratively describes the HTML you wish to produce. Within the annotation you have placeholders, such as `{0}` at ❸, which relate to parameters in the method declaration—the `String` title in this case.

Within the constructor of the cell you must use the `GWT.create` method to create an instance of `Template` to tell the compiler to take the defined interface and annotation and create the necessary implementation:

```
public PhotoCellWithTemplate() {
   super(BrowserEvents.CLICK);
   if (template == null) {
      template = GWT.create(Template.class);
   }
}
```

This is deferred binding, which we look at in more detail in chapter 17.

When it comes to rendering the cell, the render method is simple compared to the previous version. After checking that the data provided is not `null`, you `append` the result of applying data to the template to the `SafeHtmlBuilder` passed in from the cell widget ❺.

Can you go one step better toward a complete declarative definition? Sure, from GWT 2.5 onward you can declare cells using UiBinder (see chapter 6 if you want to get some more background on UiBinder).

RENDERING HTML VIA UIBINDER

We're fans of UiBinder's declarative approach that allows separation of UI layout from functionality, and so we were pleased when this capability came to cells in GWT 2.5. But it's marked as experimental, so the following might need tweaking as GWT stabilizes in the future (though we hope not by too much).

How does it work? You start by defining a declarative GUI template in the normal way (`PhotoCellWithUiBinder.ui.xml`).

Listing 10.4 The declaration GUI of the `PhotoDetails` cell

```
<ui:UiBinder xmlns:ui='urn:ui:com.google.gwt.uibinder'>

<ui:with field='title' type='java.lang.String'/>
<ui:with field='img' type='java.lang.String'/>
<ui:with field='date' type='java.lang.String'/>
```

❶ Indicating data from Java code

```
<table ui:field="theCell">
   <tr height="40px">
      <td width="80px" rowspan="2" bgcolor="{img}"></td>
      <td><ui:text from='{title}'/></td>
   </tr>
   <tr>
      <td>Taken: <ui:text from='{date}'/></td>
   </tr>
</table>
</ui:UiBinder>
```

❷ Using data from Java code

NOTE You can't include GWT widgets or panels in a UiBinder declaration that will be used for a cell (because cells don't handle widgets and panels).

The declaration is standard, with two things to note:

- A number of `<ui:with>` declarations to indicate where text is coming from ❶.
- The use of `<ui:text>` to insert data into the template ❷

On the Java side, you use the template in a similar way to a normal UiBinder, though you need to extend `UiRenderer` instead.

Listing 10.5 Using the UiBinder declaration in the cell

```
public class PhotoCellWithUiBinder extends AbstractCell<PhotoDetails> {

   interface MyUiRenderer extends UiRenderer {
      void render(SafeHtmlBuilder sb, String title,
                  String img, String date);
   }

private static MyUiRenderer renderer = GWT.create(MyUiRenderer.class);

public PhotoCellWithUiBinder() {}

@Override
public void render(com.google.gwt.cell.client.Cell.Context context,
                   PhotoDetails value, SafeHtmlBuilder sb) {
   if (value != null)
      renderer.render(sb, value.getTitle(),
                          value.getLargeUrl(),
                          CalendarFactory.getDisplayFormatter()
                                         .format(value.getDate());
}
}
```

❶ Declaring the cell's class

❷ Declaring the UiRenderer

❸ Creating the GUI

❹ Using the GUI

You declare the `UiRenderer` code in a similar manner to `UiBinder` code ❷, noting that you need to extend `UiRenderer` in this case and provide the `render` method as described.

BE CAREFUL The parameter names that you use in the render interface declaration will be mapped to the `UiRender ui:with` declarations—make a typo, and you might not get data you are looking for.

It should also be noted that in GWT 2.5, unlike UiBinder, the associated declarative XML file should be named after the outer class ❶, not the interface name ❷. (This may change in the future to bring things into alignment.)

Then, as normal for the declarative approach, you create an instance in ❸ using the `GWT.create` method. The renderer is used in ❹, passing in the necessary parameters—stick the result in a cell widget, and you're off and running.

HANDLING EVENTS

Events happen on the cell widget that the cell is associated with but are handled by the cell itself. For a GWT widget, events are internally handled by sinking the events the cell will handle and overriding the `onBrowserEvent` method with the necessary functionality.

The same approach is followed with cells, though in a slightly different way. Events are sunk by calling the parent constructor with their native names (assuming you're extending `AbstractCell`, as you should).

In our two non-`UiRenderer` versions, that means you write something similar to the following:

```
public PhotoCellWithBuilder() {
    super(BrowserEvents.CLICK);
}
```

You can either pass in a list of strings, for example, `super(BrowserEvents.CLICK, BrowserEvents.MOUSEDOWN, BrowserEvents.MOUSEUP)`, or provide them as a `Set<String>` object.

The next step is to override the `onBrowserEvent` method, as shown in the following listing to handle the events.

Listing 10.6 Overriding the `onBrowserEvent` method in a cell to handle events

```
public void onBrowserEvent(Context context, Element parent,
                           PhotoDetails value, NativeEvent event,
                           ValueUpdater<PhotoDetails> valueUpdater){

   super.onBrowserEvent(context, parent, value, event, valueUpdater);

   if (BrowserEvents.CLICK.equals(event.getType())) {
      valueUpdater.update(value);
      Window.alert("You clicked the cell with Index: " + context.getIndex());
   }
}
```

❶ Play nice
❷ Handle event
❸ Indicate an update

Within the handler you call the parent's method ❶ to play nice, and then you check if the received event is the one you're after ❷; if so, you do the necessary functionality. In a real system, an event could mean an update to the cell's data, so you fire the `update` method on the `valueUpdater` ❸. Because we're testing our example in a `CellWidget`, which seems to not allow a `ValueUpdater` to be added, you also fire up an alert window so you know it's working, as in figure 10.9.

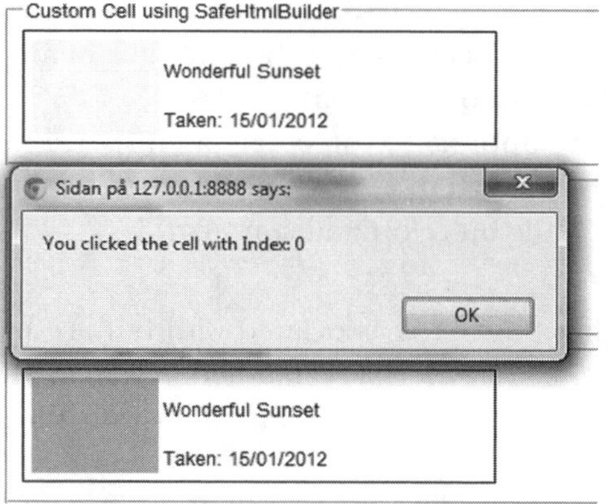

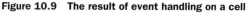

Figure 10.9 The result of event handling on a cell

To handle events in the declarative manner, you apply a similar approach but with some subtleties.

HANDLING EVENTS IN UIBINDER

From GWT 2.5 you can set up event handling through the declarative UI process, as shown next.

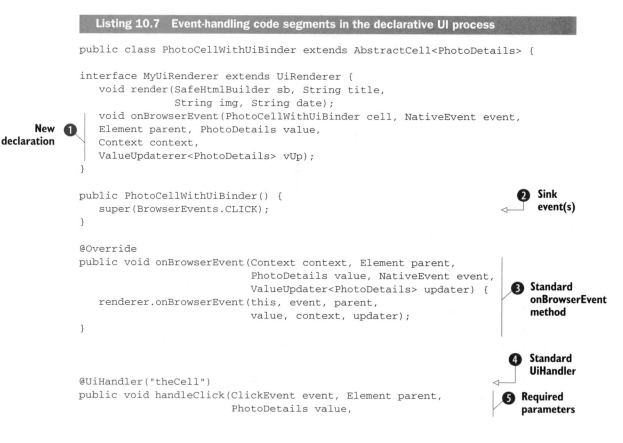

Listing 10.7 Event-handling code segments in the declarative UI process

```
public class PhotoCellWithUiBinder extends AbstractCell<PhotoDetails> {

interface MyUiRenderer extends UiRenderer {
   void render(SafeHtmlBuilder sb, String title,
               String img, String date);
   void onBrowserEvent(PhotoCellWithUiBinder cell, NativeEvent event,      ❶ New declaration
   Element parent, PhotoDetails value,
   Context context,
   ValueUpdaterer<PhotoDetails> vUp);
}

public PhotoCellWithUiBinder() {
   super(BrowserEvents.CLICK);                                             ❷ Sink event(s)
}

@Override
public void onBrowserEvent(Context context, Element parent,
                           PhotoDetails value, NativeEvent event,
                           ValueUpdater<PhotoDetails> updater) {          ❸ Standard onBrowserEvent method
   renderer.onBrowserEvent(this, event, parent,
                           value, context, updater);
}


@UiHandler("theCell")                                                     ❹ Standard UiHandler
public void handleClick(ClickEvent event, Element parent,                 ❺ Required parameters
                        PhotoDetails value,
```

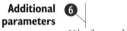

```
                                    Context context,
                                    ValueUpdater<PhotoDetails> valueUpdater){
      Window.alert("You clicked the cell with Index: " + context.getIndex());
   }
}
```

Additional parameters ❻

Let's start by looking at what we hope are the familiar parts. ❷ is the constructor where you sink the events this cell is going to manage, and ❸ is the standard cell `onBrowserEvent` method. But notice that you don't put in the event-handling code ❸; rather you make a call to the renderer's `onBrowserEvent` method.

That renderer's `onBrowserEvent` method is declared in the `UiRenderer` interface ❶, and it's important here to note the parameters. The first four parameters must be provided and must be in the order shown: cell type, event, parent element, and value (whose type is the cell's underlying data object). You can then add any other parameters you like, which become important in the next step.

Those parameters, minus the cell type, are passed to all `UiHandlers` defined in the code, such as that at ❹. The required parameters go first ❺, followed by the optional ones ❻. Because you want to update the `ValueUpdater` and display some data from the `Context`, you included them in the declaration at ❶, the call at ❸, and finally here in the `UiHandler` declaration at ❻.

The only thing left to do is tie the `UiHandler` to the declaration. In ❹ you said it's tied to `the Cell ui:field`, which you defined in the `UiRenderer` declaration in the usual way:

```
<table ui:field='theCell'>
```

As you've seen, cells need to reside within a cell widget, and so far we've only looked at the simple `CellWidget`. Now it's time to look at the other types of cell widgets.

10.3 Reviewing GWT's cell widgets

In general, cell widgets act as shown in figure 10.10 where, typically, one or more cells are arranged in columns and rows. Entries in each row of a column will have the same cell type, but there's no requirement for every column to have same cell type.

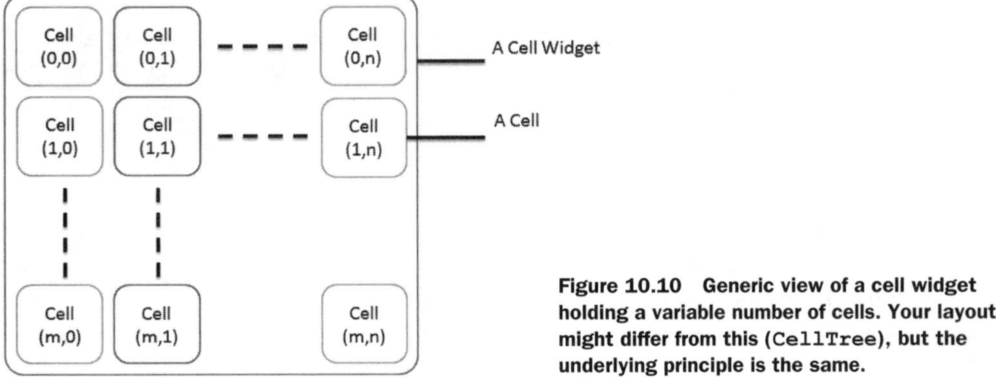

Figure 10.10 Generic view of a cell widget holding a variable number of cells. Your layout might differ from this (`CellTree`), but the underlying principle is the same.

Six different types of cell widgets come with GWT, each giving a different type of functionality, one of which is likely to meet your needs:

- `CellWidget`—You've already seen this earlier in the chapter. It allows one cell to be managed.
- `CellList`—Holds a vertical list of cells, all with the same type.
- `CellTree`—A tree structure of cells. Cells of the same level need to have the same type, but there's no requirement for different levels to have the same cell type (for example, level 0 could be a `TextCell`, level 1 a `SafeHtmlCell`, level 2 an `ImageCell`, and so on).
- `CellBrowser`—A Miller Columns-style component.
- `CellTable`—Each cell in a column must be of the same type, but there can be many different types across a row. Any header and footer provided will scroll with the screen.
- `DataGrid`—Like a `CellTable`, but any provided headers/footers are static, and data scrolls in between them.

DEFINITION `CellPanel` (in the package `com.google.gwt.user.client.ui`) isn't a cell widget in the sense of this chapter—it's used to support widgets that are table based, such as `DockPanel`, `HorizontalPanel`, and `VerticalPanel`.

Up until now we've been using the simple cell widget called `CellWidget`. This takes a single cell and provides the necessary `Context` and `SafeHtmlBuilder` within which the cell will render itself.

Cell context

A cell widget provides the context for a cell; it includes the following:

- *The column number*—A column index of the cell (zero if there's only one column in the cell widget).
- *A key*—A unique key that represents the row value of the widget (usually provided by a `KeyProvider`).
- *An index*—An absolute index of the cell.
- *An optional subindex*—If the row value renders to a single row element, then this will be zero; else it may be greater than zero (depending on the implementation).

We're now ready to start our dive into the various types of `CellWidgets` and any subtleties associated with them. Because we've already covered `CellWidget` in the first half of the book and it's not yet that interesting, let's start with `CellList`. (You may wish to have the code examples with you when you read because we have a lot to cover and nothing is better than seeing the full code and playing with it as you read.)

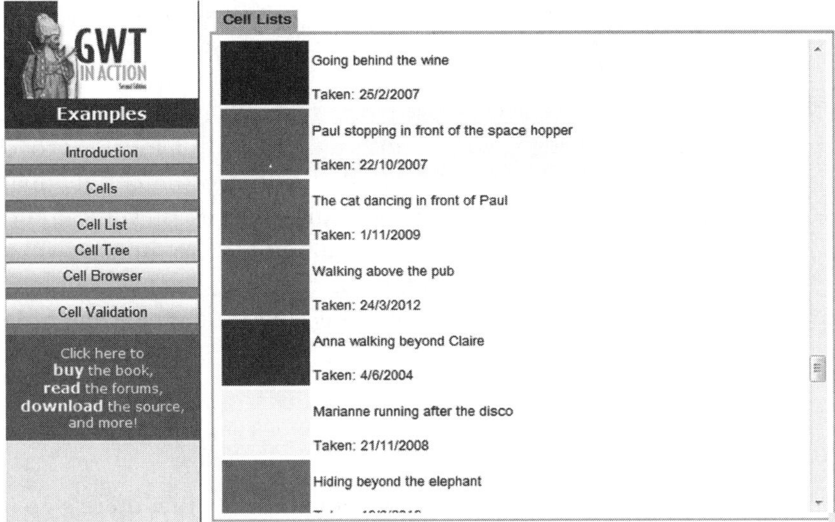

Figure 10.11 A simple `CellList` containing a list of photo cells

10.4 Looking at a CellList

`CellList` is probably the second simplest of the cell widgets, after `CellWidget`, because it holds a list of cells all of the same type. Figure 10.11 shows the `CellList` of photo cells that we'll use in this section's example (which you can find in the `com.manning.gwtia.ch10.client.celllist` package).

Because `CellList` is so simple, it gives us a good opportunity to look at how you create one, several ways to populate it, and the concept of paging.

10.4.1 Creating a CellList

Creating a `CellList` is done by passing the type of cell that the list will hold into the constructor, for example:

```
CellList<PhotoDetails> photoList =
           new CellList<PhotoDetails>(new PhotoCellWithUiBinder());
```

> **Using cell widgets with UiBinder**
>
> To use cell widgets in UiBinder you need to include the necessary namespace (shown in bold):
>
> ```
> <ui:UiBinder xmlns:ui='urn:ui:com.google.gwt.uibinder'
>     xmlns:g="urn:import:com.google.gwt.user.client.ui"
>     xmlns:cell="urn:import:com.google.gwt.user.cellview.client">
> ```
>
> Then you can refer to cell widgets in your declaration, for example:
>
> ```
> <cell:CellList ui:field=""></cell:CellList>
> ```

Once the widget is created, you need to populate it with data. That can be done in one of several ways that we'll look at next.

10.4.2 Populating data

Data to populate the cell widget can be inserted via one of four approaches. The direct approach is the equivalent of shoving the data into the cell manually and is probably the least interesting in most real applications. To use it, you call the `setRowData` method on the widget and pass in the row number where the data will start to be entered and a `List` of the data. For example, the following would result in two photo cells being shown for the two `PhotoDetails` objects in the list, starting at index 0 in the `photoList` `CellList` widget:

```
List<PhotoDetails> data = Arrays.asList(new PhotoDetails(...),
                                        new PhotoDetails(...));
photoList.setRowData(0, data);
```

TIP No data? You can set an empty list widget to indicate that there's no data to display through the `setEmptyListWidget(widget w)` method.

It's much more interesting if you can tell the `CellList` to keep an eye on a model and reflect any changes. You do that with a `DataProvider`, and there are three:

- `ListDataProvider`—Any changes to a backing list held on the client side are reflected in the widget.
- `AsyncDataProvider`—Data is retrieved usually from a server source.
- `CustomDataProvider`—You manually handle any `RangeChangeEvents` from the widget.

The first two are illustrated in figure 10.12. We'll look at them in more detail, starting with the list approach.

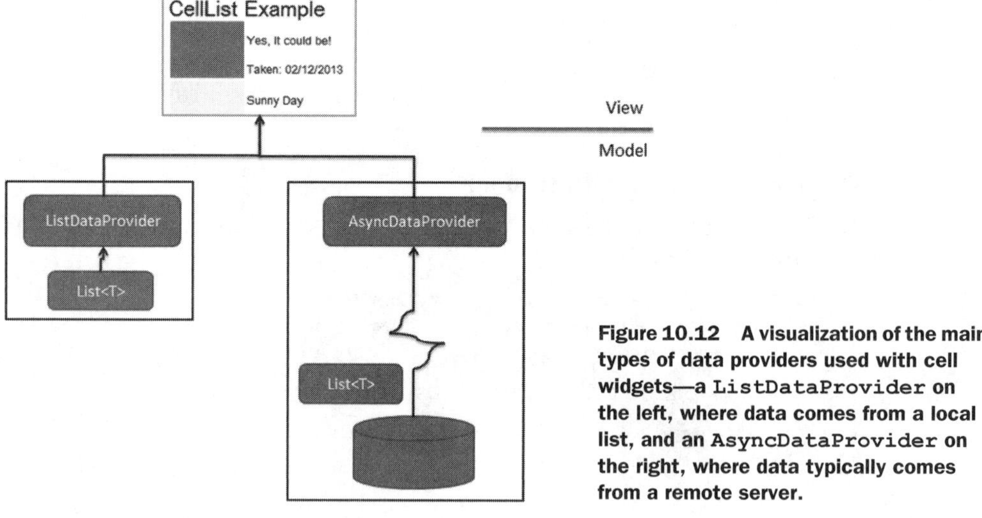

Figure 10.12 A visualization of the main types of data providers used with cell widgets—a `ListDataProvider` on the left, where data comes from a local list, and an `AsyncDataProvider` on the right, where data typically comes from a remote server.

LISTDATAPROVIDER

A `ListDataProvider` is a model that holds a `List` of objects. You can access that list and add or update data, which is then reflected by the widget in the view:

```
ListDataProvider<PhotoDetails>
          dataProvider = new ListDataProvider<PhotoDetails>();
dataProvider.addDataDisplay(photoList);
```

This code creates a new `ListDataProvider` (an empty model) with a `type` parameter indicating it will hold `PhotoDetails` objects. The view (your cell widget) is then added to the list via the provider's `addDataDisplay` method. When you want to update or add data to the model now backing the `CellList` widget, you retrieve a `List` representation of the model from the `ListDataProvider`:

```
List<PhotoDetails> theList = dataProvider.getList();
```

Then make the necessary updates.

It's not always the case that the data you need for the model is held in the client already. Most likely the required data sits on a server, and in that case, you should use an `AsyncDataProvider` instead.

ASYNCDATAPROVIDER

If the data will come from a server, then you need to take into account the fact that it will be asynchronously provided. Luckily the `AsyncDataProvider` handles this for you.

> **TIP** Loading data? You can change the loading display if you wish through the `photoList.setLoadingIndicator(widget)` method.

Listing 10.8 contains a summary of the `AllDataAsyncDataProvider` class we implement for the cell list example (in the package `com.manning.gwtia.ch10.client.dataproviders`).

Listing 10.8 Defining one of the `AsyncDataProviders` used in this chapter's examples

```
public class AllDataAsyncDataProvider
             extends AsyncDataProvider<PhotoDetails> {        ❶ Extending the interface

   private PhotoAlbumServiceAsync rpcService;

   public AllDataAsyncDataProvider() {
      rpcService = GWT.create(PhotoAlbumService.class);      ❷ Getting RPC service
   }

   @Override
   protected void onRangeChanged(HasData<PhotoDetails> display) {   ❸ Handling range change
      final Range range = display.getVisibleRange();     ❹ Getting new range

      rpcService.getPhotoList(range.getStart(),          ❺ Making server call
                              range.getLength(),
                              new AsyncCallback<Vector<PhotoDetails>>() {   ❻ Creating async callback
         public void onSuccess(Vector<PhotoDetails> result) {
```

```
            updateRowData(range.getStart(), result);        ⑦ Pushing new
         }                                                     data to widget

         public void onFailure(Throwable caught) {
            Window.alert("Error" + caught.getMessage());
         }
      });
   }
}
```

The first thing to do is create a class that extends the AsyncDataProvider abstract class ❶ that's appropriately typed with the underlying data object (PhotoDetails in the case of this example). Because you're going to get data from an RPC call (see chapter 7), you set up for that in the constructor ❷.

Within the new class you need to implement the onRangeChanged method ❸, which is passed an object that implements the HasData interface—the CellList in this case. Inside the method you query the widget for the range it now wishes to display ❹ and then call the server for the new data ❺, creating the necessary AsyncCallback object inline ❻.

The server-side code is responsible for returning the data within the range required, which is why you pass on that data in the call. You'll see when we look at CellTable that the server-side code is also responsible for sorting the data.

Assuming everything goes okay with the call to the server, you'll retrieve a list of new photos in the onSuccess method of the callback. To display these, you call the updateRowData method ❼ indicating the index where the update should start (for example, the start of the range) and the data itself. If there's a failure, then you'd deal with it as appropriate in the onFailure method of the callback.

We won't go into the example's server-side code now, beyond saying it loads a number of photos from a file and serves back the appropriate subset of those photos as requested. It's not an industrial-strength approach, where you'd normally have some type of database backend, but it's short and simple and works for our examples.

Up until this point in our discussion we haven't explained how to limit the data shown. Yes, we've mentioned range, but if you were to implement the system now, the range would be the whole data set. You can fix that, to make your display more efficient, by applying paging.

10.4.3 Paging

Paging allows you to look at subsets of your data at a time. This is particularly useful for large data sets arriving from a server—you don't want to have to load everything before you start displaying. Instead you'd commonly display items 1 to some page size and have an ability for the user to say they now want to look at the next page (containing data some page size + 1 through 2*some page size), and so on.

To achieve this, you'd update two values on the cell widget—the page size and the row count—and then associate one or more pagers to the cell widget. You can see that happening in the next listing.

Listing 10.9 Setting up paging on a CellList

```
CellList<PhotoDetails> photoList =
          new CellList<PhotoDetails>(new PhotoCellWithUiBinder());
ListDataProvider<PhotoDetails>
         dataProvider = new ListDataProvider<PhotoDetails>();
dataProvider.addDataDisplay(photoList);
List<PhotoDetails> theList = dataProvider.getList();
int PAGE_SIZE = 6;
photoList.setPageSize(PAGE_SIZE);                              ❶ Setting page size
photoList.setRowCount(theList.size(), true);                   ❷ Updating row count
SimplePager pager = new SimplePager();                         ❸ Creating pager
pager.setDisplay(photoList);                                   ❹ Applying page
```

❶ sets the page size by passing an integer to the setPageSize method; in this example you set the page size to 6, so the widget will display a maximum of six cells at a time. If you're using a ListDataProvider, then you can reasonably set the row count to be the size of the list, as you do in ❷. By passing the setRowCount method the value true as the second parameter, you're saying this value is accurate. Any pager widget can then say "showing 1–6 of 200." Using an AsyncDataProvider might mean you're less sure of the end value at the start, so you could set that to false or make a new call to the server to get the total data size.

Now the system knows there are pages and the size of those pages, but you still need to show that to the user and provide them a means to control which page is shown. That's done with a pager widget, such as the one shown in figure 10.13.

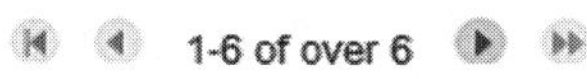

Figure 10.13 A simple built-in pager widget that you can apply to cell widgets

This is a SimplePager instance ❸ whose display is set to be the cell widget we wish it to control, ❹ Once it's inserted onto the page, the user can click the pager's forward/back buttons to navigate through the pages in the display.

It's possible to add more than one pager to a cell widget. In the example code you add not only the SimplePager but also, as shown in figure 10.14, a PageSizePager that appears at the bottom of the cells and allows the user to request to see more or fewer rows per page.

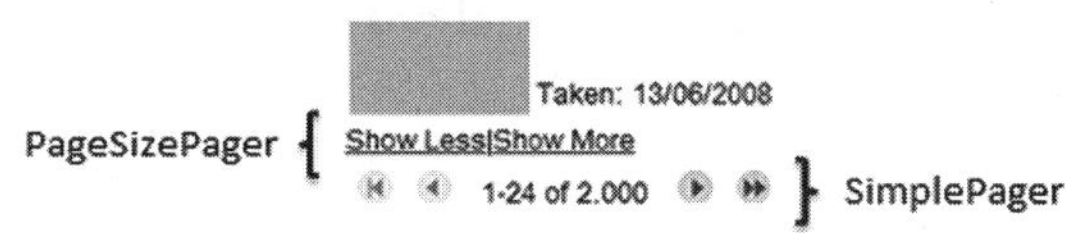

Figure 10.14 A look at how to apply two pagers to one cell widget

You can implement your own pager if you wish. Extend the AbstractPager class, and implement the onRangeOrRowCountChanged method.

Now that the user can efficiently see data and page between subsets, they're likely to start making some updates to the data.

10.4.4 Handling user updates

Handling updates on cells in a CellList is generally done through an attached ValueUpdater. Remember that we enabled the clicking of the check box on a photo cell to trigger the `ValueUpdater` when we discussed how cells handle events? Now it's time to harness that. Add the following `ValueUpdater` to the `photoList CellList` widget:

```
photoList.setValueUpdater(new ValueUpdater<PhotoDetails>(){
   @Override
   public void update(PhotoDetails value) {
      Window.alert("Handling update on photo: "+value.getTitle());
   }
});
```

When a user now clicks the `CellList`, the cell widget determines which cell has been clicked and then directs the event to that cell along with the widget's `ValueUpdater`. The cell, if you remember, had an `onBrowserEvent` method that took the event and a `ValueUpdater`, and you implemented the method so that the `ValueUpdater`'s `update` method was called, passing in that cell's underlying data object. (If you click generally on the cell, then the click is handled by the other code we included in the cell.)

In a full-blown application, this is the point where you'd probably update the database with the changed value(s).

> **NOTE** You can also preview events on cell widgets by adding a `CellPreviewEvent.Handler` to the cell widget through the `addCellPreviewHandler` method. This allows you to preview events and handle them before they get to the cell (you could, if you wish, cancel them so the cell doesn't see them).

You probably also noted that the cell's background color changed during/after the handling of the update—the cell was selected. You can set up different models for selection.

10.4.5 Managing data selection with SelectionModels

Cell widget views use a `SelectionModel` to determine if an item is selected and to provide the rules for selection. (Can only one item be selected? Are multiple items selectable?)

In the simple `CellList` example only one cell can be selected at a time by default. You can change that to allow multiple selections and check how many selections are being made (figure 10.15 shows the example with multiple selections allowed but with a five-maximum policy).

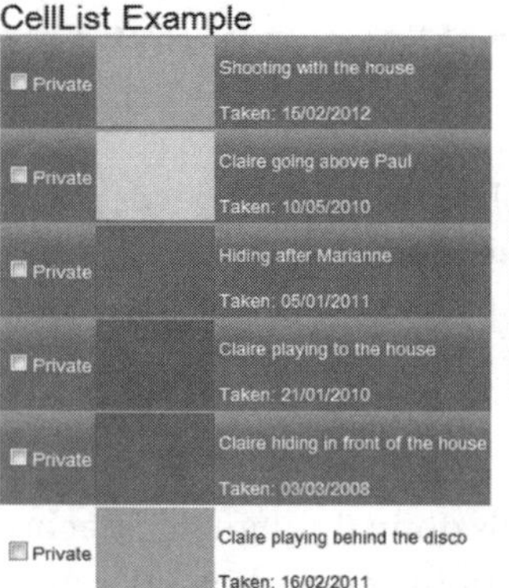

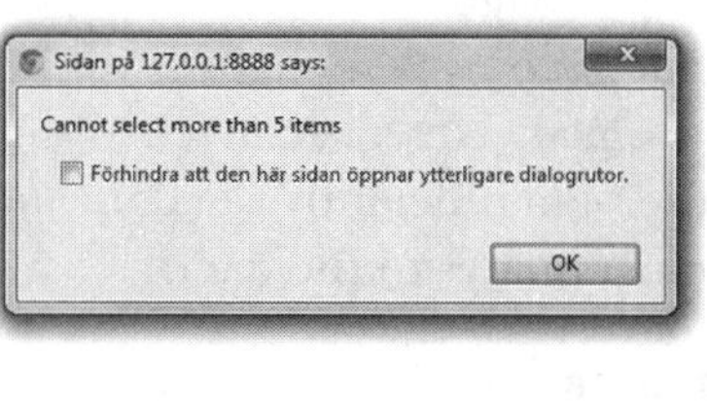

Figure 10.15 Multiselect model in action—the user is allowed to make multiple selections across pages. We've also restricted the user to selecting a maximum of five cells in the widget; in this example they've selected six and so a warning is displayed.

The following listing shows how you achieve this.

Listing 10.10 Applying a multiselect model to a CellList

```
CellList<PhotoDetails> photoList =
           new CellList<PhotoDetails>(new PhotoCellWithUiBinder());
:
:
final MultiSelectionModel<PhotoDetails> selModel =
                             new MultiSelectionModel<PhotoDetails>();   ◁ 1 New selection model
photoList.setSelectionModel(selModel);                                  ◁ 2 Applying the model
selModel.addSelectionChangeHandler(new SelectionChangeEvent.Handler() {   3 Handling selection change
   @Override
   public void onSelectionChange(SelectionChangeEvent event) {
      if(selectionModel.getSelectedSet().size()>5){                     ◁ 4 Checking how many selected
         Window.alert("Cannot select more than 5 items");
         selectionModel.setSelected(                                      5 Unselecting a selected item
           selectionModel.getSelectedSet().iterator().next(), false);
      }
});
```

❶ creates a new selection model (`MultiSelectionModel`), which is then applied to the cell widget through the `setSelectionModel` method at ❷. That's all that's needed to change the selection model, and now multiple cells could be selected in our example.

To restrict the number of selections, you add a `SelectionChangeEvent.Handler` ❸ to the selection model, and that's triggered whenever the selection is changed. In the body of that handler, you check to see how many items are already selected and whether it's more than five ❹. It's worth noting that selection works over pages, so if you select three cells on one page and another three on another page (using Ctrl+click), then the warning you set up will appear.

Finally, you programmatically deselect a selected cell in ❺ (it so happens when we tested this that the first element in the selected set was the last selected cell, but it's not clear that can be relied on).

10.4.6 Managing the keyboard

Cell widgets react to some keyboard events automatically when a selection is made. You can set a keyboard-selection policy from table 10.4 using

```
CellList<PhotoDetails> photoList =
           new CellList<PhotoDetails>(new PhotoCellWithUiBinder());
:
photoList.setKeyboardSelectionPolicy(KeyboardSelectionPolicy.ENABLED);
```

Table 10.4 The available keyboard selection policies in GWT 2.5

Value	Description
BOUND_TO_SELECTION	Selection is bound to the selection model.
ENABLED	Selection via keyboard is enabled (for example, Ctrl+click or Shift+click).
DISABLED	If the user navigates to the end or beginning of the page, then the range is increased.

You can also indicate what to do when the user presses the up/down arrow keys (or Home, End, Page Up/Down) through one of the keyboard-paging policies shown in table 10.5 using the following:

```
CellList<PhotoDetails> photoList =
          new CellList<PhotoDetails>(new PhotoCellWithUiBinder());
:
photoList.setKeyboardPagingPolicy(KeyboardPagingPolicy.CHANGE_PAGE);
```

Table 10.5 The available keyboard paging policies in GWT 2.5

Value	Description
`CHANGE_PAGE`	Cursor keys can be used to navigate to the next/previous page.
`CURRENT_PAGE`	The cursor is constrained within the existing page.
`INCREASE_RANGE`	Increase range is displayed if the user navigates to the end or beginning of the page.

So far we've looked at how to create a `CellList` widget, how to populate it with data, how paging works, and what selection models are. All these aspects are applicable to most cell widgets in one form or another. With that in mind, let's continue our exploration of the other cell widgets GWT provides by moving on to the `CellTree`.

10.5 Walking through a CellTree

A `CellTree` provides a tree-like structure to data representation, as in figure 10.16. Be careful, though, not to confuse it with the more basic `Tree` widget (if possible, you should use `CellTree` over `Tree`). In our `CellTree` example we'll be able to navigate a list of photos, dropping down the hierarchy of year, month, and date, in that order.

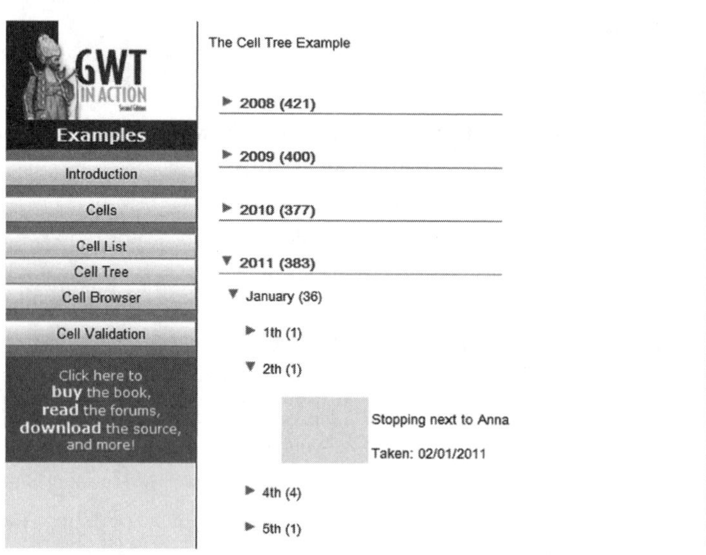

Figure 10.16 Example of the `CellTree` widget in action.

Creating a `CellTree` is done this way:

```
CellTree photoList = new CellTree(treeViewModel, open_node);
```

Typically the node to show (second parameter) is set to `null`, and that will reveal the tree's root nodes (that's how the `TreeViewModel` is typically set up), though there's nothing stopping you from opening the tree at a known lower-level node by passing that in instead.

A `TreeViewModel` explains to the widget how the tree works, so let's take a moment to look at that in some more detail. The purpose of the `TreeViewModel` is two-fold; it lets the cell widget know

- What to do when the user tries to open a node
- When the user has navigated to leaf nodes (that is, there are no more nodes to open)

Creating a model requires the implementation of the `TreeViewModel` interface together with the `getNodeInfo` and `isLeaf` methods. It's not overly challenging to do this, but it can be daunting the first time around given the heavy reliance on type parameters. In the next section we'll look at how we've done it for the example.

10.5.1 Opening a new node (with an asynchronous data provider)

The `getNodeInfo` method provides the children of the value passed to it. Our example will have nodes for years, months, days, and photos, with the intention being that when a year node is opened, the months that have photos for that year are shown, and so on. Figure 10.17 shows this visually, together with some information about each

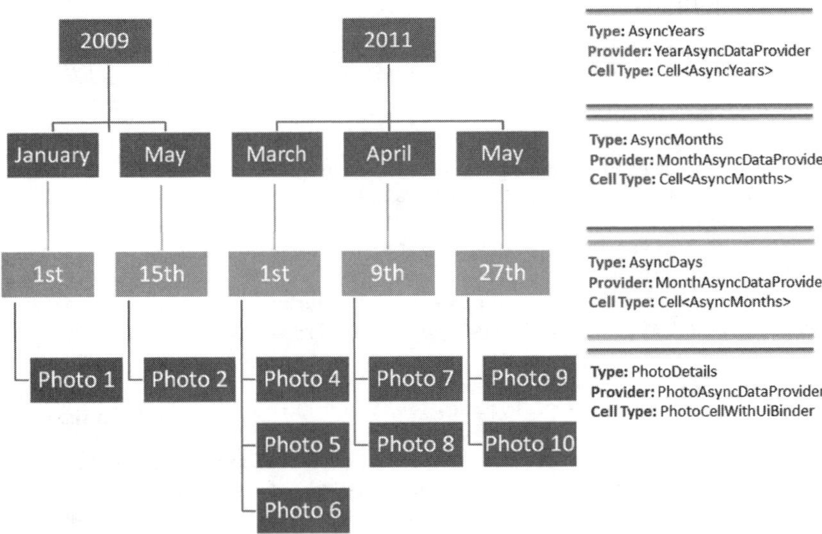

Figure 10.17 A view of the layers in our tree with associated underlying data types, data providers, and cell types

level such as the underlying data type of the node, the data provider used (assuming the example's `AsyncTreeViewModel` is used), and the associated cell.

At the root are the cells that displays the year, then in the next level the months, then the days, and finally the photos. Although years, months, and days might be integers, you wrap them in their own types (`AsyncYears`, `AsyncMonths`, and `AsyncDays`) to allow you to differentiate when you implement the `getNodeInfo(T value)`.

The basic pattern within `getNodeInfo(T value)` is to check some property of the `value` parameter, create an appropriate `DataProvider` (list or asynchronous depending on your approach), and then return a new `DefaultNodeInfo` object created from the new provider and the type of cell in which that data will be displayed.

Table 10.6 shows how you'll do this for the example—this, we hope, is slightly easier to read than the parameterized stream of code coming up in listing 10.11.

Table 10.6 Mapping the parameter value to the results of the `getInfoNode` method

Value of parameter	Purpose of the return object from `getInfoNode` is to show...
`== null`	...cells containing the available years (`AsyncYears`)
`instanceof AsyncYears`	...cells containing the available months for the year (`AsyncMonths`)
`instanceof AsyncMonths`	...cells containing the available days for the month/year (`AsyncDays`)
`instanceof AsyncDays`	...cells containing the photos for the day/month/year (`PhotoDetails`)

If you don't like complicated parameter typing in Java, now is the time to look away. if you are still with us, then listing 10.11 shows how table 10.6 is implemented in the `getNodeInfo` method of our example.

Listing 10.11 `AsynTreeViewModel` used in the `CellTree` and `CellBrowser` examples

```
package com.manning.gwtia.ch10.client.treeviewmodel;

public class AsyncTreeViewModel implements TreeViewModel {
public <T> NodeInfo<?> getNodeInfo(T value) {
   if (value==null){
      yearDataAsyncProvider = new YearDataAsyncProvider();
      Cell<AsyncYears> cell = new
                              AbstractCell<AsyncYears>(){...}
      return new DefaultNodeInfo<AsyncYears>(yearDataAsyncProvider,
                                             cell);)
   } else if (value instanceof AsyncYears){
      currYear = ((AsyncYears)value).getYears));
      monthDataAsyncProvider = new
                               MonthDataAsyncProvider(currYear);
      Cell<AsyncMonths> cell = new AbstractCell<AsyncMonths>(){...}
      return new DefaultNodeInfo<AsyncMonths>
      ➥ (monthDataAsyncProvider, cell);)
   } else if (value instanceof AsyncMonths){
      :
```

Annotations:
1. At the root of the tree
2. Create provider
3. Create new cell type
4. Bind provider and cells
5. User has clicked a year so show valid month
6. Store the year info for later
7. User has clicked a month, so show valid days

```
    } else if (value instanceof AsyncDays)[
      :
    }

public boolean isLeaf(Object value) {
   return (value instanceof PhotoDetails);
}
}

    :
AsyncTreeViewModel treeViewModel = new AsyncTreeViewModel();
CellTree photoList = new CellTree(treeViewModel, null);
    :
```

❽ **User has clicked a day, so show valid photos**

❾ **Determining if we're at a leaf node**

When the widget is first shown, it's generally passed a `null` value to the `getNodeInfo` method—this you can take to mean "show the root nodes of the tree" ❶ (in our example case, the years). You get those years by creating an `AsyncDataProvider` ❷ in the same way you did in the `CellList` example. At ❸ you create an inline cell type to show year information—the definition in the downloaded code will be quite familiar if you've read the first half of this chapter (it extracts the necessary value from the `AsyncYears` object and uses it in the cell's `render` method).

Next, you create a `DefaultNodeInfo` object that takes the provider and cell types you've created and returns them from the method ❹. The `CellTree` widget then uses this to construct the view presented to the user when the asynchronous call returns.

If the value parameter is not `null`, then you check to see what type has been passed via `instanceof` checks (this is why you wrapped the simple integer of year, month, and day to distinguish among them). In ❺ you look to see if the tree node to expand has an underlying data type of `AsyncYears`; if so, then you'll create a `MonthAsyncDataProvider` for the months, as well as a cell for showing months, and return the appropriate `DefaultNodeInfo` object. You pass that `MonthAsyncDataProvider` the current year in its constructor so it knows what to use in the server-side request (and you also save the current year ❻ for use later in the tree navigation when the user clicks months and days).

Similarly at ❼ you check to see if the value is a month and then set up to display the days, and at ❽ you check to see if the value is a day and if so set up to display the relevant photos.

> **NOTE** At first glance it might not make much sense to have paging in trees, but it's useful if the nodes you have at one level are of substantial length. `CellTree` comes with a built-in pager that's deactivated unless you call the tree's `setDefaultNodeSize(int size)` method. Once you do that, then the widget will display nodes up to certain size and then display a Show More link so the user can select more data.

`TreeViewModel` with a `List` data provider is a similar process, although generally it involves building a model of linked data types at the start and traversing through that (for example, an object holding a year might have a list holding all the months in that year with each month holding all the days, and so on). The example code can be configured to use its `ListTreeViewModel` if you want to explore this in more depth.

The typing of data also helps with knowing if you're at the leaf, which is the second function that you must implement in a `TreeViewModel`.

10.5.2 *Determining if you're in the leaves*

If each layer in the tree is underpinned by a different data type (`AsyncYears`, `AsyncMonths`, `AsyncDays`, and `PhotoDetails` in our example), and one of those types represents leaf nodes, then implementing the `isLeaf` method is simple: you return whether the parameter is of the leaf type or not.

It doesn't get much simpler than that. If the object passed into the method in our example, ❾ in listing 10.11, is of the type `PhotoDetails`, then it's a leaf—that is, it can't be further opened; if it isn't, then it isn't a leaf.

The only thing we want to highlight about `CellTree` is that it's possible to react to node open (`OpenEvent<TreeNode>`) and close (`CloseEvent<TreeNode>`) events either through the standard `UiHandler` approach if using UiBinder or `addOpenHandler/ addCloseHandler` methods.

Next, we'll take a quick look at `CellBrowser`, which is a close cousin to `CellTree`.

10.6 *Browsing a CellBrowser*

`CellBrowser` is an implementation of Miller Columns, allowing for quick navigation of tree-like data via a series of columns—each column contains all the nodes of a particular level in the tree. Figure 10.18 shows this in action.

Creating a `CellBrowser` is similar to creating a `CellTree` but slightly different. You still need to create a `TreeViewModel` as in the `CellTree` (and our `cellBrowser.CellBrowserExample` example uses exactly the same one as the `CellTree` example), but you don't directly create a `CellBrowser` object. Instead, you create a `Builder` object whose type parameter is the type of the `CellBrowser`'s root nodes together with the nodes to show, and you create the `CellBrowser` from that:

```
Builder<AsyncYears> cellBrowserBuilder =
                new Builder<AsyncYears>(model, null);
CellBrowser photoList = cellBrowserBuilder.build();
```

Figure 10.18 A `CellBrowser` widget in action

As with the tree, the second parameter is the node in which to open the view, and it's typically set to `null` to show the root(s).

This builder approach allows easier access to change the inner workings of the functionality, such as paging. A `CellBrowser` contains a `Pager` per column—you'll see this if your data in a column exceeds 25 items because it acquires a Show More link after the 25th item. You can alter this value in the builder object by calling the `pageSize` method and passing an integer for the length you want:

```
cellBrowserBuilder.pageSize(PAGE_SIZE);
```

You can also use the `pagerFactory` method to supply a different pager to be used in each column if there's more data than the defined page-size limit:

```
cellBrowserBuilder.pagerFactory(new PagerFactory(){
   @Override
   public AbstractPager create(HasRows display) {
      return new SimplePager();
   }
});
```

If you want to get rid of the pager, then it's simplest to set the page size to a huge value unlikely to be met by your data size: `Integer.MAX_VALUE` is probably sufficient.

Next, we'll look at `CellTable`, which allows us to explore a cell widget with more than one column and sorting.

10.7 Constructing a CellTable

The `CellTable` is exactly what you probably think it is—a table made up of cells. Each column has the same type of cell, and you can place headers and footers on the table (spanning several columns if required). Tables can have pagers applied to them, and, interestingly, you can apply ascending/descending sorts on columns and create custom renderers that allow you to have expandable rows/data spanning across columns.

In this section we'll concentrate on creating a table using the default renderer and how to apply sorting with both list and asynchronous backed data. We'll hold off on

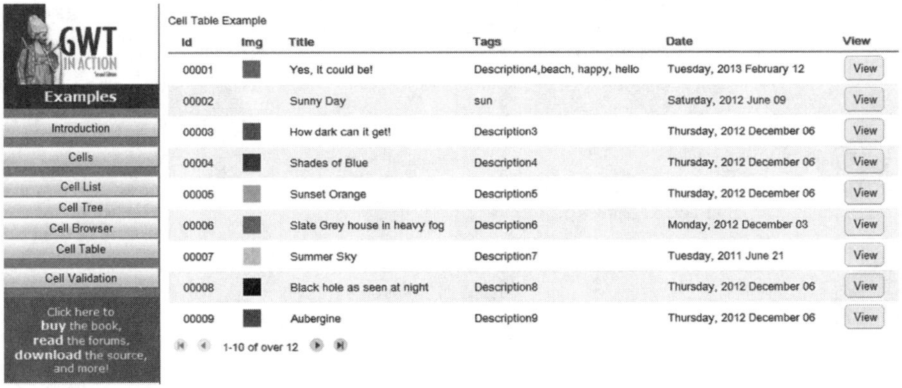

Figure 10.19 This chapter's example `CellTable` in action

the custom rendering until the next section on DataGrid. Figure 10.19 shows the example CellTable created for this section.

The first thing we'll do is look at how to create the table, then how to apply headers and footers, and finally, how to implement sorting (for both a list and an asynchronous data provider).

10.7.1 Creating a table

At its heart, a GWT CellTable is a set of columns that each hold cell widgets; in the default table, each column holds the same type of cell. Creating a table consists of creating the set of columns, adding them to the CellTable widget in the order you wish them to appear, and associating the data provider. The following listing shows the outline of how to build our example's CellTable.

Listing 10.12 Defining columns and adding them to a CellTable

```
private Column<PhotoDetails, String> buildColumnTitle() {
   columnTitle = new Column<PhotoDetails, String>(new EditTextCell()) {      // 1 Creating a new column
   @Override
   public String getValue(PhotoDetails photo) {
      return photo.getTitle();                                               // 2 Implementing the getValue method
   }
};
columnTitle.setDataStoreName(COLUMN_NAME_TITLE);                             // 3 Setting the data store name
columnTitle.setFieldUpdater(new FieldUpdater<PhotoDetails, String>() {      // 4 Adding a Field-Updater
   @Override
   public void update(int index, PhotoDetails photo, String value) {
      photo.setTitle(value);
      savePhoto(object);                                                     // 5 Implementing the update method
   }
});
return columnTitle;
}

private void createWithAsyncDataProvider() {
   dataProviderAsync = new CellTableAsyncDataProvider();
   dataProviderAsync.addDataDisplay(cellTable);                              // 6 Creating AsyncDataProvider
   dataProviderAsync.updateRowCount(24, false);
   addColumnSortAsyncHandling();                                             // 7 Setting up for sorting
}


:
columnTitle = buildColumnTitle();
columnTag = buildColumnTags();
:
cellTable.addColumn(columnTitle, buildHeader(COLUMN_NAME_TITLE),
                                 detailFooter);
cellTable.addColumn(columnTags,  buildHeader(COLUMN_NAME_TAGS),              // 8 Adding columns to table
                                 detailFooter);
:
createWithAsyncDataProvider();                                               // 9 Using AsyncDataProvider
```

❶ is where the definition of the column is made. You can see that it's defined with two type parameters—`Column<PhotoDetails, String>`: the first indicates the underlying data object, `PhotoDetails`, and the second is the cell contents, `String`. You provide the cell as the parameter to the constructor. In this example you do that inline by creating an `EditTextCell` whose `getValue` method returns the `title` from the `photo` passed to it ❷. Note that you're not defining each row individually, only the pattern for a cell in that column.

That's all that's necessary to define a column, but it's useful to set a data-store name for the column ❸. This is a text string that remains associated with the column and is useful, among other reasons, later to understand which column has been selected for sorting.

In previous cell widgets you'd apply a `ValueUpdater` to manage updates in a cell. For `CellTable` you use a `FieldUpdater` instead, applied to the column, as in ❹. A user updates a cell in the column, and the column's `FieldUpdater`'s `update` method is invoked ❺, being passed the backing object and cell value from the cell that was updated. (If you wish to do some more complicated analysis, you can retrieve the row the action happened on through the `index` parameter of `update`.)

Making CellTable more efficient in IE8

From GWT 2.5 you can disable some styling functionality to make cell tables more efficient in IE.[a] Try using the following three methods on the table:

```
setSkipRowHoverCheck(false);
setSkipRowHoverFloatElementCheck(false);
setSkipRowHoverStyleUpdate(false);
```

a. `CellTable` efficiency in IE8: http:://mng.bz/9YLu.

Columns are added to the table through the `addColumn` method ❽. You could use the simpler `cellTable.addColumn(columnTitle)` method, but we wanted to add some headers and footers to the table to make it more meaningful and so have used the alternative version with the two additional parameters. Ordering is important when you add columns: in this example the title column will appear to the left of the tag column.

Applying a data provider is done in the same manner as for other cell widgets and is applicable to the whole table. It can be either a list or an asynchronous version, as created in ❻ and applied at ❾, or a list provider (our example is configurable for both, the asynchronous provider being `dataproviders.CellTableAsyncDataProvider`).

Later in this section we'll look at how the sorting method, ❼, is implemented, but for now we'll jump to seeing how to apply headers and footers to the table.

10.7.2 Applying headers and footers

Any meaningful table is likely to need headers, and some might require footers too. To create these, you create a `Header` or `Footer` object, in the same style as creating columns. You use a helper method in the example to build headers that contain only a String:

```
private Header<String> buildHeader(final String text) {
   Header<String> head = new Header<String>(new TextCell()) {
      @Override
      public String getValue() {
         return text;
      }
   };
   return head;
}
```

Footers are similarly created but by creating a Footer object. If you apply the same header or footer to more than one cell, then it's assumed that those cells share the same object, and so it's only displayed in one column (you can see that for the detail footer in our example).

> **TIP** Looking for resizable and draggable headers? They aren't implemented in GWT yet (as of v2.5). But an issue has been raised and there have been some useful community solutions.[1]

Having meaningful headers is useful to help the user understand what the data is and also provides the mechanism to allow the user to sort the data.

10.7.3 Sorting the view

Cell tables allow the user to request a sorting of the data by clicking column headers of columns that are sort enabled. The mechanism for sorting is about the same as for list and asynchronous data providers, but the functionality is spread about differently. Let's start by looking at the asynchronous approach.

WITH AN ASYNCHRONOUS DATA PROVIDER

Sorting using an asynchronous data provider requires a little more work for the developer than using a list provider (which you'll see later) but is the more usual use case. The code in listing 10.13 comes from this chapter's CellTable example. Note that you still have to implement code in the asynchronous data provider and the server side.

Listing 10.13 Implementing sorting in the CellTable view

```
private void addColumnSortAsyncHandling() {
   columnId.setSortable(true);
   columnTitle.setSortable(true);
   columnDate.setSortable(true);

   ColumnSortEvent.AsyncHandler columnSortHandler
         new ColumnSortEvent.AsyncHandler(cellTable);
   cellTable.addColumnSortHandler(columnSortHandler);
}
```

1 Enabling columns as sortable
2 Creating the sort handler
3 Adding sort handler to table

[1] Draggable and resizable headers: http://mng.bz/9QXe.

To let the user sort columns, you need to declare them as sortable, and that's done for the example's `id`, `title`, and `date` columns in ❶ using the `setSortable` method on the column.

With the columns declared as sortable, you create a `ColumnSortEvent.AsyncHandler` in ❷ and add it to the table in ❸. This handler is responsible for handling sort events (the user clicks sortable column headings) and calls the cell widget's `setVisibleRangeAndClearData` method, which in turn fires the data provider's `onRangeChanged` method in the normal way.

In the asynchronous data provider's (`dataproviders.CellTableAsyncDataProvider`) `onRangeChanged` method, we've added some additional code compared to previous providers that determines details about the requested sorting.

Listing 10.14 Implementing code in the asynchronous data provider to support sorting

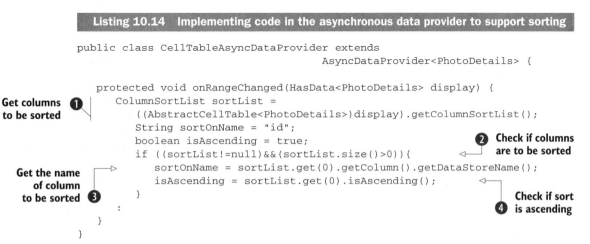

```
public class CellTableAsyncDataProvider extends
                                      AsyncDataProvider<PhotoDetails> {

   protected void onRangeChanged(HasData<PhotoDetails> display) {
      ColumnSortList sortList =
         ((AbstractCellTable<PhotoDetails>)display).getColumnSortList();
      String sortOnName = "id";
      boolean isAscending = true;
      if ((sortList!=null)&&(sortList.size()>0)){
         sortOnName = sortList.get(0).getColumn().getDataStoreName();
         isAscending = sortList.get(0).isAscending();
      }
     :
   }
}
```

❶ Get columns to be sorted
❷ Check if columns are to be sorted
❸ Get the name of column to be sorted
❹ Check if sort is ascending

First, you get a `ColumnSortList` from the table ❶. You cast the `display` parameter as `AbstractCellTable` type because you'll use this provider for both `CellTable` and `DataGrid` examples. Then ❷ you check to see if you have columns to sort on in that list. If so, you grab the data-store name of the first column in the list ❸ so you know which column it is. Finally, you check to see if the sort request is for ascending or descending order ❹ (the user clicks the column header to toggle this).

That's all you need to do in the data provider because you now pass this data on to the server-side component to get the data in the right sort order based on the column to sort, starting at the right point in the range of data and ending at the right end point. On success, you update the data rows in the table as normal through the provider. The server-side code to return the appropriate data can be seen in the code download.

Things are marginally simpler if the backing data is managed by a `List` data provider.

WITH A LIST DATA PROVIDER

With a `List` data provider, all of the data is in memory on the client side, so any sorting can be performed there. GWT also provides built-in functionality to do that, and it's used as shown in the following listing.

Listing 10.15 `List` data provider sorting (in CellTableExample.java)

```
private void addColumnSortListHandling() {
    columnId.setSortable(true);
    columnTitle.setSortable(true);
    columnDate.setSortable(true);
    ListHandler<PhotoDetails> columnSortHandler =
        new ListHandler<PhotoDetails>(dataProviderList.getList());
    cellTable.addColumnSortHandler(columnSortHandler);
    columnSortHandler.setComparator(columnTitle,
                                    new TitleComparator());
    columnSortHandler.setComparator(columnId, new IdComparator());
    columnSortHandler.setComparator(columnDate, new DateComparator());
    cellTable.getColumnSortList().push(columnId);
}
```

❶ Enabling columns as sortable
❷ Creating the sort handler
❸ Adding sort handler to table
❹ Setting column comparators
❺ Pushing the first sort

❶, ❷, and ❸ are the same as you saw in listing 10.13, except you have a `ListHandler` instead of `AsyncHandler`. In ❹ you set some comparators for the columns; these are the same `Comparator` objects for `PhotoDetails` that you used in the server-side code (and can be found in the `shared` package). All we're saying here is that the `ListHandler` should use, for example, the `DateComparator` when sorting the date column.

And that's it for sorting on a `List`. If the user clicks a column header, then the sort event `ListHandler` is fired; it selects the appropriate comparator, sorts the list, and returns the appropriate range automatically. The last thing you do, ❺, is force a sort on the Id column initially (that's not required, but it shows that it can be done).

In our last widget we'll use all the things you've seen so far, plus we'll look at how to custom-build rows.

10.8 Building a DataGrid

A `DataGrid` is essentially a `CellTable` but one where any header and footer are fixed in position and data in the widget scrolls between them. You can see this situation in figure 10.20.

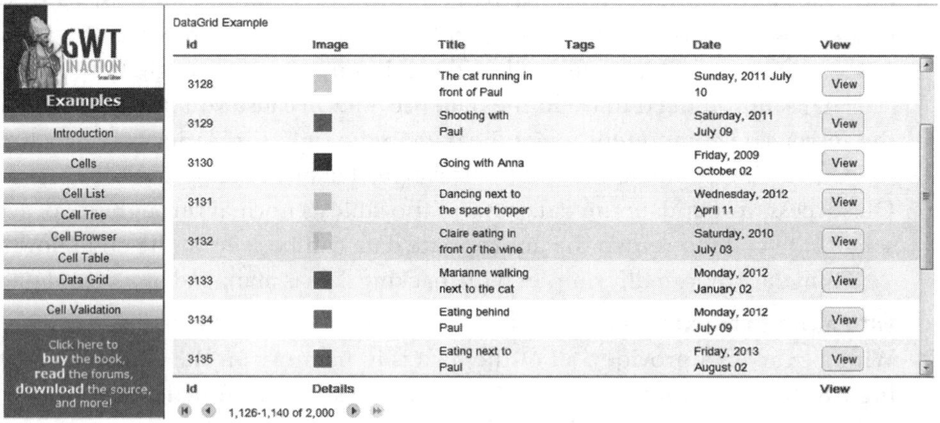

Figure 10.20 The photos shown in a `DataGrid`

The other point to note about a `DataGrid` is that it needs to be placed in a layout panel of some form to ensure it can resize as necessary (we used a simple `ResizeLayoutPanel` in the example code). Beyond that, you can consider a `DataGrid` the same as a `CellTable`.

One thing that you can do with `CellTable` and `DataGrid` is provide alternative builders—this is useful if you wish to have, for example, expandable rows or some rows that span across columns.

10.8.1 Custom `CellTable` building

In our `DataGrid` example, clicking the Edit Tags button of a photo expands a set of rows, one for each tag and an extra row for adding a new tag, as shown in figure 10.21. To achieve this you have to construct a custom `CellTable` builder, as shown in the next listing, which thankfully isn't as difficult as it sounds.

Listing 10.16 Implementing a `CustomCellTableBuilder` with expandable rows

```
public class CustomCellTableBuilder extends
                          AbstractCellTableBuilder<PhotoDetails>{      // 1

   public CustomCellTableBuilder(AbstractCellTable<PhotoDetails> cellTable)
   {
      super(cellTable);
      Style style = dataGrid.getResources().style();                   // 2
      selectedRowStyle = " " + style.selectedRow();
   }

   @Override
   protected void buildRowImpl(PhotoDetails rowValue, int absRowIndex) {  // 3
      buildStandardRowImpl(rowValue, absRowIndex);                      // 4
      if (itemsToExpand.contains(rowValue)){
         for(int index=0;index<rowValue.getTagsList().length;index++)
            buildTagRowImpl(rowValue, index, absRowIndex);              // 5
         buildNewTagRowImpl(rowValue, absRowIndex);                     // 6
      }
   }
}
```

1. Implementing the required interface
2. Setting up styling
3. Must implement this on your own
4. Building a standard row
5. Optionally building a tag row
6. Optionally building a new tag row

Listing 10.16 shows the outline of the custom `CellTable` builder you use in the `DataGrid` example. It extends the `AbstractCellTableBuilder` class ❶ and is parameterized with the underlying data type of the grid—`PhotoDetails` as usual in our examples.

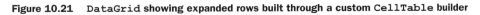

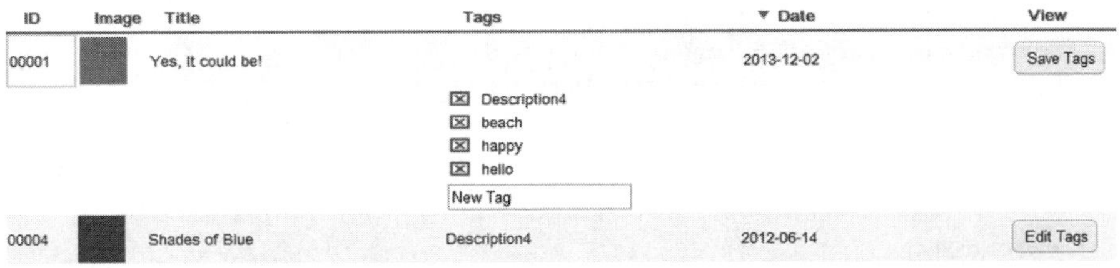

ID	Image	Title	Tags	▾ Date	View
00001		Yes, It could be!		2013-12-02	Save Tags
			☒ Description4		
			☒ beach		
			☒ happy		
			☒ hello		
			New Tag		
00004		Shades of Blue	Description4	2012-06-14	Edit Tags

Figure 10.21 `DataGrid` showing expanded rows built through a custom `CellTable` builder

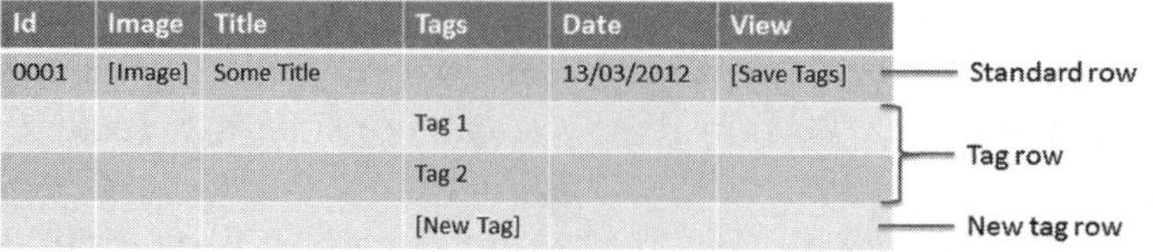

Figure 10.22 Layout of table structure when tags are expanded—not the empty cells that will need to be drawn in the standard, tag, and new-tag rows

You're responsible for styling the widget, and it's simplest if you replicate what the other table widgets do in the constructor ❷ to capture styles from a client bundle.

The key function to implement is ❸: `buildRowImpl`. This is where you're responsible for building the HTML for the rows. Our example has three types of rows, as shown in figure 10.22: a standard row that's always visible ❹, an optional set of rows that displays tag values ❺, and an optional row that displays a mechanism for adding new tag values ❻.

`DataGrid` will call `buildRowImpl` for each data object in the list to be displayed, and for clarity we provide a submethod that builds each of those row types.

One thing to note is that you store a list of photos that should be expanded in the `itemsToExpand` object. Each time an Edit Tags button is clicked on a row, the underlying `PhotoDetails` object is added to this `itemsToExpand` set so that when you draw the rows, if the current row is in the list, then you draw the optional rows. We call them "expandable" rows but they aren't dynamically expandable; you have to redraw the cell widget to show them—but because the cell widget is highly efficient, this isn't noticeable to the user.

Let's look at how those rows are drawn, starting with the standard row.

BUILDING STANDARD ROWS

Because you're writing a custom `CellTable` builder, you have to put the code in to build a normal row (which GWT gave for free in the default builder). Building a row means creating a HTML table row whose TD elements contain the cells, as in this listing.

Listing 10.17 Rendering a standard row for the `DataGrid` custom `CellTable` builder

```
protected void buildStandardRowImpl(PhotoDetails rowValue, int absRowIndex) {

   TableRowBuilder row = startRow();                          // ❶ Creating a row
   determineStyle(rowValue,absRowIndex);                      // ❷ Setting up styling
   row.className(trClasses.toString());
                                                              // ❸ Creating a cell holder
   TableCellBuilder idTD = row.startTD();
   this.renderCell(idTD, createContext(0),                    // ❹ Rendering a cell
                  dataGrid.getColumn(0), rowValue);
   idTD.endTD();
                                                              // ❺ Closing a cell holder
   :

   row.endTR();                                               // ❻ Closing a row
}
```

You create a `TableRowBuilder` to help build a row ❶. First, you determine the row's style (is it an odd/even row, or is it a selected row?) and then add the determined style to the row ❷. From the `TableRowBuilder` you then create a `TableCellBuilder` for each cell ❸ and call the cell's `renderCell` method ❹ to ask the cell to render itself. With the cell rendered, you end the `TableCellBuilder` ❺. Steps ❸, ❹, and ❺ are repeated for each cell in the table (that's not shown in listing 10.17). Once you've finished with all cells you end the `TableRowBuilder`, and the row is built.

To the `renderCell` method ❹ you pass four parameters:

- *The* `TableCellBuilder`—So the cell knows where to build itself.
- *The* `context` *of the cell*—Which you create by passing in the column number (in listing 10.17, we show how to build the first column, hence a value of 0. If you look in the downloaded code example, you'll see the next column has `createContext(1)`, and so on).
- *A* `HasCells` *object*—In the case of the default row, you'll take this from the column that has been previously built, as you saw in the `CellTree` example. You get that by calling the `getColumn` method on the `DataGrid` object. You'll see that you use something different here when you're building the other types of rows.
- *The* `rowValue`—The underlying data object for this row in the table.

A variation on this process is used for building the alternative rows.

BUILDING ALTERNATIVE ROWS

Data for the alternative rows (for example, expanded data) comes from the same underlying `PhotoDetails` object, but you choose to display different aspects. You construct the rows in exactly the same manner, but where you wish to not show data you use a `TableCellBuilder` that doesn't render anything:

```
TableCellBuilder idTD = row.startTD();
idTD.endTD();
```

Where you wish to render a different type of cell than the column's cell type, you provide the new cell instead.

Listing 10.18 Rendering a tag row for the `DataGrid` customer `CellTable` builder

```
protected void buildTagRowImpl(PhotoDetails rowValue,
int tagIndex, int absRowIndex){
   TableRowBuilder row = startRow();

   TableCellBuilder idTD = row.startTD();           ❶ Render an
   idTD.endTD();                                       empty cell

   :

   TableCellBuilder tagsTD = row.startTD();
   HasCell<PhotoDetails, String> cell = new TagCell(tagIndex);     ❷ Render cell
   this.renderCell(tagsTD, createContext(3), cell, rowValue);        not of
   tagsTD.endTD();                                                   column type
```

```
    :

    TableCellBuilder dateTD = row.startTD();
    dateTD.endTD();

    row.endTR();
}
```

In your alternative row in listing 10.18 you render empty cells where you don't wish to show data ❶, and then where you wish your tag to be shown you render a new `TagCell` ❷ (which is a wrapping of a `IconCellDecorator` showing an indexed value from the `PhotoDetails String[]` of tags). Rendering the cell that allows new tags to be added is done in the same manner, except a `TextInputCell` is used in the tag column position.

It's also possible to build custom headers and footers by implementing the `CustomHeaderBuilder` and `CustomFooterBuilder` classes, which extend `AbstractHeaderOrFooterBuilder`, in a similar manner to the row builder we've been examining—we won't go into that for reasons of space.

You create the data grid in a similar manner to the table in the last section by creating columns and adding them in the order you wish. The only additional thing you need to do is tell the table about the custom builder using the `setTableBuilder` method:

```
DataGrid<PhotoDetails> dataGrid = new DataGrid<PhotoDetails>();
:
CustomCellTableBuilder tableBuilder =
                       new CustomCellTableBuilder(dataGrid);
dataGrid.setTableBuilder(tableBuilder);
```

And, you're finished.

10.9 Summary

We've come to the end of a "quick" romp through cell widgets. We've looked at the types of cells that GWT provides as well as how to build your own custom cells (either as composite cells or from scratch). Along the way, you saw how to handle events and to harness `UiRenderer` in GWT 2.5 to create declarative cells in the manner of `UiBinder`'s declarative interfaces.

With a good background on cells, we moved on to the objects that those cells live inside: cell widgets. These form the highly efficient framework for displaying vast amounts of data in your interfaces. Putting them together with paging means you can make efficient navigation of large data sets a reality for users. We also covered how to add data into these widgets from a client-side `List` or by using a more realistic asynchronous data provider getting data from a server component.

As we cranked up the complexity of cell widgets, you learned how to create trees and column browsers with the help of a `TreeViewModel`, which guides the widget in understanding what needs to be displayed when nodes are open and when it has reached the leaves of the tree.

With tables, you saw not only how to display data efficiently and how to apply paging but also how you can mark columns as sortable and then sort the data set appropriately. If you're using asynchronous data providers, then that sorting is done on the server side, but it can also be done on the client side if you're using a `List` data provider.

Finally, we went back to basics with `DataGrid` and examined how to create a custom renderer, allowing you to build expandable rows when users interact with the widget.

In the next chapter we'll get right under the hood of GWT and start looking at interacting directly with JavaScript through the JavaScript Native Interface (JSNI).

11 Using JSNI—JavaScript Native Interface

This chapter covers

- Defining JSNI, including when and how to use it
- Creating JavaScript overlays and quick JSONP handling
- Wrapping JavaScript libraries and using them in GWT
- Exposing your application as an API

Until now we've been looking at the various enhancements and help that GWT brings to web application development. We've covered widgets, panels, handling events, creating your own widgets and applications, and communicating with the server. Along the way we've been using the great tool support that comes with Java, and consequently GWT, such as integrated development environments, code completion, syntax and semantic checking, and debugging.

Whether you knew it or not, GWT has been protecting you from problems typically associated with web application development: issues such as managing browser differences in implementation and securing against the introduction of memory leaks (a typical problem around event handling).

Most everything you could want to do in an application is possible using standard GWT. In this chapter we'll look at what happens when you step away from the protection of GWT and start hammering the metal yourself with JavaScript. Let's look at a few reasons why you might want to do this:

- Low-level integration with the browser (for the limited occasions when GWT doesn't provide a direct approach)
- Integration with existing JavaScript code and libraries, particularly third-party libraries, or simple handling of web API JSON results
- Exposing your application functionality as an API to external JavaScript users

In these cases you'd use JavaScript integration, and in GWT you'd do this through the JavaScript Native Interface (JSNI). If you see Java code in a GWT application looking similar to this

```
public native boolean someFunction() /*-{
   $wnd.alert("using JSNI! ");
   return true;
}-*/;
```

then you're seeing JSNI in action.

> **TIP** Don't use JSNI because you think it's the easier way. Most of the time, GWT already provides what you need, but you may need to dig a little deeper. The benefit to staying within Java is the tool support and reliance on GWT to solve typical web application development problems; step into JSNI and JavaScript and you become responsible for that.

Think of using JSNI as similar to how you might access assembly code directly in a high-level language. That is to say it's not wrong to do so, but it's only rarely that you'd have to, and most applications wouldn't require this.

> **NOTE** JSNI is applicable only to client-side aspects of your application, because (generally) JavaScript doesn't run on the server side. It's therefore not possible to use JSNI code in any server-side code or to pass an object over remote procedure calling (RPC) to the server and expect to be able to execute any included JSNI code server side.

You'll find that the emphasis of this chapter is a little different than the others. On the one hand we want to discourage you from using the topic we're covering—our point is that you can usually find what you want in plain GWT. Want to manipulate the page? Use the `DOM` class and the methods within `Element`. Want to create DOM elements? Use widgets and panels instead. Want to interact with the browser for cookies or getting window heights? Use the GWT `Window` class, and so on.

On the other hand, if you want to do any of the things we suggested a moment ago—interacting with existing third-party JavaScript libraries and objects, wrapping a

JSON return call from web API, or exposing an API yourself—then JSNI is the way to go, which is why we'd better look at how to use it.

Without a doubt the Google Plugin for Eclipse will help if you find you need to use JSNI. It will, as you'll see, help you avoid making some common mistakes that a normal IDE won't catch in JSNI.

So, with our warnings in place, let's get started by looking at what exactly JSNI is.

11.1 What is JSNI?

In the introduction we gave an analogy on using JSNI, saying you should use it in a similar way to how you'd use assembly language in modern program development—that is, it's not wrong to do so, but most of the time you don't need to. GWT takes that analogy one step further and uses the Java mechanism for calling native code, called Java Native Interface (JNI),[1] to interact with JavaScript code—it calls this approach JavaScript Native Interface.

Using JSNI you can include JavaScript code in your program, call other pieces of JavaScript, or provide hooks into your program that can be called externally. But just as a program is eventually compiled down to assembly language in the non-web world, making our GWT applications become JavaScript, this approach seems natural.

JSNI is a method defined like any Java method but using a specific syntax. As an example, here's a simple JSNI method that creates a DOM `Button` element and returns it to the GWT code:

```
public native ButtonElement createButtonElement(Document doc, String type)
/*-{
    var e = doc.createElement("BUTTON");
    e.type = type;
    return e;
}-*/;
```

You must abide by the following rules for a JSNI method declaration:

- It must be declared as `native`.
- It must have an empty body and be terminated with a semicolon.
- It must provide any (JavaScript) code to be used within the special comment block that starts with `/*-{` and ends with `}-*/` . The comment block is placed between the end of the parameter list of the method declaration and the closing semicolon.

Because the JavaScript code is contained within a comment block, the Java compiler sees only the following:

```
public native ButtonElement createButtonElement(Document doc, String type);
```

This causes no issue for the Java compiler and is exactly the format it would expect to see for a native JNI method call (the Java compiler would expect to find an instruction

[1] Java Native Interface documentation if you're interested (it isn't necessary to understand JSNI): http://docs.oracle.com/javase/1.5.0/docs/guide/jni/.

to load the library code, and the linker would match the library code to the native method).

Within the GWT approach you don't direct the compiler and linker to load any libraries in the linking phase. Instead, the necessary JavaScript functionality is either of the following:

- Provided directly in the special comment block
- A call to a function in a JavaScript library loaded by the browser as the result of, for example, a `<link>` element in the application's web page put in the comment block

During GWT compilation, the GWT compiler will see both the native method declaration and the JavaScript code provided in the special comment tag and will weave that into the compilation output.

This exposes one of the weaknesses of JSNI not present in normal GWT—it's not until runtime that there's any checking for the existence of any library code called from a JSNI method. This results in issues within your program if the library code is missing (unavailable or hasn't loaded at the time your GWT application makes a call to it). You'll need to defend against these problems, and you'll see some ways of doing that later in this chapter.

Two interesting aspects of JSNI that you may have noticed in the previous code are

- The JavaScript code can use Java objects (in this case passed in as parameters).
- The object created in JavaScript can be returned to the Java code.

In addition, you'll see later in this chapter that not only can you reference Java objects passed in as parameters, but you can access any Java object visible to the GWT compiler through a special syntax.

We're on record saying we discourage you from using JSNI, so before we look at how to use JSNI, here's why.

11.2 Should you use JavaScript Native Interface?

This is a question that can lead to some heated debates. It normally revolves around whether or not you have a background as a Java or JavaScript developer when you come to GWT. In the same way that many years ago a debate persisted about assembly versus high-level languages, some JavaScript developers continue to dispute the need or reason for GWT, and some GWT developers still can't fathom why anyone would use JavaScript.

We'll sit on the fence for a little while. Clearly we think GWT is the best approach, but we do recognize that in rare occasions JSNI is needed. We'll look at the reasons why, in general, you shouldn't use JSNI in your applications as well as where it might make sense. Let's start with why you shouldn't.

11.2.1 No, JSNI can quickly limit the benefits of using GWT

We'll offer the view that you're using GWT because the abstraction it provides gives you the benefits mentioned at the start of this chapter that we spread throughout this book. Doing something that limits those benefits, such as using JSNI, is probably something you wouldn't want to do unless you have to.

Using JavaScript also means that you lose the benefit of GWT's optimizations for that code. The Java-to-JavaScript compiler can't optimize your JSNI code as it does your Java code when producing its output. This means, among other things, there'll be no pruning of unused JavaScript code and no obfuscation of that JavaScript code for size optimization. The more JavaScript you include, the less GWT will be able to shrink your application size.

Like a bad infomercial, we can say, "But wait, that's not all." Memory leaks are the bane of web applications. Unless you're an extremely good JavaScript developer, you can easily introduce leaks when coding in JavaScript. If you stay in the GWT Java world, the chances of you introducing a memory leak are quite low because GWT does memory management for you (and in the rare case GWT springs a leak, when it's fixed you automatically benefit the next time you compile).

For example, if you follow a standard GWT approach, GWT will ensure event handlers you add are removed when widgets are removed. Over in JSNI land, it's up to you to carefully manage things like this. Perhaps this isn't such an issue if your JSNI is simple, but if you had larger amounts of JavaScript, you'd need to work harder. This is another hint that if you have to use JSNI, you need to keep it as small and simple as possible.

Our advice on using JSNI is as follows:

1. Avoid using JSNI:
   a. Check to make sure GWT doesn't provide a way of doing what you want first (for example, look at the `Widget`, `UIObject`, `DOM`, and `Window` GWT classes).
   b. See if you can use `JavaScriptObject` instead of accessing other JavaScript code.
2. If you have to use JSNI:
   a. Minimize the amount you write.
   b. Avoid situations where you need to manage code per browser.
3. If you can't avoid code per browser, use deferred binding to manage differences.

Let's have a look at the circumstances where you might use JSNI.

11.2.2 Yes, in these circumstances

We aren't totally negative about JSNI. It's a powerful technique, but one you should use only when needed. We can think of four situations where JSNI is your best, or only, option:

- Interacting with browser functionality that hasn't been provided by GWT (yet). We'll look at the JSNI implementation of a `getComputedStyle` function that interacts with the DOM (an alternative might be to use the GWT 2.5 Elemental library, as discussed in chapter 4).
- Handling JavaScript objects for use in your program, particularly to introduce JavaScript overlay objects, makes wrapping existing code and JSON data simple.

- Wrapping functionality of one of the many third-party JavaScript libraries you might want or need to use (including calling back into Java from JSNI); we'll also look at wrapping Cooliris functionality.[2]
- Exposing an API to your own GWT application.

If you determine that you need to write JSNI methods, then we recommend you use Eclipse and the Google Plug-in for Eclipse because they provide a lot of support that you wouldn't otherwise get.

11.3 Benefiting from the Google Plugin for Eclipse

Without the Google Plugin for Eclipse (GPE), writing JSNI in your IDE is similar to writing a book with a chisel. Support from your IDE for JSNI code is nonexistent. Look at figure 11.1, which shows a JSNI method in Eclipse without the GPE installed.

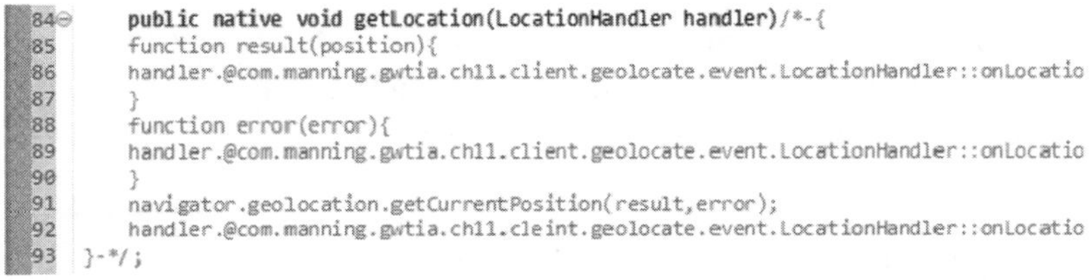

```
84  public native void getLocation(LocationHandler handler)/*-{
85  function result(position){
86  handler.@com.manning.gwtia.ch11.client.geolocate.event.LocationHandler::onLocatio
87  }
88  function error(error){
89  handler.@com.manning.gwtia.ch11.client.geolocate.event.LocationHandler::onLocatio
90  }
91  navigator.geolocation.getCurrentPosition(result,error);
92  handler.@com.manning.gwtia.ch11.cleint.geolocate.event.LocationHandler::onLocatio
93  }-*/;
```

Figure 11.1 Writing JSNI without the use of Google Plugin for Eclipse—it's hard to spot the syntax error.

The JavaScript code is treated like a comment in figure 11.1 without the GPE. There's no formatting applied, no hints that parts relate to parameters, and so on. Worse, it's almost impossible to see that the code contains a syntactic error that will break the code during execution—can you spot the error? We'd be impressed if you did.

Figure 11.2 shows the same code, only this time we're looking at it in Eclipse with the GPE installed. You can immediately see the error, highlighted on row 92, and that it has something to do with the package name (we've misspelled `client` as `cleint`).

```
84  public native void getLocation(LocationHandler handler)/*-{
85  function result(position){
86        handler.@com.manning.gwtia.ch11.client.geolocate.event.LocationHandler::onLocationFound(l
87  }
88  function error(error){
89     handler.@com.manning.gwtia.ch11.client.geolocate.event.LocationHandler::onLocationError(Lco
90  }
91  navigator.geolocation.getCurrentPosition(result,error);
92  handler.@com.manning.gwtia.ch11.cleint.geolocate.event.LocationHandler::onLocationSearch()();
93  }-*/;
```

Figure 11.2 Writing JSNI using the Google Plugin for Eclipse—now the IDE has highlighted a syntax error in the package name (and if this book wasn't printed in black and white, you'd also notice the syntax colorization).

[2] The Cooliris functionality that we'll wrap in a JSNI library in this chapter is found at www.cooliris.com/desktop/.

If you're reading the electronic version of this book, you'll also see that the JSNI code has helpful syntax coloring in the same style as normal Java code as well as having some indentation applied. The benefits of GPE for JSNI include the following:

- Error detection (as shown previously)
- Auto completion
- Validation of Java objects you're referencing in JavaScript code
- Method body autocompletion—useful for JavaScript `Overlay` objects
- Refactoring support

If you start using JSNI, you'll see how beneficial this is, and we can't emphasize enough how huge a potential problem refactoring (for example, renaming classes) is with JSNI. When refactoring, you need to ensure that all package names are updated—a process wide open to errors in JSNI code if done manually; with GPE it's automatically part of the standard refactoring process.

We won't bore you by showing pictures of each feature of the GPE relating to JSNI because it's constantly being improved and would quickly, we hope, be out of date. We'll conclude by saying if you have to use JSNI, the GPE is a welcome addition to the toolset.

Debugging JavaScript

Unfortunately you can't, at the time of writing, set a debug step in your JSNI code in Eclipse and step through it. What you can do, though, is put the JavaScript construct `debugger` in the code where you wish to start debugging. Then, if you have a JavaScript debugger in your browser, such as Chrome does, or an add-in that provides a debugger, you could see results similar to figure 11.3 when running your application (either in development mode or in web mode).

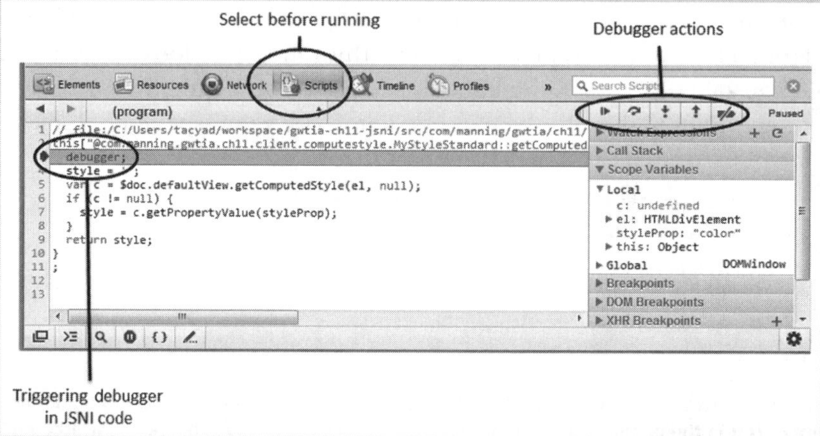

Figure 11.3 The built-in JavaScript debugger in Chrome in action, triggered by the `debugger` statement in the JSNI code. In Chrome, at least, you need to start the programmer's tools and select the Script tab and reload the application to get the debugger to trigger.

Now that you're armed for dealing with JSNI, let's start looking at the four cases where it makes sense to use it, starting with interacting with the browser.

11.4 Interacting with the browser

Where you'd use JNI in Java to access operating system functions, you (or rather GWT) use JSNI to access the web browser. Luckily, the version of GWT you have provides most of this already, so you can use GWT Java classes and be oblivious that underneath they're using JSNI and managing all the awkward browser differences for you:

- Through the `Window` class (in `com.google.gwt.user.client`), you can raise alert and confirmation windows, open new browser windows, set browser titles, enable and disable window scrolling, and get all of the browser dimensions you could want. For example, `Window.alert("hello");` pops up a JavaScript alert window containing the text `hello`.
- The `Window` class also gives access to managing window close, resize, and scroll events—you can write `Window.addResizeHandler(new ResizeHandler() {...});` to react to browser window resizing.
- The `UIObject` class in `com.google.gwt.user.client.ui` (of which `Widget` and `Panel` are subclasses) allows some access to DOM aspects of GUI components, such as `addStlyeName`, `getOffSetWidth`, `getAbsoluteTop`, and `setSize`.
- Absolute low-level DOM functions on widgets are often accessible through the widget's `getElement()` method; for example, to set the border width of a widget you can write `widget.getElement().getStyle().setBorderWidth(2.0, Unit.PX)`—no need to go anywhere near JavaScript yourself.
- General lower-level DOM functions can be accessed through the `DOM` class in a (to you) browser-agnostic manner (see the various `DOMImpl` classes in the `com.google.gwt.dom.client` package and chapter 17 to understand how GWT manages browser differences).
- Browser events are abstracted out of JavaScript for you by the GWT event-handling system, substantially reducing the chances you'll accidentally create memory leaks.

But GWT does miss a few little things, at least in version 2.5. One is how to get the computed style of a DOM element (the style a browser has computed for an element that has no explicit style—therefore the style is determined by the browser cascading styles through the DOM hierarchy). That's something you can easily fix with a little JSNI.

11.4.1 Example: getting a browser element's computed style

Take a quick look at figure 11.4. It shows this chapter's computed style example.

On the right side of the figure are two text boxes telling you the color style of the text of the inner panel on the left (the orange one if you're reading in color). The top text box tells you the value of the color attribute of the inner panel. It does that by using the following pure GWT code:

```
box2.getElement().getStyle().getColor();
```

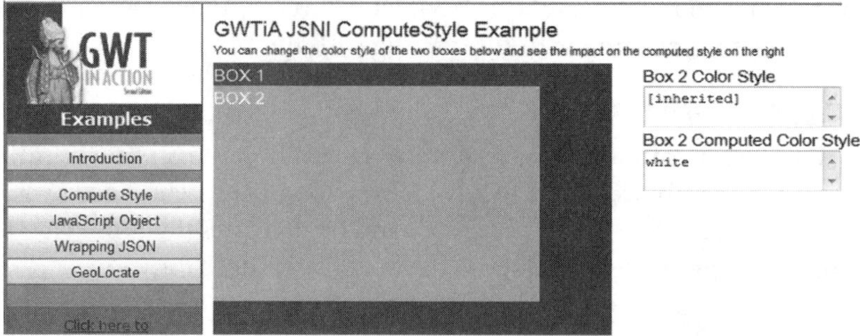

Figure 11.4 The values of GWT's `getStyle` method and this chapter's `getComputedStyle` method. Note that `getStyle` is unable to determine the text color in box 2 because it's inherited.

This code does exactly as it says: it gets the GWT object for the element of the `box2` widget; from that it gets the GWT object representing the style, and it uses that to get the value of the color attribute. If you look again at figure 11.4 you'll see that this code tells you the color style is `[inherited]`, that is, no explicit value has been set, so no value was found when making the previous call (because we wrote in the GWT application that if this code returns `null` or an empty string, then use `[inherited]`).

Although it's good to know the value is inherited, sometimes you want to know what the real value is. At the time of this writing, GWT has no way to do that, but we know the value is available through JavaScript, so we'll have to implement a JSNI method. Our first attempt might look as follows:

```
public native String getComputedStyle(Element el,String styleProp)
/*-{
   var c = el.currentStyle;
   return c[styleProp];
}-*/;
```

It looks simple, and it meets the requirements for a JSNI method we gave in section 11.1:

- It's defined as a `native` method definition.
- It has the JavaScript functionality contained within the special code block.
- Functionality wise, it will return the computed value of the style property we've requested.

But there's one problem: this code will only work for Internet Explorer. To get the computed style in standards-compliant browsers, such as Firefox, Safari, Opera, and Chrome, you need to use the following code:

```
public native String getComputedStyle(Element el,String styleProp)
/*-{
   var style = "";
   var c = $doc.defaultView.getComputedStyle(el, null);
   if (c!=null){
      style = c.getPropertyValue(styleProp);
```

```
    }
    return style;
}-*/;
```

But that code won't work for Internet Explorer before IE9. Does that mean you need to send both versions of JavaScript as well as some browser-detection code to the browser in your JSNI method?

Thankfully, no. You can use the deferred-binding GWT technique that we discuss in detail in chapter 17. We won't go into detail on how this technique works here, but suffice it to say that in the chapter's example code you'll find both computed style implementations, but shown in separate classes in the `com.manning.gwtia.ch11.client.computestyle` package. `MyStyle` class contains the IE version, and `MyStyleStandard` contains the standards-compliant version. The GWT compiler and application bootstrap code will ensure that only the correct version is sent to the browser being used.

The point to take away is that it's (another) example of the additional complexity you need to think of when using JSNI that GWT typically takes care of for you. You have to know much more about JavaScript, browsers, and DOM manipulation than you might wish or need to.

There's another subtlety to keep in mind when using JSNI, and that has to do with how you access the browser to execute functions.

ACCESSING THE BROWSER VARIABLES

In normal JavaScript, you access the browser and its properties through the `document` and/or `window` JavaScript objects. You may have noticed if you were paying abnormal attention that in the code, rather than write

```
document.defaultView.getComputedStyle(el, null);
```

we wrote

```
$doc.defaultView.getComputedStyle(el, null);
```

Using `$doc` instead of `document` is necessary in JSNI code because a GWT application could be (and usually is) loaded into a frame within the browser. This means that the visibility of the `document` variable isn't guaranteed. GWT provides the `$doc` JavaScript variable instead, which it guarantees to link to the standard `document` variable regardless of how the application is loaded into the browser. It's the same rationale behind why you should use GWT's `$wnd` object instead of the JavaScript `window` object in your JSNI code.

> **TIP** In JSNI you should use the `$wnd` and `$doc` variables instead of the normal JavaScript `window` and `document` ones.

You may have noticed two other slightly magical things going on in the code example:

- Inside the JSNI code we directly referenced the Java native method's parameters without the need for any strange syntax or mapping.
- The return value of the JavaScript code is the return value of the Java native method, again without the need for any strange syntax or mapping.

The passing in and out of Java objects to JSNI code is a feature made possible as the end product of GWT compilation in a JavaScript application. But there are a number of rules associated with this feature to ensure safety and consistency.

11.4.2 Passing data in to a JSNI method

A JSNI method declaration is a standard Java one. You can use any type of parameter you would expect: Java primitives (for example, `int` or `char`), objects (for example, `String` or `Vector` or user-defined objects), and even the `varargs` construct.

In our computed style example two Java objects were used as the parameters—an `Element` and a `String`:

```
public native String getComputedStyle(Element el,String styleProp)
```

And we referenced them quite naturally in the JavaScript code:

```
var c = el.currentStyle;
return c[styleProp];
```

At first this may seem strange: Java is a strongly typed language, JavaScript isn't, and how do we know an `Element` in Java is an `Element` in JavaScript? Well, we don't have to as long as we adhere to a small number of rules and trust the GWT compiler to ensure a consistent compilation and mapping. Table 11.1 shows the mapping from Java to JavaScript.

Table 11.1 How Java types map into JavaScript values

Java type	JavaScript representation
`boolean`	Maps to a JavaScript `boolean` value, for example, `var b = true;`.
`char, int, double, float, short, byte`	Maps to a JavaScript numeric value, for example, `var n = 17;`.
`long`	The primitive `long` type isn't allowed (explained in the text).
`String`	Maps directly to a JavaScript string, for example, `var s = "A String";`.
Java array	An opaque value, that is, it can't be changed in JavaScript code.
`JavaScriptObject`	A special GWT object used to wrap JavaScript objects when handled in Java, explained more in section 11.5. When passed from Java to JavaScript it becomes the JavaScript object again.
Any other Java object	An opaque value, the contents of which can be accessed in JavaScript code within a JSNI block via a special format we'll cover in section 11.5.

Most of the Java primitives and `String` behave as you'd expect, becoming simple variables within JavaScript and copying across the value into that new variable. Only the Java primitive `long` causes problems—it can't be passed as a parameter or returned as a result. This restriction is because JavaScript can't implement the Java `long` primitive.

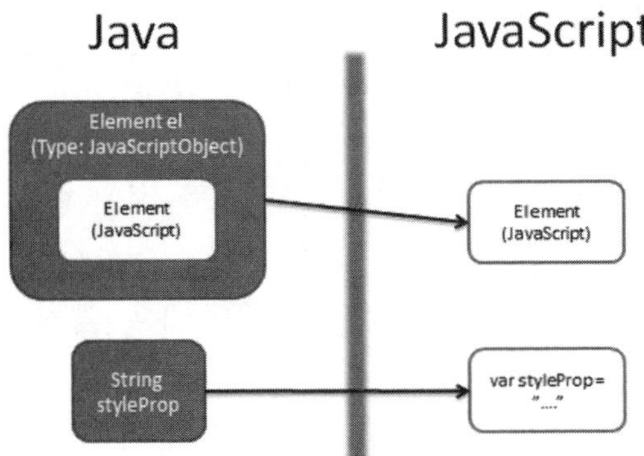

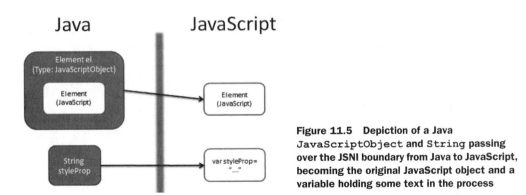

Figure 11.5 Depiction of a Java `JavaScriptObject` and `String` passing over the JSNI boundary from Java to JavaScript, becoming the original JavaScript object and a variable holding some text in the process

GWT already knows this, and so it emulates a Java `long` as an opaque data structure. The GWT documentation suggests four options to solve this primitive `long` problem:

- If you know the number will always be small enough to fit within the Java primitive `double`, then use that instead of the Java primitive `long`.
- If the `long` value is used in a calculation, rearrange your code so the calculation happens in Java instead of JSNI JavaScript code.
- If the `long` passes through the method unchanged, then wrap it in a `Long` object because `Long` in JSNI has no restrictions.
- If you're convinced you know what you're doing, you can add the annotation `@UnsafeNativeLong` to the method, which directs the compiler to allow the Java primitive `long` to be passed and returned from the JSNI method. It's still an opaque data type, so it can only be passed back to Java.

The final two items in table 11.1—`JavaScriptObjects` (a Java object that specifically represents or wraps an underlying JavaScript object) and normal Java objects—are worthy of their own sections in this chapter, so we'll hold off on discussing them in detail until then (see sections 11.5 and 11.6).

As you've seen, the computed style example shows this passing of Java objects into JavaScript JSNI code in action, and we can depict what happens visually in figure 11.5. We pass in an `Element` object (which is a `JavaScriptObject`) and a `String` as parameters. The Java `Element el`, as a `JavaScriptObject`, loses its Java wrapper and becomes the underlying JavaScript object again, allowing us in JavaScript to get the DOM property `el.currentStyle` through a normal JavaScript call. The second parameter, which is a `String`, becomes a JavaScript variable with the value from Java, which we then use in the JavaScript code `c[styleProp]`.

As you'd expect, the reverse happens when a value in JavaScript code is returned to Java in the GWT application.

11.4.3 Passing data out of a JSNI method

A mapping (see table 11.2) exists for when a value in JSNI JavaScript code is returned to Java (and it's the reverse of table 11.1).

Table 11.2 How JavaScript values map to Java types

JavaScript return value	Java type
`boolean` value, for example, return `false`;	Maps to a Java `boolean` primitive.
JavaScript numeric value	Java primitive type.
`long`	Not allowed.
JavaScript `String`	Maps to a Java `String`.
A Java array	Mostly maps to an array.
`JavaScriptObject`	A special GWT object called `JavaScriptObject`, explained more in section 11.5.
Any other Java object	It's not possible to create a Java object inside JSNI code, but you can use a special syntax to have altered instance fields either directly or via calling instance methods. We look at this in section 11.6. If the return is an object that was passed in as a parameter, then it can be returned.
`undefined` or `null`	`null`.

GWT will try type-checking objects as they pass from JavaScript to Java. If you've defined your JSNI method to return a particular Java type, and it returns another one, then an exception is thrown in development mode. You do need to be careful to check for this during testing because neither the compiler, nor your IDE, nor the GPE will pick up this error, at present, so you'll run into application problems in production if it lurks.

We can visualize the passing back of an object from JavaScript to Java in the computed style example, as shown in figure 11.6.

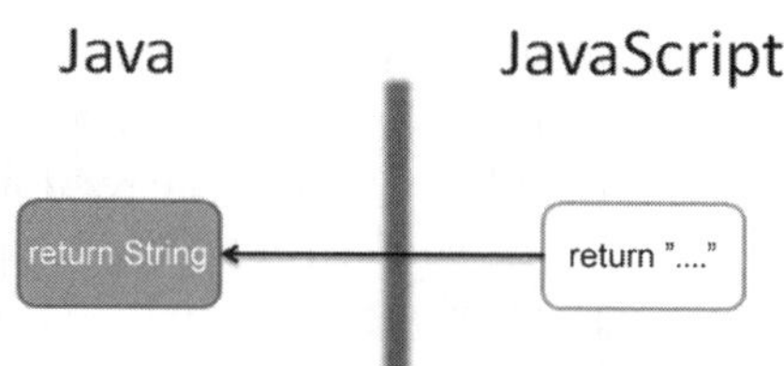

Figure 11.6 Depicting the passing back of a JavaScript variable holding some text to Java through JSNI `return`, where it becomes a Java `String` in the process

As you saw in table 11.2, simple items in JavaScript become the primitive types when passed back to Java. The figure shows a string in JavaScript being returned to Java, where it becomes a `String` object. This is what happens in our computed style example; we pass back to Java the JavaScript string value of the computed style of the DOM element passed in as a parameter. Back in Java we're free to use that `String` as we would any other `String`.

We haven't shown a JavaScript object being passed back from JavaScript in figure 11.6 (compare it to figure 11.5), but we have said they become a quite a special type: a `JavaScriptObject`. Let's rectify the fact that we haven't discussed them much yet, because they're useful objects.

11.5 Handling objects from JavaScript

Our last example didn't create anything while in the JSNI call, that is, no JavaScript objects, for example, but we did say the first parameter passed in was a `JavaScript-Object`, and now is the time to explore that further.

A `JavaScriptObject` is a Java object representing an object that's been created in JavaScript. For example, the GWT Java `Element` object represents a DOM element created in JavaScript deep in the bowels of GWT when it creates a widget. We can't create a `JavaScriptObject` object ourselves in Java code, that is, no `new JavaScript-Object()` calls; it can only be created automatically as the JavaScript object passes across the boundary from JavaScript to Java.

You can use `JavaScriptObject` in two different ways:

- *Directly*—It acts as an opaque reference, which means that you can't see into it and access any values. You'd use this approach if you don't want to access or manipulate its content on the Java side. All you can do is pass it around the Java code, and you must move it back over to JavaScript if you wish to do any processing on it.
- *Extend it*—Now any JavaScript object passed back to Java is assigned to the extended object. You'd call it an overlay object and use this approach if you want efficient access to its contents (such as when wrapping JSON, as you'll see later).

To show the differences in both these approaches and their implications, we'll introduce the example shown in figure 11.7 that allows us to manipulate a `Person` JavaScript object. That `Person` JavaScript object holds a person's name and career, plus it has a function associated with it that enables the career to be changed (you can find the example code in the `com.manning.gwtia.ch11.client.javascriptobject` package). To get the example to work, we've created a mini JavaScript library (OK, a function) by putting some JavaScript code into a person.js file in the deployable part of the application, and we'll load it into the browser during runtime (see section 11.6.1 for how we do that). We've wrapped that code in a JavaScript `createPerson` function so

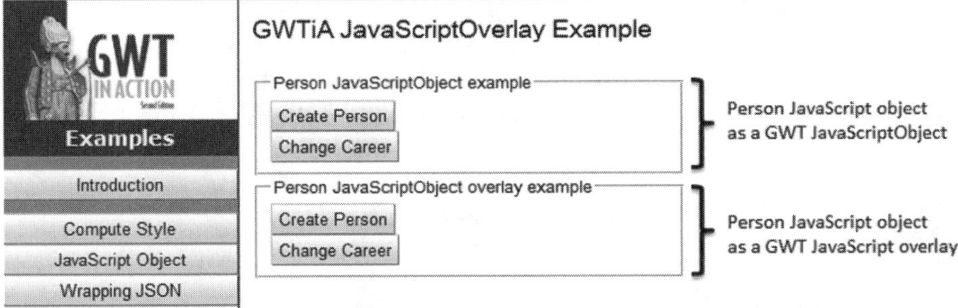

Figure 11.7 The JavaScript `Person` example showing the two parts—an upper part that handles the JavaScript object as a GWT `JavaScriptObject` and the lower part that handles another instance of the JavaScript object as a GWT JavaScript overlay object

we can call it from within our Java program to create a person—Åsa, a typical Swedish name—who happens to be a scientist at the time we create her. In the first part of the example we'll handle Åsa as a pure JavaScriptObject.

11.5.1 Example: using a JavaScriptObject

We create Åsa in a JSNI method, calling our library's single function, and return her as a JavaScriptObject:

```
public native JavaScriptObject getPerson()/*-{
   return $wnd.createPerson();
}-*/;
```

(Remember, we have to use the $wnd variable to get to the function instead of the more normal JavaScript window, as we do in JSNI.)

When Åsa comes back across the JSNI-to-Java boundary, she becomes a JavaScriptObject, which we illustrate in figure 11.8. On the Java side we show that the original JavaScript object is wrapped in a box to become the GWT JavaScriptObject. The box helps us visualize that although we have the original JavaScript object on the Java side, we can't get into it—it's opaque. This means we can't access the values of fields, which we know are there, from Java code—we have to construct a JSNI method, pass the JavaScriptObject into it, extract the name in JavaScript, and return it as the method's return value:

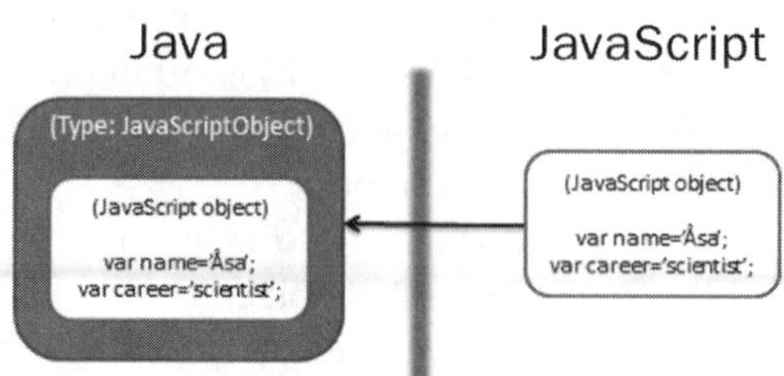

Figure 11.8 How the Person JavaScript object comes across the boundary to Java as a JavaScriptObject

```
public native String getName(JavaScriptObject person)/*-{
   return person.name
}-*/;
```

Figure 11.9 shows the top part of the example using this approach.

Once we created Åsa, by clicking the Create Person button, we called two JSNI methods to get her name and career; we had to write two methods to get her name and her career and one to change her career. To display her name and career together, we called both JSNI methods and then put them together in a string. We had

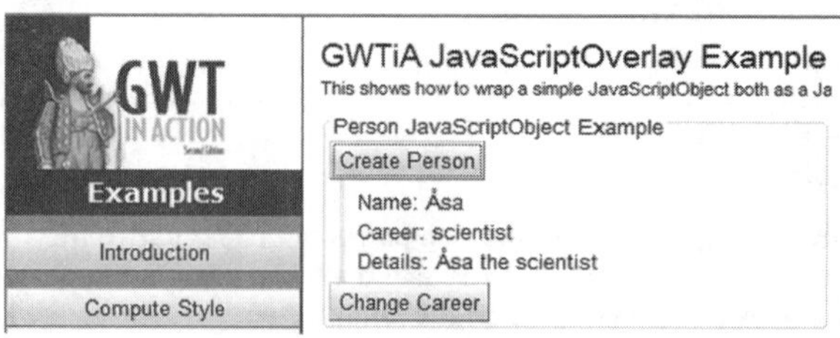

Figure 11.9 Showing the data created from JavaScript for a person via a simple JavaScript object

to do that outside the JavaScriptObject, so we're not encapsulating that functionality, which isn't good design.

Changing her career is another trip across the JSNI boundary, passing the JavaScriptObject in as a parameter along with the new career:

```
native JavaScriptObject changeCareer(JavaScriptObject person,
                                     String newCareer)/*-{
   person.changeCareer(newCareer);
}-*/;
```

It's all a bit clumsy, right? You might find legacy code that takes this approach, or you might even find it's the best way for you in your implementation if you don't need to dig into the contents. But we'll show you a better way. You can use the JavaScriptObject as an overlay.

11.5.2 Example: extending a JavaScriptObject (an overlay)

Instead of creating a person and returning a JavaScriptObject, we can define the createPerson Java method to return an object that extends JavaScriptObject, such as the following:

```
private native PersonJavaScriptOverlay makePersonOverlay()/*-{
   return $wnd.createPerson();
}-*/;
```

Now we're returning a PersonJavaScriptOverlay, the definition of which is shown in the following listing.

Listing 11.1 JavaScript overlay of a person object

```
public class PersonJavaScriptOverlay extends JavaScriptObject   <- Extending JavaScriptObject
                                     implements Person{         <- Implementing an interface
    protected PersonJavaScriptOverlay(){}                       <- An empty protected constructor (1)

    final public native Person changeCareer(String newCareer)/*-{
        this.changeCareer(newCareer);
        return this;
    }-*/;

    final public native String getCareer()/*-{                  <- Getting data
        return this.career;
    }-*/;

    final public native String getName()/*-{
        return this.name;
    }-*/;


    final public String getDescription() {                      <- (2) Getting enhanced data
        return getName() + " the " + getCareer();
    }
}
```

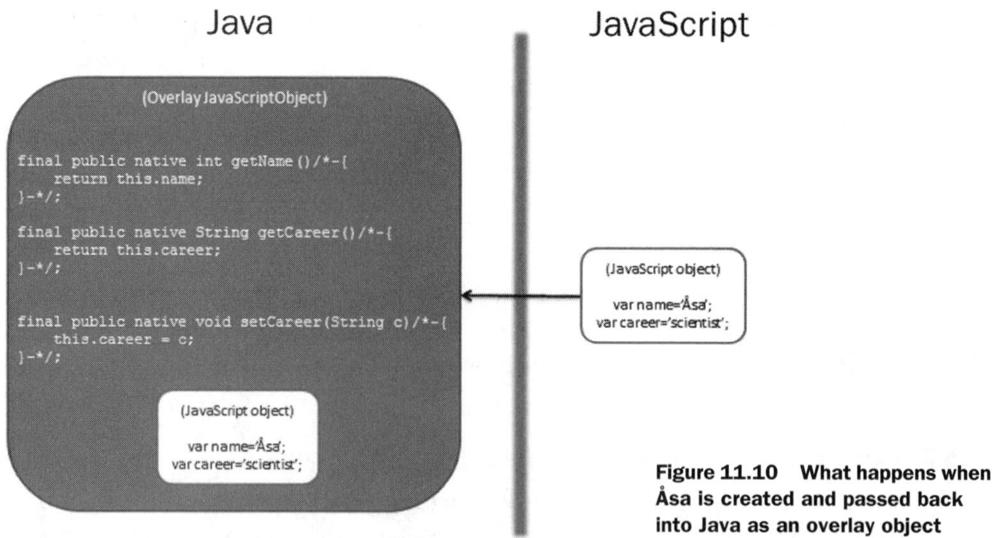

Figure 11.10 What happens when Åsa is created and passed back into Java as an overlay object

We're sure you'll agree listing 11.1 looks and feels much more natural. The methods are simpler, such as `getCareer` ❶, which returns values directly from the object. You can also encapsulate all of the functionality of a person in one object and build more natural methods such as `getDescription` ❷. Figure 11.10 shows the situation now as the JavaScript item passes into Java as an overlay.

It gets better. By using the overlay approach, you get minimal overhead in compiled code—because you no longer have to pass objects around and create JSNI methods in order to access internal items.

This flexibility comes with some high-level rules that you must follow; these are listed in the sidebar.

High-level rules for using overlay objects

1. An overlay must have only one protected, empty, no-argument constructor.
2. Instance methods must either be explicitly declared as final, be declared in a final class, or be marked as private.
3. Although you can provide additional functionality in an overlay type beyond the underlying JavaScript object, you can't have any instance fields.
4. Any nested overlay types must be defined as static.

The first rule for overlays—that you can't yourself create one—is quite important to understand. These aren't ordinary objects; they directly represent an existing JavaScript object. Without such a JavaScript object, you can't have an overlay.

We can subvert the first rule slightly to use some GWT/JSNI magic, but it has a limitation. We'll take a brief moment to discuss this magic and the limitation. Later, in the third-party wrapping example, we'll use a FlashVars overlay, which we show the relevant part of here.

Listing 11.2 Part of FlashVars overlay circumventing the first overlay rule

```
public class FlashVars extends JavaScriptObject{

   protected FlashVars(){}

   public static FlashVars newInstance() {
      return JavaScriptObject.createObject().cast();    ❶ Creating a JavaScript object
   }
}
```

You still can't write new FlashVars() because the constructor is protected, but note ❶ in listing 11.2. Here you use the underlying JavaScriptObject's createObject method to create an empty JavaScript object that you then cast to a FlashVars overlay. This does the job; you get a JavaScriptObject that you can treat as a FlashVars overlay, but the underlying JavaScript object is floating around and unable to be referenced in JavaScript. That might not be a problem to you, but you'll see that it is in section 11.6.2's example (where we want to pass an object to another JavaScript library—but there's also a solution we show there).

Another aspect of an overlay is that it can implement an interface, and we've taken that opportunity to make PersonJavaScriptOverlay implement the Person interface (as you saw in listing 11.1). You would create and implement an interface for overlays for the same design reasons as for other classes.

The use of an interface comes with a restriction—it may only be implemented by one overlay type (although it may also be implemented by one or more non-overlay types). To help indicate this, you can mark the interface with the @SingleJsoImpl annotation. This requires you to indicate which class implements it. The following is our Person interface from the example, showing the appropriate value in the annotation as the first line:

```
@SingleJsoImpl(value = PersonJavaScriptOverlay.class)
public interface Person {
    public String getName();
    public String getCareer();
    public String getDescription();
    public Person changeCareer(String newCareer);
}
```

Implementing interfaces

Don't forget to use the @SingleJsoImpl(value = XXXXX.class) annotation on your interface that will be implemented by class XXXXX.

If your overlay implementation will be created through a generator (see chapter 18), then you should use the @SingleJsoImplName annotation instead of @SingleJso-Impl, because you won't yet know the implementing class name.

The other restriction is that if the interface that extends a `@SingleJsoImpl` interface is a nontrivial interface, then that superinterface must also have the `@SingleJsoImpl` annotation.

Overlays are great for when you need to dig into components of a JavaScript object in a nice and efficient way. As you'll see next, there's one useful consequence of the overlay approach when looking at JSONP data that could come from a web service call.

11.5.3 Example: overlaying JSONP data

GWT has a set of JSON parsing classes that in certain circumstance are useful. But you can apply overlays to the structured JSON data to get fast and obvious access to the contained data, with minimal overhead, and reduce compile-sized code.

In the next few pages and in the example code (`com.manning.gwtia.ch11.jsonp` package), we'll handle data returned from querying the public photos on the Picasa web service. If you make the following call to Google's Picasa web service API

```
https://picasaweb.google.com/data/feed/api/all?max-results=6&alt=json-in-script
```

it will return a JSONP data object covering the first six public images. We've requested it as JSONP format (JSON with padding) rather than JSON, because it allows us to use GWT's `JsonpRequestBuilder` to request the data and handle it in a simple manner. We cover `RequestBuilder` in chapter 10 if you want to know more about how the basics work; `JsonpRequestBuilder` is a simple extension to that.

JSONP also allows us to work around the so-called cross-site scripting and same-site origin restriction (aka SSO). This is usually a bad idea, and you have to 100% trust that where you get the JSONP from won't inject malicious code into your application. Assuming you trust Google and Picasa, let's continue.

The point of using JavaScript Object Notation (JSON) is the JavaScript part—the return data is a nested set of JavaScript objects. And for each JavaScript object, you can overlay a GWT overlay. Figure 11.11 shows a manipulated-for-space version of data returned from this call to the Picasa API, annotated with the overlays we'll use.

```
gdata.io.handleScriptLoaded(
{  "version":"1.0",
   "encoding":"UTF-8",
   "feed":{
      "xmlns$exif":"http://schemas.google.com/photos/exif/2007",
       "id":{
         "$t":"https://picasaweb.google.com/data/feed/api/all"},
      "title":{"$t":"Search Results", "type":"text"},
      "entry":[{
            "id":{"$t":"…"},
            "title":{"$t":"DSC04941.JPG","type":"text"},
            "content":{
                    "type":"image/jpeg",
                    "src":"https://LOCATION/PHOTO.JPG"
            },
            "gphoto$access":{"$t":"public"},
            "gphoto$width":{"$t":"1600"},
            "exif$tags":{
               "exif$fstop":{"$t":"3.5"},
               "exif$make":{"$t":"SONY"},
               "exif$model":{"$t":"DSC-T90"}
            }
         }]
    }
})
```


Figure 11.11 JSONP object annotated with the JavaScript overlay objects we'll use to access the internals: `Feed`, `Entry` (there will be many of these), `Content`, and `EXIF` data objects.

From a design perspective, we can try to cover the whole response as one overlay class or, more sensibly, break out each nested element as its own overlay, allowing for simpler compartmentalized changes when someone inevitably makes them. Our recommendation is to take the latter approach, and you can see in figure 11.11 how we'll break out the JSON data into several overlay objects, nested as follows:

- `Feed`
- `Entry`
- `Content`
- `EXIF`

The first overlay is a simple `Feed` class:

```
public class Feed extends JavaScriptObject{
    protected Feed(){}

    public final native JsArray<Entry> getEntries()/*-{
          return this.feed.entry;
    }-*/;
}
```

All this class does is to allow access to the array of `Entry` objects through the `getEntries` method. When returning an array of objects, as we are here, you must use the special generic `JsArray` object. If you're returning other items, you could use one of the `JsArrayInteger`, `JsArrayBool`, `JsArrayNumber`, or `JsArrayString` objects depending on the underlying item. Each of these objects provides a `get` method that you use to pass in the index and retrieve the corresponding object. If the JavaScript array will contain values of different items, then the `JsArrayMixed` should be used; this provides methods `getNumber`, `getBoolean`, `getObject`, and `getString` to cope with the fact that different items can be returned.

Inside the `Entry` overlay, we use the approach shown with our person example a while back and can start returning values:

```
public class Entry extends JavaScriptObject{
    protected Entry(){}

    public final native Content getContent()/*-{
        return this.content;
    }-*/;

    public final native String getTitle()/*-{
        return this.title.$t;
    }-*/;
}
```

As well as providing simple lookups, such as the `getContent` method, we can dig a little deeper into the hierarchy. The `getTitle` method, for example, returns the title of our photo, which is a `String`, but if you look at the hierarchy in figure 11.5, you'll see that we have to drill down a level of the `title` object to get to the text. The `title` object holds two components, one of which is `$t`. By writing `title.$t` we jump

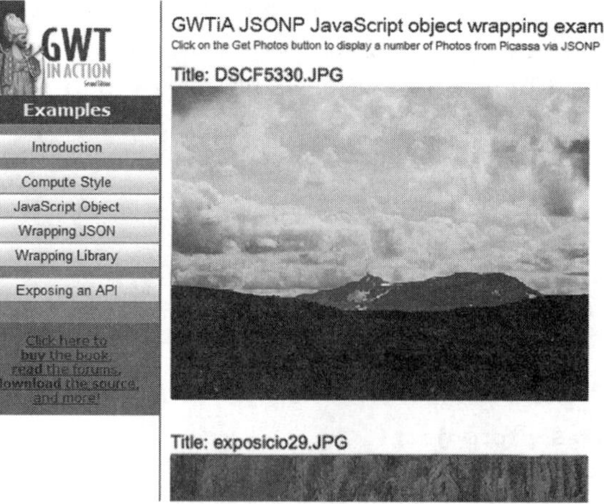

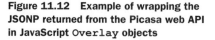

Figure 11.12 Example of wrapping the JSONP returned from the Picasa web API in JavaScript `Overlay` objects

straight to that nested value rather than bothering to create another overlay object (the `$` is the syntax Google has used in the data and nothing special).

In the example's code you'll see that we quickly use these overlay objects to pull out titles and URLs of images and give ourselves a simple photo viewer, shown in figure 11.12.

`JavaScriptObjects`, either directly or extended, also underpin approaches to wrapping more complex JavaScript libraries if you match them with JSNIs ability to call back into the Java part of a GWT application.

11.6 Wrapping a third-party library

If you need to wrap a third-party JavaScript library, you're probably in for some serious JSNI development. You're going to have to wrap all of the objects that could be created as `JavaScriptObjects` or as overlays; you'll need to hook up event handling and duplicate, in GWT Java code structure, those API methods you wish to expose.

In this section we'll do this with the Cooliris API.[3] You may be familiar with the wall of pictures that can be created, as shown in figure 11.13.

Through the chapter's photo wall example we can highlight three things:

- Ensuring the library is loaded before using it
- Calling the application's Java code from JSNI
- Accessing the application's Java fields from JSNI

We'll only do the bare minimum of third-party wrapping to enable us to discuss these items. If you're interested in seeing some serious JavaScript library wrapping, then you can check out the GWT Google API project, which wraps a number of Google's APIs.[4]

---

[3] Cooliris API: www.cooliris.com/developer/.

[4] GWT Google API: http://code.google.com/p/gwt-google-apis/. It seems to be in a state of flux at present, with APIs such as Maps not currently updated, although promising work is progressing on automatically generating bindings: http://mng.bz/z198.

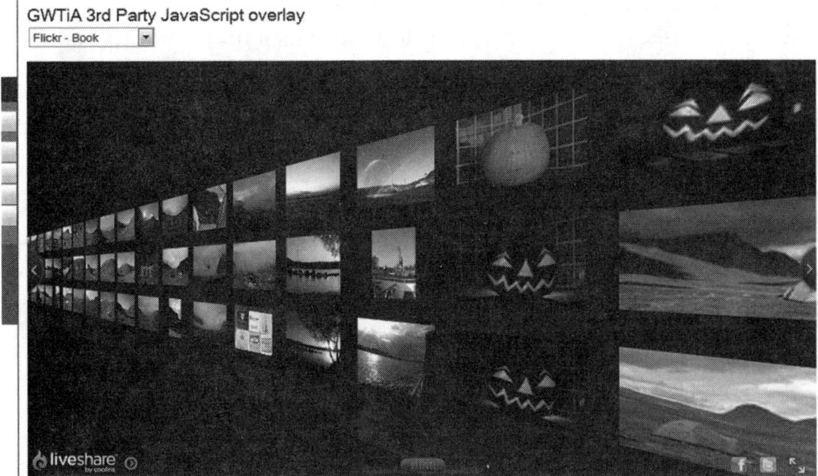

Figure 11.13 A Cooliris photo wall embedded in a GWT application

The first item we'll look at is the issue of ensuring the library code is available before using it.

11.6.1 *Ensuring the library is loaded*

To access a third-party library you must first load it, and you can do that in a few ways:

- You can load it through a `<script>` link in the application's HTML file. The problem with this is, you hit a race condition. How do you know your JavaScript library is loaded before your GWT application tries to use it?
- To prevent that race condition, you could include the entire library's code directly inside a `<script>` tag in the HTML. This may not be a pretty solution if the library is large or may not even be possible if it comes from another server.
- You can include a GWT `<script>` tag in the application's module file. This way, GWT's bootstrapping process guarantees that the JavaScript is loaded and available before your application starts. The downside of this is that it may delay the startup of your application, particularly if the code is large or you have many files to load this way and some GWT linkers (note that it isn't possible to do this if you're using the cross-site iFrame or Direct install linkers).
- An alternative is that if the library provides a callback when it's loaded, you can use that in your application to start/enable functionality.
- You can use GWT's `ScriptInjector` object to inject the script at runtime and include a callback to know when the script is injected.

The choice of how to load the code is up to you and how you wish to present the application, with perhaps some restrictions on how you can access the codebase. Let's look at what we do for our example photo wall application and compare it to what we did for our previous JavaScript overlay example.

EXAMPLE: LOADING COOLIRIS THROUGH THE MODULE FILE

In our example application we have two dependencies that need to be loaded before we can safely use the system:

- A JavaScript library stored at Google that safely handles Flash components
- The Cooliris Flash component

The swfobject library that we'll download from Google has no callback to tell us when it's loaded and ready, and we need it to be there in order to load the Flash component. So, in the list of loading options we previously looked at, only one option is the safest in guaranteeing the library is downloaded and ready for our application start, and that's including it in the application's module file. It's small in size, so that's exactly what we do—PhotoWall.gwt.xml has the following contents:

```
<?xml version="1.0" encoding="UTF-8"?>
<module>
   <script
     src="http://ajax.googleapis.com/ajax/libs/swfobject/2.2/swfobject.js">
   </script>
</module>
```

When we run the application and inspect the DOM (for example, through Firebug in Firefox or the built-in tools in Chrome/Safari), we see that the original head content of the application's HTML changes from the following,

```
<head>
   <title>gwtia-ch11-jsni</title>
   <script type="text/javascript" language="javascript"
           src="gwtia_ch11_jsni/gwtia_ch11_jsni.nocache.js"></script>
</head>
```

which has only the GWT application's bootstrap code, to what's shown in figure 11.14.

With this JavaScript library loaded and available, our application can start, and one of its first tasks is to use this library to insert the Cooliris Flash file and start it. Because it's a Flash file we're dealing with, we might not be able to know when it's loaded. But

```
Elements  Resources  Network  Scripts  Timeline  Profiles  Audits  Console
<!DOCTYPE html>
▼<html>
  ▼<head>
     <title>gwtia-ch11-jsni</title>
   ▶<script type="text/javascript" language="javascript">…</script>
     <script type="text/javascript" language="javascript" src="gwtia_ch11_jsni/gwtia_ch11_jsni.nocache.js"></script>
     <script language="javascript" src="http://ajax.googleapis.com/ajax/libs/swfobject/2.2/swfobject.js"></script>
     <script defer="defer">gwtia_ch11_jsni.onInjectionDone('gwtia_ch11_jsni')</script>
  </head>
```

GWT inserted scripts to load JavaScript library and wait until loaded before starting application

Figure 11.14 Looking at the scripts GWT has inserted into the HTML file because of a `<script>` directive in the module file—GWT will ensure the JavaScript file we indicated in the module file is loaded before starting the application.

luckily, the Flash movie calls a prenamed JavaScript function when it's loaded (or embedded, as the Cooliris API calls it).

We create a Cooliris JavaScript overlay that will allow two-way communication with the Flash object through a JavaScript variable, `cooliris`. You can either create that variable yourself in the HTML file or use some GWT code to do that. We've chosen to define the variable directly in the body of the HTML file and retrieve it using a `get` method in the `Cooliris` class, to avoid tinkering with it, but we have coded the `addHandlers` function to cope if it isn't yet defined.

It isn't necessary to know what the `addHandlers` function does at the moment, beyond knowing that it tries to add something to the JavaScript `cooliris` variable—if it doesn't exist, then we need to wait and try again. We achieve that by using a GWT `Timer` object as shown in the following listing.

Listing 11.3 GWT `Timer` in action

```
Timer timer;

private void addBaseHandlers(){
   if (theWall!=null){                                          ❶ Check if object exists
      theWall.addHandlers(initializeHandler, itemSelectedHandler);
      if (timer!=null){                                         ❷ Cancel Timer if it exists
         timer.cancel();
         timer = null;
      }
   } else {
      if (timer==null){                                         ❸ Create Timer if not existing
         timer = new Timer(){
            public void run() {                                 ❹ What to do when Timer finishes
               addBaseHandlers();
            }
         };
      }
      timer.schedule(5);                                        ❺ Run Timer
   }
}
```

Within the `addBaseHandlers` method, you check to see if the variable `cooliris` exists by seeing if the GWT object `theWall` isn't `null` ❶. If it exists, you perform the necessary functionality and then tidy up the `Timer` ❷ by canceling and setting it to `null` if the `Timer` was already defined.

If the `cooliris` variable doesn't exist, then you should keep trying the functionality until it does. To do that, you create a `Timer` ❸, if you haven't already done so. In ❹ you add to the `run` method what should happen when the `Timer` completes. That means you should rerun the `addBaseHandlers` method. Point ❺ is where you kick off the `Timer` by scheduling it to run in 5 milliseconds—a bit aggressive, perhaps.

You can see that we've had to do a fair amount of work to get the library loaded and deal with the asynchronous nature of things. Back in the Java overlay example, we loaded our JavaScript "library" in a slightly different way.

Timer, Scheduler, or Duration?

An alternative to `Timer` is `Scheduler`, though you should be aware of a conceptual difference between the two.

You'd use a `Timer` to run something in the future at a determined point—for example, in 500 milliseconds—or to repeatedly do something at determined intervals—such as every 1 second. The typical pattern is as follows:

```
Timer theTimer = new Timer(){
   public void run(){
      // Put functionality here
   }
};
theTimer.schedule(delay_in_milliseconds);
theTimer.scheduleRepeating(delay_in_milliseconds);
```

You'd use a `Scheduler` if you want to defer something to the immediate future—and by that we mean giving the browser's event loop a chance to run before your scheduled code. This could allow the browser to complete a layout drawing, for instance. The typical pattern is this:

```
Scheduler.get().scheduleDeferred(new Command() {
   public void execute () {
      // Put functionality here
   }
});
```

You can also schedule code to run before the next browser loop or after the next loop finishes. `Scheduler` also allows you to avoid slow/unresponsive script warnings by using `scheduleIncremental` instead of `scheduleDeferred`—in this case you break down the large amount of work that you need to do into steps in a `RepeatingCommand`, and the browser loop runs in between.

If you're interested in how long something is taking, use `Duration`. Creating a `Duration` object captures the current time, in milliseconds, and then you can find the elapsed time, since creation, by calling the `elapsedMillis` method.

EXAMPLE: LOADING PERSON.JS THROUGH SCRIPTINJECTOR

Back in the JavaScript overlay discussion, we mentioned that we created our own little example library and injected it at runtime. We use GWT's `ScriptInjector` object to do that, and this allows us to inject JavaScript either directly via a string or from a URL. The next listing shows how to do it from a URL for that example (the code is in the constructor of `JSOverlayExample`).

Listing 11.4 Code used to inject person.js at runtime in the JavaScript overlay example

```
ScriptInjector.fromUrl(GWT.getModuleBaseURL()+"../"+PERSON_SCRIPT)     ❶ Code source
          .setWindow(ScriptInjector.TOP_WINDOW)                        ❷ Where to place it
          .setCallback(new Callback<Void, Exception>(){                ❸ Handle injection
               @Override
               public void onFailure(Exception reason) {
```

```
            Window.alert("Script injection failed");
        }
        @Override
        public void onSuccess(Void result) {
            createPerson.setEnabled(true);
            createPersonOverlay.setEnabled(true);
        }
    })
    .inject();
```

❹ **Inject it**

You'll have four things to do in listing 11.4—two are required and two are optional. You use the static `fromUrl` method ❶ of `ScriptInjector` to indicate you're going to get the script from a URL, and you use the `inject` method ❹ to insert it. Without those two methods, you don't have any functionality.

Optionally, you also set where the script should be injected ❷ and put a callback in place ❸. The default location for script injection should be into the top window of the browser, but we've found it's safer to always explicitly tell the script injector to do that.

The callback is a simple object that's called by the `ScriptInjector` object once the script is loaded and available for use, or else it has failed to load. You use the old trick of disabling function buttons by default and enabling them in the callback on a successful attempt.

The two-way communication we mentioned through the `cooliris` variable is the topic of the rest of this section, and you'll see why you should stay in Java as much as possible; you'll learn how to access Java class fields from JavaScript (to get variables needed to set up the Flash object) and how to call Java methods from JavaScript (to call event-handling code when the Flash object embeds itself and when a photo is selected). Let's start with accessing fields.

11.6.2 Accessing Java fields from JSNI

To get the photo wall to show, you have to call the previously loaded JavaScript library's `embedSWF` function and pass in several parameters. The call is made by embedding a script element into the HTML page through DOM manipulation. You can do that manipulation in GWT, and we do so in the `PhotoWallWidget` class:

```
public void embed(){
   Element bodyElement = RootPanel.getBodyElement();
   Element script = DOM.createElement("script");
   script.setInnerText(buildIt(vars,params));
   bodyElement.appendChild(script);
}
```

This class gets the body element of the page, creates a script DOM element, sets the inner text of that element, and then appends that script element into the body—the JavaScript we set in the inner text is executed, and that kicks off the Flash movie.

But there's a little problem: two of the parameters to the `embedSWF` function are themselves JavaScript objects. We need to treat them as objects rather than text elements, and that means jumping across to JSNI. If we're in JSNI, we might as well access all the other values we need that we've stored in the PhotoWallWidget class. What do we mean? Take a quick look at the following listing.

Listing 11.5 JSNI methods and fields used to create the call to embed the Flash movie

```
SimplePanel container;
final String EL_ID = "wall";
final static String CODE_SRC =
        "http://apps.cooliris.com/embed/cooliris.swf?t=1307582197";
final String CODE_VERS = "9.0.0";
String DEFAULT_FEED = "api://www.flickr.com/";
FlashVars vars = FlashVars.newInstance();                    <- 1 An overlay
Params params =  Params.newInstance();

private native String buildIt(FlashVars vars,  Params params)/*-{
   $doc.t_vars = vars;                                       <- 2 Storing the overlay
   $doc.t_params = params;
   var text = "swfobject.embedSWF(\""
   +@com.manning.gwtia.ch11.client.photowall.PhotoWallWidget::CODE_SRC    <- 3 Accessing static field
   +"\",\""
   +this.@com.manning.gwtia.ch11.client.photowall.PhotoWallWidget::EL_ID  <- 4 Accessing object field
   +"\",\""
   +this.@com.manning.gwtia.ch11.client.photowall.
   ➥ PhotoWallWidget::container.@com.google.gwt.user.
   ➥ client.ui.UIObject::getOffsetWidth()()                  <- 5 Calling a method on an object field
   +"\",\""
   +this.@com.google.gwt.user.client.ui.UIObject::getOffsetHeight()()
   +"\",\""
   +this.@com.manning.gwtia.ch11.client.photowall.PhotoWallWidget::CODE_VERS
   +"\",\""+"\","
   +"document.t_vars"                                        <- 6 Using stored overlay
   +","
   +"document.t_params"
   +");";
   return text;
}-*/;
```

Listing 11.5 looks more complicated than it is—basically it's a bunch of field definitions followed by a JSNI method that puts them altogether in a String that represents a call to a JavaScript method that will use the fields as parameters. Some subtleties exist, not the least of which is the odd syntax that's being used.

Before we get to that syntax, let's clarify what's going on. The fields we've noted are all used in the buildIt method in some way, and some are defined as static and some not—there's no overall rationale for that beyond the fact that it helps us explain the various JSNI syntaxes briefly. Most fields are Strings, one is a GWT SimplePanel panel, and the final two ❶ are JavaScript overlays that hold parameters and variables that will be used by the Flash object.

Inside the buildIt JSNI method the first thing you do is deal with the JavaScript objects passed in as parameters. Because these were created directly from the GWT overlays, they're floating and not currently within the browser's knowledge. To fix that you store them in the browser's document variable (remember, that's accessed via the

GWT `$doc` variable ❷). Next, you have a large text concatenation to build up the call, which results in something like the following:

```
swfobject.embedSWF(
   "http://apps.cooliris.com/embed/cooliris.swf?t=1307582197",
    "wall",
    "1079",
    "324",
    "9.0.0",
    "",
    document.t_vars,
    document.t_params);
```

To get this, you need to extract, among other things, the following information from the Java class within the JavaScript:

- The value of this object's EL_ID field
- The value of the static field CODE_SRC
- The JavaScript overlays that we added to the `$doc` variable
- The offset width of this object's container field (the `SimplePanel`)

You access the first three through the special JSNI syntax, which allows you to refer to fields in Java instances. Figure 11.15 shows the format of the syntax.

Getting the EL_ID field is quite simple ❹. You know that its name is `EL_ID`, that it's in the class `com.manning.gwtia.ch11.client.photowall.PhotoWallWidget`, and that it's in the current instance, also known in JSNI as `this`. Following the format in figure 11.15, you access the field as

```
this.@com.manning.gwtia.ch11.client.photowall.PhotoWallWidget::EL_ID
```

It's similar for the static field CODE_SRC ❸. Again, you know its name and the class it's in, but what instance is it in? Because it's static, it's not in an instance, so you don't need to write anything for that part of the syntax, and you access it as

```
@com.manning.gwtia.ch11.client.photowall.PhotoWallWidget::CODE_SRC
```

(Note that when accessing a static field you have no instance and no preceding "." before the `@` symbol.)

Remember that you stored the JavaScript overlays that were passed in as parameters to the method in the `$doc` variable? When you refer to them in the method text you're building, you need to refer to the `document` variable ❻ (because when that code is executing, the `$doc` variable isn't known because you're outside of GWT). If

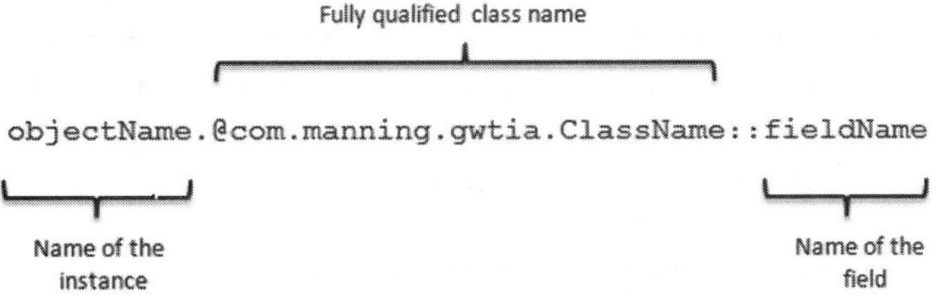

Figure 11.15 Accessing a Java field from JSNI code

Elements Resources Network Scripts Timeline Profiles Audits Console

```
▼Uncaught ReferenceError: $doc is not defined
    (anonymous function)
    @com.google.gwt.dom.client.Node::appendChild(Lcom/google/gwt/dom/client/Node;)
    __gwt_jsInvoke
    (anonymous function)
    @com.google.gwt.core.client.impl.Impl::apply(Ljava/lang/Object;Ljava/lang/Object;Ljava/lang/Object;)
    __gwt_jsInvoke
    __gwt_javaInvokes.(anonymous function)
    (anonymous function)
    (anonymous function)
>
```

Figure 11.16 A JavaScript error that's visible in the Chrome Developer's tools while running the application in development mode

you don't do that you'll get an error—and it's useful to use the development tools in Chrome/Safari or Firebug in Firefox to see these—see figure 11.16.

The final thing to look at is getting the width of the `container` (`SimplePanel`) ❺. You access `container` through the same syntax. It's a named field in a named class within the instance `this`. So you get access to the field as

```
this.@com.manning.gwtia.ch11.client.photowall.PhotoWallWidget::container
```

But once you have the `container` field, you want to call some methods on it, and to do that we need to look at the syntax for calling Java methods from JSNI code.

11.6.3 *Calling Java methods from JSNI*

Unsurprisingly, the syntax for calling methods in Java classes from JSNI is rather similar to accessing Java fields, but you also have to deal with parameters. Figure 11.17 shows diagrammatically how a call would be built up.

The instance name and fully qualified class name parts are exactly the same as for accessing a field; following that you have the method name you wish to call and then the different starts. You need to provide the signature definition of the parameters followed by the parameters themselves.

In the case where no parameters exist, such as the call to `getOffsetWidth` in listing 11.3, the call would have an empty parameter signature and parameter section, for example,

```
[instance]@com.google.gwt.user.client.ui.UIObject::getOffsetWidth()()
```

where `[instance]` follows the rules you saw before: it can be static or nonstatic, it can be `this`, or it can be a field. If it's a field, then you chain together the syntax for

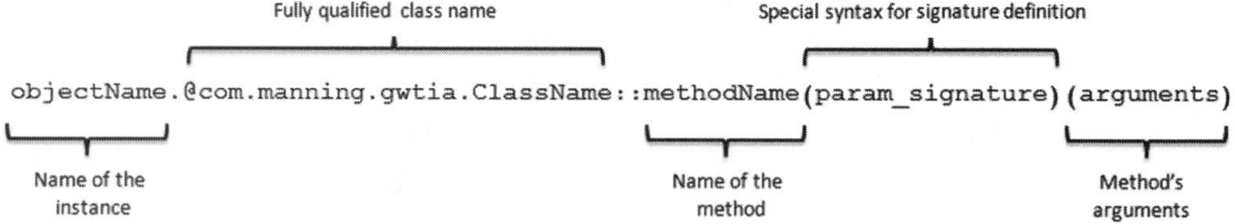

Figure 11.17 Explanation of the JSNI method used to access a method in a Java object

accessing the field with syntax for the method call. In our example of calling getOffsetWidth on the container from within JSNI, the syntax would be

```
this.@com.manning.gwtia.ch11.client.photowall.PhotoWallWidget::container
    .@com.google.gwt.user.client.ui.UIObject::getOffsetWidth()()
```

The first part accesses the container object onto which you chain the call to getOffsetWidth method. We've used the underlying UIObject class to give the fully qualified class name for the getOffsetWidth method.

It's simple for parameterless methods, but most methods have parameters, so sooner or later you're going to have to deal with signature definitions. To determine the appropriate signature for a method, you need to consult table 11.3.

Table 11.3 Java type signature for various Java types

Type signature	Java type
Z	boolean
B	Byte
C	char
S	short
I	int
J	long
F	float
D	double
Lfully qualified class; (for example, Ljava/lang/String;)	A Java object
[type	type[] (an array)

Let's jump to the addHandlers method in the Cooliris overlay class to see signature definitions in action. The purpose of this method is to tie together events from the Flash object to event handlers that you define in GWT. The Cooliris API isn't the prettiest at doing this, but the important part for our discussion is the code in listing 11.6.

Listing 11.6 JSNI code linking a Cooliris event to a GWT event handler call

```
public final native void addHandlers(InitializeHandler handler,
      ItemSelectedHandler handler2)/*-{                    ❶ Passing in handlers
   $wnd.onItemSelected = function(item){                   ❷ Inserting JavaScript function
   if (item==null){}else{
     handler2.@
       com.manning.gwtia.ch11.client.photowall.event.ItemSelectedHandler::
       onItemSelected
       (Lcom/manning/gwtia/ch11/client/photowall/jsoverlay/Item;)   ❸ Signature
       (item);                                             ❹ Parameters
   }
   }
-*/}
```

This code in listing 11.6 takes a couple of our own defined GWT handlers ❶ as parameters that will be used later in the code. At ❷, inside JSNI, you attach a new function called `onItemSelected`, taking an item as a parameter that will be called by a Cooliris Flash movie when a photo is selected. Our definition of this function is that it calls the `onItemSelect` method of a GWT `ItemSelectedHandler`, passing it the same `item` object ❹ it was given.

Of interest here is the signature definition ❸. The parameter is `item`, and because it's a Java object, then according to table 11.3 its signature definition will be `L` followed by the fully qualified class name, followed by a semicolon:

```
Lcom/manning/gwtia/ch11/client/photowall/jsoverlay/Item;
```

> **WARNING** Remember, there's a distinction between Java primitives and objects that can trip you up when defining a JSNI call's signature. For example, the signature for the primitive `int` is `I`, and for the object `Integer`, it's `Ljava/lang/Integer;`.

If there were more parameters, then the signature would be longer. The order in the signature must match the order of the arguments. So if you had a method that took two primitive integers and a `String` object and a `boolean`, then the signature would be the somewhat confusing `IILjava/lang/String;Z` (the points to note here are that the order matches our description and that there are no separators between the signature components—the semicolon is part of the definition of the `String` object signature).

> **Trick or trap?**
>
> Using JSNI notation, it's possible to circumvent the visibility restrictions on Java objects. This isn't usually a good thing to do, but you may on occasion need to do this.
>
> One of us used it once to directly access the widget held by a `Composite`, which is inaccessible for some good reasons from the API. But a little JSNI such as `return param.@com.google.gwt.user.client.ui.Composite::widget;` was enough to spring it free.

The way our photo wall functionality handles a click on a photo is this:

1. A user clicks a photo in the photo wall.
2. A Cooliris Flash movie calls the JavaScript function `onItemSelected`.
3. We have defined, in a JSNI method, the `onItemSelected` JavaScript function so that it calls the `onItemSelected` method of a Java `ItemSelectedHandler`.

We previously touched briefly on creating JavaScript objects from within GWT code—we used that approach to create the `FlashVars` in this section's example—and now we'll look at the opposite: creating Java objects from inside JSNI code.

11.6.4 Creating Java objects within JSNI

There will be the odd occasion where your JavaScript code will need to create a new Java object of some type. We don't need to do so in our Cooliris example, but if we had to, then the syntax of doing so is similar to what you've already seen.

Let's imagine you have the following class that you'll need to construct from with JSNI code:

```
package somePackage
public class MultiSelect{
      public MultiSelect(){}
      public MultiSelect(int start){}
      public MultiSelect(int start, int end){}
}
```

If you're interested in creating instances of `MultiSelect` within JSNI, you could write any of the following depending on which constructor you want to use:

```
@somePackage.MultiSelect::new()()
@somePackage.MultiSelect::new(I)(12)
@somePackage.MultiSelect::new(II)(12,35)
```

The format is similar to what you've already seen. You don't have an instance, you do have a qualified path for the class, and the only thing different from calling a method is that you use the method name `new` to run the constructor—defining the signature parameter as normal. It's similar if you want to create some static inner class, say `Start` in the following:

```
package somePackage
public class MultiSelect{
   public static class Start{
      public Start(){}
   }
}
```

Then you create it as expected:

```
somePackage.MultiSelect.Start::new()();
```

There's a subtlety when creating a nonstatic inner class, say `End` in the following:

```
package somePackage
public class MultiSelect{
   public class End{
      public End(int i){}
   }
}
```

To create `End` there has to be an instance, say `someInstance`. In Java you'd write

```
new someInstance.End(5)
```

But in JSNI you have to write the rather more long-winded

```
@somePackage.MultiSelect.End::new(LsomePackage/MultiSelect;I)(someInstance,5)
```

You have to include the instance as a parameter to the `new` method when constructing an inner class of an instance. It's also possible to handle exceptions.

11.6.5 Handling exceptions

Just as exceptions can happen and be handled in your Java code, so they can be raised in JavaScript code. Because we have an interface between Java and JavaScript, it's reasonable that exceptions raised in JavaScript come across that interface. Indeed they can, though it's strongly recommended that JavaScript exceptions be handled in the JavaScript segments of the JSNI method and that Java methods be handled in Java code.

The reason for this recommendation is that a JavaScript exception that's handed back over the JavaScript boundary into Java becomes, and can only become, an object of type `JavaScriptException`. You don't necessarily lose information about the original JavaScript exception, because you can use the `getName()` and `getDescription()` methods to return `String` values about it. But relying on these methods leads to messy code requiring the use of a `String` comparison to handle the exceptions, whereas they can be handled more gracefully in the JavaScript code.

Now it's time to look at how the techniques we've discussed can be harnessed for the final situation where you might use JSNI: exposing an API for your application.

11.7 Exposing an API to JavaScript

You can pull together all that you've learned in this chapter to expose parts of your GWT application as an API that other JavaScript code can call. You might want to do this if you're building an application others can embed—your own version of Google Maps, for example—or if you're gradually replacing the embedded functionality of an existing web page. We'll create an application that allows for enrolling in various long-distance races held within Sweden, as shown in figure 11.18.

The trick to exposing an API is to use JSNI to set up some JavaScript functions in the `$wnd` namespace and to have those functions call internal GWT code through the JSNI syntax.

In our example we'll expose two API methods:

- `getRace`, which allows the top JavaScript application in figure 11.18 to retrieve the race selected in the GWT `ListBox` in the bottom half

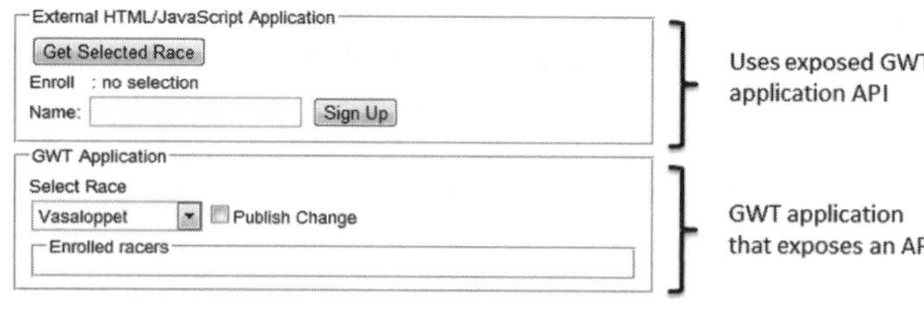

Figure 11.18 Example of a GWT application exposing an API that other JavaScript applications can call

- enrollRace, which allows the top JavaScript application in figure 11.18 to enroll an entered name in a selected race

In the GWT application, we have two simple Java methods. The first is to get the text of the selected race:

```
public static String getRace(){
  return race.getItemText(race.getSelectedIndex());
}
```

And the second is to add a new label to the Enrolled Racers area containing two text strings:

```
public static void enrollRace(String name, String race){
   enrolled.add(new Label(name + " (" + race +")"));
}
```

We could call these methods from within GWT, but our aim is to call them externally. To do that we need to set up some JSNI:

```
private native void setUpAPI()/*-{
   $wnd.getRace =
      $entry(@com.manning.gwtia.ch11.client.api.APIExample::getRace());
   $wnd.enrollRace =
      $entry(@com.manning.gwtia.ch11.client.api.APIExample::enrolRace
         (Ljava/lang/String;Ljava/lang/String;));
}-*/;
```

This JSNI puts two JavaScript functions—getRace and enrollRace—in the $wnd context, and both these JavaScript functions make calls back into the Java class methods using the syntax you've previously seen.

The only new thing here is wrapping these two functions in the GWT-specific $entry function. This is a re-entrant safe function and should be used when you're exposing GWT-compiled code that could be accessed by a non-GWT application (if you want to dig into this, check out the definition of entry in the Impl class in the com.google.gwt.core.client.impl package).

If you look in the application's HTML file, you'll see that we define a JavaScript function that calls the API and runs some functionality:

```
<script type = "text/javascript" language="JavaScript">
   getRaceName = function(){
      document.getElementById('raceName').innerText = getRace();
   };
</script>
```

Inside our example's UiBinder definition, we declared an HTMLPanel, which holds our external HTML application. Within that, we defined a standard HTML button that calls the previous function:

```
<button onClick='getRaceName();return false;'>Get Selected Race</button>
```

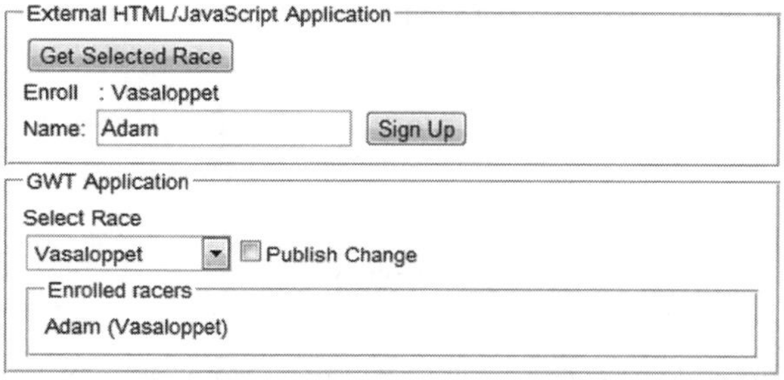

Figure 11.19 The result of calling the GWT application's API to get a race into the HTML application and then enroll a person in that race

Figure 11.19 shows the result of calling the API to get the selected race name and then enroll a person in that race.

Now we've finally finished our whirlwind tour through JSNI, and it's time to sum up what we've covered before zooming on to the next exciting chapter.

11.8 Summary

JSNI, in particular the overlay type approach, is a powerful way to interface with existing JavaScript libraries and fill in the gaps where GWT may not yet have the functionality you need. In this chapter you've seen how to move data between Java and JavaScript, how to access a Java object's methods and fields from within JavaScript code, how to integrate with third-party libraries and easy wrappers around JSON objects, and how to let JavaScript access your applications by exposing an API.

This power comes with some heavy caveats. Using JSNI can limit your ability to harness GWT goodness such as tool support, code-size reduction, type checking, and protection from memory leaks.

Going back to our view from the start of the chapter, you're using GWT because the abstraction it provides gives you the benefits mentioned, among others. Doing something that starts to limit those benefits, such as using JSNI, is probably something you wouldn't want to do unless you must.

Our final advice is to avoid using JSNI as much as possible—most of the time GWT offers a better way to do it (check the event handling and the `UIObject`, `Widget`, `DOM`, and `Window` GWT classes). Where you have to use JSNI, minimize the amount you use and try to avoid having to manage browser differences (and if you have that issue, use deferred binding).

Next we're going to jump to a topic that we've left until quite late in our discussions but which was one of the first components to start using Ajax back in the day: server communication. We've deliberately left it until later because we want to show that GWT is much more than classic Ajax and handling of forms. In the next chapter we'll look at the various ways we can communicate from the client to the server.

12 Classic Ajax and HTML forms

This chapter covers

- Using RequestBuilder to communicate with the server
- Parsing JSON and XML messages
- Sending form data to the server using HtmlForm

In chapter 7 we introduced you to GWT-RPC, which is great for greenfield projects, but for most of us the baggage that comes with many projects constrains us. Project requirements sometimes make using GWT-RPC impossible. This chapter is about those times where GWT-RPC just won't fit.

A good example of this incompatibility is when you don't control the data, and in this age of mash-ups this is somewhat common. In this chapter the majority of our examples will use Google's YouTube video data as a data source. This data is made available in several formats, and we'll explore different ways to get this data into an application.

We'll begin the chapter by looking at RequestBuilder, a tool that allows you to fetch a text file from your server and act on the returned contents. A related tool that we'll look at is JsonpRequestBuilder, a tool that has the same job as

`RequestBuilder` but is specific to working with JSONP[1] web services. If you haven't heard of JSONP, it's an acronym for JavaScript Object Notation with Padding, and this chapter will cover its use in detail.

In addition we'll explore GWT's data-handling tools for JSON and XML. JSON, or JavaScript Object Notation (without the padding), is a simple data format that has become popular because of how easy it is to parse a message in JavaScript. It has in essence become the XML of Web 2.0.

XML has been with us for over 10 years now, which means if you're integrating with a legacy application you may well need to deal with it. GWT provides some basic tools for working with XML—and although they're nothing like the tools we have available on the server, they're usually enough for the tasks you'll encounter.

Finally, we'll look at the virtual grandfather of browser and server communication, the HTML form. HTML forms may seem antiquated in a Web 2.0 world, but they still have their place, and GWT has some great support for using them.

But before we dive into all of this tooling we need to bone up on the basics, which is where we begin our journey.

12.1 Understanding the underlying technology

To begin using the tools in this chapter, it's useful to understand the foundations of the underlying protocols, formats, and browser APIs we'll be using. Specifically, we're talking about Hypertext Transport Protocol (HTTP), JavaScript Object Notation (JSON), JSON with Padding (JSONP), and the `XMLHttpRequest` JavaScript object. If you're already familiar with these, you can safely skip this section without missing any important details.

Understanding the inner workings of these will aid in troubleshooting, and the rest of this chapter assumes knowledge of these topics. We begin with the most basic of these protocols, the Hypertext Transport Protocol.

12.1.1 Understanding how HTTP works

The Hypertext Transport Protocol is the delivery vehicle for the web and is defined in a specification called RFC 2616.[2] It defines the commands used by your browser to get web pages, sends form data, and indicates what the response codes returned from the server mean. It's the language your browser uses to request pages from a web server.

In order for your browser and the server to communicate, HTTP provides a *request message* and a *response message*. Your browser sends the request message to the server, and the server uses the response message to provide the page or data requested. Both the request and response have a header section and a body section. The header provides control information, and the body contains the content.

---

1 Wikipedia maintains a good article on JSONP that you can find at http://en.wikipedia.org/wiki/JSONP.

2 RFC 2616 is published by the IETF and defines HTTP version 1.1. You'll find the specification at http://tools.ietf.org/html/rfc2616.

For example, a simple request message that your web browser might send to fetch the GWT project page (http://code.google.com/webtoolkit/) would look similar to the following:

```
GET /webtoolkit/ HTTP/1.1
Host: code.google.com
User-Agent: Mozilla/5.0 (Windows) Gecko/20100722 Firefox/3.6.8
Accept: text/html,application/xhtml+xml,application/xml;q=0.9,*/*;q=0.8
Accept-Language: en-us,en;q=0.5
Accept-Encoding: gzip,deflate
Accept-Charset: ISO-8859-1,utf-8;q=0.7,*;q=0.7
Keep-Alive: 115
Connection: keep-alive
```

As you can see, the browser sends a lot of information, including what type of browser it is, what types of files it can accept, and HTTP control information that's used to enable certain features of HTTP. All of that aside, the most important piece of the request is the first line, which provides the server with the URL of the resource being requested along with the *request method*. The method allows the requestor to indicate how the request should be handled on the server. Typically the only implemented methods on most web servers will be `GET`, which indicates you're getting a resource, and `POST`, which indicates that you're sending data to the server to be acted upon.

This can be a little confusing because although `GET` and `POST` were meant to be used for different things, they're often used interchangeably. The only important difference between the two is that `GET` allows you to send variables, known as *request parameters*, as part of the URL, whereas with a `POST` the request parameters are delivered in the body of the request. Table 12.1 shows a side-by-side comparison of what the HTTP request might look like if you want to pass two request parameters (`query` and `page`) to the server. Both send the same data to the server, one providing the query in the URL and the other providing it in the message body.

Table 12.1 Two examples of an HTTP request, one using `GET` and the other using `POST`.

The `GET` method	The `POST` method

`GET /search?query=GWT&page=1 HTTP/1.1`
`Host: www.example.com`
	`POST /search HTTP/1.1`
	`Host: www.example.com`
	`Content-Type: application/x-www-form-urlencoded`
	
	`query=GWT&page=1`

Under most circumstances they're interchangeable, with the exception of sending data other than request parameters, in which case a `POST` is required. You might need to do this if you want to send a file to the server, send an XML document, or send some other data.

For the return trip back to the browser, the following snippet shows the response that you'd see if you searched for "GWT" at Google.com:

```
HTTP/1.1 200 OK
Cache-Control: private, max-age=0
Date: Sun, 22 Aug 2010 16:53:31 GMT
Expires: -1
Content-Type: text/html; charset=UTF-8
Content-Encoding: gzip
Transfer-Encoding: chunked

<!doctype html><head><title>gwt - Google Search</title>
...a lot of HTML code...
```

The response, like the request, includes a lot of control information. Some of the header values are used to tell the browser how the content may be cached, any compression used on the response body, and the content type so that the browser knows how to display the data. But as with the request we want to focus only on the first line of the header, which includes the response code.

The response code is a three-digit code that indicates what happened. A code that starts with 2xx indicates success, a code starting with 3xx indicates that the browser needs to perform some type of action, 4xx indicates a client error, and 5xx indicates a server error. Table 12.2 provides a list of the more common response codes, and you can find a full list in the HTTP specification.[3]

Table 12.2 Common HTTP response codes

Code	Name	Meaning
200	OK	The request was handled, and content is being returned to the browser.
301	Moved Permanently	The location has moved, and the new URL is provided in the response.
302	Found	The location has moved, and the new URL is provided in the response.
304	Not Modified	The contents of the page haven't changed, and no content is returned.
400	Bad Request	The request couldn't be understood by the server.
401	Unauthorized	You're not authorized to make this request; credentials are required.
404	Not Found	The URL requested doesn't exist.
405	Method Not Allowed	The method used (for example, GET/POST) isn't allowed.
500	Internal Server Error	Something failed on the server (poor coding, DB error, and so on).

[3] A list of response codes and their meanings can be found in section 10 of RFC 2616, http://tools.ietf.org/html/rfc2616#section-10.

HTTP GETs and POSTs have been around since the beginning of the web, but in order to use them you had to write code using a system programming language. Over time this changed, and in 2000 Internet Explorer was released with a new scriptable object called `XMLHttpRequest`.

12.1.2 Understanding Ajax and the XMLHttpRequest object

The `XMLHttpRequest` object is a scriptable object found in all popular modern browsers, allowing a developer to make HTTP calls from JavaScript. The popularity of using `XMLHttpRequest` began in 2005 when Jesse James Garret coined the term *Ajax* to define this new style of architecture.[4] Within months of Jesse's essay, everyone was talking about this new style of web application design.

The primary difference between an Ajax and a non-Ajax application is how the web page is updated with new content. In a non-Ajax application the browser requests a page, the request goes to the server, which generates a result, and the content in the browser is refreshed. For each request, the entire page is sent back to the user. The implication of this is that the content only changes when the user performs an action (for example, clicks a link), and the user needs to wait for the new page to load before they can do anything else.

Ajax, on the other hand, is about using JavaScript to update parts of the page without ever refreshing the page. This is where the `XMLHttpRequest` object fits in. When a user performs an action (for example, clicks something), the JavaScript code uses the `XMLHttpRequest` to send a request to the server. The server then sends the requested data, which could be HTML, XML, or any other text content, back to the JavaScript code. JavaScript is then used to alter the structure of the web page to include the received content. In addition, JavaScript can be used to continually poll the server without user intervention, so updated data can be displayed without the user needing to request it.

An important aspect of using `XMLHttpRequest` is that it's asynchronous, meaning that the call to the server doesn't block. We covered this in chapter 7 when we discussed the asynchronous nature of GWT-RPC, but a recap is in order.

If you've ever bought something online, you've participated in asynchronous behavior. The first step is to go to an online store like Amazon and purchase something, perhaps the latest edition of *GWT in Action.* The second step is to wait for it to arrive. But until it arrives you don't sit out at the mailbox; you do other stuff. And when it arrives, then you deal with it. That's asynchronous behavior.

In GWT we deal with this behavior by using a callback routine that's executed when the "package comes in the mail." We'll discuss this soon enough, but right now we need to move on to JSON, which is a popular message format that we'll use in our examples.

---

4 Ajax was introduced in an essay titled "Ajax: A New Approach to Web Applications," found at www.adaptivepath.com/ideas/essays/archives/000385.php.

12.1.3 Understanding JSON

JSON is an acronym for JavaScript Object Notation. It's a data format, similar to XML, but with a twist that makes it extremely easy to parse. JSON is executable JavaScript code!

The JSON message format makes use of the JavaScript language to define a data structure that's easily parsed. In JavaScript it can be parsed by executing the message, and in other languages a parser is relatively simple to create. If you visit the home of JSON, www.json.org, you'll find APIs for dozens of languages.

If you know JavaScript, then the JSON format will be easy to understand. The following listing provides an example of a JSON message, which we'll explore.

Listing 12.1 A sample JSON data message

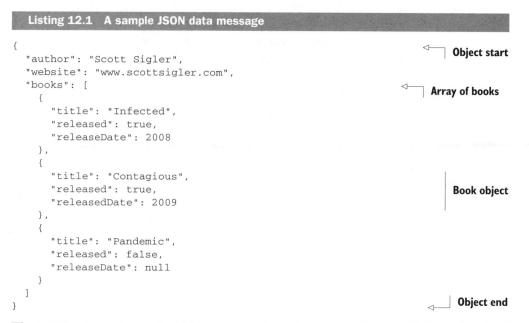

```
{                                                  <-- Object start
  "author": "Scott Sigler",
  "website": "www.scottsigler.com",
  "books": [                                       <-- Array of books
    {
      "title": "Infected",
      "released": true,
      "releaseDate": 2008
    },
    {
      "title": "Contagious",
      "released": true,                            Book object
      "releasedDate": 2009
    },
    {
      "title": "Pandemic",
      "released": false,
      "releaseDate": null
    }
  ]
}                                                  <-- Object end
```

The JSON message in the listing represents data about an author, and it includes all of JSON's available data types. In the listing you can see `{}` used to delimit objects, and within those objects are key/value pairs separated by a colon. For example, this entire message is an object, with properties for the `"author,"` `"website,"` and more.

Arrays are denoted with `[]`, with the values within separated by a comma. In the example, the `"books"` property of the root object is an array, which in turn contains three objects.

Besides objects and arrays, JSON data is limited to strings, numbers, and booleans (`true` and `false`), and `null` is used to represent an undefined value. In the example you'll see that a string like "Scott Sigler" is in quotes, numbers like 2008 are unquoted, and both boolean and `null` values use specific JavaScript keywords.

If you're interested in the exact semantics of JSON you can visit www.json.org. There you'll find detailed diagrams of the composition of a JSON message.

Because JSON is easily consumed by JavaScript applications running in the browser, it's often the message format of choice. But there's a limitation if you want to consume a JSON message from another web service, like Yahoo[5] or Google.[6] This limitation has to do with the *same-origin policy*.

12.1.4 Solving same-site-origin policy issues with JSONP

The same-origin policy is a security policy built into web browsers that prevents `XMLHttpRequest` from requesting URLs that lie outside the domain where the page running the JavaScript came from. You can use `XMLHttpRequest` to request pages from your site but not from another site. This presents a problem if you want to use a web service from Google or some other provider.

One exception to this policy is the use of `<script>` tags. It's possible for a `<script>` tag to be dynamically added to a web page, which in turn executes the remote-site JavaScript code. JSON with Padding (JSONP) takes advantage of this by padding the JSON data with a method call that calls back into your JavaScript application.

By way of example, let's assume that we want to load JSON author data provided by a remote web service. We'd first need to create a callback in JavaScript that would read the data and do something with it:

```
function printData (data) {
  // do some stuff with the data
}
```

Then we'd need to load the data by creating a `<script>` element, setting the `source` attribute, and dynamically adding it to the page with JavaScript. Notice how the URL to the external JavaScript includes a `callback` parameter set to the name of our local function:

```
var script = document.createElement("script");
script.setAttribute("src",
    "http://example.com/bookdata?callback=printData");
script.setAttribute("type", "text/javascript");
document.body.appendChild(script);
```

This will cause the remote JavaScript to be loaded and executed within the web page, but what we need is for the remote JavaScript to call our `printData` function. This is where the "padding" comes in:

```
printData(
  { "author": "Scott Sigler", "website": "www.scottsigler.com" }
);
```

As you can see, the JSON data has been wrapped as a parameter of a method call. More specifically, it's the method that we defined in our own code. In essence, the remote JavaScript code is calling our local method with the requested data.

---

5 Information on using Yahoo! web services with JSON can be found at http://developer.yahoo.com/javascript/json.html.

6 Google's GData protocol JSON messages, details of which may be found at http://code.google.com/apis/gdata/docs/json.html.

A word of warning is in order if you use JSONP. When using JSONP, you're bypassing the security provided by the same-origin policy, which is meant to protect the user viewing your page. That doesn't mean that you should avoid using JSONP, but make sure that the website serving up the JSONP content has a good reputation.

And with that we conclude our technology primer, and we'll now jump right into using the most basic of GWT's communication tools, the `RequestBuilder`.

12.2 Using RequestBuilder

In GWT, the `RequestBuilder` is an abstraction built on top of the JavaScript `XMLHttpRequest` object. This abstraction makes the underlying JavaScript API somewhat easier to work with, not to mention that it allows us to use Java idioms.

To start, you should create a new GWT project, the name and package of which don't matter. We'll then do all of our coding in the entry point so that we can focus only on the tool. In previous chapters we explained how to do this both with and without the Google Plugin for Eclipse. The method you use to create your project doesn't matter.

As discussed previously in this chapter, you need to abide by the same-origin policy that your browser will enforce. So once you've created a new GWT project, you'll need to create a file named testdata.txt in the war directory of your project and populate it with some sample text. We chose to use the sample data "Hello World."

Now let's write some code to read the file.

Listing 12.2 An example of using `RequestBuilder` to fetch a file

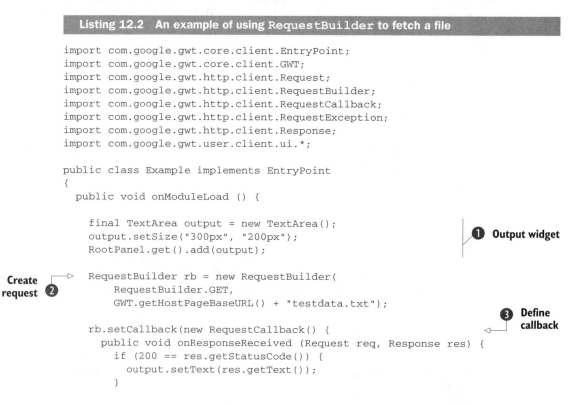

```
import com.google.gwt.core.client.EntryPoint;
import com.google.gwt.core.client.GWT;
import com.google.gwt.http.client.Request;
import com.google.gwt.http.client.RequestBuilder;
import com.google.gwt.http.client.RequestCallback;
import com.google.gwt.http.client.RequestException;
import com.google.gwt.http.client.Response;
import com.google.gwt.user.client.ui.*;

public class Example implements EntryPoint
{
  public void onModuleLoad () {

    final TextArea output = new TextArea();
    output.setSize("300px", "200px");
    RootPanel.get().add(output);

    RequestBuilder rb = new RequestBuilder(
        RequestBuilder.GET,
        GWT.getHostPageBaseURL() + "testdata.txt");

    rb.setCallback(new RequestCallback() {
      public void onResponseReceived (Request req, Response res) {
        if (200 == res.getStatusCode()) {
          output.setText(res.getText());
        }
```

1 Output widget

2 Create request

3 Define callback

```
        else {
          output.setText("ERROR CODE:" + res.getStatusCode());
        }
      }

      public void onError (Request req, Throwable e) {
        output.setText("SERVER ERROR: " + e.getMessage());
      }
    });

    try {                                                    ❹ Make request
      rb.send();
    }
    catch (RequestException e) {
      output.setText("FETCH ERROR: " + e.getMessage());
    }
  }
}
```

It's hard to miss the fact that this is a lot of code for such a simple example. This is a product of the Java language, which does provide many benefits to developers but can sometimes be fairly verbose. If you're using a good IDE, the IDE should be able to create a lot of this code for you by using the IDE's autocompletion and template features.

This example can be broken into four distinct parts. In the first part ❶ you create a `TextArea` instance and add it to the `RootPanel`. You'll use this to display the contents of the file that you're loading with `RequestBuilder`.

Next, you create an instance of the `RequestBuilder` class ❷. Two constructors are available; the one you use here uses the constant `RequestBuilder.GET` to specify that you want to send an HTTP `GET` request. The other constructor allows you to pass the HTTP method as a `String` instead of using a constant. The second argument to the constructor is the URL that you want to fetch. The GWT object has several static methods that will allow you to get the base locations of the HTML page that contains the GWT application as well as the base path to the GWT application files. Using these base locations when specifying the URL is always preferable to hard-coding the absolute path because it allows for flexibility when deploying your code. But that isn't a hard-and-fast rule because each deployment is a little different.

Next, you need to provide a callback ❸. Because calls to the server are asynchronous, you need to provide the code that will be called when the response from the server is eventually received. The callback could be constructed as separate class, or you could have this class implement the callback interface, or as we've done here it could be provided as an inline anonymous class. The callback implements the `RequestCallback` interface, which includes the methods `onResponseReceived` and `onError`. The `onError` method is called when an error occurs, but you need to define what an error is in this context. An error occurs when the call to the server can't be completed. This could occur if the server is down or isn't accessible because of a network error. An error indicates that the request could not be completed normally.

The `onResponseReceived` method is called under all other circumstances. This includes not only a successful response but error responses as well. An error response from the server could indicate that the requested resource was not found, that you don't have permissions to access that resource, or perhaps some sort of error on the server. These potential error conditions correspond to the HTTP status codes that we covered in section 12.1.1. In the example you account for this by checking the response code by calling `getStatusCode()` on the `Response` object. When the status code indicates success (200), you call `res.getText()` so that you can display it in the `TextArea`; otherwise, you display the status code that was received.

With the callback defined, the last step is to make the call ❹. Again you need to handle errors. It's possible for the underlying `XMLHttpRequest` object to immediately throw an exception when the call is made, and that's what will trigger an exception here.

Now when you run this, if all goes according to plan, the results of the text file will be loaded and displayed in the `TextArea`, as shown in figure 12.1. This works fine for the purposes of our example, but in real life things can sometimes be a little more complicated. Fortunately, `RequestBuilder` allows for this.

Figure 12.1 When you run the code in listing 12.2, the application will load the testdata.txt file from your project and display its contents.

For instance, if your server requires HTTP basic authentication, you'll want to make use of `RequestBuilder`'s `setUser()` and `setPassword()` methods to pass the authentication information. Or maybe you need to pass custom HTTP headers to the server, in which case you'd use `setHeader()`.

A more common case will be when you need to send data to the server in the body of the message.

12.3 Posting data with RequestBuilder

Now that you understand the basics of using `RequestBuilder`, let's explore how you can use it to use the HTTP `POST` method to send data to the server. We'll use the same example that we did in the previous section with some minor modifications. Listing 12.3 reproduces that example but without the code for the callback. If you're following along, you can copy the callback code from listing 12.2.

Listing 12.3 Using `RequestBuilder` to `POST` data to the server

```
public class Example implements EntryPoint
{
  public void onModuleLoad () {
    final TextArea output = new TextArea();
    output.setSize("300px", "200px");
    RootPanel.get().add(output);
```

```
    RequestBuilder rb = new RequestBuilder(          ❶ Construct builder
        RequestBuilder.POST,
        GWT.getHostPageBaseURL() + "echo.jsp");

    rb.setRequestData("test1=data1&test2=data2");    ❷ Set data payload

    rb.setCallback(...omitted...);

    try {
      rb.send();
    }
    catch (RequestException e) {
      output.setText("FETCH ERROR: " + e.getMessage());
    }
  }
}
```

The example in listing 12.3 is relatively unchanged from the example we used in the previous section with the exception that you're constructing `RequestBuilder` using ❶ `RequestBuilder. POST` as your method type and targeting echo.jsp instead of a static text file (which you'll create in a moment). In addition, you're now sending data to the server ❷ by calling the `setRequestData()` method. The data you're passing to the server is `"test1=data1&test2=data2"`, which is URL-encoded data.

There's a hidden problem with this example in that it doesn't specify the content type of the data that you're sending, so by default `RequestBuilder` will inform the server that the content type is "text/plain," which isn't exactly accurate. But before we discuss how the content type affects handling of the data on the server, you need to look at echo.jsp.

Listing 12.4 A test JSP file echoing the data it receives

```
<%@page import="java.util.*, java.io.*"%>
<%

Enumeration names = request.getParameterNames();          Print request params
for (; names.hasMoreElements();) {
    String key = (String) names.nextElement();
    response.getWriter().write(
        key + "=" + request.getParameter(key) + "\n");
}

%>
<%

StringWriter output = new StringWriter();
InputStream is = request.getInputStream();
InputStreamReader input = new InputStreamReader(is);
char[] buffer = new char[1024];
int n = 0;

while (-1 != (n = input.read(buffer))) {                  Print input stream
    output.write(buffer, 0, n);
}
response.getWriter().write("stream=" + output + "\n");

%>
```

The echo.jsp page does two things. First, it iterates over the request parameters, printing out the key/value pairs, and then it prints the contents of the request input stream. In a JSP or Java servlet, the way incoming data is handled is dependent on the content type that's sent by the call. As we mentioned, the default content type sent by `RequestBuilder` is "text/plain."

Given the default content type, if you try to run the example it should be no surprise to you that the request object has no request parameters. As shown in the following output, the unparsed data is available in the input stream:

```
stream=test1=data1&test2=data2
```

Passing data to the server as a stream makes sense if you needed to send a document to the server. It could be an XML document, JSON, or a big blob of text. But in most circumstances you'll want the server to recognize this data as URL-encoded data that's then parsed and made available to calls to `request.getParameter()`.

In order to do that you need to pass the content type "application/x-www-form-urlencoded." This is the content type that your browser will normally send to the server when it's submitting form data. The following line of code can be added to our example between the construction of the `RequestBuilder` instance and the call to `rb.send()`:

```
rb.setHeader("Content-Type", "application/x-www-form-urlencoded");
```

This will add the content type header to the request and override the default. Now if you run the example again, the echo.jsp script will return the following content:

```
test1=data1
test2=data2
stream=
```

As you can see, the data was parsed and made available to the `request.getParameter()` calls. Also notice that the stream is now empty. When the incoming data can be parsed, the stream will always be blank.

Generally speaking, if you're sending parameters to the server, you should set the content type to "application/x-www-form-urlencoded"; otherwise, the default is usually the correct choice.

One last useful bit of information is that if you're sending the data as URL encoded, be sure that it's properly encoded. This is a common mistake, particularly when the user has provided the data being sent to the server. Encoding data with a call to `com.google.gwt.http.client.URL.encodeQueryString()` takes care of the problem:

```
rb.setRequestData("p1=" + URL.encodeQueryString(data1)
 + "&p2=" +URL.encodeQueryString(data2));
```

You'd use this to encode any values that you can't be sure don't contain reserved characters, like `&` and `=`. Here you call it twice: once to encode the value of `p1` and once to encode the value of `p2`.

By now you should have a good understanding of how to use `RequestBuilder`. Now we move on to a different type of request builder, one that specializes in using JSONP.

12.4 Using the JSON API and JsonpRequestBuilder

In the last section we loaded content from our own website, but what if you want to load data from a remote site? In this age of mash-ups it's useful to be able to load content from well-known content providers like Yahoo and Google using JSONP.

We covered the technical details of how JSONP works in section 12.1.3, so let's get right into how to use the API. To begin, you should create a new project, and again the project name and root package don't matter.

Next, you need to inherit two GWT packages so that you'll have access to the JSONP tools. Add the following two lines to your module configuration file:

```
<inherits name='com.google.gwt.json.JSON'/>
<inherits name='com.google.gwt.jsonp.Jsonp'/>
```

The `JSON` module contains the JSON parser and objects that mirror the JSON data types. The `Jsonp` module includes the `JsonpRequestBuilder` and support classes.

In the example that follows we'll fetch some video data from YouTube and extract some specific details. The YouTube JSONP feed makes use of Google's `GDATA` API. The full details of using `GDATA` are beyond the scope of this book, but you can find out more at http://code.google.com/apis/gdata.

We'll begin by presenting the code example in listing 12.5, which will be followed by discussion and an example of what the output looks like. In this example we fetch video data from YouTube using JSONP and display a list of video titles in a `TextArea`.

Listing 12.5 Fetching YouTube data with `JsonpRequestBuilder`

```
import com.google.gwt.core.client.*;
import com.google.gwt.json.client.*;
import com.google.gwt.jsonp.client.JsonpRequestBuilder;
import com.google.gwt.user.client.rpc.AsyncCallback;
import com.google.gwt.user.client.ui.*;

public class Example implements EntryPoint {

  public void onModuleLoad () {
                                                            ❶ Output display
    final TextArea output = new TextArea();                 <-
    output.setSize("400px", "200px");
    RootPanel.get().add(output);
                                                            ❷ YouTube query
    String url = "http://gdata.youtube.com/feeds/api/videos?"  <-
      + "author=DisturbedTV"
      + "&max-results=5"
      + "&orderby=published"
      + "&v=2&alt=json";
                                                            ❸ Create builder
    JsonpRequestBuilder rb = new JsonpRequestBuilder();     <-
```

```
    rb.requestObject(url, new AsyncCallback<JavaScriptObject>() {    ❹ Execute

      public void onSuccess (JavaScriptObject jso) {
        printData(output, jso);
      }

      public void onFailure (Throwable caught) {
        output.setText("ERROR");
      }
    });
  }

  private void printData (TextArea output, JavaScriptObject jso) {
    output.setText("OK");
  }
}
```

Again, as with the previous example, we put all of the listing 12.5 code in the `EntryPoint` to simplify the example and focus on the API. You start off by creating a `TextArea` ❶ and attaching it to the `RootPanel`. You'll use this to display the data you get from the JSON feed.

Next, you define the `GDATA` URL string ❷. Here you're only looking for results for DisturbedTV, which is the username of a popular rock band. You're requesting the first five results, ordered by publish date. The last two parameters indicate that you're using version 2 of the `GDATA` API and are requesting back JSON data. In short, this will return the last five published video entries to DisturbedTV.

Next, you create an instance of `JsonpRequestBuilder` ❸ followed by a call to `requestObject()` ❹, which executes the request. You pass the `requestObject()` call the target URL and an `AsyncCallback`. If you recall from section 12.1.3, we discussed the different JSON data types, one of them being object. With `JsonpRequestBuilder` you need to know ahead of time what will be returned by the remote server, and in this case Google returns a JSON object, so you need to call `requestObject()`. The `JsonpRequestBuilder` has specific request calls for boolean, double, integer, and string in addition to object.

Of interest is the type parameter you use for the `AsyncCallback`, which is `JavaScriptObject`, although a subclass of `JavaScriptObject` would have also been fine. The type parameter is specific to the request call, and in this case you called `requestObject()` so you get a `JavaScriptObject` in return.

In the `onSuccess` method, you don't do much yet other than call `printData()` and print "OK" in the `TextArea`. So if everything is working right, running the application will display a satisfying "OK." Now let's modify `printData()` to read through the JSON data and print out the titles of the videos.

Listing 12.6 An updated `printData` method to print video titles

```
private void printData (TextArea output, JavaScriptObject jso) {    ❶ Create
  JSONObject objResult = new JSONObject(jso);                          from JSON

  JSONObject feed = (JSONObject) objResult.get("feed");             ❷ Get field
  JSONArray entries = (JSONArray) feed.get("entry");
```

```
    for (int i = 0; i < entries.size(); i++) {

    JSONObject entry = entries.get(i).isObject();
    JSONObject group = entry.get("media$group").isObject();
    JSONString title = group.get("media$title").isObject()
      .get("$t").isString();

    String titleStr = title.stringValue();

    output.setText(output.getText() + titleStr + "\n");
  }
}
```

❸ **Test and read**

❹ **Extract value**

In the updated printData() method you begin by creating a new JSONObject ❶, passing the JavaScriptObject that contains the YouTube data that you fetched. If you recall, when we discussed JSON data we explained that JSON is a valid JavaScript value, and here all you're doing is passing a JavaScriptObject that represents a JavaScript value into JSONObject, so JSONObject isn't doing any parsing. We point this out because if you had acquired the JSON data as plain-old text, you would have needed to use the JSONParser class to parse it. Using JSONParser was common prior to the introduction of JsonpRequestBuilder but is less common now.

With the JavaScriptObject now wrapped inside a JSONObject, you can start investigating the content. First, you drill down on the "feed" object key and then "entry," which is a JSONArray ❷. Here you need to cast the object to the proper class. Calling get() returns a JSONValue object, which is the superclass of the individual JSON type objects. But having to cast each time you want to get a child object can make for pretty messy code, so the JSONValue superclass has some utility methods to help you out.

As you loop over each of the values in the JSONArray, you use these utility methods ❸. In the example you call isObject() on the JSONValue instead of casting it to JSONObject and call isString() instead of casting to JSONString. These methods will return null if the value isn't of the specified type, so they could also be used for data-validation checks to verify the correct contents of a data structure.

Now that you have the video title stored in a JSONString, you need to convert it to a Java String so that you can use it. You do this by calling stringValue() on the JSONString ❹. Each of the JSON type objects has a method like this to get to the underlying value.

When you run the example now, you should see the last five video titles in the TextArea display:

```
Decade of Disturbed - Extended Trailer
Disturbed Dissected Trailer
Disturbed - John's Update from the Road
Disturbed Live - On Tour Now!
Disturbed - "Asylum" Official Music Video
```

As you can see, it took a bit of code to get to the video titles, and you only needed to extract a single field. Earlier in this chapter, we presented an example of an Author JSON object, which had top-level fields and a nested object array. Reading each of the

`Author` fields and nested objects would require a lot more code, and as the complexity of your JSON objects increases, so does the code required to traverse it. What if instead you could use JavaScript to extract this data? If you used JavaScript, you could replace the four lines of code used to extract the title to a one-liner.

You might recall that we specified that the callback to the `JsonpRequestBuilder` took a `JavaScriptObject` *or* a subclass of it. In the next section we'll revisit our example, but instead of trying to extract the data, we'll subclass the returned JSON object and make heavy use of JSNI in our subclass.

12.5 Using JSON with JS overlay

In chapter 11 we talked about how you can create a class that wraps a native JavaScript object with what we referred to as a JavaScript overlay type. In this section we'll use it in practice to simplify our access to JSON data. Our example in this section is the same as the one used in the previous section, which is to fetch video data from YouTube and display the titles in a `TextArea`.

Listing 12.7 presents the example, which has only minor changes from the previous listing.

Listing 12.7 Fetching YouTube data using a JS overlay

```
public class Example implements EntryPoint
{
  public void onModuleLoad () {

    final TextArea output = new TextArea();
    output.setSize("400px", "200px");
    RootPanel.get().add(output);

    String url = "http://gdata.youtube.com/feeds/api/videos?"
      + "author=DisturbedTV"
      + "&max-results=5"
      + "&orderby=published"
      + "&v=2&alt=json";

    JsonpRequestBuilder rb = new JsonpRequestBuilder();
    rb.requestObject(url, new AsyncCallback<Feed>() {           ❶ Creates callback

      public void onSuccess (Feed jso) {
        printData(output, jso);
      }

      public void onFailure (Throwable caught) {
        output.setText("ERROR");
      }
    });
  }

  private void printData (TextArea output, Feed feed) {
    for (int i = 0; i < feed.entryCount(); i++) {
      output.setText(output.getText()                           ❷ Gets data
          + feed.getEntry(i).getTitle() + "\n");
    }
  }
}
```

This is the same example that we presented in the last section, so we'll only explain what's different when working with JS overlay. In listing 12.7 you can see that when you create your callback ❶, you no longer get back a `JavaScriptObject` and instead receive a `Feed` instance. `Feed` is a class that we've created and is a subclass of `JavaScriptObject`. We'll look at the `Feed` class in a moment.

The only other change is to the `printData()` method ❷, which contains much less code than when you used the JSON objects to get at the video titles. You can see that the API provided by `Feed` is extremely simple. A call to `feed.entryCount()` returns the count of entries, and `feed.getEntry(i)` returns a single `Entry`. `Entry` is an inner class of `Feed` that encapsulates a single entry from the JSON data that you get back from YouTube, and it also has a simple interface. Calling `getTitle()` on the `Entry` returns the data you're after.

Now let's look at both the `Feed` and `Entry` classes.

Listing 12.8 Feed.java—wrapping YouTube JSON data

```
import com.google.gwt.core.client.JavaScriptObject;

public class Feed extends JavaScriptObject
{
  protected Feed () { }                                    <-- Protected constructor

  public final native int entryCount ()                    <-- Methods are final
  /*-{ return this.feed.entry.length }-*/;

  public final native Entry getEntry (int index)
  /*-{ return this.feed.entry[index] }-*/;

  public static class Entry extends JavaScriptObject       <-- Inner classes are static
  {
    protected Entry () {}

    public final native String getTitle ()
    /*-{ return this.media$group.media$title.$t }-*/;

    public final native String getDesc ()
    /*-{ return this.media$group.media$description.$t }-*/;

    public final native String getImage ()
    /*-{ return this.media$group.media$thumbnail[0].url }-*/;

    public final native String getLink ()
    /*-{ return this.link[0].href }-*/;
  }
}
```

In chapter 11 we explained that when you subclass a `JavaScriptObject`, you can use the JavaScript keyword `this` in JSNI code to reference the underlying JavaScript object. You see a lot of that in this example. For example, to get the count of entries, you return the value of `this.feed.entry.length` in the `entryCount()` method. The fact that you can create methods for only the information you need greatly simplifies the interface to the data. And because using native JavaScript made it so easy to navigate the underlying data, you add getters for not only the video title but for several other video attributes as well.

In the example we point out a few requirements of creating a `JavaScriptObject` subclass. First, the constructor must take no arguments (it's empty) and be `protected`. All methods must be declared as `final`. And inner classes must be declared as `static`.

In general, when you need to decide whether to use the JSON classes to navigate the data or to use a JavaScript overlay, the decision should be made based on the data. If the data structure is simple, then using JSON objects should work out fine. But if the data is complex, as it was in our example, using a JavaScript overlay will make your life easier.

Although JSON has gained a lot of popularity in the last few years, it isn't the only game in town. Sometimes, for one reason or another, you need to go old school. In this next section we'll look at GWT's XML capabilities.

12.6 Using the XML API and RequestBuilder

We can think of plenty of reasons to use XML instead of JSON, which is why GWT provides at least a minimal amount of support. The XML classes in GWT provide the capability of parsing, reading, and creating XML documents. By *minimal support* we mean that there's no XML namespace support and no XML validation. But still, if you need to handle XML data, it gets the job done.

In this section we'll be grabbing YouTube data yet again, but this time it will be returned as an XML document. Because of the browser's same-origin policy, we can't fetch the XML document from Google directly and will need to use a proxy.

12.6.1 Developing a server-side proxy

It's fairly common to want to draw data from external websites into your application, and a common solution is to deploy a proxy on your server. Because the proxy lives on your server, it allows you to bypass security restrictions built into the browser, and it can also be used to get around network restrictions. For example, many corporate networks allow an external web user access to the web server but restrict access beyond that. By deploying a proxy on your web server, you could, for example, proxy requests to internal web services.

With this comes some responsibility. You should never deploy an open proxy that can hit any site on the internet. You should develop your proxy such that it will only proxy requests to external sites that you want your application to access. If you fail to do this, don't be surprised when your proxy is abused and used in a manner that you didn't intend. But enough about security; let's write some code. The following listing presents our proxy code, which is followed by a detailed explanation.

Listing 12.9 A simple proxy servlet

```
package com.manning.ch12.xml.server;

import java.io.IOException;
import javax.servlet.ServletException;
import javax.servlet.http.*;
```

```
import org.apache.http.client.HttpClient;
import org.apache.http.client.ResponseHandler;
import org.apache.http.client.methods.HttpGet;
import org.apache.http.impl.client.BasicResponseHandler;
import org.apache.http.impl.client.DefaultHttpClient;

@SuppressWarnings("serial")
public class Proxy extends HttpServlet
{
  @Override
  protected void doPost (HttpServletRequest req, HttpServletResponse resp)
    throws ServletException, IOException {

    String url = req.getParameter("url");                    <-- Grab
    if (!url.startsWith("http://gdata.youtube.com/"))        ❶ requested URL
      throw new ServletException("not on whitelist");
                                                             ❷ Create client
    HttpClient client = new DefaultHttpClient();             <--
    HttpGet method = new HttpGet(url);
    ResponseHandler<String> handler = new BasicResponseHandler();

    String responseBody = client.execute(method, handler);   <-- Execute
    resp.getWriter().write(responseBody);                    ❸ the request

    client.getConnectionManager().shutdown();
  }
}
```

In order to use this servlet, you'll need to download HttpClient from http://hc.apache.org. HttpClient has several dependencies, so you'll want to download the distribution that includes the dependencies. Copy the jar files from the distribution to the /war/WEB-INF/lib/ folder of your project, and add all of them to the classpath of your IDE. As of this writing we're using HttpClient 4.0.1.

Surprisingly, you need only a few lines of code to proxy a request. The first step, and perhaps the most important, is to grab the target URL that you're requesting data for ❶ and validate it. As shown in the example, you use the request parameter `url` to specify the page for which you'll be acting as a proxy, and then you verify that the target URL is for gdata.youtube.com, rejecting all other URLs.

This validation is extremely important. If you don't validate the URL, you're opening your proxy to target any site. This could be used by a malicious hacker to use your proxy to target unscrupulous sites, potentially harming your users. So be safe, and restrict your proxy to a specific set of white-listed URLs.

Next ❷, you create a new `HttpClient`, create a `GET` request, and set up a handler to receive the result. We're using the `DefaultHandler`, which suits our needs. You then ❸ execute the request and send the contents of the received page back to the caller. If the page can't be returned for whatever reason, an error will be thrown back to the client. Again, this suits us fine for this example, but if you need more robust error handling on the server, you should consult the HttpClient documentation.

So that's it. The servlet receives a URL parameter and then fetches and returns that page. Now we need to configure our servlet in the web.xml. The next listing shows how to do this.

Listing 12.10 Adding the proxy servlet to the web.xml

```
<?xml version="1.0" encoding="UTF-8"?>
<!DOCTYPE web-app
    PUBLIC "-//Sun Microsystems, Inc.//DTD Web Application 2.3//EN"
    "http://java.sun.com/dtd/web-app_2_3.dtd">

<web-app>

  <servlet>
    <servlet-name>proxy</servlet-name>
    <servlet-class>com.manning.ch12.xml.server.Proxy</servlet-class>
  </servlet>

  <servlet-mapping>
    <servlet-name>proxy</servlet-name>
    <url-pattern>*.proxy</url-pattern>
  </servlet-mapping>

  <!-- ...other stuff omitted... -->

</web-app>
```

The web.xml is located in the /war/WEB-INF/ directory of your GWT project. You add the `<servlet>` and the `<servlet-mapping>` that maps a URL to that servlet. When you add a new servlet to the web.xml, the `<servlet-name>` in both the servlet definition and the mapping need to be the same. That's what links the two parts together. You can have multiple mappings for a servlet, but in this case one is sufficient.

The `<url-pattern>` for a servlet takes only a few specific forms. Here you use the extension pattern that matches anything ending with ".proxy". The benefit of using this wildcard match over an exact match is that it simplifies your deployment. Our GWT application can use absolutely any URL, as long as it ends with ".proxy". If you've ever struggled with mappings, you'll understand the effort that this can save.

OK, now that we have our proxy servlet written and mapped in the servlet container, it's time to write our GWT client.

12.6.2 Calling the proxy from GWT

Calling the proxy from GWT is going to look similar to the `RequestBuilder` example from the beginning of this chapter. If you missed that discussion, you can read all about it in section 12.2.

As we've done in the previous examples, we begin by presenting the code for the proxy client, followed by an explanation.

Listing 12.11 Reading and parsing XML content

```
package com.manning.ch12.xml.client;

import com.google.gwt.core.client.EntryPoint;
import com.google.gwt.http.client.*;
import com.google.gwt.user.client.ui.RootPanel;
import com.google.gwt.user.client.ui.TextArea;

public class XmlExample implements EntryPoint
{
  public void onModuleLoad () {

    final TextArea output = new TextArea();
    output.setSize("400px", "200px");
    RootPanel.get().add(output);

    String youTubeUrl = "http://gdata.youtube.com/feeds/api/videos?"
      + "author=DisturbedTV"
      + "&max-results=5"
      + "&orderby=published"
      + "&v=2";
                                                          ❶ Create builder
    RequestBuilder rb = new RequestBuilder(
        RequestBuilder.POST, "xml.proxy");

    rb.setRequestData("url=" + URL.encodeQueryString(youTubeUrl));        ❷ Configure for POST
    rb.setHeader("Content-Type", "application/x-www-form-urlencoded");

    rb.setCallback(new RequestCallback() {
      @Override
      public void onResponseReceived (Request request, Response res) {
        if (res.getStatusCode() == 200) {
          printData(output, res.getText());
        }
        else {
          output.setText("ERROR CODE:" + res.getStatusCode());
        }
      }

      @Override
      public void onError (Request request, Throwable e) {
        output.setText("SERVER ERROR: " + e.getMessage());
      }
    });

    try {
      rb.send();
    }
    catch (RequestException e) {
      output.setText("FETCH ERROR: " + e.getMessage());
    }
  }
                                                          ❸ Print output
  private void printData (TextArea output, String content) {
    output.setText(content);
  }
}
```

If you've been reading this chapter straight through, this code example should look familiar. Because we already explored nearly this same example in section 12.2, we'll only describe what's different about it. If you need a refresher on any parts of this example, you should revisit listing 12.2, where we covered it in detail.

The first portion to note is when you create the `RequestBuilder` instance ❶. Previously you used the `GET` method, but this time you'll use a `POST`. You need to use `POST` because you only implemented the `doPost()` method in the servlet, so you need to send a `POST` request so that the `doPost()` method receives it. In addition, you request the resource xml.proxy. This matches the pattern you used to map the servlet in the web.xml.

Next, you configure some of the settings in the `RequestBuilder` instance ❷. The first is to set the content of the `POST` by passing your data to the `setRequestData()` method. Notice that you use `URL.encodeQueryString()` to URL encode the parameter value. This will encode any unsafe characters. It's important to note why you don't use `URL.encode()`, which has different semantics. Specifically, `URL.encode()` tries to encode any unsafe characters in an entire URL. This sounds like a good idea, but in practice it won't encode special characters in a URL like & and =,[7] even when you need it to. In this case you're passing a full URL as a parameter value, which includes both & and =, and you need them properly encoded.

You need to configure the `RequestBuilder` instance to send a "Content-Type" header with a value of "application/x-www-form-urlencoded." This signals the server how to consume the data. In the case of servlets, this will allow you to read the data using `request.getParameter()`.

The rest is exactly as you saw when we looked at `RequestBuilder`, which is to create a callback and send the request. When you receive the data back from the request, assuming the server sent a 200 status code, you call `printData()` ❸. If you run this as it is right now, it will dump the entire contents of the XML message received via the proxy servlet to the output `TextArea`.

The XML content returned in the `TextArea` is fairly complex and contains a lot of information. For this example all you're interested in are the video titles. Removing all of the superfluous content from the XML gives you something like the following:

```
<?xml version='1.0' encoding='UTF-8'?>
<feed>
<entry>
<title>Disturbed - Thank You For Making Asylum #1</title>
</entry>
<entry>
<title>Disturbed - Mike's Drum Cam</title>
</entry>
...
</feed>
```

Now that you can see what you need to do, let's do some XML parsing.

7 `URL.encode()` will encode all nonalphanumeric characters except /, ?, :, @, &, =, +, $, and #.

12.6.3 Parsing XML content

In order to be able to use the `XMLParser` and other XML classes, you'll need to add the XML module to your module configuration. Here's our complete module file for this project, which includes the GWT XML module:

```
<?xml version="1.0" encoding="UTF-8"?>
<module>
    <inherits name="com.google.gwt.user.User" />
    <inherits name="com.google.gwt.xml.XML" />
    <source path="client" />
    <entry-point class="com.manning.ch12.xml.client.XmlExample" />
</module>
```

Your module configuration may differ depending on the package name you used, or perhaps you've added a theme or added other GWT modules. The important part is the addition of the `<inherits>` element that pulls in the XML module. This will give you access to the classes in the package `com.google.gwt.xml.client`.

Now that you've included the XML package, you can update your `printData()` method, as shown next, to parse the XML content and print the video titles.

Listing 12.12 Updated `printData()` and `extractText()` for handling XML content

```
import com.google.gwt.xml.client.XMLParser;
import com.google.gwt.xml.client.Document;
import com.google.gwt.xml.client.Element;
import com.google.gwt.xml.client.Node;
import com.google.gwt.xml.client.NodeList;

...other imports and code ommitted...

private void printData (TextArea output, String content) {

  Document doc = XMLParser.parse(content);                          ❶ Parse the XML

  NodeList nlEntries = doc.getElementsByTagName("entry");           ❷ Find entry element

  for (int i = 0; i < nlEntries.getLength(); i++) {                 ❸ Iterate subelements
    Element eEntry = (Element) nlEntries.item(i);
    Element eTitle =
      (Element) eEntry.getElementsByTagName("title").item(0);       ❹ Extract title value
    String title = extractText(eTitle);

    output.setText(output.getText() + title + "\n");
  }
}

private String extractText (Node node) {                            ❺ Extraction helper
  StringBuilder result = new StringBuilder();

  NodeList children = node.getChildNodes();
  for (int x = 0; x < children.getLength(); x++) {
    Node child = children.item(x);
```

```
      if (child.getNodeType() == Node.TEXT_NODE) {
        result.append(children.item(x).getNodeValue());
      }
      else if (child.getNodeType() == Node.CDATA_SECTION_NODE) {
        result.append(children.item(x).getNodeValue());
      }
      else if (child.hasChildNodes()) {
        result.append(extractText(children.item(x)));
      }
    }

    return result.toString();
  }
```

As listing 12.12 shows, you begin the updated printData() method with a call to XMLParser.parse() ❶. The parse() method takes a String as input and returns a Document instance. If you're familiar with the XML Document Object Model (DOM), this should look familiar because the XML support in GWT is the DOM API. If you aren't familiar with the DOM, the Document encapsulates the XML content and provides methods to traverse the content via the API.

> **NOTE** Some of the classes used in the example are used in other Java packages as well, so make sure that you're using the right ones. Specifically we make use of Document, Element, Node, and NodeList. Be sure that you use the ones from the com.google.gwt.xml.client.* package.

Next, you use one of the find methods ❷ by calling getElementsByTagName("entry") on the Document. This returns a NodeList. A NodeList is a collection of Nodes, and a Node is the most basic type in the DOM. A node can be an element, a comment, an attribute, an XML entity, or a piece of text. The Node class has several constants that can be used to test what type of node it is. We'll look at an example of this when we explore the extractText() method.

Now you iterate over the nodes that are returned ❸. You know that these nodes are Element instances because they were retrieved via a call to getElementsByTagName(), which only returns elements, so you can cast them without doing any testing. Element is a subclass of Node and is meant to encapsulate a single element within the XML document. The Element may in turn contain child nodes that can include text, other elements, comments, and the like.

Because all <entry> elements in this XML document contain exactly one <title> element, you can call getElementsByTagName("title") on the entry Element ❹ to get the one title child Element. As you can see, because you know this returns exactly one element, you can call item(0) and cast to Element without needing to perform any checks. You might have guessed that this code would quickly get ugly if you did need to perform those checks. The point is that the DOM API is extremely verbose. In the Java space, this has led to the creation of simpler-to-use tools like JAXB and JDOM, to name a couple. Unfortunately, we don't have these tools in GWT, so often you'll need to write your own helper routines.

The `extractText()` method ❺ in the example is one of those helper routines. The `extractText()` method is an attempt to extract all text content within a given element. What that means is that it takes the element that it's passed and iterates over the element's child nodes. If the child is an element, it calls the `extractText()` method to recursively extract nested text. If the node is instead of type `Node.TEXT_NODE` or `Node.CDATA_SECTION_NODE`, both of which are text content, you add it to the result. A CDATA node is any content within the XML file that uses the CDATA notation from the XML specification. The CDATA notation is used to escape content that might contain unsafe characters, such as < or >.

> **TIP** If you want to know more about XML node types, like CDATA and Processing Instructions (PI), you should take a look at the XML specification. You can find the XML 1.1 specification at http://www.w3.org/TR/2006/REC-xml11-20060816/.

Running this example now will extract the title text from the XML document and display it in the output `TextArea`. Voila! You have the titles you were after:

```
Disturbed - Thank You For Making Asylum #1
Disturbed - Mike's Drum Cam
Disturbed - Asylum Unleashed
Disturbed - Asylum Available Now
Decade of Disturbed - Extended Trailer
```

> **WARNING** XML parsing in GWT is largely handled by the web browser, and implementations between browsers will differ. What this means is that your XML parsing might work in the latest version of Firefox but not Internet Explorer 8, and it might be quirky in Chrome. The reason why GWT uses the browser's functionality is that XML parsing is a complex task, and doing this in JavaScript would be rather slow. So when consuming XML data, be sure to test that it works in all of the browsers that you need to support.

At this point we've covered a lot of ways to fetch content from an external server, but we still have one more to go. Of all the ways to fetch content, this one will likely be the most familiar. It's GWT's take on the old-fashioned, tried and true HTML form.

12.7 Using FormPanel

The `FormPanel` is GWT's own take on the HTML form. It's a subclass of `SimplePanel`, which means you can place only one widget inside the `FormPanel`. Typically this would be a `VerticalPanel`, a `Grid`, or some other widget where you can lay out the individual form elements.

The form elements consist of any widget that's rendered as a standard HTML form element. At the time of this writing this includes the widgets `CheckBox`, `RadioButton`, `FileUpload`, `Hidden`, `ListBox`, `SimpleCheckBox`, `SimpleRadioButton`, `TextArea`, `TextBox`, and `PasswordTextBox`. All of these widgets, including the `FormPanel`, are in the package `com.google.gwt.user.client.ui`.

Using FormPanel is like using a regular HTML form in all but one respect, and that's that the page never reloads when the form is submitted. The default behavior is that when you submit a FormPanel the results are sent to a hidden <iframe> in the page, which can then be used for whatever purpose is needed.

For example, you could take the results that were returned into that hidden frame and display them in a pop-up. In this section we'll do exactly that. We'll use the form to post a registration to the server and show the results in an alert box.

We begin by designing our form and then show the Java code that enables it.

12.7.1 Designing a FormPanel registration form with UiBinder

When using the FormPanel you could use it the old-fashioned way, which is to construct everything in code, but instead we're going to simplify things. For our example we'll use UiBinder, which we introduced in chapter 6. This will reduce the amount of code needed to produce the desired result.

Let's begin by looking at our template in the following listing, which will provide both the structure and widgets that we'll use in the form.

Listing 12.13 RegistrationForm.ui.xml—a registration form UiBinder template

```
<!DOCTYPE ui:UiBinder SYSTEM "http://dl.google.com/gwt/DTD/xhtml.ent">
<ui:UiBinder xmlns:ui="urn:ui:com.google.gwt.uibinder"
  xmlns:g="urn:import:com.google.gwt.user.client.ui">

  <g:FormPanel ui:field="form" method="post" action="register.jsp">    ❶ FormPanel container
    <g:HTMLPanel>

      <div>Your Name
        <g:TextBox ui:field="txtName" name="name" />                    ❷ TextBox widget
      </div>

      <div>Your EMail
        <g:TextBox ui:field="txtEmail" name="email" />
      </div>

      <div>I agree to the terms
        <g:CheckBox ui:field="chkTerms" name="terms" formValue="yes" />   ❸ CheckBox widget
      </div>

      <div>
        <g:Button ui:field="btnRegister" text="Register" />              ❹ Button widget
      </div>

    </g:HTMLPanel>
  </g:FormPanel>

</ui:UiBinder>
```

In the template you use a FormPanel as the root element ❶ and set several properties of the widget. As you saw in the UiBinder chapter, each attribute maps to a method on the class. So the method attribute maps to FormPanel's setMethod() method, which sets the HTTP method to use when submitting the form. In addition, you set the `action` to register.jsp, which is the JSP page that will handle the request and return a result message. We'll create that JSP page shortly. You also use `ui:field` to set the variable name to which you'll bind this widget in your class.

Next, you create a `TextBox` ❷ and set the `name` property. Setting the name is important to do, because this is the parameter name that will be used when the value is sent to the server. This is the same as using a plain-old HTML form. Again you use `ui:field` to map the widget to a variable in your class. This will be used to validate the contents prior to sending it to the server.

You then have another `TextBox` for an email address followed by a `CheckBox` ❸ that asks you to agree to the terms of service. Again you specify the name, and for the `formValue` property you use the word "yes."

You follow this with a `Button` widget ❹, which you'll use to submit the encapsulating `FormPanel` when it's clicked.

> **NOTE** When submitting an `HtmlForm` you can use either a `Button` hooked up to a handler or `SubmitButton`. `SubmitButton` would be less code, but at the time of this writing using `SubmitButton` creates an issue when canceling the form-submission event in development mode. You'd want to cancel the event, for example, if you included form validation and it failed. You can view the current status of this issue at http://mng.bz/fDR2.

So now we have a `FormPanel` and several widgets. But what about validation? And how do we display the results? We'll look at that next.

12.7.2 Adding behavior to the FormPanel

At this point we've created a UiBinder template that defines our registration form, using `FormPanel` as the root widget. The next step is enable it by adding behavior for validation, submission, and handling the server response. The following listing presents the `RegistrationForm` widget class to which we'll bind our template.

Listing 12.14 Registration.java—a registration form widget

```
package com.manning.ch12.form.client;

import com.google.gwt.core.client.GWT;
import com.google.gwt.event.dom.client.ClickEvent;
import com.google.gwt.uibinder.client.*;
import com.google.gwt.user.client.Window;
import com.google.gwt.user.client.ui.*;
import com.google.gwt.user.client.ui.FormPanel.SubmitCompleteEvent;
import com.google.gwt.user.client.ui.FormPanel.SubmitEvent;

public class RegistrationForm extends Composite
{
  interface Binder extends UiBinder<FormPanel, RegistrationForm> {}
  private static Binder uiBinder = GWT.create(Binder.class);
```

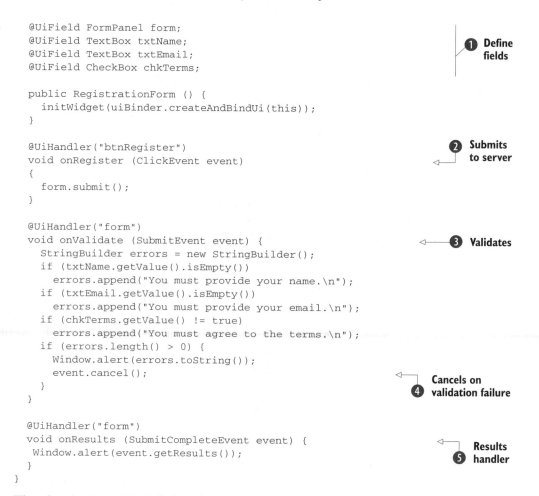

```
  @UiField FormPanel form;
  @UiField TextBox txtName;
  @UiField TextBox txtEmail;
  @UiField CheckBox chkTerms;

  public RegistrationForm () {
    initWidget(uiBinder.createAndBindUi(this));
  }

  @UiHandler("btnRegister")
  void onRegister (ClickEvent event)
  {
    form.submit();
  }

  @UiHandler("form")
  void onValidate (SubmitEvent event) {
    StringBuilder errors = new StringBuilder();
    if (txtName.getValue().isEmpty())
      errors.append("You must provide your name.\n");
    if (txtEmail.getValue().isEmpty())
      errors.append("You must provide your email.\n");
    if (chkTerms.getValue() != true)
      errors.append("You must agree to the terms.\n");
    if (errors.length() > 0) {
      Window.alert(errors.toString());
      event.cancel();
    }
  }

  @UiHandler("form")
  void onResults (SubmitCompleteEvent event) {
   Window.alert(event.getResults());
  }
}
```

❶ Define fields

❷ Submits to server

❸ Validates

❹ Cancels on validation failure

❺ Results handler

The class begins with defining the UiBinder interface definition and the creation of the class that will implement it. The details of how this works are spelled out in chapter 6, so we won't repeat them here. This is followed by defining the four fields your form widgets will be bound to ❶. It's useful to note that you won't be using these to submit their values to the server, because the `FormPanel` can do this without your help. As you'll see shortly, you'll only be using them to validate their contents.

The fields are then followed by a constructor that binds this class to the widgets defined in the template, along with two `FormPanel` event handlers.

The first handler, which is defined in the method `onRegister()` ❷, is used to submit the form to the server when the button in the interface is clicked. We could have also done the validation here, but we decided to separate that out into its own `onValidate()` method ❸, which handles the `FormPanel` submit event. The `SubmitEvent` occurs when form submission is activated. This could be triggered by clicking a `SubmitButton` widget in the form, pressing the Enter key while one of the form fields has focus (this only works if you use `SubmitButton` in the interface), or calling `submit()` on the `FormPanel` instance as you do in this example, in other words, all the usual ways that a regular HTML form can be submitted.

The validation is fairly simple; you test each of the fields to ensure the user entered some information, including checking off the agreement to the terms of service. You test each field individually and gather a list of error messages so that you can show them all together in an alert box. And perhaps the most important step here is that if there's an error, you call `event.cancel()` ❹, which will cancel the form submission.

The last handler, `onResults()` ❺, receives the `SubmitCompleteEvent`, which occurs after the results have been received from the server. This event provides access to the content returned from the server, and here you display it in an alert window.

Now that we have our client completed, we need to write the code on the server that will handle our form submission. Create a new file in the war directory of your project named register.jsp, with the following content:

```
Dear <%=request.getParameter("name")%>,
your registration is being processed.
Once processed we will send a confirmation
email to <%=request.getParameter("email")%>.
```

If you recall, we specified register.jsp in the `action` attribute for our `FormPanel`, so it will submit to this JSP page. This JSP page in return sends a message back to the client, using the name and email address sent in for form data to personalize the message.

One important rule to remember when sending data back to the client is that it must use the content type "text/html." That isn't to say that you can't send plain text (that is, content type of "text/plain") back to the client, but the browser may tweak it a bit. This occurs when the browser parses the returned content, as if it was HTML, and stores it in its own internal format.

For example, if you add the directive `<%@page contentType="text/plain"%>` to the top of the register.jsp example, Chrome will automatically wrap the content in a `<pre>` HTML element.

This will work as long as the content returned doesn't include any special HTML characters. XML content, in particular, will be parsed and potentially modified. A way to get around this is to URL encode the content before sending it to the client. This will replace characters like < and >, which could be parsed as HTML, with encoded values like `%3C` and `%3E`. You can encode the content by using `java.net.URLEncoder`, as in this example:

```
String encoded = URLEncoder.encode("< don't parse me! >", "UTF-8")
```

On the client side, you can reverse the encoding by using GWT's URL utility, passing the encoded content into the `decodeQueryString()` method, as in this example:

```
String decoded = URL.decodeQueryString(event.getResults())
```

Getting back to our example, if you run it now you'll see a form like the one shown in figure 12.2.

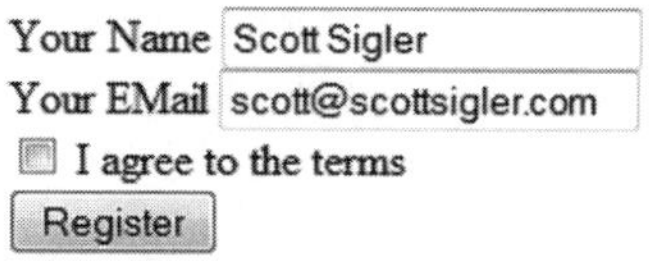

As you can see, FormPanel is a valuable tool, particularly if you're already well versed in handling HTML form data. And this holds true regardless of what language you're using on the server. This also makes it valuable as a transition tool, in some cases allowing you to use your existing backend code.

Your Name Scott Sigler
Your EMail scott@scottsigler.com
I agree to the terms
Register

Figure 12.2 The registration form displayed in a browser, partially filled out with sample data

Unfortunately, too many scenarios exist to say for sure which tool is right for a given project, which is why GWT provides several tools with a lot of overlapping capability. It's our hope that this chapter has provided the mental building blocks to help you determine the right tool for your job so that your project can succeed. And this leads us into our summary.

12.8 Summary

When we began this chapter, we touted it as a chapter of flexibility, for those times when GWT-RPC doesn't fit. As the first argument for our case we showed you RequestBuilder, the general all-purpose tool for reading files from your web server. When we combined that with the JSON and XML tooling found in GWT, we were able to read data from the server, parse it, and display its content.

As our second argument for flexibility we showed you JsonpRequestBuilder, a tool that you can use for reading JSONP data from not only your web server but also any web server on the internet. This is a big win for developers because when GWT can talk directly to a remote server that means less work for you, eliminating the need to develop a proxy service.

As our closing argument we showed off GWT's FormPanel. But this isn't the outmoded HTML form you remember; it's been upgraded. FormPanel submits its data to the server and then holds the results for you in a hidden iFrame. You can then use the returned content to update the display. The most important feature of FormPanel is that the browser page doesn't need to reload, which is a usability win over old non-GWT forms.

So when it comes to flexibility, GWT is a virtual ballerina. Case closed. Now that we've shown GWT's flexibility when it comes to client/server communication, we'll explore the tools that make our planet "a small world."[8] Up next, internationalization.

[8] "It's a Small World" is an attraction at Walt Disney parks all over the world: http://en.wikipedia.org/wiki/It%27s_a_Small_World.

13 Internationalization, localization, and accessibility

This chapter covers

- Making your user interface as widely usable as possible
- Handling pluralization and user-defined differences in messages
- Presenting times, dates, currencies, and numbers as users expect

In this chapter we'll explore how to make your application as familiar to as many people as possible, through internationalization and localization. Using those techniques, you can present the interface in a user's own language—with familiar date, time, and currency formats—and even display it in the expected direction (some users may read from right to left).

We'll look at both of GWT's provided approaches to internationalization (i18n)—static and dynamic—as well as how it supports localization (L10n). The static approach is preferred because it allows the compiler to remove unused information (making the download as small as possible, thereby improving user experience), whereas the dynamic approach is more useful when you have legacy data. Finally, we'll quickly cover some tips on making your application more accessible—supporting visually impaired users.

If you have the chapter's example application loaded into Eclipse, then it's time to start looking at how to make the user interface as familiar to the user as you can.

13.1 Making a user feel comfortable

If your application is available in only one language (or *locale* if we use the standard lingo), then you limit your reach. Certainly, some languages may feel they're the de facto ones on the web, and these may be the ones you want. But we suspect that most of you want your applications today to have a global reach, and to do that you should make it as easy for the user to use as possible, and present the user interface in a familiar manner to them.

What do we mean by *familiar manner*? One answer is obvious, and some answers have subtleties:

- *User's language*—This is probably the thing that comes to mind. Whereas a French person might expect to see French words and phrases, a Spaniard would expect Spanish ones, and so on.
- *User's dialect*—You might want to cater to the differences in spelling within the same "language"—an English person might be happier to see the word *tyres* instead of *tires*; a Canadian might want the option to choose between Canadian French and Canadian English.
- *Reading direction*—Some users read from left to right, and others read from right to left. Presenting a user interface in Arabic (read right to left) in a left-to-right manner will be confusing—and this applies to widget placement as well as to text in those widgets.
- *Plurals*—Your interface should probably take care of plural forms of messages, making sure nouns match to a count, for example, "*0 people are* viewing," "*1 person is* viewing," or "*5 people are* viewing." (English has three forms: 0, 1, and *n*; some languages have more and some less.) And maybe the interface should cope with other variations, such as "she is" and "he is."
- *Date, times, currency, number formats*—What does the date 10/07/2012 mean—the 10th of July or the 7th of October? Or the number 1,500—is that fifteen hundred or one point five to three decimal points?
- *Other resources*—Do you also need to change other resources, such as images, for different locales; is there more that needs doing?
- *Accessibility*—What if the user is visually impaired? GWT tries to support the ARIA approach to annotating DOM elements so that screen readers can attempt to interpret the screen for users.[1] You can also harness client bundles to provide more accessible styling options.

[1] Accessibility and GWT: http://mng.bz/IZ9P.

Making user interfaces more familiar to your user is more in depth than it might casually appear. Luckily, GWT has two standard approaches baked in that will help you: static and dynamic. You only need to use a couple of simple techniques in your GWT code, and the world will open up to you. The cost is low, but the benefits are high.

> **DEFINITIONS** *Internationalization*—Usually shortened to i18n, internationalization refers to differences in text between locales.
>
> *Localization*—Often shortened to L10n, localization addresses date, number, and currency types of subtleties.
>
> *Accessibility*—Often shortened to a11y, accessibility is all about making your interface usable by users with disabilities such as visual impairment, hearing loss, or limited dexterity.

In this section you'll see what you need to do at a minimum to use i18n in a project to address the issues we've mentioned. We'll also look at L10n in a GWT application to steer date, time, currency, and number format, as well as how you can harness the static approach to i18n to solve the challenge of other resources (through localization of client bundles, as we discussed in chapter 5).

The driving force behind all of the approaches to i18n and L10n is *locale*, and because it's so important, it's the thing we'll look at first.

13.1.1 What is a locale?

In GWT, as with many other toolkits and frameworks, a locale is a string representing the language, with optionally the country, script, and any dialect. GWT is moving toward using BCP47[2] language tags to represent locales, such as those shown in figure 13.1.

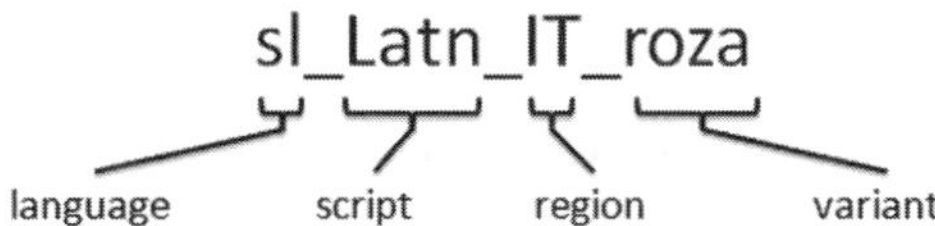

Figure 13.1 An example complex language tag showing the language, script, region, and variant components

The language component of a language tag is mandatory and is always first. Everything else is optional, occurring once at most. In quick summary, the fields are as follows:

- *Language*—A value from ISO 639-1,[3] such as `en` (English), `fr` (French), `hi` (Hindi), `zh` (Chinese), or other registered value.
- *Script*—A value from ISO 15924, such as `Cyrl` for Cyrillic or `Latn` for Latin. For example, Bulgarian is usually written in Cyrillic script but can be transliterated to Latin; a script component can distinguish between these two forms.
- *Region*—A value from either ISO 3166-2,[4] which is an alpha string such as `CA` for Canada, or United Nations UN M.49,[5] which is numeric, such as `262` for Djibouti.
- *Variants*—Usually restricted by language codes.

---

2 BCP47: www.rfc-editor.org/rfc/bcp/bcp47.txt.

3 ISO 639-1: http://en.wikipedia.org/wiki/List_of_ISO_639-1_codes.

4 ISO 3166-2: http://en.wikipedia.org/wiki/ISO_3166-2.

5 UN M.49: http://unstats.un.org/unsd/methods/m49/m49.htm.

Typically, a GWT locale consists of the mandatory language component and optionally, the region component. You'll see locales such as `en_US` for U.S. English and `en_GB` for UK English or just `fi` for Finnish. Older versions of GWT didn't mandate BCP47, but locale tags were the same as you've just seen, for example, `fi` or `en_US` (so in practice you don't need to worry about legacy code).

What does this mean? Let's look at a few examples of this chapter's static i18n example in different locales, starting with `en_US` locale (U.S. English), as shown in figure 13.2.

Figure 13.2 The title and description of our i18n example application in the American English locale—note the word *Internationalization*, the American flag, and the statement of locale

Changing the locale to `en_GB`, for British English (which you can do from the drop-down box at the bottom of the example), we obtain figure 13.3—spot the difference?

Figure 13.3 The title and description of our i18n example application in the British English locale—note the word *Internationalisation*, the UK flag, and the statement of locale

The difference is quite subtle, and if you didn't spot it, it's that *internationalization* is spelled with an *s* in British English. Sometimes the locale will drive more obvious differences—look at figure 13.4, which is in the Finnish locale. Now the difference should be quite obvious.

Figure 13.4 The static i18n example in the Finnish locale—quite a difference

An implication of using locales is that your application will probably be using letters beyond the 26 found in the English language—perhaps the åöä from Swedish, àçê from French, ąůč from Czech, the Russian БЖЮ, the Greek ζλε, or the Chinese 好运气. This means you need to do a couple of things in your IDE to enable support of those characters.

13.1.2 Setting up to use internationalization

When internationalizing an application, you must encode your GWT application in UTF-8 format to avoid having little square boxes all over the UI instead of real characters. You need to do two things to remedy this: encode project files in UTF-8 format, and let the browser know this.

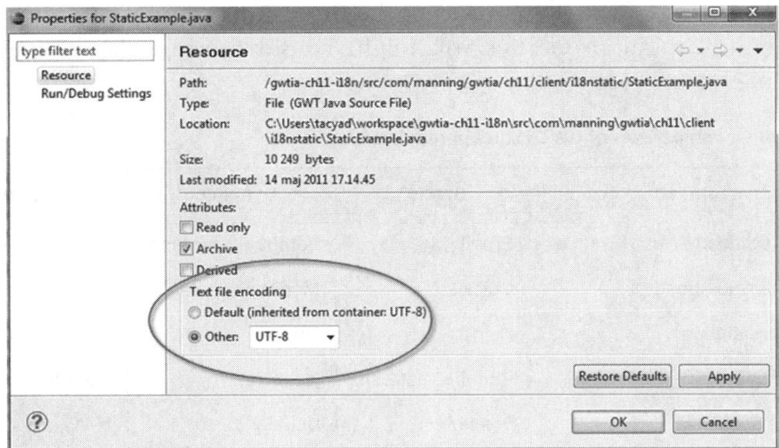

Figure 13.5 Setting the project files to have UTF encoding in Eclipse

ENCODING PROJECT FILES IN UTF-8 FORMAT

In Eclipse you can encode all of your project files in UTF-8 format by opening the project's properties and setting the resource Text File Encoding value, as shown in figure 13.5 (you can do something similar in other IDEs), and clicking Apply.

With the project source files in UTF-8, the next thing you need to do is let the browser know that the application is coming in UTF-8 format.

LETTING THE BROWSER KNOW

If you don't tell the browser your application is coming as UTF-8 encoded files, it will try to guess and potentially get it wrong (giving your UI that square-box look). By adding the following meta tag to your application's HTML file's head section, all will be OK:

```
<meta http-equiv="content-type" content="text/html; charset=UTF-8">
```

Now you're set up for i18n, and your next step is to decide which of the two built-in approaches you should use, or if the third approach that we briefly mentioned is a better option.

13.1.3 The three types of GWT internationalization

GWT provides two methods for handling local differences, a static approach and a dynamic approach, and we can also imagine a third, the reactive approach.

Although the dynamic approach might sound more exciting, the static approach is the preferred method. This is because it uses the compiler's power to statically analyze what's used. It therefore reduces download size by removing unused strings, and it removes runtime errors related to string unavailability. Dynamic means everything is sent to the browser, and what to use is determined at runtime.

We also mentioned a third, reactive approach that uses an online translation API to translate text on the fly. You have no control over the success, the quality, and sometimes the cost of these APIs. Google had a free API for this, but it's also a pay-to-use service now.

Table 13.1 gives a quick comparison of the three i18n approaches and how they stack up against typical properties you might consider using, depending on the approach you choose.

Table 13.1 Quick comparison of GWT i18n approaches

I18n approach	Static	Dynamic	Reactive
Application download size	Small	Potentially largest	Potentially smallest
Application startup speed	Quick	Medium	Quick
Accuracy of translation	High	High	Low to medium
Changing locale	Requires refresh	No refresh	No refresh
Reuse legacy data	Possible	Usually	N/A
Potential for runtime errors	None	Yes	Yes
Handle new locales during execution	No	No	Yes

We've simplified our guidance on which approach to use into the following three points:

- If you're building an application from scratch, use the static approach.
- For integration with legacy code, you can choose either static or dynamic.
- If you don't know the locales in which your application will be used, you aren't too bothered about accuracy of translation, and you can afford any potential license costs for API usage (plus a way of using it), then the reactive approach is a viable choice.

We're going to concentrate on the two standard GWT approaches, starting with the static way.

13.2 Using static string internationalization

This approach uses a set of property files containing key/value pairs, one for each locale. It's called the static approach because the GWT compiler uses a technique called *static analysis* to ensure the output includes only those values in use in the application. This has two benefits:

- Your download doesn't include unused values, minimizing code size.
- You'll have no missing values at runtime, removing potential for errors.

Not only are unused values removed, but the compiler also produces an output per locale used that contains only the set of strings for that locale. That is to say, a French locale output (or *permutation*, as it's known) wouldn't have to carry the text for English and Persian and so on, so that's the smallest possible download/quickest startup speed.

This takes the compiler a little longer to produce, and you end up with more files to deploy (multiply the number of locales you have by six—the number of supported rendering engines (browsers)—and you get an idea of the number of permutations). But this shouldn't be an issue, for the following reasons:

- With hosted mode, compilation isn't needed, so you miss this impact.
- When deploying, you only need to compile once: when you're ready to deploy.

But if you use continuous integration techniques, you may run into issues as compilation time increases. An option is to limit the locales extended in the GWT property to one and only extend to the full set nearer to deploy time.

The only real potential downside to static i18n occurs when the user needs to change locales in the application—they have to wait a short time for the new version of the application to come from the server, and the state of the application could be lost if you haven't somehow stored or encoded it in the request.

In our experience, most users don't switch locale on a minute-by-minute basis. Even if they do, the aggressive caching of GWT means that after the first-time use of a locale, the time to change back to it is quick. The benefit of small download size and no runtime errors should outweigh this drawback. If you find this is a huge problem for your application and you're comfortable taking the hit of larger downloads, then you can employ the trick of collapsing properties (see section 17.4.2), for example, adding the following to your module file:

```
<collapse-property name="locale" values="*" />
```

Figure 13.6 shows what the static string i18n part of this chapter's example application includes.

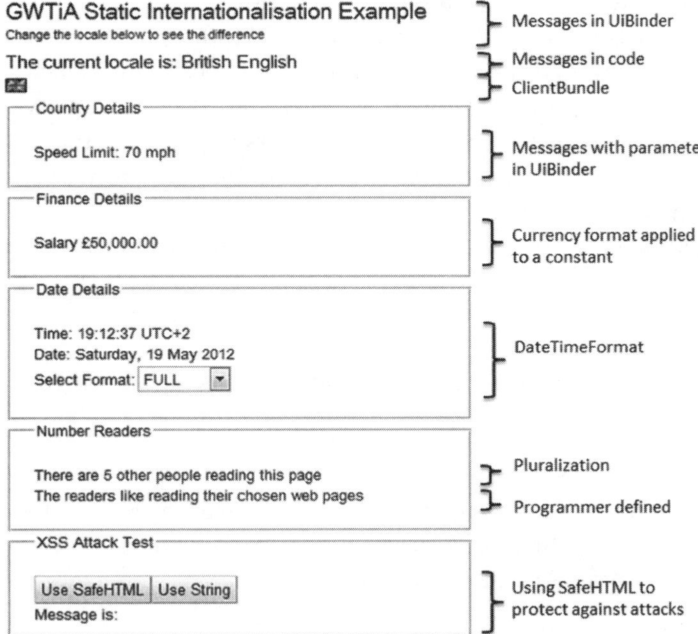

Figure 13.6 The static i18n example application listing techniques in use

In our static i18n example we use every approach we can, to give some examples—your application will probably be more efficient using only what's necessary. We'll cover the following:

- Using `Messages` within a UiBinder template with and without parameters to display the title and speed limit details.
- Displaying differing flags by harnessing i18n techniques and `ClientBundles` (from chapter 5).
- Using some data titles and values, for example, Speed Limit and its value, that come from `Constants`.
- Testing `NumberFormat` to localize the currency value used in the salary display.
- Manipulating `DateTimeFormat` to show times and dates; overall formats are specific to a locale, but within a locale you can dynamically choose various format options, such as full, medium, or short.
- Using alternate messages, you can present plural texts to show the right text depending on the number of users reading the page.
- Also using alternate messages to alter the message when only one user is reading the page, based on the gender of that person.
- Finally, covering an important aspect related to security—you'll see how GWT's `SafeHtml` type can help you protect against script-injection attacks in messages.

Typically, extending the `Localizable` interface drives the static-string i18n mechanism, and using deferred binding creates instances of those interfaces. Linking the interface to properties files causes the compiler to automatically generate code for you by taking into account any related annotations in use.

You'll see more on code generation and deferred binding in later chapters; for now you only need to know that when the compiler comes across an interface extending `Localizable`, or more specifically for i18n, `Constants`, `ConstantsWithLookup`, or `Messages`, it will try to create a new class. That new class implements the found interface, and the GWT compiler will bind method names in that class to values it finds in the properties files you've provided.

Before we dig into all the details, let's look at an example that shows how to use static i18n.

13.2.1 The basics

To use GWT's approach to i18n, you must inherit the GWT I18N module in your application's module file:

```
<inherits name='com.google.gwt.i18n.I18N'/>
```

This module defines a `locale` property that you need to extend with the locales to be available (we cover locales in the next section). For example, to add the American and British English locales to the French locale, you write

```
<extend-property name='locale' values='en_US, en_GB, fr'/>
```

You can add as many locales in one definition as you need, or add additional tags. You should also define a locale that will be used as a fallback, to be used if GWT can't determine the locale. If you don't define a locale, then GWT will use its own `default` value. But that can have unexpected results (particularly with L10n). Let's pick French as our fallback:

```
<set-property-fallback name='locale' value='fr'/>
```

In your Java code you'll provide interface(s) that extend one of `Constants`, `ConstantsWithLookup`, or `Messages`. There will be a method declaration (accessor method) for each key you'll use. Let's take `Constants` for a quick example, with `Hello` and `Farewell` methods:

```
public interface HelloWorldConstants extends Constants{
    public String Hello();
    public String Farewell();
}
```

These method names are expected to match keys in one or more properties files you now need to provide (although you'll see later that you can use annotations to give some flexibility).

> **NOTE** Which package should you use? GWT 2.5 saw the start of supporting i18n on the server side as well as in client code. For this reason, some types are duplicated in `client` and `server` packages (such as `Messages`), and some are now in the `shared` package (a deprecated version, annotated to suppress the deprecation so it's not visible in your IDE, is in the `client` package, for example, `Localizable`). Be careful to use the relevant package, or be aware if you're using the deprecated versions that they may disappear in the future.

Properties files will go in the same package as your interface definition and will contain key/value pairs in the format of a standard Java properties file.

These properties files follow a strict naming convention. First, there's a file that has the same name as the interface that contains values that will be used if not provided in other files—think of this as the default file. For our simple example, it would be called HelloWorldConstants.properties and could be defined with the following content:

```
Hello = Hi
Farewell = Bye
```

It's possible to skip providing this default file by defining the values via annotations in the interface. We'll cover that when we look at the interfaces themselves shortly.

Other locale properties files are named the same interface name but with the appropriate language tag appended to the name; for example, the American English locale properties file would be called HelloWorldConstants_en_US.properties and a British English one HelloWorldConstants_en_GB.properties. If there were values common to both American and British English, they could be defined once in a file called HelloWorldConstants_en.properties. GWT knows to look through a locale hierarchy to find values, ending up at the default locale as a last resort.

Because we defined a fallback locale previously, to be used if GWT can't determine what locale the user wants, we must provide at least that properties file. The locale was `fr`, so the filename will be HelloWorldConstants_fr.properties and could have these contents:

```
Hello = Bonjour
Farewell = Au revoir
```

Notice that the key stays the same, because it's meant to match the method name in the interface, but the value is now in French.

Beware when using some characters

Some characters are treated specially and need to be backslash escaped to be used; for example, the double quote " should be written \". The same is true for commas. See http://mng.bz/ONVB for more.

If your locale uses a single quote, for example as in the French word *l'heure*, you must use two single quotes together, '', to represent it and avoid an unmatched quote error from the GWT compiler, that is, use *l''heure*.

In our application code we create an object of the interface type using the `GWT.create` deferred binding method, for example:

```
HelloWorldConstants constants = GWT.create(HelloWorldConstants.class);
```

We can then get the necessary values by calling the relevant method name, for example:

```
String helloText = constants.Hello();
```

That's the basics of static i18n; now it's time to look at the details. As we said, everything is driven by the `Localizable` interface, which is therefore a good place to start.

13.2.2 The Localizable interface

Any class or interface that extends the `Localizable` interface, and is instantiated using the `GWT.create` method, will be processed by the GWT compiler through a generator in the i18n package called `LocalizableGenerator. Constants` and `Messages` are two such interfaces.

The `LocalizableGenerator` generator takes the source interface along with the locale related to the current permutation under compilation and produces a locale-specific class that's then passed to the compilation. In this way, appropriate values in relevant properties files or other `Localizable` resources are bound to classes that are then used in the compilation of your application. The locales that are used in the determination of permutations are precisely those that are defined in your GWT module file's `extend-property` definition for the `locale` property.

Let's walk through this with a simple example. If the `LocalizableGenerator` generator is passed a class, `X.class`, and locale, `y_z`, then it will try to match each method

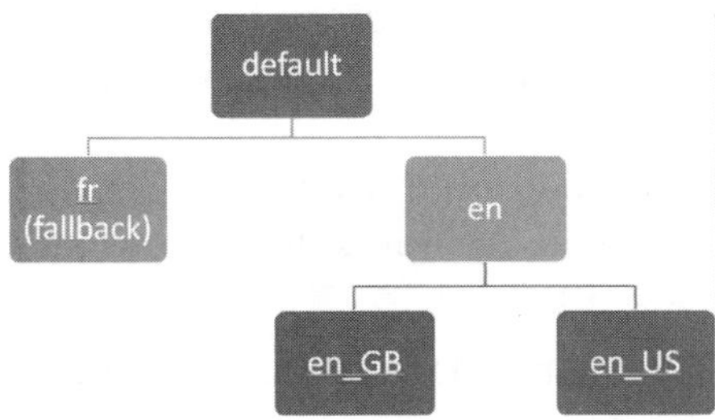

Figure 13.7 Overview of locale hierarchy: default locale, locales with only the language component of the language tag, locales with the language and region components of the language tag

in `X` against keys in the file called X_y_z.properties. If it doesn't find a match, then it will look for the key in the file X_y.properties; if not there, it falls back to default values provided either in a default properties file or as annotations to the interface method names.

Figure 13.7 shows how this hierarchy of locales might look for some of the locales we used in our earlier example.

Let's say the current permutation under compilation is for locale `en_GB` and source file X.class has a method `welcomeBack`. If there's no `welcomeBack` key in the X_en_GB.properties file, the generator will look in the X_en.properties file, if it exists, and if not there, it will look in the X.properties file or any default annotation on the interface method (throwing an error if then not found).

It's important to note that although the French locale is indicated as the fallback locale in our little example, this means it's used if GWT can't determine what locale to present to the user. It's not used in the binding discovery process to provide values for unfound keys (except in its own hierarchy).

We've mentioned the default properties file a couple of time now, and yes, you can create it yourself, but it's often clearer or better to annotate the interface methods with default values. In the next section we'll look at how to do that annotation, as well as a couple of other annotations that are available.

13.2.3 Localizable annotations

A number of useful annotations are provided in the `LocalizableResource` interface, which extends the basic `Localizable` interface and is itself extended by `Constants` and `Messages`. Three of these annotations could be applied to the accessor methods, for example:

```
@Key("TheColdWetBit")
@Meaning("The magnetic pole")
@Description("Co-ordinates of North Pole in WGS84 co-ordinate")
public String northPole();
```

Let's take each annotation in turn and see what they mean.

ANNOTATION: @KEY

Normally the generator will try to match the method name to key values in properties files. Using the `@Key` annotation, you can direct the generator to look for a different key name.

In the previous example, the generator would normally look for `northPole` as the key, but the `@Key("TheColdWetBit")` annotation changes that to look for `TheColdWetBit`.

You'll find this useful if your properties files use, for example, legacy taxonomy and you want to provide more meaningful names in your code.

ANNOTATION: @MEANING

If you intend for someone else to provide translations for you, you'll find the `@Meaning` annotation useful. Here you can provide a particular meaning of a key, which will be required if you have several different meanings.

Because the phrase "north pole" could refer to one of several different locations, we use this annotation in the example to indicate we're talking about the magnetic north pole (as opposed to the geographic north pole).

ANNOTATION: @DESCRIPTION

Use the `@Description` annotation on an accessor method to provide a textual description of the key or value.

You can also apply a few annotations to the interface/class definition: `@DefaultLocale`, `@Generate`, `@GenerateFrom`, and `@GenerateKeys`. We'll cover those a little more in the section on UiBinder and i18n.

We don't use `Localizable` or `LocalizableResource` directly; rather we extend one of `Constants`, `ConstantsWithLookup`, or `Messages`. These are where you'd keep constants and messages—which we'll soon define—and they also provide some additional annotations that help you. We'll continue our journey by looking at these three interfaces, beginning with `Constants`.

13.2.4 Internationalizing constants

In GWT, an i18n constant is a constant value that can be of the following types:

- Simple types: `String`, `int`, `float`, `boolean`, `double`
- Complex types: `String[]`, `Map` (strictly `Map<String, String>`)

Extending the `Constants` interface indicates that the accessor methods defined in the interface will return a constant value, of one of these types.

In the chapter's static i18n example, we've defined the following interface to provide information shown on the screen:

```
public interface CountryDetails extends Constants{

    @DefaultStringValue ("mph")
    public String speedUnits();

    @DefaultIntValue (60)
    public int speedLimit();

    @DefaultFloatValue (50000)
    public float averageSalary();
}
```

This would have a corresponding set of property files defining the keys/values, for example:

```
speedUnits = km/h
speedLimit = 120
averageSalary = 50000
```

As we mentioned, constants come in two types: simple and complex.

SIMPLE CONSTANTS

For constants of type `String`, `int`, `float`, `boolean`, and `double`, the GWT compiler will perform some type checking between the constant values and accessor method definition.

COMPLEX CONSTANTS

`String`, `Arrays`, and `Maps` are slightly more complicated, but not hugely so. If one of your properties files was to define

```
months = Jan, Feb, Mar, Apr, May, Jun, Jul, Aug, Sep, Oct, Nov, Dec
```

then defining `String[] months()` in the interface would allow you to write `constants.months[0]` in your code (which would return `"Jan"`).

Maps require a little more work. First, you define the keys/values in the properties file, for example:

```
Q1End = Mar
Q2End = Jun
Q3End = Sep
Q4End = Dec
```

Then you define your mapping key/value using those keys. If you want a mapping of quarter ends, you could write

```
QtrEnds = Q1End, Q2End, Q3End, Q4End
```

Back in your interface file, you'd create the following accessor method:

```
Map<String, String> QtrEnds();
```

From the `Constants` interface you can use a number of annotations to provide default values for the accessor methods.

ANNOTATION: @DEFAULT*XXXX*VALUE

You can use one of several annotations provided in the `Constants` interface to define default values for constants, rather than writing a default properties file. This is useful because it keeps the original definition together in one place.

For constants, GWT defines the following annotations for simple types: `@DefaultIntValue`, `@DefaultBooleanValue`, `@DefaultFloatValue`, `@DefaultDoubleValue`, and `@DefaultStringValue`. In the example introducing this section, you can see some of those in use.

When it comes to the two complex constants, you use @DefaultStringArrayValue, as follows:

```
@DefaultStringArrayValue({"Jan", "Feb", "Mar", "Apr"})
public String[] months();
```

Note the use of the curly brackets to surround the data.

For the string map, you can use @DefaultStringMapValue:

```
@DefaultStringMapValue ({"Q1End", "Mar", "Q2End", "Jun"})
public Map<String, String> QtrEnds();
```

This maps Q1End to Mar and Q2End to Jun in the default locale.

As we mentioned earlier in this chapter, one of the big benefits of using static i18n is that the compiler will remove any strings that aren't used when it produces the output. In the rare occasion when you don't want this to happen, you can use the ConstantsWithLookup interface instead.

13.2.5 Constants with lookup

Extending the ConstantsWithLookup interface instead of Constants will prevent the GWT compiler from pruning any unused constants. You can still access constants as you would with the Constants approach, but you also have a number of methods such as getString and getBoolean that return values based on the method names provided as a parameter. If GWT can't provide the value, then it will do so through a MissingResourceException, which you should handle.

We haven't used this approach in our examples because we prefer to let the compiler prune as much away as possible.

Constants are good, and we've shown how they can be used. Sometimes, though, they aren't enough—what happens if you want to have a more variable piece of text? You might want to write "The current locale is *<locale_name>*" and substitute *<locale_name>* with some text you only know at runtime. To do that, you use Messages.

13.2.6 Messaging the user

Messages are those strings of texts that are inserted at runtime into placeholders. To use them, you extend the Messages interface and provide the required methods. The differences from constants are as follows:

- The messages in properties files will contain zero or more placeholders.
- The methods in the interface will have zero or more parameters.

Typically, the number of placeholders in a message will match the number of parameters in the corresponding method. It's not allowed to have more placeholders than parameters, though there may be more parameters than placeholders.

Our chapter example defines most of our messages in the ExampleMessages interface, a snippet of which is

```
public interface ExampleMessages extends Messages{
   public String locale(String locale);
}
```

Here we have one message that takes a `String` parameter. The text of the message in a properties file would be

```
locale = The current locale is: {0}
```

Just like constants, we have the key followed by a value. This time, though, the value includes a placeholder, `{0}`. At runtime GWT will put the parameter value in the method call into the placeholder position and display the complete message.

If you have more parameters than one, then you'll require additional placeholders. For example, if you have two parameters, your message in a properties file will be

```
accessorName = {0} are bigger than {1}
```

In these two examples, the parameter passed in is directly inserted into the message template without any formatting. You can easily control that.

MESSAGE PARAMETER FORMAT

Because the message used in GWT i18N follows the Java `MessageFormat` object, you can provide further formatting information. The parameter can be written in one of the following three ways:

```
{argument index}
{argument index, format type}
{argument index, format type, format style}
```

The `argument index` is the parameter number, such as 0, 1, or 2. If you use the `format type`, then it can be one of `number`, `date`, `time`, or `choice` or a GWT special: `list`.

When using a `format type`, you can also provide a `format style`. The Java documentation gives the complete definition of what can be combined with what,[6] but as an example, you could say the parameter `0` should be formatted as a full date by writing

```
{0,date,full}
```

This also means the parameter in the method declaration must also have type `java.util.Date`.

There might be occasions when you have more parameters than you might use in a message (more often some locales will use all parameters and others not). In that case, you need to annotate the parameter(s) that might not be used.

ANNOTATION: @OPTIONAL

The compiler will complain when it comes across the situation where not all parameters are used in any message in the locale hierarchy. To overcome that, you must mark the potentially unused parameter(s) with the `@Optional` annotation.

Let's say we have the following accessor method

```
public String property(String propName,
                       @Optional String size,
                       String propValue);
```

---

6 See http://mng.bz/SS3Q.

where at least one property message won't use the `size` parameter, for example:

```
something = Property {0} has value {2}
```

Because we've marked the parameter that would have gone into placeholder `{1}` as `@Optional`, we won't have a problem during compilation.

Just as with constants, you can define a value for the message in the default locale using an annotation in the interface file.

ANNOTATION: @DEFAULTMESSAGE

Using the `@DefaultMessage` annotation on the accessor method in the interface file allows you to specify the message in the default locale without having to put it in a separate properties file:

```
@DefaultMessage("The current locale is: {0}")
public String locale(String locale);
```

There can be only one default message per accessor method, but you'll see later that you can provide alternate messages for certain situations.

HANDLING LISTS OF VALUES

GWT can also handle lists of values—passed in either as an array or a `java.util.List` object. Maybe you want to pass in a list of people who are logged into the system. You could define

```
@DefaultMessage("These people are logged in: {0,list}")
public String lists(List<String> elements);
```

The `{0,list}` in the default message is saying that parameter `0` is a list and should be displayed as text (remember, we spoke earlier about formats for the parameter). If you call it as

```
Window.alert(msgs.lists(Arrays.asList("Adam", "Anna", "Jason", "Rob")))
```

then you'll see the alert box shown in figure 13.8, in which GWT is displaying the alert message in English.

You can add further qualifiers; for example, a list of numbers could be defined as `{0,list, number}` in the annotation.

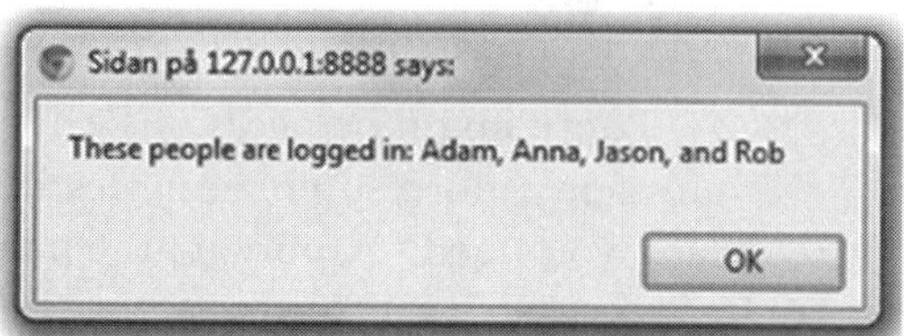

Figure 13.8 Displaying a list of items in a message

> **Note on message parameter qualifiers**
>
> These extra qualifiers aren't required to be used, and you'll see that most of our examples in this chapter don't use them, and there's no ill effect.
>
> But for lists, if you don't include the `list` qualifier on the `message` parameter, then GWT automatically assumes you mean the length—so you'll see a number displayed instead of your list.

A problem with messages is that the text might need to change depending on the value of the parameter passed in. The most common example of that is when dealing with pluralization.

13.2.7 Dealing with plurals

In most languages, the text used for singular and plural messages is different. For example, in English you'd say, "There is 1 *person* using the site," but if you have more than one user, say five, you'd say, "There are 5 *people* using the site" (the same construct is used for 0 users). English uses different forms for 1 and more than one (with 0 treated as plural).

Other languages have different patterns—Japanese has no plural forms, whereas Slovakian has different plural forms for 1, 2, 3, 4, and more than 4.

GWT static i18n has built-in support for this, and we show it working in our chapter example. Let's take a message we've defined in our static example in the `ExampleMessages` interface:

```
@DefaultMessage("There are {0} other people reading this page")
public String currentReaders(int numberReaders);
```

This will display a number of other people reading this application (in our example we use a made-up number of readers that we can change at the bottom of the interface). To make this handle plural text, we make two changes to the interface file and one to any properties file that we also wish to implement plurals.

In the interface file we'll introduce the annotations `@PluralCount` and `@AlternateMessage`.

ANNOTATION: @PLURALCOUNT

We need to tell GWT which parameter is indicating the plurality of the message. We do that by annotating the parameter with @`PluralCount`:

```
public String currentReaders(@PluralCount int numberReaders);
```

Next, we need to provide the alternate message(s) for plural forms.

ANNOTATION: @ALTERNATEMESSAGE

In English we need to distinguish between when `numberReaders` is 1 and other values. We have a default message defined:

```
@DefaultMessage("There are {0} other people reading this page")
```

And that fits well for plurality of 0 or more than 1. When `numberReaders` is 1, we want to use an alternative message that has the correct agreement of verb and subject ("is" and "person"). We provide that message in an `@AlternateMessage` annotation that takes a value plus the alternate message:

```
@AlternateMessage({"one", "There is {0} other person reading this page"})
```

The value `one` used in the alternate message is a predefined constant. In locales where you have to deal with other combinations, you can use one or more of these pluralization constants: none, one, two, few, or paucal (the count ends in 2 or 4 but is not 12, 14, 22, or 24). You can also use other, which maps to the default message.

If the language you're using needs additional alternate messages, then you include them in the one annotation, that is, {"one", "message for one", "two", "message for two"} and so on.

You can check out the types of rules that are allowed by looking at the classes in the com.google.gwt.i18n.client.impl.plurals package.

For example, the DefaultRule_fr class tells us "Plural forms for French are 1 and n, with 0 treated as singular." Because we're providing French as a locale, we have to capture that in the MessagesExample_fr properties file. We do that as follows:

```
currentReaders = Il y a {0} personnes qui lisent cette page
currentReaders[one] = Il y a {0} personne qui lit cette page
```

Providing the alternate messages in a properties file is just a case of appending the pluralization constant to the key.

But beware: if you try to use a plural count that doesn't exist in the language, for example, none in English, then you'll be shown a warning in development mode, and the default message will be used. You can get around this by using "exact" values.

EXACT VALUES IN PLURALIZATION

If you can't use plural counts that don't exist in a locale, say none in English, then how can you change a message from "there are 0 users reading this page" to the easier-to-read "there are no users reading this page"? You use exact counts:

```
@DefaultMessage("There are {0} other people reading this page")
@AlternateMessage({"one", "There is {0} other user reading this page",
                   "=0", "There are no other users reading this page"})
public String currentReaders(@PluralCount int numberReaders);
```

You've just seen the first part of this definition; what's new is the alternate message with key "=0". Now when the plural count argument is zero, the appropriate message is shown.

There's another trick you can play with alternate messages, and that's to harness the underlying approach to pluralization to your own advantage.

13.2.8 Selecting an alternate message based on a user-defined value

In our static i18n example we pretend that a user is logged in and that we know their gender. If they're the only user reading the page, then we want to display messages such as "she likes..." or "he likes...."

The following listing contains the code used in this chapter's static i18n example to do that.

Listing 13.1 User-defined selection of alternate messages within static i18n

```
enum Gender {MALE, FEMALE}
@DefaultMessage("The readers like reading their pages")
```

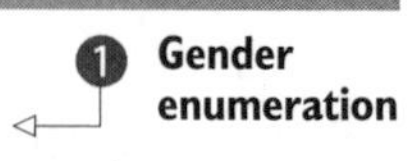

```
@AlternateMessage({"one|MALE", "{0} likes reading his pages",
                   "one|FEMALE", "{0} likes reading her pages"})
public String likesReading(@Optional String name,
                           @Optional @PluralCount int num,
                           @Optional @Select Gender gen);
```

❸ Alternate message

❹ Driving the selection

The pattern should look familiar now—a default message is given for multiple readers ❷, and then two alternate messages are given ❸. The new bit is the selection criteria in the alternate messages and the annotation `@Select` ❹ on the parameter.

ANNOTATION: @SELECT

This annotation indicates to GWT that the parameter should be used in selecting the default message or one of the alternate messages. It needs to be an enumeration, in our case defined in ❶ of listing 13.1 (we've simplified this here compared to the real code).

We've marked all the parameters as `@Optional` because none appear in the default message and only one in the alternate message.

With the parameter annotated with `@Select`, we can use it in the alternate message values. We made the example a little more complicated than necessary because we wanted to show how to combine selection criteria. In this case our alternate messages are selected only if the plural count is 1, and which of the two alternate messages is picked depends on the value of the `Gender` parameter.

One risk with messages occurs if you're going to use something the user has typed in as one of the parameters. If so, you need to think about securing yourself against hack attacks.

13.2.9 Securing against hack attacks

If you're worried about potential hacking attacks through i18n—and who wouldn't be?—then you can start securing your `Strings` by returning `SafeHtml` objects instead of standard `String`. For example, if you define

```
@DefaultMessage("<b>{0}</b>")
public String hackAttackString(String code);
```

with the intention of getting user input and displaying it in bold on the screen using a HTML panel

```
TextBox input = new TextBox()
:
HTMLPanel test = new HTMLPanel(msgs.hackAttackString(input.getText()));
```

then it all looks quite innocent so far. But what if the user types the following in the text box?

```
<img src=\"gwtia_ch13_i18n/clear.cache.gif\"
     onload=\"window.alert('You've been attacked');\">
```

Then you'll get attacked, as shown in figure 13.9. (You can simulate this in the running example by clicking the Use String button in the attack test section.)

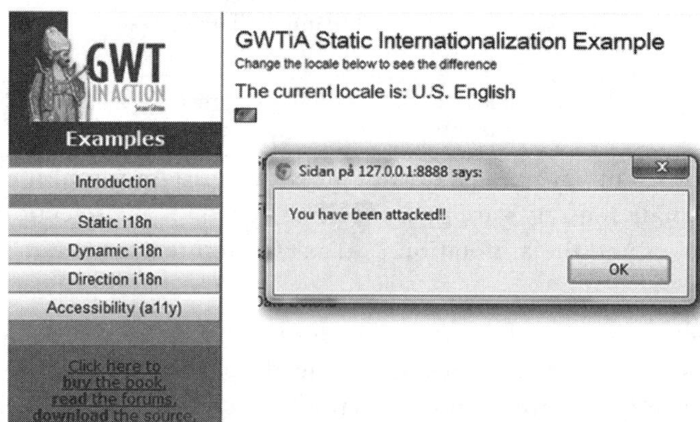

Figure 13.9 A hacking attack through an i18N message—this can happen because we're returning a `String` for the message and then putting that `String` directly into an `HTMLPanel`.

Naturally, a true attacker's code would be more malicious than just popping up a window. You can protect yourself by making a simple change to the message definition and returning a `SafeHtml` object instead of a `String`:

```
@DefaultMessage("<b>{0}</b>")
public SafeHtml hackAttackSafeHTML(String code);
```

Now you just get a simple text and no action in the application; as shown in figure 13.10, we've neutralized this attack.

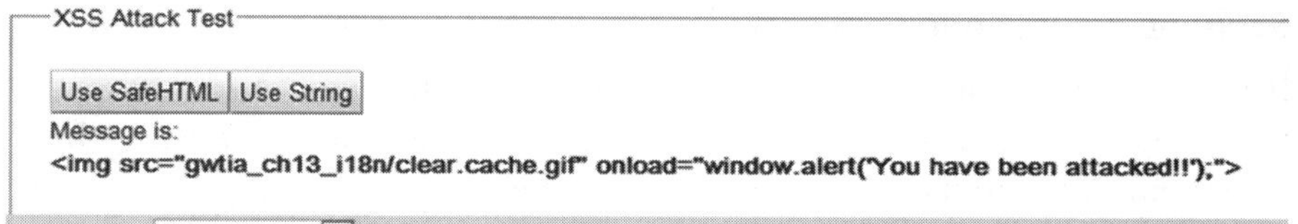

Figure 13.10 Using `SafeHtml` is a way of neutralizing the potential XSS attack shown in figure 13.9. Now the message is sanitized and can no longer execute.

If you already have a properties file, then you can generate the Java interfaces using the i18nCreator script that comes with GWT,[7] though it can be easier to hand-code it yourself.

Wow, that's been quite a hike through some functionality—and if you've been reading in one go up until now, it's probably time for a `@DefaultMessage("cup of tea")`. After that, we look at how to use static i18n in our preferred manner of building user interfaces with UiBinder.

13.3 Using static-string i18n with UiBinder

UiBinder allows you to define string constants and messages in the UI declaration. The approach is quite simple but with some gotchas along the way.

---

7 i18nCreator tool: http://mng.bz/2br7.

Let's look at how to use string constants in UiBinder, which are messages with no parameters, and after that, we'll discuss what changes to make for using messages with parameters.

13.3.1 Constants with UiBinder

Our example's UiBinder declaration, StaticExample.ui.xml, has a label

```
<g:Label>GWTiA Static Internationalization Example</g:Label>
```

to which we'd like to apply i18n techniques.

We need to make one small change to the definition: wrap the text we wish to be translated with a <ui:msg> tag, so it becomes

```
<g:Label>
   <ui:msg>
      GWTiA Static Internationalization Example
   </ui:msg>
</g:Label>
```

We also want GWT to treat the text in our declaration as the default text and create the relevant default properties file for us (we need it to do that because it needs to generate the keys to keep things consistent). The following listing shows the attributes we need to add to our declaration to get this done.

Listing 13.2 ui:UiBinder tag attributes that drive default messages file generation

```
<ui:UiBinder xmlns:ui='urn:ui:com.google.gwt.uibinder'
  ui:generateFormat='com.google.gwt.i18n.rebind.format.PropertiesFormat'    <- File format
  ui:generateKeys="com.google.gwt.i18n.rebind.keygen.MD5KeyGenerator"       <- Key generation
  ui:generateLocales="default"                                              <- (1) Produce default file
   xmlns:g="urn:import:com.google.gwt.user.client.ui">
```

(1) tells UiBinder to generate the default locale for you using values wrapped by <ui:msg> in the declaration. The other two attributes you don't need to know much more about, apart from saying that they tell GWT to create the default locale file in the properties format and to use an MD5 algorithm to create the file.

The first time you run or compile the application, GWT will create the default locale file. Unfortunately, it also hides the file!

To find it, you need to provide the `extra` flag to the compiler and indicate a directory to store it in. We recommend defining a directory, such as extras or tmp, in your existing project. For this chapter's example, we called it extras and set it up in the arguments section of the run configuration (providing the full path, for example, C:\...\workspace\gwtia-ch10-i18n/extras).

After running development mode or compiling for the first time—and refreshing the project in Eclipse—the project structure looks like figure 13.11.

That long filename you see in figure 13.9's extras/gwtia_ch13_i18n folder is the automatically created default properties file. If you look in that file, you'll see that it has generated a key and mapped it to the text we surrounded with the <ui:msg> tag, for example:

```
4F8408CF782FAE2D0F51ACB1138EE91B=GWTiA Static Internationalization Example
```

gwtia-ch13-i18n
test
src
JRE System Library [jre6]
JUnit 4
GWT SDK [gwt2.4 - 2.4.0]
extras
gwtia_ch13_i18n
rpcPolicyManifest
com.manning.gwtia.ch13.client.i18nstatic.StaticExampleStaticExampleUiBinderImplGenMessages.properties
gen
gwt-unitCache
war

Figure 13.11 The generated properties file shown in the extras folder after providing the `extra` flag to the compiler

Keys are generated using the class indicated in listing 13.2; at the time of writing, the options are

- `MD5KeyGenerator`, as we indicated
- `MethodNameKeyGenerator`
- `FullyQualifiedMethodNameKeyGenerator`—any user-provided implementation of the `KeyGenerator` interface

In the non-UiBinder world, you can change the key-generation method using the `@GenerateKeys` annotation in a `LocalizableResource` interface file.

We're not quite finished yet. Although GWT has generated the default file for us, we need to provide the translations, and they must use the same key as the generated file.

The simplest approach is to copy the file from the extras folder into the package where the UiBinder template is; then you can rename it, appending the locale to the end of the copy. There's one subtle difference—you no longer need to keep the full qualified class name in the filename. Figure 13.12 shows some of the static i18n examples properties files, so you can see what we mean.

In figure 13.12 you can see the copied default properties file along with 12 locale-specific translations that have been created. Don't forget to set the encoding of the properties file to UTF-8 for things to work.

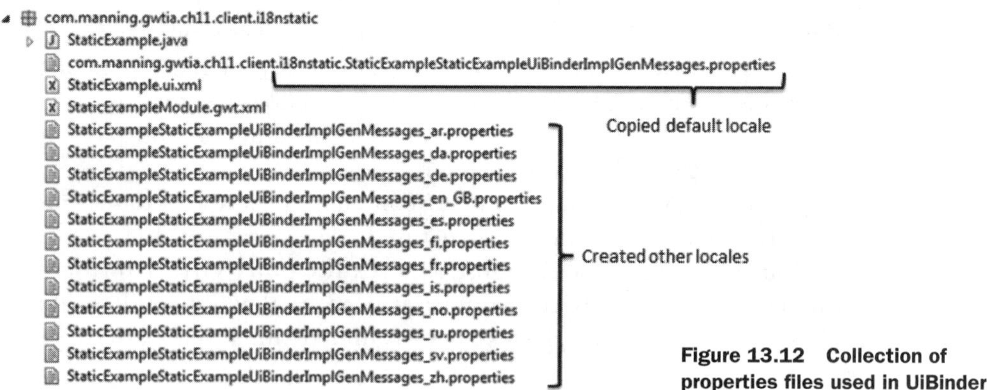

Figure 13.12 Collection of properties files used in UiBinder

Gotchas

If you add new `<ui:msg>` tags in UiBinder, then to provide translations you need to go into the generated file in the extras directory and copy the new key/value pairs to your other local files (they won't appear in the copy of the default file automatically).

If you change the text in an existing `<ui:msg>` tag and are using the MD5 key generation, then GWT will recalculate the key. This makes your existing translations useless until you copy the new key from the generated default file into your translation files.

As you can see, constants are relatively simple, and UiBinder treats them as messages with no parameters, but we have some tinkering to do: copying files and being aware if we change things. It's when we start adding parameters that things get a little more interesting.

13.3.2 Parameterized messages with UiBinder

Using parameterized messages with UiBinder requires us to rethink a little what we're doing, because we don't end up with an interface extending messages being created. That, together with the fact that our interface is declarative rather than programmatic, makes it hard to create messages such as `msgs.getAMessage(param1, param2)`.

Instead, we have to think about a parameterized message as a template in HTML. Our static i18n example prints a country's speed limit to the screen. Without i18n and parameters, we could write this in a label as follows:

```
<g:Label>Speed Limit: 30 km/h</g:Label>
```

If we want this to be an i18n message with the value and units as parameters, then we have to replace the label with HTML. The best approach is to use an `HTMLPanel`, wrap our message with the `<ui:msg>` tag to indicate it's translatable, and where we have parameters, put them in a uniquely identifiable `span` element. We'd rewrite the speed limit label as

```
<g:HTMLPanel>
   <ui:msg>
      Speed Limit: <span ui:field="speedLimit"></span>
   </ui:msg>
</g:HTMLPanel>
```

UiBinder will output something similar to the following in the default properties file:

```
EB905D17E7F6AF5EC999D62A4708EF93=Speed Limit\:{0}{1}
```

You might notice that it has inherited two placeholders instead of the one you might be expecting. Not to worry, these placeholders are internal to GWT's implementation and relate to the start and end tags of the `<span>` element. You can ignore them, but make sure you don't delete them!

Unlike messages outside the UiBinder approach, where you could call a method to generate the message with parameters, you need to set the content of the `ui:field` with values explicitly.

Because we've named the span using the attribute `ui:field="speedLimit"`, we can refer to it in our code (see the chapter on UiBinder if you need to follow what we're doing here):

```
@UiField SpanElement speedLimit;
```

Then we set the inner text of this span with the data we want—in this case, two values from a normal GWT `Constants` interface:

```
CountryDetails det = (CountryDetails)GWT.create(CountryDetails.class);
speedLimit.setInnerText(det.speedLimit()+" "+det.speedUnits());
```

We can also indicate within the UiBinder template properties such as the description and meaning. To do so, the attributes are added to the declaration; for example

```
<ui:msg description="value plus unit of speed limit"
        meaning="top speed limit in country">
    Speed Limit:
    <span ui:field="speedLimit">Ouch</span>
</ui:msg>
```

would result in the following definition in the default generated messages file:

```
# Description: value plus unit of speed limit
# Meaning: top speed limit in country
# 0=htmlElement1Begin (Example: <tag>), 1=htmlElement1End (Example: </tag>)
01A894D89AFE45B1D016FA068330579F=Speed Limit\: {0}Ouch{1}
```

Et voila. We're more than halfway through the chapter, and we've completed our look at the static approach. It's the preferred approach because it supports everything you've just seen and aggressively gets rid of extra unneeded stuff from the download, and we can be comfortable that the static analysis means we aren't missing anything (so no runtime errors).

We hope you agree that static i18n is an awesome approach, but we still have one problem we haven't solved—how to determine the locale!

13.4 Determining the locale for static-string internationalization

All the talk of constants and messages per locale is great, but without knowing what locale the user is requesting, you're not going to see a difference.

Locale determination is performed during the bootstrapping of the GWT application in the browser. Once the locale is determined, the appropriate locale-specific implementation is downloaded. The determination is performed by something called a *property provider*, which is a segment of JavaScript code defined either directly in a GWT module or by a property-provider generator referenced in a GWT module. For static i18n, it's the latter, defined in the I18N module that you inherit to use i18n.

Older versions of GWT had a fixed approach to locale determination that waterfalled through, looking in the URL for a parameter, then for a specific meta tag in the HTML file, then for a user-defined script, and finally determining the fallback locale if nothing else was determined.

From GWT 2.2, this has become much more flexible and dynamic!

13.4.1 Where to find the locale

From GWT 2.2 you can indicate which of several places GWT should look for the locale and in which order it should do that. There's the new ability to use the browser's headers to determine the locale, but the ability to use a user-defined script from earlier GWT versions is gone.

This increased flexibility is supported by five *configuration properties* that can be set in your module file. For now you just need to know that these pass information to the compiler (see chapter 18 if you want to know some more detail about configuration properties). Unlike GWT deferred-binding properties (see chapter 17), such as the `locale` property, they won't make the compiler create additional permutations of code. You set them by writing something like the following in your GWT module file:

```
<set-configuration-property name='property_name' value= 'property_value'/>
```

The first four configuration properties are shown in table 13.2 and relate to setting up the approaches that can be used to determine the locale.

Table 13.2 GWT configuration properties involved in determining the locale

Name	Default value	Description
`locale.queryparam`	`locale`	The query parameter name where the locale could be found in the URL. Its value defaults to `locale` for backward compatibility with older code, but if you wish to use a different value in your application, you'd set it using this configuration property.
`locale.cookie`	`<blank>`	New for GWT 2.2. You can check for the locale in a cookie, and this configuration property is used to identify the name of that cookie. By default it's blank and so is not effective in the determination of the locale.
`locale.useragent`	`N`	Also new for GWT 2.2. You can use the browser's headers to determine the locale. This functionality may or may not be useful. If you're sure that the locale of all users can be determined from headers, then this is great—but think of the case when you go abroad and try to use your application. Do you want your locale or that of where the browser was built shown first? By default this is set to `N` so that it isn't used.
`locale.usemeta`	`Y`	Indicates if GWT should look in the meta tags of the HTML page for a meta tag showing the locale. By default it's turned on for backward compatibility.

On top of the four configuration properties given in table 13.2, there's an additional configuration property: `locale.searchorder`. The value in this configuration property is an ordered list of which approach to use and in what order. Valid values are `queryparam`, `cookie`, `meta`, and `useragent`, and by default this is the order they're used in.

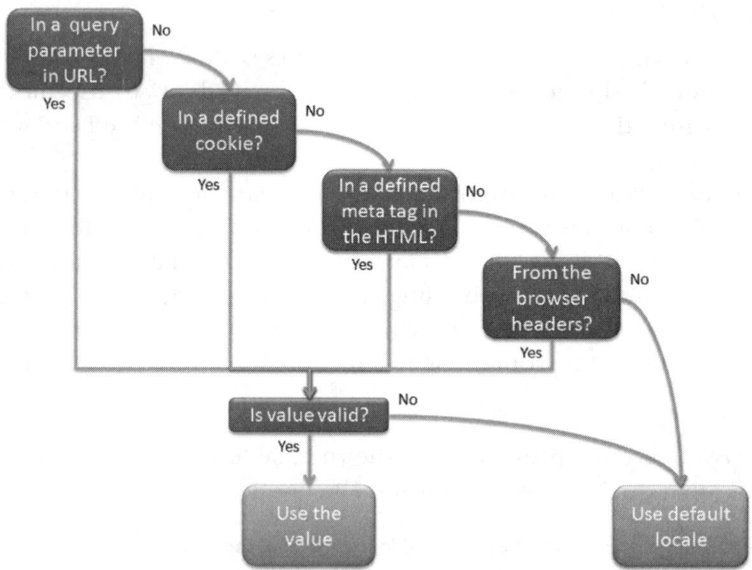

Figure 13.13 Waterfalling through the locale-determination algorithm

By default, GWT has defined the waterfall shown in figure 13.13. Let's say that you want to change this, so that GWT searches for the query parameter called `lang`, then a cookie also called `lang`, and finally at the browser's user agent but not the meta tag. You'd write the following in your application's module file:

```
<set-configuration-property name='locale.cookie' value= 'lang'/>
<set-configuration-property name='locale.useragent' value= 'Y'/>
<set-configuration-property name='locale.queryparam' value= 'lang'/>
<set-configuration-property name='locale.searchorder'
                           value= 'queryparam,cookie,useragent'/>
```

You must place your definitions after the inheriting of the I18N module because that's where these properties are defined.

In the next three sections, we'll look at how to set the locale so it's picked up by this property provider. We'll start at the top of the waterfall, looking for the locale in the URL.

13.4.2 Searching the URL

You can ask GWT to look in the URL for a specific query parameter and use the value there as the locale. By default that query parameter is called `locale`, and so, for example, the Swedish locale, `sv`, would be represented as

```
http://www.gwtinaction.com/MyApp.html?locale=sv
```

Setting the locale in the URL makes it simple to change the locale through the user interface. The most common way is to present the user a series of flags they can click; each will be a link to your application with a different value for the `locale` parameter.

You might wish to create that link dynamically so you preserve any other parameters and information. One such way is to use an `UrlBuilder` object to update the parameter name and then reload the page:

```
void changeLocale(String localeParamName, String newLocale) {
   UrlBuilder newUrl = Window.Location.createUrlBuilder();
   newUrl.setParameter(localeParamName, newLocale);
   Window.Location.assign(newUrl.buildString());
}
```

Alternatively, as we do in our chapter example, you can present all the available locales and let the user select, as shown next.

Listing 13.3 Changing locale through the URL

```
final ListBox locales = new ListBox(true);
for (String localeName : LocaleInfo.getAvailableLocaleNames()) {
   locales.addItem(
        LocaleInfo.getLocaleNativeDisplayName(localeName));
}
locales.addChangeHandler(new ChangeHandler(){
   public void onChange(ChangeEvent event) {
      locales.getItemText(locales.getSelectedIndex());
      String[] ls = LocaleInfo.getAvailableLocaleNames();
      String newLocale = ls[locales.getSelectedIndex()];
      changeLocale("locale", newLocale);
   }
});
```

❶ Build list of locales

❷ Change locale

You get a list, in ❶, of all the locales used when extending the `locale` property using the `LocaleInfo.getAvailableLocaleNames` method. It's also possible to get a text description of the locale using the `LocaleInfo.getLocaleNativeDisplayName` method, so that you can display the more useful British English text instead of `en_GB` to the user.

> **TIP** Need to know the current locale? GWT provides the `LocaleInfo` object that can be used to programmatically find information about the current locale, the available locales, and readable names for the locales.

When the user selects a new locale, you determine which one was selected in ❷ and then call the previously defined `changeLocale` method.

That's it for the query parameter, but you might want to find the locale in a cookie.

13.4.3 Digesting a cookie

Locale can be found from a cookie, if it exists. If you add the following to your GWT module file

```
<set-configuration-property name='locale.cookie' value= 'lang'/>
```

then GWT bootstrapping will look for the cookie named `lang` (assuming it hasn't found the locale using a previous method).

Using a cookie is less transparent to the user, and some users block cookies for security reasons. But it does have the advantage of not cluttering up your web address (with the disadvantage that sharing the URL won't keep the locale choice).

It's easy to set a cookie in GWT; you use the `setCookie` method from the `com.google.gwt.user.client.Cookies` package. For example, to set the cookie with name `lang` to have value `sv` you write

```
Cookies.setCookie("lang", "sv");
```

You'll need to refresh the page to see any changes as a result of setting a cookie. You might also want to use the `setCookie` methods that add an expiration date or domain for security reasons rather than the simple version we've just used.

Next, we'll look at the two approaches that are somewhat less dynamic—using the meta tag and the browser's headers.

13.4.4 Finding a HTML meta tag

Setting the locale in a meta tag in the HTML page is a more hardcoded approach than the previous URL way. Writing a meta tag in the header of the HTML page takes care of this, as follows:

```
<meta name="gwt:property" content="locale=fi">
```

Here we're saying to set the locale as Finnish.

If you use an HTML page, then this is a static approach. But if you change your HTML page to a more dynamic JSP page or something similar, you could set the meta tag dynamically on the server. But perhaps the approach in the next section is what you want if you're thinking of doing this.

13.4.5 Letting the browser decide

An alternative approach, supported from GWT 2.2, is to select the locale based on the value the browser indicates. This can be a useful approach, and it gives the user the "right" locale from the first download (rather than them downloading the default locale and then having to download another locale once they've selected it).

But it can also be a negative experience. Say you're American and log into the application from Finland using a browser on a Finnish machine. Will you appreciate seeing the interface first in Finnish?

Using this approach is a design decision you'll need to make, based on your needs and analysis. To enable it, enter the following into your module file:

```
<set-configuration-property name="locale.useragent" value="Y"/>
```

Now you know how to use static i18n and how GWT determines which locale to display. Before we leave the topic and move on to dynamic i18n, we have one last trick to look at. GWT can use the i18n approach within client bundles.

13.5 Internationalizing client bundles through static internationalization

Back in chapter 5, we looked at the great things you can do with client bundles and how they reduce the number of round-trips to servers. We can now further reveal that because they implement the `Localizable` interface, you can easily harness the i18n approach. This allows you to create and manage resource bundles specific to locales.

In our static i18n example, we show this in action to create a client bundle holding a flag broadly representing the locale. Although we don't get any great advantages with just one image, it's easy to envisage this approach extending to cover other resources such as documents and other locale-specific images.

We start off by creating a `ClientBundle` as you saw in chapter 5:

```
public interface LocaleFlags extends ClientBundle{
    @Source("flag.gif")
    public ImageResource getLocaleFlag();
}
```

For the sake of convenience, we've annotated the `getLocalFlag` method so that it maps to a more sensibly named flag.gif, rather than the getLocalFlag.gif file.

You use it as you would any client bundle:

```
LocaleFlags flags = (LocaleFlags)GWT.create(LocaleFlags.class);
Image flag = new Image(flags.getLocaleFlag());
```

Up to this point there's no difference at all from what you've seen before. You saw in chapter 5 what goes on in the background for the client bundle when GWT assimilates the resources for you.

But if you've inherited the I18N module, then when the client bundle is put together, GWT looks for resource filenames in a way similar to properties files. That is to say, if GWT is compiling the `en_GB` locale, it will first look for flag_en_GB-gif; then if that's not found, it will look for flag_en.gif, and if that's not found, it will use flag.gif.

We use this functionality in our chapter's static i18n example to display the most appropriate flag for the locale, as in figure 13.14.

The current locale is: British English

Figure 13.14 Flags provided by the localized client bundle

OK, that truly is it for static i18n. You've seen that static i18n is a useful technique with all the optimizations and runtime protection. But sometimes it makes sense to not have these and to use the dynamic approach to i18n, which is what we look at next.

13.6 Dynamic string internationalization

Outside the world of GWT, it's common to provide i18n translations as JavaScript objects that are used either on the server side or in the client. If you're incrementally building a GWT application, or even sharing i18n files with other applications, you might already have these assets that you want to reuse.

This is where GWT's dynamic i18n approach comes in. You load translations into the application as JavaScript objects and access them via GWT's `Dictionary` class.

What you lose is access to the compiler stripping out unused data and confidence that there will be no missing data at runtime, and you have to build all of the support for pluralization and selection that you got for free in the static approach.

Let's peek at how to do this (together with discussing some ways around the drawbacks) and then see the impact of UiBinder for this approach.

13.6.1 The basics

To use GWT's `Dictionary` class, include the I18N module in your application:

```
<inherits name='com.google.gwt.i18n.I18N'/>
```

The i18n data needs to be provided as a JavaScript associative array, and it's typically included within the HTML file to ensure that it's available when your application asks for data. In our dynamic i18n chapter example, we have the following simple object holding the strings for the title and description in the application's HTML file:

```
<script>
var labels = {
    title : "GWTiA Dynamic String Internationalization Example",
    description : "Change locale below to see this text change"
};
</script>
```

Unsurprisingly, it shows up on the screen as in figure 13.15.

Figure 13.15 GWTiA Dynamic String i18n example as shown when it starts

Values are accessed by creating a `Dictionary` object

```
Dictionary theLabels = Dictionary.getDictionary("labels");
```

and retrieved using the `get` method:

```
theLabels.get("title");
```

But, because we have no static analysis, we need to guard against runtime errors such as missing values. The `get` method throws a `java.util.MissingResourceException` if a value is not found, so we can build the setting of a label into a Java `try` statement:

```
final String TITLE = "title";
String theTitle="";
try{
   theTitle = theLabels.get(TITLE);
} catch(MissingResourceException e){
   theTitle = "Missing Title";
} finally {
   titleWidget.setText(theTitle);
}
```

To support multiple locales, we've included an object per locale in the HTML file; for example, our Swedish locale is given as

```
var labels_sv = {
   title : "GWTiA Dynamisk String Internationalisering Exempel",
   details : "Ändra locale nedan för att se denna text förändring"
};
```

Changing locale is swift and requires no refresh. You create a `Dictionary` with the new JavaScript object you wish to take values from.

In our example, we provide JavaScript objects for our locales made from the variable name `labels` appended by locale—we're manually emulating the static i18n approach.

But you have to build your own code to determine the locale and then grab the correct JavaScript object. There's also no support for any locale hierarchy that you saw in the static approach. If a certain locale is missing a value, you can't look higher in a hierarchy; you have to display your default text. Try the French or Spanish locales in the dynamic example; each is missing one element of text (figure 13.16 shows the Spanish locale where the title is missing).

Missing Title
Cambiar configuración regional de abajo para ver este cambio de texto

Figure 13.16 The dynamic i18n example in the Spanish locale showing the result of missing data in the JavaScript object fed to the `Dictionary` class

That's all we need to cover on the dynamic approach: provide the JavaScript object, access it through a `Dictionary` object, and be careful of missing data at runtime. It has a number of restrictions, but you might be willing to, or have to, live with those, depending on the environment your application is in.

One other often-cited issue with the dynamic approach is that you have to send all of the strings to the browser for all locales and then determine what to use on the browser side. We'll cover some ways around that, as you'll see next.

13.6.2 Enhancing the standard approach

The main downsides to the dynamic approach are that the download size increases, slowing down application startup, and it doesn't hook into the GWT locale. Although we won't provide a code example in this section, you might wonder if you can minimize those restrictions.

For a start, if you use a JSP page (or your favorite server-side code) to create the application's HTML page, then you can insert a JavaScript object when the page is created that includes only one locale's data. You can retrieve that locale from the URL's parameter.

Alternatively, when changing the locale in the application, you could dynamically load the appropriate JavaScript object from the server, insert it into the current HTML page via DOM manipulation, and, when you're sure it's loaded, start using it. We can even imagine a mechanism that deals with not finding a key in the `en_GB` locale by dynamically loading the `en` JavaScript object and looking there.

Neither of these approaches gives you the safety of knowing a `String` will be available at runtime or the aggressive removal of extra code that the static approach provides, but they're alternatives you might want to explore if you have to use the dynamic approach.

There's one other little problem when considering the dynamic approach, and that's its use in UiBinder.

13.6.3 Using with UiBinder

Quite simply, you can't use the dynamic i18n approach with UiBinder inside a template. The best you can do is create a `Label` in the UI and then insert the text from the `Dictionary` into it in the code, similar to what we did in section 13.3.1.

We've covered the two GWT approaches to i18n, but we still need to consider two things to make the user feel absolutely comfortable: display things such as dates in a way they're familiar with, and make sure the text is written in the right direction.

In the next section, we'll move from i18n to L10n, which is all about localization (presenting dates, times, numbers, and currencies in the way a user expects).

13.7 Localization of dates, times, and currencies

If you've lived in only one locale, the idea that dates, numbers, and times might be written and read by users in a different way than you do might come as a surprise. But we've got plenty of examples. Start writing times as 4:15 P.M., and although it's understandable, most Europeans will have to take an extra brain cycle to realize you mean 16:15; whereas write 16:15, and most Americans will need that extra brain cycle to realize you mean 4:15 P.M. Similarly, is the date 8/2 the 8th of February or August 2? Or, would an English speaker understand that the number 50.000 000 presented in German is 50 million and not 50 to 6-decimal precision?

Although we can all cope with things written differently than what we expect, if we remove the need for those extra brain cycles our interfaces become much easier for the user. Localization, written L10n, is the technique you can use to address these different presentational aspects.

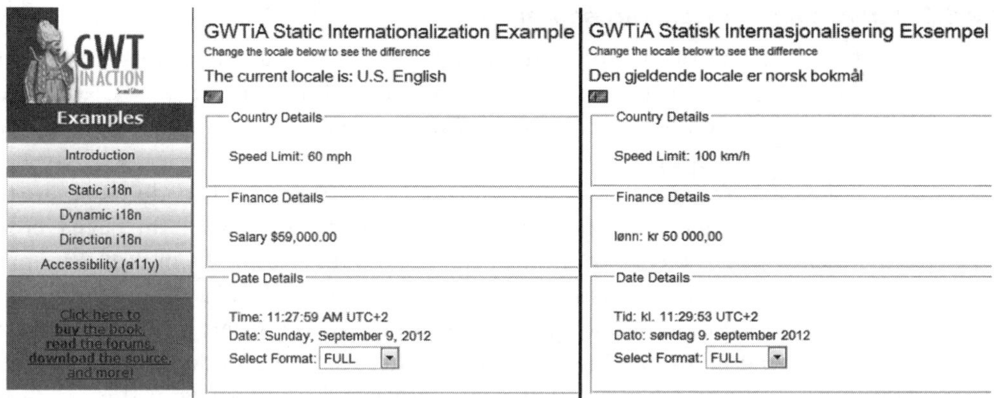

Figure 13.17 Differences of L10n applied to currency, time, and date fields in our chapter's example

Figure 13.17 shows how we've used L10n in our example.

We're using GWT's localization of numbers and currency to show salary details (notice that the number has different separators) and the time/date localization for the Date Details (12-hour versus 24-hour clock, and where the day number comes).

Setting up for localization is familiar if you've read the previous sections. You inherit the I18N module and then start using the various format classes we'll look through next.

13.7.1 Displaying numbers and currency values

`NumberFormat` is used in displaying the salary value. We write something similar to the following in our code:

```
NumberFormat fmt = NumberFormat.getCurrencyFormat();
String theSalary = fmt.format(50000);
```

`NumberFormat` selects the appropriate currency symbol to display for the current locale (it doesn't convert the value for us; GWT isn't that clever yet). It's not visible in figure 13.17 because it's the same for both locales, but `NumberFormat` also knows if the currency symbol is displayed before or after the number.

You can also get formatters for decimal, percent, and scientific from `NumberFormatter` and use them in a similar way.

Potential localization gotcha

What currency should the locale `es`, Spanish, have?

To a European, at least at the time of writing this edition, the answer is obvious: euros.

To someone on the American continent, like the Google team, set it to Argentinean dollars.

The point is, don't make assumptions about locale information based on your experience or expectations. To get euros for Spanish, you need to use the locale `es_ES`.

Let's look at time and date formats.

13.7.2 Displaying times and dates

You can display times and dates in a familiar manner similarly, but through the `DateTimeFormat` object. Four short formats for dates and times are also available in each locale by appending one of the following to the date or time: `FULL`, `LONG`, `MEDIUM`, or `SHORT`. You use it as follows:

```
Date today = new Date();
String theDate =
     DateTimeFormat.getFormat(PredefinedFormat.DATE_FULL).format(today);
String theTime =
     DateTimeFormat.getFormat(PredefinedFormat.TIME_SHORT).format(today);
```

Here is a quick example of the four date styles in American English:

- FULL: Sunday, October 24, 2010
- LONG: October 24, 2010
- MEDIUM: Oct 24, 2010
- SHORT: 10/24/10

The cool thing is that you don't need to know anything about how Swedish dates are written; GWT handles it all for you. The Swedish grammatical rules, which say that days and months are all in lowercase, and that specify the long/short names for a month, and that say short dates are written year-month-day, we let GWT worry about (and assume it's correct, or corrected by someone, because anyone can contribute to GWT).

The last thing we wish to cover in this chapter is how to display the user interface in the right direction for the locale.

13.8 Displaying the right direction

We're now using a specific user language and displaying times, dates, and numbers in the corresponding format familiar to that user. But we have one thing left to do, and that's to get our widgets displaying and reacting in the right direction.

We're sure text such as "etaD" and "timiL deepS" isn't so easy for you to read. You might spot that it's written backward and so read it with a little trouble, but if the entire interface was like this, you'd give up.

This isn't such an unusual situation, because some languages are written and read from right to left. If you've gone to the trouble to translate your interface, you should at least present it in the right direction.

GWT knows whether a locale is left to right (LTR) or right to left (RTL), and you can find that out using this method:

```
LocaleInfo.getCurrentLocale().isRTL();
```

You'd need to know this if you're building a widget such as our question/answer widget from chapter 4. You might remember that it showed a question and allowed an answer to be typed, such as shown in figure 13.18.

The Question | The Answer

Figure 13.18 Question and answer widget in left-to-right mode

You might build your widget without thinking about L10N and so would use a FlowPanel and add the question part as a Label first, followed by the answer part as a TextBox. If you're supporting a RTL language, that would be wrong because you'd be reading the answer before the question.

The widget would use the isRTL method to determine whether it adds the Label before the TextBox or the other way around, for example:

```
if(LocaleInfo.getCurrentLocale().isRTL()){
   add(textbox);
   add(label);
} else {
```

```
    add(label);
    add(textbox);
}
```

When you have a widget that supports keyboard navigation, you might also need to think how that works with direction. The Tree widget, for example, allows you to open and close branches using the left- and right-arrow keys. It has built-in support to know that in a LTR locale, the right arrow should open a branch, but in a RTL locale it's the left arrow that should do that.

On top of this, you need to set the direction of the Label and TextBox. Normally they'll inherit direction from the panels they're added to. But both implement the HasDirectionEstimator interface, so you can provide a DirectionEstimator for them. This means heuristics will be applied and the appropriate direction selected when used. If you write

```
theQuestion = new Label();
theQuestion.setDirectionEstimator(WordCountDirectionEstimator.get());
```

the direction will be determined by the direction of most of the words—because you've supplied a WordCountDirectionEstimator. This allows you, for example, to write a question using one foreign word. The direction selected will be based on your question language, ignoring the one foreign word (assuming you have more than two words in the question).

For the answer, you might allow a user to write in a language different than the question. If you want the direction to switch from LTR to RTL on typing the first RTL character, then you'd use an AnyRtlDirectionEstimator object:

```
theAnswer = new TextBox();
theAnswer.setDirectionEstimator(AnyRtlDirectionEstimator.get());
```

Typing an Arabic answer into the direction example in the LTR locale shows the result of this code—you can see it in figure 13.19.

The LTR locale in the figure is indicated by the message under the widget saying the Right-to-Left locale is false. But we've typed the Google Translates answer for "Hello" in Arabic. Because we added a direction estimator, that has resulted in the answer part of the widget being switched automatically to RTL mode.

In previous versions of GWT, you were able to set the direction of the text in a widget via setDirection methods. This is now deprecated in favor of the direction

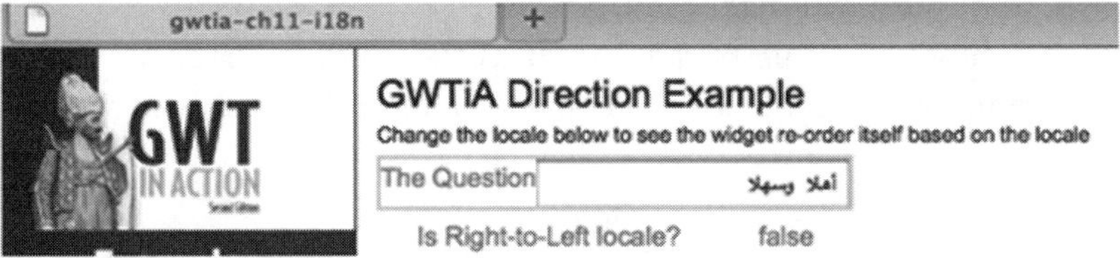

Figure 13.19 The direction example showing the question/answer widget in a LTR locale but with the answer in an RTL language. Notice how the answer is written RTL.

estimator approach just discussed. You can, though, provide a direction for the text when you use the setText method. If you write

```
Label myLabel = new Label();
myLabel.setText("Some text", Direction.LTR);
```

then you explicitly set the direction of the label to LTR (the other options are RTL and DEFAULT).

To quickly recap, you've now seen almost everything about making your application available to the widest possible audience. We've changed the language to a user's locale; we've presented numbers, dates, and times in a way they would instantly recognize; and we've had the text flowing in the correct direction. Next, we'll look at some tips on making your application accessible.

13.9 Accessibility

At this point we've looked at how to make the application available in a wide range of languages and dialects; how to present numbers, currencies, and time/dates is a way users will quickly understand; and how to make sure things flow and appear in the right direction.

All of this was focused on users who have no impairment when reading the web page. But that's not the case for everyone. In the following subsections, we'll consider what you can do to make your applications more accessible.

13.9.1 Using alternative text for images

Don't forget to provide alternative text for your images. Use the setAltText method programmatically:

```
Image myImg = new Image();
myImg.setAltText("description of Image");
```

Or use the altText attribute in the UiBinder approach:

```
<g:Image src="x.png" altText="description of image" />
```

You should also ensure that the way widgets get focus is correct when the user presses the Tab key.

13.9.2 Setting up a tab index

Ensure that the tab ordering—the movement between widgets when user presses the Tab key—of your application makes sense.

Widgets that subclass FocusWidget,[8] such as TextBox, DoubleBox, CheckBox, and Button, all have a setTabIndex method that you should use, passing in the integer value for its place in the order:

```
Button myButton = new Button("Click Me");
myButton.setTabIndex(4);
```

[8] http://mng.bz/uQ5C.

In UiBinder, use the tabIndex attribute:

```
<g:Button tabIndex="4">Click Me</g:Button>
```

For widgets that don't subclass FocusWidget but that you wish to include in the tab order, wrap them in a FocusPanel. To keep focusable widgets out of the tab order, set their tab index to -1.

The Tab key isn't the only key that's useful to manage.

13.9.3 Establishing keyboard shortcuts

Keyboard shortcuts are useful to allow quick access to functionality, and they're useful beyond the accessibility case. We look at how to manage shortcuts in chapter 14, so we're a little ahead of ourselves here! There's a working group[9] that's trying to standardize keyboard shortcuts for use in website widgets.

You can also think about providing an alternative styling for users.

13.9.4 Providing alternative styling

You can harness GWT to provide alternative styling to be applied for specific cases. You might want to have a slightly larger font or perhaps change the color scheme you've applied.

You could use conditional CSS statements in a ClientBundle with a user-defined deferred binding property. OK, that's a bit of a mouthful. What we mean is, you can create a new deferred-binding property (see chapter 17) that allows you to distinguish between standard and accessible. For example

```
<define-property name="a11y" values="standard, accessible">
```

means you could write your CSS used by a client bundle as

```
@if a11y standard{
      body{text: 12pt;
      color: red;
      background-color: green;
   }
} else {
      body{text: 18pt;
      color: black;
      background-color: white;
   }
}
```

Finally, let's look at supporting screen readers through ARIA.

13.9.5 Using ARIA

ARIA is the W3C accessibility initiative,[10] and it defines, in essence, the addition of well-defined roles and states as DOM attributes to widgets. These roles and states are readable by screen readers and can, for example, be read aloud to the user.

---

[9] DHTML Style Guide Working Group: http://dev.aol.com/dhtml_style_guide.

[10] ARIA: www.w3.org/WAI/intro/aria.

When creating your own nonstandard browser widget, you should define what type of ARIA role it will have. Roles indicate how the widget will behave—for example, will it behave like a button (`ButtonRole`) or an alert (`AlertRole`)?

Coupled with roles are states. States are expected to change in reaction to user interaction. If your new widget has a `ButtonRole`, then clicking something on it should presumably change its state to `pressed`.

Listing 13.4 shows a quick code example of using ARIA in GWT 2.5[11] on a new widget that we'd like to have the behavior of a button (pre version 2.5, an alternative approach through an `Accessibility` class was used).

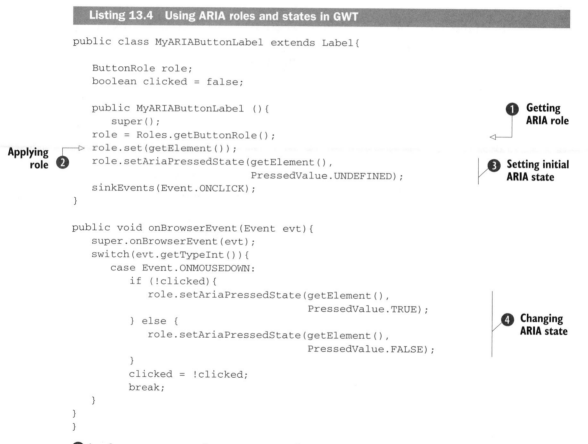

Listing 13.4 Using ARIA roles and states in GWT

```
public class MyARIAButtonLabel extends Label{

   ButtonRole role;
   boolean clicked = false;

   public MyARIAButtonLabel (){
      super();
      role = Roles.getButtonRole();                       ❶ Getting ARIA role
      role.set(getElement());                              ❷ Applying role
      role.setAriaPressedState(getElement(),
                               PressedValue.UNDEFINED);    ❸ Setting initial ARIA state
      sinkEvents(Event.ONCLICK);
   }

   public void onBrowserEvent(Event evt){
      super.onBrowserEvent(evt);
      switch(evt.getTypeInt()){
         case Event.ONMOUSEDOWN:
            if (!clicked){
               role.setAriaPressedState(getElement(),
                                        PressedValue.TRUE);
            } else {
               role.setAriaPressedState(getElement(),
                                        PressedValue.FALSE);   ❹ Changing ARIA state
            }
            clicked = !clicked;
            break;
      }
   }
}
```

❶ is where you access the `ButtonRole` from GWT's ARIA support classes, and then you apply that role to this widget's element in ❷. The last thing you do in the constructor, ❸, is set the initial ARIA pressed state for the widget (`unpressed`).

11 ARIA in GWT: http://mng.bz/IZ9P.

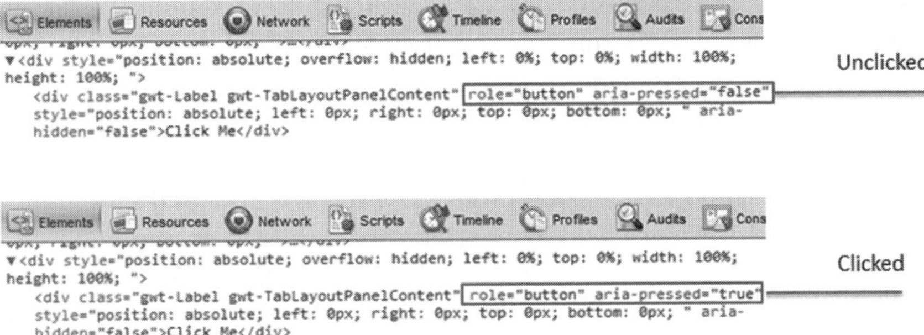

Figure 13.20 Examining the DOM to see the impact of using ARIA role and state in a widget. At the top the widget has not been clicked, whereas the bottom shows that the state has changed to reflect a mouse click on the widget.

You override the widget's event-handling method (`onBrowserEvent`) so that you can change the widget's ARIA state when an `onclick` event is received ❹. If the widget has not already been clicked, you set the ARIA state to `pressed`; otherwise you set it to `unpressed`. In a real widget you'd also change the display of the widget to indicate whether it's pressed.

If you don't have a screen reader to check out the impact of your ARIA setup, you can always inspect the DOM; see figure 13.20. But it's easier to check with a screen reader, and nowadays you can install browser extensions such as ChromeVox to act in that capacity.

Using all these options and a general good design, you should have an application usable by as many people as possible.

13.10 Summary

We covered quite a lot in this chapter—a testament to the flexibility of GWT in addressing the internationalization (i18n) and localization (L10n) questions.

Out of the three techniques for i18n, we recommend the static approach as the one you should adopt. It provides the greatest guarantee that there will be no runtime errors while ensuring the smallest code download for the user.

If you can't use the static approach, then the dynamic approach is the next preferable. You might defer implementing the static approach if you already have a large number of legacy translation files—in which case you can use the `Dictionary` class to access the data.

With GWT's approach to L10n, you can make sure currency, numbers, dates, and times are all shown in the way that a user is most likely to recognize without having to spend extra time converting them in their brain. It might not seem like an important issue to you at the moment, but making a user interface as familiar as possible will help in the long run.

Along the way you've seen that static i18n is quite usable in the UiBinder approach, as long as you remember to add the `-extra` flag to the hosted mode/compiler so that the generated properties file is available for you to copy and use.

Now your application is easier for almost everyone everywhere to use, because they understand it.

This is the last chapter in this part of the book. When you've had a moment to relax, we'll jump into the advanced part of the book by getting into the details of events. We'll look at how to create your own types of events, and then break open the toolbox used to create industrial-strength applications as we begin to explore event buses.

Part 3

Advanced

This part looks at some of the advanced aspects of GWT. We need to point out that these are not advanced because of their complexity, but rather they're the tools and techniques you'd use when pushing beyond the simplest of GWT applications and your concerns turn to group development, maintenance, and a deeper understanding of the user experience.

In part 3 we cover using architectural patterns such as MVP, employing dependency injection, creating your own events, and using event busses. We look at how to handle differences with deferred binding and how to reduce the amount of boilerplate code developers need to write. Finally, we look at collecting performance metrics from your application and how to split your application into smaller chunks of code to improve both load and execution time.

As with the previous part, there's no right order in which to read these chapters, and although the dependency-injection chapter uses the same code base as the MVP chapter, it's still sufficiently independent that it could be read first.

14 Advanced event handling and event busses

This chapter covers

- Creating user-defined events
- Browser-agnostic handling of events
- Previewing events and stopping their propagation
- Using event busses

Our first topic in the advanced part of this book is a deeper look at events and event busses.

Before we get to event busses, we'll reaffirm the brief description from chapter 3 of what events are and then look at how GWT handles the differences between Internet Explorer and standards-compliant browsers in event handling. This is useful because it means we only have to worry about handling events in one way and not how, say, Firefox handles them compared to IE.

We'll also show how to preview events so you know what event has been raised before any item gets to handle it. Previewing events means you can cancel them if you want, so that they don't get handled, or you can use the preview to implement keyboard shortcuts in your application. In addition to previewing events, we'll also

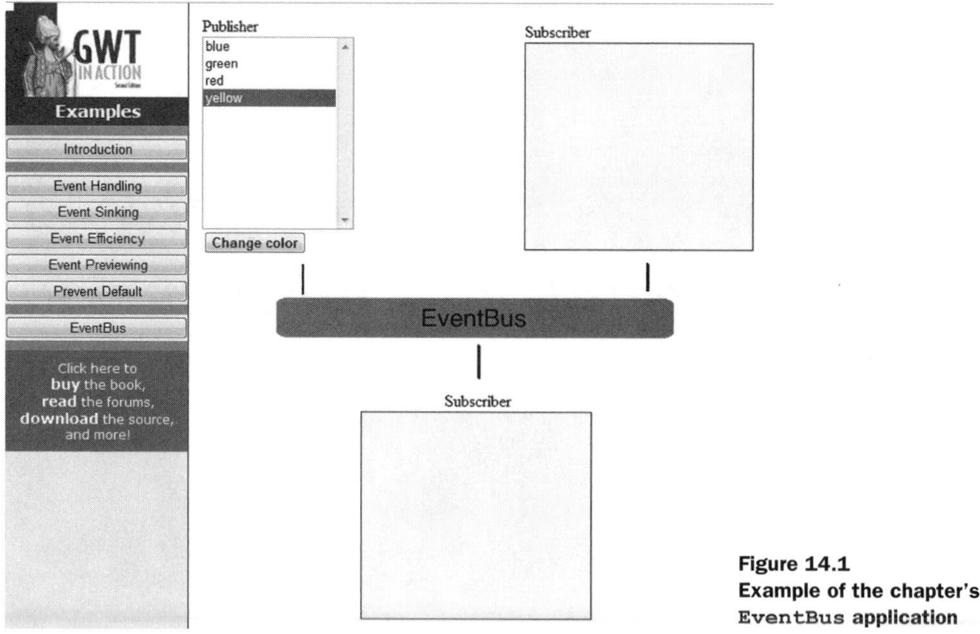

Figure 14.1 Example of the chapter's `EventBus` application

look at preventing the browser from doing its default action—for example, if you drag an image to the location bar it will load only that image, which you might not want to happen.

After looking at how to use existing events, you'll create your own event. This is useful when you want to make events more meaningful to your application and when using event busses. You create and use your own events in exactly the same manner as standard GWT events. But it's rather cumbersome to do this because you have to provide the event plus a couple of interfaces, and make sure it all ties together; but you'll see how to do that later.

Armed with a good grounding knowledge in events, we'll investigate the `EventBus` (part of the Google bindery functionality). Event busses are useful in decoupling applications, and the reference MVP implementation (see chapter 15) uses them. We'll look at how you can use the different types of event busses in the fun application shown in figure 14.1.

Let's start the chapter with trying to understand events within GWT.

14.1 Understanding events

Because you're this far into the book, we're going to assume you're familiar with adding event handlers to widgets and panels (back in section 3.7 we discussed this). You've probably written code similar to the following:

```
Button save = new Button("Save");
save.addClickHandler(new ClickHandler(){
   public void onClick(ClickEvent event){
```

```
        Window.alert("Saving");
    }
});
```

Or you may have used the UiBinder equivalent, such as the following:

```
@UiHandler("save")
void saveInformation(ClickEvent event){
    Window.alert("Saving");
}
```

Order of event handlers

If you add two event handlers for the same event to a widget, they're fired in the order in which they're added.

In the UiBinder approach, the ordering is taken from the order of `@UiHandler` definitions in the code in a top-down manner.

To remove an event, you need to store the `HandlerRegistration` that's returned from adding an event handler to an object, for example:

```
ClickHandler clicker = new ClickHandler(){
    public void onClick(ClickEvent event){
        Window.alert("Saving");
    }
};
HandlerRegistration theClickHandler = myButton.addClickHandler(clicker);
```

With access to the `HandlerRegistration`, calling the `removeHandler` method removes an event:

```
theClickHandler.removeHandler();
```

In chapter 3 we defined an event as an indication that something had happened, and we're sticking to that definition.

The indication might be that an image has loaded, a user has clicked a button, some HTML 5 media that was playing has ended, a user has touched the mobile Safari area with a finger, a widget's value has changed, or perhaps a user is closing a browser window. These are all examples of events that can be raised within an application, and we can think of many more; you can even create your own events that make sense for things that are happening within your own application—maybe a "user has logged on" event.

Events come in two types: those raised by the DOM—so-called *native events*—and those that are more *logical events*, such as a selection handler that indicates a particular tab has been selected.

14.1.1 Native events

Native events are those that the DOM raises. If you come from a JavaScript background, these are the types of events for which you'd have directly added an event handler to the DOM element.

Within GWT there's a further subdivision of native events into bit and bitless. This distinction comes from legacy GWT versions and how memory leaks were avoided. The bit events are associated with a numerical value, for example, 4 for a mouse down and 64 for a mouse move. The `Event` class in `com.google.gwt.user.client` shows the bit values for those bit-related events.

Those events that are bitless are only in newer browsers and don't suffer as much from memory leaks (which means the additional code that goes with managing bit events isn't needed). We'll come back to this point in section 14.2.3 when we look at the GWT event model.

You can find the full list of native events in the `com.google.gwt.event.dom.client` package, and in the following list we'll highlight a broad selection of them:

- Focus events: blur, focus
- Change event
- Mouse events: click, double-click, move, down, up, out, over, wheel
- Scroll event
- Progress event
- Key events: key up, key down, keypress, key code
- Load: load, error
- Touch events: start, end, move, cancel
- Gesture: start, end, change
- Drag/drop: drag end, drag enter, drag leave, drag over, drag start, drop
- Media: can play through, ended

All of these events extend the `DomEvent` class, which in turn extends the `GwtEvent` class. But not all events may be fired by all browsers—in particular, the gesture and touch events require a browser that can fire those events (usually a browser that runs on a mobile device), and the drag-and-drop and media events require a browser that supports these HTML 5 aspects.

As we've mentioned, beyond the native events, we also need to discuss the logical events.

14.1.2 Logical events

Logical events are those that aren't DOM events but still indicate something has happened—a value may have changed, a widget may have been attached, a window has been resized, and so on.

All of the events in this group extend the `GwtEvent` directly rather than `DomEvent`. You can find the standard ones that GWT defines in the `com.google.gwt.event.logical.shared` package. These include the following:

- Attach event
- Selection events: before selection and selection

- Highlight event
- Initialize event
- Open event
- Resize event
- Show range event
- Value change event

Various widgets can fire these events, such as the `TabLayoutPanel`, which will fire a `BeforeSelection` event as a user selects a new tab and before it changes to that tab, and a `Selection` event as the new tab is shown. `ValueChange` events are raised by a few widgets but are also at the heart of GWT history management.

It's to this group of logical events that we'll usually add our own created events to represent happenings in our own applications—you'll see more about that in section 14.6.

Now that you know what an event is and have examples of the types of events, we should look at how GWT manages those events in the context of the browser and an application.

14.2 How GWT manages events

Like most areas of DOM, browsers aren't consistent in how they manage events, plus some substantial issues exist with leaky implementations that GWT needs to work around. As usual, GWT does manage to hide nearly all of those differences for us, leaving us to program against one model and expect consistency across all browsers. In this section, we'll look at how GWT does that, starting with how it deals with the main inconsistency in browser implementations—the difference between event bubbling and capture.

Once you know how GWT will generally handle events, we'll dig into how you can stop events from propagating, if you want to do that. Then we'll look at how to tell the GWT event-handling mechanism that a particular widget will be able to listen to particular events. In that discussion we'll look at why some events are known as bit events and some as bitless, and how event handlers are registered with the GWT event system.

The last thing we'll look at in this section on how GWT manages events is how to introduce some efficiency into your event handling. Through the use of a matrix of buttons, you'll see how to add one handler to manage all click events on the buttons, rather than adding an event handler per button.

As we mentioned a moment ago, the first thing we'll look at is how GWT handles the different ways browsers can handle events.

14.2.1 Dealing with browser differences

Take figure 14.2, which shows three nested panels. What do you think should happen when you click the innermost panel (the green one, if your version of this book is in color)?

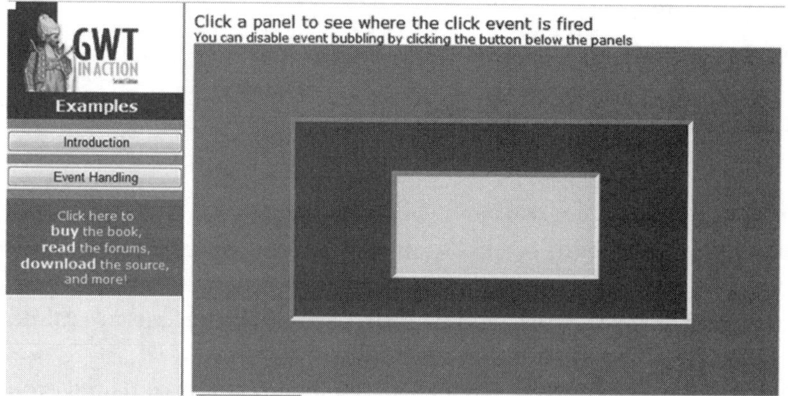

Figure 14.2 Screenshot of the example application's event-handling mechanism that allows you to see how events are propagated in GWT

If this is your first time thinking about events in DOM, then you'd most likely say that the event is fired on that innermost panel. And you'd be correct. But the event is also fired on the other two panels because the innermost panel is nested inside the middle (blue) panel and the outer (red) panel.

The order in which you'd expect those panels to receive the event will be clouded by whether you're used to Internet Explorer or the standards-compliant browsers (you'll add to the confusion if you start thinking about whether IE9 is standards compliant).

The difference in propagation of events in various browsers is whether events are *bubbled* or *captured* through elements.

EVENT BUBBLING

In IE, the normal model is *event bubbling*. The innermost panel would be the first to receive notification of the click, followed by the middle panel, and then the outer panel (and over time the DOM `Document` itself)—you can see this situation simplified in figure 14.3.

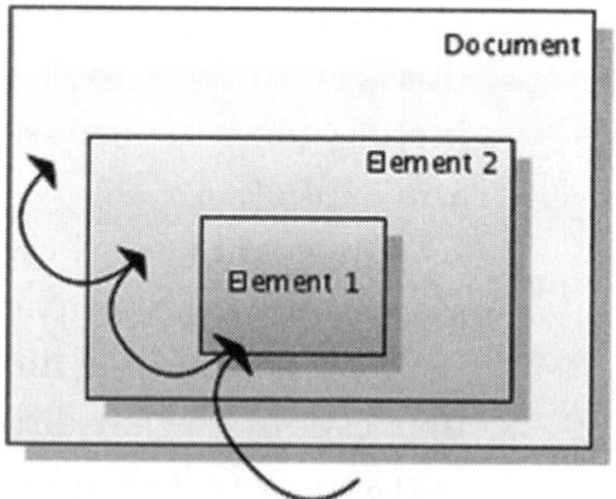

Figure 14.3 Summary of the process of event bubbling (the IE model). Clicking Element 1 fires the event there; then it bubbles to Element 2 and then to the `Document`.

To quote from the W3C recommendation:

> Bubbling events will then trigger any additional event listeners found by following the `EventTarget`'s parent chain upward, checking for any event listeners registered on each successive `EventTarget`. This upward propagation will continue up to and including the `Document`.
>
> —W3C Document Object Model (DOM) Level 2 Events Specification

Standards-compliant browsers, on the other hand, use a model called *event capturing*.

EVENT CAPTURING

In the capturing model, the DOM `Document` is the first component to receive notification when the innermost panel is clicked, followed by the outer panel, then the middle panel and finally the innermost panel (see figure 14.4 for a simplified view of this capturing).

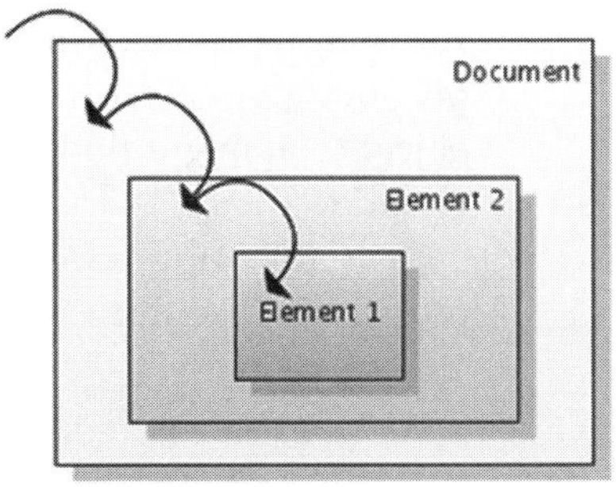

Figure 14.4 Summary of the process of event capture. Clicking Element 1 means the event is captured on the `Document` first, then Element 2, and eventually Element 1.

To quote from the W3C:

> Event capture is the process by which an `EventListener` registered on an ancestor of the event's target can intercept events of a given type before they're received by the event's target. Capture operates from the top of the tree, generally the `Document`, downward, making it the symmetrical opposite of bubbling.
>
> —W3C Document Object Model (DOM) Level 2 Events Specification.

Clearly, having two models is a recipe for disaster. Therefore, let's look at how GWT protects us from that.

THE GWT VIEW

Luckily, under the hood, GWT manages all these differences for us, and we can rely on the fact that the GWT event model follows the perhaps more natural IE approach. For the technically minded, GWT can do this by overlaying its own event-handling structure onto DOM elements to make it consistent, as we'll discuss a little later when we talk about sinking events.

For standards-compliant browsers, the event modeling is forced to be the bubble model, and for IE that's the default approach anyway. Each DOM element that will handle an event in a GWT application has a single event listener added to it, which points to a global GWT event handler.

The result, then, of clicking the innermost green panel in our example application is a bubbling up of the event through the panel hierarchy. You see that at the bottom of the chapter's first example, as shown in figure 14.5.

You may have times when you click the innermost panel and you don't want any click handler on the next panel to be triggered. To achieve that, you need to stop the propagation of the original event.

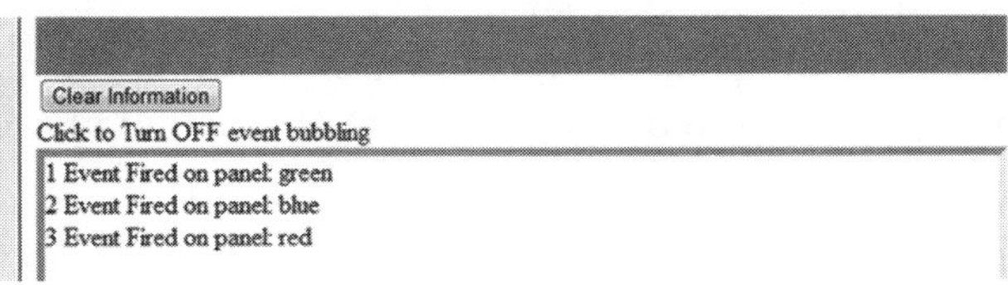

Figure 14.5 The order of event bubbling through the panels in the event-handling part of this chapter's example application, once the innermost green panel is clicked

14.2.2 Preventing event propagation

You may have occasions when you don't want the event propagation to happen. GWT provides an easy way to do that; you call the `stopPropagation` method on the event object (you might find legacy GWT code that uses the now-unavailable `cancelBubble` method).

The following is how you'd write the basic version of the code to stop the event propagating from the innermost panel, in the UiBinder approach:

```
@UiHandler("innermost")
void showInnermostEventHandling (ClickEvent event){
   event.stopPropagation();
}
```

If you're "old school" and not using the UiBinder approach, then you'd add the code inside your defined handler, for example:

```
FocusPanel innerMost = new FocusPanel();
innerMost.addClickHandler(new ClickHandler(){
   public void onClick(ClickEvent event){
      event.stopPropagation();
   }
});
```

Now that you know how GWT solves the issue of bubbling versus capturing and how to prevent an event from propagating, we'll turn to the topic of how GWT ensures prevention of memory leaks in this notorious area of event handling.

14.2.3 Sinking events

The event handling in GWT is complicated to follow through the classes within GWT code. As we've mentioned before, GWT builds its own scaffolding around events in order to make all browsers react the same way—all you need to do is register, and then a widget will sink an event (that is, it will handle events of that type itself).

We won't go into detail on how to do this, but it starts in the DOM implementation classes where some JavaScript global event handlers are set up to capture events and walk through your application's DOM structure looking for DOM elements that the event handlers are listed against (the so-called dispatch methods).

We say handlers "listed against" rather than registered because GWT doesn't register JavaScript event handlers against associated DOM elements; rather, they're sunk—a tag is made on the `Widget`'s DOM element saying that a particular GWT handler exists. This is done to prevent a well-known memory-leak issue, primarily in versions of Internet Explorer.[1]

When a widget is attached to the DOM, then the GWT DOM method `setEventListener` is called to register this widget as being an item involved in event management. Similarly, when a widget is removed, the `setEventListener` method is again

[1] A good reference is http://mng.bz/H6SW.

called with the value `null` to remove the widget from the event system—and avoid any memory leak.

You can handle events in two ways: either internally to a widget (that is, with no visibility outside the widget boundary) or by adding external handlers to the widget.

INTERNAL EVENT HANDLING

In older GWT code, you always had to sink events—indicating that this widget was going to listen to the GWT event-handling system for specific events—and then react when those events happened.

Nowadays you only have to sink if you're going to internally handle the event within the widget. Sinking is easy; you call the `sinkEvent` method, usually in the constructor, passing in the integer value of event you'll be sinking. The following listing shows the event sinking and the next step (handling) for an imaginary widget.

Listing 14.1 Sinking and handling an event internal to a widget

```
public class MyButton extends Label{

   MyButton(){
      super();
      sinkEvents(Event.ONCLICK);          ❶ Sinking event
   }

   public void onBrowserEvent(Event evt){
     switch(evt.getTypeInt()){
        case Event.ONCLICK:                ❷ Handling event
           Window.alert("Hello!");
           break;
     }
     super.onBrowserEvent(evt);
  }
}
```

In ❶ of listing 14.1 you sink the `click` event; that is, you tell the GWT event system that this widget will be reacting to click events itself. The new part is in ❷ where you override the widget's `onBrowserEvent` class. This is called by the GWT event-handling system, and there you switch on the integer value of the event type received. If that event type has the value `Event.ONCLICK`, then you pop an alert.

Table 14.1 shows events that can be sunk this way.

Table 14.1 Events that can be sunk in the GWT `sinkEvents` method

Mouse events	Gesture events	Touch events	Focus events
ONMOUSEDOWN	ONGESTURESTART	ONTOUCHCANCEL	ONFOCUS
ONMOUSEUP	ONGESTUREEND	ONTOUCHEND	ONBLUR
ONMOUSEMOVE	ONGESTURECHANGE	ONTOUCHMOVE	ONSCROLL
ONMOUSEOUT	ONLOAD	ONTOUCHSTART	ONPASTE
ONMOUSEOVER	ONERROR	ONKEYUP	ONCONTEXTMENU

Table 14.1 Events that can be sunk in the GWT `sinkEvents` method *(continued)*

Mouse events	Gesture events	Touch events	Focus events
ONMOUSEWHEEL	ONCHANGE	ONKEYPRESS	KEYEVENTS
ONCLICK	ONDBLCLICK	ONKEYDOWN	

An alternative is to use one of the `Widget` class's `addHandler`, `addDomHandler`, or `addBitlessDomHandler` methods and pass it a newly created handler object. That manages the sinking for you, whereas the underlying GWT code ensures the appropriate handler is executed.

The difference between these three methods is that the first, `addHandler`, is for logical events, and the other two are for native (DOM) events. The native events are split into two types: those that require a bit mask on the element's tag and those that don't (events that are common only to new browsers that don't have the memory leak issue). Again, you don't need to know about this split of native events into two types.

But these methods are normally wrapped by higher-level methods specific to event types and exposed outside the widget so that users of the widget can be notified when events occur. This is external event handling.

EXTERNAL EVENT HANDLING

How do you use the various add handler methods in a widget? Well, let's build a widget, inventively called `MyWidget`, that will handle a native event that requires bits (mouse clicks), a native event that's bitless (a touch start), and a logical event (value change). It could be defined as follows.

Listing 14.2 Part of `MyWidget` showing the three types of handler registration

```
public class MyWidget extends Widget
                      implements HasDragStartHandlers,
                                 HasClickHandlers,
                                 HasValueChangeHandlers<String>{

   @Override
   public HandlerRegistration addClickHandler(ClickHandler handler) {
      return addDomHandler(handler, ClickEvent.getType());
   }

   @Override
   public HandlerRegistration
          addDragStartHandler(DragStartHandler handler) {
      return this.addBitlessDomHandler(handler, DragStartEvent.getType());
   }

   @Override
   public HandlerRegistration
          addValueChangeHandler(ValueChangeHandler<String> handler) {
      return addHandler(handler, ValueChangeEvent.getType());
   }
```

Annotations: ❶ Native event handling; ❷ Native bitless event handling; ❸ Logical event handling

```
    public MyWidget(){
        setElement(Document.get().createDivElement());     ❹ Creating widget
    }

    public void setText(String text){
        this.getElement().setInnerHTML(text);
        ValueChangeEvent.fire(this, text);                  ❺ Firing ValueChange event
    }
}
```

The MyWidget is simple. It has a <div> element ❹ on which you can set text; doing so fires a ValueChange event ❺, the handler for which is added in ❸. You can click the widget, which fires a Click event handled by the handler added in ❶. And if some of the text is selected and you're using a HTML 5–capable browser, then you can drag that text and fire the DragStart event, which is handled by any handler you've added through ❷. All of these events are recorded underneath the example, as shown in figure 14.6.

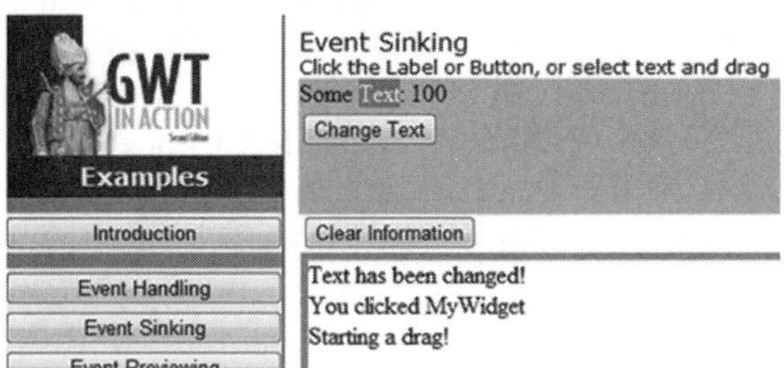

Figure 14.6 Three events fired when interacting with MyWidget in the chapter's Event Sinking example

Event handling is much simpler in the current GWT, and you can even create your own logical events and use the same framework—we'll do that a little later in this chapter. Before we discuss some other things you can do with events, we'll take a quick look at some event-handling efficiency.

14.2.4 Event-handling efficiency

Often, adding handlers as anonymous inner classes is inefficient; for example, our Event Efficiency example shown in figure 14.7 has 16 buttons. Adding 16 different event handlers, 1 per button, is going to eat into memory.

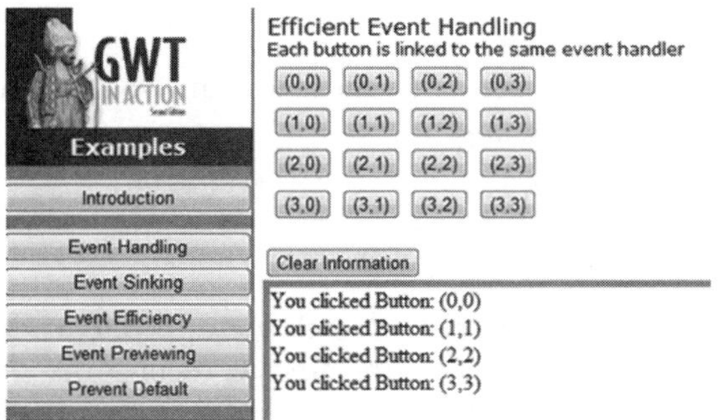

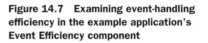

Figure 14.7 Examining event-handling efficiency in the example application's Event Efficiency component

As figure 14.7 shows, every button's text is written to the text window as a result of each button press.

Rather than have 16 event handlers, we've defined one.

Listing 14.3 Event handler for 16 buttons

```
@UiHandler({"butt00", "butt01", "butt02", "butt03",
         "butt10", "butt11", "butt12", "butt13",
         "butt20", "butt21", "butt22", "butt23",
         "butt30", "butt31", "butt32", "butt33",})
void handleClick(ClickEvent click){
   Button sender = (Button) click.getSource();
   addMessage("You clicked Button: "+sender.getText());
}
```

❶ Handling multiple widgets

❷ Determining widget-raising event

Listing 14.3 works because widgets register themselves as the source of the event. This means that you can use the `getSource` method ❷ to get the widget and either compare it against a set of known widgets to determine which fired it or, in our example, get the text from the widget for displaying.

In the UiBinder approach, you can add a handler to multiple widgets by passing them in as an array to the `UiHandler` annotation ❶. Outside UiBinder, you'd define the handler as a variable and then add that to all of the `Button` widgets.

Now that you've directly handled events, let's see what else you can do with them, starting with previewing them before they trigger any action.

14.3 Previewing and canceling events

Previewing events is useful if you want to do something before the event gets handled—maybe you want to cancel it. We'll look at both those topics in this section.

To preview events, you add a `NativePreviewHandler` to the `Event` object. In our example application we use a `NativePreviewHandler` similar to the following:

```
NativePreviewHandler previewer = new NativePreviewHandler(){

   @Override
   public void onPreviewNativeEvent(NativePreviewEvent event) {
      String eventType = get_event_type(event);
      Label theEvent = new Label(counter++ + "  "+BASE_COMMENT+ eventType);
      comment.add(theEvent);
   }
}
```

It implements one method, `onPreviewNativeEvent`, where we handle any event that's being previewed. In the simplistic view, we write:

```
Event.addNativePreviewHandler(previewer);
```

And the native events that are previewed are written to our example's screen.

> **NOTE** If you add two native preview handlers, they work the opposite of normal handlers. That is, the last-added handler is the first to receive the preview, and the first added is the last to preview.

WARNING GWT registers `NativePreviewHandlers` in the browser's window—this means if you have two or more GWT applications on a page that preview events, they can interfere with each other (one application may cancel an event before the other one gets to preview it).

But previewing uses a lot of resources—you get absolutely everything that's happening anywhere in your application. A way to minimize this is to wrap the content in which you're interested in a `FocusPanel` and then add and remove the event previewer as the mouse enters and leaves that panel.

That's exactly what we do in our example; to add the previewer, we write

```
@UiHandler("wrapper")
void startPreviewingEvents (MouseOverEvent event){
   previewerHandler = Event.addNativePreviewHandler(previewer);
   previewingStatus.setText("Previewing Events: ON");
}
```

To remove the previewer, we call the standard `removeHandler` method on the `HandlerRegistration` we obtained when adding the native event handler to the `Event` object:

```
@UiHandler("wrapper")
void stopPreviewingEvent (MouseOutEvent event){
   previewerHandler.removeHandler();
   previewingStatus.setText("Previewing Events: OFF");
}
```

Running the example gives output similar to figure 14.8, where some mouse moves have been seen as well as a keypress (which results in three events: key down, keypress, and key up events).

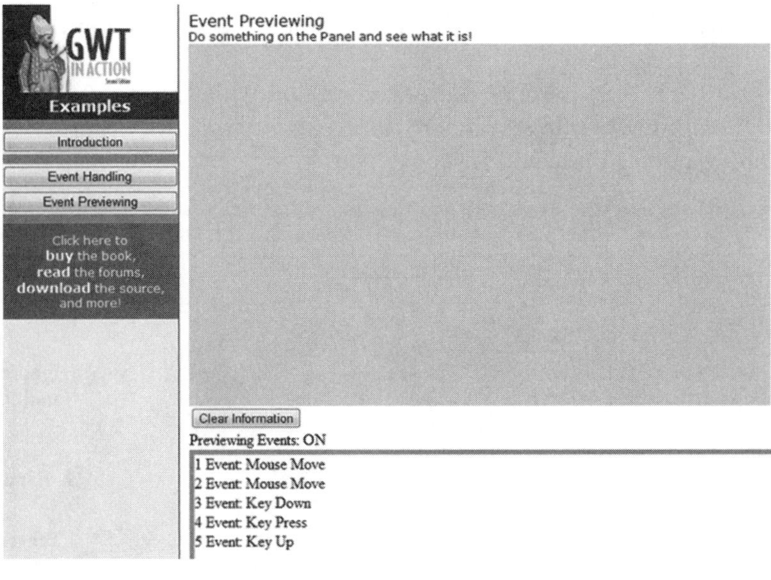

Figure 14.8 Previewing events on the target panel in the Event Previewing example application

In addition to previewing events, you also can cancel them. If you're previewing an event, it's because you want to do something before the event is handled. Either you might want to stop the event from propagating, as you saw earlier, or you might prevent the default browser action from happening, as you'll see in the next chapter, or you might cancel the event so that it isn't handled.

Canceling an event is simple. When you have the event object, you write

```
event.cancel();
```

and it will no longer be available for the event handlers.

Maybe canceling the event is too drastic an action. You might want to prevent the browser from taking its default action.

14.4 Preventing default actions

The browser is quite happy to handle some events by itself—press the Enter key when you're in a form, and the browser will generally submit it; drag an image to the location bar, and the browser will reload it; press Ctrl+N in most browsers, and a new browser window will open.

Sometimes these default actions are useful, and sometimes not. In the example application from chapter 3 we prevent the logo image from being dragged to the location bar by overriding the onBrowserEvent method when we create it:

```
logo = new Image(GWT.getModuleBaseURL() + "../" + LOGO_IMAGE_NAME){
   public void onBrowserEvent(Event evt){
      evt.preventDefault();
      super.onBrowserEvent(evt);
   }
};
```

By calling the preventDefault method on the event, we prevent the default browser action. We call the parent's onBrowserEvent method to allow the widget to play nicely with the event system. The image is added to the chapter 3 application the same way any image is.

Another approach is to prevent the default action while previewing events. You might do this for implementing keyboard shortcuts in your application. The basic implementation is quite simple and is shown next.

Listing 14.4 Implementing keyboard shortcuts in an application

```
NativePreviewHandler keyboardShortcutHandler = new NativePreviewHandler(){

@Override
public void onPreviewNativeEvent(NativePreviewEvent event) {
   if(event.getTypeInt()==Event.ONKEYPRESS||
      event.getTypeInt()==Event.ONKEYUP) return;            ❶ Ignore multiple events
   NativeEvent ne = event.getNativeEvent();
   if (ne.getCtrlKey()){
     String text="";                                        ❷ Handle Ctrl+S
      if (ne.getKeyCode()=='s' || ne.getKeyCode()=='S'){
         ne.preventDefault();                               ❸ Prevent default action
```

```
            text="Handling Ctrl+s";
         } else if (ne.getKeyCode()=='n' || ne.getKeyCode()=='N'){      ◁┐ Try to
            ne.preventDefault();                                          │ handle
            text="Handling Ctrl+n";                                     ❹ Ctrl+N
         }
         Label theEventLabel = new Label(text);
         comment.add(theEventLabel);
      }
   }
};
```

When previewing events in listing 14.4, you ignore ONKEYPRESS and ONKEYUP events ❶; otherwise you'll get multiple firings. Next, you check to see if the Ctrl key and S or s are pressed ❷; if so, you prevent the default action of the browser for this keypress combination ❸ and implement your own (in this case setting the value of the text string, which we then display on the screen. Figure 14.9 shows Ctrl+S and Ctrl+N being pressed, but watch out for a gotcha, as described in the following sidebar.

Be aware with keypresses

Our example offers the opportunity to show that not even GWT can protect you from all the browser differences. Currently, the implementers of Chrome have decided that the Ctrl+N key combination, and some others, won't be passed through to the renderer.[a] This means that the code in ❹ will never be triggered in Chrome—try the example in IE and Google, and you'll see the difference (and this is also why Google apps tend to use Ctrl+M for creating new slides, and so on).

a. See Chromium issues 84332, 13891, and 5496 (for example, http://mng.bz/S4VK

The last action with events that we want to look at is how to programmatically fire them.

14.5 Programmatically firing events

You likely won't have many occasions where you want to programmatically create native events. Most often it's in test cases for your own widgets. (Because Google constantly tests GWT widgets, there's limited benefit in testing them yourself. In fact, it's

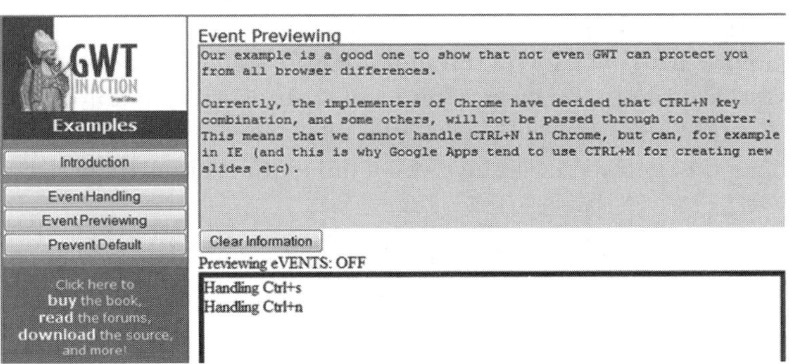

Figure 14.9 Implementing keyboard shortcuts in GWT in action in the Prevent Default part of this chapter's example application

positively encouraged not to test GWT widgets because UI testing is heavy compared to functionality testing—that could be a whole chapter on its own!)

But if you find yourself in a situation where you have to programmatically fire native events, then you do so as follows. First, you need to get the event from the `Document`; for example, the following listing shows firing a keypress event on a `TextBox`.

Listing 14.5 Programmatically firing a keypress event on a `TextBox`

```
TextBox name = new TextBox();
boolean ctrlKey = false;
boolean altKey = false;
boolean shiftKey = false;
boolean metaKey = false;
char charCode = 'a';
NativeEvent nE = Document.get().createKeyPressEvent(ctrlKey,
                      altKey, shiftKey, metaKey, charCode);
DomEvent.fireNativeEvent(nE, name);
```

❶ Create event
❷ Fire event

First, you create the event from the `Document` object ❶, and then you can fire it through the `DomEvent` object ❷.

> **TIP** If you need to programmatically fire a click event on a `Button`, it's much simpler—you use the `click()` method on the `Button`.

If you want to fire logical events, that's much easier. Logical events all have a `fire` method, and that's what you call. For example, here's how to fire a `ValueChange` event:

```
ValueChangeEvent.fire(this, text);
```

The last thing we want to cover on events before moving on to event busses is how to create your own events. You might like to do that in your application for a better understanding of what's happening.

14.6 Creating your own events

The great thing with the current approach to GWT events is that you can create your own events and have them handled in exactly the same way as all other GWT events. Unfortunately, you have to write a disproportionate amount of code: the event, a handler, and another interface! Maybe the Google Plugin for Eclipse will someday have a wizard, but for now it's all by hand.

In this section we'll create a logical event to indicate a change of color, which we'll use in the next section about `EventBus`. The act of creating a user-defined event is simple, but it's a bit cumbersome and open to a lot of opportunity for typing something wrong. Creating a user-defined event involves defining things in two steps:

- The event class
- The various interfaces related to handling the event: the `Handler` and `HasHandler` interfaces

The first thing you need to do is create the event.

14.6.1 Defining your own event

The following listing shows a new logical event that indicates a change of color has happened.

Listing 14.6 The Event class

```
public class ChangeColorEvent extends GwtEvent<ChangeColorEventHandler>{

   public static final Type<ChangeColorEventHandler>
                     TYPE = new Type<ChangeColorEventHandler>();

   @Override
   public Type<ChangeColorEventHandler> getAssociatedType() {
      return TYPE;
   }

   public static Type<ChangeColorEventHandler> getType() {
      return TYPE;
   }

   private String color;

   public ChangeColorEvent(String color) {
      this.color=color;
   }

   public String getColor() {
      return color;
        }

   @Override
   protected void dispatch(ChangeColorEventHandler handler) {
      handler.onChangeColor(this);
   }
}
```

❶ Extending the base event
❷ Dealing with event type information
❸ Constructor
❹ Dispatching an event

The new event needs to extend `GwtEvent` ❶ (not `DomEvent`, because you're creating a logical event). It also needs some standard code that provides unique type information about the event that GWT will use. You need all three bits marked ❷. When you create your own events, you can copy this code, ensuring the type parameters are correct with respect to your event handler.

At ❸ you provide the constructor of this event. In this case it has one argument, the color, but you can also define constructors with zero arguments.

You provide two more methods related to handling this event. The first is the `dispatch` method used by GWT in its handling process ❹; the second is the static `fire` method that can be used to programmatically fire the event.

To hook up the event handling, we need to define two handler interfaces.

14.6.2 Providing the related interfaces

The event-handler interface is simple to define. It's an interface that you expect to be implemented by the user to handle the event you've created. You'll notice that this interface is used heavily as a type parameter in the definition of the event. Here's our definition for `ChangeColorEventHandler`:

```
public interface ChangeColorEventHandler extends EventHandler{
      public void onChangeColor(ChangeColorEvent event);
}
```

Notice also that the method declaration matches that used in the `dispatch` method of the event.

> **NOTE** Some developers prefer to define the event handler inside the event class; this is merely a matter of style.

Your user will implement this interface if they want to provide code to handle `ChangeColor` events—perhaps they'll show the user a message saying the application is busy. It will always extend the `EventHandler` interface, which is currently a marker interface.

We also need to define another interface that objects (usually widgets) can implement to indicate that handlers can be added to them—the `HasHandlers` interface:

```
public interface HasChangeColorEventHandlers extends HasHandlers {
  public HandlerRegistration
         addHasChangeColorEventHandler(ChangeColorEventHandler handler);
}
```

These interfaces always extend the `HasHandlers` interface, which declares the `fireEvent` method (that's implemented by the `Widget` class). The method declaration given in the `HasChangeColorEventHandlers` interface must return a `HandlerRegistration` object so that it ties in with the event-handling system and allows a user to remove the handler at a later point.

With these three types in place, we can now create a widget that can handle and raise such an event:

```
public MyOtherWidget implements HasChangeColorEventHandlers{

   public HandlerRegistration
     addHasChangeColorEventHandler(ChangeColorEventHandler handler){
      return addHandler(handler, ChangeColorEvent.getType());
   }

   public void somethingHappened(){
      ChangeColorEvent.fire(this, "red");
   }
}
```

Although you can handle events inline within your code, sometimes it's useful to decouple your components. An easy way to do that is to use an event bus—you drop events from one component onto an event bus, and other components register to handle those events. In the next section you'll find out all about event busses and even see our just-created event type in use.

14.7 Event busses

When building complex and large web applications, it's common that widgets share the same information. Objects that are dependent on the same data are affected whenever a change occurs to the data they depend on. This means that modules have to carry references to each other in order to react appropriately whenever changes happen. This could result in to tight coupling or even circular dependencies among the widgets or application subsystems. Two important rules when it comes to building code that doesn't break easily are high cohesion (keep dependencies locally in the module) and low coupling (interdependency between modules). Tight coupling and circular dependencies contribute to spaghetti code; consider figure 14.10.

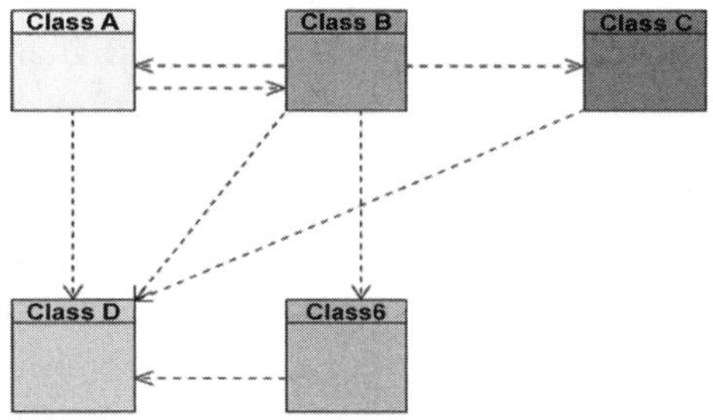

Figure 14.10 High coupling; components are dependent on each other.

It requires skilled architects to design code where this type of coupling between objects is circumvented. It also requires frequent refactoring activities, which take time.

You can eliminate evil coupling from arising between different parts of an application by using an event bus. The `EventBus` technique is built on top of GWT's `HandlerManager` and is a mechanism for passing and subscribing to events. We can rearrange figure 14.10 to use `EventBus`, as shown in figure 14.11.

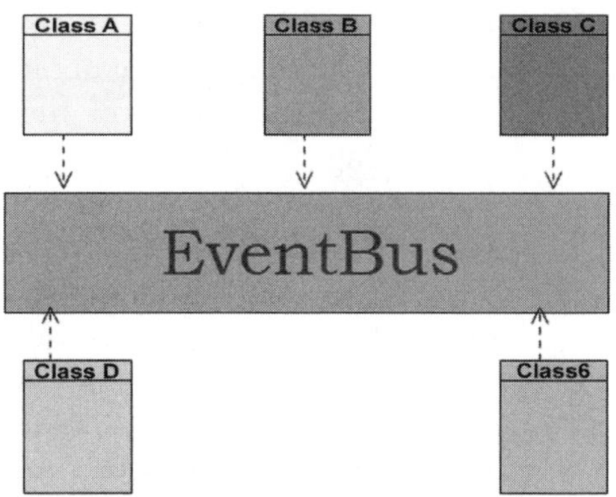

Figure 14.11 Low coupling; components interact over an event bus and don't need dependencies.

Components can react to the same event without carrying references to each other. The main activities are first that the publisher fires an event. The event could contain data; any kind of data could be passed from publisher to subscriber. The subscriber in turn defines a handler that's associated with the particular event. When a publisher fires an event on the `EventBus`, all of the registered subscribers to the same event will be invoked. The associated handler code will then be executed. Note that a publisher can also be a subscriber to events from itself or other components, and a subscriber can publish events that it's responsible for.

Sharing events instead of having references to all of them makes applications more robust, and changes can be done faster. You also avoid unexpected behavior, which is common with tangled code.

Is EventBus good for all situations? No: there are cases where events are useful and some where they aren't. A good rule is that an event bus should transport events that have several components that are interested in their state.

So let's define an event bus.

14.7.1 What is an event bus?

The EventBus implementation is related to the Observer design pattern, in which the subject (EventBus) keeps a list of its observers (subscribing classes) and notifies them when state changes occur by invoking one of their methods (the registered handler). The result is distributed event handling and a high level of decoupling between the participating components.

EventBus implements the HasHandler interface, which means it has a collection of EventHandlers associated with it. It has the capability to fire events to the event handlers listening to a given event. The event handlers are associated with a specific event type. When a publisher fires an event on the event bus, the bus loops through its list of associated handlers and invokes its method by passing the event to the handler.

Figure 14.12 gives a simplified view of the event bus that distributes an event from a publisher to the subscribers.

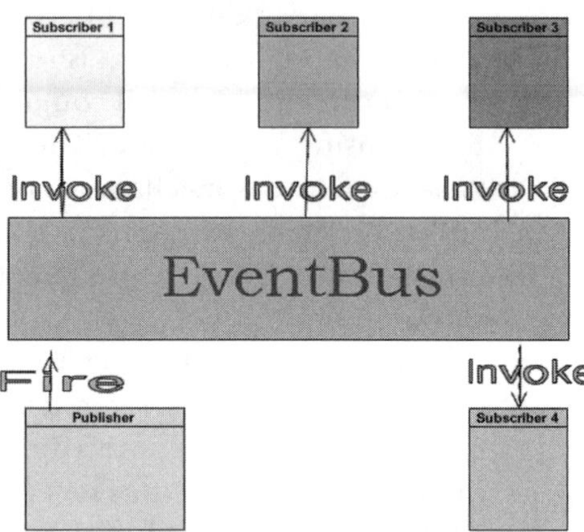

Figure 14.12 Event bus with subscribers

Building your application around an event bus is handy and helps you keep your code clean. Does that mean that an event bus should handle all events? The answer is no; this type of communication isn't suitable for all types of events.

Putting all of your events on the event bus could make your application unpredictable. If you put every mouse click on the bus, your application will end up handling events instead of doing what it should. You also have to write a large number of classes that define handlers and source these events. It's time consuming. The code won't be coherent and you'll lose control over the application.

The events you distribute with the event bus should be application-wide. For example, if you have a view where you're listing a bunch of contacts, then this particular widget should be interested in changes in any of the contacts. If a user edits a contact somewhere else in the application and the result is an RPC call to save the edited contact, then it's appropriate to fire an event to update the contact in the listing view. The conclusion is to use one event bus per application and only for general event handling.

There are several types of event busses. The types you'll find are SimpleEventBus, ResettableEventBus, CountingEventBus, and RecordingEventBus. Let's look at the details of how these busses could be helpful.

14.7.2 Types of event busses

All busses extend the abstract type `EventBus`. The base class requires implementation of four methods from the subclasses that provide the basic event-handling behavior. The key functionality for the bus is to keep a list of handlers correlated to an event; the methods `addHandler` and `addHandlerToSource` add handlers to the list:

```
public abstract <H extends EventHandler> HandlerRegistration
       addHandler(GwtEvent.Type<H> type, H handler)
```

`H` is the type of handler, and `type` is the event type associated with this handler. The return value is the `HandlerRegistration` object; it can be stored in order to be removed when suitable. This method registers the handler to receive events of this type from all sources.

There's also the method `addHandlerToSource`, which does almost the same thing; the difference is that it only accepts events from a given source:

```
public abstract <H extends EventHandler> HandlerRegistration
     addHandlerToSource(GwtEvent.Type<H> type,
                        java.lang.Object source, H handler)
```

There are two methods to fire events, `fireEvent` and `fireEventFromSource`. With the following method, an event can be fired from any source. All registered handlers for this event will receive it:

```
public abstract void fireEvent(Event<?> event)
```

With the method `fireEventFromSource`, an event can be fired from any source. All registered handlers for this source and event will receive it:

```
public abstract void fireEventFromSource(<?> event,
                                         java.lang.Object source)
```

The abstract base class `EventBus` offers functionality for dispatching and sourcing events. As you've seen, the remaining bus behavior is implemented by the subclasses. All types are quite basic and are easy to use. If you look briefly at the different types, you'll see that `SimpleEventBus` provides a basic `EventBus` implementation. Almost inevitably, `SimpleEventBus` is the one you'll use. Table 14.2 gives a brief summary of the busses.

Table 14.2 The different types of event busses

Type of `EventBus`	Description
`SimpleEventBus`	The basic event bus, which we'll use in this chapter's example.
`ResettableEventBus`	If you want a bus with the possibility of resetting all of its handlers at once, you could use the `ResettableEventBus`. The bus's `removeHandlers` method removes all handlers from the bus.
`CountingEventBus`	This bus keeps track of the number of handlers for particular events registered with it. You acquire this value by the `getCount` method, where the parameter is the event type you're interested in. This is mostly helpful for implementing testing classes.

Table 14.2 The different types of event busses *(continued)*

Type of `EventBus`	Description
`RecordingEventBus`	You should use this bus if you need to keep track of fired events. Its specialty is to give information as to whether a specific event has been fired or not. You could get that information by using the method `wasEventFired` by passing the event you're interested in.

Let's continue with the `SimpleEventBus`, and we'll employ a straightforward example to illustrate how to use it.

14.7.3 Using SimpleEventBus

The type `SimpleEventBus` gives, as mentioned earlier, basic `EventBus` behavior. Our simple example constitutes of a *publisher* with the main purpose of firing events of the change-color type. This publisher is a widget where the user can choose a color, and this color is propagated to some *subscribers*, which when receiving a change color event immediately change their background color to the chosen color. Figure 14.13 shows the example application we'll use in this section.

We defined the event and its supporting interfaces earlier in this section. What we'll do now is fire it across an event bus from the publisher to the subscribers. To do that, we have to perform the following steps:

1. In the subscriber(s), give an implementation of the event handler that takes actions when the events are fired.
2. In the subscriber, attach the handler to the event bus.
3. In the publisher, fire the event from the appropriate location.

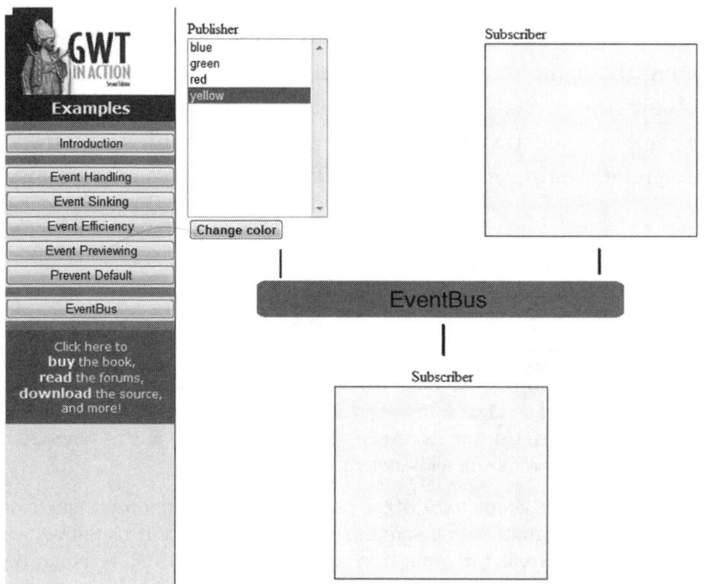

Figure 14.13 Screenshot of the `EventBus` example in action

The next steps are to define the implementation of the event handler in the subscriber widget and finally add the handler to the global event bus, which is shown in the following listing.

Listing 14.7 Subscriber class

```
public class EventSubscriberWidget2 extends Composite{
.
.
 SimpleEventBus eventBus;
                                                                    ❶ Global event bus
   public EventSubscriberWidget2(SimpleEventBus eventbus) {     <--
      this.eventbus = eventbus;
                                                                    ❷ Add handler to the event bus
      eventbus.addHandler(ChangeColorEvent.getType(),           <--
                          new ChangeColorEventHandler() {
         @Override
         public void onChangeColorSent(ChangeColorEvent event) {    ❸ Implementation
            String col = event.getColor();                            of ChangeColor-
            changeColor(col);                                         EventHandler
         }
      });
   }
```

When you create a component in the application, you pass in the `EventBus` to the constructor ❶. This ensures that each component has a reference to the same event bus; otherwise, the bus would be pointless. You don't have to do it in the constructor; you could provide a separate method, such as `setEventBus`, but then you run the risk of the event bus not being set up before the application runs. (In chapter 16 we'll look at how this can be done via dependency injection instead of manually ensuring it as we do for now.)

Inside the component, you need to subscribe to the color-change events that will be published to the event bus. You do that via the event bus's `addHandler` method in ❷. This takes two parameters—the event type and the handler. To get the event type, you use the event's `getType` method, and the handler you have to create.

In ❸, you create the handler as an anonymous class, as you saw earlier in the chapter. When handling the event, you retrieve the new color from the event object and then use a helper method that uses GWT DOM access to change the color of the widget that represents this subscriber.

On the publisher side, you react to the user updating the chosen color by firing a `ChangeColorEvent` on the event bus:

```
String color = getChosenColor();
this.eventbus.fireEvent(new ChangeColorEvent(color));
```

Here you retrieve the chosen color from the user interface, create a new `ChangeColorEvent` object and pass in the color (remember from section 14.6 that we need that for this event type), and use the event bus's `fireEvent` method to fire it on the event bus (which will then be handled by all of the subscribers to this event type that are listening to the bus).

The entry point to our application is where we create the event bus as well as the other application components, for example:

```
SimpleEventBus eventBus = new SimpleEventBus();
Controller contr = new Controller(eventBus);
AppComponent a1 = new AppComponent(eventBus);
AppComponent a2 = new AppComponent(eventBus);
AppComponent a3 = new AppComponent(eventBus);
```

In this section you learned the major activities needed to define and use an event bus. We hope you've realized by now how powerful the event bus mechanism is, particularly for large applications where it's easy to lose control over the code. It helps you keep decoupled code and reduce the amount of refactoring needed to maintain good structure. Keep in mind, though, that `EventBus` isn't suitable in all occasions and that a good rule is to only use it for situations where you have several interested parties located in different parts of the application.

The various event bus types are similar with small deviations. What's common for all of them is that you perform some easy-to-learn steps that give you the most useful functionality.

14.8 Summary

You can build advanced event handling with GWT. You can create your own events and have them handled in exactly the same way as all other GWT events.

Unfortunately, you have to write a disproportionate amount of code: the event, a handler, and an interface. You have two types of events: those raised by the DOM—so-called native events—and those that aren't DOM events, called logical events. Previewing events is useful if you want to do something before the event gets handled, or maybe cancel an event.

Browsers aren't consistent in how they manage events, but GWT builds its own scaffolding around events in order to make all browsers react the same way. You can program against one model and expect consistency across all browsers.

You can eliminate evil coupling between different parts of an application by defining your own events that can be fired on an event bus. The event bus keeps a list of subscribers interested in a particular event, and whenever a publisher fires the event on the event bus, the bus notifies the subscribers. The result is distributed event handling and a high level of decoupling between the participating components.

Another good way to write structured code is to use the MVP, or Model-View-Presenter, pattern, which is suitable when you're building large-scale applications. In the next chapter we'll talk about how to build MVP-based applications with GWT.

15 Building MVP-based applications

This chapter covers

- What the MVP approach is and why it's useful
- How to hand-code the MVP approach in GWT
- How to use GWT's `Activity` and `Place` objects

One of GWT's main selling points is that it allows you to use an industry-grade language, with an industry-grade set of tools, to build, well, industry-grade web applications. But, as with any large-scale development project, you can easily paint yourself into a corner. Far too many times when building GWT-based applications, you may find yourself slinging code wherever necessary to make the application work and (sometimes more important) look good.

This makes your code development and, perhaps worse, your code maintenance a nightmare. No longer are you able to push the boundaries of web applications because you're spending all of your time and budget fixing bugs and scratching your head wondering why now that it's fixed *here*, it's suddenly all going wrong over *there*. And why, when you're trying to add new functionality, it never comes in anywhere near the on-budget number.

Fortunately, these problems have well-known engineering and architectural solutions. One of these is to build your applications around the model-view-presenter (MVP) paradigm (or pattern, if you want to call it that).

In this chapter we'll quickly review MVP to make sure we agree we're talking about the same thing (or, if we disagree, then at least you'll understand where we're coming from). Once we've finished our MVP review, we'll look at how to implement it, in two ways: first we'll hand-code it, and then we'll use GWT's `Activity` and `Place` objects. This might sound like double the effort, and it is, but we want to make the point that although GWT provides a built-in way to implement MVP, you're not forced to use it—and vice versa, because you can instead use `Activity` and `Place` objects, without implementing an MVP paradigm.

As usual, we've included some code samples that go along with this chapter—although, this time around, you have the added bonus of three projects to look at:

- *gwtia-ch15-mvp*—A basic photo application using a hand-coded approach to the MVP paradigm.
- *gwtia-ch15-mvp-enhanced*—The same as the previous project, but we're showing off by easily swapping out the view layer for another one and implementing code splitting to minimize the initial download.
- *gwtia-ch15-mvp2*—The project that contains the photo application built using `Activity` and `Place`.

If you've downloaded the samples, let's start this chapter by defining MVP.

15.1 What is MVP?

As we wrote in the introduction, we should agree on what we're talking about when we say MVP. It's an approach to dividing code into layers that solves a number of issues with code, which can occur if you build an application on an ad hoc basis. Projects built in an ad hoc manner suffer from four intrinsic problems:

- Adding new features will take an order of magnitude longer.
- They're impossible to optimize.
- They're extremely difficult to test.
- Fixing and debugging can be a nightmare (fixing something in one place can lead to something else breaking that seems completely unrelated).

MVP aims to provide a "separation of concerns" of logic:

- *Model*—Contains only data
- *View*—Contains only UI code
- *Presenter*—Drives and manages the views while updating the models when necessary

By ensuring there's no leakage between these MVP components, systems become easier to test, maintain, upgrade, and optimize. You can see how these interact in figure 15.1, which shows a version of MVP also known as MVP (Passive View).

Looking at the figure, you can see that there's a direct two-way connection between the view and the presenter: the presenter populates the view, and the view calls actions on the presenter as a result of user commands on the view.

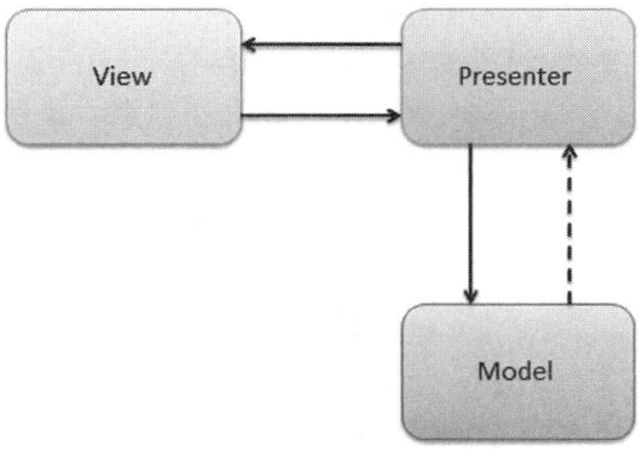

Figure 15.1 Visualization of how the MVP paradigm works. (The dotted line from model to presenter indicates that the model has no action on the presenter but the presenter does take the data from the model.)

You'll also see a direct connection between the presenter and the model, because the presenter updates the model, usually in response to actions of the user in the view—see how it's all connected? The dotted line from the model to the presenter indicates that the presenter pulls information from the model rather than the model directing the presenter, and it can sometimes imply that changes in the model by external entities are notified to the presenter.

In this MVP (Passive View) approach, the interaction with the model and view is exclusively performed by the presenter. There's another version of MVP called the MVP (Supervising Controller) approach, which we'll cover in section 15.6 when we look at how editors and data-presentation widgets fit into the MVP model.

It's worth exploring the relationship between views and presenters because it might look strange, even if you're used to MVP.

15.1.1 The two-way presenter/view relationship

At the heart of the MVP pattern is the relationship between your presenters and views. Presenter classes should contain all of your complex application logic and no widget code or references. Completely inverse to that, your views should contain nothing more than widgets and should avoid any application logic wherever possible.

Why? For two reasons:

- Fast testing with increased code coverage
- Maximum code reuse when porting to other Java-based platforms, for instance, Android (written carefully in the MVP paradigm, you can reuse the application logic of a GWT application, and all you need to do is replace the view component)

If you look at testing, enforcing this split between presenters and views offers another way to save more time, money, and development frustration. Whenever you need to test functionality within your application that relies on widgets or JavaScript Native Interface (JSNI), you'll need a browser context. This means you'll need to run it within a `GWTTestCase`, which means, you guessed it, it's going to take a long time to run that test because you have to fire up a headless browser instance each time. So how do you fix this? Simple. Don't test at all—if you make the view as dumb as possible, by moving all of your application logic out into the presenter, you should be left with a view that contains nothing more than GWT widgets. Given that these are continuously tested by the GWT team, doing so in your own tests is redundant and not required. And honestly, where you do need to test your views, those tests should be few and far between, and in many instances with integration testing being driven by Selenium (or some Selenium-like testing suite).

> **A quick note on connecting views and presenters**
>
> The more contemporary MVP setup you may have read about in previous articles, blog posts, and so on would indicate that the presenters register to receive events raised from the view's widgets. But you'll see that you specifically make the presenter register itself in the view, and that the view notifies the presenter by calling appropriate registered presenter methods when events are raised. This is a subtle difference that we'll discuss in this chapter.

Now that we agree on moving the application logic out of the view, you have to move the view logic out of the presenter. More specifically, you have to make sure your presenters are solely relying on plain-old Java code. This is to ensure that they can be tested using a vanilla JUnit test (which runs in ~1/1000th of the time of a `GWTTestCase`).

But you're also making the relationship between view and presenters slightly different from what you might expect. As we noted, the more contemporary MVP setup you may have read about would indicate that presenters register to receive events from the view's widgets.

But you'll see in our examples that we specifically make the presenter register itself with the view via the view's `setPresenter` method, and that the view listens for events and then calls the appropriate method in the presenter—figure 15.2 shows what we mean for the detailed photo functionality of the photo application.

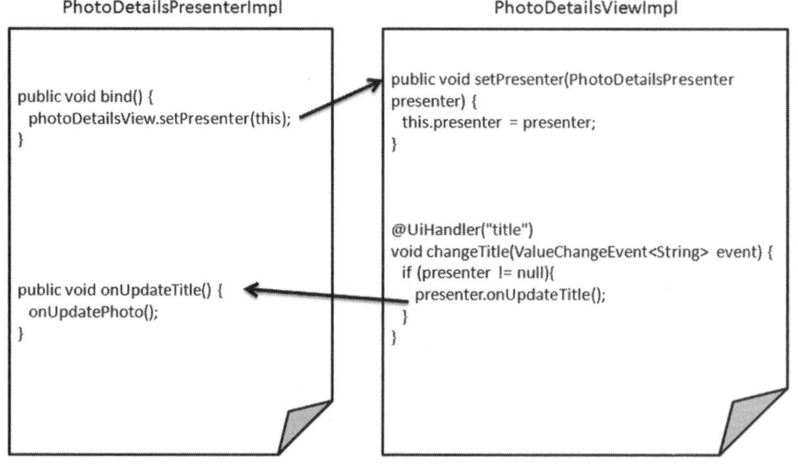

Figure 15.2 The coupling between presenter and view in our photo application

Technically, you don't have to make the presenter listen for events from the view widgets. But allowing the view to call back into the presenter makes using the UiBinder approach easy, as you can see in figure 15.2.

We've talked about the problems you may encounter when you're not using MVP, so let's discuss the benefits of using it.

15.1.2 Benefits of MVP

Many books, papers, articles, and web blogs have been written that explain the benefits of the MVP approach. We'll highlight five points:

- Makes testing simpler and more efficient and focused
- Enables swapping out of layers without major code overhauls
- Supports a modular approach to development
- Readily supports development by teams
- Makes using and benefiting from GWT code splitting a simple task

Are there downsides? Sure, you have to write a little more code, and you have to be disciplined in your development to keep the separation of logic in place. But with the benefits we've mentioned, you'd have to come up with a strong argument (or your application is too simple and will never be reused or enhanced—you've heard that before, right?) for the downsides to outweigh the benefits.

As we go forward, keep these two things in mind:

- Avoid being rigid in your design decisions. The MVP framework is a guide, and at times you'll need to bend the rules.
- `GWTTestCase(s)`, compared to standard JUnit tests, are expensive and should be avoided at all cost. What you want are JUnit-testable presenters that rely on nothing more than vanilla Java code and dumb views that need minimal testing (if any at all).

Why are those things important? Because sometimes we get too stuck focusing on the rules when a little flexibility makes things simpler, but other times we forget about the separation, and so testing becomes more complicated.

With those two points in mind, let's look at an overview of the `PhotoApp` that we'll be building in this chapter.

15.2 Looking at the PhotoApp's MVP foundations

Architecting your GWT-based applications to take advantage of the MVP paradigm provides the foundation and rails necessary to avoid some common pitfalls. Let's first look at how the user sees the application and then how we'll implement it from an MVP perspective.

15.2.1 From the user's perspective

If you fire up any of the example projects for this chapter, then you, as a user, will see the same application (which is good news, because making the types of changes you

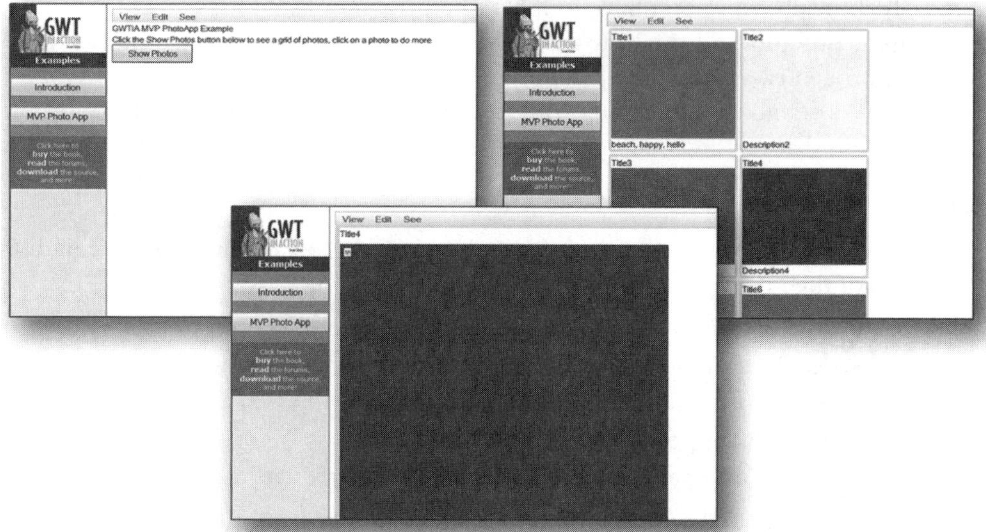

Figure 15.3 The three views in the photo application. The user starts at the `WelcomeView`, clicks a button to see the `PhotoListView`, and then clicks a photo to bring up the `PhotoDetailsView`.

want without impacting the application is one of the benefits we previously mentioned). Figure 15.3 shows the three main screens you'll find in the applications.

When you start the application, you're taken to a welcome screen (top left in figure 15.3), from where you can request a list of photos (top right) by clicking the Show Photos button or going through the menu bar options. Our photographer seems to have been in one of her abstract moods for this photo set, because they're all blocks of color.

You can click one of the photos to show a larger version, and that's where you can edit the title through an editable label that saved the new title back to the server if requested.

When any server requests are ongoing, such as getting a list of photos, seeing an individual photo's details, or saving updated photo information, the user will see a busy message display.

We won't claim this application is going to topple Picasa, Flickr, PhotoBucket, or any other photo-sharing site, but it's a nice application in which to explore MVP. You'll also gain a good appreciation of how GWT supports your building of industry-grade web applications by seeing how easy and neatly divided your solution can become (and we'll use the same application in the next chapter to see dependency injection in action).

15.2.2 From the MVP perspective

At its core, when you apply the MVP paradigm to the photo application, it breaks the app into the components listed in table 15.1.

Table 15.1 Components of the MVP paradigm

MVP component	Description

Model	The data objects that are presented and acted upon within the UI. The number and granularity of models is a design decision. In our photo application, we'll have one simple model:
	`PhotoDetails`
	Our model holds data about a photo, including the title, some tags, a couple of URLs, the date it was taken, and so on:
	`public class PhotoDetails implements IsSerializable {`
	`    String title;`
	`    String tags;`
	`    String id;`
	`    String thubnailUrl;`
	`    String largeUrl;`
	`    String date;`
	`    public PhotoDetails() {}`
	`}`
	In the application, the model has data served to it from a file on the server. Implementation-wise, we give a simple implementation that isn't robust enough for production use but serves our purposes. On first use, the model is read in from a file, and any changes made result in the whole model being rewritten to the same file.

View	It's not necessary to have a view per model—you may have a view that uses several models or several views for one model. We'll keep things simple for our photo application and use three views: `WelcomeView`—A simple welcome page `PhotoListView`—Displays a list of thumbnail photos and their title `PhotoDetailsView`—Displays the photo together with title and other data and allows the user to change some of those details (In the mvp2 example, we'll introduce a fourth view to show how you might use the MVP Supervising Controller model when showing a GWT Data Presentation widget.)
Presenter	The presenter will hold the complex application and business logic used to drive UIs and changes to the model. It also has the code to handle changes in the UI that the view has sent back. For each view, there will be an associated presenter. This could be a one-to-one mapping, or there could be many views driven by a presenter. In our photo application we'll have the following three presenters: `WelcomePresenter`—Pushes the welcome screen in front of the user and handles the jump to `PhotoListView` `PhotoListPresenter`—Drives the thumbnail view `PhotoDetailsPresenter`—Drives the view of the original photo The mvp2 example uses `Activity` instead of presenters and has a fourth one for the fourth view we mentioned.

We hope that gives a good overview of what the photo application will look like in our code. Now it's time to look at how it's built. We'll do that first using the approach of building the MVP code ourselves (and then see how easy it is to swap out the GUI for another version as well as see how easy it is to implement code splitting); then we'll look at how to build exactly the same application using `Activity` and `Place`.

We advocate using `Activity` and `Place`, because they're built into GWT, make the use of the MVP paradigm more obvious, and don't require you to build a lot of boilerplate code for handling tokens. But you don't have to use them, so let's start with implementing the MVP code ourselves to get used to the principles.

15.3 Building MVP yourself

Because MVP is a set of design rules, you can implement it in your GWT application by applying those design rules. You can download two versions of our chapter example following this approach. The first is a basic implementation in the `gwtia-ch15-mvp` project; the second is an enhanced version in `gwtia-ch15-mvp-enhanced`, where we've swapped the basic views for UiBinder versions and implemented code splitting.

Navigation to a new view is performed when the URL in the browser is updated—which can be either by the application updating the URL in the browser as a result of the user doing something or the user clicking the Forward/Back button. The application will react to changes in the browser's URL, creating the appropriate presenter, which creates/shows the associated view. We'll call the function that does this the application controller or `AppController` for short.

We'll also make use of an event bus, which you saw in chapter 14. We'll use this to raise application-wide events. To keep to the MVP paradigm, we need to be careful that these events don't cause changes in the model. What is their use, then? In our application we'll allow various presenters to raise `ApplicationBusy` and `ApplicationFree` events (these are user-defined events) when, for example, starting and completing communication with the server. These events will be dropped onto the event bus by the presenters, and the `AppController` will listen for them and react by showing or hiding a busy message on the screen (here's an example of us breaking out of the MVP paradigm where it makes sense—because the busy message can appear at any time, we could either add it to each view or create a new area of a screen as a view that's controlled by all presenters or only control the message showing from the `AppController`).

Using a ClientFactory

Throughout the two photo application projects you'll see us use a `ClientFactory` object. It will provide access to common objects across the application. For example, it provides access to our views as singleton objects (this improves efficiency because views contain DOM calls, which are expensive) and access to the common application's event bus.

There's no requirement to use a `ClientFactory` in the MVP paradigm, but it's helpful if you're thinking of enterprise-wide development.

> ***(continued)***
>
> A `ClientFactory` also helps us swap layers simply. We define `ClientFactory` as an interface and provide implementations that contain the necessary classes. Using deferred binding (a `replace-with` tag in the MVP module file), we tell the compiler which `ClientFactory` implementation to use. We'll cover this a little more later in the chapter.
>
> In the next chapter, we'll take the next logical step and replace `ClientFactory` with dependency injection.

Between a presenter and its view, there's a strong connection but loose coupling. Nice words, but what do they mean? Let's crack open some of the photo application's code and have a look.

15.3.1 Creating views

Remember that views should have no application logic in them at all. They should be UI components from which the presenter can set or get values.

All of our views will consist of an interface that we'll refer to elsewhere in the code (allowing future flexibility when it comes to implementations) and a separate implementation. We'll begin by looking at the interfaces.

VIEW-SPECIFIC INTERFACE

All of our view interfaces, which we store in the `com.manning.gwtia.ch15.client.mvp.views` package, will start as an interface that extends the `IsWidget` interface. This indicates there's a widget implementation of the view accessible through the `asWidget` method.

Here's the `PhotoDetailsView` interface:

```
public interface PhotoDetailsView extends IsWidget{
      HasValue<String> getPhotoTitle();
      HasValue<String> getPhotoTags();
      void setPhoto(String largeUrl);
      void setPresenter(PhotoDetailsPresenter presenter);
}
```

Because our view implementations will be `Composite` widgets, we're good to go with no additional effort (`Composite` already implements `asWidget`, returning itself). We'll also require any view implementation to implement the `setPresenter` method, allowing us to set up the two-way view<->presenter interaction we've previously discussed.

Each view needs to provide access to its UI components, allowing the associated presenter to get and set values as required. In the previous code you can see this in the title and tags areas. Both of these are accessed via methods that return a `HasValue<String>` interface (which indicates the presence of getter and setter methods), so in our presenter we can write things such as

```
photoDetailsView.getPhotoTitle().setValue("new Title");
```

Our example application has three views, and you can find the three interfaces in the source code in the com.manning.gwtia.ch15.client.mvp.views package. All that's left to do for views is provide the implementation.

IMPLEMENTING THE VIEWS

Our implementation of the PhotoListView interface, which we imaginatively call PhotoListViewImpl, is simple (you'll find it in the com.manning.gwtia.ch15.client.mvp.views.hardcoded package). It, as do our other views, implements the setPresenter method to register the parameter as this object's presenter, as follows:

```
public void setPresenter(PhotoListPresenter presenter) {
  this.presenter = presenter;
}
```

The view also constructs the GUI in code—hence dropping it in a package with hardcoded in its name. It creates a couple of DockLayoutPanels, an Image, and some labels and adds them all together, resulting in something similar to figure 15.4.

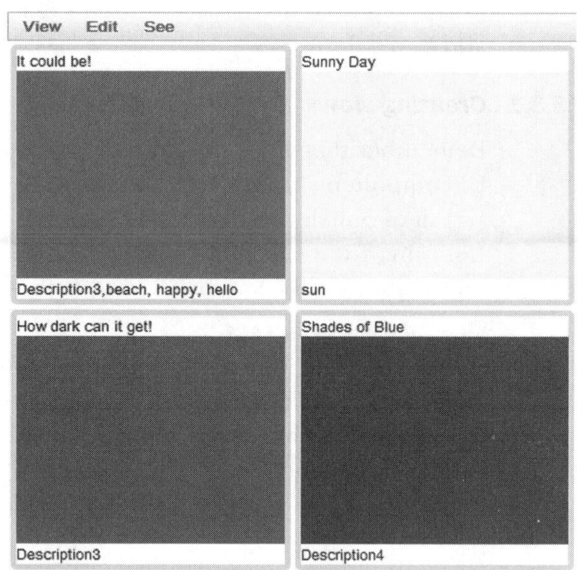

Figure 15.4 The visual result of building the PhotoListView implementation

We also set up event handling in the GUI to enable reactions to user commands. The guiding principle here is that any command that would result in a model change is sent to the presenter to manage. For example, over in the PhotoDetailsView we add a ValueChangeHandler to the title widget that calls the onUpdateTitle method of its presenter:

```
title.addValueChangeHandler(new ValueChangeHandler<String>(){
   public void onValueChange(ValueChangeEvent<String> event) {
      if (presenter != null){
         presenter.onUpdateTitle();
      }
   }
});
```

So our views are dumb and contain zero application logic. That's because we agreed that all logic should appear only in the presenter; and this brings us nicely to the discussion about those presenters.

15.3.2 Presenters

Presenters are where the application logic sits, and they have no UI components (those are all in the view, as you've seen). In a similar way to views, we provide interfaces (in the `com.manning.gwtia.ch15.client.mvp.presenters` package) and implementations (in the `presenters.impl` package). First, we provide a root interface that all presenters need to implement.

THE ROOT OF ALL PRESENTERS

There's no requirement to create interfaces, but it's good engineering practice to do so (they disappear during compilation, so you're not bloating your application's code). Here's our basic interface for presenters, declaring two methods that all presenters will need to implement:

```
public interface Presenter{
  public void go(final HasWidgets container);
  public void bind();
}
```

The `go` method takes the widget in which we wish the view associated with this presenter to be displayed. All we require of that widget is that it implement the `HasWidgets` interface, that is, it's a panel of some kind.

A presenter will also implement a `bind` method. In our design, this is where the presenter will listen to any application-wide events it's interested in (for example, this is where it hooks into the event bus) as well as where it calls the associated view's `setPresenter` method to bind the view to itself.

Each view will have an associated specific interface.

PRESENTER-SPECIFIC INTERFACE

The specific functionality of each presenter is given in a new interface that extends `Presenter`. Remember, the view is responsible for reacting to UI events, but it will call methods on the presenter for the actual business logic. Here you see the `PhotoDetailsPresenter` interface:

```
public interface PhotoDetailsPresenter extends Presenter{
    public void onUpdateTitle();
    public void onUpdateTags();
}
```

What we're saying here is that we expect the `onUpdateTitle` method to be called when the title is updated in the view, and similar for `onUpdateTags`.

Now that we have the specific presenter interface in place, we should implement it.

IMPLEMENTING SPECIFIC PRESENTERS

Our presenters are merely implementations of the specific presenter interfaces. For example, `PhotoDetailsPresenterImpl` implements the `PhotoDetailsPresenter` interface.

This means it needs to implement the go and bind methods from Presenter as well as the onUpdateTitle and onUpdateTags methods from PhotoDetails-Presenter. The following listing shows the skeleton of our implementation.

Listing 15.1 Implementing PhotoDetailsPresenter

```
public class PhotoDetailsPresenterImpl implements PhotoDetailsPresenter {

   private ClientFactory clientFactory = GWT.create(ClientFactory.class);
   public PhotoDetailsPresenterImpl(final PhotoDetailsView photoDetailsView
                                   , final String id) {
      this.rpcService = clientFactory.getPhotoServices();          ❶ Getting shared
      this.eventBus = clientFactory.getEventBus();                    resources
      this.photoDetailsView = photoDetailsView;
      eventBus.fireEvent(new AppBusyEvent());                      ❷ Firing application-wide event
      rpcService.getPhotoDetails(...)                              ❸ Making a server call
      bind();
   }

   public void bind() {
     photoDetailsView.setPresenter(this);                          ❹ Binding presenter to view
   }

   public void go(final HasWidgets container) {                    ❺ Implementing the go method
      container.clear();
      container.add(photoDetailsView.asWidget());
   }

   public void onUpdateTitle() {                                   Called from view when title updated
      rpcService.savePhotoDetails(...);
   }
}
```

The first thing that's done in the constructor is to make your life a bit easier by getting hold of some common resources from the ClientFactory ❶. For example, you grab the RPC service and the event bus—you might as well share the RPC service for efficiency, and you have to share the event bus; otherwise it wouldn't be system wide.

Once you've grabbed your resources from the factory, you make a call to get the details of the photo ❸ after you've fired off a system-wide AppBusy event ❷. The intention here is that some other component will inform the user that the application is busy in some way—you don't care at this point how that's done in the presenter (but see figure 15.5 for what it looks like on the screen). Not shown in listing 15.1 is the fact that an AppFree event is fired within the RPC return-handling code so that the user is notified the application is no longer busy.

Figure 15.5 Indicating that the application is busy by displaying this message when an AppBusy event is received over the event bus

Within the constructor you also call the bind method from the Presenter interface. For this implementation you call the view's setPresenter method, ❹, to register this presenter with that view. Other implementations may register on the event bus if it has to handle application-wide events.

In ❺ you implement the Presenter's go method. This clears the container widget passed in as the parameter and then adds the associated new view as the widget in the container. In the application controller, which we'll discuss shortly, we'll create presenters in the following manner

```
new PhotoDetailsPresenterImpl(clientFactory.getDetailsView())
                              .go(container)
```

where container is the widget in which we wish the view to be presented by the presenter.

That's it for the model, views, and presenters. But we still have no way of knowing which presenter to request (so we have no idea which view to show) or how to react to the user changing views. We need to control the application.

15.3.3 Controlling the application

We need a mechanism for changing views in our application. The most common one is to indicate in the browser URL the new view required, usually via a token on the URL, and then to react to that. If you remember back to chapters 2 and 3, this is exactly what the standard history support in GWT can do, so that's what we'll use.

In our presenters we'll change the history token to an appropriate value to indicate a view change is required:

1. The user clicks a photo in the photo list view.
2. The click is handled by a ClickHandler in the view, which calls the presenter's onSelectPhotoClicked method.
3. That method sets a new history token:

   ```
   public void onSelectPhotoClicked(String id) {
      History.newItem(Tokens.DETAIL + "&" + id);
   }
   ```

4. GWT's history subsystem picks up the change in the token and fires up the appropriate presenter, which fires up the new view.

For example, if we're interested in photo number 00004, then our development mode URL becomes what you see in figure 15.6.

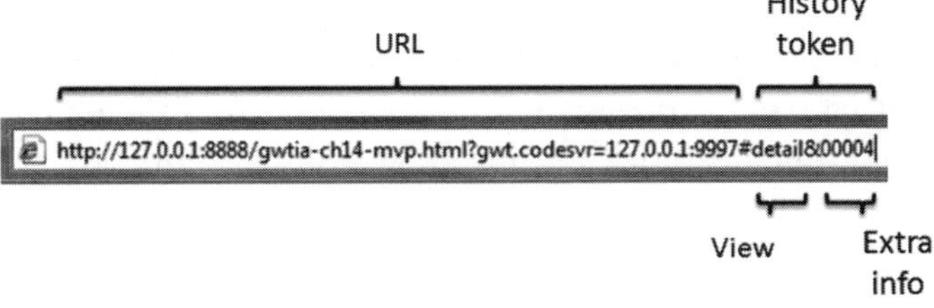

Figure 15.6 Development mode URL after photo 00004 has been selected for showing in the detailed view

Because we're using GWT history to store tokens, we must set up our GWT history management to handle when these tokens change and take the appropriate action—in this case to fire up the required presenter (which in turn drives the new view). We do that in a class called `AppController`, as shown next.

Listing 15.2 `AppController` showing `bind()` to `History` and other events

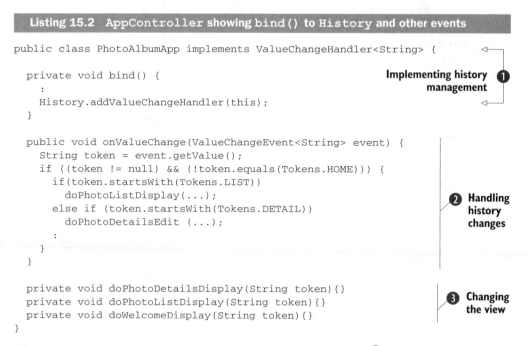

```
public class PhotoAlbumApp implements ValueChangeHandler<String> {

  private void bind() {
    :
    History.addValueChangeHandler(this);
  }

  public void onValueChange(ValueChangeEvent<String> event) {
    String token = event.getValue();
    if ((token != null) && (!token.equals(Tokens.HOME))) {
      if(token.startsWith(Tokens.LIST))
        doPhotoListDisplay(...);
      else if (token.startsWith(Tokens.DETAIL))
        doPhotoDetailsEdit (...);
      :
    }
  }

  private void doPhotoDetailsDisplay(String token){}
  private void doPhotoListDisplay(String token){}
  private void doWelcomeDisplay(String token){}
}
```

❶ Implementing history management

❷ Handling history changes

❸ Changing the view

The `AppController` binds itself to listen to history events in ❶ by implementing the `ValueChangeHandler` interface as well as adding itself as the `ValueChangeHandler` in the `History` object (see chapter 2 if you wish to recap this).

You must implement the `onValueChange` method ❷, which is called when the history changes by GWT's history subsystem. This method we set up to parse the history token to determine what view is requested and then is required and will call one of the `do` methods in ❸ if the history token is recognized and an action can be determined.

These `do` methods are responsible for creating the view and presenter and then calling the presenter's `go` method. For example, if we've changed to the situation in figure 15.6, then the `onValueChange` method determines that the value `detail` means it needs to call the `doPhotoDetailsDisplay` method. This action shows the user the new photo details view with the requested image, while the `AppController` sits there waiting for the next history change.

We mentioned that among the benefits of using the MVP paradigm in GWT were the abilities to swap out layers and engage GWT's code-splitting functionality. We'll group these together under the heading "altering an MVP application."

15.4 Altering an MVP application

We hope you'll remember that a while back we listed five benefits of the MVP paradigm. It was far from a comprehensive list, but it included the following:

- Readily supports development by teams (supports a modular development approach)
- Makes testing simpler and more efficient/focused
- Enables swapping out of layers without major code overhauls
- Makes using and benefiting from GWT code splitting an extremely simple task

All these benefits are arrived at because of the clean separation of logic between layers and the use of interfaces to code against. Various teams can work on different components without fear of interfering with each other.

Testing GWT applications can easily be done using the built-in support for JUnit; but, testing user interfaces is an expensive effort requiring the use of `GWTTestCase` (which instantiates a headless browser). If we assume that the GWT developers have already extensively tested GUI components and how they're constructed together, then why should we test them again?

Because views are isolated, we can swap them out for a layer that emulates user interaction but doesn't create GUI components, therefore avoiding the expensive `GWTTestCase` approach, and we can instead use lightweight and efficient JRE tests—you can see this pictorially in figure 15.7.

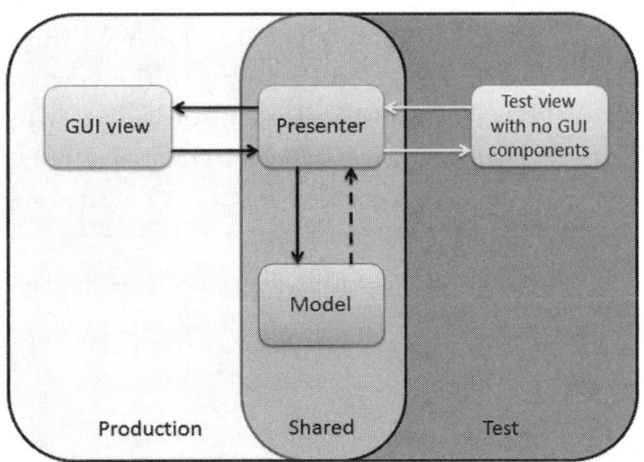

Figure 15.7 Visualization of components involved in an MVP application in production versus testing (to avoid use of the expensive `GWTTestCase` approach)

It's not only for testing that we can swap out layers. In the first version of this chapter's example, we're using the legacy approach to user interface development by creating it in code. In the next section you'll see how easy it is to swap that for another user interface (and after that we'll come to the interesting topic of code splitting).

15.4.1 Swapping out layers

You saw that you might want to swap out layers, perhaps for efficiency of testing, perhaps for presenting a brand-new view (it's conceivable you'll have one view for desktop web applications and one for mobile applications—but the underlying presenter and model are the same).

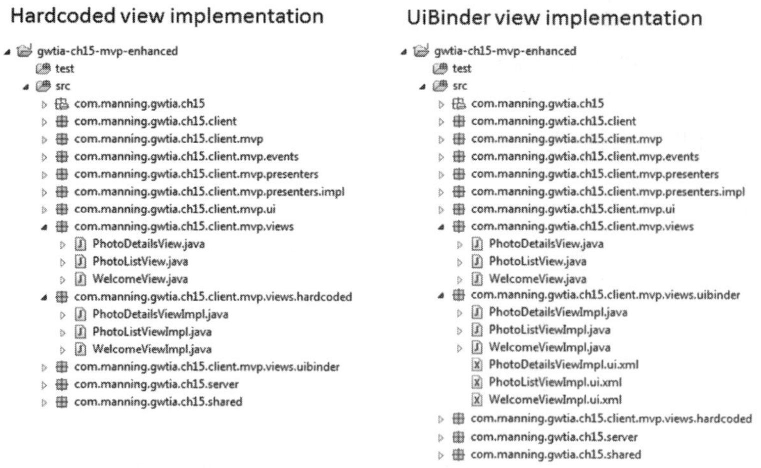

Hardcoded view implementation

```
gwtia-ch15-mvp-enhanced
  test
  src
    com.manning.gwtia.ch15
    com.manning.gwtia.ch15.client
    com.manning.gwtia.ch15.client.mvp
    com.manning.gwtia.ch15.client.mvp.events
    com.manning.gwtia.ch15.client.mvp.presenters
    com.manning.gwtia.ch15.client.mvp.presenters.impl
    com.manning.gwtia.ch15.client.mvp.ui
    com.manning.gwtia.ch15.client.mvp.views
      PhotoDetailsView.java
      PhotoListView.java
      WelcomeView.java
    com.manning.gwtia.ch15.client.mvp.views.hardcoded
      PhotoDetailsViewImpl.java
      PhotoListViewImpl.java
      WelcomeViewImpl.java
    com.manning.gwtia.ch15.client.mvp.views.uibinder
    com.manning.gwtia.ch15.server
    com.manning.gwtia.ch15.shared
```

UiBinder view implementation

```
gwtia-ch15-mvp-enhanced
  test
  src
    com.manning.gwtia.ch15
    com.manning.gwtia.ch15.client
    com.manning.gwtia.ch15.client.mvp
    com.manning.gwtia.ch15.client.mvp.events
    com.manning.gwtia.ch15.client.mvp.presenters
    com.manning.gwtia.ch15.client.mvp.presenters.impl
    com.manning.gwtia.ch15.client.mvp.ui
    com.manning.gwtia.ch15.client.mvp.views
      PhotoDetailsView.java
      PhotoListView.java
      WelcomeView.java
    com.manning.gwtia.ch15.client.mvp.views.uibinder
      PhotoDetailsViewImpl.java
      PhotoListViewImpl.java
      WelcomeViewImpl.java
      PhotoDetailsViewImpl.ui.xml
      PhotoListViewImpl.ui.xml
      WelcomeViewImpl.ui.xml
    com.manning.gwtia.ch15.client.mvp.views.hardcoded
    com.manning.gwtia.ch15.server
    com.manning.gwtia.ch15.shared
```

Figure 15.8 Comparing the photo application with a hardcoded view and a UiBinder view

In the second example of this chapter (`gwtia-ch15-mvp-enhanced`), we swap out the old hardcoded GUI of `gwtia-ch15-mvp` for a UiBinder approach; everything else stays the same, as you can see in figure 15.8.

It's a bit anticlimactic. The view interfaces remain the same, and we end up providing new implementations of the view interfaces, which instead of creating the GUI by hardcoding the creation of widgets, only have the UiBinder create code in the standard way. We also have to change the event handling to fit the UiBinder approach; for example, for `PhotoDetailsViewImpl` we update the title-change code as follows:

```
@UiHandler("title")
public void changeTitle(ValueChangeEvent<String> event) {
   if (presenter != null){
      presenter.onUpdateTitle();
   }
}
```

We use the `ClientFactory` to indicate which set of views to use by providing two implementations:

- `ClientFactoryUIBinderImpl`—Uses UiBinder views, for example:

  ```
  public PhotoListView getListView() {
     if (listView == null) listView = new

  com.manning.gwtia.ch15.client.mvp.views.uibinder.PhotoListViewImpl();
      return listView;
  }
  ```

- `ClientFactoryHardCodedImpl`—Uses old hardcoded MVP views, for example:

  ```
  public PhotoListView getListView() {
     if (listView == null) listView = new
  com.manning.gwtia.ch15.client.mvp.views.hardcoded.PhotoListViewImpl();
      return listView;
  }
  ```

And we set the necessary `replace-with` tag in the MVP module. By default, MVP-enhanced uses the UiBinder views, and so we bind the `ClientFactory` interface to the `ClientFactoryUIBinderImpl` class:

```
<replace-with
      class="com.manning.gwtia.ch15.client.mvp.ClientFactoryUIBinderImpl">
   <when-type-is class="com.manning.gwtia.ch15.client.mvp.ClientFactory"/>
</replace-with>
```

You can swap back to the old hardcoded views by changing the `replace-with` tag for the commented-out text in the example's module and commenting out the previous lines.

That's it—remarkably simple but powerful. A similar anticlimax is implementing code splitting using an MVP paradigm.

15.4.2 Optimizing with code splitting

If you're reading this book in chapter order, then you haven't gotten to code splitting yet. It's described in chapter 19, but we want to quickly talk about it here and how simple it is to implement in MVP. Code splitting is the idea that you identify segments of your code that can be downloaded on an as-needed basis and wrap them in a `GWT.runAsync` code block. Why download the entire application at the start if you're not going to use it?

The problem with code splitting is that if you have spaghetti code, it's the hardest optimization to implement because references that are strewn all over the place make it nearly impossible to identify where to split the code. But we're using MVP, so that makes it easier, right?

Remember our `do` methods in the application controller? They seem an excellent place to split the code. You only call a `do` method when you want to fire up the presenter, which then fires up a view. Because you're using MVP, you know that you have clear separation of logic between presenters, so you can have confidence that no dependencies to other places exist, which makes code splitting safe.

If you weren't using the MVP approach, it would be much easier for dependencies to creep into the code that you can't see, and so the code splitting could become less efficient (in the worst case, you'd end up with no code split, even though you asked for it).

All you need to do is wrap the `do` method contents in a `GWT.runAsync` block and you're finished. You can see this in action in the following listing.

Listing 15.3 One of our methods wrapped efficiently as a code-split point

```
private void doPhotoDetailsDisplay(final String photoId) {
   GWT.runAsync(new RunAsyncCallback() {
      public void onFailure(Throwable reason) {}

      public void onSuccess() {
         new PhotoDetailsPresenterImpl(clientFactory.getPhotoView(),
                                       photoId).go(container);
      }
   });
}
```

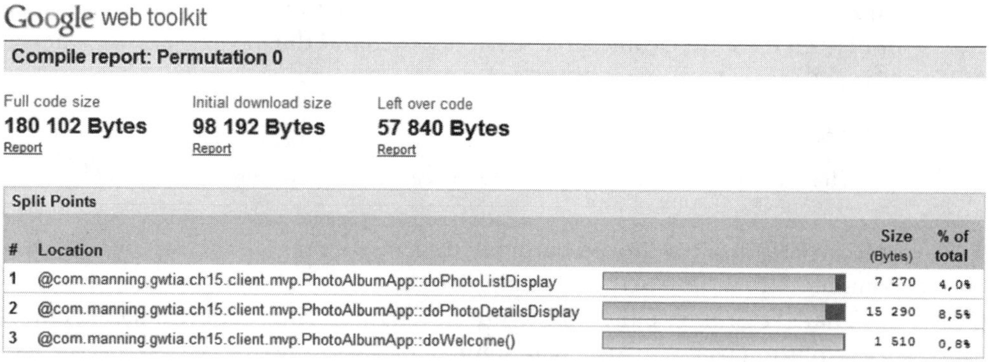

Google web toolkit

Compile report: Permutation 0

Full code size	Initial download size	Left over code
180 102 Bytes	**98 192 Bytes**	**57 840 Bytes**
Report	Report	Report

Split Points

#	Location	Size (Bytes)	% of total
1	@com.manning.gwtia.ch15.client.mvp.PhotoAlbumApp::doPhotoListDisplay	7 270	4,0%
2	@com.manning.gwtia.ch15.client.mvp.PhotoAlbumApp::doPhotoDetailsDisplay	15 290	8,5%
3	@com.manning.gwtia.ch15.client.mvp.PhotoAlbumApp::doWelcome()	1 510	0,8%

Figure 15.9 The compiler report for the enhanced version

If the `runAsync` call is successful, then the code segment has been downloaded to the browser and the presenter can be started.

We warned you that this would be anticlimactic, and it is. You can see code splitting in action in the `gwtia-ch15-mvp-enhanced` project. The compiler will do all the work for you, creating the split point and code segments.

To bolster the point, figure 15.9 shows the compiler report for the enhanced photo application (see section 19.2.1 for how to turn on this report). You can see that the initial download is now 98 KB as opposed to the full code size of 180 KB—a near twice speedup in getting the application running in the user's browser the first time.

The report also shows we have only three split points on the `do` methods, which is exactly what we're expecting (if our code was more spaghetti-like, then we could have more or fewer split points and a real mess shown in the report). The "left-over code" is code shared between split points, so if we call `doPhotoDetailsDisplay` we'll download 15 KB for that split point plus the 57 KB of left-over code.

Now we have reached the end of the first part of this chapter. You've seen how to implement the MVP paradigm in GWT from the ground up, and you have a couple of example applications in your hands to play with.

We had to write a fair amount of code ourselves to deal with history management, creating and parsing tokens, and so on. It would be much nicer if we could do MVP in GWT without needing to directly worry about that boilerplate stuff. And we can. In the second part of this chapter we'll explore GWT `Activity` and `Place`, which can be seen as GWT's reference implementation of MVP.

15.5 Activity and Place (GWT's reference MVP approach)

You can find plenty of implementation libraries on the internet for supporting MVP and even a few GWT-specific libraries from third parties. GWT itself provides what it calls `Activity` and `Place`, and these can be seen as supporting GWT's reference MVP implementation.

In this section, we'll take our familiar photo application from earlier and reimplement it using `Activity` and `Place`. You'll find the resulting application in the `gwtia-ch15-mvp2` chapter example project.

> **Don't forget**
>
> To use `Activity` and `Place`, you need to inherit the following two modules in your application's module file:
>
> ```
> <inherits name='com.google.gwt.activity.Activity'/>
> <inherits name='com.google.gwt.place.Place'/>
> ```

You don't have to use `Activity` and `Place` to implement MVP, as you saw in the first part of the chapter. Similarly, you don't have to architect your application around MVP to use `Activity` and/or `Place`; you may find other uses for them. But because they're made for each other, we're going to use them for MVP. Let's take a quick look at how they and a few other objects plug together to give our photo application functionality.

15.5.1 How objects plug together

In the earlier versions of `PhotoApp`, we hooked into GWT history to react to changes and pull out history tokens in the URL to determine which presenter to initiate. Sometimes we needed to parse those history tokens to find various data, for example, when retrieving the photo ID to show in the detailed view.

If you use activities/places, the user functionality is essentially the same, but you don't need to worry about the underlying implementation so much. You have a much more declarative way of describing what happens.

> **A place**
>
> A place represents a bookmark-able location in an application, that is, somewhere to go. It's a URL in which the user will enter the place in the browser's location bar. For example, our photo application has three places:
>
> - *A Welcome place*—http://127.0.0.1:8888/gwtia-ch15-mvp2.html#WelcomePlace:null
> - *A Photo List place*—http://127.0.0.1:8888/gwtia-ch15-mvp2.html#PhotoListPlace:0
> - *A Detailed Photo place*—http://127.0.0.1:8888/gwtia-ch15-mvp2.html#showPhotoNumber:00001
>
> Arriving at a place starts one or more activities.

Now the user will enter a place into the browser's location (an encoded URL), and GWT will kick off one or more activities that controls a specific piece of the user interface.

The activity has a lifecycle—starting, canceling, and stopping—and can react if you try to stop it, perhaps asking the user if they're sure they wish to stop it when they attempt to change the current place. Loosely speaking, the activity is the presenter of our previous examples.

> **An activity**
>
> An activity represents something the user is doing—writing an email, changing the email folder, creating an expense item, or even editing the details of a photograph. Many activities can be going on at once, though it should be a sensible number.
>
> Usually, an activity has an associated view and is related to a place such that when a user navigates to the place, the associated activity is started.

If you take a quick peek at the project structure between our old example and the first using this new approach, you'll see that it looks quite familiar (see figure 15.10).

You're free to use the concept of place or activity independent of an MVP approach. A place, with its neat way of encoding and decoding tokens, might be an interesting or better way for you to handle normal GWT history if you're not using the MVP approach. Or maybe the lifecycle support of an activity is useful in some way to your application without the need for dealing with places or MVP.

But we want to look at harnessing `Place` and `Activity` to support an MVP implementation. This means we need to provide a few other objects to get things linked together:

- A `PlaceHistoryMapper` that maps a URL to a place and encodes/decodes data into tokens in that URL
- One or more `ActivityMappers` to tell what activity to start for each place
- An `ActivityManager` that keeps track of activities running in a particular GUI component
- A `PlaceController` that keeps track of places our application could call

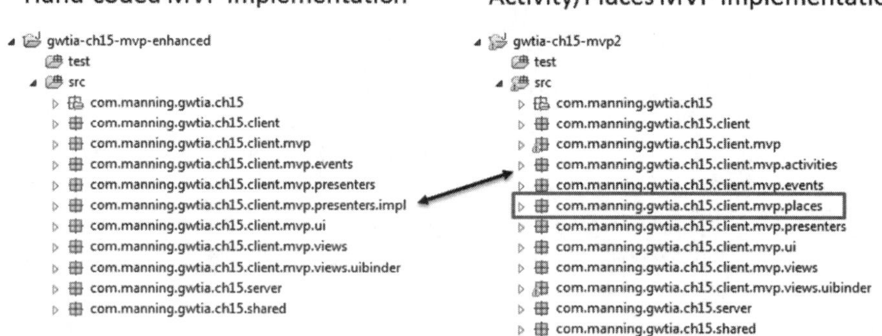

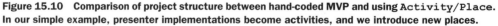

Figure 15.10 Comparison of project structure between hand-coded MVP and using `Activity/Place`. In our simple example, presenter implementations become activities, and we introduce new places.

These objects firing events across an event bus perform most of the controlling of your application that the other objects are listening for and react to—but that's mostly in the background, and you don't need to be conscious of the mechanism. Let's look at the bits that are involved in some more detail, starting with activities.

15.5.2 Activity

An activity represents something the user is doing: writing an email, creating an expense item, or looking at a list of photos. It shouldn't contain any UI code itself, although it's responsible for controlling a specific UI component of the application.

This component is close enough to the concept of presenters we previously discussed that you can consider them the same. There's some ongoing discussion in the developer community as to whether activities and presenters are equivalent or if an activity should create a presenter. For our discussion, think of an activity and a presenter as the same.

`Activity` is managed by an `ActivityManager` and has four lifecycle methods: `start`, `onCancel`, `mayStop`, and `onStop`, which the `ActivityManager` calls in that order (see figure 15.11). In addition to the four lifecycle methods, you can think of initialization as another function.

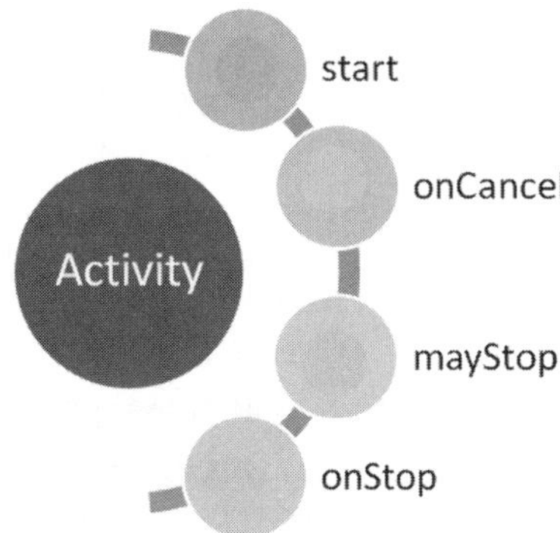

Figure 15.11 The lifecycle methods on `Activity` that are called by an `ActivityManager`

We'll update our photo application to use `Activity` and `Places`. In the `gwtia-ch15-mvp2` project, you can find a simple implementation of this chapter's example, and we'll begin digging into it by looking at the lifecycle methods of an `Activity`.

DEFINING

Any activity must implement the `Activity` interface to ensure the necessary lifecycle methods are put in place. For the photo application, we'll also make sure the activities implement the same presenter interfaces we defined for the earlier versions. For example, the `PhotoDetailActivity` (in `client.mvp.activities`) is declared:

```
public class PhotoDetailsActivity implements
                                    Activity,PhotoDetailsPresenter
```

(We won't get into a discussion on how we've named activities—they should be more descriptive and action-like, for example, `editPhoto`, but then we'd lose the link back to the earlier implementations, so we'll upset some purists and keep calling it `PhotoDetailsActivity`.)

Sometimes you'll have an activity that doesn't need most lifecycle methods. Our `WelcomeActivity` (in `client.mvp.activities`) is such an activity—there's nothing for it to do when starting (apart from showing the view), canceling, and checking if it can stop or is stopping. In these cases you can extend AbstractActivity, which conveniently provides empty implementations of these methods, and you override the start method to show the view—anything for an easier life!

Once you've declared the activity, the first thing that will happen is that it's created or initialized, like any Java object.

INITIALIZATION

Unlike the expensive view, an activity is designed to be disposable and so is created each time it's needed and may be disposed of when you're finished with it.

Initialization happens in constructor of the activity, which is typically passed the place that triggered the start of the activity. You store that place so you have access to values in it now or later. If you look at PhotoDetailsActivity in the example, you'll see that we get the photo ID from the place and store it for later use:

```
public PhotoDetailsActivity(PhotoDetailsPlace place,
                            ClientFactory clientFactory){
    this.id = place.getPhotoId();
    this.clientFactory = clientFactory;
    this.appEventBus = clientFactory.getEventBus();
    this.rpcService = clientFactory.getPhotoServices();
}
```

In our older version of the application, we had to build our own code to parse history tokens; here we call a method on the place.

We're still using the familiar ClientFactory to provide access to application event busses and views/presenters, so we pass it in here and store the required elements locally. In the previous code segment you'll see that we also prepare ourselves for some server-side calls by retrieving the RPC service we'll be using.

Usually we'll defer creating views and making server calls until the start stage of the Activity lifecycle for reasons of efficiency (why request a UI to be built if it's not used yet?).

STARTING AN ACTIVITY

An activity is started when the ActivityManager calls the activity's start method, which is declared as

```
public void start(AcceptsOneWidget panel, EventBus eventBus)
```

The ActivityManager passes in the widget that the activity controls as well as the event bus that the Activity/Place subsystem is using (this event bus may be different from the one your application is using).

You put creating views, extracting model data, and inserting the view into the widget that Activity controls in the start method. Notice that the activity expects this widget it controls to accept only a single widget, which means anything you create must be either a simple or composite widget.

If you look at PhotoDetailsActivity, you'll see that we get the relevant view from the client factory and then fire the busy event on the application's event bus, followed by an asynchronous call to get the photo's details; see the following listing.

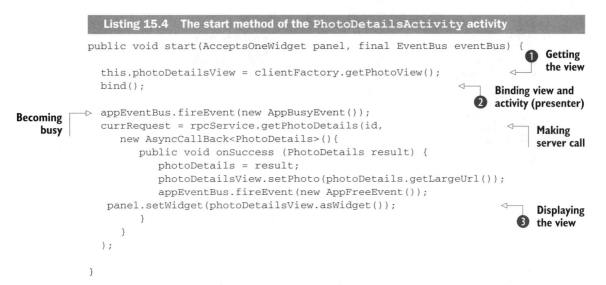

Listing 15.4 The start method of the `PhotoDetailsActivity` activity

```
public void start(AcceptsOneWidget panel, final EventBus eventBus) {

  this.photoDetailsView = clientFactory.getPhotoView();
  bind();

  appEventBus.fireEvent(new AppBusyEvent());
  currRequest = rpcService.getPhotoDetails(id,
     new AsyncCallBack<PhotoDetails>(){
        public void onSuccess (PhotoDetails result) {
           photoDetails = result;
           photoDetailsView.setPhoto(photoDetails.getLargeUrl());
           appEventBus.fireEvent(new AppFreeEvent());
   panel.setWidget(photoDetailsView.asWidget());
        }
     }
  );

}
```

Annotations: ❶ Getting the view; ❷ Binding view and activity (presenter); Becoming busy; Making server call; ❸ Displaying the view

Because views are expensive, due to the DOM calls, you retrieve the view from the `ClientFactory` as you did in the previous version ❶. The views in this version are exactly the same as the previous one—we're highlighting the benefit of the MVP approach, even in different MVP implementations. You still call the `bind` method as you did in our old version ❷, which at a minimum still calls the `setPresenter` method on the view to give the two-way communication between view and activity.

One thing to recognize here is that a view can outlive the activity, which is why in our example we set the URL of the image before we put the view in the activities panel ❸ (so we cleared the old photo before displaying).

During the start, you kick off an RPC call to get the photo's details. If your RPC call is successful, you set the widget of the panel that's passed in to the view's widget (the `ActivityManager` handles clearing the previous widget in the way that our old `go` method did).

We've made the asynchronous RPC return a `Request` object instead of the usual `void`, and we'll use that returned object in the `onCancel` lifecycle method.

MANAGING AN ACTIVITY ONCANCEL

The `ActivityManager` calls this method if the user is trying to go to another place before this activity has completed its `start` method. You can use it to clean up any initialization that's under way, if needed.

In `PhotoDetailsActivity` we stored the `Request` object of the RPC call so we can use it now:

```
public void onCancel() {
   if ((currHttpRequest!=null)&&(currHttpRequest.isPending())){
      currHttpRequest.cancel();
      Window.alert("Cancelling RPC");
   }
}
```

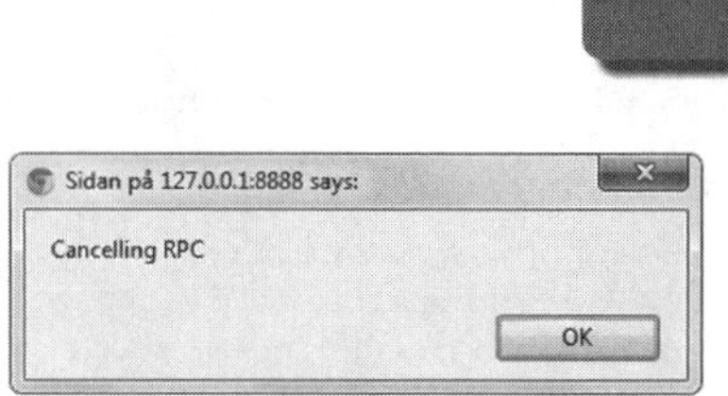

Figure 15.12 The `PhotoDetailsActivity`'s `onCancel` method in action. Here it's reporting that a pending RPC request has been canceled.

We check to see if there's a pending request and, if so, we cancel it (and for the sake of verifying to ourselves that it works, we throw an alert onto the screen). It's a bit hard to test this in development mode without cheating and introducing a delay into the server-side code's `PhotoAlbumServiceImpl` class. If we do so, then you can see the cancel working, as shown in figure 15.12.

Assuming the activity has started and has not been canceled before the `start` method has completed, then we're now into the part of the code that progresses any activity.

PROGRESSING THE ACTIVITY

The user will now be busy interacting with our application, clicking buttons, choosing menu options, updating text, and so on. As with the presenter in our previous approach, the activity will now react to those interactions and update the model as necessary. Events will be captured in the view, which has a reference to the activity (presenter) and will call methods there that we've created to update the model or navigate to new places—for example, clicking a photo in the `PhotoListActivity` will take the user to the place for that particular photo (`PhotoDetailsPlace`).

In our old approach, navigating to a new view required us to create a history token, stick it on the location, and wait for GWT's history subsystem to pick it up, parse it, and then fire up a new presenter. To navigate to a new view, we had to create a history token for the browser's location bar.

Things are much easier with activities and places. You create a new `Place` within the `Activity` and call the `PlaceController`'s `goTo` method. Say the user clicks a photo in the `PhotoListActivity` and then the view captures the click event and calls the activity's `onSelectPhotoClicked` method:

```
public void onSelectPhotoClicked(String id) {
   goTo(new PhotoDetailsPlace(id));
}
```

That creates the new `Place` and calls a local `goTo` method, which in turn calls the `PlaceController`'s `goTo` method:

```
public void goTo(Place place) {
   clientFactory.getPlaceController().goTo(place);
}
```

Under the hood, GWT is doing something similar to what we did in our old version, but in the new code it's much clearer conceptually.

Once you've indicated you're going to a new place, then the `ActivityManager` will check with the current activity to see if that activity may stop.

CHECKING IF AN ACTIVITY MAY STOP

Once the activity is started, if the user indicates they're moving to a different place, then the `PlaceController` fires a `PlaceChangeRequestEvent`, which the `ActivityManager` reacts to by calling the `mayStop` method on the current activity it is managing.

If the `mayStop` method returns `null`, then nothing happens, that is, the new place is navigated to straight away. But if a non-null `String` is returned from this method, then the user will be shown that message and asked to confirm going to the new place (see the section on `PlaceController` for some options around this display).

One enhancement we make over the previous version of the example is to ask the user if they're sure they want to go to a new place when they navigate away from the `PhotoDetailsPlace` and they've made some changes to the title or tags.

We use the `mayStop` method to achieve this by overriding it and returning a `String`:

```
public String mayStop() {
  if (madeEdits) return "Are you happy with the edits "
                      + "made to the photo?";
  else return null;
}
```

Doing that means that when the `ActivityManager` receives a `PlaceChangeRequest-Event`, it gets the text from the activity and updates that event's warning text. The result for the user is similar to figure 15.13. GWT will only show a standard JavaScript confirm dialog for this functionality (see the section on `PlaceController` for why). If the user clicks Cancel, then the navigation is canceled, but if they click OK, then we jump to the final part of the activity's lifecycle: stopping.

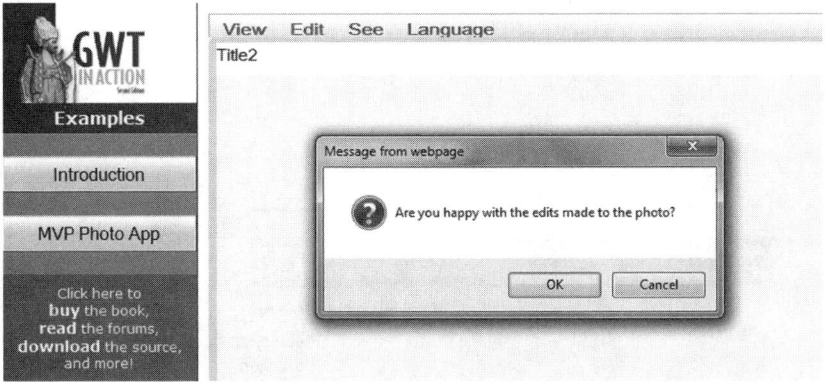

Figure 15.13 The alert shown to the user if a value is returned from the `mayStop` method in `PhotoDetailsActivity`

STOPPING AN ACTIVITY

After an activity has been stopped by the ActivityManager and the widget removed from the display, the onStop method is called. If you provide an implementation, it will now run. But be aware that at this point all event handlers the activity has registered will have been removed.

We use this method in the project's PhotoDetailsActivity to clear the image from the view to ensure there's no old image flashing momentarily when the view is reused for the next photo:

```
public void onStop(){
  if(photoDetailsView!=null)photoDetailsView.setPhoto("");
}
```

Before we jump on to looking at the other aspects involved, we'll take a diversion to consider how many activities you have per page.

> **How many activities per page?**
>
> You can have many activities on the page, and not all need to be visible at the same time. (You might use the start and stop lifecycle methods to make the views associated with activities visible or invisible.)
>
> Each ActivityManager drives the activity (which you'll see later in this chapter).

That's it for Activity. Now let's look at the other part of the Activity/Place approach.

15.5.3 Places

At its most basic, a place represents a bookmark-able location in an application, that is, somewhere to go to. When arriving at a new place in an MVP setup, GWT will start all the necessary activities.

To the user a place is a URL. To the application it's a URL made up of a location plus a GWT history token that's itself made up of a place prefix, a divider character (by default a colon, :) and a place-specific token. Figure 15.14 shows a place representing the same photo as was referenced in figure 15.6.

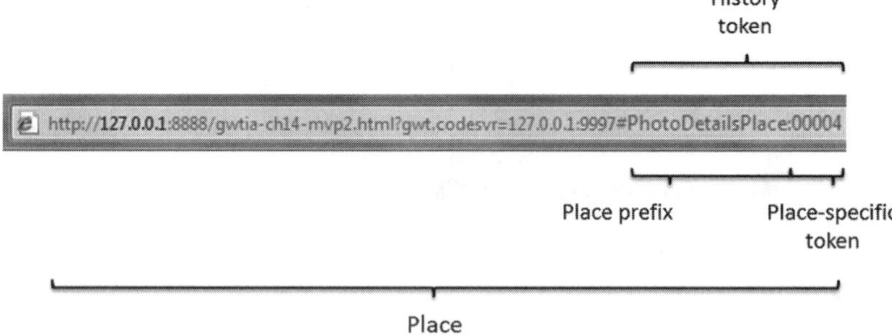

Figure 15.14 A place as shown in the browser navigation bar. The annotation above the browser location box denotes how a place looks if we think of it as a pure URL; the annotations below the browser location box show the interpretation of the URL as a place.

By default the prefix in figure 15.14 is the name of the place—`PhotoDetailsPlace` in figure 15.6—but it can be changed to more user-expressive text. The last part of the place is the place-specific token. In our example that specific information relates to the ID number of the photo, but it can be a more complicated encoding of state if appropriate.

How do you define a place in your code? You create a Plain Old Java Object (POJO) that extends the `Place` class and that can store and retrieve the relevant data, as in the next listing.

Listing 15.5 `PhotoDetailsPlace`

```
public class PhotoDetailsPlace extends Place{

    private String photoId;

    public PhotoDetailsPlace(String photoId){
        this.photoId = token;
    }

    public String getPhotoId() {
        return photoId;
    }
}
```

Listing 15.5 shows that `PhotoDetailsPlace` is a simple object. A `PhotoDetailsPlace` can be constructed by passing in the photo ID as the token, and there's a getter method for retrieving that `photoId`.

More complicated places will have more variables in the constructor and more getter objects to access those variables. You don't normally provide setters for the variables because you'd create a new place through the constructor rather than tweaking an existing one.

We need a way of translating a place POJO to the place URL and vice versa. That's performed by place tokenizers.

15.5.4 Place tokenizers

It's common, but not required, to define the relevant tokenizer as an inner class in the place. You'll see that we've done that in our project's code.

You can call the tokenizer whatever you want; in our application we're spectacularly uninventive and call it `Tokenizer`. It needs to implement the `PlaceTokenizer` interface using the associated place as the parameter—that is, our tokenizer in for `PhotoDetailsPlace` implements `PlaceTokenizer<PhotoDetailsPlace>`. You can see the basic approach next.

Listing 15.6 `PhotoDetailsPlace`'s tokenizer (inner class in `PhotoDetailsPlace`)

```
public static class Tokenizer implements PlaceTokenizer<PhotoDetailsPlace>{

  public PhotoDetailsPlace getPlace(String token) {      <-- Creating a place
    return new PhotoDetailsPlace(token);
  }
```

```
  public String getToken(PhotoDetailsPlace place) {      Getting
    return place.getPhotoId();                           the token
  }
}
```

Listing 15.6 shows the case where the token encodes only one piece of information. If it was to encode more, then the `getPlace` method would be responsible for parsing the token into the constituent parts and then passing it on to the `Place` constructor. Similarly, the `getToken` method would be responsible for building the single-token `String` from the various variables.

Remember our place prefix from figure 15.14? Well, we can make it a little more user friendly if we want by using an annotation.

CHANGING A PLACE'S PREFIX

The default prefix used in a place is the place name. This is probably OK for some applications, but you might have a need to change this. Maybe you wish to have more descriptive URLs or not have the prefix at all. To change the place prefix, you can use the `@Prefix` annotation on the `PlaceTokenizer` class.

In the photo application, we've decided that for the `PhotoDetailsPlace` we'd rather have a prefix of `showPhotoNumber` than `PhotoDetailsPlace`. Here's the code to achieve that:

```
@Prefix("showPhotoNumber")
public static class Tokenizer implements
        PlaceTokenizer<PhotoDetailsPlace>{.....}
```

Now the URL that we used back in figure 15.14 changes to that shown in figure 15.15.

http://127.0.0.1:8888/gwtia-ch14-mvp2.html?gwt.codesvr=127.0.0.1:9997#showPhotoNumber:00004

Figure 15.15 `PhotoDetailsPlace` when prefixed with `showPhotoNumber` instead of the default prefix

There might be occasions where you don't wish to have the prefix at all. That's possible by using the annotation `@Prefix("")`. But you should note that this also removes the `:` before the place-specific token.

Now that you know about activities and places, you need to see how you get from a place typed into the browser's location bar to the actual activity. That starts with mapping the history token to a place, through the `PlaceHistoryMapper` object.

15.5.5 PlaceHistoryMapper

The `PlaceHistoryMapper`'s purpose is to indicate where the tokenizer(s) that can map a place to a history token and back can be found in your code. It does this through annotations to a simple interface that extends `PlaceHistoryMapper`.

Here's the implementation used in the photo application:

```
@WithTokenizers({   WelcomePlace.Tokenizer.class,
                    PhotoListPlace.Tokenizer.class,
                    PhotoDetailsPlace.Tokenizer.class})
```

```
public interface AppPlacesHistoryMapper extends PlaceHistoryMapper{
}
```

As you can see, we provide the three tokenizer classes we have (which were defined as inner classes in the relevant place) into the `@WithTokenizers` annotation.

At runtime (in development mode) or compile time, a generator will link everything together and provide the necessary implementation. This generator is called `PlaceHistoryMapperGenerator` if you're interested in digging in to see what it does.

> **Not happy with using : in the token?**
>
> If the default way of tokenizing and mapping history tokens to places doesn't work for you, then you can extend the `PlaceHistoryMapperWithFactory` interface and use that instead.
>
> You lose GWT automatically building and linking things for you—such as grabbing the information from the `@Prefix` and `@WithTokenizers` annotations—but you do gain some flexibility that might be useful for your circumstances. We won't look into this in any more detail.

Now that you can map the history token in the browser URL to a place, you need to be able to map that place to an activity, and that's where the `ActivityMapper` comes in.

15.5.6 *ActivityMapper*

The `ActivityMapper` is the final piece in the jigsaw of getting from a URL to determining the activity to start. You create a class that implements `ActivityMapper` and implements the `getActivity` method.

That method receives a `Place` and is a large `if-then-else` statement checking the `instanceof` the `Place` and returning the appropriate `Activity`, if it can determine one, or `null` otherwise. The following listing shows our photo application's implementation, mapping the three places we've defined to the three activities.

Listing 15.7 Photo application's implementation of `ActivityMapper`

```
public class AppActivityMapper implements ActivityMapper{
  public Activity getActivity(Place place) {
    if (place instanceof WelcomePlace)
      return new WelcomeActivity((WelcomePlace)place, clientFactory);
    else if (place instanceof PhotoListPlace)
      return new PhotoListActivity((PhotoListPlace)place, clientFactory);
    else if (place instanceof PhotoDetailsPlace)
      return new PhotoDetailsActivity((PhotoDetailsPlace)place,
     clientFactory);
    else return null;
  }
}
```

Mapping place to activity

If a basic activity mapper doesn't float your boat, you could look at two wrappers that GWT provides—the CachingActivityMapper and the FilteredActivityMapper. Both take your defined ActivityMapper in their constructor. The CachingActivityMapper keeps track of the last place visited, so if the user goes immediately back there, some efficiency savings can be realized.

The FilteredActivityMapper allows one place to be interpreted by another; for example, you could implement this so that if a user goes to the PhotoDetailsPlace, they get sent to the PhotoListPlace. You could perhaps use this to redirect the user when your site is in maintenance (though it's probably simpler to do that via server configuration).

The ActivityMapper doesn't need to have a one-to-one mapping of aplace to an activity. For the BreadCrumb in the gwtia-ch15-mvp2-multi project we define getActivity to return the BreadCrumb activity regardless of the place:

```
public Activity getActivity(Place place) {
    return new BreadCrumbActivity(place, clientFactory);
}
```

Now that you've seen almost all the chunks, it's time to look at how they're pulled together when starting our application.

15.5.7 Managing the activities

If you remember, in the first version of the photo application we had to initialize history management, provide code for navigating to different views depending on which tokens we found, and so on. We also said a little earlier that place and activities help make this all look much cleaner in our code. Now it's time to see if we were right.

In the photo application we pull everything together in the PhotoAlbumApp class. First, we create the ActivityMapper and pass it into a new ActivityManager, along with a required event bus (we're using the one we previously created to be consistent across the whole application):

```
ActivityMapper activityMapper = new AppActivityMapper(clientFactory);
ActivityManager activityManager =
                      new ActivityManager(activityMapper, eventBus);
```

Then we tell the ActivityManager which part of the GUI it will be starting activities in, that is, where the views will be added (remember, this must implement the AcceptsOneWidget interface, that is, it must be a simple panel of some kind):

```
activityManager.setDisplay(appWidget);
```

Next, we start dealing with the places. We create our PlaceHistoryMapper and pass it into a newly created PlaceHistoryHandler. The history mapper has to be created through the deferred binding call (GWT.create) in order to get the compiler to run the generator and create and link the various parts together:

```
AppPlacesHistoryMapper historyMapper=
                          GWT.create(AppPlacesHistoryMapper.class);
PlaceHistoryHandler historyHandler =
                            new PlaceHistoryHandler(historyMapper);
```

15.5.8 *Controlling the place*

Now that we have the bits we need for places and activities, we introduce a new object called the `PlaceController`. This controls where the user is in that application as well as firing `PlaceChangeEvents` (which are picked up by the `ActivityManager`):

```
PlaceController placeController = clientFactory.getPlaceController();
```

After defining a default place

```
private Place defaultPlace = new WelcomePlace();
```

(we chose `WelcomePlace` because it fits, as well as being the place first shown to the user when starting the application), we're ready to register it and the place controller with our `PlaceHistoryHandler` object:

```
historyHandler.register(placeController, eventBus, defaultPlace);
```

Then we kick off our application by handling whatever place the user has arrived at when the application has been launched:

```
historyHandler.handleCurrentHistory();
```

Changing how confirm works

You might wish to replace the standard `Window.confirm` box that will display the result of the `mayStop Activity` method—and you may even have spotted that you can add a `Delegate` to the `PlaceController` during creation and override the standard `confirm` method.

Unfortunately, the only way to block the `confirm` method from returning is to use the `Window.confirm` approach, ugly on the screen as it is (and this is unlikely to change anytime soon; see GWT issue 6228[a]).

If you don't need to block the navigation—maybe you'll have a Gmail-like "undo" for some activity—then you should provide an implementation of the `Delegate` object when creating the `PlaceController` that has an appropriate `confirm` method.

a. http://mng.bz/s892.

Last, we'll look at the views.

15.5.9 *Views*

There's zero difference in views compared with our earlier version—but that's great news, isn't it?

We're finished. As you use the application and interact with it, places are changed and activities are stopped and started; the code is carefully, cleverly, and cleanly divided into various logical components so that testing, maintenance, and upgrading are a dream.

15.5.10 Code splitting with activities and places

Unfortunately, it's not so easy to implement code splitting in your application when using `Activity` and `Place` as it was with the hand-coded MVP approach. It's possible to do, if you want to, but we'd suggest waiting for the GWT team to put an implementation into the standard download. If that hasn't put you off, then you can follow the discussion in GWT's issue manager under issue 5129[1] to find out the latest thoughts on this topic.

If you've read chapter 9 on editors or chapter 10 on data-presentation widgets, you may be wondering how they fit into this approach.

15.6 Fitting editors/data-presentation widgets into MVP

At first glance you might feel that editors (see chapter 9) and data-presentation widgets (chapter 10) don't fit into this model. They typically imply a tight coupling from user interface to model, bypassing the presenter—you could consider that the presenter and view are together in the view.

There's a "little cheat" or "inspired architecture approach," depending on your view. The MVP paradigm we've discussed so far is also known as the MVP (Passive View) approach. In the passive view, the interaction with the model and view is exclusively performed by the presenter. There's another version of MVP called MVP (Supervising Controller), which is the same as the passive view except it acknowledges that the view can interact directly with the model for simple data binding—as shown in figure 15.16.

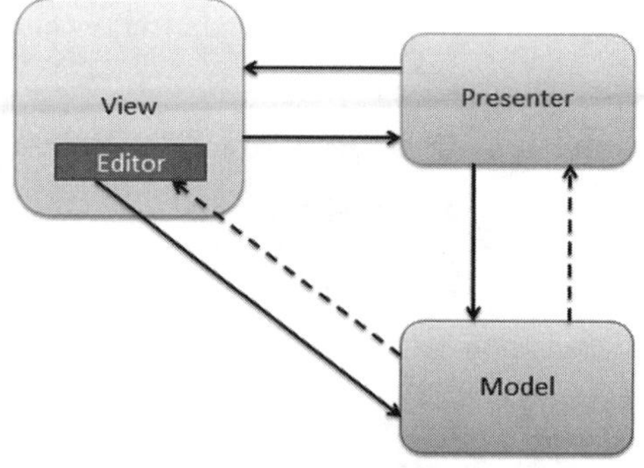

Figure 15.16 MVP (Supervising Controller). This variation of MVP is applicable when you're using editors or data-presentation widgets in an MVP paradigm application.

In the supervising controller approach, the main MVP paradigm is kept and the presenter will drive most of your user interface. But a small amount of simplistic data binding is allowed directly between view and model—this is a perfect description of using editors or data-presentation widgets in an MVP application.

For fun, you'll see this in action in figure 15.17, where we've added an extra view to the photo application, which shows all of our photos' details in a `CellTable` widget. We reuse the `PhotoListPresenter` interface for our new `PhotoListTextActivity` presenter, which fires up the view that contains the `CellTable` in the normal way. But it's the widget in the view that's now responsible for getting data from the model through its own data provider (see chapter 10 for more details on data-presentation widgets).

---

[1] http://mng.bz/MBz3.

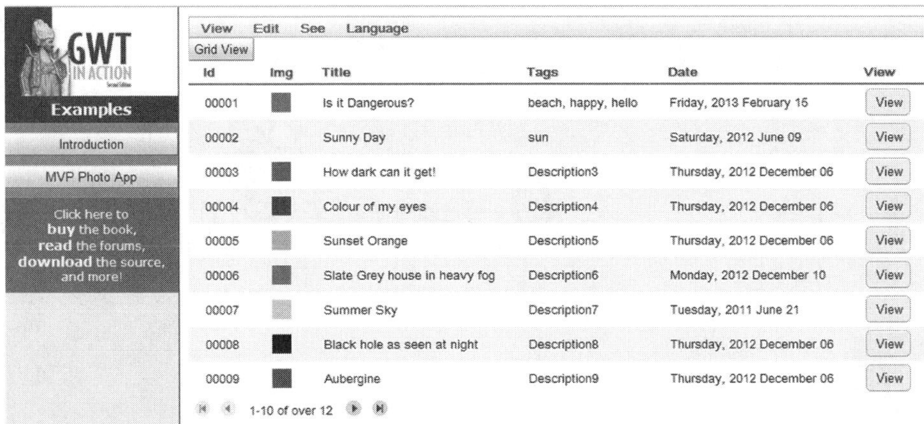

Figure 15.17 Using the MVP (Supervising Controller) version of MVP to integrate a `CellTable` data-presentation widget into an MVP-based application

Data-presentation widgets don't provide synchronization back to the model, unlike editors (see chapter 9). Therefore, you use the functionality in the presenter to save changes back to the model and server.

And with that, we're officially finished with the MVP pattern and how it can be used and how it helps your development of GWT applications.

15.7 Summary

We hope, with this chapter under your belt, that you've become a firm believer in the MVP pattern being extremely useful when building large, web-based applications with GWT. Not only does it help make code more readable, and subsequently more maintainable, but it also makes it much easier to implement new features, optimizations, and automated testing. Speaking from experience, we can't stress the testing benefits enough. It's a fundamental part of writing real-world applications, but oftentimes it's overlooked because it's left until the end and is too much of a pain to integrate. When your application is developed using the MVP pattern, test cases are a piece of cake, so much so that you'll want to write them first. Remember, test-driven development is your friend.

GWT doesn't force you into using MVP, and even if you take a `Place/Activity` approach, you're not forced to conform to the MVP paradigm; but we hope this chapter has shown that this paradigm should be implemented if it's appropriate for your application.

Throughout the chapter, we've been using the slightly mysterious `ClientFactory` to give us consistent access to objects in various levels. In the next chapter you'll see that we can swap this out and use dependency injection instead to inject those objects where needed.

16 Dependency injection

This chapter covers

- Defining dependency injection (DI)
- Using GIN for DI, and why it doesn't work for GWT client side
- Using GUICE for GWT client-side DI

Dependency injection (DI) is a technique that allows you to describe dependencies between items and inject relevant objects into your code (rather than having to code their creation yourself).

Why is this useful? It makes your upgrade path simpler, and your ability to support different devices is instantly accessible. Need to test with mock-ups? Simple, swap your functional implementation with a mock-up. Most of the time, you can do this in DI with a one-line change of code.

DI also allows you to remove a bunch of boilerplate code used in object creation, as hinted at in figure 16.1. But be careful with DI, because the removal of the boilerplate code makes it possible to lose yourself and others in dependency graphs—the result being that no one is quite sure what is created where, which

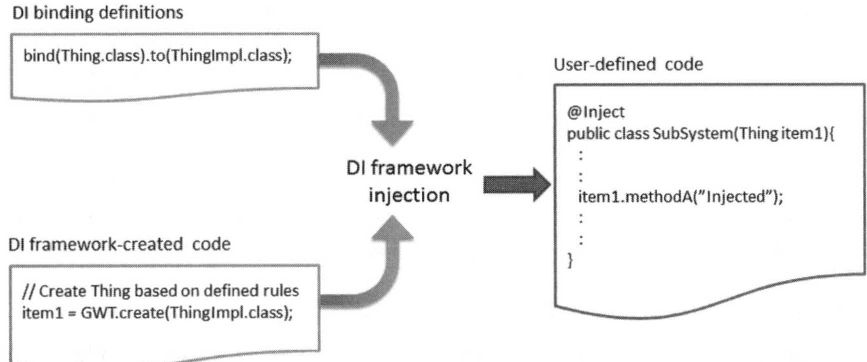

Figure 16.1 A schematic of dependency injection in action. Here "Thing" isn't created in our code; rather, an implementation is created and injected into our code by the DI framework in use based on a set of binding definitions.

leads to a maintenance issue. Like any technique, you must use it in the right place, use it carefully, and use it well.

This chapter is about using DI in your GWT applications, focusing eventually on client-side GWT code. We're going to take the photo application from the last chapter and apply DI to it. We'll as quickly as possible review what DI is, with reference to the *Guice* library—a common DI framework for Java, which can be used for DI on GWT's server side if you're using Java.

Then we'll look at how things are slightly different for DI in the GWT client-side world than normal Java. That leads us to use the *GIN* (GWT Injection) framework for GWT client-side code, and we'll explain why—but don't worry, GIN is built on Guice so what you'll learn first is still useful!

An alternative framework to keep an eye on that supports, among other things, DI is the JBoss ERRAI[1] framework (we won't cover that in this book because we focus on Guice and GIN, but the ideas you'll get from this chapter are equally applicable in ERRAI).

If you haven't read the previous chapter and so don't know the photo application we built, it's not a problem. All you really need to know about the photo application is the following:

- It has three user interface views (screens, in this case)—a welcome view, a view that shows a list of photos, and a view that shows details of a particular photo.
- Each view is dumb, that is, it has no business logic and is driven by an associated presenter object that can get/set data in the user interface.
- We implement an event bus for communicating global events (such as indicating that the application is busy talking to the server).

---

1 JBoss ERRAI framework: www.jboss.org/errai/.

In this chapter you'll see how to inject all the necessary views, the presenters, and the event bus and asynchronous server communication into the application, as well as how easy it is to swap out one view implementation for another using DI.

You can find the chapter's example code in the `gwtia-ch16-di` project from the book's download site.

We can't completely get away from defining what DI is, so the first thing we need to do is agree on what dependency injection is, what it means in a GWT application, and why there are occasions when you might not want to use it.

16.1 Dependency injection—the fundamentals

One of the goals in coding these days is to minimize the amount of code written. Sure, less code is easier to maintain, but let's be realistic; the slickest code is the code that isn't written at all. Boilerplate be gone, you could say.

Dependency injection allows us as developers to work with interfaces, and it lets code generators (and custom class loaders) provide the concrete class types. This technique works well in the following situations:

- Working with a framework or subsystem that has multiple versions
- Maintaining a multiplatform application (for example, a windowing interface on one platform might share the same interface as another platform, but their implementations are completely different)
- Mocking out your tests

Dependency injection itself isn't a terribly complex concept. That said, the way this is implemented within a GWT app is marginally different than other ways of doing so and can be a bit confusing.

We'll first look at the fundamentals, starting with how we'd have built things with no dependency injection, then how we could use the factory pattern (as we did in the photo application in chapter 14), and then how we could use DI for real.

In its base form, dependency injection is the ability to code to interfaces without having to worry about, or clutter your source with, specific implementations. It abstracts the lower-level services and implementations, allowing you to write clean, readable code that's easier to maintain and test.

Let's assume we wanted to build a computer. To begin with, the computer would need a hard drive to store data. It doesn't know how to install the hard drive itself and instead would rely on an outside service to do so.

The Java example in the following listing helps outline some of the dependencies that naturally evolve in this situation.

Listing 16.1 Example interfaces for a computer and a hard drive

```
public interface HardDrive {
    public long getFreeBytes();
    public void writeBytes(byte[] bytes);
}
```

```
public interface Computer {
    public void saveFile(String filename);
    public long getFreeSpace();
}
```

Two simple interfaces are defined: one representing a computer that can save a file and get the free space of a storage device; the other a hard drive that can indicate how many free bytes it has, as well as write a number of bytes to its media.

16.1.1 At the beginning of time

The straightforward, non-dependency-injection way of interacting with these components would be to create some implementation classes and directly rely on them, sort of like figure 16.2.

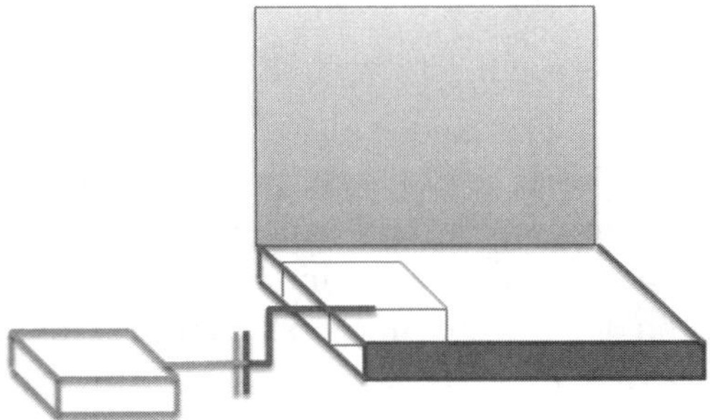

Figure 16.2 Implementing a computer directly

Code-wise, this could look similar to the following listing.

Listing 16.2 Example implementations of computer and hard drive interfaces (no DI)

```
public class HardDriveImpl implements HardDrive {          <-- Implementing the hard drive
  long freeBytes = 0;
  public long getFreeBytes() {
    return freeBytes;
  }

  public void writeBytes(byte[] bytes) {
    :
    freeBytes -= bytes.length;
  }
}

public class ComputerImpl implements Computer {            <-- Implementing the computer
  private HardDrive hardDrive;
  public ComputerImpl(HardDrive hardDrive) {
    this.hardDrive = hardDrive;
  }

  public void saveFile(String filename) {
    byte[] bytes = new byte[];
    :
```

```
    hardDrive.writeBytes(bytes);
  }

  public long getFreeSpace() {
    return hardDrive.getFreeBytes();
  }
}
```

We won't go into too much detail on these implementations. You shouldn't see any surprises, but our main point is that they're implementations of the previous interfaces. To use them in an application, you'd create an instance of the computer implementation and use its methods:

```
public class MyApp {
    public static void main(String[] args) {
        Computer computer = new ComputerImpl(new HardDriveImpl());
        computer.saveFile(("some file name");
        long freeSpace = computer.getFreeSpace();
    }
}
```

To get the `Computer`, you'd create a new instance of `HardDriveImpl` and pass it to the constructor of `ComputerImpl`. As the app grows, you'd need to make sure you pass around the interfaces and not the concrete types for maximum flexibility.

You can do better by looking at the dependency injection pattern. The DI pattern typically talks about three entities: the dependent consumer (something that needs to achieve something, for example, our main application shown previously), a list of the dependencies, and an injector (something that can create the dependencies ready for use in the dependent consumer).

Your first step from the simple implementation is to start using a factory class.

16.1.2 Straight from the factory

The injector for DI can be implemented manually as a factory class. Doing it this way allows you to abstract the notion of concrete types within your application and abstract the instantiation. This factory class would be capable of building the computer for you, as well as installing the appropriate hard drive, as could be envisaged in figure 16.3.

Figure 16.3 Using a client factory to instantiate and build our computer. If we need a different configuration, then we'll need to retool the factory.

Here's an example of how this could be done in code:

```
public class ComputerFactory {
  public static Computer buildComputer() {
    return new ComputerImpl(new HardDriveImpl());
  }
}
```

Again, nothing too complicated, and in the main code you'd now use this factory class instead of the direct objects you used before:

```
public class MyApp {
  public void main(String[] args) {
    Computer computer = ComputerFactory.buildComputer();
    computer.saveFile("some file name");
  }
}
```

This is definitely a step in the right direction, because your application doesn't have to know how to build a computer in order to use one. If you have to use a different process to build a computer or create hard drives, then you could provide a different implementation of `ComputerFactory`.

If you've read the previous chapter on MVP, then you'll remember that this is the way we left our implementation of the photo application. We created a `ClientFactory` object that was responsible for returning the various views, the event bus, and the asynchronous service for server communication.

We took it a step further in the photo application because we suggested that you can use GWT's deferred-binding `replace-with` construct in a module (`MVP.gwt.xml` in this case) to bind an implementation to a `ClientFactory` interface. Doing that makes it easy to swap out complete implementations of `ClientFactory`, for example, to provide test views or something similar.

The factory pattern is nice, but it still contains some boilerplate code that will inevitably grow as our app does. That code is unnecessary and ultimately creates more overhead than we'd like.

What we'd like to do is get away from this boilerplate code and manual injection and go to a world of automatic injection.

16.1.3 Automatically injecting dependencies

If we could somehow just tell the code where something needs injecting and let a framework do that work for us, then we'd remove all the boilerplate code for creation plus the need to manually inject things. Imagine writing something like the following:

```
public class ComputerImpl implements Computer {

  @Inject
  public ComputerImpl(HardDrive hardDrive) {
   :
  }
}
```

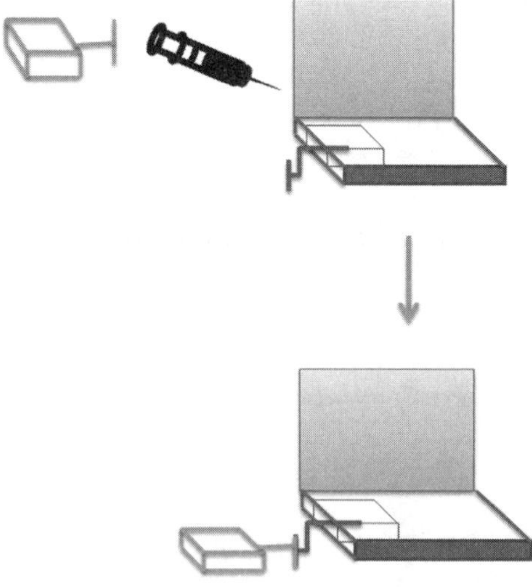

Figure 16.4 Injecting the hard drive into the computer as part of a dependency injection approach to construction

Some framework knows that the `@Inject` annotation means it needs to generate some boilerplate code that creates a `HardDrive` object based on a list of bindings held somewhere else, as in figure 16.4.

For example, that binding could be defined as

```
binder.bind(HardDrive.class).to(HardDriveImpl.class);
```

saying that `HardDrive` is implemented by `HardDriveImpl`.

We mentioned that a benefit of DI is that you can easily swap out implementations. What if you need to run some tests on a computer using a `HardDriveMockup`? Well, you'd just change the binding to

```
binder.bind(HardDrive.class).to(HardDriveMockup.class);
```

It may sound like a dream, but it's indeed possible through the use of a dependency injection framework. To look at that, we'll need a whole new section.

16.2 Guice—a Java dependency injection framework

There are several such DI frameworks in the world; one is called Guice, and we'll be using that in this book. Guice[2] is a popular Java DI framework that we can easily use for any server-side Java code we might have. Importantly for us, Guice underpins the GIN framework that we need to use for GWT client-side dependency injection.

We'll discuss why we need an additional framework for GWT client-side code a little later, but first we'll use Guice to go through dependency injection frameworks in some more detail. After all, it can still be used for any Java server-side code we have, and the principles we'll examine in Guice are in GIN.

[2] http://code.google.com/p/google-guice/.

Although you can download Guice 3.0 (at the time of writing) from the Guice website, we'll be using the version of Guice that comes with the GIN download, just to escape any dependency issues.

Every DI framework needs a way of defining dependencies and provides different ways of performing an injection, and we'll look at both of those now.

16.2.1 Defining the dependencies

Because we're going to discuss Guice, we'll define dependencies in the Guice way, and that means writing a class that implements `AbstractModule` (other frameworks might describe dependencies in an XML file). Guice's use of Java means, among other things, that our IDE will spit out errors if we make spelling mistakes, which can only be another good thing in our aim of minimizing errors.

For our computer, we want this dependency injection module to bind the implementation classes we have with the interface. That way, we can refer to the interface mentioned in our code, annotate its use, and let the dependency injection framework knows what class it needs to inject.

The dependency injection module is defined in the following listing.

Listing 16.3 Defining dependencies in Guice

```
import com.google.inject.AbstractModule;
import com.google.inject.Module;

public class MyAppModule extends AbstractModule {          ❶ Extending AbstractModule
  protected void configure() {
    bind(Computer.class).to(ComputerImpl.class);           ❷ Binding implementation classes
    bind(HardDrive.class).to(HardDriveImpl.class);
  }
}
```

In listing 16.3 you create a `MyAppModule` class that extends `AbstractModule` ❶. This lets the dependency injection framework know that this is a set of dependencies. Inside the class you implement the required `configure` method. It's also in there that you indicate the bindings between implementation class and interface, for example, at ❷.

The bindings are simply defined and almost in plain English. As you can see in ❷, you bind `Computer.class` (the interface) to `ComputerImpl.class` (the implementation). There's other verbiage you could use, such as `in(Singleton.class)` to indicate that a bound instance should be of the singleton pattern (one instance across the injector).

NOTE In this chapter we use a limited set of Guice bindings and scopes: just "to" and "in." For more details of what can be used, see the Guice documentation at http://code.google.com/p/google-guice/wiki/Bindings.

With the list of dependencies in place, you can start using them. The first thing to do is bootstrap the dependencies as early in the program as possible. The following code segment shows how to do that in the main method of a normal Java application:

```
import com.google.inject.Guice;
import com.google.inject.Injector;

public class MyApp {
  public static void main(String[] args) {
    Injector injector = Guice.createInjector(new MyAppModule());   // 1 Bootstrapping the injector
    Computer computer = injector.getInstance(Computer.class);      // 2 Getting a computer instance
    :
  }
}
```

In this example, you create an Injector object ❶ based on the dependency injection module MyAppModule. Then you request a Computer object from the Injector object created in the bootstrap. This type of injection is called *on demand*, and it's pretty much like the factory class we previously looked at. On-demand injection is just one of the types of injection that we're interested in.

16.2.2 Types of injection

Dependency injection frameworks usually provide several ways of injecting objects. Guice allows on-demand, constructor, field, and method (also known as setter) injection, as well as ways to provide further information, that is, providers. Let's go through each in turn.

ON-DEMAND INJECTION

If you call methods in the injector, then Guice refers to this as on-demand injection. Guice will see it and will resolve, through the MyAppModule, that objects of type Computer should be bound to the ComputerImpl class. Guice will therefore create an instance of ComputerImpl for use in the application.

On-demand injection is useful for initializing things, particularly if you're injecting singleton classes.

> **NOTE** Unlike standard Java, where a singleton class is unique across the JVM, in Guice, it's only unique across the injector. If you have two injectors, you'll get two instances. By using on-demand injection first, you can ensure that subsequent injections are the same object.

You may recall, though, that ComputerImpl requires a HardDrive to be passed to its constructor, and you don't see that happening in ❷ in the previous listing. Fear not; this is where we can introduce the other types of injection, starting with constructor injection.

CONSTRUCTOR INJECTION

Constructor injection is used when you define those objects that need to be injected in the constructor of the class. You know that the ComputerImpl object needs a HardDrive, so you can indicate that the constructor parameter needs to be injected by the DI framework. You do that in Guice by annotating the constructor with `@Inject`, as shown in the following snippet:

```
public class ComputerImpl implements Computer {
  private HardDrive hardDrive;

  @Inject
  public ComputerImpl(HardDrive hardDrive) {
    this.hardDrive = hardDrive;
  }
}
```

1 Constructor injection

Using constructor injection **1** drives Guice to create the necessary objects in the constructor and make them available. Guice uses the rules defined in our DI module class to identify that it needs to inject a `HardDriveImpl` object when it sees the `HardDrive` interface.

Constructor injection is the preferred approach from a Guice perspective—it's straightforward and clear to see what's being injected. But sometimes you might need superclasses in your code, and so method injection might be your preference.

METHOD INJECTION

Method injection (which can sometimes be called setter injection) uses injection on methods as opposed to on the constructor. A function so annotated is automatically executed after the constructor has been executed. For example, you could rewrite the `ComputerImpl` as follows:

```
public class ComputerImpl implements Computer {
  private HardDrive hardDrive;

  @Inject
  public void setHardDrive(HardDrive hardDrive){
    this.hardDrive = hardDrive;
  }

  public ComputerImpl(){}
}
```

Method injection

Now when a `ComputerImpl` is created, the constructor is executed as normal, followed by an automatic call to the `setHardDrive` method (because it's annotated as a method injection).

The way Guice works, you can even perform injection on a field.

FIELD INJECTION

Because Guice only cares about finding an `@Inject` annotation, you can use that directly on a field, for example:

```
public class ComputerImpl implements Computer {
  @Inject private HardDrive hardDrive;

  public ComputerImpl() {
  }
}
```

Field injection

This is functionality equivalent to the constructor and method injection in the previous section, but it's generally seen as harder to test and so is the least common/least preferred use case.

Sometimes an object to be injected needs some initialization code to execute; you can do that via the `@Provides` annotation.

PROVIDING THE INJECTION

These injection methods are fine if there's no setup or initialization required. If some is required—maybe you're injecting an object that will connect to a database and so need to set up that code before it can be used—then you'll need to rely on a `Provides` element, defined in the dependency injection's module file.

Providing the code is a case of defining a method in the dependency injection module that returns the type expected and is annotated with `@Provides`.

To keep with our example, let's assume that when we create a computer, we also want to stamp it with the manufacturer that inspected it. We'll update `MyAppModule`, as shown in the following listing.

Listing 16.4 Guice description for provider injection

```
import com.google.inject.client.AbstractModule;
import com.google.inject.Provides;

public class MyAppModule extends AbstractModule {

  protected void configure() {
    bind(HardDrive.class).to(HardDriveImpl.class);     // Binding implementation classes as normal
  }

  @Provides                                            // (1) Indicating a Provides element
  Computer provideComputer() {
    Computer computer = new ComputerImpl();            // (2) Providing a Computer
    computer.setManufacturer("Acme Computing");
    return computer;
  }
}
```

You define a `provideComputer` method (2), which returns a `Computer` type and is annotated with `@Provides` (1). When injecting a `Computer`, Guice will find this method and inject the result. Notice as well that the bind on `Computer` to `ComputerImpl` has been removed from the `configure` method, because it's now performed by the `provideComputer` method.

So that's DI, and it's exactly how you could use DI on the server side of your GWT application if you're using Guice. If you're using a different framework or language, then you'd just follow its rules. All of them will have a way of defining the dependencies, and all perform the injection at runtime, usually through Java reflection.

Ahh! That last part of that last sentence is where the issue comes in for GWT. At runtime, your application isn't Java and doesn't support runtime class loading or reflection. So it would seem that DI doesn't work for GWT on the client side.

Luckily, the GIN library, built on top of Guice, allows you to work with this limitation.

16.3 GIN—how DI differs in a GWT application

Guice relies heavily on the runtime reflection ability of Java. This is great for server-side GWT code because reflection is available there. But runtime reflection isn't available on the client side of GWT (because it comes at the cost of, for example, compiler optimizations). With no runtime reflection, standard Guice just won't work for client-side GWT injection.

Luckily, step forward the GWT Injection (GIN) library, which performs the necessary injections at GWT compile time, where reflection is supported (for the compiler).

To get a bit more specific, Guice uses tricks such as implementing a custom class loader to inject the necessary classes, whereas GIN injects the necessary intermediate forms that are then compiled into the resulting application.

> **Problems with GIN?**
>
> We mean the GWT Injection library here, not the drink—though we're not going to say no to a nice Bombay Sapphire, tonic, and lots of ice on a sunny balcony.
>
> But back to IT. GIN has a readily accessible issue list that you can review if you're having problems and add to if yours is unique. You can find it here: http://code.google.com/p/google-gin/issues/list.

Beyond that, the two frameworks are almost identical, and GIN uses Guice under the hood—so all you've learned earlier in this chapter is still relevant. But using GIN instead of Guice means you have to take note of the following three differences:

- You must use `AbstractGinModule` instead of `AbstractModule`.
- You must provide a `Ginjector` interface definition rather than relying on the runtime reflection Guice `Injector`.
- You need to use `GWT.create` to create your `Ginjector` instance in order to drive GWT's generators (see chapter 17) to create bindings and the like.

You also need to set up your GWT application to be able to use GIN.

16.3.1 Setting up for GIN

To use DI in client-side GWT, at the time of writing this chapter, you need to download and add the following libraries to your build path:

- gin-1.5.jar
- guice-snapshot.jar
- guice-assistedinject-snapshot.jar
- aopalliance.jar
- javax.inject.jar

You can get all these in a zip file to be downloaded from the GIN website.[3]

> **Beware**
>
> There are two gin-1.5 jar files:
>
> - *gin-1.5-pre-gwt-2.2.jar*—For use with GWT version 2.2 and below
> - *gin-1.5-post-gwt-2.2.jar*—For use with GWT above version 2.2 (GWT 2.5 was the latest release at the time of writing, so it's most likely the jar that you'll use)
>
> Make sure you use the right version; otherwise you'll get lots of errors because the underlying compile-time reflection in GWT changes between version 2.2 and later versions.
>
> If you navigate to the Guice website, you could download the latest Guice and replace the guice-assistedinject-snaphot, aopalliance, and javax.inject jars in the GIN download with those latest versions, but you'd have to check to make sure they're still compatible.

Place the jar files anywhere you like, but remember to make sure they're included on your classpath. If we're only doing client-side dependency injection, our preference is to create a lib folder in the project and store these jar files there (they don't need to be in the WEB-INF directory because they won't be deployed to the server, which they would be if you had server-side dependency injection).

> **Don't forget**
>
> You also need to add the following definition to one of your GWT module files to give GWT access to the necessary classes and generators:
>
> ```
> <inherits name="com.google.gwt.inject.Inject"/>
> ```
>
> You need to make sure that compiled Java classes are available to GWT at compilation time. You do that by making sure your war/WEB-INF/classes directory is added to your classpath.

Now that your IDE is set up to use GIN, you'll start using it, beginning with defining the dependencies.

16.3.2 Defining the dependencies

The definition of a GIN dependency injection module will look familiar from the Guice definition but with one slight difference: it extends `AbstractGinModule` rather than `AbstractModule`.

TIP If you want to make a GIN module available as a Guice module, you can use the `GinModuleAdapter` class.

---

[3] http://code.google.com/p/google-gin/.

Let's jump at this point from our computer example to a more substantial application: our photo application. If you've read the previous chapter on MVP, then this will be familiar to you. If you haven't, then don't worry too much; you just need to know that we have a number of views (user interface screens) that are linked to a number of presenters (that control the data in the views), all of which are controlled by an application, with an event bus running throughout.

We'll inject views into presenters, and presenters into the application, and the event bus into almost everything. The next listing is a snippet of our `PhotoAppGinModule` class, which resides in the `com.manning.gwtia.ch16.client.di` package.

Listing 16.5 Defining some of the photo application dependencies

```
public class PhotoAppGinModule extends AbstractGinModule{

   @Override
    protected void configure() {
       bind(WelcomeView.class).to(WelcomeViewImpl.class).in(Singleton.class);
        bind(EventBus.class).to(SimpleEventBus.class).in(Singleton.class);
      bind(PhotoDetailsPresenter.class).to(PhotoDetailsPresenterImpl.class);

        :
    }
}
```

Listing 16.5 extends `AbstractGinModule`, as you'd expect, and provides just the `configure` method. This method is the same as what you'd define using Guice, though there are some restrictions on what methods can be used in GIN compared to Guice (see the following sidebar).

GIN/Guice compatibility

For the latest on the compatibility between GIN and Guice, including what configuration and runtime functionality of Guice is available in GIN, it's best to check out the GIN project home page: http://code.google.com/p/google-gin/wiki/GuiceCompatibility.

In our example the binding module just binds some implementations to the view, presenter, and event bus interfaces used in the photo application. You can also optionally define methods annotated with `@Provides` in the module that do the same as you saw in Guice.

The point of interest in the definition is that the views and event bus are defined in the singleton scope; that is, they have `.in(Singleton.class)` as part of their definition and so will be injected as singleton classes, but the presenters won't. This is a design decision, which makes sense for our application but for two different reasons.

The event bus is used across components, so we need to ensure that every injection uses the same thing—otherwise components would be putting messages on individual event buses that aren't linked and so defeat the purpose!

Our rationale for creating views in the singleton scope is that they're expensive UI items to build. Once they're built, we shouldn't waste our time building them again; we can just refresh the data in them if they're shown again. By creating them in the singleton scope, we achieve just that.

You might notice in the example's code that there are two definitions for binding of `PhotoListView`, one of which is commented out. We'll come back to this in section 16.5 when we discuss how easy it is to swap views using DI.

So the definition of dependency injection modules between Guice and GIN isn't too different. Where you do see greater differences is in the bootstrapping process. In Guice you could just access the `Injector` class directly passing in a class, and then Guice would use runtime reflection to get the appropriate object. You can't do that in GWT, so it's a little more of a manual process.

16.3.3 Bootstrapping the injection

In GIN you must create a `Ginjector` interface yourself, because of the lack of runtime reflection, whereas you may remember that it gets created automatically in Guice. Within the interface you need to write a number of getter methods for the objects that will be injected.

The following listing shows the photo application's `Ginjector`.

Listing 16.6 The photo application's injector interface

```
@GinModules(PhotoAppGinModule.class)                          ❶ Pointing to DI module
public interface PhotoAppGinjector extends Ginjector{         ❷ Extending Ginjector
    EventBus getEventBus();                                   ❸ Getting the event bus
    PhotoAlbumServiceAsync getPhotoServices();
    PhotoDetailsView getPhotoView();
    PhotoListView getListView();                              ❹ Getting a view
    WelcomeView getWelcomeView();
    WelcomePresenter getWelcomePresenter();
    PhotoListPresenter getPhotoListPresenter();
    PhotoDetailsPresenter getPhotoDetailsPresenter();         ❺ Getting a presenter
}
```

This meets the requirements placed in `Ginjector` definitions—it uses the `@GinModules` annotation ❶ to point to the module file you've already created; it extends the `Ginjector` interface ❷, and it provides a number of getter functions for the objects you'll inject, for example, ❸, ❹, and ❺.

Internally, GIN will use the deferred binding `GWT.create` method to instantiate objects being injected during compile time. This means the GIN generator will get to work creating the required Java class, resolving dependencies recursively.

Because GIN uses the `GWT.create` method, there's an additional subtlety that's often to your benefit. If GIN can't find a binding in the dependency module file for an object you're injecting, say it can't find `bind(MyImages.class).to(MyImagesImpl.class)`, then it falls back to creating the object as just `GWT.create(MyImages.class)`.

Now if MyImages is a ClientBundle, then GIN automatically calls the standard deferred-binding functionality for client bundles (see chapter 5). This is equally true if you're injecting a GWT-RPC asynchronous call—as you'll see later—or a static internationalization object, or it can be developer defined if the developer has set up GWT in a way that harnesses GWT.create.

The dependency injection bootstrapping should be upgraded from the Guice version to use GWT.create method to create an instance of PhotoAppGinjector. Your application could look something like this:

```
public class PhotoAlbumApp implements EntryPoint {
  private final PhotoAppGinjector injector =
        GWT.create(PhotoAppGinjector.class);

  public void onModuleLoad() {
    this.eventBus = injector.getEventBus();
    :
  }
}
```

❶ **Bootstrapping GIN injector**

❷ **On-demand injection**

Calling GWT.create() with a PhotoAppGinjector.class ❶ will bootstrap your injector class, which you can then use to on-demand inject an EventBus ❷. The actual injector class is created at compile time by a generator within GIN, but because we're using interfaces here, the code is syntactically correct.

Just as in the Guice example, the act of injecting various objects will, in turn, inject all of its dependencies and so on. Let's see that in action as we look at where else in the photo application we employ dependency injection.

16.3.4 Types of injection

GIN has the same types of injection as Guice: on-demand, constructor, method (setter), and field. We'll use each of those dependency-injection methods in our photo application. Specifically, we'll inject the following:

- Presenters into the application via *on-demand injection*
- Views into the presenters as singleton classes via *constructor injection* in the presenters (they use DOM calls and so are expensive but only need creating once)
- The data services via *method injection*
- The event bus across the application via *field injection*

In a real application you probably wouldn't use all types of injection, but because we're in the business of showing how things work, we will. You can see the result in the gwtia-ch16-di project in this book's downloads on the website, so let's look through what we've done.

ON-DEMAND INJECTION

Inside the photo application, you've already seen some on-demand injection because we bootstrapped the injector in the startup code, but we'll also use on-demand injection to inject our presenters. The relevant parts of the application are shown in the following listing.

Listing 16.7 Dependency injection in the photo application

```
public class PhotoAlbumApp implements ValueChangeHandler<String> {

  EventBus eventBus;
  HasWidgets container;
  private final PhotoAppGinjector injector =
                           GWT.create(PhotoAppGinjector.class);

  private void doPhotoListDisplay(final String page){
    PhotoListPresenter pres = injector.getPhotoListPresenter();   // Injecting the presenter ❶
    pres.onNewPhotosNeeded();
    pres.go(container);
  }
}
```

At ❶ you on-demand inject one of the presenters, in this case the `PhotoListPresenter`, which is responsible for controlling the photo list view.

If you're familiar with this from previous chapter, you'll probably remember that there we needed to create a view and pass that in as a parameter to the presenter as we created that. This is missing in listing 16.7 because we'll use constructor injection in the presenter to inject it.

CONSTRUCTOR INJECTION

Injection in the constructor is probably the most common approach. Just like in the Guice example, you annotate the constructor and let GIN inject all the parameters. Here's how the `PhotoListPresenterImpl` does this:

```
public class PhotoListPresenterImpl implements PhotoListPresenter {
:
   @Inject
   public PhotoListPresenterImpl(PhotoListView photoListView) {
     this.photoListView = photoListView;
     bind();
  }
}
```

When GIN runs, it will find the binding between `PhotoListView` and `PhotoListViewImpl` in the dependency module and therefore inject it into the presenter's code.

The point to note here is that when you on-demand inject `PhotoListPresenter` in the main application, GIN injects the presenter and further sees that the presenter has a constructor dependency on the view, which it also injects.

You can also use method (setter) injection approach.

METHOD INJECTION

Method injection is simply set up as per Guice, that is, you annotate the appropriate method with `@Inject`. As soon as the constructor is executed, this method is executed.

We use that functionality in our example to set up the presenter's RPC services:

```
public class PhotoListPresenterImpl implements PhotoListPresenter {
  :
  @Inject
  protected void setUpRPC(PhotoAlbumServiceAsync rpcService){
     this.rpcService = rpcService;
  }
  :
}
```

In our example the `setServices` method sets up the RPC services that the presenter will use to get information about photos from the server.

You might have noticed that we didn't define a binding for the RPC services in our dependency module. This means that when GIN tries to build the injection object, it won't find a binding. In these cases, GIN will fall back to using `GWT.create(PhotoAlbumService.class)` to create the object. This is exactly what we want here because RPC objects need to be created this way (see chapter 7 on RPC if you wish to refresh your memory on this). GIN gives us this for free.

Finally, you'll use field injection to set up the presenter's event bus.

FIELD INJECTION

Field injection can be performed in GIN. Just annotate the field as shown here:

```
public class PhotoListPresenterImpl implements PhotoListPresenter {
    :
    @Inject private EventBus eventBus;
    :
}
```

This injects the event bus into the presenter. But it only does this after the constructor has executed, so we need to make sure that the constructor doesn't attempt to use it!

That's all there really is to moving the photo application from the previous chapter to one that uses dependency injection. If you look at the code, pulled together in the following listing, it should be simple to see what's happening and where the dependencies are.

Listing 16.8 `PhotoList` presenter using dependency injection

```
public class PhotoAppGinModule extends AbstractGinModule{

  @Override
  protected void configure() {
    bind(PhotoListView.class).to(PhotoListViewImpl.class)
                             .in(Singleton.class);
    bind(EventBus.class).to(SimpleEventBus.class).in(Singleton.class);
  }
}

public class PhotoListPresenterImpl implements PhotoListPresenter {

  @Inject private EventBus eventBus;
```

Listing bindings

Field injection

```
    @Inject
    private void setServices(PhotoAlbumServiceAsync rpcService){
      this.rpcService = rpcService;
    }

    @Inject
    public PhotoListPresenterImpl(PhotoListView photoListView) {
      this.photoListView = photoListView;
      bind();
  }
}
```

Method injection

Constructor injection

You can swap out views with other views or mock-ups (to speed up testing, for example) by updating the dependency binding in `PhotoAppGinModule`, and that's the beauty of dependency injection, as you'll see next.

16.3.5 Swapping components

We've talked about one benefit of DI being the ability to quickly swap out component implementations for other implementations. Most often this is useful in testing, particularly when user interfaces are so expensive in terms of computation.

Perhaps you've been through the previous chapter and saw that we swapped views in the photo application by providing a different `replace-with` tag in the application's module file. We do something similar with real dependency injection: look closely at the `PhotoAppGinModule`, and you'll see there are two definitions for `PhotoListView` binding (the second one commented out):

```
bind(PhotoListView.class).to(PhotoListViewImpl.class)
                         .in(Singleton.class);
bind(PhotoListView.class).to(PhotoListViewImpl_TEST.class)
                         .in(Singleton.class);
```

These are just to show how quick and simple it is to swap components. If you run the application with the second binding commented out, then `PhotoListViewImpl` is used; with the first binding commented out, `PhotoListViewImpl_TEST` is used.

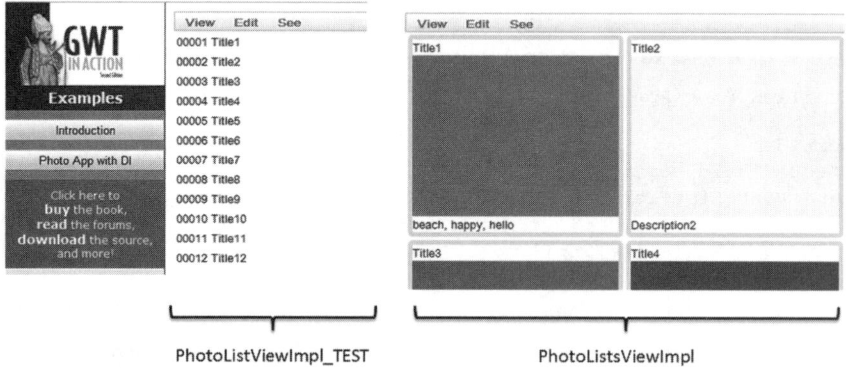

Figure 16.5 Comparison of photo list view implementations—it's easy to swap between them by making a single change in the GIN module.

That's how simple it is. Swapping between the implementations just requires commenting out one of the bindings and stopping and then restarting the GWT development mode. If you do that, then you'll see the results shown in figure 16.5.

`PhotoListViewImpl_TEST` could have been written to not have any GWT GUI components in at all, but that wouldn't have made for a great diagram in the book, so instead it just lists a text representation of the photos on the screen, whereas the original `PhotoListViewImpl` shows our photos in a block.

So far we've looked at the goodness of DI, but we should also consider when not to use it.

16.4 When to avoid DI

We have nothing against using the latest technologies and techniques, but any good developer will weigh the pros and cons before incorporating them into their overall design—and it wouldn't be unreasonable to assume these decisions are driven by a trained system architect. This is especially true of technologies such as cloud computing, libraries such as Hibernate, and techniques such as dependency injection. Although dependency injection has its benefits, there are several drawbacks that should be noted for the sake of completeness and should be taken into consideration when architecting your application.

First is the fact that dependency injection can lead to less-manageable and less-readable code. Sure, it removes the boilerplate code that we all hate writing, but it's that same boilerplate code that provides insight as to what the method or class is intended to do. When you're a new developer coming on to a large project, staring at 100,000 lines of code without the ability to track down what instantiates what or how you've arrived at some call site is enough to drive you mad. Good developers don't let other developers become DI junkies.

There are other subtleties as well, such as the inability to declare injected member variables final. Take, for example, the following declaration:

```
public class ComputerImpl implements Computer {
  @Inject private final HardDrive hardDrive;

  public ComputerImpl() {
  }
}
```

This will generate an error stating that the final field `HardDrive` may have not been initialized. If your goal was to guarantee that this variable was set once and only once (basically acting as a static variable that can be initialized with one of *(n)* values based on application state), then you're out of luck. No big deal, you say? True, if you're building a small-scale application. But if it's a large-scale application, consisting of multiple components and development teams, inevitably someone will come along later on in the project and without any contextual knowledge will write the following:

```
public void replaceHardDrive(HardDrive newHardDrive) {
   this.hardDrive = newHardDrive;
}
```

Your `Computer` object shouldn't be replacing its own `HardDrive`; the factory installs the hard drive when it builds the computer, and if there are any issues, it should be the one to replace the hard drive. See how programming constructs can parallel human language?

But we're getting off on a tangent here. The goal isn't to reiterate the uses of basic programming constructs and semantics. It's to make you, the developer, completely think through the ramifications of your design. And in the case of the previous example, there's a simple fix—use constructor injection rather than setter injection:

```
@Inject
public ComputerImpl(HardDrive hardDrive) {
    this.hardDrive = hardDrive;
}
```

In architecture circles there's discussion about the different types of injection methods. Field injection is typically avoided because it causes issues for testing, and in GIN's case the concern is that the injection happens only after the constructor completes.

The choice between method and constructor injection often comes down to whether you're from the Spring school or the Guice school. Both are valid, but method injection can obfuscate flow whereas constructor injection can lead to an expanding number of objects in the constructor.

As with any architecture technique, you should have good training in how to apply it, create and stick to application rules, and use it only where it's appropriate.

Finally, and above all other reasons, be pragmatic. Dependency injection is a powerful and useful technique when your application is highly configurable or is intended to run on other platforms or within other environments. If you find yourself reaching for dependency injection in cases where these aren't part of the application requirements, where you have no intention of utilizing multiple implementations, you may be simply drinking the "dependency injection Kool-Aid." In these cases the cons will quickly outweigh the pros. Good application design and architecture are a result of good object-oriented practices, well-defined responsibilities, intuitive interfaces, and abstraction that benefits the current developer, the future developer, as well as the user.

16.5 Summary

You've seen that dependency injection is a powerful technique that allows developers to write applications such that new contexts and configurations have minimal (if no) impact on the resulting codebase. At the same time, it removes the boilerplate code associated with class factories that provide concrete implementations and class constructors that serve as a bridge for passing values between components.

Various, sometimes passionate opinions abound regarding the use of dependency injection. They all have their basis, but more often than not, it's the way and degree to which dependency injection is used that causes developers to have a negative view of it. And honestly, we can't blame them. Staring at 100,000 lines of code with `@Injects`, `@Provides`, and `binds.to`, and so on would drive us all to the brink of insanity.

Think about it this way: dependency injection is like a steroid for abstraction, and when your abstraction grows too large too fast, you're all but guaranteed to create unmaintainable and inefficient code. But sensible use of dependency injection with Guice on the server side and GIN on client side can make code more readable and maintainable by removing that boilerplate code, which could otherwise obfuscate the real, functional code.

Dependency injection separates the dependencies for you, making it simple to swap out implementations for others, which, as long as they fulfill your defined interfaces, will work seamlessly.

For GWT client side, you must use GIN because of the lack of client-side runtime reflection. This brings a few minor changes in the way that injection is set up, but overall the concepts in GIN are the same as in Guice.

GIN makes heavy use of two advanced GWT techniques: deferred binding and generators. We'll look in detail at both of those techniques in the next two chapters.

17 Deferred binding

This chapter covers

- Understanding deferred binding and its properties
- Managing code differences with deferred binding
- Determining property values with a property provider

What do you do when you want to provide different code implementations depending on a particular condition?

For example, you need to access the browser DOM, and you know that Internet Explorer needs different code than the other browsers (like our computed-style example in the JSNI chapter). Or you're implementing internationalization and have different text for different locales. Or you want logging in one situation but not in another—the list can go on and on.

You could send all possible combinations of implementations to the user's browser: some code for Internet Explorer with Finnish language text, some for Firefox with Italian, a WebKit user (Safari/Chrome) who prefers the Canadian dialect of French text, and so on. You'd also need to send some additional code in your application to be able to select the right bits to use to handle each difference.

You already can see, we hope, the challenges you'd encounter trying to implement any of these examples—but despite the many more we could list, we want to highlight these two:

- Your users will have to download much more code than they need, which will slow down their experience (enjoyment of your application).
- You can (will?) quickly introduce maintenance and debugging nightmares—did you remember to fix all the variations in the `if/then/else` spaghetti? Why, when you've fixed it here, does it still fail there (or worse, start failing over there when it worked fine before)?

Deferred binding efficiently handles differences

You use deferred binding when you need to handle differences in code. The most common difference you'll need to handle is the various implementations of DOM in the assorted browsers. (GWT hides most of these differences from the programmer by making heavy use of deferred binding, as you'll soon see.)

GWT provides a way of solving both of those problems: *deferred binding*. It harnesses the power of Java to manage differences in your source code (reduces the maintenance and debugging problem), and the GWT compiler automatically creates several JavaScript versions of your application, called *permutations*. These permutations each contain only the code for one combination of differences (smaller code download equals an enhanced user experience). The compiler also produces some bootstrapping code that determines which permutation the user requires based on resolution of one or more properties. Differences are identified by the use of a *property* that can have one of several predeclared values. In the GWT bootstrap code the compiler inserts a *property provider*—a segment of JavaScript that determines the precise value of the property for this implementation—and downloads the appropriate permutation.

You'll already have experienced deferred binding in GWT when you compiled your application. GWT, by default, creates a permutation for each of the rendering engines (browsers) supported—that's why you see several *.cache.html files as a result of compilation.

Strictly speaking, deferred binding is used in GWT to refer to the content of this chapter (handling differences) and the next chapter (generators), but we'll stick to handling differences for now.

By the end of this chapter, you'll have a good idea of how to use all of the aspects involved in deferred binding. To get there, we'll break the chapter into three parts. First, we'll quickly look at what we mean by deferred binding, and then we'll show how to use it. After that, we'll look in some detail at two key aspects: properties and property providers.

Let's get started with looking quickly at what deferred binding is.

17.1 What is deferred binding?

Let's jump straight into an example of deferred binding in action through the GWT compiler. You might remember in chapter 11 that we used JSNI to determine the computed style of an element (the style the browser has computed).

The challenge was that we needed two implementations: one for standards-compliant browsers and one for the others (IE versions before version 9). The solution was to use deferred binding, and in chapter 11 we were more interested in discussing the JSNI aspects of the code, so we skipped what that meant. Now we're going to get into it. You don't need to have read the JSNI chapter to follow what we're discussing here because we're looking only at the deferred binding aspects in this chapter.

Figure 17.1 shows the components involved in deferred binding for our computed style example. In ❶ we have a small amount of code in an application that creates a button, adds it to the browser, and then gets the computed style of the button's color.

So what's going on in the figure? We'll note several things:

- We store implementation differences in a class hierarchy, ❷ in the figure.
- We provide a way of identifying differences, if any. GWT itself defines a deferred binding property, `user.agent`, along with the values it can take, ❹, which we can use.

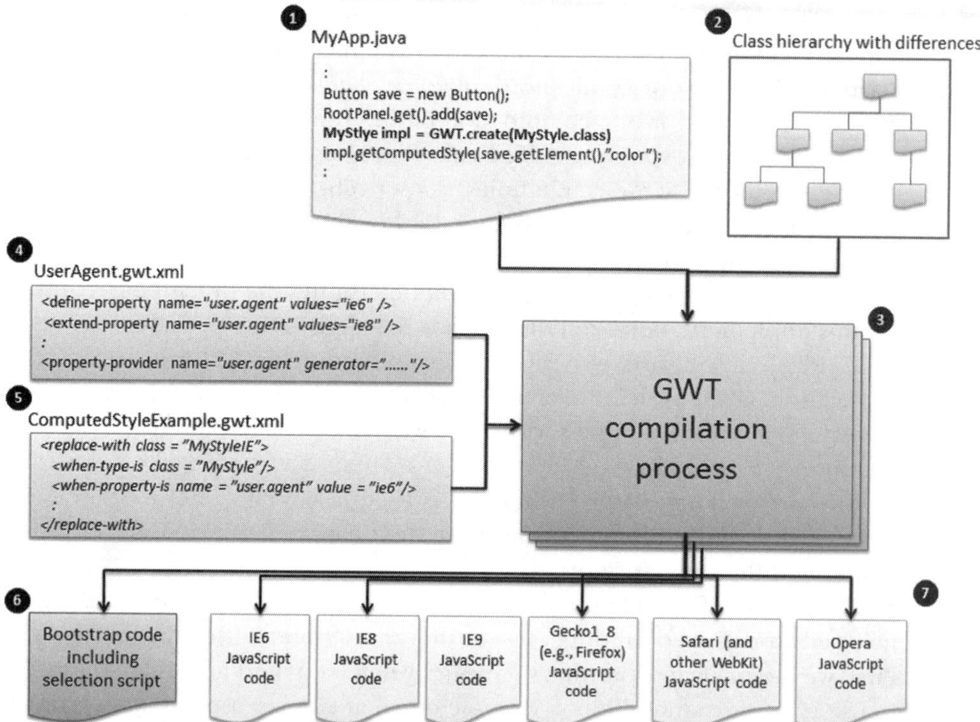

Figure 17.1 Deferred binding in action. The GWT compiler takes a number of Java files defining variations of functionality plus some replacement rules in a GWT module file and outputs your application in a number of permutations—each permutation matches a particular set of values for the properties.

- We inform the GWT compiler which class from the hierarchy to use for the `replace-with` instructions when the property has a particular value ❺.
- We tell the GWT compiler it needs to pick a difference by using the special `GWT.create` construct when creating the object ❶.

Based on these instructions, the GWT compiler will compile ❸ several permutations of JavaScript code ❼, each one meeting a particular value of the property given in `replace-with` definitions. You'll always get a minimum of six permutations because GWT uses deferred binding for DOM handling, and it knows of six different rendering engine types.

If you have more properties in play, say locales from internationalization, then the number of permutations will increase: for example, 4 locales with 6 rendering engines means 24 permutations (although we'll cover ways to potentially reduce this so-called permutation explosion later in the chapter).

Along with the permutations of code, the compiler will output the method of determining the current value of a property (or properties) into the bootstrap code ❻. The code determination of the value of a property is a segment of JavaScript code returning relevant values—this is known as a property provider. For the `user.agent` property, this is given by GWT in the `UserAgent` module ❹.

Let's look at these items in more detail by examining how they're used in the `ComputedStyle` example.

17.1.1 Storing implementation differences in a Java class hierarchy

Our computed style method determines the style value for a DOM object that it inherits through the DOM hierarchy; put a `div` inside another `div`, and the inner `div` will inherit the outer `div`'s styles unless it has them explicitly set (for example, set the text color for the outer `div` to be white, and the inner `div`'s text will be white unless you explicitly make it a different color). In the introduction we said that we needed two implementations for this: one for standards-compliant browsers and one for IE6 through IE 8. Both of these you can see in action in figure 17.2.

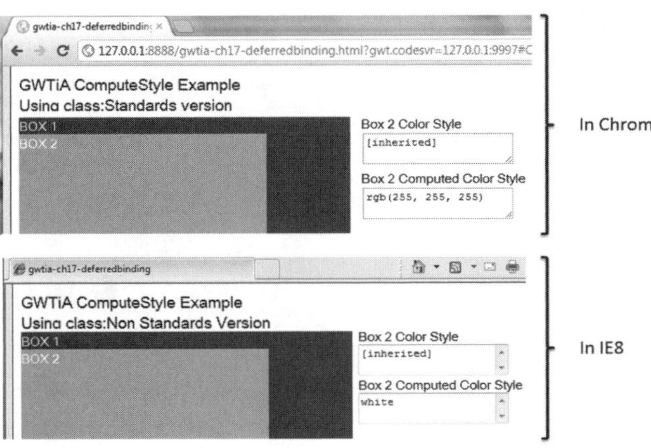

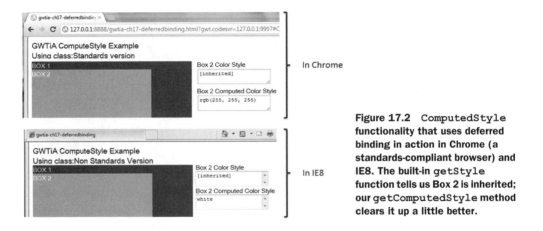

Figure 17.2 `ComputedStyle` functionality that uses deferred binding in action in Chrome (a standards-compliant browser) and IE8. The built-in `getStyle` function tells us Box 2 is inherited; our `getComputedStyle` method clears it up a little better.

We could provide these implementations in a single code block in the JavaScript and include some sort of determination code, for example:

```
var browser = getRenderEngine();
if (browser = "ie6" || browser = "ie8"){
   // IE version of getComputedStyle
} else {
   // Standards compliant version of getComputedStlye
}
```

The problem with this approach is, what do you do when a new browser comes along, or IE decides its next version is going to do something different than IE6/8 and standards compliance? (OK, IE9 is more standards compliant, but who knows about IE10?) You'd need to add more and more `if/then/else` statements. And you'll need to remember to add them everywhere in your code where there might be differences, which is a lot of places if we're talking about the differences because of DOM.

You could move the problem to a library of code to help a little with the maintenance, but the size is still an issue. And that library approach only works with a small number of variables driving the permutations. Once you get above anything trivial, the maintenance overhead becomes silly—you end up with a bunch of spaghetti or different techniques for each problem. All of this is easy to make errors in, and you'd need to go through all of the code to find any errors that happen—not a pleasant day at the office.

Java almost includes a way to solve this problem. If you think about it, we're talking about a set of common defined functionality with different implementations for variants of a property. Sounds a bit like inheritance, right? And indeed, inheritance through a class hierarchy is a great way to capture these variations. In our computed style example, we have one class, `MyStyle`, for standards-compliant browsers, and one for the rest, `MyStyleIE`, as shown in the following listing.

Listing 17.1 GWT approach to our DOM `getComputedStyle` method

```
package com.manning;
public class MyStyle{
   public native String getComputedStyle(Element el, String prop)/*-{
      style = "";
      var c = $doc.defaultView.getComputedStyle(el, null);
      if (c!=null){
         style = c.getPropertyValue(prop);          Standards-compliant
      }                                             browser code ❶
      return style;
   }-*/;
}

package com.manning;                                ❷ Extending MyStyle
public class MyStyleIE extends MyStyle{
   public native String getComputedStyle(Element el, String prop)/*-{
      stlye = "";
      var c = el.currentStyle;                      IE code ❸
```

```
        style = c[prop];
        reutrn style;                                    IE code ❸
    }-*/;
}
```

The IE version ❷ extends the standard version ❶ but overrides the `getComputedStyle` method with IE6/8-specific code ❸. OK, our example here is simple because there's only one method, but we can easily find more complications—look at GWT's DOM class hierarchy, shown in figure 17.3, and you can see that the class hierarchy is much more comprehensive.

The figure shows that leaf classes are available for all of the rendering engines that GWT supports: Mozilla (refers to Gecko rendering engine used in Firefox), Opera, WebKit (used in Safari and Chrome), IE6, IE8, and IE9. If you were to dig into these classes, you'd see each subclass providing specific implementations of DOM functions as necessary, inheriting common functionality where appropriate.

Now when a new browser version or even a new browser comes along, all that's needed is to implement a new class that inherits from the most appropriate parent class. We've highlighted the IE browser versions in figure 17.3 to point this out—note how IE9 sits over on the `DOMImplStandard` branch, reflecting its more standards-compliant approach compared to IE6 and IE8, which need to sit under the separate `DOMImplTrident` branch.

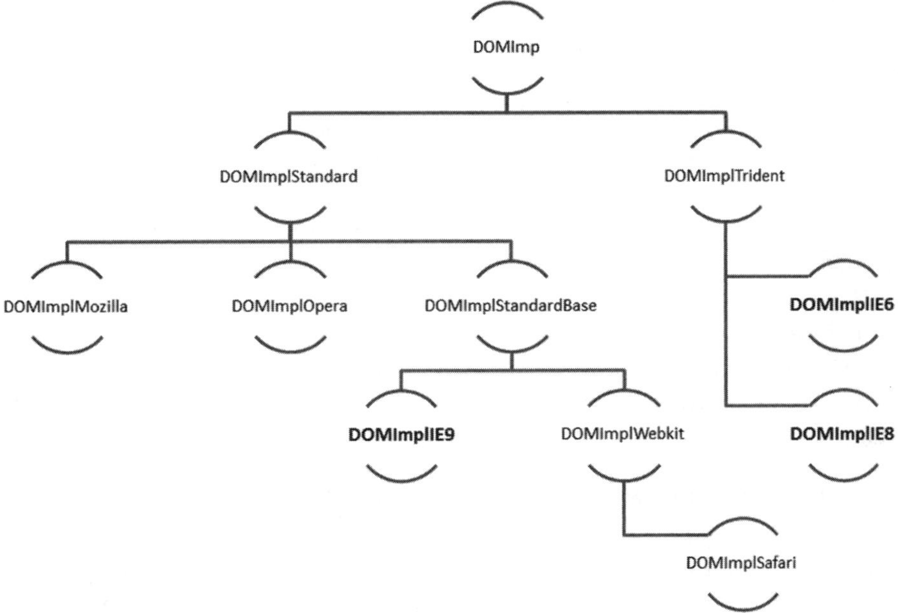

Figure 17.3 Hierarchy of `DOMImpl` classes within GWT. These classes provide the interface between GWT and browser DOM implementations. Deferred binding is used in the code to refer to the `DOMImpl` class, which is replaced during compilation with a browser-specific implementation in the leaf nodes for each permutation of compilation.

You can have code differences for more than the browser-rendering engine. If you've gone through the internationalization chapter, then you've seen that we have code differences because of locales. You can even create your own differences based on existing properties or some new property that's important to you. Having the hierarchy is good, but you need a way of identifying when you'll have a difference—you don't want to write several versions of the code yourself, each one using a different class from the hierarchy; you want the compiler to do that for you. To identify that there will be differences, you use deferred-binding properties.

17.1.2 Identifying differences via deferred-binding properties

The ranges of differences that can be in a GWT application is defined by a set of property values and the values they can take. You're free to define your own properties, which we'll look at in section 17.3, but you have some built-in ones as well, such as for browser rendering engines and locales.

Our computed style example is dependent on the rendering engine, so it makes sense for us to use the built-in `user.agent` deferred-binding property that identifies that there will be differences for rendering engines. This is defined in the `UserAgent`[1] module, which is inherited by the `User` module, which all GWT applications must inherit.

Referring to figure 17.1, ❹ shows part of the definition of the `user.agent` deferred-binding property. The full definition, in GWT 2.5, has six possible values:

```
<define-property name="user.agent" values="ie6" />
<extend-property name="user.agent" values="ie8" />
<extend-property name="user.agent" values="gecko1_8" />
<extend-property name="user.agent" values="safari" />
<extend-property name="user.agent" values="opera" />
<extend-property name="user.agent" values="ie9" fallback-value="ie8" />
```

Line 1 defines the property and says it can have value `ie6`. Lines 2–5 extend the property so that it could have values `ie8`, `gecko1_8`, `safari`, or `opera` in addition to `ie6`. Line 6 completes the definition by adding `ie9` as an option and saying that it falls back to `ie8` (you can find out more on what *fallback* means in chapter 13).

Now we need a way of telling the GWT compiler that a specific subclass in the hierarchy should be used when the property is determined to have a specific value. To do that, we need to write some more definitions in module files.

17.1.3 Informing the GWT compiler which class to pick

With implementation differences captured in a class hierarchy, and a deferred binding property defined that allows us to understand there will be differences, we now need to link those together to tell the GWT compiler what class it should pick under what circumstances.

---

[1] In GWT2.4 and earlier versions, this is in the `com.google.gwt.user` package; in GWT 2.5 it still exists but as a passthrough to a same-named file in the `com.google.gwt.useragent` package.

In the computed style example we'll use the rules in table 17.1 to determine which class in the hierarchy to use for each rendering engine (the value of the `user.agent` deferred-binding property).

Table 17.1 Mapping which class in the `MyStyle` hierarchy will be used for which value of the `user.agent` deferred-binding property

Value of `user.agent`	Class to use
ie6	MyStyleIE
ie8	MyStyleIE
ie9	MyStyle
opera	MyStyle
safari	MyStyle
gecko1_8	MyStyle

We capture the rules in table 17.1 within a series of `replace-with` tags in a module file visible to our GWT application. The definition of these rules requires us to apply a little common sense. Looking at table 17.1, it's obvious that `MyStyle` is the class most used and that `MyStyleIE` only needs to replace `MyStyle` in two circumstances (for IE6 and IE8). Therefore we can assume the user will create `MyStyle` and only needs to replace it in two situations, that is, we only need to define one `replace-with` statement. In figure 17.1, ❺ shows part of our computed style example's module file—part of the `replace-with` definition is repeated as follows:

```
<replace-with class="com.manning.gwtia...computestyle.MyStyleIE">      ❶ Use this type...
  <when-type-is class="com.manning.gwtia...computestyle.MyStyle"/>     ❷ ...instead of this type
  <when-property-is name="user.agent" value="ie6"/>                    ❸ ...if this is for IE6
</replace-with>
```

This tells the GWT compiler that when it's compiling the permutation where `user.agent` equals `ie6` ❸, it should replace the `MyStyle` class ❷ with the `MyStyleIE` class ❶. When making these types of definitions, you have to provide the fully qualified class names (which because of space limitations we haven't here).

If you were to look into the `UserAgent` module, then you'd see a `replace-with` definition for each `user.agent` value for replacing the `DOMImpl` class for the rendering engine. This is why every GWT application produces a minimum of six JavaScript permutations. If you ever create a widget in your application, which 99.999 percent of applications do, then you'll have six DOM implementations for that, so six JavaScript permutations are created.

But it's a bit excessive to have to write `replace-with` tags for every class for every value the property can take—particularly for our computed style example with only two classes.

Luckily, we can fine-tune the tag with the conditionals <any>, <all>, and <none>. The <any> tag implies that at least one of the conditions is true, <all> requires all the conditions to be true, and <none> acts as a not. The following listing enhances our definition—in it we're saying to replace `MyStyle` with `MyStyleIE` for either `ie6` or `ie8`.

Listing 17.2 Simple deferred binding replacing a class if dealing with an IE browser

```
<replace-with class="com.manning.MyStyleIE">
   <when-type-is class="com.manning.MyStyle"/>
   <any>
      <when-property-is name="user.agent" value="ie6"/>
      <when-property-is name="user.agent" value="ie8"/>
   </any>
   <none>
      <when-property-is name="user.agent" value="ie9"/>
   </none>
</replace-with>
```

❶ Replacing for IE6 or IE8

❷ But not for IE9

Here you use the <any> tag to make the `replace` condition `user.agent = ie6` or `ie8`. But you also need to make sure you don't replace for IE9, because it is standards compliant in this area—so you include the <none> tag. In the example we're only including `ie9` for completeness of definition. If we hadn't included it, it still wouldn't have replaced `MyStyle` because of the way we're using `MyStyle` as the default case.

In section 17.2.4, we look at how we can use conditional properties to make this even clearer.

> **WARNING** If you're using deferred-binding code you've found on the internet or elsewhere, make sure it handles IE8 and IE9 as a user agent. The IE8 property value is new as of GWT 2.0, and IE9 is new as of GWT 2.2. Some old code might miss those definitions—that would mean your code wouldn't run as expected.

The result of all this is the generation of a set of JavaScript permutations. You can see an example of output files from a compilation of a GWT application in figure 17.4, which shows the six cache.html files—the JavaScript permutations of our application that we're expecting because of the DOM classes. Four of these would have our standards-compliant code for computed styles and two our IE version.

One sometimes-heard criticism of GWT is the number of permutations it creates. But because these are created by the compiler, this criticism tends to be more emotional than real. Because you typically use development mode when developing, you don't need to wait for the compiler to produce all versions before you can test.

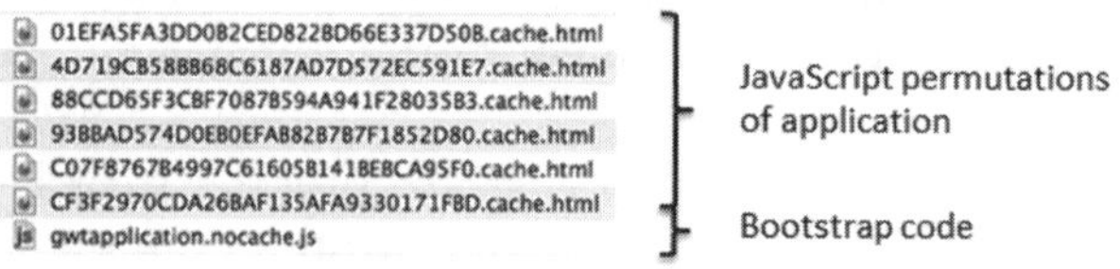

Figure 17.4 Example of the compiler output of a simple GWT application showing six HTML files containing permutations of JavaScript together with the nocache.js selection script

It's only if you're using continuous-compilation methods that you might need to be concerned. A large number of permutations, or an unexpected permutation explosion, might mean your compilation isn't complete before the next cycle starts. We'll discuss the techniques for managing permutation explosions in section 17.4.

The last thing we need to look at from a code perspective is how to tell the GWT compiler it needs to perform some extra work but keep the code Java compliant. Step forward a special GWT construct: `GWT.create()`.

17.1.4 Telling the GWT compiler to make a choice

Normally you create new instances of Java objects using the `new` construct, such as

```
MyStyle impl = new MyStyle();
```

This is fine for the Java compiler to parse and generate code from, but it ignores the hierarchy and `replace-with` rules we've set up. Remember that in the case of IE6 and IE8, you want to use `MyStyleIE` instead of `MyStyle`.

So for objects that you know should involve deferred binding, you use the GWT-specific `create` construct instead:

```
MyStyle impl = GWT.create(MyStyle.class);
```

To a Java compiler, this appears exactly the same as writing `new MyStyle()` because `GWT.create(SomeObject)` looks like it returns the result of `new SomeObject`. But to the GWT compiler running development mode, this construct indicates that it should start rebinding using the `replace-with` rules to get the correct implementation.

The final challenge is at runtime: to get your application to select the right permutation.

17.1.5 Selecting the right difference (permutation) at runtime

Now that the compiler has created several permutations of your application, you need a sensible way of determining which one to download when your application runs. This challenge is solved by property providers—segments of JavaScript code that are defined directly in a module `property-provider` tag (from GWT 2.3, you can alternatively refer to a Java class that will generate the JavaScript code at compilation time). Your imagination is the only limit on what to include in this code.

Some property providers are already given for you. For example, the `user.agent` property provider determines its value from the browser's user agent object; the `locale` property can look in cookies, meta tags, or URL parameters. We'll take a little look at that in a moment.

During compilation, the property providers relating to properties used in your application are copied to the application's bootstrap code (❻ in figure 17.1 if you can remember that far back). The bootstrap code is the first code downloaded when the user runs your application. It determines values for all the properties required for

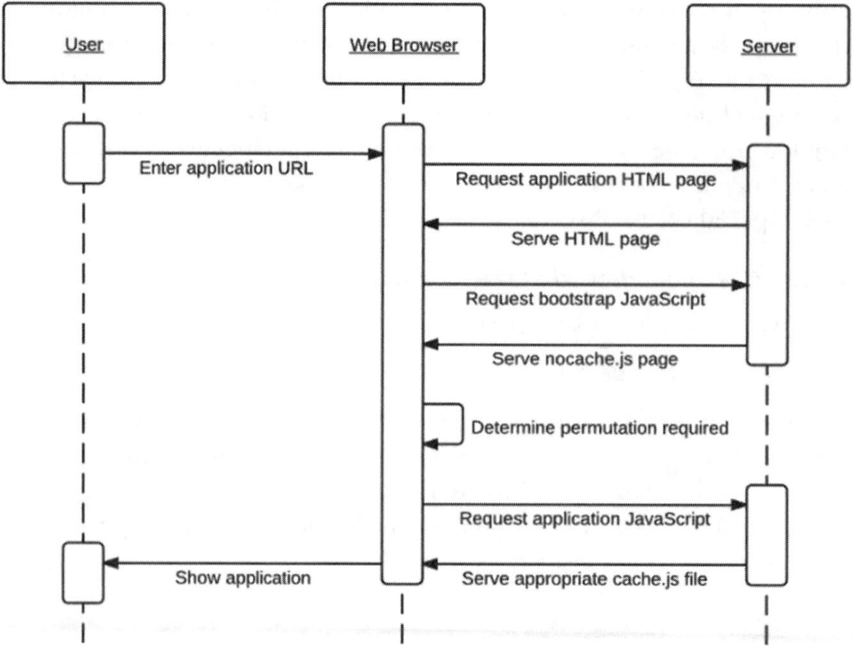

Figure 17.5 A view of the bootstrapping process in GWT applications. The user requests the application's HTML file, which requests the bootstrap code, which then determines and requests one permutation of the application to run.

your application. From that, the bootstrap code selects the appropriate JavaScript permutation. The process of bootstrapping is shown in figure 17.5.

The user requests your application's HTML page, which requests the bootstrap nocache.js file. That bootstrap file runs in the browser and determines the values of the properties required to select a permutation.

Once all the properties used have determined values, the bootstrap code requests the filename of the appropriate permutation of your application from the server. This is returned, usually as JavaScript code wrapped in an HTML file that's loaded into an iFrame; once that's loaded, the bootstrap calls the application's `onModuleLoad` function, and your application is running.

That's all the details; let's take a quick look at how it's all pulled together.

17.2 Pulling it all together

We can summarize the steps involved to use deferred binding as follows:

1. Write a number of classes in an inheritance structure that contain the functional permutations—for example, `SomeClass` and its subclass `SomeOtherClass`.
2. Define one or more `<replace-with>` tags in a module file that will be inherited by your application (or in the application's module file directly) that indicate

what property values would determine that `SomeClass` should be replaced by one of its subclass during compilation, for example:

```
<replace-with class="com.manning.SomeOtherClass">
   <when-type-is class="com.manning.SomeClass"/>
   <any>
      <when-property-is name="someProperty" value="someValue"/>
      <all>
         <when-property-is name="otherProperty" value="otherValue"/>
         <when-property-is name="aNewProperty" value="aNewValue"/>
      </all>
   </any>
</replace-with>
```

This `replace-with` tag says to replace `SomeClass` with `SomeOtherClass` when the following is true: `(someProperty=someValue OR (otherProperty=otherValue AND aNewProperty=aNewValue))`.

3 Use the `GWT.create(class literal)` construct in your application to create an instance of the class:

```
SomeClass impl = GWT.create(SomeClass.class)
```

You then use your new object as a normal Java object, for example, calling methods on it: `impl.someDefinedMethod()`.

Common gotchas

If you're trying to use deferred binding in your own application but don't see the results in the output code, double-check that you're using the `GWT.create(YourClass.class)` structure and not `new YourClass()`. The latter approach won't make the compiler use your replacements.

If you've defined the `replace-with` rules and/or properties in a different module than your main module, make sure you've inherited it.

This covers the mechanics of deferred binding, and you've seen that properties and property providers are key items. In the next two sections, we'll look in more detail at how you use properties in your code along with some of the properties GWT provides and how you can attempt to control the explosion of permutations in certain circumstances.

17.3 Using GWT properties to drive deferred binding

GWT properties are defined in a module XML file. They're in some ways a combination of a Java enumerations and a variable at the same time—we can list the possible values for a property and define what value it has.

> **Deferred-binding property vs. configuration property**
>
> You might notice `<define-configuration-property>` tags in a module file. For example, the `UserAgent` module defines `user.agent.runtimeWarning` as a configuration property.
>
> These don't define deferred binding properties, that is, differences the compile needs to manage and result in permutations. Rather, they're properties you can set before your application runs or is compiled—in a way they're a little like flags in a normal program.
>
> They're more often used in generators and linkers, so we'll keep our detailed discussion until chapter 18, but we note them here because you can use deferred-binding and configuration properties together in `replace-with` rules.

We're going to cover both the enumeration and variable views of a property in this chapter, starting with its enumeration view—where you define what a property is and what values it can take (either initially defined or when extended). After that, we'll look at how to set the value a property should have, by setting it directly or conditionally. Let's start at the obvious point of defining a deferred-binding property.

17.3.1 Defining properties

To define a property and the set of values it can take, you use a `<define-property>` tag. For example, the GWT-provided `user.agent` property is defined in the `UserAgent` module as

```
<define-property name="user.agent" values="ie6" />
```

It then extends the property with the additional values it can take: `ie8`, `ie9`, `gecko1_8`, `safari`, and `opera`—we look at extending properties in the next section.

You can define several values at the same time if you want, all separated with commas, for example. Pre GWT 2.3, GWT defined `user.agent` with the following values:

```
<define-property name="user.agent"
                 values="ie6, ie8, gecko, gecko1_8, safari, opera"/>
```

Which approach you take is a matter of style or personal choice (as an aside, notice that GWT 2.3 has different values than currently; this is because `ie9` is now supported and older versions of `gecko` no longer are—we wonder at what point `ie6` will go the same way).

The set of values in `user.agent` isn't expected to be altered by the programmer—though you might do so if you want to support a different rendering engine yourself. On the other hand, the `locale` property used in internationalization is defined in the `I18N` module (in package `com.google.gwt.i18n`):

```
<define-property name="locale" values="default" />
```

And it's expected that the programmer will add the locales they're using to this property to tell the GWT compiler to create locale-specific permutations. You do this by extending the property.

17.3.2 Extending properties

If you've read chapter 13 on internationalization, then you might recall that to introduce a new locale, you extend the `locale` property using the `<extend-property>` tag in your application's module file. Adding the French, country-independent locale is achieved by using

```
<extend-property name="locale" values="fr" />
```

This means you have now two values for the `locale` property in your application: `default` and `fr`. You can extend the property with as many values as you like. Each value added increases the permutation space.

Now that we've defined what values a property could hold, that is, when it acts as an enumerated set, we need to look at how to make a property act as a variable and set the value(s) it will have.

17.3.3 Setting properties

As well as defining a list of possible values for a property (where it acts similar to a Java enumeration), a property can hold a particular value (now it acts similarly to a variable). The value can be set either directly in a module file or programmatically at runtime.

Setting a property value directly is done in a module file by using the `<set-property>` tag. It doesn't make sense to set the `user.agent` directly because you don't know what browser the user is using, nor does it make sense to set a `locale` because you typically want a property provider to do that.

> **An old tip**
>
> Before GWT 2.0's web mode browser plug-ins, testing your code in a browser that wasn't built into your operating system version of GWT meant compiling your code. That could take some time because you have at least six permutations. To make things quicker, you could limit the permutations by using the `set-property` tag. Adding the following to your application's module file limits browser permutations to Opera:
>
> ```
> <set-property name="user.agent" value ="opera"/>
> ```
>
> It's unlikely you'll need to do this for GWT 2.0, because you'll use the plug-in in your chosen browser.

Instead, we'll quickly look at another GWT-provided property: `gwt.enableDebugId`. This property is provided in the `Debug` module in the `com.google.gwt.debug` package. It enables you to give widgets particular ID values in the DOM so you can see what's going on in your application more easily in a DOM inspection tool.

We get the result shown in figure 17.6 if we write the code

```
Label aLabel = new Label("Check this Label's ID");
aLabel.ensureDebugId("DEBUG LABEL");
```

and turn on the enable-debug ID functionality of GWT by setting the `gwt.enableDebugId` property to `true` as follows in a module of our application:

```
<set-property name="gwt.enableDebugId" value="true"/>
```

Figure 17.6 is a GWT application as seen through a DOM inspection tool (such as Firebug or the one built into WebKit browsers). You can see that our `Label` is the `div` element in the body, and that the element has been given the ID we requested, prefixed with the text `gwt-debug`. If we had set `gwt.enableDebugId` to `false`, this ID wouldn't appear (the code for it would have been compiled out by the compiler). By default, `gwt.enableDebugId` is set to `true`, but because we don't typically use the `ensureDebugId` method in our code, we don't see the result in the DOM.

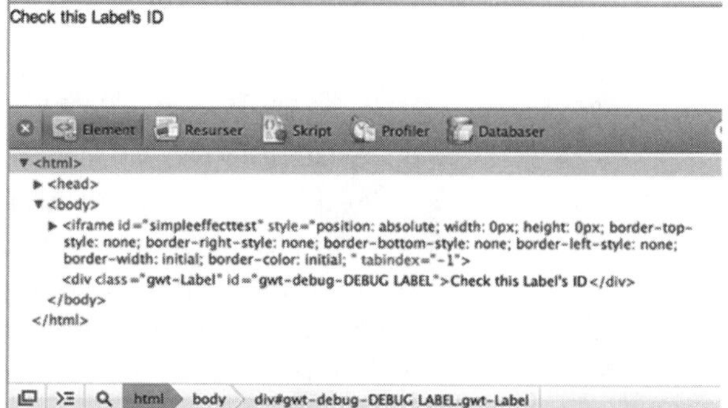

Figure 17.6 A GWT `Label` displayed in Safari, with Safari's Web Development tool open showing HTML—in particular the `div` representing the `Label` shows our debug ID of `gwt-debug-DEBUG LABEL` as the `div`'s ID value.

> **Unhappy with debug IDs in GWT?**
>
> From GWT 2.5 it's possible to alter the prefix used for debug IDs (`DebugInfo. setDebugIdPrefix(String prefix)`) and even what attribute they're put in (`DebugInfo.setDebugIdAttribute(String attribute, boolean asProperty)`). You should call these methods before setting debug IDs to see the impact.

One thing to note is that GWT always uses the last definition in module files, so you need to be careful of order. If you have the following two lines in your module, then the `locale` will have value en because it's written second:

```
<set-property name="locale" value="fr"/>
<set-property name="locale" value="en"/>
```

The same issue arises when inheriting GWT modules. If there's a module `MyModule` that sets the `locale` to `fr` and a module `MyOtherModule` that sets it to `en`, then `local` will be still be set to `en` if you have the following order of module inheritance:

```
<inherits name="com.manning.gwtia.MyModule"/>
<inherits name="com.manning.gwtia.MyOtherModule"/>
```

This ordering might sometimes cause an issue if you don't have a clear view of what's being set where, but it can be used to your advantage—you're able to set properties conditionally, adding some more capability for you to look at and potentially use.

17.3.4 Conditionally setting a property

It's possible to set a property value conditionally, based on the value(s) of other properties. This is useful for several reasons, including creating derived properties and minimizing the number of permutations produced.

GWT uses this approach for HTML 5 widgets such as audio, video, and canvas—look at the following listing, which comes from the audio widget's module definition (Media.gwt.xml in com.google.gwt.media).

Listing 17.3 Conditional property setting underpinning GWT's approach to HTML 5 widgets

```
<define-property name="audioElementSupport" values="maybe,no" />   ❶ Defining property
<set-property name="audioElementSupport" value="maybe" />          ❷ Setting property

<set-property name="audioElementSupport" value="no">

   <any>
      <when-property-is name="user.agent" value="ie6" />
      <when-property-is name="user.agent" value="ie8" />            ❸ Conditionally setting property
   </any>
<set-property>
```

Parts ❶ and ❷ should be fairly familiar now. You define a property called audioElementSupport and set its value to maybe. ❸ is where the conditional setting is made. It says to set the value of the audioElementSupport property to no, if the value of the user.agent property is ie6 or ie8.

Because GWT runs through these definitions in order, it will first set the value of audioElementSupport to maybe and then reset it to no if the user.agent is ie6 or ie8.

Conditions can be grouped together to indicate various boolean conditions using the tags <any>, <all>, and <none>. The <any> tag implies that at least one of the conditions is true, <all> requires all the conditions to be true, and <none> acts as a not (or nor if multiple conditions are contained).

Using the new conditionally set property allows you more logical definitions; you can readily understand the following:

```
<replace-with class="Audio.AudioElementSupportDetectedMaybe">
   <when-type-is class=" Audio.AudioElementSupportDetector" />
   <when-property-is name="audioElementSupport" value="maybe" />
</replace-with>
```

It says that AudioElementSupportDetector is replaced by AudioElementSupportDetectorMaybe when audioElementSupport has the value maybe.

Now we've reached the end of our section on using GWT properties for deferred binding. If you remember back to the start of the section, we talked about there being a minimum of six permutations because of the different browsers. And if you were to use 4 locales, plus our `dev.mode` property, then all of a sudden you're asking the compiler to produce 6 × 4 × 2 = 48 permutations. It's easy to see this number of permutations exploding if you add more locales or if another property comes into play; then your compilation time could take forever. Luckily, you have ways to manage this explosion if you're careful, which we'll discuss next.

17.4 Managing explosive permutation numbers

You've already seen that a basic application will have 6 permutations for the `user.agent`; add in some locales, say 10, and the number multiplies. Throw in some more properties, and the number of permutations can rapidly explode.

Compiling all of those permutations leads to long compile times. This is mitigated because development mode reduces the need to compile until you're ready to deploy (unless you're using a continual-compilation approach). You can further minimize the impact by using two compiler flags: `-localWorkers` and `-draftCompile`. The first allows you to harness multi-cores on your machines, and the second reduces the number of checks the GWT compiler makes, giving a faster compile time.

Over the years, GWT has become more efficient at determining the permutations required—there was a time when it would compile a new permutation for every possible combination of values, regardless of whether some produced the same output.

For example, imagine you wish to include a property that tells you if the layout engine is on a smartphone or not. You could define a new property `mobile.user.agent` that allows you to know if you're on an Android or iPhone device or on neither:

```
<define-property name="mobile.user.agent"
                 values="android, iphone, not_mobile" />
```

If you had a deferred-binding class for `not_mobile` and another for `android/iphone`, then how many permutations would be created?

Under previous versions of GWT you could expect 18 permutations, because you have 6 permutations that are driven by the `user.agent` property, covering the DOM differences, and you've defined 3 values for `mobile.user.agent` (6 × 3 = 18).

Currently, GWT is a bit cleverer. You're stuck with at least six permutations because it's still driven by DOM differences. But GWT can determine from your module file definitions that there's no difference between the permutation for, say, Safari on Android and Safari on iPhone. Therefore it doesn't need to create two permutations; only one, which is used twice, is sufficient. So GWT needs to create only 12 permutations. If there were differences between `android`, `iphone`, and `not_mobile`, then 18 permutations would pop out.

It's possible to further improve on the number of permutations by taking one of two approaches: conditional properties or soft permutations. Let's see how it would be done with both approaches.

17.4.1 Using conditional properties

Let's say that you know that only the WebKit rendering engine, which GWT knows as Safari, will ever be on mobile devices. Then you could conditionally set the `mobile.user.agent` to be `not_mobile` for all non-Safari property values:

```
<set-property name="mobile.user.agent" value="not_mobile" >
   <none>
      <when-property-is name="user.agent" value="safari" />
   </none>
</set-property>
```

By creating this definition, you indicate to the GWT compiler that everything except Safari has only one permutation for the `mobile.user.agent` property. Figure 17.7 is taken from the application's nocache.js bootstrap file.

```
unflattenKeylistIntoAnswers(['android', 'safari'], '32C248B22B5085AF7B5A86A23174DAF4');
unflattenKeylistIntoAnswers(['iphone', 'safari'], '32C248B22B5085AF7B5A86A23174DAF4');
unflattenKeylistIntoAnswers(['not_mobile', 'ie6'], '383F73C29B2317FFEFC995C887DF1BD9');
unflattenKeylistIntoAnswers(['not_mobile', 'ie8'], '55B16BFEFC6616C504FC68DCA614A048');
unflattenKeylistIntoAnswers(['not_mobile', 'ie9'], '81CD7710DFEC6310DDA42CDC5A4952A0');
unflattenKeylistIntoAnswers(['not_mobile', 'safari'], 'A44700F1E424B9BF34B1641DE0DB31E8');
unflattenKeylistIntoAnswers(['not_mobile', 'opera'], 'A52BEA59B2ECB84EAD39AB2D4F675AA6');
unflattenKeylistIntoAnswers(['not_mobile', 'gecko1_8'], '27AC07D8DE117DC64B2098862C86BFBC');
```

Figure 17.7 The seven files and eight permutations in the bootstrap script created using a conditional property deferred-binding strategy. (To see this in a human-readable form, as shown here, you need to compile in pretty mode.)

You can see only seven permutations output—six for `user.agent` and `not_mobile` plus one permutation for Safari on Android or iPhone (although you see eight permutations of properties in figure 17.7, note that the top two point to the same code permutation).

An alternative approach to reducing the number of compiler-produced permutations through conditional properties is to use soft permutations. As you'll see next, this means moving some of the permutation decisions until runtime, which means a larger code download.

17.4.2 Using soft permutations

Soft permutations break a few things we've discussed already—you don't get a permutation for each property value. Rather, you collapse a number of property values together and leave the selection of functionality until runtime. This means that more code is sent to the browser than perhaps necessary, but compilation time is increased and the user doesn't need to wait for a new permutation to be downloaded if they're changing the property.

You use the `<collapse-property>` tag to inform the compiler what needs to be resolved at runtime. Let's say you want to resolve Android and iPhone at runtime; you could write

```
<collapse-property name="mobile.user.agent" values="android, iphone"/>
```

```
unflattenKeylistIntoAnswers(['android', 'opera'], '021F2393C0D5A6EE23831CC995E0E2C7');
unflattenKeylistIntoAnswers(['iphone', 'opera'], '021F2393C0D5A6EE23831CC995E0E2C7' + ':1');
unflattenKeylistIntoAnswers(['android', 'safari'], '1ECC25B0B0719AC1504A22FBC112FDED');
unflattenKeylistIntoAnswers(['iphone', 'safari'], '1ECC25B0B0719AC1504A22FBC112FDED' + ':1');
unflattenKeylistIntoAnswers(['not_mobile', 'gecko1_8'], '27AC07D8DE117DC64B2098862C86BFBC');
unflattenKeylistIntoAnswers(['not_mobile', 'ie6'], '383F73C29B2317FFEFC995C887DF1BD9');
unflattenKeylistIntoAnswers(['android', 'gecko1_8'], '42FA00DB61BE093A8056F2E6270516EF');
unflattenKeylistIntoAnswers(['iphone', 'gecko1_8'], '42FA00DB61BE093A8056F2E6270516EF' + ':1');
unflattenKeylistIntoAnswers(['not_mobile', 'ie8'], '55B16BFEFC6616C504FC68DCA614A048');
unflattenKeylistIntoAnswers(['not_mobile', 'ie9'], '81CD7710DFEC6310DDA42CDC5A4952A0');
unflattenKeylistIntoAnswers(['android', 'ie6'], '83FFEA3BE432ACDA098E693FDED40B5C');
unflattenKeylistIntoAnswers(['iphone', 'ie6'], '83FFEA3BE432ACDA098E693FDED40B5C' + ':1');
unflattenKeylistIntoAnswers(['not_mobile', 'safari'], 'A44700F1E424B9BF34B1641DE0DB31E8');
unflattenKeylistIntoAnswers(['not_mobile', 'opera'], 'A52BEA59B2ECB84EAD39AB2D4F675AA6');
unflattenKeylistIntoAnswers(['android', 'ie9'], 'C08511C8B6636E664C396806DC3D0312');
unflattenKeylistIntoAnswers(['iphone', 'ie9'], 'C08511C8B6636E664C396806DC3D0312' + ':1');
unflattenKeylistIntoAnswers(['android', 'ie8'], 'C37869A2A097F9845D45E15552B321E5');
unflattenKeylistIntoAnswers(['iphone', 'ie8'], 'C37869A2A097F9845D45E15552B321E5' + ':1');
```

Figure 17.8 The 12 files in 18 permutations in the bootstrap script with the `mobile.user.agent` property collapsed—notice that the `android/iphone` values have the same filename.

You'll take away the conditional property from before and indicate that Android and iPhone have different implementations, so you should expect 18 permutations. Collapsing the properties as shown, you end up with only 12 permutations (though you still have 18 entries in the bootstrap)—see figure 17.8.

It may not be easy to see immediately in the figure, but look for the `android` and `iphone` permutations for a particular `user.agent`, such as the first two entries. You can see that the filename for both of these is the same, but one has a ':1' suffix so GWT can track the soft permutations.

The increase in performance you get during compilation is deferred to runtime when more code is sent to the browser and runtime selection is done. You can move more decision making to runtime by using wildcards in the `<collapse-property/>` tag. Let's say for some reason you want to move the permutations for `user.agent` to runtime; you could say

```
<collapse-property name="user.agent" values="*" />
```

You can even use partial mapping in the values. If you've read the internationalization chapter, you'll remember that you can have region locales, for example, `en_GB` for British English and `en_US` for American English—and they will generate their own permutations. Write the following

```
<collapse-property name="locale" values="en_*" />
```

and those permutations relating to those locales disappear from the compiler output and become runtime chosen instead.

We have one final trick—if you want to cut down the compile time to the smallest possible, that is, produce only one permutation where all various properties and paths are determined at runtime, you can use the `<collapse-all-properties>` tag in your application's module file. The result is shown in figure 17.9. Now you have only one code permutation from the compiler, but all decisions on what needs to run are made during runtime.

```
unflattenKeylistIntoAnswers(['android', 'gecko1_8'], '0CA3B2C46F5A50BF970FAFE22CFA67E4');
unflattenKeylistIntoAnswers(['android', 'ie6'], '0CA3B2C46F5A50BF970FAFE22CFA67E4' + ':1');
unflattenKeylistIntoAnswers(['iphone', 'opera'], '0CA3B2C46F5A50BF970FAFE22CFA67E4' + ':10');
unflattenKeylistIntoAnswers(['iphone', 'safari'], '0CA3B2C46F5A50BF970FAFE22CFA67E4' + ':11');
unflattenKeylistIntoAnswers(['not_mobile', 'gecko1_8'], '0CA3B2C46F5A50BF970FAFE22CFA67E4' + ':12');
unflattenKeylistIntoAnswers(['not_mobile', 'ie6'], '0CA3B2C46F5A50BF970FAFE22CFA67E4' + ':13');
unflattenKeylistIntoAnswers(['not_mobile', 'ie8'], '0CA3B2C46F5A50BF970FAFE22CFA67E4' + ':14');
unflattenKeylistIntoAnswers(['not_mobile', 'ie9'], '0CA3B2C46F5A50BF970FAFE22CFA67E4' + ':15');
unflattenKeylistIntoAnswers(['not_mobile', 'opera'], '0CA3B2C46F5A50BF970FAFE22CFA67E4' + ':16');
unflattenKeylistIntoAnswers(['not_mobile', 'safari'], '0CA3B2C46F5A50BF970FAFE22CFA67E4' + ':17');
unflattenKeylistIntoAnswers(['android', 'ie8'], '0CA3B2C46F5A50BF970FAFE22CFA67E4' + ':2');
unflattenKeylistIntoAnswers(['android', 'ie9'], '0CA3B2C46F5A50BF970FAFE22CFA67E4' + ':3');
unflattenKeylistIntoAnswers(['android', 'opera'], '0CA3B2C46F5A50BF970FAFE22CFA67E4' + ':4');
unflattenKeylistIntoAnswers(['android', 'safari'], '0CA3B2C46F5A50BF970FAFE22CFA67E4' + ':5');
unflattenKeylistIntoAnswers(['iphone', 'gecko1_8'], '0CA3B2C46F5A50BF970FAFE22CFA67E4' + ':6');
unflattenKeylistIntoAnswers(['iphone', 'ie6'], '0CA3B2C46F5A50BF970FAFE22CFA67E4' + ':7');
unflattenKeylistIntoAnswers(['iphone', 'ie8'], '0CA3B2C46F5A50BF970FAFE22CFA67E4' + ':8');
unflattenKeylistIntoAnswers(['iphone', 'ie9'], '0CA3B2C46F5A50BF970FAFE22CFA67E4' + ':9');
```

Figure 17.9 The one permutation in the bootstrap script created when collapsing all properties

The thing to remember in all this collapsing is that you aren't removing the permutations but are changing where you're making the decision. The more you move to runtime, the less you benefit from the GWT compiler making your application download as small as possible, but you may benefit from fewer permutations.

We hope you can see that using these techniques can help you manage any permutation explosion you might be having. One approach means you need to think through your properties in a little more detail beyond naïvely defining them; the other approach collapses values, making the resulting code larger. You'll need to decide if any permutation explosion is a problem for you, and if so, what strategy you'll apply.

What we'll look at next is how to determine what value(s) the property should have in order for the bootstrapping code to request the appropriate permutation for execution.

17.5 Determining a property value

It's the act of defining properties, extending them, and providing one or more `replace-with` tags in module files that drives the generation of permutations of your application. But all of that's pointless if you can't determine the value(s) the property should have. If you can't do that, then the bootstrap code has no idea which permutation to request.

There are two ways to set the value(s) of a property. You can either set it directly in a GWT module file, or you can try to dynamically determine it at runtime through a property provider. In this section we'll look at both of these approaches.

We'll split the discussion on property providers into three parts: understanding what a property provider is, how to handle property-provider errors, and how to create your own property provider. Directly setting a value is much simpler, though perhaps less useful, so we'll start with that way.

17.5.1 Directly setting a property value in a module file

The simplest way for a developer to set a property is to use the `<set-property>` tag in a module definition. You've seen that this is as simple as writing the following:

```
<set-property name="someProperty" value="someValue"/>
```

That works for certain types of property that can be set at compile time.

Sometimes you can't set the property in a module file at compile time. This might be because you want the user to choose the value (as in i18n's `locale` property) or you don't know the value until the application is running (as in the case of `user.agent`). Fortunately, you can set a property value programmatically. To do that you use a property provider.

17.5.2 Understanding property providers

A *property provider* is a segment of JavaScript code that determines the value of a property. In former versions of GWT, it was directly defined within a `<property-provider>` tag and was included, by the GWT compiler, in the selection script sent to the browser as part of the application's bootstrapping process when a user started the application. The general pattern of that approach is shown in the next listing.

Listing 17.4 General structure of a property provider that returns one of several values

```
<property-provider name="property-name">
   <![CDATA[
      try{
         if (condition1 == true) return propertyValue1;
         if (condition2 == true) return propertyValue2;
           ...
         else return propertyValuen;
      } catch(e) {
         alert("Some error message: "+ e);
         return propertyValuex;
      }
   ]]>
</property-provider>
```

During compilation, the JavaScript code provided in the CDATA segment is copied into the application's nocache.js file (if using the standard linker) and executes as part of the bootstrapping mechanism.

From GWT 2.2, there's a move to use a Java class to generate the property provider's JavaScript code during compilation/linking, and from 2.4 it seems this is the only way GWT is built. The result is the same in that the generated JavaScript is inserted into the application's nocache.js file (if using the standard linker), and it still executes as part of the bootstrapping mechanism. We'll look only at this generator approach because it's the way GWT is going.

To use the generator approach to property providers means you write a Java class that implements `PropertyProviderGenerator`, say `SomeClass`, and reference that class in the property-provider definition for the `propertyName` it will work for:

```
<property-provider name="propertyName" generator="SomeClass"/>
```

Typical selection code will try to access a browser variable, a value in the URL, or a meta tag value set in the HTML file for the condition checking. For example, the internationalization property provider goes through all the steps we looked at in chapter

13—looking in the URL, looking for a meta tag in the HTML page, and finally looking for a user-defined JavaScript function to execute. But because it's JavaScript, your imagination on how to determine a value for your property is free to roam.

Let's take a look at how to generate a property provider within your code.

17.5.3 Generating a property provider

You can define a property provider that's generated at compile time. A user agent property provider is generated this way, and GWT's internationalization functionality uses this same approach but in a more interesting and complex manner.

The internationalization property provider can allow a number of approaches to be used for determining the locale, as well as determine the order in which they should be used. The approaches used are defined in an ordered list as a configuration property called `locale.searchorder`. By default, this is defined as the following:

```
<set-configuration-property name='locale.searchorder'
                              value= 'queryparam,cookie,meta,useragent'/>
```

This ordering indicates that GWT should look at the query parameter first, followed by the meta tag, then a cookie, and finally the browser headers.

Because this ordering and the methods included are user definable, it's not possible to provide a hardcoded property provider the way it used to be done in previous versions before compilation. Rather, the `I18n` module defines the property provider as the following:

```
<property-provider name="locale"
   generator="com.google.gwt.i18n.linker.LocalePropertyProviderGenerator"/>
```

This tells the compiler that the property provider must be created by executing the code in the `LocalePropertyProviderGenerator` class. That class implements the `PropertyProviderGenerator` interface, which is intended to create the necessary JavaScript to be used in the property provider through a call to the `generate` method:

```
String generate(TreeLogger logger, SortedSet<String> possibleValues,
    String fallback, SortedSet<ConfigurationProperty> configProperties)
    throws UnableToCompleteException;
```

The `generate` method takes a `TreeLogger`, a list of possible values for the property, a fallback value to use if one can't be determined, and the set of configuration properties in the compilation context.

In implementing the `generate` method, you construct the necessary JavaScript property-provider code as a `String` and use that as the return value. The best way to see it in action is for us to define our own `isWeekend` property that allows us to change the application if the date it knows about is a Saturday or a Sunday:

```
<define-property name="isWeekend" values="workhard,partytime"/>
<property-provider name="isWeekend"

    generator="...ch17.linker.WeekendPropertyProviderGenerator"/>
```

Figure 17.10 shows the application when the property provider has determined the isWeekend property is equal to workhard, that is, it's a normal day—you'll see in a short while what happens on the weekend.

To get this, we need to build the WeekendPropertyProviderGenerator property provider.

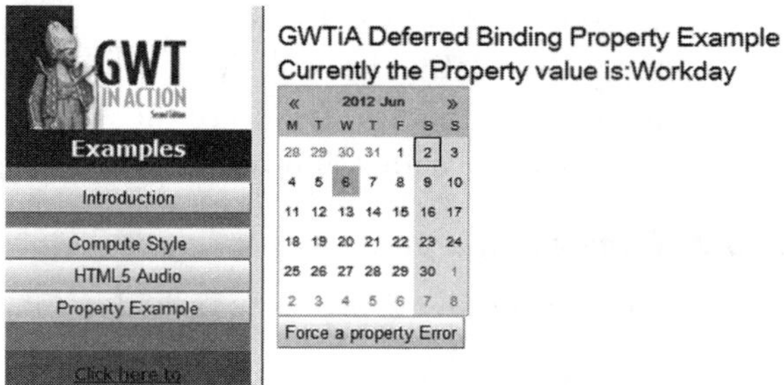

Figure 17.10 The property example during a normal working day (date has been set to June 6)

17.5.4 Defining your own property provider

Defining your own property provider is a case of deciding where you're going to get the value from and writing a property provider for it. For our weekend functionality, we'll grab it from the URL if it exists as a parameter or get the current date from the browser if it doesn't:

```
http://www.myapplication.se/?date=2010/06/02
```

Our property provider would need to search the URL for our parameter date and then parse the value to see if it's a weekend or not. The JavaScript shown in the following listing can achieve this.

Listing 17.5 Properties and conditional setting, debug- and production-mode compilation

```
{
  var isWeekend = "workhard";                                  <- Default value
  var queryParam = location.search;
  var datum = "";
  var qpStart = queryParam.indexOf("date=");                   <- Searching for parameter
  if (qpStart >= 0) {
    var value = queryParam.substring(qpStart + 5);
    var end = queryParam.indexOf("&", qpStart);
    if (end < 0) {
      end = queryParam.length;
    }
    datum = queryParam.substring(qpStart + 5, end);            <- Extracting parameter if found
  }
  var d = new Date();                                          <- Starting date calculation
  if (isNaN(datum) && datum != null && datum != ''){
    var currTokens = datum.split( "/" );
    if (currTokens.length > 0)
        d.setFullYear(currTokens[0],currTokens[1]-1,currTokens[2]);
  }
  isWeekday = !(d.getDay()==0||d.getDay()==6);
  if (!isWeekday) isWeekend = 'partytime';                     <- Is it a weekend?
  return isWeekend;                                            <- Returning the property value
}
```

What you need to do is somehow get a Java class to write that code. In our module definition, we've written

```
<property-provider name="isWeekend"
                  generator=
       "com.manning.gwtia.ch17.linker.WeekendPropertyProviderGenerator"/>
```

in which we're saying that our property provider generator is in the class `WeekendPropertyProviderGenerator`. (Note that we've put it in a `linker` package outside of the client package—this is because we don't want the GWT compiler trying to compile this class.)

The generator follows a couple of simple rules. Take a quick look at this listing, which shows the framework (the full listing is in this chapter's example download).

Listing 17.6 Our own generator for a property provider

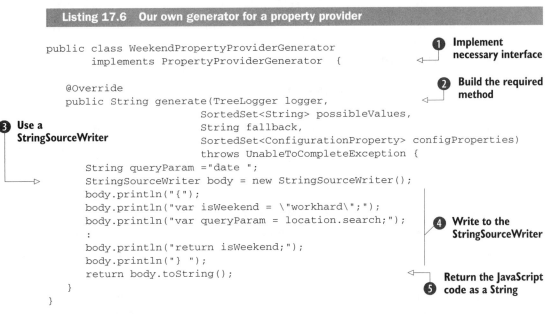

```
public class WeekendPropertyProviderGenerator
       implements PropertyProviderGenerator  {

   @Override
   public String generate(TreeLogger logger,
                          SortedSet<String> possibleValues,
                          String fallback,
                          SortedSet<ConfigurationProperty> configProperties)
                          throws UnableToCompleteException {
      String queryParam ="date ";
      StringSourceWriter body = new StringSourceWriter();
      body.println("{");
      body.println("var isWeekend = \"workhard\";");
      body.println("var queryParam = location.search;");
      :
      body.println("return isWeekend;");
      body.println("} ");
      return body.toString();
   }
}
```

❶ Implement necessary interface

❷ Build the required method

❸ Use a StringSourceWriter

❹ Write to the StringSourceWriter

❺ Return the JavaScript code as a String

The property-provider generator must implement the `PropertyProviderGenerator` interface ❶, which requires it to provide an implementation of the `generate` method ❷. It's convenient to use a `StringSourceWriter` object ❸ in which to write the JavaScript code using `println` methods ❹. This object also has `indent` and `outdent` methods, allowing you to give some readability to the output (the code in listing 17.6 comes from our provider when using the pretty mode of the compiler, so you can see that it works). All you need to do once you've created the JavaScript code in the `StringSourceWriter` object is to return it as a `String` from the method ❺.

During linking of your application, GWT calls this `generate` method to get the JavaScript code that it needs to insert into the bootstrapping code. If you compile in pretty mode, then you see all your JavaScript code in full glory in the application's bootstrap (nocache.js) file—which is helpful if you need to debug it.

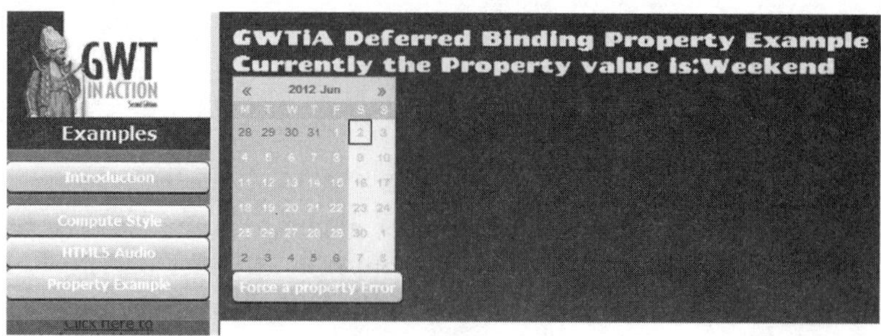

Figure 17.11 The property example running when the date is a weekend (June 2)

If everything works fine and the time you run the application is a Saturday or a Sunday, or you force the date through the picker to be one of those, then you'll see the weekend version (as in figure 17.11).

We've nearly finished with properties, but what happens if for some reason you encounter an error when trying to determine the property? Well, there's a catch-all process; it's not pretty, but at least it might help your user or provide some diagnostics.

17.5.5 *Handling failure to get a property value*

Most (nearly all?) of the time, you won't have a problem getting the property values you want, and if you do, you would have remembered to program defensively, so there's always a correct fallback, right? OK, but for that 0.00001% of the time where something has gone catastrophically wrong and your fallback/defensive programming hasn't worked, the last thing you want is for your user to have the web equivalent of the blue screen of death.

You can define a JavaScript function in the HTML page of the application that can at least acknowledge something has gone wrong. The first thing to do is define a meta tag as follows:

```
<meta name='gwt:onPropertyErrorFn' content='handlePropError'>
```

GWT bootstrapping code will call the function you name in the `content` attribute when it comes across a property error. You can put any JavaScript you want in that function, but you can't fix the error. In our example, we'll report the wrong value and the values that could have been used; in production, you might try to log the problem and inform the user in a more user-friendly way.

Here's the definition of our simple error-handing function:

```
<script>
    function handlePropError(propName, allowedValues, badValue){
    alert("Property Error for: " + propName +
          "\n Value was: "+badValue +
          "\n you could have: "+allowedValues);
    }
</script>
```

It's passed three parameters: the name of the property where the error happened; the value, if any, that was determined; and the allowed values.

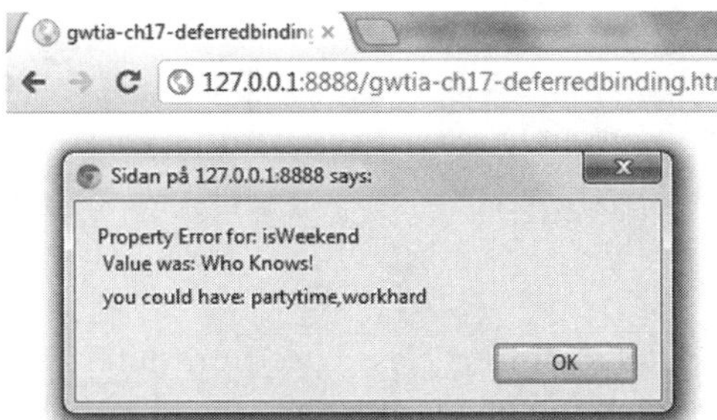

Figure 17.12 The last-chance-saloon error-handling functionality for GWT deferred-binding properties

Clicking the Force a Property Error button in our example will trigger the property provider to return an unknown value and so fire up this function, resulting in figure 17.12.

Before we finish, let's catch up on a situation where deferred binding on its own is not quite enough—handling HTML 5 widgets.

17.6 Coping when deferred binding isn't enough

Way back in section 17.3.4, we briefly looked at a new property introduced for HTML 5 widgets that allows you to defer binding out the widget in IE6 and IE8 because you know those two browsers don't support HTML 5 widgets, such as `Audio`.

But it's not so clear cut that all the other browsers do. Certainly the later versions do, but in earlier versions the support is patchy and inconsistent across the different browser versions. You could break up `user.agent` into smaller and smaller granularity until you're at point releases—but then you'd have a huge number of permutations.

Instead, the `Audio` widget uses this property to select the correct version of an inner class—`AudioElementSupportDetector`—that tells the widget if the browser may support HTML 5 audio. That inner class provides two methods:

- `isSupportedRunTime`—Used to check runtime availability of the `Audio` element
- `isSupportedCompileTime`—Used at compile time to check if the `Audio` element is supported

The `isSupportedRunTime` method checks to see if a passed-in `Element` is an `AudioElement` (meaning that version of the engine supports it) or `null` (that version of the engine doesn't support it) and returns an appropriate boolean value. In comparison, the `isSupportedCompileTime` method knows at compilation if the element will be supported or not.

What this means in practice is that you don't create `Audio` widgets in the normal way; you use the `createIfSupported` method, which you can see copied next.

Listing 17.7 `createIfSupported` method used to create HTML 5 `Audio` widgets

```
public static Audio createIfSupported() {
   if (detector == null) {
      detector = GWT.create(AudioElementSupportDetector.class);
   }
   if (!detector.isSupportedCompileTime()) {
```

❶ Get instance of detector

❷ Is Audio not supported?

```
         return null;
      }
      AudioElement element = Document.get().createAudioElement();   ❸ Try creating it
      if (!detector.isSupportedRunTime(element)) {                  ❹ Did it work?
         return null;
      }
      return new Audio(element);
   }
```

First, ❶ it gets a copy of the correct detector inner class based on deferred binding and then runs a compile-time check to see if the element is supported ❷. This will fail for IE6 and IE8 because you'll be using the `AudioElementSupportDetector` inner class due to the following deferred-binding definition in GWT's Media.gwt.xml file (Audio.gwt.xml if pre GWT 2.5):

```
<replace-with class="Audio.AudioElementSupportDetectedNo">
   <when-type-is class="Audio.AudioElementSupportDetector" />
   <when-property-is name="audioElementSupport" value="no" />
</replace-with>
```

That makes `isSupportedCompileTime` return `false`. That's as far as you need to go for IE 6 and IE 8.

For other browsers it returns `true`, so you fall through to trying to create the element ❸ and then checking if it has been created properly at runtime ❹. If it hasn't been created, then that point release of the browser doesn't support it. If it has, then the result is as shown in figure 17.13.

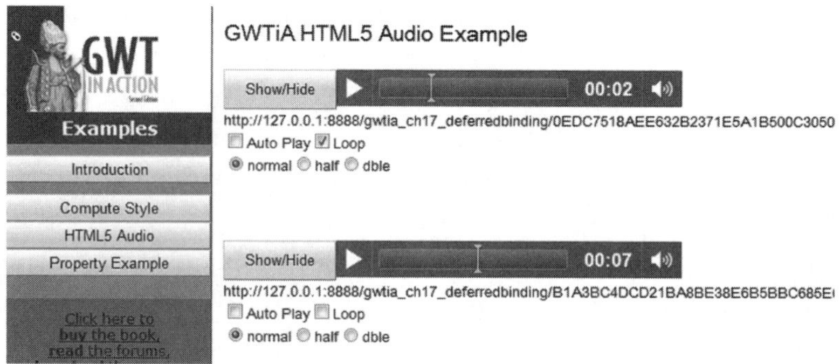

Figure 17.13 The result of conditional properties on the HTML 5 `Audio` element in a browser where it's supported

Figure 17.14 shows the same application running in IE 8, where the HTML 5 widget isn't supported.

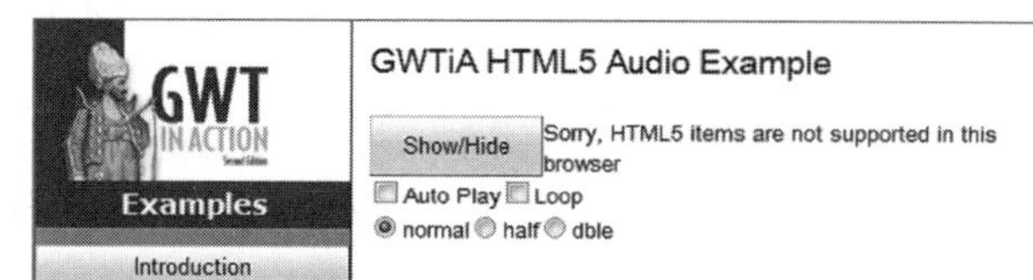

Figure 17.14 The result of conditional properties on the HTML 5 `Audio` element in a browser where it's not supported

And that's it; we're finished with deferred binding in the basic case. In the next chapter we'll look at how the plumbing of deferred binding helps you generate code at compile time, but for now, it's time to sum up this chapter.

17.7 Summary

You've seen how you can use deferred binding when you need to implement a piece of functionality in several different ways, and the way used is dependent on a particular property. Deferred binding helps maintenance and debugging because each implementation difference is encapsulated in its own class. Your users benefit because they have only the code necessary for their situation downloaded, making it a quicker download and therefore quicker startup time. As a developer you get no overhead in using deferred binding; rather it helps foster good engineering principles.

The one potential downside is the explosive growth of permutations as you add more properties and property values. You saw that you can control some of that growth by using conditional properties to reduce the space.

You also saw that using soft permutations allows you to reduce the permutations produced by the compiler—which will speed up compilation—by collapsing properties. But that comes at the expense of sending more code to the user and allowing the decision to be made at runtime about which functional implementation is used. The ultimate case is collapsing all properties, at which point all permutation decisions are made at runtime and all code combinations are sent to the user.

The key thing to remember when using deferred binding is to create your objects that use deferred binding through the `GWT.create` method rather than `new`. If you don't, then all of the work you put in defining functionality in different classes and creating your `replace-with` tags and your property provider will be ignored.

One of the things that came with GWT 2.2 was the ability to generate the property provider at compile time. This gives you real flexibility to minimize or alter the functionality of the property provider.

It's not only property providers that you can generate at compile time; you can also generate whole chunks of your application automatically. You do that through something called generators, and they're the subject of our next chapter.

18 Generators

This chapter covers
- Examining generators
- Exploring configuration properties
- Creating and using a generator

Wouldn't it be nice if your toolkit could write your code for you? Imagine, you provide a few instructions and, voila, your code is produced. Although you can't (yet) do this for a whole application, GWT gets close to this idea in a number of areas.

If you've used RPC, internationalization, JUnit, UiBinder, client bundles, or even dependency injection (as we described a couple of chapters ago) in your GWT application, you've experienced this, maybe without realizing it.

For example, with internationalization you write an interface and one or more properties files whose name(s) follow a specific naming convention. At compile time, GWT will automatically generate a set of classes that implements the interface, each class containing methods that return values from the properties file for a specific locale. These generated classes are then used in the compilation of your application, giving you a multilingual application.

The item that generates the classes in internationalization is a GWT generator. Generators can do much more than create classes to implement an interface. They can manipulate types (classes/interfaces), methods, fields, annotations, and so on, of source files; determine values of deferred binding and configuration properties; and access or manipulate other external resources (such as images, properties files, and the like) in the compilation space as you're compiling.

DEFINITION A *generator* runs at compile time, takes specific resources in your source code, and generates new replacement resources that are used in the compilation instead of the original.

We'll look at generators in this chapter, divided into two parts. In the first part we'll look at what generators are, what aspects of your project they can work on, and how you invoke them. When you're comfortable with that, we'll then jump into the heavier work of building our own generator, which will take every widget we use in this chapter's example and generate a new subclass widget that logs every constructor and method invocation. Along the way we'll look at how to prepare your IDE to help debug, as well as all of the components you'll use.

You can see the results of the generator we'll build in this chapter in figure 18.1, where at the bottom of the Logging window, among other things, you can see that a `Label` has been created and its `setText` method called (this is the result of the user clicking the Add A Label button in the application).

Note that generators harness the same GWT components as deferred binding and are sometimes thought of as a variant of deferred binding. We, though, will keep the two as separate aspects because they achieve different things.

Let's start the first part of this chapter by looking at what generators do.

18.1 What does a generator do?

We'll jump straight into what a generator does in this section by looking at the generator used by internationalization. A little earlier we discussed what this generator

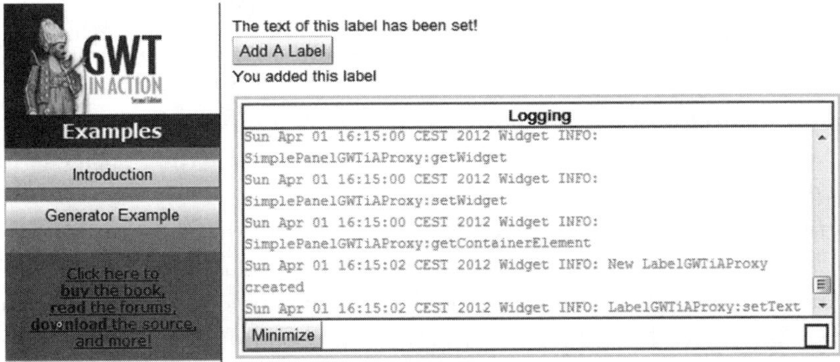

Figure 18.1 The result of the generator built in this chapter. In the Logging window you can see various method calls to the methods of a `FlowPanel`, a `Label`, and a `Button`.

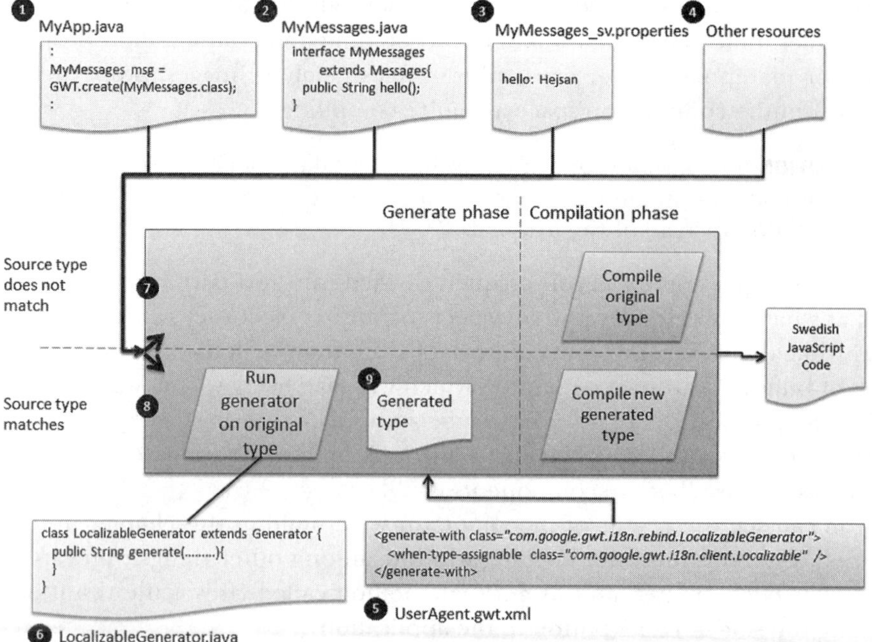

Figure 18.2 A depiction of what happens in internationalization, which uses a generator to merge the MyMessages interface file with the MyMessages_sv properties file, when compiling the Swedish locale, to create a new internally generated class that's then used in the compilation phase instead of the original interface

does, and figure 18.2 shows what's happening diagrammatically when we're compiling several source types for an imaginary application, `MyApp`, for the Swedish locale. At first glance, the figure can seem rather overwhelming. We're doing the following:

- Compiling the source files for our application, which currently consists of `MyApp` ❶, which uses an interface `MyMessages` ❷ and perhaps some other resources ❹. Note that the `MyMessages` interface has no implementation (at the moment).
- Indicating to the GWT compiler that it needs to do something additional when creating a `MyMessages` type by constructing it using the special `GWT.create` method in ❶.
- Defining (although GWT has defined it) a generator ❻ that will take the `MyMessages` interface and create an implementation class using strings in the associated MyMessages_sv.properties file ❸ as return objects in the class's methods.
- Providing the rules to the GWT compiler that it should run a specific generator when it comes across the given type created using the `GWT.create` method (the `<generate-with>` tag in the module file ❺).

When the compiler sees `GWT.create(MyMessages)`, it's directed by the `generate-with` tag in the module file ❺ to run the `LocalizableGenerator` generator on `MyMessages` because it's assignable to the `Localizable` type (for example, `MyMessages` extends `Localizable`—this isn't so obvious in this case, but `MyMessages` implements the `Messages` interface, which in turn extends some other interfaces until you find at the bottom of the stack that it all implements `Localizable`).

So, when compiling the `MyMessages` interface, the compiler will go through the path ❽. That is to say, the `LocalizableGenerator` will take the `MyMessages` interface, and because we're compiling for Swedish locale in this iteration, it will find the MyMessages_sv.properties file and/or other files in the internationalization hierarchy (see chapter 13) in order to find the necessary strings to be returned in the generated class methods. If the type is not assignable, then the compilation goes through the path ❼; that is, the original type is used with no alterations.

This new class, like all the other items the compiler can see, is known as an *artifact* and is made available to the compiler by the `generate` method returning its name—which must be different from any existing artifact. But the new artifact isn't normally visible to you as a programmer because it's transient (it will be re-created each time the compiler runs).

> **TIP** Normally, the output of the generator is hidden from view. You can add the `-gen someDirectory` switch to the development mode or the compiler to see the result of your generator in the someDirectory folder.

The resultant type from the generator is fed into the GWT compiler for compilation instead of the original type. A similar process happens in development mode, where the browser plug-in gets access to the generated artifact.

We hope you agree this is pretty neat—you can save yourself a lot of time and effort and remove a lot of boilerplate code if you provide generators in sensible places. You may be wondering what else a generator can do. Good, because that's what we'll cover next.

18.2 What can a generator do?

In addition to internationalization, which we briefly discussed, you can find GWT using generators in the following areas:

- Remote Procedure Call (RPC) proxy code and serialization/unserialization code
- Declarative user interfaces (UiBinder)
- RunAsync proxy code (for deferred loading of code)
- Internationalization and localization
- Client bundles
- Benchmark tools
- Editors
- Places
- SafeHtml
- Validation (when it makes it to the trunk)
- JUnit testing

Not all of these take a properties file and map the contents to methods in an interface, as the internationalization generator does. In this section, we'll look briefly at what some of the standard GWT generators do for your code and see what they can access and manipulate.

The internationalization generator might already have given you some hints that you can access types and their components in the compilation, so let's briefly look at that.

18.2.1 Accessing code

In internationalization, the generator is used to bind values in properties files to newly created classes that are then used by the compiler as deferred-binding entities in the compilation of locale-specific application permutations. This is beneficial because the developer only needs to worry about providing an interface for constants and messages. Leaving the properties files independent from the code means that they can be sent out to translators to get perfect translations (and they don't have to care how the code works).

But how does the generator know what properties file to look for and what text to find in those files? The generator has access to all sorts of information about the type under compilation, including its name, what it imports, subclasses, the methods and fields it holds, and so on. It does this through a `TypeOracle`, which we'll discuss in section 18.7.4.

The internationalization generator uses the interface name passed to it by the compiler as the base name for the properties file to use. It uses the `TypeOracle` to get access to the method names in the interface and then looks up the matching key in a properties file to get the text to be used.

You might remember from the internationalization chapter that you can indicate via an annotation that the properties file uses a different name for the key than the interface method name. Luckily, a generator can also read annotations and their values.

18.2.2 Reading annotations

Instead of looking only at internationalization, let's look at another generator that reads annotations for information. The generator used in a Remote Procedure Call is responsible for creating the boilerplate code implementation behind the server RPC code. If you've read chapter 7, then you might remember the Twitter example we created, which defined a `TwitterService` interface:

```
@RemoteServiceRelativePath("service")
public interface TwitterService extends RemoteService{
    public ArrayList<FeedData> getUserTimeline(String screenName)
        throws GTwitterException;
}
```

At compile time the `RpcServiceGenerator` generator, defined in package `com.google.gwt.rpc.rebind`, will be invoked because the `TwitterService` interface extends the `RemoteService` class (because this is the direction given in the `generate-with` definition in the RPC module). This generator creates the proxy code for calling the server-side code, as well as the code for serializing and deserializing your data objects (for a good explanation of what we're talking about here, see the first part of chapter 7). If the generator was not there, you'd have to write all that code.

The generator accesses the annotation on the type (`@RemoteServiceRelativePath("service")`) to understand the path to the server code to use when it plumbs the client/server communication together.

Remember the deferred-binding properties from the last chapter? Generators can access them as well.

18.2.3 Accessing properties

If we jump back to internationalization, you'll likely recall a deferred-binding property called `locale`, which lists the locales the compilation should run through, such as `en` for English or `sv` for Swedish. The compiler will create a permutation for each locale (and `user.agent` property) and will get the appropriate translations for text from the appropriate properties file.

You saw earlier that internationalization used the `TypeOracle` to access method names to use as keys to find in the properties file(s) and the name of the interface to find in the base properties file. But for the Swedish locale, you don't want the generator to use MyMessages.properties; instead you'll use MyMessages_sv.properties. That means you need to let the generator know what `locale` property the compiler is currently compiling for, and it gets that information through the `PropertyOracle`.

Using the `PropertyOracle`, a generator gets access to all the available deferred-binding properties in a compilation context. It can see what particular values the compiler is currently working with, plus what values are possible. You'll also see later in this chapter that the `PropertyOracle` provides access to configuration properties.

You've seen briefly from internationalization that generators can use resources (the properties files), so let's examine a little more how they do so.

18.2.4 Using resources

Another GWT generator is dedicated to constructing a whole user interface worth of Java code from a simple XML definition. For UiBinder (chapter 6), we provide some XML declaring a widget and an associated widget class. If you want to create the widget shown in figure 18.3, you'd use the declaration and code shown in listing 18.1.

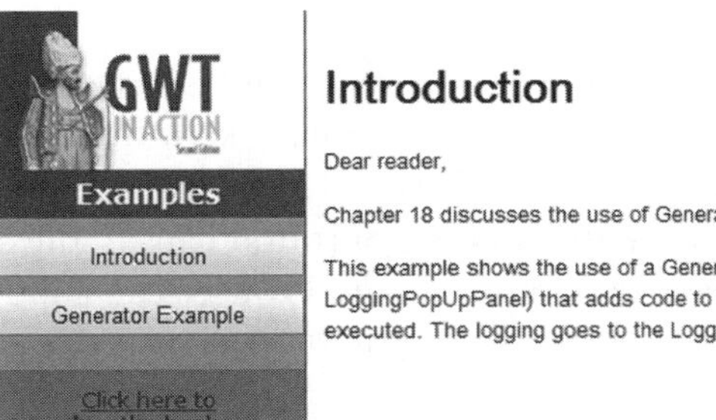

Figure 18.3 The result of generating the chapter 18 example's UI from its UiBinder declaration through the UiBinder generator

The following listing shows the components used to create the widget in the previous figure.

Listing 18.1 Example XML and Java class components used in UiBinder functionality

```
[ExamplePanel.ui.xml]                                          ❶ XML definition's filename
<ui:UiBinder xmlns:ui='urn:ui:com.google.gwt.uibinder'>
<g:DockLayoutPanel unit="PX">
   <g:west size="180">
      <g:SimplePanel>
         :
</ui:UiBinder>

[ExamplePanel.class]
  :
  interface ExamplePanelUiBinder extends
                      UiBinder<Widget, ExamplePanel> {}
  private static ExamplePanelUiBinder uiBinder =               ❷ Triggering the generator
                      GWT.create(ExamplePanelUiBinder.class);
  :
```

`UiBinderGenerator` in the `com.google.gwt.uibinder.rebind` package binds the declaration in the ExamplePanel.ui.xml file to the `ExamplePanel` implementation. It knows to look for an XML file whose name ❶ starts with the class name ❷ under compilation and that that resource is outside the Java code.

Access to resources is via a `ResourceOracle`. We'll look in a little more detail at this `ResourceOracle` later in the chapter, along with the `TypeOracle` and `PropertyOracle`, when we're building our own generator.

The client-bundle generator goes a step further than only accessing resources. It can manipulate them, creating a new resource that's used in the application rather than the original ones.

18.2.5 Manipulating resources

You saw that a generator can access the contents of an external resource, but it can also manipulate those resources and/or create new ones. A good example of this is client bundles.

In the case of client bundles, the generator can perform one of two optimizations. Assuming none of the images in the client bundle are animated GIFs, the generator will automatically stitch them together to create a single image. This can significantly reduce the number of round trips to the server for images, speeding up your application. In addition, if the browser can support it, the resulting image is turned into an inline data URL; if not, then a cacheable output file is produced by the generator, cutting the trips to the server yet again.

The generator does this using a third-party image-manipulation library, which indicates that you aren't restricted in the Java you use in a generator (unlike client-side GWT code). Typically, the generator code is placed in a `rebind` package outside the `client` package so that the GWT compiler doesn't attempt to compile it.

As you can see, a generator is a powerful thing. It can access annotations, class/interface names, and method names of the class under compilation; see the values of all properties that drive this permutation of compilation; access external resources; and call external functionality that might even manipulate those external resources. A generator can likely do much more, limited only by your imagination and needs.

One thing we still need to look at is how you tell GWT when to use a generator and when not to, because you might not want it running for everything.

18.3 Indicating what generator to use and when

In your code we tell the GWT compiler that it needs to do something extra by using the `GWT.create` method to construct your objects. But you also need to tell the GWT compiler what that extra work is: in this case, what generator to use and when.

This is done by providing a `generate-with` tag definition in a module file. For internationalization, that's done in the `I18N` module, which you inherit in your application's module file. The definition is given in the `I18N` module in GWT 2.5 as follows:

```
<generate-with class="com.google.gwt.i18n.rebind.LocalizableGenerator">
  <when-type-assignable class="com.google.gwt.i18n.shared.Localizable" />
</generate-with>
```

(Pre GWT 2.5, the `Localizable` class was in `com.google.gwt.i18n.client`; that's now deprecated in favor of the shared package version.)

If you read chapter 17 on deferred binding, then you'll see that defining a generator in a module file follows a similar pattern. Don't worry if you haven't, because all the definition says is to run the `LocalizableGenerator` generator on the class given in the `GWT.create` call if that class is type assignable to (is, extends, or implements) `Localizable`.

In the case of internationalization, we extend `Messages` and `Constants` interfaces; they themselves extend `Localizable` in their type hierarchy, so they can be said to be type assignable to `Localizable`. Figure 18.4 shows this hierarchy for `Constants`.

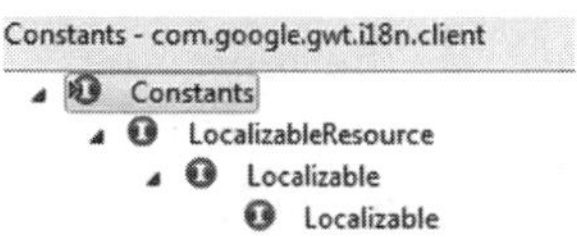

Figure 18.4 The type hierarchy of `Constants` showing that it's type assignable to `Localizable`

You can make the module definition of a generator as complicated as needed to deal with the situation at hand. It can even include GWT properties and logical operations. The following listing shows the more complicated setup that GWT uses for client bundling.

Listing 18.2 Partial generator definition using conditional properties

```
<generate-with class="com.google.gwt.resources.rebind.context.
                        InlineClientBundleGenerator">          ❶ Defining the generator to use
  <all>
    <when-type-assignable class="com.google.gwt.resources.client.
                                   ClientBundle" />            ❷ Type assignable
```

```
        <when-property-is name="ClientBundle.enableInlining"
                          value="true" />                        ❹ Logical OR
Inlining ❸  <any>
enabled       <when-property-is name="user.agent" value="safari" />
              <when-property-is name="user.agent" value="opera" />      Correct
              <when-property-is name="user.agent" value="gecko1_8" />   rendering
              <when-property-is name="user.agent" value="ie8" />     ❺ engine
              <when-property-is name="user.agent" value="ie9" />
            </any>
          </all>
        </generate-with>
```

Listing 18.2 directs the compiler to use the `InlineClientBundleGenerator` ❶ if the type is assignable to `ClientBundle` ❷, the `ClientBundle.enableInlining` configuration property is set to `true` ❸, and the rendering engine being compiled for is Safari (or WebKit, for Safari, Chrome, and so on), Opera or Gecko (Firefox and the like), or Internet Explorer 8 ❺.

Note that the use of <any> in ❹ acts as a logical `OR`. You could also use `<all>` as a logical `AND` and <none> for negation. We covered deferred-binding properties in some detail in section 17.3 because they're a substantial component of deferred binding. They're also usable in generator definitions, as you've seen through the use of the `user.agent` deferred binding property.

One thing you saw introduced in listing 18.2 is a new type of property, the configuration property.

18.4 Configuration properties

You saw in chapter 17 that deferred-binding properties have a set of values that are enumerable (for example, a set of browser agents or a set of locales), which can drive the generation of permutations of JavaScript code.

What if you want to turn on or off some generator functionality during compile, much like the inlining of client bundles discussed previously? If you use a deferred-binding property, then you'll double the number of permutations created—one set of permutations when the property is off and one for when it's on. This probably isn't what you wanted. Or what if you need to pass the generator a particular filename not included as an annotation? That's not possible using deferred-binding properties.

To solve these types of problems, GWT has the configuration property. You can perform three operations with configuration properties: define them, set them, and extend them.

18.4.1 Defining a configuration property

Configuration properties are defined in a module file. They're used to pass one or more values to a generator (usually when it doesn't make sense to do so via a deferred-binding property).

WARNING Don't confuse deferred-binding properties with configuration properties. Deferred-binding properties generally drive permutations of the compiler; configuration properties are for passing some information to a generator (or linker) when it's not sensible or possible to do so via a deferred-binding property, and those values don't change between permutations.

You can use the `<define-configuration-property>` tag to define a configuration property. For example, let's define a `gwtia.debugWidgets` configuration property that you'll use later when you create your own generator:

```
<define-configuration-property name="gwtia.debugWidgets"
                                is-multi-valued="false" />
```

The definition gives a name to the configuration property and indicates whether it's permitted to have multiple values or not. For this example, you want it to represent a simple yes/no flag, so you say that its `is-multi-values` attribute is `false`.

An example of a configuration property that's multivalued is the set of runtime locales in internationalization, which we'll come back to momentarily.

Once a configuration property is defined, you can set its value.

18.4.2 *Setting the value of a configuration property*

Unlike deferred-binding properties, you need to explicitly set the value of a configuration property. This is done through the `<set-configuration-property>` tag:

```
<set-configuration-property name="gwtia.debugWidgets" value="true" />
```

Before GWT 2.0

Configuration properties were introduced in GWT 1.6, although at that time you weren't required to use the `<define-configuration-property>` tag—you used a `<set-configuration-property>` tag to create the property.

In GWT 2.0 you can still do this, but it's likely to be dropped in the future. Our advice is to always use the `<define-configuration-property>` tag and follow up with the `<set-configuration-property>` tag.

If a configuration property is multivalued, then you might want to extend it to add additional values.

18.4.3 *Extending the value of a configuration property*

You can extend a configuration property as you did the deferred-binding properties. To do so, you use the `<extend-configuration-property>` tag. But extending a configuration property where `is-multi-valued` is set to `false` will fail.

For internationalization runtime locales, you extend the `runtime.locale` configuration property in the `I18N` module with the locales that you wish to be changeable at runtime. This functionality is useful where translated messages are the same but things such as currency symbols or number formatting are different. For example, the following

```
<extend-configuration-property name="runtime.locales" value="fr"/>
<extend-configuration-property name="runtime.locales" value="fr_BE"/>
<extend-configuration-property name="runtime.locales" value="fr_CA"/>
<extend-configuration-property name="runtime.locales" value="fr_CH"/>
<extend-configuration-property name="runtime.locales" value="fr_FR"/>
<extend-configuration-property name="runtime.locales" value="fr_LU"/>
<extend-configuration-property name="runtime.locales" value="fr_MC"/>
<extend-configuration-property name="runtime.locales" value="fr_SN"/>
```

would ensure that all the region-specific variances for the French language are available at runtime.

What's the point in these configuration properties? The generator can access them through the `PropertyOracle`, which we'll discuss later in this chapter when we build our own generator.

Before we get into the details of creating our own generator, we'll take a moment to review the steps involved in using a generator in your code.

18.5 Pulling it all together

We can summarize the steps involved to use a generator as the following:

1. You write a Java class, `SomeGeneratorClass`, that extends the `Generator` class of the `com.google.gwt.core.ext` package. By convention this class will be in a `rebind` package.
2. In a module file, you provide a `<generate-with>` tag that defines when the generator should be applied:

   ```
   <generate-with class="com.gwtbook.rebind.SomeGeneratorClass">
      <when-type-is class="com.gwtbook.client.SomeType"/>
   </replace-with>
   ```

3. You define `SomeTypeToBeGenerated`, which will extend or implement a trigger type (an interface or class—let's call it `SomeType`).
4. You see, or use, the following code in a GWT application, which implies that a form of deferred binding is going to happen:

   ```
   SomeTypeToBeGenerated impl = GWT.create(SomeTypeToBeGenerated.class)
   ```

   In the application's code, `impl` is used like any other class in Java—even if it's an interface, it's syntactically correct to call methods on it.

Now we'll move on from what generators do and how you use them to creating your own generator. The first leg of our journey is to look at some steps that will make development and debugging a little easier.

18.6 Preparing to write a generator

Our generator is going to be fairly simple. It will take all the widgets and panel classes used in our example application and generate new classes that log each constructor

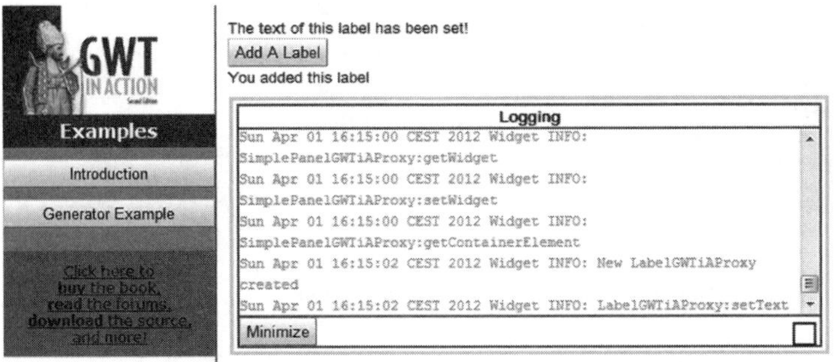

Figure 18.5 The result of the generator built in this chapter. In the Logging window you can see various method calls to the methods of a `FlowPanel`, `Label`, and `Button`.

and method invocation to the GWT dialog-based logger (which is available from GWT 2.1 onward) if the configuration property `gwtia.debugWidgets` is set to `true`. Figure 18.5 shows the result of all the logging in action.

In the figure, the user has clicked the Add A Label button, and as a result the Logging window, at the bottom, shows messages such as `New LabelGWTiAProxy created` and `LabelGWTiAProxy:setText`. These are messages from the generated version of GWT's `Label` that's printing out the actions it has taken.

Before you start creating a generator, you have a couple of preparatory steps to take. One is mandatory; the other is optional but highly useful.

You must add the gwt-dev jar to your classpath, because it includes all the classes and interfaces, such as the oracles, classes representing classes, methods, and so on, that you'll be using in the generator.

> **NOTE** When developing a generator, you must add the gwt-dev jar to the classpath because it includes all the necessary classes.

It's also useful, during development, to tell the compiler where to place the generated classes. If you remember, the compiler treats them as transient files by default, so you don't see them. You will see lots of errors if you get something wrong, so not being able to see the output file will make debugging a nightmare!

To rectify that debugging issue, you can pass the `-gen` flag to the compiler or development mode along with a directory where you wish the generated files to be placed. You can send them to any location; we prefer to send them to a folder name within the existing project structure that we name: generated. That allows us to view them directly within Eclipse by refreshing the project—as you can see in figure 18.6.

You'll need to look inside this generated folder to see your generated classes—and will probably have to refresh the project (in Eclipse, highlight the project and press F5) to see the files. As you can see in figure 18.6, the generated code you're interested in sits under the path com/google/gwt/user/client/ui, but you also have other code under other paths. This should be expected because this generator isn't the only one running.

With your environment set up for building a generator, we should now turn our attention to doing precisely that.

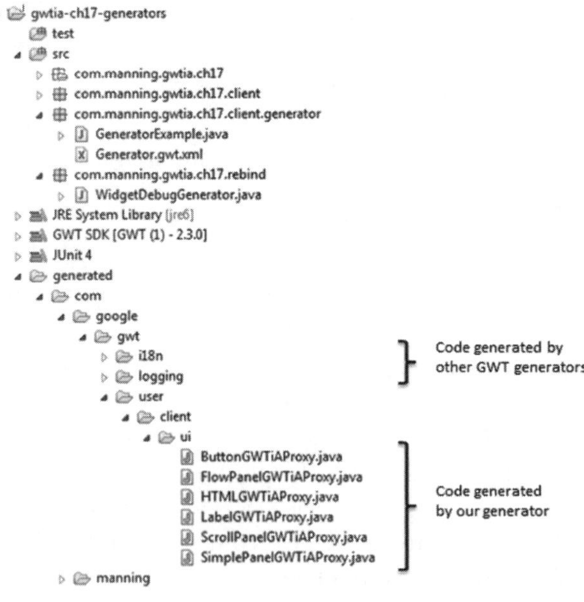

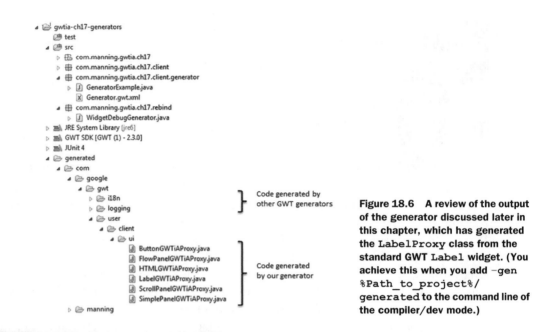

Figure 18.6 A review of the output of the generator discussed later in this chapter, which has generated the `LabelProxy` class from the standard GWT `Label` widget. (You achieve this when you add `-gen %Path_to_project%/generated` to the command line of the compiler/dev mode.)

18.7 Creating your own generator

It's much simpler to write your own generator than you might imagine. We find the hardest part is the amount of code you have to write and dealing with the strings when writing your new class.

Typically, you write a generator taking the stepwise approach shown in figure 18.7. Every generator follows the same pattern: extending the `Generator` interface and implementing the `generate` method. So it makes sense that we look at that first. Then you'll need to create a new output type (usually a new class) and start writing content into it. That content will most likely be based on other artifacts of the compilation (resources, types, properties, and so on) that you can access through one of three GWT-provided oracles.

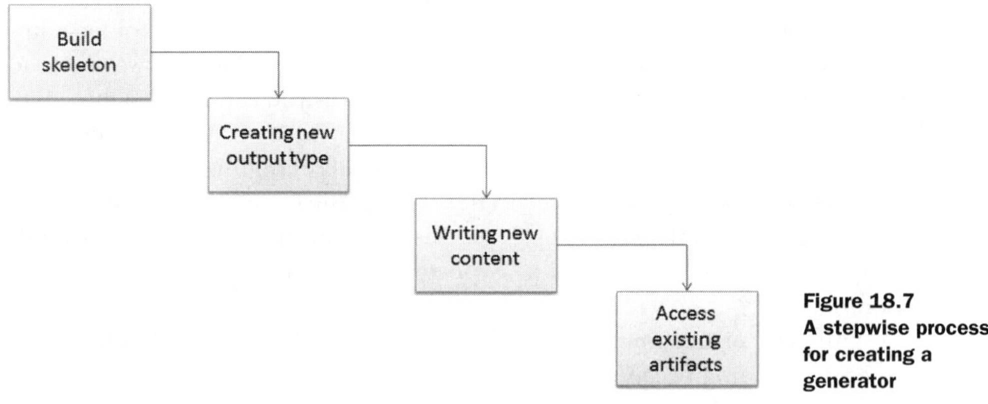

Figure 18.7 A stepwise process for creating a generator

In this section we'll walk through all of these steps, and along the way we'll show how they're used in our chapter's example generator code, starting with the skeleton of a generator.

18.7.1 The generator skeleton

All generators extend the `Generator` class in the `com.google.gwt.core.ext` package (in the gwt-dev jar). By convention, generators are stored in a `rebind` package at the level in the package structure that's most relevant.

Unlike your client code, a generator has no restrictions on the Java it can use; for example, classes such as those in `java.io` are useable by a generator. This means your generator should not be in a subpackage of the `client` package—otherwise, the GWT compiler will try to compile it and will complain. By convention, it's usually stored under a `rebind` package. In our example code, it's in the package `com.manning.gwtia.ch18 .rebind`.

Every generator will follow the same pattern, with the simplest containing only one method, `generate`, and returning a `null` object, as you can see in the next listing.

Listing 18.3 The template of a generator

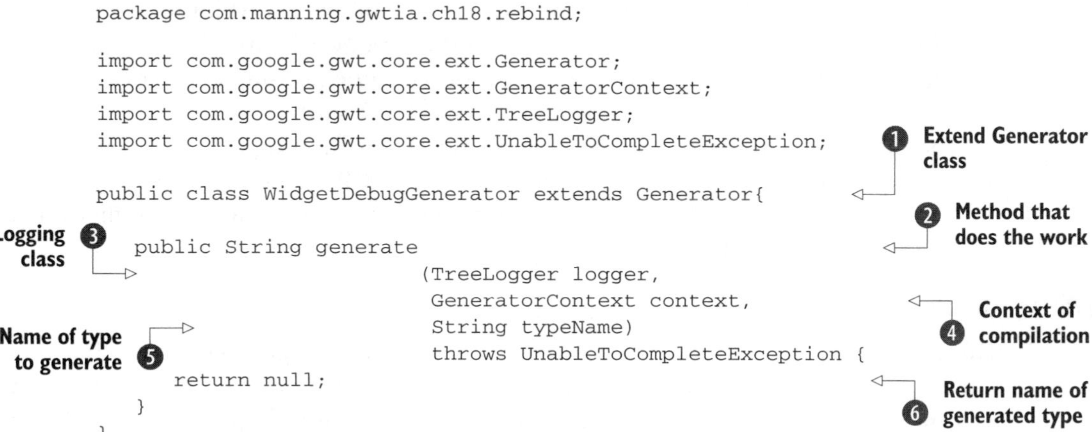


```
package com.manning.gwtia.ch18.rebind;

import com.google.gwt.core.ext.Generator;
import com.google.gwt.core.ext.GeneratorContext;
import com.google.gwt.core.ext.TreeLogger;
import com.google.gwt.core.ext.UnableToCompleteException;

public class WidgetDebugGenerator extends Generator{

   public String generate
                          (TreeLogger logger,
                           GeneratorContext context,
                           String typeName)
                           throws UnableToCompleteException {
      return null;
   }
}
```

The entry point to a generator class, called by the compiler, is the `generate` method ❷ required as you implement the `Generator` interface ❶. When it's finished, the generator returns either the fully qualified class name of the type it has created, which the compiler will then use instead of the original type, or `null`, as in ❻, in which case the compiler assumes nothing has been generated and will use the original type.

As you can see in listing 18.3, the compiler passes three objects to the generator. The first ❸ is the logger that the compiler is currently using. You can use that logger to emit any log messages you want or even create a child of it and emit your messages there, during compilation. Because our generator is running in the context of the compilation, it makes perfect sense to attach any log messages to that compiler's logger. Typically the logger passed in from the compiler is the console, either the

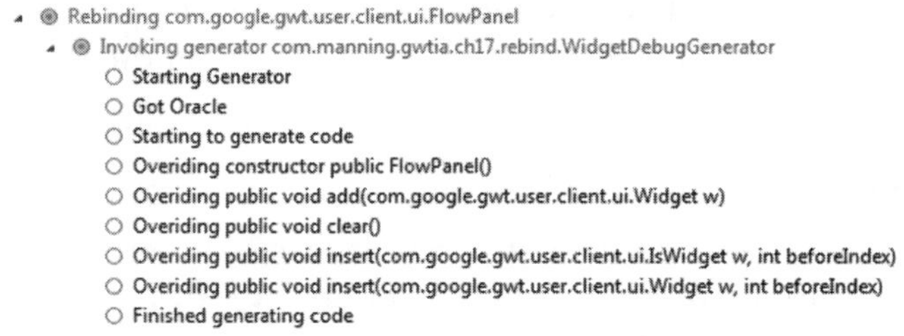

- Rebinding com.google.gwt.user.client.ui.FlowPanel
  - Invoking generator com.manning.gwtia.ch17.rebind.WidgetDebugGenerator
    - Starting Generator
    - Got Oracle
    - Starting to generate code
    - Overiding constructor public FlowPanel()
    - Overiding public void add(com.google.gwt.user.client.ui.Widget w)
    - Overiding public void clear()
    - Overiding public void insert(com.google.gwt.user.client.ui.IsWidget w, int beforeIndex)
    - Overiding public void insert(com.google.gwt.user.client.ui.Widget w, int beforeIndex)
    - Finished generating code

Figure 18.8 Our example generator's log output as it generates the proxy class for `FlowPanel`

command line or console area of your IDE. In our generator example, we log the methods and constructor we're overriding, leading to output similar to that shown in figure 18.8.

The second object passed into the generator is the context of the compilation ❹. This includes all the artifacts that the compiler can see—all your application's types, resources, and properties (for example, what locale is currently being compiled, the set of possible locales, and configuration properties). These artifacts are accessed via the three generator-specific oracles—the `TypeOracle`, the `ResourceOracle`, and the `PropertyOracle`.

The third parameter to the generator ❺ is the name of the type that's being passed in for generation by the compiler. Typically the generator code will use this value to retrieve a Java representation of the type from the `TypeOracle` and then create a new type. It can also be used as the start part of a resource name (as you saw when using i18n to find property files named after the class followed by country code).

The generator shown in a moment in listing 18.4 is the simplest possible; it does nothing apart from return `null`, for example, tell the GWT compiler to use the original class. Let's now look at how you'd improve on that to make it do something by first looking at how you create a new type.

18.7.2 Creating a new type

The `SourceWriter` object creates a new type, but before you get to creating the type, you need to establish the qualified name of your new type. In our example generator, we want the new type to be in the same package as the input type, plus its name should be the input type's name appended with `GWTiAProxy`. For example, `com.google.gwt.user.client.ui.FlowPanel` generates `com.google.gwt.user.client.ui.FlowPanelGWTiAProxy`.

This is quite simple to achieve, but it takes the few steps shown here.

Listing 18.4 A basic generator framework

```
public String generate(TreeLogger logger, GeneratorContext context,
             String typeName) throws UnableToCompleteException {
   try {
      TypeOracle types = context.getTypeOracle();
      JClassType type = types.getType(typeName);
      String packageName = type.getPackage().getName();
      String simpleClassName = type.getSimpleSourceName();
```

❶ Get input type info

```
      String proxyName = simpleClassName + "GWTiAProxy";
      String qualifiedName = packageName + "." + proxyName;

      return qualifiedName;
   } catch (NotFoundException e) {
      throw new UnableToCompleteException();
   }
}
```

❷ **Create output type info**

❸ **Handling issues**

First, in the `generate` method, you need to get hold of information about the input type ❶. You get the `TypeOracle` object from the context, and from that you get a `JClassType` object that gives you access to information about the input type. You use that object to get the name of the package and the simple source name of the input class.

You now ❷ use that information to create the name of your generated type. By adding `GWTiAProxy` to the simple class name and then the result of that to the package name, you achieve what you want.

Using the `TypeOracle` is analogous to introspection in standard Java: you have classes for each type of Java construct, and you use the methods in these classes to access components of the source code. If you jump ahead to section 18.7.4, you'll see these in more detail.

This version of the `generate` method uses a simple `try/catch` construct in case information about the input type isn't available ❸.

To complete your final `generate` method definition, you have to build the output type—so far you've only created its name. You do that by creating a `SourceWriter` object and writing the code into it; once the `commit` method is called on that `SourceWriter`, you have a type the GWT compiler can use.

The route to getting a `SourceWriter` is slightly convoluted and is best placed in its own method to aid maintainability and readability. Our version is shown here.

Listing 18.5 Creating the `SourceWriter` object

```
SourceWriter getSourceWriter(TreeLogger logger ,GeneratorContext context
                             , String packageName, String className
                             , String superclassName
                             , String... imports){
   PrintWriter printWriter = context.tryCreate(logger,
                                                packageName,
                                                className);
   if (printWriter == null) return null;
   ClassSourceFileComposerFactory composerFactory =
       new ClassSourceFileComposerFactory(packageName, className);
   for (String imprt : imports)
      composerFactory.addImport(imprt);
   if (superclassName!=null)
      composerFactory.setSuperclass(superclassName);
   return composerFactory.createSourceWriter(context, printWriter);
}
```

❶ **Create PrintWriter**

❷ **Handle when new type already exists**

❸ **Get new ClassSourceFileComposerFactory**

❹ **Add imports**

❺ **Set superclass**

❻ **Create SourceWriter**

The SourceWriter is created in a ClassSourceFileComposerFactory from the compilation context and a created PrintWriter object. This is step ❻ in listing 18.5. To get there, you first try to create a PrintWriter object ❶.

If you're unsuccessful in creating a PrintWriter, for example, you get null as the result of ❶, it's because the type you're trying to create already exists ❷—most likely you either have your package and source names wrong for the new type or you've already generated the class and there's no point in doing it again. The latter case is quite possible, because the compiler builds multiple permutations of your application due to of deferred binding. If the generated type isn't dependent on the factors driving the permutation, then it will be created the first time and null will be returned each subsequent time. Looking back at listing 18.4, you can see that if getSourceWriter returns null, then you still return the new type's qualified name, because the new type exists.

Assuming you have the PrintWriter object and it's not null, then in ❸ you get a new ClassSourceFileComposerFactory object and start adding the imports passed in as parameters to getSourceWriter to it ❹. We've added this because the generated class may use imports not in the original. In our example generator this is true because we'll import the Logger class in the proxy classes, and that isn't used in the input type.

The new type needs to extend the source type, and so you do that in ❺. If you don't do that, then you're likely to have compilation errors around type mismatches.

We're assuming in our generator that we're creating a class, which is the default in the composer factory. If you wish to generate an interface instead of a class, then you should additionally call the makeInterface method on the composer factory.

With all that done, the SourceWriter is created from the factory using the PrintWriter and the context in ❻. The result inside the SourceWriter, in our example for a Label, would be the following:

```
package com.google.gwt.user.client.ui;
import java.util.logging.Level;
import java.util.logging.Logger;

public class LabelGWTiAProxy extends Label {
}
```

We told you it was quite an effort.

Now you have a new LabelGWTiAProxy class that's returned to the generate method and ultimately to the GWT compiler to use instead of the original Label class. It still doesn't do anything more than the original Label. What you need to do is start writing some overridden constructors, methods, and new variables into the class.

18.7.3 Writing the new content

If you were successful in getting a SourceWriter object in the previous step, then you can begin filling out the details of the generated class. If the previous step returned a null, then the generated class is already written, so there's nothing more to do but return the fully qualified class name to the generator.

At least once, though, you'll have to write the generated class. This is an easy task but again not the prettiest. Thinking about our example where the generated widget needs to log things to the logger, one of the tasks you'll need to do is create the logger that will be used. You want the resulting class to look like the following:

```
package com.google.gwt.user.client.ui;
import java.util.logging.Level;
import java.util.logging.Logger;

public class LabelGWTiAProxy extends Label {
  /**
   * Logger that is used in class
   */
  Logger logger = Logger.getLogger("Widget");
:
}
```

The following listing shows the code for writing the class variable for the logger (you already included the import in the previous step).

Listing 18.6 Code for writing the new logger variable in the generated class

```
public void writeLoggerCode(TreeLogger logger, SourceWriter writer){
   writer.beginJavaDocComment();
   writer.println("Logger that is used in class");          ❶ Writing some Javadoc
   writer.endJavaDocComment();
   writer.println("Logger " + LOGGER_VAR_NAME + " =
                                Logger.getLogger(\"Widget\");");   ❷ Writing some code
}
```

You start off by writing a Javadoc comment for the variable ❶ and end with writing the code to create the logger variable itself ❷. As we said, it's simple to do, but all these `println` statements make it a little messy to keep track of where you are (particularly if you have to escape additional quote marks).

It's worth writing out Javadocs as well as using the `indent()` and `outdent()` methods to format the output class, because that's going to help with readability if you need to debug the generator by looking at the outputted code.

In writing generated classes, you'll heavily rely on entities called *oracles* to get information about the type (as you've seen in this section), or properties used in the permutation being compiled, or even other resources in the system.

You can see the same pattern appearing in the code that creates overridden methods in our example, such as `writeUpdatedAddMethod` and `writeUpdatedConstructor`. In the case of methods, you create an overridden method for each original method and top it with a Javadoc comment. During the building, you use a helper method, `determineParams`, which takes a method declaration, such as

```
public void myMethod(String arg1, int arg2)
```

and returns the text `(arg1, arg2)`. The purpose is to allow you to take a method's declaration and create a call to the parent's method; for example, by appending the result of `determineParams` to the text `super` and the original method name, you get

```
super.myMethod(arg1, arg2)
```

Because this call is included in your new type, which is a subclass of the original, this calls the original class's method. Once you add in the code to log the type and method name, then you have the new method created and move on to the next method until all methods are overridden in this way.

To put it more concretely, the original `Label`'s `setText` method becomes that shown here.

Listing 18.7 Output of generator for the `Label` widget's `setText` method

```
/**
* Overides Widget's setText method          *      ❶ Generated Javadoc
**/
public void setText(java.lang.String text)        ❷ Generated method declaration
{
   logger.log(Level.INFO, "LabelGWTiAProxy:setText");   ❸ Generated logging
   super.setText(text);                                  ❹ Generated method call
}
```

In listing 18.7 you can see the generated Javadoc code ❶, the generated method declaration built from the source type ❷, the generated logging code to log the class and method ❸, and the call to the parent `setText` method ❹. Note that in this case the logger refers to the GWT logger in the application, not the generator's logger.

We've touched briefly on accessing the structure of code, and you may guess from this example that you need a way of accessing methods, constructors, arguments to method calls, and so on. This is possible through the first of three oracles—the `TypeOracle`.

18.7.4 Accessing types through the TypeOracle

The `TypeOracle` gives you access to the compiler's view of the class under compilation and everything else it knows about your code (such as other classes). Like the other two oracles we'll look at later, it's created from the compiler `context` that's passed into the `generate` method by the compiler. You get access to it as follows:

```
TypeOracle types = context.getTypeOracle();
```

Access to the type oracle gives access to all the code in the compiler's view. This is the way that introspection works in GWT (although it's introspection at compile time). You can't use normal Java introspection in GWT; instead, you access the code structure through a number of classes and methods in the `com.google.gwt.core.ext.typeinfo` package (remember to look in the gwt-dev jar file for these).

You've seen some of this in action already. When you created the name for your new type back in section 18.7.2, you used the `JClassType` to get the package name of the type being generated. From the `JClassType` class you can also access constructors, methods, the classes' visibility, and many other things.

For our example generator, you want to override all of the methods, so you use the following to get access to the existing methods in a class:

```
TypeOracle types = context.getTypeOracle();
JClassType type = types.getType(typeName);
```

```
for (JMethod method: type.getMethods()){
   if (!method.isStatic())
  writeUpdatedAddMethod(logger, srcWriter, proxyName, method);
}
```

The call to `getMethods` returns an array of `JMethod`, covering all of the methods in the class. Within the `if` statement you check to see if each method isn't static, and if not, you write your overridden method in the new class through the previously mentioned `writeUpdatedAddMethod` method in the generator.

You do something similar for the constructors but using the `type.getConstructors()` method instead. Also, within the previously mentioned `determineParams` method, you use an array of `JParameter` obtained from a call to the relevant `JMethod`'s `getParameters()` method.

You can access all aspects of source code through this approach, the objects of which you can find in the `typeinfo` package. Rather than spending a lot more pages of this book going through them, we'll point you to figure 18.9, which shows these classes and how they relate. The figure might look a little intimidating. It shows all of the types you can use to introspect over one of your application types. For example, `JArrayType` is a subclass of `JClassType`, which itself is a subclass of `JType`.

Using the `TypeOracle` you can retrieve any class that's in the compilation context, and then you use the classes in the `typeinfo` package to introspect on them. It's these

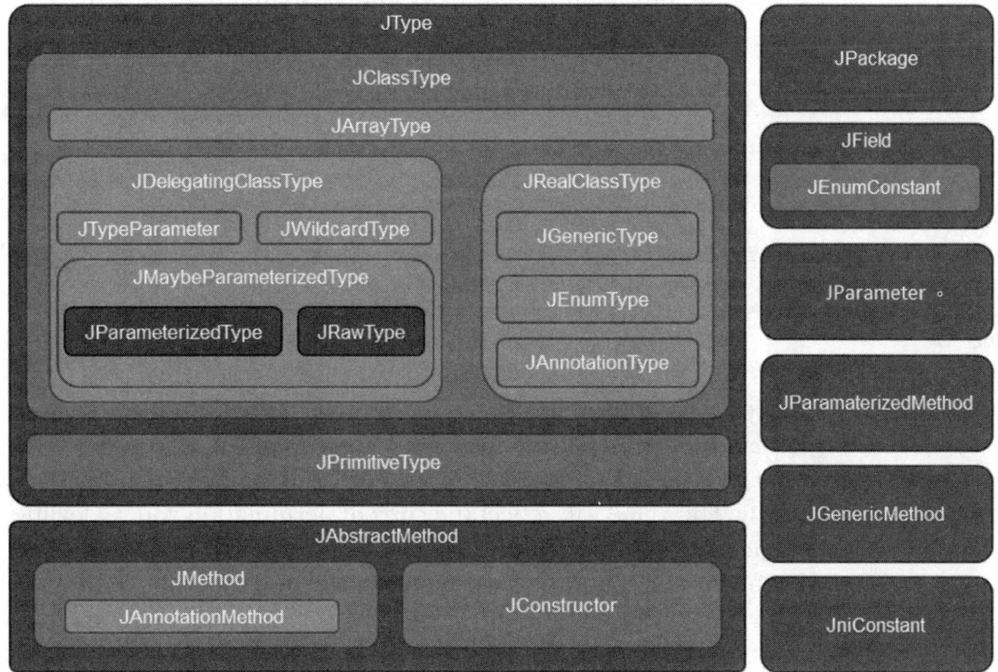

Figure 18.9 The classes available in the `com.google.gwt.dev.javac.typemodel` package (in gwt-dev.jar), which are used in GWT's form of introspection through the `TypeOracle` class

classes that allow you to get method names you might look up in properties files or the value of annotations to use further.

When generating, you might also want to get access to the deferred-binding or configuration properties relating to the compilation—internationalization does that to get the locale currently being compiled for in order to search for an appropriately tagged properties file. Access to properties is through the next oracle we'll look at, the `PropertyOracle`.

18.7.5 Accessing properties through the PropertyOracle

The `PropertyOracle` provides access to both deferred-binding and configuration properties. To obtain the `PropertyOracle`, you retrieve it from the `context` parameter of the `generate` method:

```
PropertyOracle props = context.getPropertyOracle();
```

Once you have access to the `PropertyOracle` object, you can request two further objects. The first gives access to the deferred-binding properties, which were discussed in chapter 16, and is retrieved through the `getSelectionProperty` method. The second gives access to the configuration properties we discussed earlier in this chapter, via the `getConfigurationProperty` method. Both of these methods may raise `BadPropertyValueException` exceptions, if for any reason they can't get the objects, so they need to be surrounded by a `try/catch` construct.

Let's say you're interested in the `locale` deferred-binding property. The code in the following listing shows you how to access it and what you can do with it.

Listing 18.8 Accessing various deferred-binding properties

```
PropertyOracle props = context.getPropertyOracle();                  // ❶ Accessing PropertyOracle
try {
   SelectionProperty selectProp =                                     // ❷ Selecting deferred-binding property
         props.getSelectionProperty(logger, "locale");
   String currVal = selectProp.getCurrentValue();                     // ❸ Getting current value
   String fallbackVal = selectProp.getFallbackValue();                // ❹ Getting fallback value
   SortedSet<String> possValues = selectProp.getPossibleValues();     // ❺ Getting possible values
} catch (BadPropertyValueException e) {
}
```

❶ is where you request an instance of the `PropertyOracle`. With access to the `PropertyOracle`, you can ask for the object that holds all of the deferred-binding properties relating to locale ❷. That object allows you to request the current value ❸ of the property. This value will reflect the current permutation you're dealing with.

The `PropertyOracle` can also tell you the fallback value the property has ❹ (defined in the module file) and a sorted set of `Strings` covering all the possible values the property could have ❺. You can also get the name of the property using the `getName` method, if you've forgotten it since the call to `getSelectionProperty`.

If the generator is interested in the configuration properties of the compilation context, like our example is, then it can access information about them from the object returned from the getConfigurationProperty method. Listing 18.9 shows how you use this at the start of our example's generate method to see if you want to generate the proxy class.

Listing 18.9 Accessing various configuration properties

```
PropertyOracle props = context.getPropertyOracle();          <- Accessing PropertyOracle
try {
   ConfigurationProperty useGenerator =
      getConfigurationProperty(logger, context,"gwtia.debugWidgets");
   if (useGenerator != null){                                 <- 1 Selecting configuration property
      List<String> values = useGenerator.getValues();         <- 2 Getting values
      if(values.contains("true"))) {                          <- Check for value
      }
   }
} catch (BadPropertyValueException e) {
}
```

Configuration properties are a little simpler than deferred-binding properties—they don't change because of the permutation. Therefore, after accessing the property ❶, the only method available returns all the values the property holds ❷—getValues. A single-valued configuration property will only ever have one entry in the List<String> return object.

You'd typically use the values of a configuration property to invoke certain functionality in the generator. We've cheated a little in our example. Because you're using a configuration property to determine whether to run the generator or not, it would have made more sense to include the check in the generate-with definition, but then we wouldn't have been able to show how to programmatically access it in the code.

The value of the deferred-binding property might be used to access particular resources. That's what the internationalization generator does. Once it knows the locale of the compilation context, it looks for a properties file whose name is suffixed with that locale. To do that, it must use the ResourceOracle, which is the subject of our next section.

18.7.6 Accessing resources through the ResourceOracle

You can find resources—text files, images, and so on—within a compilation context through the ResourceOracle. It's created from the context parameter passed to the generate method of the generator:

```
ResourceOracle resrs = context.getResourcesOracle();
```

With access to the ResourceOracle the generator can now look up resources, as shown in the following listing.

Listing 18.10 Using the methods in the ResourceOracle to access resources

```
ResourceOracle resrs = context.getResourceOracle ();   <- 1 Accessing ResourceOracle

String thePath = "com/manning/gwt/client/GWTinAction.pdf";   <- 2 Defining a path
```

```
Map<String, Resource> resourceMap = resrs.getResourceMap();
Resource book_1 =  resourceMap.get(thePath);
```
❸ **Mapping path to a resource**

```
Set<Resource> resources = resrs.getResources();
```
❹ **Getting resource set**

```
Set<String> pathName = resrs.getPathNames();
for(String str : pathName){
    Resource book_2 = resourceMap.get(str);
}
```
❺ **Getting path set**

You can do three things with a `ResourceOracle` ❶, each revolving around the path to a resource. The path is the location of a resource in some arbitrary namespace, constructed using / between name elements and ending in a valid filename. At ❷ you can see a path to a GWTinAction.pdf file that's in a `com.manning.gwt.client` package.

If you know the path, then you can grab the `resourceMap` ❸ and use the `get` method to obtain a reference to the appropriate resource. Be careful to always check that a `null` object isn't returned from `get` (`null` means the resource isn't found). Alternatively, you can get all the resources ❹ and walk through them or get all the paths and walk through them ❺. Naturally, these collections are unmodifiable by the generator.

Getting a resource is one thing, but what can you do with it once you have it? A generator can request three bits of information: the last-modified timestamp (`getLastModified` method), the location (`getLocation` method), and the path (`getPath` method). The location is a URL-like location of the resource that's valid only if the resource is truly available via a URL.

Far more interesting is that the generator can open and read the resource contents. It does that through the `openContents` method, which is shown in action in the next listing.

Listing 18.11 Accessing the contents of a resource in a generator

```
ResourceOracle resrs = context.getResourcesOracle();
Resource res = resrs.getResourceMap().get("GWTinAction.pdf");
if (res != null){
   InputStream stream = res.openContents();
   int data;
   try {
      while ((data = stream.read()) != -1){
         System.out.println(data);
      }
   } catch (IOException e) {
   }
}
```
Opening

Reading

The `openContents` method retrieves a Java input stream. You can read that byte for byte as before (maybe you're going to manipulate images), or you can wrap the input stream up in a `BufferedReader`, in the standard way, if you want to read it line for line (perhaps to read a properties file).

The final thing we wish to discuss in this section is how to log messages from the generator.

18.7.7 Logging in the generator

The compiler passes a TreeLogger to the generator that represents the compiler's current logger. You can use that to log any messages that you want to while your generator is executing. Typically, this will be the console window that has started the compiler (or development mode). You perform logging as shown next.

Listing 18.12 Performing logging in a generator

```
logger.log(TreeLogger.ERROR                              ❶ Type of log message
           , "An Error Message"                          Error message
           , new Exception()                             An exception
           , new HelpInfo(){                             For more help, see...
               public String getAnchorText(){return null;}
               public String getPrefix(){return "More Info: ";}
               public URL getUrl(){return null;}
           });
```

Logging-level values ❶ come from the TreeLogger class and include the levels ALL, DEBUG, ERROR, INFO, SPAM, NULL, TRACE, and WARN. These levels are in a hierarchy, similar to Log4J levels.

> **TIP** If you use a logging level lower than INFO, you'll need to change the -logLevel parameter when you run GWT web mode or the compiler; otherwise, you won't see the messages.

Now that your generator is defined, we should look at how you define when it's used.

18.8 Using your new generator

You want to use your generator on all widgets. To do that, you need to define the <generate-with> tag as follows:

```
<generate-with class="com.manning.rebind.MyGenerator">
   <when-type-assignable class="com.google.gwt.user.client.ui.Widget"/>
</generate-with>
```

But there's a problem. Such a simple definition allows your generator to run on UiBinder code itself, and that unfortunately causes some issues. You won't normally have this problem because it's unlikely you'll run a generator on widgets, but because you are, you have to exclude UiBinder code. You'll also hit a conflict issue with the Logging window from GWT, so you need to exclude that too.

Luckily, these are easy to exclude by adding some conditionals in your <generate-with> tag. The following is our final definition:

```
<generate-with class="com.manning.gwtia.ch18.rebind.WidgetDebugGenerator">
   <all>
      <when-type-assignable class="com.google.gwt.user.client.ui.Widget"/>
      <none>
```

```
        <when-type-assignable class=
                 "com.google.gwt.uibinder.client.UiBinder"/>
        <when-type-assignable class=
                 "com.google.gwt.logging.client.LoggingPopup"/>
     </none>
   </all>
</generate-with>
```

We could have included a condition in this definition around the configuration property `gwtia.debugWidgets`, but then we wouldn't need the code in the generator to check for its value, and it was important to show that in action.

That's it; we're finished with generators.

18.9 Summary

You've seen that generators are capable components in GWT development, able to access all aspects of a type during compile time and build a new type from that type or other resources through type and resource oracles. You can even alter the generated class based on deferred-binding properties or configuration properties.

A typical developer is unlikely to need to create generators on a daily basis. But designers of any serious application should consider whether they can use generators to reduce the need to implement certain repeated or boilerplate functionality or to reduce the burden on developers.

The key thing to take from this chapter is that generators should sit outside the GWT compile path because they aren't restricted by GWT compiler restrictions (as your client code is). They're the closest you'll get at present to introspection of Java classes, even if it can feel a little clunky having to write each line of the new type yourself.

You must remember, though, that to trigger your generator you need to have the appropriate `<generate-with>` tag in an accessible module file and use the `GWT.create` method to create the object meeting the tags constraints.

Our example generator, included in the chapter code, is useful to see what methods are being called and when. It can also help you see if you can make efficiencies in your code. But GWT can be optimized in many other ways, and that's the topic of the next chapter.

19 Metrics and code splitting

This chapter covers

- Gathering statistics with lightweight metrics
- Generating and understanding the GWT Compile Report
- Using code splitting to decrease load times

Throughout this book we've covered everything you need to know to build massive GWT applications that will rival anything found on the desktop. But perhaps your massive application is a little too massive. Perhaps it feels slow and bloated. Perhaps you know that you need to optimize your application, but you aren't sure exactly where to start.

You can break optimization into two parts. First, you need to be able to measure performance metrics, and then, based on these metrics, you'll be able to dig into the code to target those parts that optimization benefits the most.

GWT provides two useful tools for understanding your application: lightweight metrics and the Compile Report. Lightweight metrics is a mechanism that allows you to gather performance statistics at runtime. Without adding any instrumentation to your code, you'll be able to review measurements for the startup speed of your application and the time it takes to make GWT-RPC calls to the server. In addition, you can instrument your application to measure performance as you see fit, allowing you to better understand how your application performs and where you can optimize it.

The Compile Report provides details regarding the file sizes of compiled code and what classes were compiled into that code. This data allows you to see how your design decisions affect the size of the code, with the outcome of leading you to write leaner code, which in turn results in shorter download times.

Once you have a baseline, GWT provides several tools for increasing performance. One of them is client bundles, which you learned about in chapter 5, and code splitting, which we'll look at in this chapter. Code splitting is a way to chop up the compiled GWT code into several fragments, which the developer defines. This allows for the possibility of having a smaller initial download fragment, followed by the loading of additional code fragments after the application starts. This tool is useful for large projects where your compiled code is several hundred kilobytes, because splitting up your code means faster download and startup time. This is far from automatic, but with the aid of the Compile Report you'll be able to find the right place to split your code.

So without delay, let's get into developing a better understanding of your application with lightweight metrics.

19.1 Using the lightweight metrics tool

Before we get into what are and what aren't lightweight metrics, let's discuss the promise this tool hopes to provide. When developing an application, it's often valuable to know how long an operation took to perform. This allows you to optimize a routine within the application and get hard data on how much better (or worse) it performs after the change.

Measuring the time it takes to execute an operation isn't that difficult. You could hardcode a few debug statements to print out timings to the dev-mode console or to some `TextArea` on the page. Something like the following would work in most cases:

```
GWT.log("start: " + Duration.currentTimeMillis());
someExpensiveOperation();
GWT.log("end: " + Duration.currentTimeMillis());
```

Generating timings like this is fast and easy, but sometimes you need something a little more complex. Perhaps you need to gather statistics from multiple modules in the same page. Perhaps you want to be able to turn on and/or off metrics logging, without having to recompile your code. Or perhaps you want to measure the startup time of your module, which isn't quite as easy.

This is the promise of the lightweight metrics tool, but unfortunately it isn't something you can drop into your application and start using; it takes a little effort in order to get benefit from it. So what exactly are lightweight metrics?

19.1.1 Defining lightweight metrics

In the design document[1] for lightweight metrics, you'll see four goals; verbatim from the document they are as follows:

- Provide data about the bootstrap process and RPC subsystem in code paths where user code cannot be added.
- Support multiple modules on the same page.
- Incur negligible overhead when no statistics collector function is defined.
- Minimize observer effects by allowing for data aggregation to be performed in post-processing.

If you begin to imagine how you might implement these goals in GWT, you'll likely find that it's not entirely possible. For example, you can't measure the timing of the bootstrap process from a GWT application because that occurs before the application is running. And you can't take measurements from multiple modules at the same time because GWT has no tools that allow inter-application communication.

The answer to these problems is to go outside GWT and do all of this in JavaScript. In JavaScript you can measure the speed of the bootstrap process, measure the time it takes remote calls to return, and even gather metrics from multiple modules, as long as the method of how to accomplish that is defined. And this is exactly what lightweight metrics are all about.

But the method of generating and capturing these metrics is where the design document ends, and it doesn't define a way to view the metrics. When it comes to viewing the metrics you'll find a Debug Panel for GWT project,[2] but it isn't part of GWT proper and it isn't entirely trivial to use; alternatively, you can build your own.

In this chapter we'll briefly look at the Debug Panel for GWT, which is fairly well documented, and we'll spend the majority of our time focusing on building our own basic viewer from scratch so that you can better understand how the mechanism works.

The first step in building a trivial metrics viewer is to create a global-collector function.

19.1.2 Writing the global collector

The global collector is a fancy name for a JavaScript function with a specific name. The absolute simplest global collector that you could write looks like the following:

```
window.__gwtStatsEvent = function(event) {
   return false;
};
```

As you can see, this code attaches a function named `__gwtStatsEvent()` to the `window` object. The function itself does nothing useful, which means it doesn't collect any of

---

1 You'll find the LightweightMetricsDesign document at http://mng.bz/nC3q.

2 You can find the Debug Panel for GWT project at http://code.google.com/p/gwt-debug-panel/.

the events passed to it. The only thing it does do is return `false` to indicate that the event wasn't captured. But in this section we'll write our own implementation of `__gwtStatsEvent()` that does collect events and displays them in the web page for viewing.

Before we write our implementation, let's take a look at an example event that this method would receive.

UNDERSTANDING THE COMPOSITION OF AN EVENT

An event is a plain-old JavaScript object that contains several fields. The following is an example of what an event could look like:

```
{
    moduleName : 'com.manning.gwtia.ch19.Example',
    subSystem : 'Initialization',
    evtGroup : 'initPanels',
    type : 'begin',
    millis : 1287935060700
}
```

As you can see, the event contains the `moduleName`, `subSystem`, `evtGroup`, `type`, and `millis` fields. The `moduleName` identifies the module logging the metric and is useful when you have multiple GWT modules being displayed on a single HTML page. You can get this information from within GWT by calling `GWT.getModuleName()`. The `subSystem` is, as the name implies, used to identify the subsystem logging the metric. GWT uses several `subSystem` names already, so you should avoid using any of the names in table 19.1.

Table 19.1 Values the GWT core uses for `subSystem`

`subSystem` value	Description
`Startup`	These events begin as early as possible, prior even to the selection of the correct permutation for the target browser, and end after the `onModuleLoad()` of the entry-point class has completed.
`moduleStartup`	Used to mark the start and end of the execution of the `onModuleLoad()` method of the entry-point class.
`Rpc`	Used to report on timings associated with GWT-RPC calls to the server.

The `evtGroup` in the event object is used to group metric events together, with the `type` field used to indicate the timing metric within that group. Per the design document, the `type` name can be anything that makes sense to you, but the last `type` recorded in an `evtGroup` should be `end`.

For example, if you want to record the timings between the beginning and the end of a set of `RequestBuilder` calls that load game data from the server, you might use the `evtGroup` name of `loadGameData` with the `types` `begin` and `end`. On the other hand, if loading the game data required several calls, you might use the types `loadHighScores`, `loadPlayerData`, `loadFriendData`, `loadGameMap`, and `end`. How you structure your values depends on what information you need to get, and it may take a little playing with the information before you get it right.

The last value in the event data is `millis`, which is the current time in milliseconds when the event occurred. A call to GWT"s `Duration.currentTimeMillis()` fetches this value.

So now that you know what fields are in an event, let's implement the global-collector function.

IMPLEMENTING THE GLOBAL COLLECTOR

We've designed our implementation with customization in mind, so it's broken down into several routines. Listing 19.1 shows the full implementation, which you can copy and paste into the <head> section of any HTML page that hosts a GWT application for instant results.

Listing 19.1 A base global-collector implementation

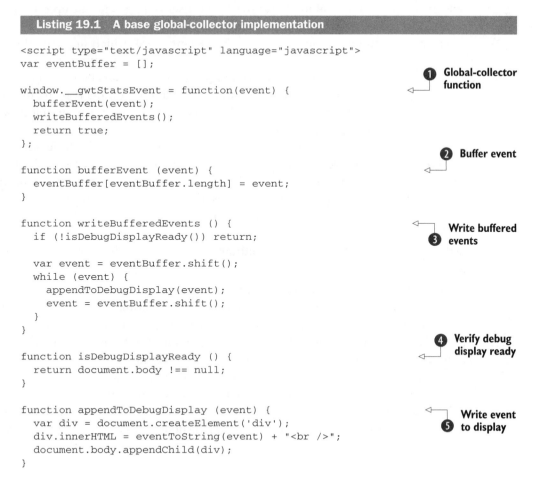

```
<script type="text/javascript" language="javascript">
var eventBuffer = [];

window.__gwtStatsEvent = function(event) {          ❶ Global-collector function
  bufferEvent(event);
  writeBufferedEvents();
  return true;
};

function bufferEvent (event) {                      ❷ Buffer event
  eventBuffer[eventBuffer.length] = event;
}

function writeBufferedEvents () {                   ❸ Write buffered events
  if (!isDebugDisplayReady()) return;

  var event = eventBuffer.shift();
  while (event) {
    appendToDebugDisplay(event);
    event = eventBuffer.shift();
  }
}

function isDebugDisplayReady () {                   ❹ Verify debug display ready
  return document.body !== null;
}

function appendToDebugDisplay (event) {             ❺ Write event to display
  var div = document.createElement('div');
  div.innerHTML = eventToString(event) + "<br />";
  document.body.appendChild(div);
}
```

```
function eventToString (event) {
  return '[' + event.moduleName + '] ' + event.subSystem + ' - '
    + event.evtGroup + ' - ' + event.type + ' | '
    + event.millis;
}
</script>
```

❻ **Convert event to String**

The listing splits the global collector into six functions and one global variable. Beginning with the `__gwtStatsEvent()` function ❶ you buffer the event, display events that have been buffered, and then return `true` to indicate that the event has been handled. The question with this method is, why do you need to buffer the event at all?

The answer is that you can't be sure that the display area has been set up at this point. For example, if the display area is a `<div>` element at the bottom of the page and this JavaScript code is placed in the `<head>` of the page, that `<div>` won't have been rendered yet by the browser. This leads us to another important point, and that's the placement of this code. This code needs to appear before the `<script>` tag that loads the GWT module. Failing to do that will cause some of the startup events, notably the events prior to the `onModuleLoad()` execution, to be missed.

The next method in the listing is `bufferEvent()` ❷, which appends the event object to the global `eventBuffer` array. This then leads to the `writeBufferedEvents()` function ❸, which does a few things for you. First, it calls `isDebugDisplayReady()` ❹, which verifies that the area where you'll write events is ready to receive them. In this implementation you verify that `document.body` returns an object, which is where you'll be displaying your events.

Assuming the debug area is ready, the `writeBufferedEvents()` function iterates through the buffered events and calls `appendToDebugDisplay()` ❺ for each of them. The `appendToDebugDisplay()` function takes the event object and displays it, which in this implementation means that it creates a new `<div>` element on the page with the event message. The event message is created with a call to `eventToString()` ❻.

The purpose of this design is to promote reuse, and in most cases, all you should need to do is modify the last three methods to suit your needs. Let's take a look at a few examples of how you can do that.

ALTERING THE GLOBAL COLLECTOR FOR USE WITH FIREBUG

When collecting metrics in a global collector, you'll ultimately want to be able to retrieve that data. One way to do that without having the collected metrics printed directly in the page is to print them to an external tool outside the browser window. Firebug[3] (or Firebug Lite for other browsers), an extremely popular Firefox plug-in among developers, includes a console that allows you to do that. Firebug makes a JavaScript object named `console` available, which includes methods for logging events to the Firebug console window. We have our events displayed here by modifying the `isDebugDisplayReady()` and `appendToDebugDisplay()` functions, as you see in the next listing.

[3] You'll find Firebug and Firebug Lite at http://getfirebug.com.

Listing 19.2 A global collector for Firebug

```
var eventBuffer = [];

window.__gwtStatsEvent = function(event) {...}

function bufferEvent (event) {...}

function writeBufferedEvents () {...}


function isDebugDisplayReady () {            <-- ❶ Provide readiness state
  return true;
}

function appendToDebugDisplay (event) {      <-- ❷ Append event to display
  if (window.console)
    console.log(eventToString(event));
}

function eventToString (event) {...}
```

In listing 19.2 you see the full global-collector code, with ellipses (...) used to denote methods that were not modified from the base global collector as shown in the previous section.

As promised, you change only two methods. First, you alter `isDebugDisplayReady()` ❶ to always return `true`. This makes sense in this case because Firebug is a browser add-on and is always available once it has been installed. Next, you modify the `appendToDebugDisplay()` function ❷ to test for the presence of Firebug's `window.console` object and then call `console.log()` if it's present. Testing for the presence of the `window.console` object ensures that you don't cause JavaScript errors when Firebug isn't installed.

Placing the modified global collector in the HTML page results in Firebug console output that looks like what you see in figure 19.1 when you start up your GWT application.

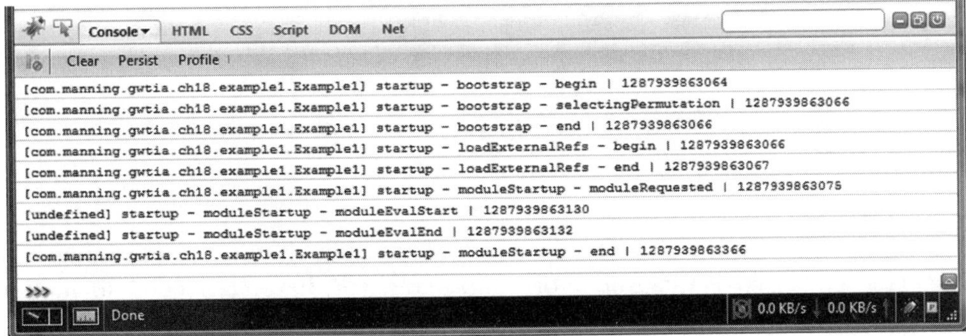

Figure 19.1 We use the Firebug console to display lightweight metrics events, as opposed to displaying them within the page.

The downside to what you've seen so far is that the output has a timestamp in milliseconds, but what you want to know is how much time it took from the `begin` event to the `end` event. Quick, what is 1287939863366 minus 1287939863064? Let's find a better solution.

ALTERING THE GLOBAL COLLECTOR TO CALCULATE ELAPSED TIME

You can determine elapsed time by making some minor changes to the global collector. You do this by capturing the `begin` time of a `evtGroup`, and then for each event with a `type` value other than `begin` you include the elapsed time in milliseconds in the output. The following listing shows the modifications you'll need to make.

Listing 19.3 A global collector that displays elapsed time

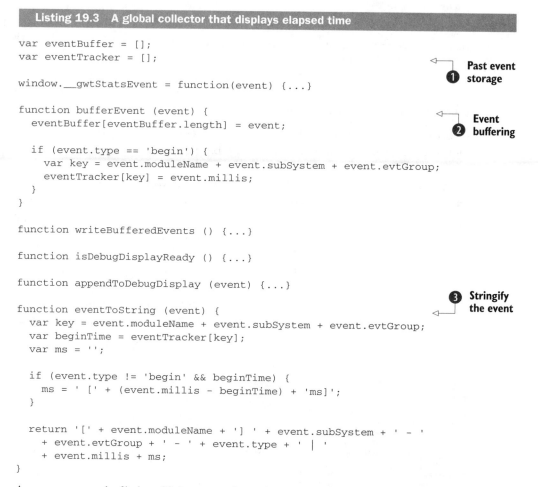

```
var eventBuffer = [];
var eventTracker = [];                                          ❶ Past event storage

window.__gwtStatsEvent = function(event) {...}

function bufferEvent (event) {                                  ❷ Event buffering
  eventBuffer[eventBuffer.length] = event;

  if (event.type == 'begin') {
    var key = event.moduleName + event.subSystem + event.evtGroup;
    eventTracker[key] = event.millis;
  }
}

function writeBufferedEvents () {...}

function isDebugDisplayReady () {...}

function appendToDebugDisplay (event) {...}

function eventToString (event) {                                ❸ Stringify the event
  var key = event.moduleName + event.subSystem + event.evtGroup;
  var beginTime = eventTracker[key];
  var ms = '';

  if (event.type != 'begin' && beginTime) {
    ms = ' [' + (event.millis - beginTime) + 'ms]';
  }

  return '[' + event.moduleName + '] ' + event.subSystem + ' - '
    + event.evtGroup + ' - ' + event.type + ' | '
    + event.millis + ms;
}
```

As you can see in listing 19.3, you only make a few minor changes from the original base global collector. And more important, you haven't needed to modify either `isDebugDisplayReady()` or `appendToDebugDisplay()`, so this change will work with both the base global collector and the Firebug version.

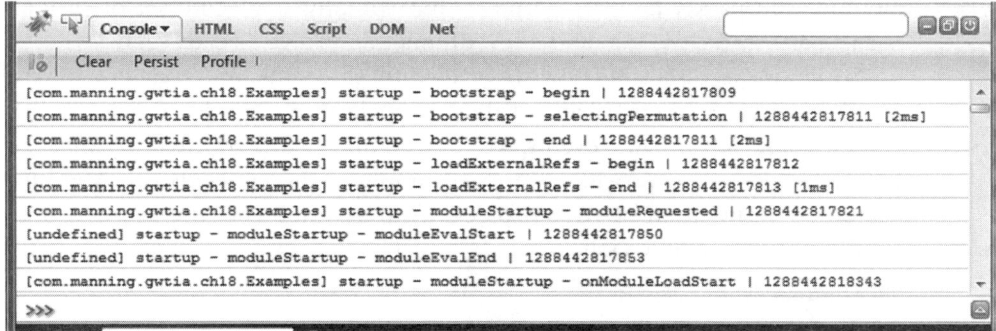

Figure 19.2 The Firebug version of the global collector with the elapsed-time modification created. Events now display the elapsed time in milliseconds since the last `begin` event for the event group.

In order to capture the begin times, you need a place to store them. You create a new array `eventTracker` ❶ for this purpose. You then alter the `bufferEvent()` ❷ function so that it now looks for events with a `type` value of `begin`, and when it's found you store the value in the `eventTracker` array. You store the value using a combined key that includes the `moduleName`, `subSystem`, and `evtGroup` values, which will keep it unique even when you have multiple GWT modules in the same web page.

And finally, you update the `eventToString()` function ❸ in order to print the elapsed time. You do this by checking to see if the `eventTracker` has a begin time, and if it does you calculate the elapsed time since the begin time so that you can include it in the output. You may also notice that you test to see if this event that you're handling is itself a `begin` event, and if it is you don't include the elapsed time because it will always be zero.

By applying these changes to the Firebug version of the global collector, you end up with the output you see in figure 19.2. You now have the elapsed time in ms displayed at the end of each event line. One issue you might spot in the figure is that the `moduleStartup` event grouping has no elapsed time shown. This is because there was no event in it with a `type` value of `begin`. This goes against the lightweight metrics design document and is the exception not the rule, so for our purposes we'll ignore it.

At this point we now have a global collector, which is perhaps the hard part. Now let's look at how we'll send events from our application.

19.1.3 Sending events to the global collector

At the beginning of this chapter we characterized lightweight metrics as a tool, but in reality we were being fairly generous when we said that. To this point we've had to write a lot of JavaScript code to be able to capture and display the time measurements, so where exactly is this tool? In reality the tool is a defined set of semantics.

The semantics of lightweight metrics are to have your GWT components make calls out to the JavaScript method `__gwtStatsEvent`, if it exists. And when calling this method, you pass a JavaScript object that contains a specific set of properties, like `moduleName`, `type`, `millis`, and a few others that you've already seen.

So far we've discussed how to receive these events, and you saw how several of GWT's own components broadcast these events, so the next logical step is to start generating some of our own events. We'll accomplish this by creating an `EventLogger` class, which not only provides a good example of the concepts involved but can also be reused easily in all of your projects. And as you'll see, the secret sauce to lightweight metrics is a little JSNI code.

CREATING AN EVENT LOGGER

As you may recall, the global collector's main JavaScript function was named `__gwtStatsEvent`, which accepts an event object as an argument. So all we need to do is create a class that creates the event object and sends it off to the global collector. The following listing provides an example implementation of this.

Listing 19.4 `EventLogger` class for logging lightweight metrics events

```
package com.manning.gwtia.ch19.client;

import com.google.gwt.core.client.Duration;
import com.google.gwt.core.client.GWT;

public class EventLogger
{
  public static void logEvent (String subsys, String grp, String type)
  {
    logEvent(GWT.getModuleName(), subsys, grp,
       Duration.currentTimeMillis(), type);
  }

  public static native void logEvent (String module, String subsys,
       String grp, double millis, String type)
  /*-{
    if ($wnd.__gwtStatsEvent) {
      $wnd.__gwtStatsEvent({
        'moduleName' : module,
        'subSystem' : subsys,
        'evtGroup' : grp,
        'millis' : millis,
        'type' : type
      });
    }
  }-*/;
}
```

❶ Abbreviated param list

❷ Interface with global collector

In listing 19.4 you implement two methods. The first `logEvent()` method ❶ takes the subsystem, event group, and event type as arguments. When we discussed the makeup of an event, you saw that an event includes these three fields plus one for the module name and the current time in milliseconds. This method gets the values for those missing fields and passes them on to the second `logEvent()` method ❷.

The second `logEvent()` method is a JSNI method that does two things. First, it checks to see if there's a defined `__gwtStatsEvent` function, and if there isn't, it does nothing. But if a global collector is defined, it creates a new JavaScript object with the event fields and passes the object to the global collector. And from there the global collector code kicks in and does whatever it was designed to do with that data.

As we mentioned, you check to ensure there's a `__gwtStatsEvent` before you send data to that. This allows you to include a global collector while you're developing and testing your application; then you can remove it when you deploy the code to production. Because you have that simple test, you'll ensure that you won't cause JavaScript errors to occur because of the missing method.

With this class in your project, you can now log metrics events with a call as simple as the following:

```
EventLogger.logEvent("animation", "rocket", "begin");
runRocketAnimation();
EventLogger.logEvent("animation", "rocket", "end");
```

So what's next? One potential enhancement is to have the global collector feed data into a second GWT application that can read that data and display it. One such example is the Debug Panel for GWT.

USING THE DEBUG PANEL FOR GWT

The Debug Panel for GWT[4] is a project developed by the GWT team along with the GWT community. It provides access to thrown exceptions, browser cookies, and lightweight metrics events. Earlier in the chapter, we mentioned that we wouldn't cover this tool in any amount of detail, and we won't, but it's a good example of feeding metrics data into a second GWT application for viewing. Figure 19.3 shows the Debug Panel for GWT in an HTML page.

As you can see, the Debug Panel for GWT makes use of a `Tree` widget to group events together, making it somewhat easier to navigate a large number of events. But like everything, it has advantages and disadvantages.

One disadvantage is that events are shown in the browser, which means it could interfere with the normal display of your application, particularly if your application

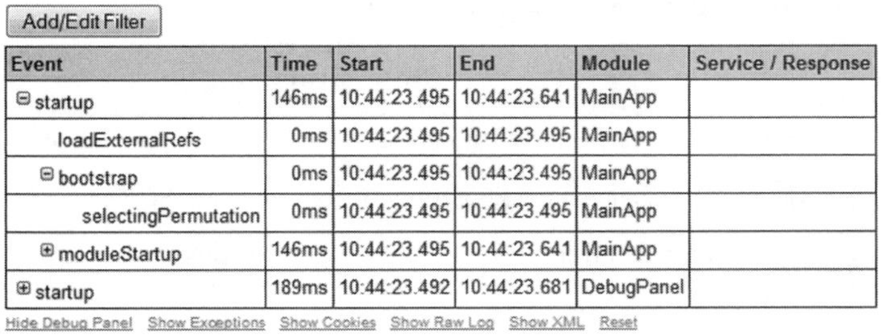

Add/Edit Filter

Event	Time	Start	End	Module	Service / Response
⊖ startup	146ms	10:44:23.495	10:44:23.641	MainApp	
loadExternalRefs	0ms	10:44:23.495	10:44:23.495	MainApp	
⊖ bootstrap	0ms	10:44:23.495	10:44:23.495	MainApp	
selectingPermutation	0ms	10:44:23.495	10:44:23.495	MainApp	
⊕ moduleStartup	146ms	10:44:23.495	10:44:23.641	MainApp	
⊕ startup	189ms	10:44:23.492	10:44:23.681	DebugPanel	

Hide Debug Panel Show Exceptions Show Cookies Show Raw Log Show XML Reset

Figure 19.3 The Debug Panel for GWT, displaying events in a tree structure, allowing for easy navigation of grouped events

[4] You can find the Debug Panel for GWT at http://code.google.com/p/gwt-debug-panel/.

takes up the full browser window. But at the same time, the tree navigation is a nice feature and may be useful to you.

In the end, you'll have to find the tooling that matches your development style. Perhaps the Debug Panel for GWT is a good fit, perhaps logging to the Firebug console, or perhaps something completely different. We hope that as we close this section you now have a good understanding of how to use lightweight metrics and a lot of ideas on how to use it.

Lightweight metrics is about getting a better understanding of performance when your application is running, but how can you better understand the compiled application? To put it another way, we have a 200 KB JavaScript file that runs our application in the browser, so that begs the question, what the heck is in there? The next section introduces the tool that will help us answer these questions, the Compile Report.

19.2 Using the Compile Report

Throughout the book, we've talked a lot about how the compiler generates a bunch of code for you, prunes out any code that isn't called, creates several versions of that code specific to each browser, runs it through a Java-to-JavaScript conversion process, and then spits it out. You can dismiss it as magic, but dismissing it won't help you understand what's in there (and what isn't).

Understanding the output is useful for a number of reasons. Perhaps you want to reduce the size of your compiled code and need to know what classes have been compiled into the output. Perhaps your users are complaining about a JavaScript error in a function named `Cb`, and you need to know to what Java method it corresponds. Or maybe you like to know exactly what you're feeding your users and exactly what's in the compiled output. Whatever your reason, the Compile Report is a useful tool, and the first step is to activate it.

19.2.1 Turning on the Compile Report

To turn on the Compile Report, all you need to do is add the `-compileReport` flag and optionally two others when compiling your code. Table 19.2 lists the compiler flags that relate to generating the Compile Report.

Table 19.2 Compiler flags used to generate the Compile Report

Compiler flag	Description
`-compileReport`	Turns on the generation of the Compile Report and supporting files
`-XsoycDetailed`	Generates additional detailed Story Of Your Compile (SOYC) files
`-extra <DIR>`	The directory in which to generate the report; defaults to extras

Turning on the Compile Report with the `-compileReport` flag will generate the report under the base directory specified by the `-extra` flag, which by default will be the extras directory.

If you're using the Google Plugin for Eclipse, you set these flags in the GWT Compile dialog. When the dialog appears, you click the Advanced label to reveal a frame that provides additional options. Here you add the `-compileReport` flag to the Additional Compiler Arguments text area prior to clicking the Compile button. Figure 19.4 shows this dialog with the Advanced options frame.

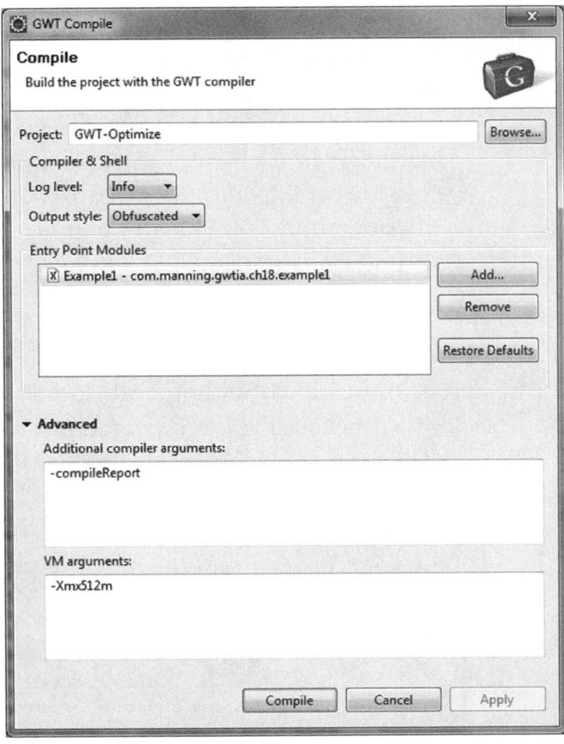

Figure 19.4 The GWT Compile dialog with the Advanced options panel opened. Add the compiler argument `-compileReport` to generate the Compile Report.

The generated files include an HTML report, RPC policy manifest, symbol maps, and XML SOYC (Story Of Your Compile) files. These files are then used to generate the HTML Compile Report, providing a user-friendly view of the data. Figure 19.5 shows the generated directories used to store these files.

Focusing on the HTML Compile Report, once you compile your application with `-compileReport` you'll find it's been generated under extras/MODULE/soycReport/compile-report. In that directory is the starting page index.html, which presents the list of compiled permutations.

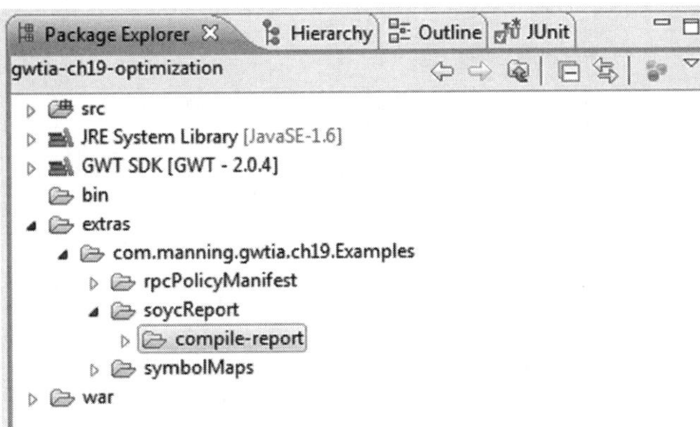

Figure 19.5 Compiling your code with the `-compileReport` flag will generate an RPC policy manifest, SOYC report, and symbol maps under the extras directory.

19.2.2 Understanding the permutation list

When you open the starting page (index.html) in your web browser, it will present you with a list of permutations. Figure 19.6 shows what this will look like, as well as the permutation home page, which you can access by following one of the permutation links.

As shown in the figure, each permutation is numbered, starting at zero, and each item in the list includes the property values that apply to that permutation. For example, Permutation 3 in figure 19.6 indicates that this permutation was created for when the property `user.agent` has a value of `ie6`:

```
Permutation 3 ('user.agent' : 'ie6')
```

Understand, though, that `ie6` is merely a well-known property value used for the purposes of deferred binding and doesn't necessarily indicate that this permutation is *only* for Internet Explorer version 6. If you dig into the GWT source, you'll find that the `ie6` permutation will be loaded by all Internet Explorer versions prior to version 8.

Looking back at figure 19.6, you'll see six permutations (four shown and two below the fold), and in this case the only differentiator between them is the value of the `user.agent` property. As we've explained throughout this book, the number of

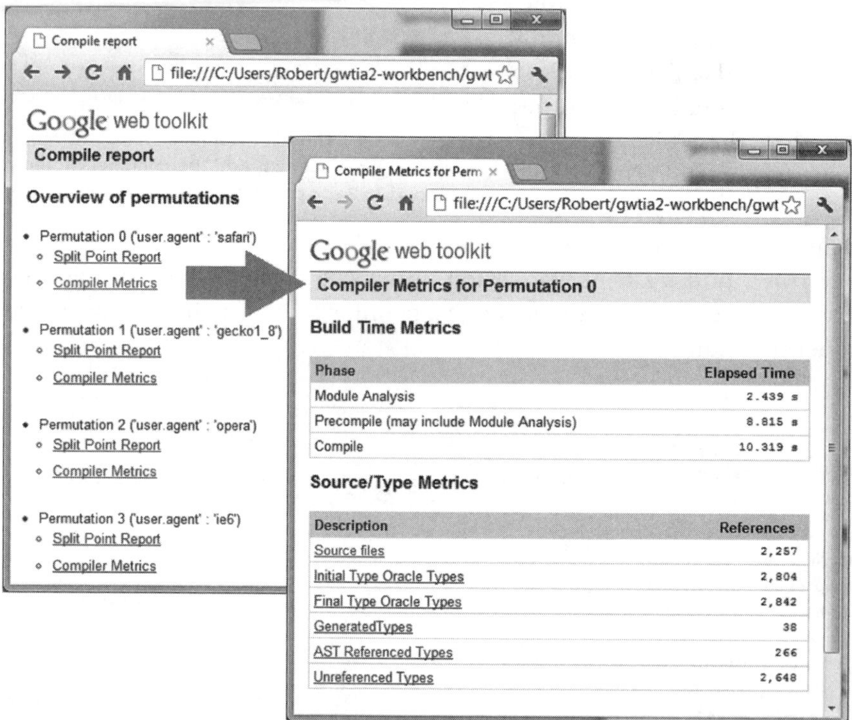

Figure 19.6 When you load the Compile Report in your browser, it lists the different permutations that were generated, and selecting one will provide you with an overview of that permutation.

permutations depends on your deferred-binding rules, which take into account not only browser differences but locale and other differences as well.

Figure 19.7 shows the first few permutations for this same application with the addition of locale support for `en_US` and `en_GB`. In this case we've taken an application with six permutations and added support for three locales (`en_US`, `en_GB`, and the default). This results in 18 total permutations, which is reflected in the updated list. As you can see, each permutation now takes into account the value of two properties, `locale` and `user.agent`, for example:

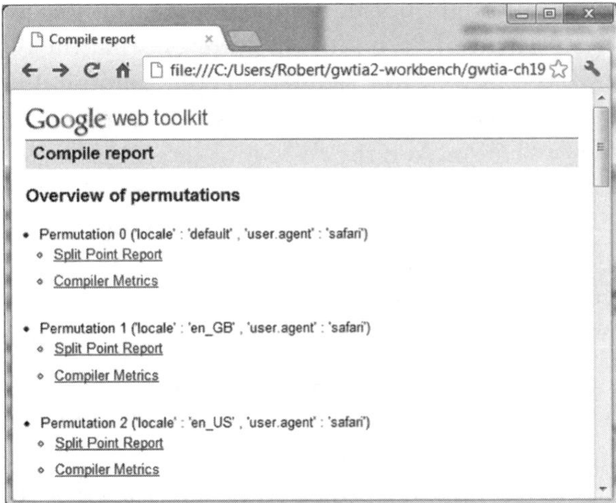

Figure 19.7 Permutations are created not only because of browser differences but also because of locale differences. Here you see the first three permutations of an application that supports two locales in addition to the default for the same user agent.

```
Permutation 1 ('locale' : 'en_GB' , 'user.agent' : 'safari')
```

To continue, click one of the Split Point Report links, which will allow you to drill down on the details of that permutation.

19.2.3 *Digging into the Split Point report*

The details about a permutation begin on the Split Points page, which provides the size of the permutation in bytes. In figure 19.8 you see this page, which shows a full code size of about 88 KB and an initial download size of the same.

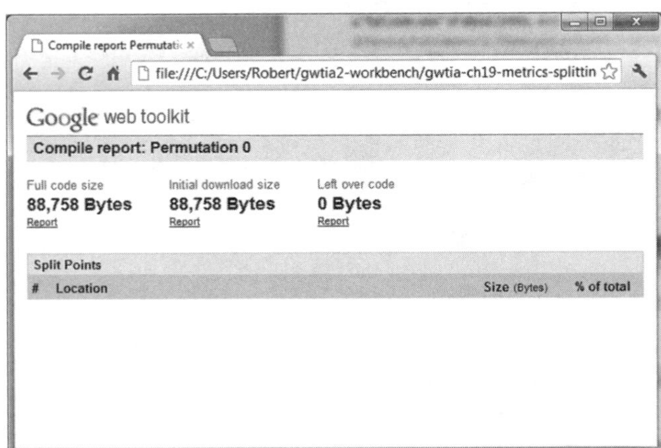

Figure 19.8 The permutation home page presents information on the size of the download along with links to further details.

It might not be completely clear at this point why the full code size and initial download size are the same or even what the difference is. Later in this chapter, we'll show you how to make use of split points, which allow you to break your application into smaller pieces. In this case we have only one piece, which is why the sizes match. If we had broken the code into several parts, the initial download size would have been less than the full code size, and the Split Points table in the previous figure would have listed each of the pieces. But more on split points shortly; first let's see what sort of details the Compile Report holds.

Each part as well as the full code will have a report link. Clicking the report link brings you to the application breakdown analysis.

VIEWING THE BREAKDOWN ANALYSIS

The application breakdown analysis presents a breakdown of the entire application by Java package as well as code type, providing size details of these divisions. The Application Breakdown Analysis page can be seen in figure 19.9.

For each division, the page displays a bar so that you can quickly identify what packages or types constitute the majority of the application size. To the right of the bar is the actual size in bytes along with a numeric percentage, which is the percentage of the total size. If you're looking at the breakdown for the full application, this is the percentage of the whole application; otherwise it's the percentage of the part.

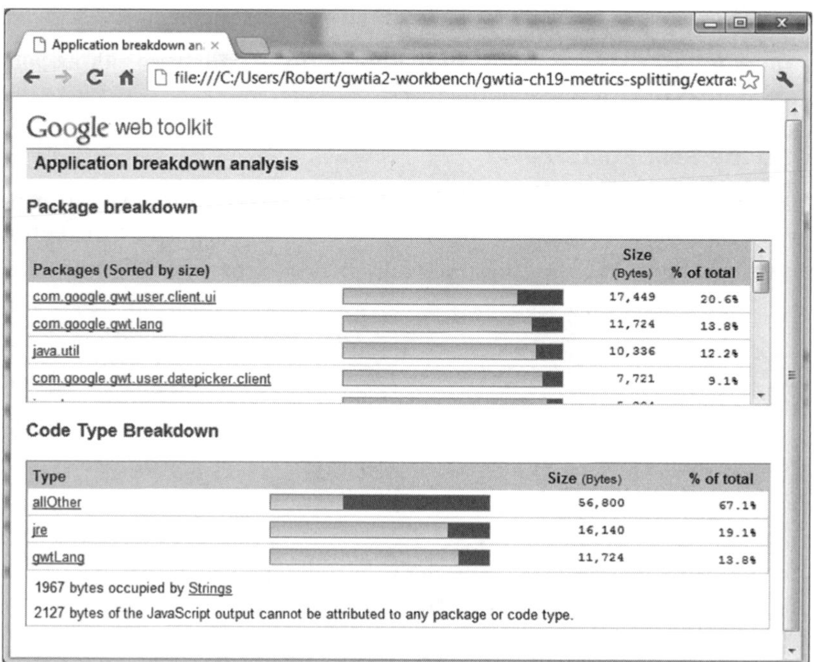

Figure 19.9 The Application Breakdown Analysis page provides a breakdown by both package and code type. For each division, it displays the size in bytes along with a percentage of the overall code size.

The breakdown by package is self-explanatory, but the breakdown by type requires some explanation. The type list includes the categories of `allOther`, `jre`, `gwt.lang`, and `Strings`. The `gwt.lang` category includes classes in the `com.google.gwt.lang` package. This includes classes like `Cast`, `Array`, `Exceptions`, and other classes that are used to emulate Java language features.

The `jre` category includes all classes in the Java runtime that have been emulated for use in GWT. This includes any classes in `java.lang` and `java.util`, such as `java.lang.String`, `java.util.Date`, and dozens of others.

The `allOther` category contains everything else. This includes all of your classes as well as any classes from the GWT API. Except in extremely rare circumstances, this is where the majority of your application size will be.

At the bottom of this report is a Strings link, which when followed brings you to our next report.

UNDERSTANDING THE STRINGS REPORT

The Strings report includes all of the string literals within your application. This includes literals from your own Java code, from the GWT standard libraries, from external libraries, and from any compiler generated code. The Strings report is shown in figure 19.10.

When you look at the Strings report for the first time, you might be surprised by the number of strings in your application. In this report you'll see HTML tag names,

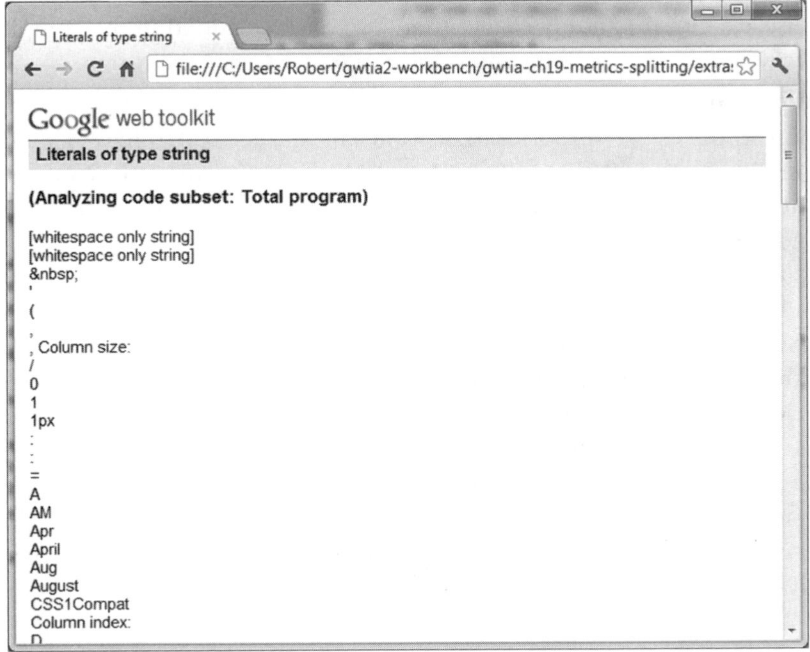

Figure 19.10 Navigating to the Strings report from the Application Breakdown Analysis page will display a list of all of the strings compiled into the application.

CSS class names, regular expressions, messages in your i18N properties file, and much more. And if you made use of image bundles, you'll even see embedded image data, as in this example:[5]


```
data:image/gif;base64,R0lGODlhEAAQAIQaAFhorldnrquz1mFxsvz9/vr6/
     M3Q2ZGbw5mixvb3+Gp5t2Nys77F4GRzs9ze4mt6uGV1s8/R2VZnrl5usFdortPV2/
     P09+3u8eXm6lZnrf///wAAzP///////////////
     yH5BAEAAB8ALAAAAAAQABAAAAVE4CeOZGmeaKquo5K974MuTKHdhDCcgOVvvoTkRLkYN8bL0
     ETBbJ5PTIaIqW6q0lPAYcVOTRNEpEI2HCYoCOzVYLnf7hAAOw==
```


This particular embedded image is the plus (+) symbol image used by the `Tree` widget. When you use image bundles, the GWT compiler will embed image data in the JavaScript code, using the data URI scheme to display it. If you've never used or heard of the data URI scheme, you aren't alone, but this is one of many optimizations that the GWT compiler delivers.

The benefit of embedding images in this manner is that it reduces the number of downloads that the web browser needs to initiate. Because of the time it takes to initiate a connection to the server, this can decrease the overall download time. But as is often the case when developing for web browsers, the data URI scheme isn't universally supported. So you'll see these embedded image strings only if the browser supports them. For example, Internet Explorer prior to version 8 doesn't support the data URI scheme, and version 8 restricts the size of the image embedded in this manner.

Now that you've seen the Strings report, let's take a step back and return to the Application Breakdown Analysis page. As discussed, the Application Breakdown Analysis page lists each of the Java packages that have been included in the compiled JavaScript. Clicking one of these links will bring you to the Classes report.

UNDERSTANDING THE CLASSES REPORT

The purpose of the Classes report is to provide a list of classes that have been included in the compile output. But this doesn't imply that the entire class was included. Because of compiler optimizations, any code that's unreachable by the application (dead code) isn't included.

An example of what you'd see when viewing this report is shown in figure 19.11. For each class, the report provides a bar graph to visually display the size of the code for that class along with the number of bytes and the percentage. Again, we want to bring up the fact that compiler optimizations can affect what you see. If the compiler detects that a given class can be optimized away, it will do so. To understand this, picture a class method that's called from only one location. In this case the compiler may well inline that method, and if that was the only method in use from the target class, it becomes subject for dead-code elimination.

At this point, if you follow one of these class links, the Method Dependencies report will be displayed.

---

[5] You can learn more about the data URI scheme on Wikipedia at http://en.wikipedia.org/wiki/Data_URI_scheme.

Classes in Total program

file:///C:/Users/Robert/gwtia2-workbench/gwtia-ch19-metrics-splitting/extras/gwtia_ch19_metrics_splitting/soycReport/compil

Google web toolkit

Classes in Total program

(Analyzing code subset: Total program)

Package: com.google.gwt.core.client	Size (Bytes)	% of total
com.google.gwt.core.client.JavaScriptException	566	57.8%
com.google.gwt.core.client.JsDate	245	25.0%
com.google.gwt.core.client.JavaScriptObject	105	10.7%
com.google.gwt.core.client.Scheduler	64	6.5%

Package: com.google.gwt.core.client.impl	Size (Bytes)	% of total
com.google.gwt.core.client.impl.StackTraceCreator$Collector	850	27.4%
com.google.gwt.core.client.impl.StackTraceCreator$CollectorChrome	591	19.0%
com.google.gwt.core.client.impl.SchedulerImpl	565	18.2%
com.google.gwt.core.client.impl.Impl	326	10.5%
com.google.gwt.core.client.impl.StackTraceCreator$CollectorMoz	295	9.5%
com.google.gwt.core.client.impl.StringBufferImplAppend	223	7.2%
com.google.gwt.core.client.impl.StackTraceCreator	193	6.2%
com.google.gwt.core.client.impl.StringBufferImpl	64	2.1%

Figure 19.11 Drilling down on a specific Java package from the Breakdown report will display a list of classes from that package that have been compiled into your application.

UNDERSTANDING THE METHOD DEPENDENCIES REPORT

The Method Dependencies report is meant to provide a means for understanding why a specific class has been included in the compiled JavaScript. If you plan on using code splitting, which we'll cover shortly, this report will be a valuable tool. An example of this report is pictured in figure 19.12.

The Method Dependencies report contains all of the methods from a single Java package, separated by class and then by method. When you follow a link to this page

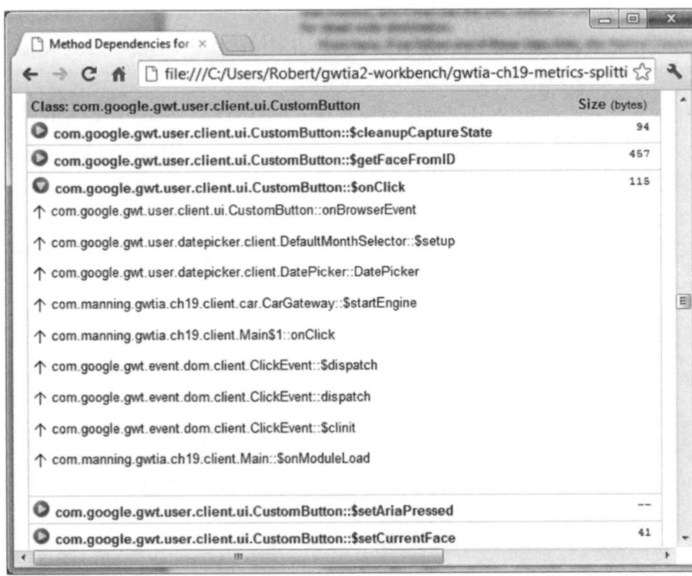

Figure 19.12 The Method Dependencies report provides a list of methods that are included in the compiled output, along with a call stack that provides clues as to why it was included.

from the Classes report, it will bring you to the section of this page where methods of that class begin.

Looking at figure 19.12 you see several methods that have been included in the report for the `CustomButton` class, along with their compiled size in bytes. In the report, each method can be clicked in order to provide the call stack that was discovered at compile time, which is the reason for that method being included. In the figure we've displayed the details for the `onClick` method, which looks like the following:

```
com.google.gwt.user.client.ui.CustomButton::onBrowserEvent
com.google.gwt.user.datepicker.client.DefaultMonthSelector::$setup
com.google.gwt.user.datepicker.client.DatePicker::DatePicker
com.manning.gwtia.ch19.client.car.CarGateway::$startEngine
com.manning.gwtia.ch19.client.Main$1::onClick
com.google.gwt.event.dom.client.ClickEvent::$dispatch
com.google.gwt.event.dom.client.ClickEvent::dispatch
com.google.gwt.event.dom.client.ClickEvent::$clinit
com.manning.gwtia.ch19.client.Main::$onModuleLoad
```

The call stack is like a stack trace, where the calls are in reverse order, with the initial call at the bottom of the stack. Here you see that this method is included in the compiled application because it's referenced from the `onBrowserEvent()` method of `CustomButton`, which is referenced by the `DatePicker` constructor, which is referenced by some user code in a class called `CarGateway`, and then can eventually be traced back to the initialization of the application in `onModuleLoad()`.

The double colons (`::`) split the class from the method, the dollar sign (`$`) usually indicates that the method is static, and constructors will have a method name that's the same as the class (for example, `DatePicker::DatePicker`).

The exception to the dollar-sign rule is that a nonstatic method may start with a dollar sign, which is normally uncommon but occurs often in GWT when code is generated by the GWT compiler. When reading this report, keep in mind that `$dispatch` could indicate a static method `dispatch()` or an instance method `$dispatch()`. The only way to know for sure is to dig into the JavaScript output.

And that brings up a good point, which is that the call stack is that of the JavaScript output and not of the original Java code. If you take even this small example and dig into the Java code for `DefaultMonthSelector`, you'll see that `DefaultMonthSelector.setup()` is *not* a static method. So why does the report show it as being static? The answer is that the compiler optimizes your Java code, and one of those optimizations is to convert instance methods to static methods.

Viewing compiler optimization details

The GWT compiler provides detailed logging of its optimizations, allowing you to see how the compiler has modified and eliminated superfluous application code. You turn this on by passing a JVM argument (not a GWT compiler argument) when running the compiler.

> ***(continued)***
>
> An example is `-Dgwt.jjs.traceMethods=DefaultMonthSelector.setup`, where the value is the simple class name and method that you want to view the optimization details for. In this case, the optimization details of `setup()` of the class `Default-MonthSelector` will be printed to the console. You may specify multiple methods by separating them with a colon.

So what good is all of this information? The primary use for this data is to provide the understanding necessary to divide your application into smaller parts. This is accomplished through code splitting.

19.3 Making use of code splitting

To reminisce a bit, back in 2006 when GWT was released it solved a lot of the traditional problems for developing large JavaScript applications. So great was the promise that developers began to produce massive GWT applications—massive enough that they started hitting a wall. The wall they hit had to do with the size of the application.

If you think about a traditional desktop application like Microsoft Word, the application has many features that you don't normally use. For instance, the Mail Merge tool within Microsoft Word is extremely useful when you need that functionality, but most users rarely use it, if at all. So the first question is, how do you load only the functionality that will be used?

Another common engineering issue was how to decrease the load time of the application. It's common for a feature-full GWT application to approach a megabyte in size. With broadband this is generally a fast download, but at the same time users have higher expectations than they did with their 56 Kbps modem. Users now judge the speed of your application in hundreds of milliseconds and not seconds. If your application takes a full second to start up, it may be considered sluggish. So how can you decrease the start time?

This is where code splitting comes in. If you can cut your code into multiple segments, you can kill two birds with one stone. A smaller initial download means faster startup, and loading less-often-accessed code only when it's needed means smaller total downloads.

In this section we begin by explaining the basics of using code splitting and then delve deeper and explore a coding pattern that has proven useful for segmenting applications.

19.3.1 Understanding code-splitting basics

Code splitting in theory is quite simple to understand. You wrap a piece of code in an asynchronous block, much as you'd do with an RPC call, and let the compiler handle the rest. Let's start with the example in the following listing so you can see what we're talking about.

Listing 19.5 An extremely simple example of code splitting

```
RunAsyncCallback callback = new RunAsyncCallback() {      ❶ Create callback

  public void onSuccess () {                               ❷ Define success handler
    doStuff();
  }

  public void onFailure (Throwable reason) {               ❸ Define error handler
    Window.alert("Error: " + reason.getMessage());
  }
};

GWT.runAsync(callback);                                     ❹ Load and execute
```

This example literally covers the entire code-splitting API, and even though it's extremely simple, we'll walk through it and provide some commentary. As shown in the example, you first create a `RunAsyncCallback` instance ❶. `RunAsyncCallback` is an interface that's similar to the asynchronous interfaces used by RPC, like `AsyncCallback` and `RequestCallback`, in that it has methods for handling success and errors.

The success handler `onSuccess()` ❷ is called when the JavaScript fragment, called a *split point*, is successfully loaded from the server and is ready to be run. This is also where the compiler determines where to split your code. It isn't quite that cut and dried because of dependencies, which we'll discuss shortly.

The error handler `onFailure()` ❸ is called when the split point fails to load. The typical cause of this would be because the network isn't available or the site isn't reachable. This could occur for mobile users, for example, where they start using your application from a Wi-Fi hot spot and then trigger a split point after leaving the hot spot. Here we show an alert pop-up, but it's probably a good idea to think about how your application should handle these errors.

Once the callback is defined, all you need to do is call `GWT.runAsync()` ❹ to trigger the loading and execution of the split point. In addition to loading the split point, there may be some leftover code that also needs to be loaded. During compiling there may be some code that doesn't fit in a single split point and instead is shared across more than one. This is called *leftover code*, and it will be loaded prior to any split-point code.

To visualize this, add a few split points to a GWT application; then compile the code and generate a Compile Report. You can turn on generation of the Compile Report by adding the compiler switch `-compileReport`. If you skipped over section 19.2 where we examined the Compile Report, we recommend that you go back and review it to get all the details.

An example of what you might see on the Compile Report if you had two split points is shown in figure 19.13. As you can see, the initial download size for this permutation is only about 24 KB, which compared to the total code size of 292 KB is a significant improvement. In addition, you'll see that there's 62 KB of leftover code. The

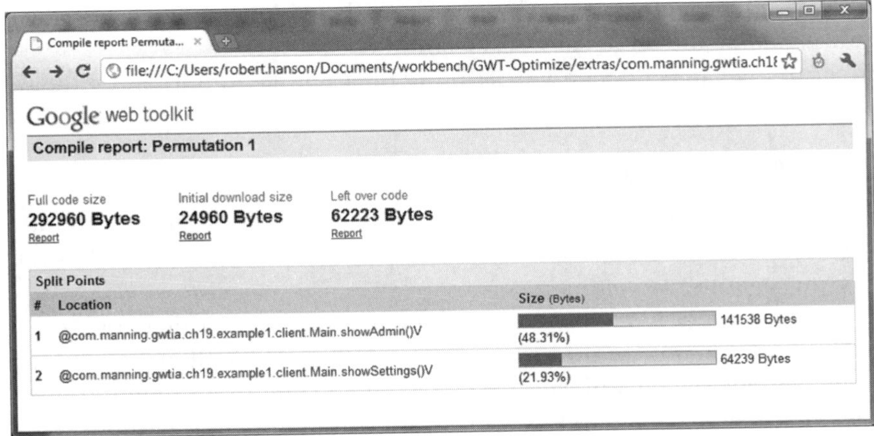

Figure 19.13 An example of a Compile Report showing two split points. It shows the size of the initial download, the two split points, and leftover code that's shared between the split points.

leftover code is code that's shared by more than one split point but isn't needed in the initial download. And finally, you have the two split points, one of 141 KB and another of 64 KB. So you have four total JavaScript files, each containing some portion of the total application.

If you drop this into one of your own applications, it's likely you won't see results quite as good as these. These results are from a simple test application where the initial download has relatively no functionality and the parts of the code within the split points have no dependencies on each other.

Unless you planned ahead, you'll likely see something closer to figure 19.14, where practically the entire application is in the initial download. But why does this happen? You may have guessed that the culprit is inter-class dependencies. Most developers

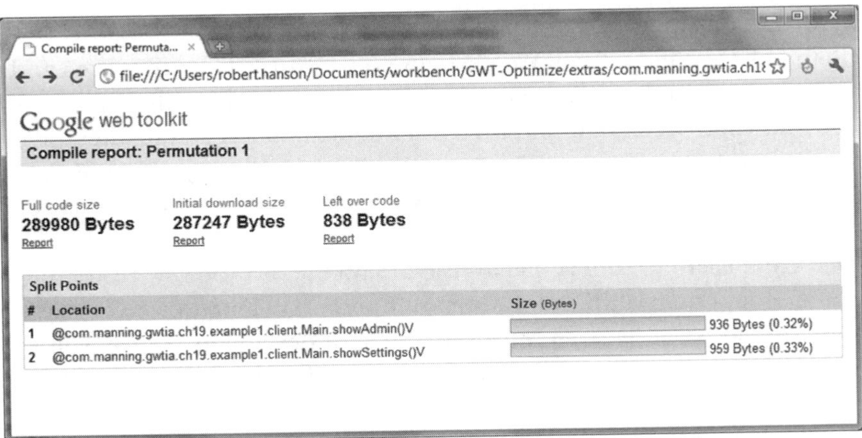

Figure 19.14 Another example of a Compile Report, but this time inter-class dependencies have caused almost the full application to be included in the initial download.

don't think about inter-class and inter-package dependencies much. Usually the focus is on inter-library dependencies (aka jars).

You can track down dependencies using the Compile Report, as we showed in section 19.2, but you can also rely on a pattern, the Async Package pattern.

19.3.2 Using the Async Package pattern

The intent of the Async Package pattern is to place collaborating classes within a Java package and then restrict access to classes within that package so that they can only be used asynchronously as split points.

The motivation is to create a split point that contains a particular segment of your code base, and you want to do so in a way that makes it difficult or impossible to create code dependencies that will cause the segmented code to be required by other segments. This is useful for development teams with multiple programmers, where you want to ensure that one developer can't undo the work done by another. This is also useful for a single developer who wants to keep the application easy to maintain, so that enhancements added months from now don't cause your split points to become dependent on each other.

If we were to boil this pattern down to a recipe, it would consist of these four points:

1. Isolate collaborating classes within a package.
2. Remove all static methods.
3. Create a single gateway class with a private constructor.
4. Instantiate the gateway within only a `GWT.runAsync()` call.

The general idea is that all access to that package must first require the creation of the gateway class using `GWT.runAsync()`. By doing this, you ensure that your split point can't be broken from users calling into the package. The first step in implementing this pattern is to isolate classes within a package from the outside world.

ISOLATING COLLABORATING CLASSES

We do this all the time in Java. We make use of keywords like `protected` and `private` to hide methods and fields from unrestricted use. By providing access where it's needed, our code becomes inherently easier to maintain. A private method can always be renamed with the assurance that it won't affect anything outside the class. And the type of a protected field can be altered, knowing that it affects only classes and subclasses in the same package.

The Async Package pattern makes use of Java's access tools by restricting access to the set of classes that will become your split point. Locking down the classes in your package should be fairly straightforward for Java developers, so we won't say much about that other than that you should use protected and default access to prevent outside access.

Ideally, you'd plan out your split points ahead of time, but like with many things you can't always predict where it makes sense to split your code. So if you already have

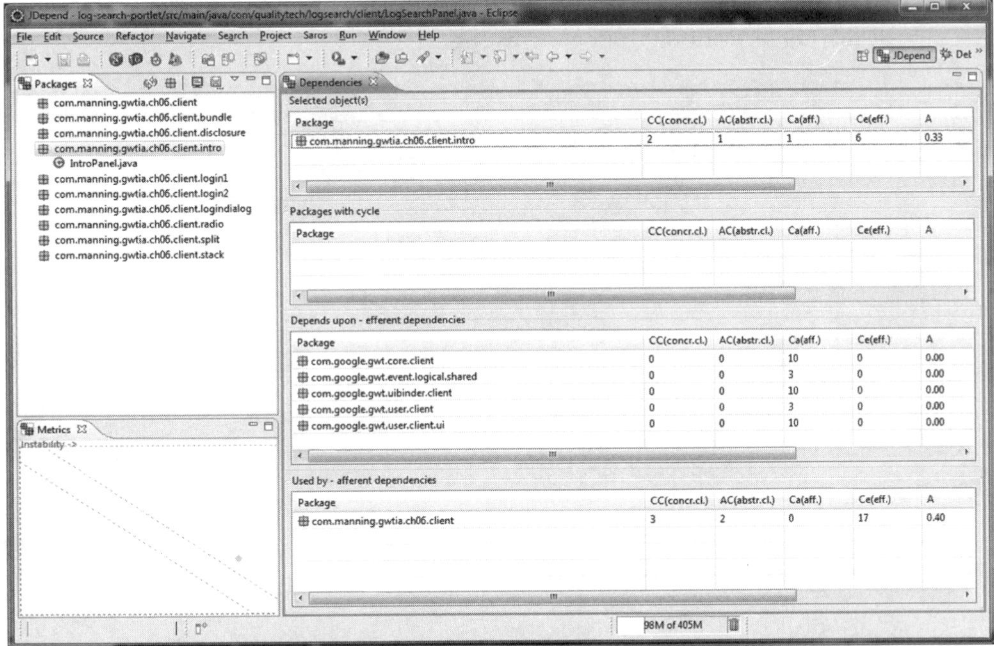

Figure 19.15 JDepend4Eclipse will analyze your Java code and allow you to review dependencies between packages and classes.

an existing application, you may wish to use a tool like JDepend,[6] which will analyze your application and report on dependencies between packages. If you're using Eclipse for your development, we recommend using JDepend4Eclipse,[7] which is shown in figure 19.15.

JDepend4Eclipse makes it easy to see dependencies, both incoming and outgoing, for both packages and classes. If you aren't familiar with JDepend, it will be worth the effort to read the overview on the JDepend website. The overview provides definitions for the terms used in the report, for example, afferent versus efferent coupling and dependency cycles.

Once you've grouped your collaborating classes in a package, it's time to create the gateway class.

CREATING THE GATEWAY

Creating the gateway class involves creating a private constructor, creating an asynchronous factory method, and implementing any methods needed by the world outside your package.

---

6 JDepend is available from www.clarkware.com/software/JDepend.html.
7 JDepend4Eclipse is available from http://andrei.gmxhome.de/jdepend4eclipse/.

We present our example gateway class for a package that encapsulates functionality for driving a car in the following listing.

Listing 19.6 An example gateway class for the Async Package pattern

```
package com.manning.gwtia.ch19.client.car;

import com.google.gwt.core.client.GWT;
import com.google.gwt.core.client.RunAsyncCallback;

public class CarGateway {

  private CarGateway () { }

  public static void createAsync (final Callback callback) {     ❶ Factory method
    GWT.runAsync(new RunAsyncCallback() {

      public void onSuccess () {                                  ❷ Success handler
        callback.onCreated(new CarGateway());
      }

      public void onFailure (Throwable reason) {                  ❸ Failure handler
        callback.onCreateFailed(reason);
      }
    });
  }

  public interface Callback {                                     ❹ Callback interface
    void onCreated (CarGateway gateway);
    void onCreateFailed (Throwable reason);
  }

  public void startEngine () { ... }
  public void setSpeed (int mph) { ... }
  public int getSpeed () { ... }
}
```

In listing 19.6 you make the constructor private, forcing callers to construct the class using the factory method `createAsync()` ❶. The `createAsync()` method takes a single `callback` argument, which is an interface that we'll define shortly. In `createAsync()` you use `GWT.runAsync()`, which will create your split point.

In the `onSuccess()` method ❷ you use the `callback` argument, calling `callback.onCreated()` and passing back a new instance of `CarGateway`.

The `callback.onFailure()` method ❸ passes the exception back to the user. As stated before, this would typically be triggered if there was a network error where the split point couldn't be loaded.

The `Callback` interface ❹, implemented by the parameter passed to the `createAsync()` method, is defined here as an inner class. You then provide some work methods that can be called, like `startEngine()` and `getSpeed()`, once the `CarGateway` instance has been constructed.

Creating a gateway class in this manner, where you force callers to use a factory method, means that the caller can't get it wrong. We'll look at some examples of that next.

USING THE GATEWAY CLASS

From the client side, use of the gateway class is unrestricted now that it can only be created via the factory method `createAsync()`. Instead of looking at the simplest use case, let's look at something you might find in the real world. Imagine that your application is heavy and you want to present a splash screen as early as possible. This is akin to when you open a web application and it says "Loading," as you might see on Gmail.

Developers do this so that the user perceives the application as loading quickly. A typical user will perceive the speed of starting the application based on how long it takes you to render those first widgets, so it's useful to display some sort of splash screen while the full application code loads.

For our example in the next listing, we'll display the simple message "Loading car data..." and then replace that message with a button to start the car once the split point is loaded.

Listing 19.7 Example client usage of an Async Package gateway

```
package com.manning.gwtia.ch19.client;

import com.google.gwt.core.client.EntryPoint;
import com.google.gwt.event.dom.client.*;
import com.google.gwt.user.client.Window;
import com.google.gwt.user.client.ui.*;
import com.manning.gwtia.ch19.client.car.CarGateway;
import com.manning.gwtia.ch19.client.car.CarGateway.Callback;


public class Main implements EntryPoint
{
  private CarGateway carGateway;

  public void onModuleLoad () {

    RootPanel.get().add(new Label("Loading car data..."));        ❶ Loading message

    CarGateway.createAsync(new Callback() {                       ❷ Load split point

      public void onCreated (CarGateway gateway) {                ❸ Handle loaded
        carGateway = gateway;
        initDisplay();
      }

      public void onCreateFailed (Throwable reason) {
        Window.alert("Error loading data");
      }
    });
  }
```

```
  private void initDisplay () {                          ❹ Initialize display
    RootPanel.get().clear();

    Button button = new Button("Start your engines!");
    RootPanel.get().add(button);

    button.addClickHandler(new ClickHandler() {
      public void onClick (ClickEvent event) {
        carGateway.startEngine();
      }
    });
  }
}
```

This example is the module entry point, and the first thing you do is add a loading message to the page in the form of a `Label` ❶. This is followed up by a call to `CarGateway.createAsync()` ❷, which will load the split point.

In the `onCreated()` method of the callback ❸ that was passed to `createAsync()`, you can initialize the application. You do this by first storing a reference to the `CarGateway` in the class field `carGateway` and then calling `initDisplay()`.

The `initDisplay()` ❹ method then uses the `carGateway` reference to create a Start Your Engines! `Button` and a `ClickHandler`, which are displayed on the page.

This example is simple, but let's look at some things worth noting. First is that you can store a reference to the gateway class. When GWT creates a split point for the gateway, it will recognize that the reference can only be `null` until the object is constructed. And because it's only constructed within a `GWT.runAsync()` call, all of the `CarGateway` methods can be included in the split point. To be specific, you can store references to the `CarGateway` and pass them around without breaking the split point.

Another thing to point out in this example is that because the loading message is a `Label`, it could have probably been hardcoded in the HTML page. Our example is small, but in a larger application you might expect to find a progress bar instead of a simple text message. A progress bar is useful to the user because they can see that something is happening, preventing them from thinking that the application has hung.

If you had several split points, you could initiate the loading of them all at the same time and increment the progress bar as each one completed. Then you could use some sort of event handler in the progress bar to initialize the application once all of the split points were loaded.

One ideal place to add a second split point in this specific application would be where you create the widgets in the `initDisplay()` method. If you could move this code into a gateway as well, it would decrease your initial download size even further, and, generally speaking, the UI code is a fairly large part of most GWT applications.

In section 19.3.1 we introduced leftover code, or code that's shared across split points. When the first split point is loaded, the leftover code is, too. Depending on how you've split your code, you may have a significant chunk of leftover code. To reduce the size of the leftover code, GWT has one more trick up its sleeve.

19.3.3 Reducing leftover code by specifying load order

The leftover download shown in the Compile Report is any code that's shared across split points. If you have a lot of split points, you may find that this chunk of code can be rather large. For example, if you have four split points, you may have 5 KB of code shared between split points A and B and a different 5 KB of shared code used by split points C and D. If you were to load split point A, you'd also be downloading the shared code for C and D, even though you might never need it.

GWT provides a mechanism to solve this problem, but in order to use it you need to be able to predict the load order of at least some of the split points. To do this you need to first give your split points an identity and then reference the identity of the split point in the module configuration. The next listing takes our example from the previous section and provides an updated `CarGateway` class.

Listing 19.8 Updated gateway class providing an identity for the split point

```
package com.manning.gwtia.ch19.client.car;

import com.google.gwt.core.client.GWT;
import com.google.gwt.core.client.RunAsyncCallback;

public class CarGateway
{
  private CarGateway () { }

  public static void createAsync (final Callback callback) {

    GWT.runAsync(CarGateway.class, new RunAsyncCallback() {     // Identity provided

      public void onSuccess () {
        CarGateway gateway = new CarGateway();
        callback.onCreated(gateway);
      }

      public void onFailure (Throwable reason) {
        callback.onCreateFailed(reason);
      }
    });
  }

  ...
}
```

In listing 19.8 we omitted most of the example to allow you to focus on the `GWT.runAsync()` call. Here you pass a class literal as the first argument to `GWT.runAsync()`. This purpose of this is only to provide a unique identity, meaning that you could have used any class literal for this purpose, but typically you'll use the class literal that's related to the split point. In this case it makes the most sense to use `CarGateway.class` as the identity.

The second part is to identify the order of the initial split points in the module configuration. This is done by extending the configuration property `compiler.splitpoint.initial.sequence`, as in this example:

```
<extend-configuration-property
  name="compiler.splitpoint.initial.sequence"
  value="com.manning.gwtia.ch19.client.car.CarGateway"/>
```

The value is where you specify the identity that you give your split point. By extending this property, you're signaling to the compiler that your split point will be the first to load following the initial download. Because of this, the compiler can include shared code that your split point uses in this split point, increasing the size of the split point and reducing the size of the leftover code.

If you can provide the order of additional split points beyond the first, you can specify them by adding additional entries in the module configuration:

```
<extend-configuration-property
  name="compiler.splitpoint.initial.sequence"
  value="com.manning.gwtia.ch19.client.car.UIGateway"/>
<extend-configuration-property
  name="compiler.splitpoint.initial.sequence"
  value="com.manning.gwtia.ch19.client.car.RoadwayGateway"/>
```

These will again reduce the size of the leftover code, increasing the code in the split points.

The downside to specifying the load order is that if your code ends up loading a split point out of order, it will need to go back and load additional split points. For example, if you declare the load order to be A B C but try to load C first, it will also trigger the loading of split points A and B.

Ordering the split points can reduce your total leftover code, but it requires some preplanning to use it effectively. And it's with that bit of advice that we wrap up our discussion of optimization.

19.4 Summary

Optimization is at the heart of GWT. Starting with the compiler, GWT literally rewrites your Java code, making it more efficient in terms of both execution time and size. As you saw in the chapter on client bundles, GWT reduces the number of files that need to be downloaded by embedding them in your application code. And let's not forget the i18N and locale support, where GWT creates a separate version of the compiled output for each supported language, as opposed to a single bloated artifact.

GWT does a lot of the optimization for you, but it can't do everything, which is why it also provides some of the tools we covered in this chapter. Lightweight metrics don't do anything by themselves, but if you use them wisely you'll gain great insight on your application's performance and, most important, where to best spend your time optimizing your code.

In this chapter we looked at the Compile Report and code splitting, a fairly new tool to the GWT stack, and one of the most anticipated. With code splitting you have, in theory, no upper limit to the size of your applications. It also lets you break out the rarely used parts to be loaded only when they're needed. Imagine a one-million-line application running in the browser, with an initial load time of less than one second. That's amazing, considering that the underlying technology, namely JavaScript, was never meant to do that.

What makes GWT such a compelling product in our minds is that it allows us to do all of these things without needing to think about the underlying JavaScript all that much. That's a good thing, because JavaScript implementations differ, and as a developer you can spend your time either learning about JavaScript implementation differences or coding your application. We prefer the latter.

In closing, we hope that this book has done justice to the tens of thousands of engineering hours that have gone into GWT, and we want to thank the GWT team for its dedication and hard work.

index

E

H

Q

R

X

Y

RELATED MANNING TITLES

The Well-Grounded Java Developer
Vital techniques of Java 7 and polyglot programming
by Benjamin J. Evans and Martijn Verburg

ISBN: 978-1-617290-06-0
496 pages, $49.99
July 2012

The Quick Python Book, Second Edition
Revised edition of The Quick Python Book
by Naomi R. Ceder

ISBN: 978-1-935182-20-7
360 pages, $39.99
January 2010

Third-Party JavaScript
by Ben Vinegar and Anton Kovalyov

ISBN: 978-1-617290-54-1
300 pages, $44.99
January 2013

Secrets of the JavaScript Ninja
by John Resig and Bear Bibeault

ISBN: 978-1-933988-69-6
392 pages, $39.99
December 2012

For ordering information go to www.manning.com